Infinite Suburbia

INFINITE SUBURBIA

Edited by
Alan M. Berger
Joel Kotkin
with Celina Balderas Guzmán

Princeton Architectural Press, New York

INFINITE

SUBURBIA

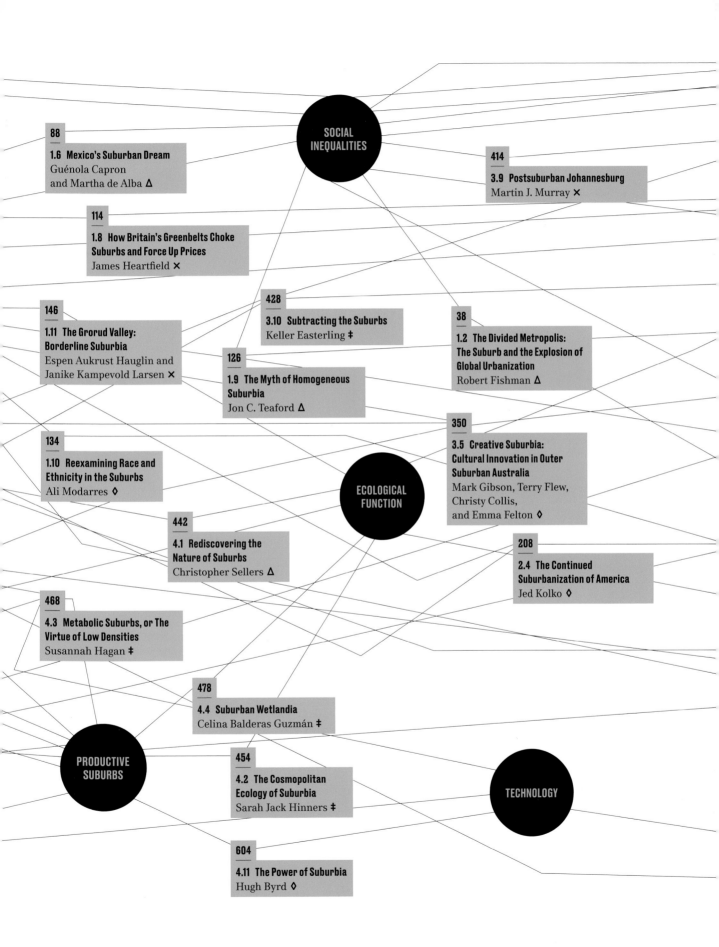

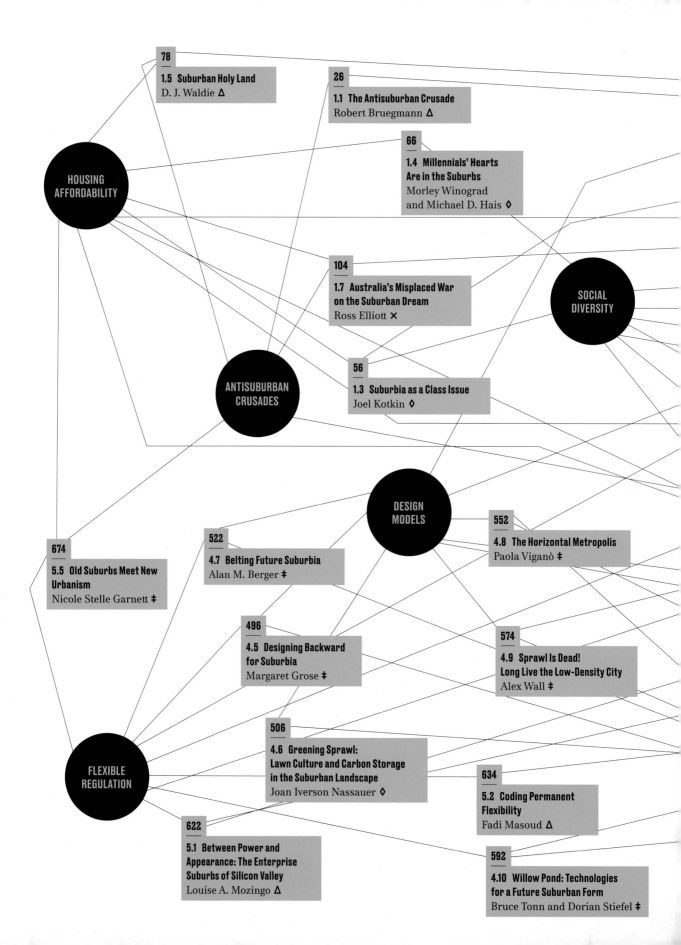

78
1.5 Suburban Holy Land
D. J. Waldie △

26
1.1 The Antisuburban Crusade
Robert Bruegmann △

66
**1.4 Millennials' Hearts
Are in the Suburbs**
Morley Winograd
and Michael D. Hais ◊

HOUSING
AFFORDABILITY

SOCIAL
DIVERSITY

104
**1.7 Australia's Misplaced War
on the Suburban Dream**
Ross Elliott ✕

ANTISUBURBAN
CRUSADES

56
1.3 Suburbia as a Class Issue
Joel Kotkin ◊

DESIGN
MODELS

552
4.8 The Horizontal Metropolis
Paola Viganò ‡

674
**5.5 Old Suburbs Meet New
Urbanism**
Nicole Stelle Garnett ‡

522
4.7 Belting Future Suburbia
Alan M. Berger ‡

496
**4.5 Designing Backward
for Suburbia**
Margaret Grose ‡

574
**4.9 Sprawl Is Dead!
Long Live the Low-Density City**
Alex Wall ‡

506
**4.6 Greening Sprawl:
Lawn Culture and Carbon Storage
in the Suburban Landscape**
Joan Iverson Nassauer ◊

FLEXIBLE
REGULATION

634
**5.2 Coding Permanent
Flexibility**
Fadi Masoud △

622
**5.1 Between Power and
Appearance: The Enterprise
Suburbs of Silicon Valley**
Louise A. Mozingo △

592
**4.10 Willow Pond: Technologies
for a Future Suburban Form**
Bruce Tonn and Dorian Stiefel ‡

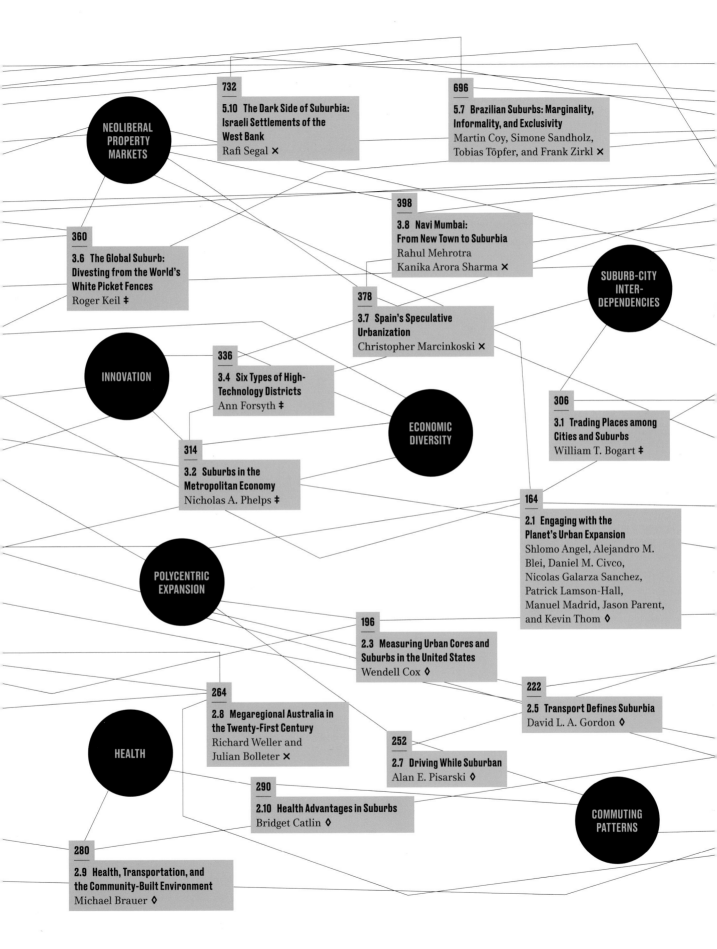

NEOLIBERAL PROPERTY MARKETS

732
5.10 The Dark Side of Suburbia: Israeli Settlements of the West Bank
Rafi Segal ✕

696
5.7 Brazilian Suburbs: Marginality, Informality, and Exclusivity
Martin Coy, Simone Sandholz, Tobias Töpfer, and Frank Zirkl ✕

398
3.8 Navi Mumbai: From New Town to Suburbia
Rahul Mehrotra
Kanika Arora Sharma ✕

SUBURB-CITY INTER-DEPENDENCIES

360
3.6 The Global Suburb: Divesting from the World's White Picket Fences
Roger Keil ‡

378
3.7 Spain's Speculative Urbanization
Christopher Marcinkoski ✕

INNOVATION

336
3.4 Six Types of High-Technology Districts
Ann Forsyth ‡

ECONOMIC DIVERSITY

306
3.1 Trading Places among Cities and Suburbs
William T. Bogart ‡

314
3.2 Suburbs in the Metropolitan Economy
Nicholas A. Phelps ‡

164
2.1 Engaging with the Planet's Urban Expansion
Shlomo Angel, Alejandro M. Blei, Daniel M. Civco, Nicolas Galarza Sanchez, Patrick Lamson-Hall, Manuel Madrid, Jason Parent, and Kevin Thom ◊

POLYCENTRIC EXPANSION

196
2.3 Measuring Urban Cores and Suburbs in the United States
Wendell Cox ◊

222
2.5 Transport Defines Suburbia
David L. A. Gordon ◊

264
2.8 Megaregional Australia in the Twenty-First Century
Richard Weller and Julian Bolleter ✕

252
2.7 Driving While Suburban
Alan E. Pisarski ◊

HEALTH

290
2.10 Health Advantages in Suburbs
Bridget Catlin ◊

COMMUTING PATTERNS

280
2.9 Health, Transportation, and the Community-Built Environment
Michael Brauer ◊

Acknowledgments

The inspiration and ideational framework for this book extend from many conversations about urbanization trends around the world and the need for better research and a more balanced approach for exploring suburban topics. The lack of a contemporary "suburban theory" to ground these discussions with our students, colleagues, and others informed the structure of the book. The curatorial nature of such an unusually large project is a combinatory effort between the three of us to include many perspectives that balance our individual knowledge and experiences.

Such a mammoth undertaking as this book would not be possible without the support of our colleagues at the MIT School of Architecture + Planning, and the MIT Norman B. Leventhal Center for Advanced Urbanism (LCAU), and especially the Leventhal Family Foundation. We are grateful for Alan Leventhal's support and leadership, and to Janet Atkins and Robert Melzer for their guidance and friendship during LCAU's launch. This book's production spanned two school deanships with Adèle Naudé Santos and Hashim Sarkis, both avid supporters of our work.

The coeditors have special acknowledgments for those who helped with intellectual trajectories, time, and resources: Alan M. Berger thanks his colleagues in the City Design and Development Program within MIT's Urban Planning Department, including Eran Ben-Joseph, Dennis Frenchman, Brent Ryan, Anne Spirn, Terry Szold, Larry Vale, and Fadi Masoud, who have supported his time codirecting LCAU over the past four years and often exchanged ideas on suburban topics; LCAU staff and researchers Prudence Robinson, Hope Stege, Alma Pellecer, Kira Intrator, Matthew Spremulli, David Birge, Sneha Mandhan, and Roi Salgueiro; Alexander D'Hooghe for early conversations about suburbia; and student research assistants Pamela Bellavita and Dennis Harvey, who helped with book production. We would also like to thank Zina Klapper for serving as our initial manuscript editor, and for insightful development of many essays.

Two courses in support of LCAU's Future of Suburbia biennial theme were held at MIT during fall 2014 and spring 2015. Twenty-two students from five different programs and four degree areas participated, including Aria Finkelstein, Claudia Bode, Joshua Eager, Ethan Lay-Sleeper, Jessica Jorge, Laura Williams, Dwight Howell, Elizabeth Galvez, Kara Elliott-Ortega, Jossie Ivanov, Dalia Munenzon, Cate Mingoya, Lizzie Yarina, Catalina Maria Picon, Tania Shamoun, Esther Chung, Bjorn Sparrman, Ellen Lohe, David Vega-Barachowitz, Jennifer Hiser, and Larisa Ovalles.

We also held a one-day workshop at MIT on the future of suburbia, with leaders in the field, including Daniel D'Oca (Interboro Partners), John Lienhard (MIT), Bradley Cantrell (Harvard-GSD), Ben Goldstein (MIT), Peter Arnold (Arid Lands Institute), Ted Nelson (Newland Real Estate Group), Sara Bronin (Center of Energy and Environmental Law, University of Connecticut), Liat Margolis (University of Toronto), Albert Saiz (MIT), Lupe Larios (United Farm Workers of America), Rafi Segal (MIT), Alex Wall (University of Virginia), Mark Weglarz (FarmedHere), Brent Ryan (MIT), Dan Adams (Northeastern University), Lorena Bello (MIT), Mary Anne Ocampo (MIT), Stephen Gray (MIT), Fred Turnier (City of Reno), and Kobi Ruthenberg. In addition, the Norman B. Leventhal Center for Advanced Urbanism would like to acknowledge and thank its members and collaborators.

We also thank the artists Matthew Niederhauser and John Fitzgerald, who collaborated with LCAU to document suburban conditions around the world in

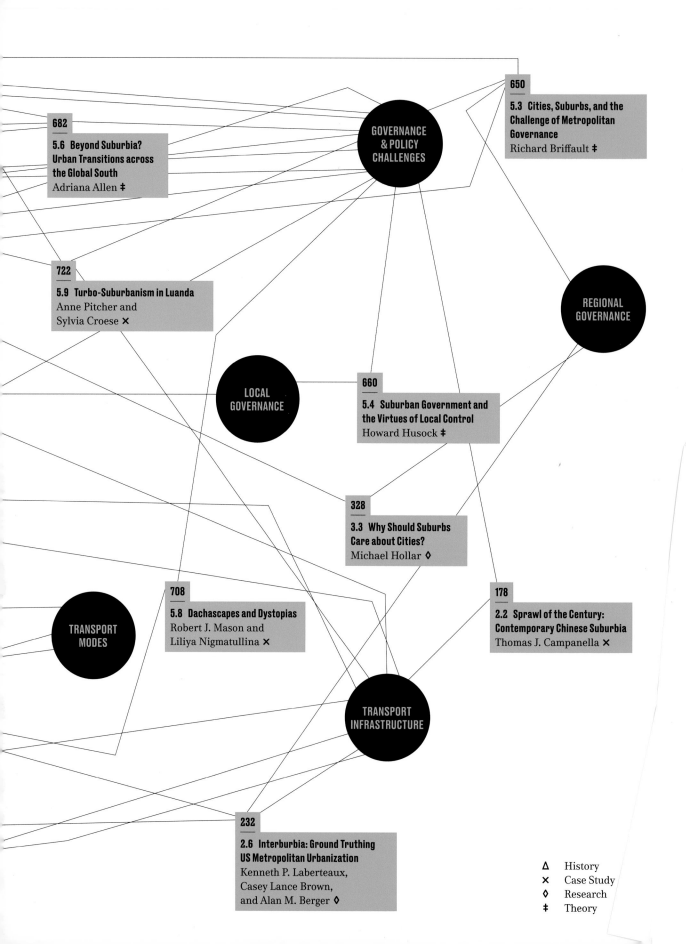

650

5.3 Cities, Suburbs, and the Challenge of Metropolitan Governance
Richard Briffault ‡

GOVERNANCE & POLICY CHALLENGES

682

5.6 Beyond Suburbia? Urban Transitions across the Global South
Adriana Allen ‡

REGIONAL GOVERNANCE

722

5.9 Turbo-Suburbanism in Luanda
Anne Pitcher and Sylvia Croese ✕

LOCAL GOVERNANCE

660

5.4 Suburban Government and the Virtues of Local Control
Howard Husock ‡

328

3.3 Why Should Suburbs Care about Cities?
Michael Hollar ◊

708

5.8 Dachascapes and Dystopias
Robert J. Mason and Liliya Nigmatullina ✕

178

2.2 Sprawl of the Century: Contemporary Chinese Suburbia
Thomas J. Campanella ✕

TRANSPORT MODES

TRANSPORT INFRASTRUCTURE

232

2.6 Interburbia: Ground Truthing US Metropolitan Urbanization
Kenneth P. Laberteaux, Casey Lance Brown, and Alan M. Berger ◊

Δ   History
✕   Case Study
◊   Research
‡   Theory

India, South Africa, China, Brazil, and the United States with aerial photography. Wherever possible, we worked with Matthew and John to capture sites discussed in our authors' essays. Some of these images are featured in full-page spreads throughout this book. With the artists, we also created four video narratives of footage that were featured in the Future of Suburbia exhibition at the MIT Media Lab in 2016. The video narratives exposed the staggering extent of suburban expansion, the polycentricity of metropolitan areas, interfaces with the natural environment, and the diversity of suburban building typologies around the world.

Joel Kotkin thanks Chapman University for its financial and intellectual contributions to the project, and its Center for Demographics and Policy for its help. This was made possible due to the vision of Chancellor Daniele Struppa and President James Doti. We also thank Christina Marshall for her assistance. Chapman students added greatly to this effort, not only with research but also by asking good questions. In particular, we would like to thank Charlie Stephens, Alicia Kurimska, Clinton Stiles-Schmidt, Nate Kaspi, Sarah Chong, Jordan Taffet, and Haley Wragg. We are also grateful for the support of our project from Joel's colleagues and the board of directors at the Center for Opportunity Urbanism.

Alan M. Berger, Joel Kotkin, and Celina Balderas Guzmán, 2017

Introduction

They have not destroyed space; they have simply rendered it infinite by the destruction of its centre (hence these infinitely extendable cities).

—Jean Baudrillard, *America*

Global urbanization is heading toward infinite suburbia. Around the world, the vast majority of people are moving to cities not to inhabit their centers but to suburbanize their peripheries.[1] Thus, when the United Nations projects the number of future "urban" residents, or when researchers quantify the amount of land that will soon be "urbanized," these figures largely reflect the unprecedented *suburban* expansion of global cities.[2] By 2030, an estimated nearly half a million square miles (1.2 million square kilometers) of land worldwide will become urbanized, especially in Asia, Africa, and Latin America.[3] In the United States alone, an additional 85,000 square miles (220,000 square kilometers) of rural land will be urbanized between 2003 and 2030.[4] Given that these figures represent the conversion of currently rural land at the urban fringe, these lands are slated to become future suburbias. Even so, many countries are already majority suburban. In the United States, 69 percent of the population lives in suburbs.[5] As late as 2010, over 75 percent of American jobs lay outside the urban core.[6] Many other developed countries are also majority-suburban. In the Global South, it is estimated 45 percent of the 1.4 billion people who become new urban residents will settle in peri-urban suburbs.[7] The sheer magnitude of land conversion taking place, coupled with the fact that the majority of the world's population already lives in suburbs, demands that new attention and creative energy be devoted to the imminent suburban expansion.

Despite all the evidence showing that the world's most prevalent and rapidly growing form of urbanization will be suburbia, the fields of Planning, and especially Design, still lack a robust, unbiased intellectual and theoretical platform to examine and debate it.[8] Not since rapid post–World War II suburban expansion in the United States was ushered in by the stewardship of landscape architecture has any design field taken the lead on suburban futures.[9] The allied Planning and Design fields have proved unable to significantly shape suburbia, which has continued unabated and in forms primarily driven by economic policies, some consumer preferences, speculation, tax policies, and lax government regulation. The results are widespread suburban models that are wasteful, unsustainable, and inequitable for many social and economic reasons, but also spreading everywhere including China, Ireland, Spain, Turkey, Panama, Dubai, Ghana, Kenya, and many other countries.

Perhaps as a reaction to our own ineffectiveness, Planning and Design have overwhelmingly vilified suburbia. As the historian Robert Bruegmann describes in "The Antisuburban Crusade," the intellectual elite has railed against suburbia primarily in three distinct waves in history, and particularly for aesthetic reasons (though the suburb has endless criticisms leveled against it). As a solution, many arguments call for a full return to high-density living, dismissing the suburbs altogether.[10] However, most of America's and many other developed countries' populations currently live in suburbs, while the developing world is undergoing massive suburbanization, too. A truly "back to the city" future, as imagined by retro-urbanists, seems highly unlikely short of imposition of draconian planning regimes.

This book is construed for an alternative discourse around suburbia that can open paths to improvement and agency,

Epigraph: Jean Baudrillard, *America* (London; New York: Verso, 1988), 99.

1   Although rarely loudly proclaimed, this phenomenon has been noted in the press as well as in scholarly literature, albeit in disparate places. One reason for the disparate sources is that global suburbanization is often called by other terms (e.g., peri-urbanization in the Global South) and studied by scholars specializing in those specific conditions. As a result, what is a global phenomenon is often divided into multiple niche topics (or specific geographies), and thus the global picture is harder to discern and figures are difficult to come by. More study on the global phenomenon is needed. Nonetheless, the dominance of suburbanization worldwide has been noted, for example, in "A Suburban World," *Economist*, December 6, 2014, http://www.economist.com/news/leaders/21635486-emerging-world-becoming-suburban-its-leaders-should-welcome-avoid-wests; Mark Clapson and Ray Hutchison, eds., *Suburbanization in Global Society* (Bingley, UK: Emerald, 2010). In 2010 the United Nations (UN) declared that "suburbanization is becoming more prevalent," and that "more and more people both in the North and South are moving outside the city to 'satellite' or dormitory cities and suburban neighborhoods." See UN-HABITAT, "State of the World's Cities 2010/2011, Bridging the Urban Divide," ix, 10–11, http://mirror.unhabitat.org/pmss/listItemDetails.aspx?publicationID=2917.

2   Within professional and popular design culture, there is a strange propagation of facts used to distort the dominance of "cities." When the UN declared that by 2030, six out of every ten

rather than condemning it altogether or trying to stop it. As Bruegmann reveals, the long history of antisuburban crusades has shown that the latter strategies always fail. Changing the discourse entails abandoning ideological biases and critically examining nuanced research on suburbia that exposes both its flaws and its opportunities. In doing so, we find that suburbia contains many opportunities to be a more productive landscape than its current condition. As the largest form of new growth and settlement globally, it is a vast frontier awaiting innovation. Suburbia could be an experimental test bed for new typological forms, environmental retrofitting, clean water, home-based employment, energy production, novel ecosystems, social programs, and many other innovations yet unimagined. Moreover, in order to find innovative solutions for suburbia, the allied Design and Planning fields need a new intellectual framework.

The *Infinite Suburbia* project began in the summer of 2014 to find the most recent, cutting-edge research on suburbia that pointed toward more productive futures. Following a literature search involving over five hundred references by a team of researchers at MIT Norman B. Leventhal Center for Advanced Urbanism, over fifty authors were invited to contribute to the publication. We allowed authors to define suburbia on their own terms. We wanted to include contrasting perspectives and have a balanced approach to show there are advantages and disadvantages to the suburban condition.

The Infinite Suburbia Roadmap

Suburbia is complex. Its production, persistence, and expansion can best be explained as a nonlinear set of interrelationships. We cannot talk about one aspect of suburbia without considering how it might affect many other social,

people would live in an urban area, and seven out of ten by 2050, they carefully defined that "there is no common global definition of what constitutes an urban settlement. As a result, the urban definition employed by national statistical offices varies widely across countries, and in some cases has changed over time within a country." See United Nations, Department of Economic and Social Affairs, Population Division, "World Urbanization Prospects: The 2014 Revision, Highlights" (United Nations, 2015), http://esa.un.org/unpd/wup/Highlights/WUP2014-Highlights.pdf. Albeit a minor conflation of language, the term *urban*, as specified by previous UN documents, was swapped out for "cities" by those outlets reporting on the UN's publications. These figures were uncritically adopted by foundations that have funded initiatives and spent hundreds of millions on this topic. See "100RC Announces Opening of 2014 100 Resilient Cities Challenge," accessed December 7, 2015, http://www.100resilientcities.org/blog/entry/. It is impossible to trace the exact origins of this conflation, but it is certainly ubiquitous now. The subtle swap in terminology has been malignant and has permeated the corporate world and popular media in an uncritical cycle of repetition. Thought leaders, such as Bill Ford, the chairman of Ford Motor Company, declared at his TED talk that 75 percent of the world will be living in cities. See Bill Ford, *A Future beyond Traffic Gridlock*, TED Talks, March 2011, https://www.ted.com/talks/bill_ford_a_future_beyond_traffic_gridlock. Hundreds of other media outlets regularly use the same statistic and incorrect language.

Consider *USA Today*'s headline "U.N.: By '09, Half the World Will Live in Cities," which incorrectly states the content of their own article and UN report! The article goes on as follows: "The (UN) report predicts that there will be 27 'megacities' with at least 10 million population by mid-century compared to 19 today, but it forecasts that at least half the urban growth in the coming decades will be in the many smaller cities with less than 500,000 people...Thus, the urban areas of the world are expected to absorb all the population growth expected over the next four decades while at the same time drawing in some of the rural population," which completely obfuscates the differences between "urban areas" and "cities." See "U.N.: By '09, Half the World Will Live in Cities," *USA Today*, February 26, 2008, http://usatoday30.usatoday.com/news/world/2008-02-26-cities-population_N.htm. Using the same family of UN reports, Fast Company reported with its own headline: "By 2050, 70 percent of the World's Population Will Be Urban. Is That a Good Thing?" The article, however, gets its content confused with terminology again, saying: "Once you get over the fact that, by 2050, both China and India will have about a billion people living in cities alone, you can mine the image for thoughtful comparison. For instance, since the 1990s, more than 75 percent of the US population has lived in cities... By 2050, somewhere between 50–75 percent of their population will live in cities." This is factually incorrect, but it is fascinating to see such a blatant misunderstanding between the use of *urban* in the headline and *cities* in all of these varied outlets. See Mark Wilson, "By 2050, 70 percent of the

World's Population Will Be Urban. Is That a Good Thing?," *Fast Company, Co.Design*, March 12, 2012, http://www.fastcodesign.com/1669244/by-2050-70-of-the-worlds-population-will-be-urban-is-that-a-good-thing.

3   Karen C. Seto, Burak Güneralp, and Lucy R. Hutyra, "Global Forecasts of Urban Expansion to 2030 and Direct Impacts on Biodiversity and Carbon Pools," *Proceedings of the National Academy of Sciences* 109, no. 40 (October 2, 2012): 16083–88.

4   Eric M. White, Anita T. Morzillo, and Ralph J. Alig, "Past and Projected Rural Land Conversion in the US at State, Regional, and National Levels," *Landscape and Urban Planning* 89, nos. 1–2 (January 30, 2009): 37–48.

5   Wendell Cox, "Measuring US Urban Cores and Suburbs," in *Infinite Suburbia* (New York: Princeton Architectural Press, 2017).

6   Elizabeth Kneebone, "Job Sprawl Stalls," Metropolitan Opportunity Series (Brookings Institute, Metropolitan Policy Program, April 2013), http://www.brookings.edu/~/media/research/files/reports/2013/04/18%20job%2sprawl%20kneebone/srvy_job sprawl.pdf.

7   Douglas Webster, *Summary of Peri-urbanization: The New Global Frontier* (Enschede, Netherlands: International Institute for Geo-Information Science and Earth Observation, 2004).

8   The start of the "suburban century" was noted in an influential article by William Schneider, "The Suburban Century Begins," *Atlantic Monthly*, July 1992, http://www.theatlantic.com/past/politics/ecbig/schnsub.htm.

9   Garrett Eckbo, Daniel Kiley, and James Rose, "Landscape Design in the Primeval Environment,"

economic, political, or ecological factors. Any study of suburbia—just as any study of urbanization at large—is not bounded by any single discipline or argument. For these reasons, instead of conforming to a linear packaging of chapters, we have chosen a more unconventional structuring of this book.

To capture the complexity and richness inherent in the book's content, we analyzed all essays to find common, reoccurring topics across authors. Initially, we identified nearly two hundred common topics creating over three hundred connections across the fifty-two essays in the book. When we mapped these topics and linked them to the book's essays, we found a rich set of interrelationships between seemingly disparate essays and topics, exposing the multidisciplinary nature of suburban studies.

We reduced the topics from two hundred to twenty-one in order to distill the most important ideas in the book. Thus, the Infinite Suburbia Roadmap was born. The Roadmap is the navigational guide to this book. It maps the book's essays and their connections to the twenty-one topics, which have been organized around five major themes: the drive for upward social mobility, polycentric metropolitan form, metropolitan economic relationships, harnessing ecological productivity, and scales of governance.

These themes are the five chapters of the book. The authors' essays are placed in the chapter that is most closely related to their theses, indicated in the Roadmap by page, chapter, and essay number, plus a symbol marking the essay type: history, case study, research, or theory. However, most essays straddle multiple themes, and the Roadmap is useful in showing the connections between one essay or topic to another. In this way, the Roadmap allows readers to take their own improvised journeys through the material, starting at a topic of interest and following the threads that unfold. We invite readers to construct unique trajectories and to form their own paths derived from the material.

Since the topics and major themes emerged organically from the book's content, they constitute the most important ideas in the book and potentially the beginnings of a new theory on suburbia. Suburbia—if not ignored altogether—has long been a niche subject within urban theory. Even when studied in its own right, suburbia has typically been geographically imagined as an extension of urban cores, which reinforces the city-suburb duality.[11] Changing such deeply embedded dualism requires envisioning suburbia not as an "explosion" away from a center but as an emergence of new centers with different, and often unique, characteristics.[12] Herein, we begin building a new theory of suburbia that is inclusive of old and new centralities. It is a theory that aims to understand the phenomenon of "complete urbanization."[13]

Related fields have parallel theories already in development. In social science, new regionalism examines the effects of regional-scale urban agglomerations in terms of economic, political, and cultural effects. New regionalism accepts the polycentric structure of modern metropolitan areas. Yet the geographer Edward Soja admits that, "unfortunately, the new regionalism in an explicit and assertive sense has remained poorly articulated in the wider literature and not well developed empirically."[14] Moreover, as a social science theory, a spatial component tends to be missing from new regionalist literature. Designers and planners need a theory that also helps to explain the spatial structure and characteristics of metropolitan areas and even larger regions to serve as a framework for agency and intervention. As many of our authors explain, little physical Design and Planning agency exists at these larger scales, even though it is one of increasing

Architectural Record 87, no. 2 (February 1940): 74–79.

10 Vishaan Chakrabarti, *A Country of Cities: A Manifesto for an Urban America* (New York: Metropolis Books, 2013).

11 Roger Keil, "Suburban," in *Urban Theory: New Critical Perspectives*, ed. Mark Jayne and Kevin Ward (London: Routledge, 2016).

12 Ibid.

13 Ibid.

14 Edward Soja, "Accentuate the Regional," *International Journal of Urban and Regional Research* 39, no. 2 (March 1, 2015): 373, doi:10.1111/1468 -2427.12176.

focus and importance in our age of environmental concerns. It is because of their horizontality that suburban surfaces still have the capacity for retrofitting large, new designed systems that can alter regional sustainability. At the same time, heavy regulatory and financial constraints in urban cores, especially the challenges of infrastructural upgrades in congested spaces, make large-scale Design and Planning an anathema.

The purpose of this book is not to unveil a fully developed new theory of suburbia; rather, our ambition is to lay out a plausible roadmap that outlines the beginnings of such a theory. We start by prioritizing contemporary issues, the critical need for larger scales of physical Design and Planning, and opening new lines of research that planners and designers interested in the physical nature of urbanization would not typically follow. We hope that other urban scholars and practitioners expand on the conversations begun in this book to eventually shape a more full-fledged theory for understanding the future of suburbia.

The Drive for Upward Social Mobility

The first chapter explores suburbia as a place of opportunity and upward social mobility for many, but also frequently a result or manifestation of social inequalities. Suburbia's power as a place of opportunity comes from its dynamic and heterogeneous nature. As Robert Fishman describes, "Nothing is more hybridized—indeed, chaotic—than morphology and land uses at the edge of a rapidly growing city." In "The Myth of Homogeneous Suburbia," Jon C. Teaford expands on the hybridity of suburbia, outlining the ways in which suburbs have been socially and economically mixed since their inception. In fact, suburbia's social diversity has radically increased over the past twenty years. Not only do 61 percent of foreign-born immigrants in America live in suburban areas of large metros, suburbia is home to more than half of all minority groups.[15] Moreover, the number of large metro areas where suburbs are majority-minority has increased from eight to sixteen since 2000.[16] In the United States, suburbs are diversifying at the national level, but the metropolitan dynamics also yield interesting insights into the movements of minority groups. In "Reexamining Race and Ethnicity in the Suburbs," Ali Modarres's research shows how minorities are continuing to move into formerly white areas in greater numbers. Where they originally inherited inner-city areas during white flight, now minorities are moving into the inner-ring suburbs vacated by white populations moving to gentrified inner-city areas. In doing so, minorities are gaining access to homeownership and amenities that enhance their quality of life.

The movement of minority groups into formerly white suburbs is more than just an American phenomenon, and adjustments need to be made to handle these migrations depending on where they are located. From Norway's Grorud Valley, outside Oslo, Espen Aukrust Hauglin and Janike Kampevold Larsen discuss in "The Grorud Valley: Borderline Suburbia" how the valley's landscape structure needs reconsideration now that new demographic groups have moved in. These groups have a different relationship to nature and recreational needs than the native Norwegians the Grorud Valley was designed for.

Contrary to popular press, millennials are also finding homes in suburbia in great numbers. Morley Winograd and Michael D. Hais, in their essay, "Millennials' Hearts Are in the Suburbs," argue that as millennials move from urban cores into suburbs, they will dramatically reshape its landscape.

And yet, while suburbia is a place of opportunity for many, it can also be the

15 Foreign-born statistic, from Jill H. Wilson and Nicole Prchal Svajlenka, "Immigrants Continue to Disperse, with Fastest Growth in the Suburbs," Brookings Institution, accessed March 5, 2015, http://www.brookings.edu/research/papers/2014/10/29-immigrants-disperse-suburbs-wilson-svajlenka; William H. Frey, "Melting Pot Cities and Suburbs: Racial and Ethnic Change in Metro America in the 2000s," State of Metropolitan America (Metropolitan Policy Program, Brookings Institute, May 2011).

16 William H. Frey, "The Rise of Melting-Pot Suburbs," Brookings Institution, May 26, 2015, http://www.brookings.edu/blogs/the-avenue/posts/2015/05/26-melting-pot-suburbs-frey.

manifestation of social inequalities of many kinds. Robert Fishman, in "The Divided Metropolis: The Suburb and the Explosion of Global Urbanization," explains the now familiar tendency to enclave the rich in suburbia, leaving the disadvantaged in the city center, as originally devised in the Anglo-Saxon model. Historically, France has done the reverse, pushing its poor to the periphery (housing them in modernist *grands ensembles*), keeping the urban core gentrified. Only Ebenezer Howard's garden city model attempts to break class divisions, but its implementation has been limited. Most other models are predicated on divisions between the rich and the poor, resulting in asymmetrical provision of infrastructure and services. Thus fragmentation in metropolitan areas arises between the rich (frequently in gated communities) and the poor (frequently in slums) that exist side by side in many developing world cities.

Mexico City is a metropolitan area known for its divisions along economic lines, in part fueled by the concerns of security and exclusivity of the upper classes. Guénola Capron and Martha de Alba's essay "Mexico's Suburban Dream" recounts how Mexico City's first middle-class suburbs emerged in the 1940s and 1950s at a time when suburbs were initially associated with poverty. They describe how the fusion of international and local architectural ideas produced the designs for the first developments, which normalized suburban middle- and upper-class development in Mexico City.

As the central parts of cities become denser, land on the fringe often provides a cheaper alternative. Housing affordability is a major driver of suburban growth, without which America risks becoming a "rentership society" with degradation of wealth and quality of life, according to Joel Kotkin in "Suburbia as a Class Issue." Kotkin argues that homeownership

is a way for Americans to achieve middle-class status, and the suburbs are the place where homes are most accessible to buyers. In "Australia's Misplaced War on the Suburban Dream," Ross Elliott explains how policymakers have sought to increase density in the urban cores by creating aggressive tax policies to curb suburban expansion, leading to record high property prices that have made it impossible for young first-time home-buyers to buy. Similarly, in the United Kingdom, strict greenbelt and rural development policies have created social costs in the form of poor housing quality and high housing prices, as explained by James Heartfield in "How Britain's Greenbelts Choke Suburbs and Force Up Prices." As Joel Kotkin reminds us, there will always be people who prefer suburban living. Kotkin and other authors see suburbanization as an innate human desire (most likely for privacy and ownership) that may be repressed, but will burgeon when given the opportunity.

Yet as suburbia has offered homeownership, amenities, and higher quality of life for the masses, the elite have consistently voiced strong opposition to suburbs:

> There are major problems with suburban development including everything from the cost of providing services to the problem of protecting species habitat. But it is hard to avoid the conclusion that the existing criticism has, more often than not, been based on traditional aesthetic notions about "proper" urban form deeply rooted in the model of the traditional European city, with its focus of power and authority at the center.[17]

While there are many valid criticisms of suburbia, Robert Bruegmann in "The Antisuburban Crusade" explains that the heart of the criticisms tend to rest on the elites' judgments of suburban aesthetics and taste, often leading to negative

17 Robert Bruegmann, "The Antisuburban Crusade," in *Infinite Suburbia* (New York: Princeton Architectural Press, 2017), 57.

characterizations about suburban neighborhoods and their residents. We rarely hear the voices of suburban residents themselves. In the rare personal narrative "Suburban Holy Land," the author D. J. Waldie shares his perspective of being a lifelong resident of Lakewood, California, a tract-house suburb that originally offered working-class families a chance to own a home and have a new life. And yet, places such as these are described as the "anti-place" or "where evil dwells" by some elite urban critics.

Polycentric Metropolitan Form

This second chapter explores the sheer scale of suburban expansion in the United States and the world, the characteristics of polycentric metropolitan areas, and the implications of this condition on mobility. For many decades, suburbia has been the predominant fabric in the United States, as well as in other countries. But exactly how much of the world is suburban? Although suburbia is the most prevalent form of urbanization, it is notoriously difficult to measure. One issue is the multiplicity of definitions of suburbia.[18] There are no universal categorizations of suburbia that define its geography. Although the term *principal city* is used by the United States Office of Management and Budget as an attempt to designate urban cores, many of our authors argue that it is inaccurate because principal cities often include places that are a mix of high and low densities (such as Irvine or Tustin, California), and often function more like suburbs than traditional core cities.[19] Instead, our authors have sought to create their own ways of capturing suburbia. David L. A. Gordon, in "Transport Defines Suburbia," discusses his pioneering methodology to more precisely categorize suburbia based on transportation modes in Canada, finding that 67 percent of the population lives in suburbs. Wendell Cox, in "Measuring

US Cores and Suburbs in the United States," also uses Gordon's methodology, finding that approximately 69 percent of the American population is suburban, 14 percent urban, and 17 percent exurban. Clearly, the vast majority of America lives in suburbia.

What kind of architecture exists in suburbia? The American Housing Survey of 2013 found that 64 percent of all occupied American homes are single-family structures.[20] Jed Kolko's analysis of suburban housing in "The Continued Suburbanization of America" shows that household growth in the United States between mid-2011 and 2014 was growing the fastest at 5.3 percent in the lowest density neighborhoods in the United States. In the same time period, urban neighborhoods grew by 2.5 percent and all suburbs by 3.1 percent. The production of this housing type, and more important, its infrastructural and landscape needs, does not appear to be slowing.

Spanning the globe, Shlomo Angel and colleagues analyze a sample of 4,245 cities, primarily in developing countries where 95 percent of future urban growth will occur. Their analysis in "Engaging with the Planet's Urban Expansion" shows that these cities between 1990 and 2000 physically expanded at an annual rate of 3.6 percent, while population growth was 1.6 percent. This horizontal growth translates to residential density declining worldwide at a rate of 2.1 percent per year. Their pending results for 2000 to 2014 suggest continued declining densities and quite drastic decreases in some developing cities such as Accra, Ghana. Angel concludes that denying suburban expansion (or peri-urbanization) leads to worse outcomes than planning for it. "Urban expansion," Angel warned in *Planet of Cities*, "must be prepared for in advance or not at all."[21]

Around the world, China's suburban development has far outpaced any

18 Ann Forsyth, "Defining Suburbs," *Journal of Planning Literature* 27, no. 3 (August 2012): 270.

19 US Census Bureau, Metropolitan and Micropolitan Statistical Areas Main, http://www.census.gov/population/metro/; http://www.census.gov/population/metro/data/def.html.

20 United States Census, "Table C-01-AH, American Housing Survey," 2013, http://www.census.gov/programs-surveys/ahs/data.html.

21 Shlomo Angel, *Planet of Cities* (Cambridge, MA: Lincoln Institute of Land Policy, 2012), 7.

other country's. According to Thomas J. Campanella in "Sprawl of the Century: Contemporary Chinese Suburbia," China's urban footprint in the 1990s increased by an area ten times that of New York City. However, he notes important differences between American and Chinese suburbia, namely, that China's suburban development and urban cores are more closely unified.

Most of the past century's suburban expansion would not have been possible without transportation infrastructure. The resultant system is dominated by automobiles and roads as the primary means of mobility. Today, the largest segment of American commuters move between two suburbs (rather than from suburb to city center), and nearly 80 percent drive alone. Alan E. Pisarski's "Driving While Suburban" shares quantitative evidence to reveal how commuting patterns are becoming increasingly complex, interacting across scales from the local to the regional, and often extending across state lines. The spatial implications of these new commuting patterns are coined into a new term *Interburbia* in the essay by Kenneth P. Laberteaux, Casey L. Brown, and Alan M. Berger titled "Interburbia: Ground Truthing US Metropolitan Urbanization." Their case studies of Denver and Atlanta outline the need for infrastructural investment that targets inter-suburban connections—where almost everyone is driving—and argues for major changes to regional governance and federal support necessary to implement metropolitan-scale transport plans, noting that most funding goes to the wrong problem.

As these new commuting patterns make clear, the vast global suburban expansion has forced a reconsideration of the regional structure of metropolitan areas, moving away from models of radial expansion away from the historic urban core toward those that acknowledge the

growing polycentricity of metropolitan areas. In the United States, the concept of polycentric metropolis was first introduced by the geographer Jean Gottmann in his 1961 book, *Megalopolis*, which focused on the Northeast corridor of the United States.[22] Regionalism later became another framework to understand metropolitan areas. In Europe, other scholars, such as Thomas Sieverts, proposed concepts such as the *Zwischenstadt* to describe the extensive, nonhierarchical expansion characteristic in Europe.[23] For Southeast Asia, Terry McGee termed the highly mixed-use peripheries of cities like Jakarta *desakota*.[24] Richard Weller and Julian Bolleter offer a new design vision for a future polycentric metropolitan fabric based on regional-scale transport in "Megaregional Australia in the Twenty-First Century." Acknowledging continuing high levels of population growth in Australia and the insufficiency of infill development, they propose an extended urban area where major cities and smaller settlements of 1.2 million people are linked together by high-speed rail with interwoven productive landscapes.

Several authors mention electric or autonomous vehicles as a potentially revolutionary change in suburbia. Michael Brauer in "Health, Transportation, and the Community-Built Environment" mentions that such technologies could substantially reduce vehicle air pollution, as well as the health impacts of noise. Echoing air quality and transportation concerns, Bridget Catlin, in "Health Advantages in Suburbs," explains that at the county level, suburbs have the highest levels of particulate matter and long commutes compared with urban and rural counties. Yet she also notes that in the County Health Rankings study, suburbs rank the highest in ten out of twenty-nine measures. The study exposes differences between urban, suburban, and rural health outcomes and behaviors. For

22 Jean Gottmann, *Megalopolis: The Urbanized Northeastern Seaboard of the United States* (New York: Twentieth Century Fund, 1961).

23 Thomas Sieverts, *Cities without Cities: An Interpretation of the Zwischenstadt* (London; New York: Spon Press, 2003).

24 T. G. McGee, "The Emergence of Desakota Regions in Asia: Expanding a Hypothesis," in *The Extended Metropolis: Settlement Transition in Asia*, ed. Norton Ginsburg, Bruce Koppel, and T. G. McGee (Honolulu: University of Hawaii Press, 1991), 3–25.

example, it is rural counties that have the highest levels of obesity and physical activity, not suburbs, as so many prejudiced urbanists and New Urbanists have purposefully misstated.[25]

If autonomous vehicle technology was adopted at a large scale in metropolitan areas, then some of suburbia's biggest negative impacts could be diminished. However, the improved efficiency of autonomous vehicles and the cut in commute times may drive suburban expansion even farther afield, as may already be the case in terms of home-based telecommuting. Some speculate that even more remote areas could be brought into the metropolitan fold.[26] More research is needed to understand the potential impacts of autonomous vehicles on metropolitan structure.

Metropolitan Economic Interrelationships

The economic complexity and significance of suburbs is often underestimated. This chapter explores the economic diversity, interconnectedness of suburbs to urban cores, and how economic policy can have substantial impacts on the spatial form of suburbs. William T. Bogart presents a theoretical essay on cities and suburbs in "Trading Places among Cities and Suburbs," describing how cities and suburbs engage in the exchange of goods and services within the metropolitan area. In "Why Should Suburbs Care about Cities?" Michael Hollar finds quantitative evidence of the economic links between urban cores and suburbs, finding that the economies of urban cores and suburbs within a metropolitan area will grow or shrink together unless they are highly specialized around one industry.

Within metropolitan areas, suburbs are economic powerhouses where the vast majority of jobs are located. Nicholas A. Phelps's essay, "Suburbs in the Metropolitan Economy," offers a nuanced look at economic activities in different kinds of suburbs, from new suburbs to inner-ring suburbs, airports, and shopping malls. Centering on one of these activities, Ann Forsyth's "Six Types of High Technology Districts" outlines the ways that such economic districts can be planned for long-term sustainability.

Mark Gibson and colleagues offer another example of suburban economic diversity and how suburbs can fuel innovation in "Creative Suburbia: Cultural Innovation in Outer Suburban Australia," which presents primary research on creative workers. Since the advent of the so-called creative class concept, investment has been pouring into urban cores, which are presumed to be hotbeds of creativity and innovation. Gibson and colleagues show that creativity in suburbs is significant and neglected. From their research, we learn that creative workers greatly value the suburbs for housing affordability, space and tranquility, amenities, and the high level of social diversity that spurs creativity. Interestingly, some of the creative workers interviewed stated that they preferred working in the suburbs because they were freer from the "pressures to conform" that "inhibit creative freedom" they would otherwise be subjected to in urban cores, which they allude to being more socially homogeneous.

With globalization, neoliberal economic policy has expanded throughout the world. Roger Keil, in "The Global Suburb: Divesting from the World's White Picket Fences," describes neoliberalism as "the privatization of economic decision-making and responsibilities over collective solutions" and lists the outcomes as increased economic segregation, boundaries between public and private spaces, and the commodification of sustainability through "green developments" such as those that New Urbanism claims as sustainable.

Multiple case studies illustrate the results of economic policies on spatial

25 As "Honorary Chair" of the Congress for the New Urbanism's 2009 and 2012 meetings, respectively, the noted urban health researchers Howard Frumkin and Richard Jackson have served as CNU's plenary speakers. Their bias was noted by the author of a critique of Frumkin and his author group in a 2012 book review from the *Berkeley Planning Journal*. The reviewer states that a "lack of clarity" pervades the book and makes the reader wonder "if they are getting the whole story" (249). The review goes on to call some of the content "overly deterministic" by jumping past the "complex web" of causation (249). For the review, see William Riggs, "Making Healthy Places: Designing and Building for Health, Well-Being, and Sustainability," *Berkeley Planning Journal* 25, no. 1 (January 2012): 248–51; original publication in Andrew L. Dannenberg, Howard Frumkin, and Richard J. Jackson, eds., *Making Healthy Places: Designing and Building for Health, Well-Being, and Sustainability* (Washington, DC: Island Press, 2012). See also the following quote by new urbanist Ellen Durham Jones: "Dr. Frumkin's work and that of his CDC colleagues have helped recognize the links between automobile-dependent development patterns and obesity, chronic diseases, injuries, and air and water quality degradation... The confluence today of the economic crisis, health-care crisis, and environmental crisis mean we can't afford to return to gas-guzzling development patterns." The Eighteenth Annual Congress for New Urbanism, titled "New Urbanism: Rx for Healthy Places" (which took place on May 19–22, 2010 in Atlanta, Georgia), explored links between development patterns and health. Available

form. Martin J. Murray, in "Postsuburban Johannesburg," explains the concept of real estate capitalism, whereby Johannesburg's suburban form and governance is dictated by private interests. Christopher Marcinkoski, in "Spain's Speculative Urbanization," tells a cautionary tale of how urbanization and infrastructure building were "instrumentalized" into an economic development tool in Spain, resulting in extensive ghost towns and underutilized infrastructure. In "Navi Mumbai: From New Town to Suburbia," Rahul Mehrotra and Kanika Arora Sharma discuss how a lack of regional planning and specific economic policies in Mumbai led to the dissolution of the original vision for Navi Mumbai. Originally intended to be an independent satellite city near Mumbai, Navi Mumbai instead became a bedroom suburb.

In the United States, a recent and palpable example of economic policy and spatial form is the foreclosure crisis of 2010, whereby the image of suburbs became associated with large areas of abandoned homes. Partly a response to this crisis, Keller Easterling, in "Subtracting the Suburbs," speculates on how relationships between spatial form and economic policy can be reconfigured to conserve the value and wealth of suburbs in times of flux. She describes a theoretical set of rules that interrelates "building and un-building" across the full fabric of cities and suburbs, which could also create resiliency in the face of new stressors such as flooding and sea-level rise.

Harnessing Ecological Productivity
The large amounts of landscape surface in suburbia create the greatest opportunity for sustainability through retrofitting and different forms of ecological production. With today's pressing challenges of climate change and natural resource constraints, this chapter exposes the ecological and productive potential of suburbs. In "The Cosmopolitan Ecology of Suburbia," Sarah Jack Hinners describes suburbs as "novel ecosystems" that are "more heterogeneous and dynamic over space and time than natural ecosystems…loci of novelty and innovation." She explains that the combination of differentiated suburban lawns (where each neighbor plants according to his or her preferences) and patches of native ecosystems of a certain minimum size has been found to yield higher biodiversity for certain species than purely native habitats alone. Other ecologists have come to similar conclusions. In the book *Welcome to Subirdia*, the ornithologist and urban ecologist John M. Marzluff finds in a study of the Seattle metropolitan area that bird diversity peaks in suburbs due to the availability of many different habitats, which echoes the ecologist Robert Blair's earlier work.[27] While undoubtedly some species will simply vanish, Hinners acknowledges, "We don't have all the answers yet, because we are still in the middle of the experiment." We see this as one of the great opportunities of suburbia's youth and open-endedness: suburban experiments can be designed to maximize biodiversity potential as well as the production of many other kinds of ecologically derived needs, such as clean and renewable energy generation, water storage, air filtration, and the metabolizing of wastes.

Landscape architects and architects have constructed many models to conceptualize the design of a future productive suburb. In "Metabolic Suburbs, or The Virtue of Low Densities," Susannah Hagan outlines how suburbs can be used to grow food and fuel, clean water, modify microclimates, and save and generate energy. Celina Balderas Guzmán, in "Suburban Wetlandia," elaborates on the potential for constructed wetlands in suburbia to improve water quality and

online at http://cnu
.civicactions.net/cnu
-news/2009/12/cdc's
-dr-howard-frumkin
-named-honorary-chair
-cnus-18th-congress.
See also Chakrabarti,
A Country of Cities.
26 Joseph Coughlin and
Luke Yoquinto, "The
Long Road Home,"
Slate, May 19, 2015,
http://www.slate.com
/articles/technology
/future_tense/2015
/05/autonomous_cars
_and_the_future_of
_the_commute.html.
27 John M. Marzluff,
*Welcome to Subirdia:
Sharing Our Neighbor-
hoods with Wrens,
Robins, Woodpeckers,
and Other Wildlife*
(New Haven, CT: Yale
University Press,
2014); Libby Sander,
"'Subirdia,'" *Chronicle of
Higher Education* 61,
no. 5 (October 3, 2014):
7; Robert B. Blair and
Elizabeth M. Johnson,
"Suburban Habitats
and Their Role for Birds
in the Urban-Rural
Habitat Network: Points
of Local Invasion and
Extinction?," *Landscape
Ecology* 23, no. 10
(September 30, 2008):
1157–69.

resiliency in metropolitan areas at large. Margaret Grose emphasizes the need to reduce unintended consequences and break disciplinary silos to arrive at better ecologically productive designs. She outlines three new conceptual techniques in "Designing Backward for Suburbia." Joan Iverson Nassauer shows how carbon sequestration by large trees in suburbia can be increased through specific development layouts, whose viability she explores through developer and homeowner preferences in "Greening Sprawl: Lawn Culture and Carbon Storage in the Suburban Landscape."

Christopher Sellers, in "Rediscovering the Nature of Suburbia," explores another antisuburban crusade, the one aimed specifically at the environment. He notes the irony of environmental critiques against suburbia today, given that the history of the environmental movement was born in the suburbs, specifically out of a desire to protect the nature enveloping suburban neighborhoods. He notes how the wealthy have always had access to lush, vegetated suburban settings, which offer better health for residents and improved ecological outcomes over the long-term. In contrast, the working class is often relegated to areas with smaller lot sizes and less vegetation, which offers them fewer health and environmental benefits.

Alex Wall, Paola Viganò, and Alan M. Berger present design models that integrate ecology into the megalopolis scale of many contemporary urban areas. Wall proposes the concept of a low-density city as a sustainable megalopolis, with high- and low-density areas and ecological areas to promote circular metabolism and ecosystem services in "Sprawl Is Dead! Long Live the Low-Density City." Viganò's "The Horizontal Metropolis" explores three examples in Europe to show how dispersed networks of water, transportation, and energy can create new hybrid spaces of multifunctionality. In

"Belting Future Suburbia," Berger revamps the outdated concept of the greenbelt into "wastebelts," or highly functional landscapes that consolidate and metabolize wastes from urban cores and suburbs and form regional connective tissues between polycentric developments. Unlike the greenbelt, the wastebelt allows metropolitan areas to continue horizontally expanding, but uses the dross of expansion to build an eloquent and sophisticated armature for environmental functions.

Harnessing the ecological productivity of suburbia will entail rethinking the way we currently use common open spaces, private lawns, and even building surfaces. Hugh Byrd, in "The Power of Suburbia," offers quantitative research on Auckland (a predominately suburban New Zealand city similar to American cities) to show how rooftop solar power in suburbia (due largely to the greater exposure of rooftops per capita) could be substantial enough to power not just suburbia but the whole metropolitan region.

Also focusing on technology, Bruce Tonn and Dorian Stiefel, in "Willow Pond: Technologies for a Future Suburban Form," offer a sociotechnological scenario of a retrofitted suburb in 2050 where climate change and volatile energy and labor markets have forced suburban neighborhoods to assemble into self-sufficient communities. Tonn and Stiefel sketch the myriad of agricultural, manufacturing, building, energy, and ecological technologies that will allow suburbs to become independent centers of production.

Ultimately, the advantage of suburbs with regard to productivity is the vast availability of space, which makes it possible to interweave functions and landscapes at a scale large enough to be effective yet in proximity to people. To accomplish this, new governance models will be needed.

Scales of Governance

Many of the issues raised up to this point in the book can be traced back to short-comings of the regulation and governance systems that underlie suburbia's form and function. In this chapter, authors outline the need for more flexible forms of regulation to improve and capitalize on suburbia's strengths. Suburbia is ripe for experimentation in part because it represents a tabula rasa with "no past, no precedent, no settled conventions," as noted by the journalist David Brooks.[28] Additionally, this chapter discusses the advantages and disadvantages to local versus regional metropolitan governance. The scale of governance is increasingly debated as issues of regional importance have emerged but the relevant governance mechanisms may not be present to address them.

Innovations in suburbia are extinguished by restricting rules and form-based code types of regulations. In "Between Power and Appearance: The Enterprise Suburbs of Silicon Valley," Louise A. Mozingo recounts how Silicon Valley's suburban zoning strategies created flexibility in building typologies that allowed businesses to flourish. Many authors argue that if suburbia is to evolve, it must accommodate new forms of production, with more flexible codes that incorporate ecological thinking. Fadi Masoud, in "Coding Permanent Flexibility," exposes how America's suburban single-use zoning tradition is based on early ecological ideas, which claim that "end states" are possible. Today, ecological thought has outgrown that notion and instead emphasizes the dynamic, ever-changing nature of ecosystems. Masoud outlines the ways that designers could explore some of these principles to create process-based codes intended to help neighborhoods adapt as ecological imperatives change.

What should the scale of governance be for metropolitan areas today? This is one of most intensely debated questions being played out in metro areas globally, as suburban areas have accumulated new wealth and inequality gaps have broadened. Depleted urbanized cores now want to share in that wealth by changing their governance structures to capture outlying suburbs. Whether or not regional or local governance is the answer to entrenched problems of social inequality, economic development, transportation planning, and environmental protection is unanswered, but is explored as part of our emerging suburban theory. On the local governance side, Howard Husock, in "Suburban Government and the Virtues of Local Control," explains the multitude of ways that independence can create healthy competition between municipalities in America. On the regional governance side, Richard Briffault, in "Cities, Suburbs, and the Challenge of Metropolitan Governance," exposes the social inequalities that emerge in fragmented metropolitan areas. Unfortunately, regional government as a model has largely failed in America, and few scholars seem convinced that it is possible to implement successfully. Instead, Briffault recommends regional governance instead of regional government, whereby agencies and partnerships are created for specific functions. Important questions remain as to which functions should be governed by regional bodies and which should be left to local governments.

Globally, governance is a major stumbling block to equitable and sustainable metropolitan planning as seen in our case studies. Martin Coy and colleagues explain the difficulties of planning at the macro-metropolitan scale in "Brazilian Suburbs: Marginality, Informality, and Exclusivity." In spite of authorities in Brazil creating agencies at this scale, they have failed to produce meaningful change due to institutional weakness, struggles about

28 David Brooks, *On Paradise Drive: How We Live Now (and Always Have) in the Future Tense* (New York: Simon & Schuster, 2004), 48; as noted in Jamie Peck, "Neoliberal Suburbanism: Frontier Space," *Urban Geography* 32, no. 6 (2011): 892.

responsibilities, political conflicts, and lack of democratic legitimization. Robert J. Mason and Liliya Nigmatullina's case study of Moscow, "Dachascapes and Dystopias," describes Russia's emerging suburbanization, noting how regional planning could secure better outcomes in terms of transport infrastructure, emissions, and local food production. In post–civil war Angola, the government funds large-scale housing projects for the working class in the periphery of Luanda with oil revenues, but fails to provide the necessary transport infrastructure to connect them to the urban core and financing mechanisms for low-income buyers. In the end, the housing shortage in Luanda persists, according to Anne Pitcher and Sylvia Croese in "Turbo-Suburbanism in Luanda."

Designers and planners may come up with more sustainable models and planning strategies for development, but how do we ensure that they are uniformly implemented across social classes? This difficulty is explained in "Beyond Suburbia? Urban Transitions across the Global South," where Adriana Allen describes how three common planning strategies for promoting sustainability in peri-urban areas in the Global South result in sustainability for the rich at the expense of the poor. Given that working classes are more numerous worldwide, meaningful change with regards to sustainability will only happen if it affects all sectors of society.

In a similar vein, Nicole Stelle Garnett, in "Old Suburbs Meet New Urbanism," explains the repercussions of New Urbanist form-based code on struggling inner-ring suburbs, which she conceives as another example of elite imposition of aesthetics. Form-based code is frequently touted as a pathway to urban regeneration, but she explains how it comes with high costs that inner-ring suburbs may not be able to bear.

Finally, Rafi Segal describes how governance mechanisms can have a direct physical manifestation. "The Dark Side of Suburbia: Israeli Settlements of the West Bank" describes how mountaintop Israeli suburbs in the West Bank are designed to reinforce territorial control and surveillance of Palestinian villages in the valleys below. This narrative of power and control is revealed through stunning drawings and photographs in his essay.

The Future Polycentric Metropolis

Suburbia's homogeneity is soundly rebutted in Jon C. Teaford's "The Myth of Homogeneous Suburbia," where he explains that "suburbia has not been a world apart from the metropolitan norm. Instead, it has been, and is, a diverse reflection of the heterogeneous world of the modern metropolis." Passages such as this remind us that the homogeneity often attributed to suburban environments comes from outsider's views of one dimension or fixated scales.

Arguably, suburbia's most digestible scale is the mesoscale, which tends to capture coherent neighborhood forms, such as the aerial obliques of the photographer William Garnett. It is plausible, through this angled view, that suburbia appears predominately homogeneous. Yet at larger and smaller scales, a vast heterogeneity exists. The heterogeneity of suburbia is a concept that arises time and time again in these essays and demands strong consideration in our developing theory: from wildlife biodiversity to social diversity, to myriad economic activities, to the multiplicity of typologies worldwide. Whether it is Hinners referring to suburbs ecologically or Keil referring to suburbs socially and typologically, both agree that suburbs are "new assemblages."

With vast global suburban expansion the polycentric metropolis unfolds, and a new convergence between urban cores and suburbs persists. As Keil states, "There are no essential differences anymore between centers and suburbs. The suburban is not a derivative."[29] Bruegmann rightly calls this phenomenon of convergence one of the ironies of the "triumph of the city" movement and the criticism of the suburbs.[30] While city centers have grown more affluent, they have also grown more socially and economically homogeneous, while suburbs are rapidly diversifying. Suburbs are experimenting with new models of sustainability, some recoding to increase pockets of density, while struggling to retain affordability. Simultaneously, many urban cores are accumulating either vacant lots or luxury high rises, squeezing out socioeconomically disadvantaged populations. There is an economic reversal happening, as Phelps argues: "American suburbs present a potentially immense laboratory in which to observe the remaking of the suburban economy, in which not only will suburbs become more urban in certain respects, but also, cities may acquire suburban attributes." Because each urban form presents advantages and disadvantages, it is not a matter of choosing one over the other. Rather, it is about exploiting the potential of each to optimize polycentric metropolitan areas.

For the landscape architect Frederick Law Olmsted, designer of several iconic suburban neighborhoods and city plans, suburbs were a natural progression of urbanization:

> It thus becomes evident that the present outward tendency of town populations is not so much an ebb as a higher rise of the same flood...It would appear then, that the demands of suburban life, with reference to civilized refinement, are not to be a retrogression from, but an advance upon, those which are characteristic of town life, and that *no great town can long exist without great suburbs.* (italics added)[31]

Olmsted challenges us to make great suburbs in order to envision the true potential of full urban life, a challenge that is even more imperative today than it was in 1868.

Alan M. Berger, Joel Kotkin, and Celina Balderas Guzmán, 2017

29 Keil, "Suburban."
30 Edward L Glaeser, *Triumph of the City: How Our Greatest Invention Makes Us Richer, Smarter, Greener, Healthier, and Happier* (New York: Penguin Press, 2011).
31 Frederick Law Olmsted, *Preliminary Report upon the Proposed Suburban Village at Riverside, Near Chicago* (New York: Sutton, Bowne, 1868), 7.

1

DRIVE FOR UPWARD SOCIAL MOBILITY

1.1
THE ANTISUBURBAN CRUSADE

Robert Bruegmann

ANTISUBURBAN CRUSADES

SOCIAL INEQUALITIES

Imagine that intelligent visitors from another planet were to visit earth several centuries hence to try to piece together the history of the vanished people who had inhabited the place in the twentieth century. They might well be perplexed by a good deal of the writing about urban development they would find in the ruins of the places earthlings called libraries. Perhaps the most confounding feature would be the vitriol heaped on the suburbs. After all, it was in the twentieth century that, for the first time in earthly history, ordinary families from the middle and working classes gained the wherewithal to move into their own homes in cities and suburbs, something almost exclusively the privilege of the rich and powerful. And move they did, in substantial numbers, all across the globe, as soon as they were able and mostly to suburbia.

Our visitors might have imagined that this suburbanization had been seen as a vast democratization of the landscape and a good thing, but they would soon discover that this was not the opinion of many of the architects, planners, intellectuals, and tastemakers of the day. They would find passages such as this one from the celebrated architectural and social critic Lewis Mumford from his famous book, *The City in History*, published in 1961:

> Whilst the suburb served only a favored minority it neither spoiled the countryside nor threatened the city. But now that the drift to the outer ring has become a mass movement, it tends to destroy the value of both environments without producing anything but a dreary substitute, devoid of form and even more devoid of the original suburban values…A new kind of community was produced which caricatured both the historic city and the archetypal suburban refuge: a multitude of uniform unidentifiable houses, lined up inflexibly, at uniform distances, on uniform roads, in

a treeless communal waste, inhabited by people of the same class, the same income, the same age group, witnessing the same television performances, eating the same tasteless prefabricated foods, from the same freezers, conforming in every respect to a common mold.[1]

What would our visitors make of this thunderbolt hurled from America's intellectual Mount Olympus? Mumford, after all, didn't live in the city when this book was published. He was what we would now consider an exurbanite, living in bucolic Amenia, New York, a place even more far-flung and lower in density than a suburb, but one that was conspicuously located on the suburban commuter train line that ran directly to Grand Central Terminal in New York City through some of America's wealthiest neighborhoods in Westchester County. Why would Mumford, who had for years been calling for decongesting and decentralizing the city, have been so vociferous when he saw it actually happening on a massive scale?

Clearly Mumford didn't like the form suburbanization had taken, what he described elsewhere in *The City in History* as "sprawl and shapelessness" or even as an "anti-city."[2] He had long called for the decongestion of the very high densities found in most industrial cities, but he envisioned the move of families out of the city into well-defined nodes of commerce and residence on the model of the British garden city; places that, he imagined, combined the economic and cultural advantages of the city with the light and air and healthy living he associated with the country. Instead, the massive development out of the city that he saw from the train into Manhattan took the form of low-density subdivisions, engulfing vast areas around New York as they did every other American city—creating what his friend the British urbanist Sir Patrick Geddes called *conurbations*.[3] He

1   Lewis Mumford, *The City in History* (New York: Harcourt, Brace & World, 1961), 506.
2   Mumford, *The City in History*.
3   Sir Patrick Geddes, "The Population Map and Conurbations," in *Cities in Evolution* (London: Williams & Norgate, 1949), 9–21.

considered it an affront to everything he believed in: an ugly and wasteful pattern that lacked the advantages of either city or country.

But that doesn't explain the degree of anger in the condemnation that poured from his pen. His image of automatons eating frozen dinners in identical kitchens in identical suburban houses is more than just a gross exaggeration. It suggests a man deeply out of sympathy with much of what he saw in the modern, middle-class world around him. And for someone who had the luxury of not having to buy groceries, cook his own meals, or even have a driver's license (he counted on his wife to do most of the shopping, cooking, and driving), his castigation of millions of Americans who lived in single-family houses, drove automobiles, watched television, and appreciated the convenience of frozen food appears mean-spirited, and uncomprehending.

Mumford's response to suburbia and suburbanites was not an isolated phenomenon. It echoes the laments of a long list of members of the Western world's twentieth-century intellectual elite—for example, the novelists Sinclair Lewis and F. Scott Fitzgerald. In *The Great Gatsby*, Fitzgerald referred to the "bored sprawling swollen towns beyond the Ohio."[4] The critic H. L. Mencken in 1922 coined the term *booboisie*, for what he saw as a poorly informed and culturally illiterate working- and middle-class American population.[5] Over the years the arguments against the suburbs have waxed and waned, and they have taken on many different forms. There have been arguments claiming that the suburbs are economically inefficient, that they are socially reprehensible, and that they are environmentally damaging. But even as these arguments have changed and mutated, there has been a constant set of class-based biases and aesthetic assumptions that has clearly been the foundation

on which much of the criticism of suburbia has rested.

In my book *Sprawl: A Compact History*, published in 2006, I described three main stages in the criticism of suburbia and sprawl in the twentieth century, corresponding with three boom periods of growth.[6] During each boom period suburban growth accelerated and the anger against it mounted, only to subside when development slowed. Of course, none of these campaigns had much effect in stopping the suburban growth and sprawl increasingly seen all over the world because the desire to move outward to lower-density and greener environments continues to attract families worldwide. Since my book appeared, there has been a further twist in the story of the antisuburban crusade. For a short period there was the thought that the economic downturn of 2008 had finally, at long last, demonstrated that the critics were right all along when a large number of suburban houses went into foreclosure. Some critics were gleefully predicting rusting SUVs sitting in front of abandoned McMansions when families in the far-flung suburbs realized their folly and decided that they could no longer afford to commute so far for work and other daily activities.[7] But already by 2015 this point of view appears to be just the latest instance in a long tradition of wishful thinking.

Three Periods of the Antisuburban Crusades

Although there has been criticism of suburbia for centuries, this criticism only seems to have become intense when, as a consequence of the increase in wealth generated by the industrial revolution, a sizeable part of society had become affluent enough to move there.[8] For this reason, it is not surprising that the first period of intense criticism of the suburbs took place in Britain in the twentieth century in the years between the two world

4   F. Scott Fitzgerald, *The Great Gatsby* (New York: Charles Scribner's Sons, 1925), 137.

5   Henry Lewis Mencken, *Prejudices* (New York: Alfred A. Knopf, 1922).

6   Robert Bruegmann, *Sprawl: A Compact History* (Chicago: University of Chicago Press, 2005); John Archer, *Architecture and Suburbia from English Villa to American Dream House, 1690–2000* (Minneapolis: University of Minnesota Press, 2005), 291–329.

7   For an example of this literature, see Christopher Leinberger, "The Death of the Fringe Suburb," *New York Times*, November 26, 2011, A19. See also the "prescriptions" for suburbia in Barry Bergdoll and Reinhold Martin, *Foreclosed: Rehousing the American Dream* (New York: Museum of Modern Art, 2012).

8   Bruegmann, *Sprawl*, 115–16, 169. For complaints against suburbia in early modern London, for example, see Robert Fishman, *Bourgeois Utopias: The Rise and Fall of Suburbia* (New York: Basic Books, 1987), 6–7.

1.1.1 Suburban developments of semidetached houses, Merton Park, outside London

9　On British suburbanization, see Elizabeth McKellar, *Landscapes of London: The City, Country, and Suburbs, 1660–1840* (London: Paul Mellon Center for British Art, 2014).

10　Among the critics of suburbia were architects such as Clough Williams-Ellis and planners like Thomas Sharp and Patrick Abercrombie. For a good example of the jeremiads of this period, see essays in Clough Williams-Ellis, ed., *Britain and the Beast* (London: J. M. Dent, 1937).

wars. British cities, and particularly London, were among the world's wealthiest cities from the late eighteenth through the mid-twentieth century and saw perhaps the greatest suburban expansion in the world during those years.[9] (fig. **1.1.1**) As the quotation from Mumford at the beginning of this essay demonstrates, when suburban residential development was largely a matter of affluent families building houses for themselves, critics like Mumford had little complaint. It was when the movement swelled into a mass phenomenon and developers started building housing for working- and middle-class families on a massive scale that the chorus of disapproval became deafening.

This conspicuous antisuburban movement emerged as a major force in planning circles and among urbanists after World War I.[10] Many critics have long wanted to believe that the worldwide low-density suburban development seen across the world today was a post–World War II American invention, fueled by widespread automobile ownership and by specific government policies, notably federal income tax deductions and

highway building. It is important for them to believe this because they would like to think that changing a few policies will reverse the dynamics of urbanization and curtail the spread of suburbia. In fact, mass suburbanization had occurred in Britain long before the end of the nineteenth century, and almost all the arguments against it—for example, the idea that such low-density development was the result of greedy developers creating economically unsustainable development, that it despoiled the countryside, that it destroyed farmland, and, above all, that it was ugly—were already widely articulated at that time without any of the conditions that supposedly created American postwar suburbia; notably, widespread automobile use and federal policies that supposedly gave preferential treatment to suburban development. This history supports the notion that the suburbanization of the last several centuries had much deeper and more profound causes than most anti-sprawl advocates would like to acknowledge.

The early British coalition against sprawl united several quite disparate groups. The first was a set of great British landowners, often descendants of the families who had obtained the land during feudal times. They were appalled by the incursion of working- and middle-class families into the countryside that they had largely controlled for centuries. They joined together with other individuals, who were often of quite different political beliefs but equally unhappy with suburban development, to form the Council for the Protection of Rural England. They and their allies decried the loss of farmland and increase in traffic due to suburbanization. They also were disturbed by the way suburban development looked, and the way it was blurring their idealized, traditional distinction between city and countryside. This loose coalition included a group of artists, intellectuals, architects, and planners—many of whom resided in London—who were ideally positioned to put many of the complaints about suburbia into print. Among the leaders of this movement were the architect Clough Williams-Ellis and the planner Thomas Sharp. Together, they made many of the arguments and crafted the rhetorical stance that has influenced the anti-sprawl movement to this day.[11] Here is Sharp on British suburbia in 1932:

> Tradition has broken down. Taste is utterly debased. There is no enlightened guidance or correction from authority. The town, long since degraded, is now being annihilated by a flabby, shoddy, romantic nature-worship. That romantic nature-worship is destroying also the object of its adoration, the countryside. Both are being destroyed. The one age-long certainty, the antithesis of town and country, is already breaking down. Two diametrically opposed, dramatically contrasting, inevitable types of beauty are being displaced by one drab revolting neutrality…The strong, masculine virility of the town; the softer beauty, the richness, the fruitfulness of that mother of men, the countryside, will be debased into one sterile, hermaphroditic beastliness.[12]

Sharp believed that this lamentable situation had occurred because standards of taste had been allowed to deteriorate since the advent of what he called "dull democracy." This shift in power from an aristocratic ruling class to a more democratic society, he believed, had allowed individuals to do what they wished without regard to the opinions of architects and planners like himself who, he undoubtedly thought, should be the arbiters of taste because they were better educated and had a better-developed sense of taste than ordinary citizens. British polemics, like those of Sharp, transmitted through figures like Sir Patrick Geddes, foreshadow Lewis Mumford's description of suburbia.

The same kind of thinking is evident in Mumford's use, in *The City in History*, of the term *sprawl*. The word had long been used as a verb, and as a noun describing a loose gathering of things, but in Britain immediately after World War I it increasingly appeared as a noun applying to the built environment. For example, in 1919, the *London Times* referred to the "vast sprawl of London over huge areas," and the paper would use the term increasingly over the next decades.[13] In 1938 Mumford used it several times in *The Culture of Cities*.[14] Even the sound of the word suggested something lazy and undisciplined. It has remained a potent polemical term in great part because it does triple duty in describing a pattern of settlement (low-density without an overall plan), a place (suburbia or, later, exurbia), and those who occupy it (suburbanites). Conveniently, all are subject to the same derision. That very looseness of definition has allowed it to morph over the years to accommodate changing circumstances

11 Peter Hall, *Cities of Tomorrow: An Intellectual History of Urban Planning and Design in the Twentieth Century* (Oxford: Basil Blackwell, 1988).

12 Thomas Sharp, *Town and Countryside Some Aspects of Urban and Rural Development* (London: Oxford University Press, 1932), 11.

13 I owe this information on the immediate post–World War I use of sprawl to David Halton, who sent me his draft manuscript "Sprawl: The Early Origins of the Epithet in London and New York, 1911–1958."

14 For example, Mumford wrote about the "sprawl and shapelessness" of the big city as it grew "in amoeboid fashion, failing to divide its social chromosomes and split up into new cells," in *The Culture of Cities* (New York: Harcourt Brace and Co., 1938), 234.

and has helped fuel nearly a century of antisuburban rhetoric.

One of the great ironies of the first generation of twentieth-century attacks on low-density sprawl and suburbia is the way the rhetoric mirrored almost exactly the complaints about the high-density industrial city: that it was ugly, dehumanizing, wasteful, and a kind of malignant biological organism. For example, the American housing reformer Lawrence Veiller described the "blight" of the central city as a cancer that needed to be cut out with a surgeon's knife.[15] Urban experts like Ebenezer Howard sought to counteract the blight of dense cities by lowering urban densities, decentralizing the city, and moving citizens from the slums out into garden cities in the countryside. Many subsequent observers, though, saw the scattered low density of the suburbs, including the garden cities and suburbs, as the great evil to be combated. They advocated higher densities, greenbelts around existing cities, and bans on building outside existing urban areas.

World War II put a temporary end to the first campaign against sprawl, at least in Britain, because the country was preoccupied by rebuilding after the destruction caused by war. In addition, immediately after the war, the Labour Party government managed to create an agreement between antisuburban planners and the great landowners, neither of whom was in sympathy with many Labour initiatives or with each other but who shared a strong desire to stop the middle-class suburbanization of the British countryside. This alliance made it possible for Parliament to create one of the most draconian sets of planning regulations ever seen in a democratic country, one that involved nationalizing all development rights. Ironically, this policy was particularly beneficial for the great landowners, who were able to not only preserve their beloved countryside

against encroachment but, despite a dramatic weakening of their economic position and the imposition of high income taxes, were also able to afford to continue living on their estates because of compensation for the loss of those development rights. It is a system that is largely still in place, and that has contributed to one of the greatest mismatches anywhere between the demand and the supply of housing. This in turn has led to some of the most expensive urban land anywhere, as James Heartfield explains.

The Second Wave

With British critics of sprawl temporarily sidelined after World War II, the second period of antisuburban rhetoric was centered in the United States, where the massive suburban development of the interwar period was only a prelude to an even greater push during the boom years of the 1950s and 1960s. (fig. **1.1.2**) It was in this era that suburban lot sizes in America reached their maximum size, one that, contrary to much popular belief, has been declining ever since.[16] William H. Whyte, a staff member at the prestigious business magazine *Fortune*, fired an important early salvo in this phase of the war of words. He convened a conference and then published a book called *The Exploding City* to argue that suburban growth was wreaking havoc on the American landscape. Whyte, Mumford, Jane Jacobs, and many other New Yorkers were especially appalled by the new urban patterns they saw in the newer cities of the American West. "Huge patches of once green countryside have been turned into vast, smog-filled deserts that are neither city, suburb, nor country," he wrote.[17] Whyte's essay makes clear that his eye was particularly fixed on Los Angeles, which became the poster child for sprawl for an entire generation because it seemed to defy every characteristic of the high-density, monocentric

15　Lawrence Veiller, "Slum Clearance," in *Housing in America, Proceedings of the Tenth National Conference on Housing* (New York: National Housing Association, 1929), 75.

16　On the history of lot sizes since World War II, see Samuel Staley, *The Sprawling of America: In Defense of the Dynamic City* (Los Angeles: Reason Public Policy Institute, 1999).

17　William H. Whyte, ed., *The Exploding Metropolis* (Garden City, NY: Doubleday, 1958), 115.

1.1.2 Postwar "raised ranch" houses in the Chicago suburb of Skokie

premodern European city with its easily legible diagram of power radiating from the center. Ironically enough, the characterization of Los Angeles as a low-density place has survived, even though the Los Angeles area always had smaller lot sizes than those in most older American urban areas, and, unlike almost all of the large, older urban areas in the world, has gotten considerably denser since World War II, making it today the densest urban area in the United States.[18]

The second generation of complaints against suburbia saw a reprise of all the particulars laid out against it in the first campaign. Suburbia supposedly ate up precious farmland that the nation couldn't afford to lose, although with the vastly increased efficiency of agriculture and huge surpluses of agricultural products, this argument was not very convincing to everyone. Low-density suburban development was also supposedly less efficient economically than more compact development, although this line of reasoning, laid out most notably in the publication *The Costs of Sprawl*, has been attacked and sharply debated.[19]

To this list was added an argument that applied most particularly to the United States. Affluent citizens, particularly white families, who supposedly turned their backs on the cities and fled to the suburbs, were depriving the city of an important part of its tax base and leaving it a place occupied primarily by the rich and the very poor, often minority, families.[20] However, blaming suburban development for the flight of affluent white residents does not explain the fact that suburbia boomed in areas with low numbers of residents just as it did for areas with extensive minorities. It also does not explain why in many other countries in the affluent world, for example, in Europe and Australia, a considerable portion of the most affluent population stayed in the city, and it was the less affluent population that moved to the suburbs.

There was also a growing worry about the environmental impact of suburban growth, as the push for limiting suburban development to protect rural land and agriculture joined concerns about population growth and automobile usage. These were the years that produced

18 The densities I refer to are population densities for urbanized areas, which is the only good measure of density because it counts the central city and all of the urbanized land adjacent to it as opposed to measures that count density according to municipal or county boundaries that are arbitrary lines on a map rather than any indication of what is functionally part of the urban area. For a good summary of the way most older American and European urban areas have declined in density while Los Angeles and most of the fast-growing younger cities of the American South and West have seen increases, see the data prepared by Wendell Cox in the section on urban area densities on his demographia.com website. For historical data, see "International Urbanized Area Data: Population, Area, and Density," Demographia, May 2, 2001, accessed November 24, 2015, http://www.demographia.com/db-intlua-data.htm. For more recent data, see "Demographia World Urban Areas," Demographia, January 2015, accessed May 10, 2015, http://www.demographia.com/db-worldua.pdf.

19 Real Estate Research Corporation, *The Costs of Sprawl* (Washington, DC: US Government Printing Office, 1974).

20 A good example of criticism of suburbs on social grounds can be seen in Robert Goldston, *Suburbia: Civic Denial* (New York: Macmillan, 1970), and in popular diatribes such as Richard E. Gordon, Katherine K. Gordon, and Max Gunther, *The Split Level Trap* (New York: Random House, 1961); and John Keats, *The Crack in the Picture Window* (Boston: Houghton-Mifflin, 1975).

the zero population growth movement and the widespread worry about the "limits to growth."[21] In planning circles, one initiative was a series of experiments with limiting growth around places like Ramapo, New York; Boulder, Colorado; and Petaluma, California. These efforts were to some extent successful in slowing suburban growth around these communities, although it could be argued that they mostly just deflected growth elsewhere.[22] Of course, no one doubted that there were environmental problems with suburban growth, but in reality, the problems of pollution, freshwater supply, and wastewater were faced by all parts of urban America and perhaps even more pressing in the central cities, where air and water pollution were more concentrated and affected more people and the cost of creating new infrastructure more expensive than at the periphery.[23]

Another environmental issue led to a growing literature condemning the automobile and urging a return to mass transit. This line of attack ignited a revolt against highway construction that eventually proved quite successful in stopping many planned urban freeways. Whatever the validity of the arguments against the automobile, however, they were not enough to overcome the fact that most of urban America had become too low in density to support a comprehensive transit system. By the end of the postwar decades, some 85 percent of American households owned an automobile, and transit had become an insignificant factor in the transportation picture outside service into a few dense American downtowns, a situation that continues to this day.[24]

For all the talk of economic, social, and environmental issues, once again the most persistent and emotional complaints were based on class-bound assumptions and aesthetic biases. One can get some idea of the emotional heat of the antisuburban campaign from a 1964 book written by the architect and journalist Peter Blake, *God's Own Junkyard*. "This book is not written in anger. It is written in fury," Blake begins. A few pages later, after describing the majestic natural landscape of the United States, he comments, "We are about to turn this beautiful inheritance into the biggest slum on the face of the earth."[25] During the postwar years, one argument after another came to the fore. What remained constant was the animus against the suburbs and against suburbanites. Bennett M. Berger commented on this fact when he wrote, in 1961, "'Suburb' and 'suburban' have replaced the now embarrassingly obsolete 'bourgeois' as a packaged rebuke to the whole tenor of American life."[26]

The second campaign against suburbia pretty much came to a halt in the 1970s, when an economic downturn sharply curtailed suburban development once again. The oil crisis of that decade convinced many observers that the great suburban boom of the postwar years was over, automobile ownership would decline, and suburban dwellers would return to the city and to public transit.[27]

The Third Wave of Criticism

Instead, of course, what happened once development bounced back in the 1980s was a resurgence in suburban building, and not just in the United States or the affluent nations of northern and western Europe. All over the world, as soon as there was a substantial middle class that could afford to move to low-density suburban locations, densities fell at the center and settlement at the edge boomed.[28] And, once again, the antisuburban forces attacked, this time on a scale much greater than anything seen heretofore. The linchpin of this third campaign, at least in debates on public policy, has been environmental, particularly the notion that low-density suburbia increases

21 Two key documents are Paul Ehrlich, *The Population Bomb* (New York: Ballantine Books, 1968); and Donella Meadows et al., *The Limits to Growth* (New York: University Books, 1972).

22 On growth controls, see Randall W. Scott, David J. Bower, and Dallas Miner, eds., *Management and Control of Growth* (Washington, DC: Urban Land Institute, 1975).

23 A good summary of attitudes toward problems of growth can be found in Scott, Bower, and Miner, *Management and Control of Growth*.

24 Among the flood of anti-automobile and antihighway books was Lewis Mumford, *The Highway and the City* (New York: Mentor Books, 1964). Other books, often with rhetoric as inflammatory as their titles, included John Keats, *The Insolent Charioteers* (Philadelphia: Lippincott, 1958); Alpheus Quinley Mowbray, *Road to Ruin* (Philadelphia: Lippincott, 1969); Helen Levitt, *Superhighway-Superhoax* (Garden City, NY: Doubleday, 1970); Richard R. Schnedier, *Autokind vs. Mankind* (New York: Schocken Books, 1972); and Ronald A. Buel, *Dead End: The Automobile in Mass Transportation* (New York: Prentice Hall, 1972). An important corrective volume was B. Bruce Briggs, *The War against the Automobile* (New York: E. P. Dutton, 1975).

25 Peter Blake, *God's Own Junkyard: The Planned Deterioration of America's Landscape* (New York: Holt, Rinehart & Winston, 1964), 8.

26 Bennett Berger, "The Myth of the Suburb," *Journal of Social Issues* 17, no. 1 (January 1961): 316. This article, an expansion of the argument in Berger's 1960 book *Working Class Suburb: A Study of Auto Workers in Suburbia* (Berkeley: University of California Press, 1960), provides a powerful

energy use, gasoline consumption, and greenhouse gases. Once again, one could argue that the target is misplaced, that what has dramatically increased energy and automobile usage has simply been affluence, and that the remedy for pollution and greenhouse gases is to reduce our dependency on fossil fuels through conservation, technological innovation, and, in the longer term, the growth of new, cleaner forms of energy.[29]

And once again, underlying much of the rhetoric of antisprawl has been a set of class, based assumptions and aesthetic preferences. James Howard Kunstler is one of the authors who have taken the place of Thomas Sharp and other prophets of suburban doom of the interwar years, using similarly overheated prose and betraying a comparable disdain for ordinary citizens. In *The Geography of Nowhere*, Kunstler describes suburbia as "a landscape of scary places, the geography of nowhere, that has simply ceased to be a credible human habitat."[30] More recently, in a TED Talk on his blog *Clusterfuck Nation*, he continued the rant: "I like to call it 'the national automobile slum.' You can call it suburban sprawl. I think it's appropriate to call it the greatest misallocation of resources in the history of the world."[31]

This third campaign against sprawl, unlike previous campaigns, did not stop with the economic meltdown of the Great Recession. As building declined sharply everywhere in the affluent world, specific criticisms of suburbia receded, but didn't disappear. They just reappeared in a different guise, as a growing chorus of observers convinced themselves that, despite all previous experience, this economic crisis had finally shown the futility of suburban development. They proclaimed a new era in which the suburbs would wither while central cities would boom.

The heralds of the new triumph of the city have cited statistics showing that young people are driving less, own fewer cars, and are more likely to rent apartments in the central city than their counterparts were a generation ago. These straws in the wind have convinced observers like the economist Edward Glaeser and the sociologist Richard Florida that the centers of big cities are the places where the economy of the future will be forged. They believe, although with very little convincing evidence, that physical proximity is what drives innovation; the result, today's antisuburban critics predict, is that the centers of big cities will thrive at the expense of the suburbs.[32] For other observers, for example as seen in the 2004 movie *The End of Suburbia: Oil Depletion and the Collapse of the American Dream* the impending crisis of "peak oil" all but guarantees that the suburban era is over.[33]

By the time of this writing in 2015, however, as the US economy has started to recover and new sources of energy have been found, these gleeful predictions of suburban doom have started to look silly. It is definitely true that many city centers across the Western world are now more attractive than they have ever been, and they are drawing an increasingly affluent population. However, there is almost no evidence that this gentrification of the city center will stop or even slow suburban growth at least in the short run. In fact, the very people who fulminate against sprawl at the edge are often the same ones who, in the name of protecting their own central neighborhood from increased congestion, traffic, and noise, reject density near themselves.[34]

Criticism of the Suburbs and the Urban Future

In some ways, the widely trumpeted "triumph of the city" is filled with irony. One of these ironies is that the gentrified city centers and the suburbs have in many ways converged. As American central cities have become more affluent, they

counterargument to the antisuburban biases of urban academics.

27 See, for example, Stewart Udall, "The Last Traffic Jam," *Atlantic*, October 1972.

28 On the worldwide decline in urban population densities, see the excellent work of Shlomo Angel, for example, *Planet of Cities* (Cambridge, MA: Lincoln Institute of Land Policy, 2012); and Shlomo Angel et al., *Atlas of Urban Expansion* (Cambridge, MA: Lincoln Institute of Land Policy, 2012).

29 An early and concise summary of environmental arguments can be found in F. Kaiden Benfield, Matthew D. Raimi, and Donald C. T. Chen, *Once There Were Greenfields* (Washington, DC: National Resources Defense Council, 1999). A good corrective for environmental alarmism can be found in Gregg Easterbrook, *A Moment on the Earth* (New York: Viking, 1995).

30 William Howard Kunstler, *The Geography of Nowhere: The Rise and Decline of America's Manmade Landscape* (New York: Simon and Schuster, 1973), 15.

31 Jim Kunstler, "The Clusterfuck Nation Chronicle," June 26, 2006, accessed May 10, 2015, http://www .kunstler.com/mags _diary17.html.

32 Edward Glaeser, *The Triumph of the City: How Our Greatest Invention Makes Us Richer, Smarter, Greener, Healthier, and Happier* (New York: Penguin Press, 2011); Richard Florida, "How the Crash Will Reshape America?," *Atlantic*, March 2009, http://www .theatlantic.com/maga zine/archive/2009/03 /how-the-crash-will-re shape-america/307293/.

33 *The End of Suburbia: Oil Depletion and the Collapse of the American Dream*, directed by Gregory Greene (Canada: Electric Wallpaper Company, 2004), DVD.

34 An excellent, albeit highly anecdotal,

have become less dense and less diverse demographically and ethnically, while the suburbs have become denser and more diverse.[35] The same is true of the kinds of economic activity found in central cities and in the suburbs. Factories have moved out of central cities, new parks have been created (often in areas that had been the densest quarters of the city), and thousands of trees have been planted, making city centers less dense and greener than their counterparts of previous generations. At the same time, suburbia has been moving in the opposite direction. Suburban lot sizes in the United States have been declining, and suburban townhouses and apartment buildings have become more common. Not surprisingly, since major developers operate in the city and the suburbs, it is now possible to see similar town houses and strip centers at the urban periphery and near the center of cities. Also, as even major cultural institutions open in the suburbs and the kind of high culture of museums, symphony halls, and used bookstores is increasingly available through the internet, the old city-suburb cultural divide has dramatically narrowed.[36]

Whither our urban areas? As city centers have become safer, greener, and healthier, it is likely that an increasing percentage of people will want to live at higher, rather than lower, densities. After all, many of the wealthiest individuals in the world, those who could choose to live anywhere, have chosen to spend their time in places like the Upper East Side of New York or the Sixteenth Arrondissement in Paris, with second houses at the seashore or in the mountains, and as the world becomes more affluent, many more families may want to follow their lead. Of course, with any major increase in the demand to live in city centers, there is likely to be a strong move by current residents and newcomers to limit this growth in an attempt to forestall any increase

in congestion and protect views and open space. Any such measures will almost inevitably lead a corresponding rise in housing prices that will limit the ability of less affluent newcomers to live there. This pattern has been visible in Paris for over a century and is now increasingly on view across the affluent world.

At the same time, there will almost certainly be families at every income level who will choose to live in very low-density exurbia even farther than they now are from city centers. It has been this exurban part of the landscape, the settlement beyond the regularly developed subdivisions at the urban fringe, which has seen the greatest increase in population in recent decades in the United States.[37]

And, finally, there will almost certainly be a great many who will either choose to live in some version of the suburbs or be forced to live there by rising prices in the gentrifying city centers. What exactly those suburbs will look like, though, is open to question. With all of the new technologies and shifting lifestyle preferences, these suburbs could, in fifty years, easily look quite different from what we see today.

Criticism of our suburbs could play an important role in what these suburbs look like and how they function. The great crusade against suburbia has undoubtedly done some good in opening up a public debate on what the good urban and suburban life can or should look like. There are major problems with suburban development including everything from the cost of providing services to the problem of protecting species habitat. But it is hard to avoid the conclusion that the existing criticism has, more often than not, been based on traditional aesthetic notions about "proper" urban form deeply rooted in the model of the traditional European city, with its focus of power and authority at the center. This class-based preference has served to

example of this can be found in an article by David Zahniser, "Do as We Say, Not as We Do," *LA Weekly,* May 30, 2007, accessed November 24, 2015, http://www .laweekly.com/news /do-as-we-say-not-as -we-do-2149098

35 On these demographic changes, see William H. Frey, "Melting Pot Cities and Suburbs: Racial and Ethnic Change in Metro America in the 2000s," Brookings Institution, May 2001, accessed May 10, 2015, http://www.brookings .edu/research/papers /2011/05/04-census -ethnicity-frey.

36 Bruegmann, *Sprawl,* 71–73.

37 Alan Berube et al., *Finding Exurbia: America's Fast-Growing Communities at the Metropolitan Fringe* (Washington, DC: Brookings Institution, October 2006), accessed May 10, 2015, http:// www.brookings.edu /~/media/research/files /reports/2006/10 /metropolitanpolicy -berube/20061017 _exurbia.pdf.

reinforce old stereotypes and, in the unrelenting push to turn back the clock to recapture the form of earlier cities, obscure the possibility of new and perhaps more satisfying urban futures.

The continuous barrage of complaints against the private automobile and agitation for more public transportation, for example, has mostly distracted attention away from the many of the most positive ways that we might be able to improve mobility for all of the population. The arrival of self-driving cars is just one instance of how some of today's most vexing problems might yield to new solutions. With these cars it is quite possible that the line separating public and private transportation would erode as users could summon vehicles of different sizes for different kinds of trips, move much more quickly along existing right-of-way because of sensors that would smooth flow, eliminate friction, and dramatically reduce the need for private vehicles or parking spaces. It is quite possible that this kind of shared vehicle, allowing direct movement from any given point A to point B would eliminate the need for most of the "big box" vehicles such as buses and trains that we currently think of as "public transportation." And, once again, as with many other advances in technology over the last century, these advances could allow people more freedom to choose exactly which kind of environment they would prefer for their residence, work, and leisure.

To make a real contribution to the emerging urban pattern, it would probably help for architects, planners, and public policy makers to move away from their fixation on the forms of the past, traditional aesthetic notions, and attempts to build cities to accommodate existing technology and ways of life. Instead, they should focus on how various parts of the population would like to live and then see what kinds of technology and urban forms could give the largest number of citizens the greatest choice and most satisfying physical environments.

1.2
THE DIVIDED METROPOLIS
THE SUBURB AND THE EXPLOSION OF GLOBAL URBANIZATION

Robert Fishman

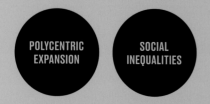

POLYCENTRIC
EXPANSION

SOCIAL
INEQUALITIES

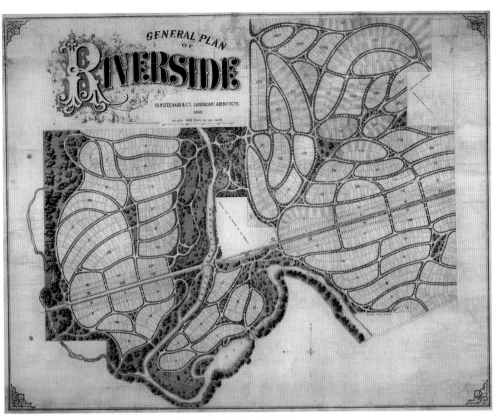

1   Olmsted, Vaux & Co., *Preliminary Report upon the Proposed Suburban Village at Riverside near Chicago* (New York: Sutton, Bowne, 1868), 7.

1.2.1 The bourgeois utopia, Olmsted & Vaux, General Plan of Riverside, 1869

In 1868 Frederick Law Olmsted published his landmark plan for the picturesque garden suburb of Riverside, Illinois, eleven miles west of Chicago. (fig. **1.2.1**) He found it necessary to emphasize, "The present outward tendency of [urban] population is not so much an ebb as the higher rise of the same flood…."[1] For him, the "flood" was the increasing concentration of a modern society's population in cities, a process that he believed was synonymous with the advance of civilization itself. Suburbanization, he argued, was not a rejection or "ebbing" of urbanization but rather "the higher rise," that is, the extension and intensification, of metropolitan growth into new districts that could potentially combine the best of the urban and the rural. To generalize Olmsted's point, we might define the suburb as the form that urban expansion takes—the place where the density and dynamism of the city encounters and transforms the still-rural periphery.

The specifics of suburban form vary radically, as different cities and cultures make fundamentally different choices for how the relatively cheap land at the edge will be used. If Olmsted's magnificently landscaped "bourgeois utopia" for the upper-middle class represents one end of a social and design continuum, the informal settlements for rural migrants at the fringe of so many megacities of the developing world represent the other. Whether a specific suburb is a landscape of exclusion defined by privilege or a landscape of poverty to which the excluded are relegated, all suburbs nevertheless embody that flood tide of urbanization that has transformed the world. From ancient to eighteenth-century cities, urban growth had been severely constrained by limitations inherent in premodern society itself: the inefficiency of agriculture that required 80 percent or more of the population to labor on the land; the inefficiency of transportation that made supplying a large city virtually impossible; and the inability to manage density that made cities synonymous with disorder, fire, disease, and early death.

Eighteenth-century London was arguably the first city to overcome enough of the constraints to growth to transform its poor, not yet policed, and unregulated suburban edges (called "liberties") into crucial sites for sustained urban expansion. In London's growth, we first see the fundamental transformation of human life that is now reaching its climax in the cities of the developing world. An agricultural revolution in the countryside increases productivity while rendering much of the peasant population redundant; the city's access to increased food supplies promises survival and perhaps a better life than the village offers; the more complex division of labor in cities somehow absorbs the migrants and creates new work and higher productivity for an ever-increasing population. In this rolling crescendo of urbanization, the land at the edge becomes the key strategic site for expansion. The core might provide a city's identity, but it is the periphery that is crucial for growth: relatively cheap, close enough to the core to be part of the larger urban economy, and open enough to support rapid building and expansion. The suburb thus becomes the key strategic terrain for the "age of great cities" that runs from the eighteenth century to the present, with an urban domain that now extends from London to cover the whole globe.

The protean forms of the evolution of the modern suburb might be expressed as a single narrative that organizes the vast variety of suburbs into three stages, with each stage characterized by a binary opposition. In the first stage, which covers roughly the nineteenth and early twentieth centuries, the basic opposition was between the early Anglo-American suburbs where the upper-middle class seized the land at the edge of the metropolis for their bourgeois utopias, versus Baron Haussmann's Paris (and the European Continent more generally), where the wealthy stayed at the core and pushed the poor to the working-class and industrial suburbs at the edge.

The second stage emerged in post-1945 North America and Western Europe, where suburbanization became a strategy for social democracy, using the cheap land at the edge of the great cities to create a new social environment of mass prosperity. In the United States and Canada, this new environment was formed by the mass ownership of detached, single-family houses as exemplified by D. J. Waldie's Lakewood. But Western Europe chose a more socialist model of planned, transit-based communities with high-rise or townhouse-style cooperative rental housing, exemplified by the Swedish new towns and the French *grands ensembles.*

Today we have reached a third and climactic stage of suburbanization in the flood tide of peripheral expansion in the cities of the developing world. As in the previous two stages, we can see a fundamental binary opposition in suburban form. The dominant form is the informal settlement at the periphery. As authorities in most of the exploding megacities have lost control of their periphery, the great flood of migrants from the countryside have been forced or permitted to house themselves, much as they have been forced or permitted to employ themselves. But the informal settlements have their binary opposites in the highly planned East Asian new towns. Derived from the post-1945 European new town but dramatically larger in scale, the East Asian new towns from the island of Singapore to the periphery of Seoul are as strict and regular in their form as the informal settlements are anarchic and ungoverned. Taken together, the informal settlements and the East Asian new towns will define the basic challenges of urbanism in our "century of cities."

These three stages and their characteristic binaries are all, of course, "ideal types" in the sense that Max Weber used the term: deliberate simplifications and accentuations of a highly complex reality.[2] In fact, nothing is more hybridized—indeed, chaotic—than morphology and land uses at the edge of a rapidly growing city. Not only does rapid urbanization clash with still-rural survival, but both ends of the social spectrum are simultaneously drawn for different reasons to the cheap land at the edge. This was true in the nineteenth century in England and in America, where picturesque bedroom-suburbs were often bordered by factory towns and workers' housing. It's also true today in Latin America, where a highly securitized gated suburb of privilege might be surrounded by informal settlements, and in China, where masses of middle-class apartment blocks often surround an "urban village" where recent rural migrants are packed into low-rise tenements.

The suburb, in both its wealthy and underprivileged forms, was historically not only the expression of urban expansion but also the paradigm for the divided metropolis, the imposition of class divisions on what had been relatively hybridized premodern cities. Cities and their citizens resisted and continue to resist these divisions. Nevertheless, the clarity of the ideal types permits us to distinctly see the underlying forces at work.

One more ideal type—although not in the Weberian sense—is the utopian model for peripheral development. Thirty years after Olmsted's Riverside, the English reformer Ebenezer Howard put forward his own ideal for suburban expansion, the garden city, which was both a critique of previous development at the periphery and a prescription for future growth. Like Riverside, the garden city

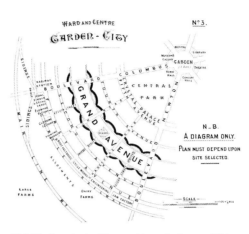

1.2.2 Utopian suburbs, Ebenezer Howard's diagram of the garden city's ward and center

was designed to combine the best of the city and the countryside. The expanding metropolis, in Howard's vision, would not simply extend indefinitely as a dense mass into the countryside, nor would it peter out in scattered development. Instead, metropolitan expansion would form a complex pattern, where newly built garden cities would be set in perpetual greenbelts of farms and other open space. These garden cities, moreover, would not be exclusive refuges for the elite, or dumping grounds for the poor, but mixed-income communities where careful planning would provide for genuine urban diversity, including a range of jobs as well as housing. The garden cities would be dense enough to be walkable and urbane, but limited enough in size to maintain a sense of community and to keep open countryside within easy reach.[3] (fig. **1.2.2**)

Howard himself founded two would-be garden cities outside London, and his followers would subsequently found or influence literally hundreds of new towns throughout the world, but we might question whether any of them truly embody the ideal. Nevertheless, Howard's garden city ideal will serve as a point of reference throughout this chapter against which to measure the social impact of extant patterns of suburban development.[4]

2   Max Weber, *Basic Concepts in Sociology*, trans. H. P. Secher (New York: Citadel Press, 1962), 14.

3   Ebenezer Howard, *Garden Cities of To-morrow* (Cambridge, MA: MIT Press, 1965).

4   Robert Fishman, *Urban Utopias in the Twentieth Century: Ebenezer Howard, Frank Lloyd Wright, and Le Corbusier* (New York: Basic Books, 1977), chaps. 2–3.

Origins of Suburbia

Two centuries ago, the middle classes in the two great Western European cities, London and Paris, faced a crisis provoked by the traditional middle-class pattern of a city core of row houses that combined workplace and residence. Massive in-migration from the countryside made these core neighborhoods dangerous, overcrowded, and unhealthy. At the same time, new ideals of family life in both England and France pointed toward homes that enjoyed a degree of privacy and emotional focus unattainable in "live-work" environments where the workplace and the home were fundamentally intertwined.

The English bourgeoisie responded first to this challenge by radically redefining their relationship to the city. As early as the mid-eighteenth century, leading London merchants and bankers began to separate their homes from their workplaces. The family business was continued in the heart of the city in houses that were now only shops and offices. And, influenced by the Evangelical movement that emphasized the religious purity of women and children over the sinful amusements and pollution of the city, these families established their home life in the healthy, uncrowded, unspoiled villages at the edge of the expanding metropolis.

The upper-middle-class elite that built large, comfortable houses around the parklike Clapham Commons to the south of London or the similarly open Hampstead Heath to the north (commuting back to London by private carriage) set in motion a revolution in urban form that continues to reverberate to this day. They redefined the edge as a place of privilege and redefined the middle-class home as a refuge from the city in the midst of nature. And, through projects like John Nash's 1823 Park Village, they created a new design language for these settlements that placed detached, single-family houses, usually of historicist design ("the village") in the midst of a picturesque landscape of lawns and trees ("the park").[5]

Although the French bourgeoisie would largely reject these innovations, the new suburbia spread widely through the Anglo-American world in the course of the nineteenth century. Suburbia both reflected and reinforced the divided metropolis of the Industrial Revolution. Working-class factory districts remained relatively close to the urban core, while the capitalist middle class was able to escape the smoky, polluted city—that they themselves had created—by using their wealth to purchase homes in the green and healthy garden suburbs at the edge. The Anglo-American industrial city thus came to possess a clear spatial logic, as innovations in transportation reinforced patterns of land use. The need to settle within walking distance of the first horse-drawn streetcar lines, and then of trolley and rail lines, meant that suburbs had a distinct center and an edge, with ample greenbelts preserved between transit lines running out from the core.[6]

The binary opposite of this Anglo-American suburbia of privilege was the French suburb, or banlieue, as it took shape in the middle of the nineteenth century around Paris. The core of the French capital was at least as overcrowded and unhealthy as any English or American city, but the French bourgeoisie never shared the Evangelical reaction against urban pleasures that characterized their Anglo counterparts. Perhaps more important, Paris in the 1850s and 1860s was governed by the authoritarian regime of Louis Napoleon and his famous Prefect of Paris, Baron Georges-Eugene Haussmann. Louis Napoleon and Haussmann were determined to remake the center of the city to make it a showplace for the regime and an exemplar of the regime's alliance with the bourgeoisie. Their favored urban design paradigm was the grand boulevard that cut through the fabric of the old city

5 Robert Fishman, *Bourgeois Utopias: The Rise and Fall of Suburbia* (New York: Basic Books, 1987), chaps. 2–3.

6 Sam Bass Warner Jr., *Streetcar Suburbs: The Process of Growth in Boston, 1870–1900* (Cambridge, MA: Harvard University Press, 1962).

to knit together the disconnected parts of the metropolis (and also to open the city to troops in the case of insurrection). Bordered by magnificent apartment houses, the grand boulevards were multipurpose infrastructure: linear parks above that also accommodated water, and sewerage below. The boulevards and apartment houses thus provided the French bourgeoisie at the center with the privacy, health, and greenery that their English counterparts could find only in the suburbs.

The massive condemnations that the boulevards required meant the destruction of housing for the poor, who were forced to seek cheaper accommodation at the edge of the city. This was "a feature[,] not a bug," because it established middle-class dominance at the core and marginalized (literally) a potentially revolutionary population. Suburbanization in France thus came to mean something very similar to what we call "informal settlements" today. The Parisian banlieue consisted of self-built housing without firm title to the land, and without the water, sewers, paved roads, lighting, or other modern services that Haussmann had provided to the boulevards at the core. But compared to the remaining central slums—the notorious *îlots insalubres* (unsanitary islands)—the banlieue provided a version of the community and informality of the rural villages that the migrants had left behind.[7] (fig. **1.2.3**)

The process of "Haussmannization" thus established a very different dynamic of suburbanization and urban expansions than the Anglo-American patterns. In Paris and the many cities in Europe, and eventually in the rest of the world that followed Paris's lead, the core was the place of privilege and exclusion; migrants from the countryside were kept at the edge to self-build their informal villages of poverty. For the Anglo-American suburb, by contrast, migrants from the

1.2.3 Suburbia, French style. Eugene Atget, *A Ragpicker's Villa*, 1912.

7   Norma Evenson, *Paris: A Century of Change, 1878–1978* (New Haven, CT: Yale University Press, 1979).

countryside were fed into the most crowded and polluted factory districts just outside the business core; skilled workers and the lower-middle class occupied better neighborhoods farther out; and the well-to-do at the suburban fringe enjoyed the benefits of extensive cheap land, ever-improving transportation to the core, and the health, beauty, and prestige of their garden suburbs. But both the Anglo-American and Parisian dynamics expressed a single underlying theme: the divided metropolis.

Social-Democratic Suburbia

The great task and the ideal of twentieth-century suburbanization was the attempt to overcome the divided metropolis that had been inherited from the nineteenth century, and to create a new, (relatively) classless world of modern housing at the edge, where mass production techniques would ensure health and comfort for all in a setting of greenery and generous public spaces. This social-democratic suburbia could not be attempted until post-1945 prosperity replaced the terrible years of war and depression for both North America and

Western Europe. Moreover, social-democratic suburbia depended on a postwar consensus that the state had a vital role in planning, and especially in home finance. The social-democratic era in suburbia lasted only from about 1950 to about 1980, before changing conditions led to very different patterns and results. But those three decades were sufficient to permanently redefine suburbia and to provide important legacies for the emerging megacities of the rest of the world.

Social-democratic suburbia, like its nineteenth-century predecessors, took two very different forms, one in the United States and the other in Western Europe. Postwar mass suburbanization in the United States was fundamentally shaped by the experience of the Great Depression and the New Deal's response to the collapse of the housing industry in 1929. Suburban developers in the 1920s had hoped that the automobile would open up cheap land in the vast peripheral territories between railroad or streetcar lines for mass suburbanization. But continued reliance on expensive, small-scale building techniques and even more expensive and wasteful high-interest, short-term mortgages meant that the single-family suburban house was still out of reach for the mass of households.

To revive the Depression-devastated building industry, the New Deal's 1934 Federal Housing Administration (FHA) revolutionized both housing construction and housing finance in order to maximize affordability. In contrast to more radical reformers who pushed for multifamily rental housing as the only modern form, the FHA very intentionally kept the model of the single-family house on a generous lot financed by an individual mortgage. But the FHA completely redesigned (and shrank) the typical middle-class suburban house so that it could be mass-produced, insofar as possible, from factory-processed lumber and other materials. The FHA also completely reengineered the home financing system to lower monthly payments by providing federally guaranteed long-term, low-interest, lowdown payment, self-amortizing mortgages through federally supervised thrift institutions. The seemingly minor ability to grant (or withhold) federal mortgage insurance gave the FHA tremendous power over the design, locale, and pace of suburbanization.[8]

These innovations had relatively small effects in the 1930s, but suburban housing after 1945 entered a classic virtuous cycle, as mass production brought down costs for a broad middle and working class whose growing incomes meant ever-increasing access to the American dream house. This virtuous cycle was most dramatically demonstrated in three key projects that embodied the scale and the designs favored by the FHA: Levittown, Long Island; Park Forest, Illinois; and Lakewood, California. (fig. **1.2.4**) All three used neighborhood unit planning that attempted to create walkable neighborhoods that included an elementary school and a small shopping center. Indeed, these early postwar suburbs came surprisingly close to the Howard ideal of the garden city. As Greg Hise has pointed out, they were often located near aircraft plants and other new industries that provided jobs for their residents.[9] And, as D. J. Waldie observes of Lakewood, the postwar suburb provided a uniquely democratic mix of working-class and middle-class households.[10]

If the social-democratic aspect American suburbanization consisted of building a democratized and streamlined version of the bourgeois utopia, European social-democratic new towns represented a more radical reimagining of the former banlieue. The model here was Sweden's People's Home movement that, like the New Deal, dates back to the 1930s. Swedish Social Democrats sought

8 Kenneth T. Jackson, *Crabgrass Frontier: The Suburbanization of the United States* (New York: Oxford University Press, 1985).

9 Greg Hise, *Magnetic Los Angeles: Planning the Twentieth-Century Metropolis* (Baltimore: John Hopkins University Press, 1997).

10 Donald J. Waldie, *Holy Land: A Suburban Memoir* (New York: W. W. Norton, 1996).

1.2.4 Aerial photograph of Levittown on Long Island, New York, in 1954

11 Peter Hall, *Cities in Civilization* (New York: Pantheon, 1998), chap. 14.

12 Brian W. Newsome, *French Urban Planning 1940–1968: The Construction and Deconstruction of an Authoritarian System* (New York: Peter Lang, 2009).

to relieve the terrible overcrowding of the slums of Stockholm with highly planned new towns to be built at still-rural stops at the end of commuter rail lines leading out of the city. As opposed to the New Deal, the Swedish model emphasized the collective both in design and in finance. The Swedish government made large, low-interest loans to nonprofit building societies that erected mid-rise rental apartment blocks and garden apartments in accordance with the larger plans. Although these rental apartments were certainly austere, even in comparison with the typical downsized postwar American tract house, the public spaces and parks of the Swedish new towns were relatively generous, and the apartments themselves designed according to the best standards of Swedish modernism.[11]

This Swedish model, an even closer approximation of Howard's ideal than American mass suburbia, had deep appeal to the generation of planners and architects who held strategic positions in Western European social democracies comparable to the role of the Levitts and other private developers in the United States. The Swedish model was adopted not only in the northern social democracies (Demark and the Netherlands) but in the British new towns, and especially in the French grands ensembles—high-rise housing projects—around Paris. As late as the 1950s, Paris was surrounded by a banlieue of poorly built villas and out-and-out shantytowns, occupied by recent French migrants from the villages or by North African immigrants. The grands ensembles that replaced them were certainly the largest-scale efforts yet at redefining the Western European suburb, combining the monumental scale of modernist high-rise construction with the promise of a new life beyond the squalor and class divisions of the past.[12] (fig. **1.2.5**)

After Social Democracy

After what the French called *les trente glorieuses*, the thirty glorious years from 1945

1.2.5 Mass suburbia, European style, Bijlmermeer, Amsterdam, 1975

to 1975, when all the Western economies experienced both a rapid rise in household incomes and rapid suburbanization, the two modes of postwar social-democratic suburbia then followed two very different trajectories. American postwar suburbia was, if anything, too successful. The spectacular growth of the early large projects led to a speculative land market where the neighborhood unit ideal was replaced by the reality of leapfrog development: scattered subdivisions connected by congested roads to strip developments, shopping centers, industrial parks, and office parks. The suburbs necessarily urbanized as their automobile-dependent population lost touch with their central cities, leading to an urban crisis, especially for black households that were not allowed to join the suburban exodus.

After 1980, incomes stagnated for most American households, but rose dramatically at the top. The metropolitan fringe segmented into highly privileged districts, often the well-preserved bourgeois utopias of more than a century ago, and a struggling, sprawling mass suburbia. By contrast, Western European planners were careful to maintain transit, and with it the dominance of central city shopping and office districts. Moreover, the European city was always a formidable competitor of the suburbs for elite residence. More seriously, the postwar new towns increasingly lost the loyalty of a middle class with growing incomes and affluent lifestyles that were no longer reflected in the aging modernist apartment blocks. This contrasted with the United States, where the individually owned frame houses could be enlarged and upgraded to reflect greater affluence, while the European rental apartments resisted change. Too many European architects and housing bureaucrats lost their idealism but continued to be obsessed with mass production, designing ever-larger and more standardized housing complexes that were never fully occupied.[13]

Only in Italy did the Ina-Casa program of social housing, conceived not simply as an employment program but also as a housing program, produce imaginative and human-scaled projects that have held their value.[14] Elsewhere, the Western European middle class opted for their own (somewhat reduced) versions of American postwar suburbia, with privately developed townhouses and condominium apartments, or for gentrified districts in the urban core or inner suburbs. Meanwhile, the social-democratic towers at the edge have increasingly been occupied by immigrants, isolated not only physically but socially from the gentrified cities and middle-class suburban developments. Haussmann's divided metropolis is back in a modernist form.

Suburbia in Developing Countries

If suburbia is, as I have argued, the form that urban expansion takes, then the historic process of suburbanization is now reaching its highest pitch of intensity in the rapidly growing megacities, as well as in the smaller cities of the developing world. None of the previous movements of population from the countryside to the cities can match the climactic force of the present migrations that are shifting the human race decisively toward urban life. As world population increases over the next thirty-five years from 7 billion to an estimated 9.6 billion, the planet's urbanized population will increase from 3.9 billion today to 6.4 billion in 2050. Whether they settle in the megacities of twenty million or in the multitude of cities of 500,000 to a million people (that are in fact projected to grow even more rapidly than the megacities), these 2.5 billion additional urbanites will inhabit places that are sure to be among the most crowded and chaotic environments in human history.[15]

Yet the logic that first propelled London above the million mark in the early nineteenth century still applies today. Agrarian innovation renders the bulk of village workers superfluous, and the cities seem impossibly overcrowded. And yet somehow, within the complex division of urban labor, the migrant finds a place in the lowest reaches of the bazaar economy, in export-oriented industries, or in marginal services, such as the *dabbawallas* of Mumbai who deliver hot lunches from middle-class suburban homes to office workers in the core.[16] The constant flood of new migrants helps to propel others a little better established into a precarious middle class.

The most characteristic form of developing world suburbanization is the informal settlement, a direct successor of the banlieue of Haussmann's time, but now scaled up to reflect the enormousness of contemporary migration. As in Haussmann's Paris, the urban core constitutes a zone of modernity and relative order to which the middle class clings. Beyond the core, the urban governments lose control of even the most basic functions of planning, services, and infrastructure. The result is Mike Davis's *Planet of Slums*, but one must also note that the anarchy to some degree liberates the poor and powerless from ineffectual and corrupt bureaucracies. The insecurity of land tenure also holds down land values at the edge, minimizing the transfer of wealth from the poor to wealthy landlords that was so much a feature of the slums of the past. Self-building in the informal settlements is counterpart to the micro-level self-employment that is the mass basis of the urban economy, particularly in megacities.[17]

East Asia's New Towns

As in our two previous stages of suburbanization, this third stage is binary, in that there is a clear alternative to the

13 Evenson, *Paris: A Century of Change*, 232–64.

14 Stephanie Zeier Pilat, *Reconstructing Italy: The Ina-Casa Neighborhood of the Postwar Era* (Farnham: Ashgate, 2014).

15 United Nations, Department of Economic and Social Affairs, Population Division, *World Urbanization Prospects: The 2014 Revision; Highlights* (New York: United Nations, 2014), 1, 16.

16 Saritha Rai, "In India Grandma Cooks, They Deliver," *New York Times*, May 29, 2007, accessed July 30, 2015, http://www.nytimes.com/2007/05/29/business/worldbusiness/29lunch.html?pagewanted=all&_r=0.

17 Robert Neuwirth, *Shadow Cities: A Billion Squatters, a New Urban World* (New York: Routledge, 2005); Mike Davis, *Planet of Slums* (London: Verso, 2006).

informal settlement as the basic form of peripheral growth. This is the East Asian new town, as seen first in Singapore and now in Korea and especially China. Here, an authoritarian government seizes and keeps control of growth at the edge, with carefully—indeed obsessively—planned developments of high-rise towers whose form owes much to the European new town tradition, but whose unprecedented scale and uniformity make even the French grands ensembles seem intimate.

This model first emerged in newly independent Singapore in the 1960s, when that city-state was in the throes of a transition from one of the poorest places on earth to becoming a thriving economic power. At independence in 1959, an estimated half of Singapore's million citizens lived either in squatter settlements or in dangerously overcrowded "shophouses" near the core. A Housing and Development Board (HDB) founded a year later made publicly built housing an integral part of a highly capitalist development strategy. The HDB initiated what became twenty-two high-rise new towns, each with average populations of over 250,000 people, erected on land obtained cheaply by eminent domain powers that ruthlessly cleared away the shantytowns and small farms. But with the HDB keeping housing costs low in the new towns, Singapore's workers could improve their living standards on modest wages, spurring further economic development. The new towns, moreover, were carefully planned to include a mix of income and ethnic groups, as well as generous public amenities surrounding the tower blocks.[18]

Today, the squatter settlements are gone and the remaining shophouse districts are tourist attractions; nearly 84 percent of Singapore's present 5.47 million people live in housing built by the HDB, now mostly condominiums rather than rental units. Although no other country has been able to match this radical upgrading of suburban housing stock, Singapore has made a deep impression on the other Asian Tigers, most notably Korea. There, a ring of Singapore-style new towns surrounds Seoul. China, though less neatly organized, has largely followed Singapore's model, with immense districts like Huilongguan, some twenty miles north of central Beijing, organized in endless superblocks around transit stations.[19] (fig. **1.2.6**)

The Suburban Challenge

The massive suburbs of the contemporary megacity seem to alternate between extremes of disorder, such as the ubiquitous favela, and order, such as the East Asian new towns. At worst, we are now seeing a kind of negative synthesis of suburban order and disorder that combines the most socially regressive features of the historic Anglo-American and French models: a periphery that consists of gated communities for the wealthy surrounded by informal settlements for the poor. The Haussmann model of pushing the poor to informal settlements at the edge had at least provided for a magnificent core that would serve as a showplace of modernity and affluence and provide impressive public spaces for the city as a whole. But as failed states lose control of both the informal settlements at the edge *and* the urban core, the public spaces and elite apartments at the core become too dangerous, unstable, and unhealthy to serve as a true center. So, as in the Anglo-American model, the elite use distance to remove themselves from the stresses of the exploding city.

But since the periphery of these cities is already largely dominated by informal settlements, this means in practice creating highly securitized "gated communities" at defensible spots at the edge. As in Sao Paulo's "Alphaville," these gated communities provide not only security but reliable electricity, water, sewage,

18 Manuel Castells, Lee Goh, and Reginald Yin-Wang Kwok, *The Shek Kip Mei Syndrome: Economic Development and Public Housing in Hong Kong and Singapore* (London: Pion Limited, 1990).

19 Thomas J. Campanella, *The Concrete Dragon: China's Urban Revolution and What It Means for the World* (New York: Princeton Architectural Press, 2008).

1.2.6 Aerial photograph of Beijing housing

1.2.7 The challenge: gated community bordered by informal settlement, Buenos Aires

and other utilities; good schools and landscaped parks; access to high-end shopping; and the illusion of freedom and security behind gates and fences worthy of a medieval fortress town. These islands in a sea of informal settlements constitute a kind of archipelago of affluence and modernity that connect, however precariously, to each other and replaces for the wealthy the now derelict public space of the city.

In such cities, the informal settlements then constitute a poverty-stricken reverse image of the spaces of affluence: a vast sea of poverty without even minimal services interrupted only by gated communities and securitized enclaves whose zones of modernity remain strictly off-limits to the vast majority of the population. These "monstrous hybrids" of the French and Anglo-Saxon models of suburbanization represent an even more devastating inscription of class divisions on the metropolis than even the worst-divided cities of the nineteenth and twentieth centuries. (fig. **1.2.7**)

Nevertheless, there is some evidence that a more complex pattern will somehow prevail, combining the human scale and spontaneity of the informal settlement with the modern services and efficient planning of the East Asian new towns.

For example, in Sultanbeyli, an informal settlement with over 250,000 people dating from the 1960s at the edge of Istanbul, a reforming mayor used modest property tax assessments to give a kind of legitimacy to informal occupation. This initiative not only provided funds for basic city services but gave the settlers enough security for them to finance significant improvement to their homes.[20]

Sultanbeyli thus might be seen as embodying a Turkish version of what Jane Jacobs in 1960s New York called "unslumming," a process of gradual improvement initiated and financed by the residents themselves that Jacobs hoped

would replace the cataclysmic clearances of urban renewal.[21] Unfortunately, the urban renewal mentality still seems as dominant throughout the developing world as it was in Robert Moses's Manhattan. Informal settlements, such as Badia East in Lagos, that occupy desirable sites are frequently slated for total clearance and replacement by planned middle-class districts.[22] Only a few cities—such as Medellín, Colombia, with its famous public escalator to the informal settlements— are attempting infrastructure investments to support rather than supplant the unslumming process.[23] And yet, as slow and chaotic as this process might be, the unslummed informal settlements might prove in the end to be more humanely habitable than the regimented suburbs of the East Asian model.

If hybrids such as Sultanbeyli take hold, they will embody some of the more positive hybrid aspects that characterized the suburbs of the past. The modern suburb that emerged in the nineteenth century was a hybrid of the village and the city, preserving through conscious design (as in Riverside) or informal practice (as in the French banlieue or Sultanbeyli) the qualities of a village that is nevertheless an integral part of the larger dynamism of the city. Olmsted's vision of suburbia as the site of urban expansion—the place where the city transforms the edge—still remains true, and perhaps serves as the very definition of suburbia, then and now.

The garden city tradition itself might be seen as a more thoroughgoing attempt at planned positive hybridization, not only in its mixture of classes but also in the environmental interplay of a relatively dense settlement with its greenbelt. So it is appropriate to give the last word on the subject to Ebenezer Howard, who wrote in 1898, "Town and country *must be married*, and out of this joyous union will spring a new hope, a new life, a new civilization."[24]

20 Neuwirth, *Shadow Cities*, 152–60.
21 Jane Jacobs, *The Death and Life of Great American Cities* (New York: Random House, 1962).
22 Alexis Okeowo, "Lagos Must Prosper," *Granta*, April 2015, accessed July 30, 2015, http://granta.com /lagos-must-prosper/.
23 Jon Henly, "Medellín: The Fast Track from the Slums," *Guardian*, July 13, 2013, accessed July 30, 2015, http:// www.theguardian .com/world/2013/jul /31/medellin-colombia -fast-track-slums -escalators.
24 Ebenezer Howard, *Garden Cities of To-morrow* (Cambridge, MA: MIT Press, 1965), 48.

Taboão da Serra, Santana de Parnaíba, São Paulo, Brazil

Sino-Singapore Tianjin Eco-City, Binhai, Tianjin, China

1.3
SUBURBIA AS A CLASS ISSUE

Joel Kotkin

HOUSING
AFFORDABILITY

SOCIAL
DIVERSITY

SOCIAL
INEQUALITIES

From the earliest days of urban settlement, suburbs have been regarded generally as less-desirable places, hence the term's origin in the Latin *suburbium*, which implies inferiority. Generally speaking, in the great cities of Europe or Asia the wealthy clustered in the urban core, while the less well-off moved outward.[1] This was particularly true in great European cities such as London, Amsterdam, and Paris, which have always had higher costs than other locales; the French historian Fernand Braudel described global cities like these as "the core of a world-economy."[2]

The urban wealthy, of course, have long had the option of living in spacious townhomes or large city apartments, as opposed to crowded ones in less appealing areas. They could also purchase country houses for a break from the pressures of urban life.[3] In contrast, the historian Robert Bruegmann argues, suburbia offered the "surest way" for broader portions of the population "to obtain some of the privacy, mobility and choice that once were available only to the wealthiest and most powerful members of society."[4] It was also in the suburbs that many long-term urban renters could at last buy their own residences.

The Importance of Homeownership

At the core of the relationship between suburbs and upward mobility is homeownership. After all, the house is the primary asset for the middle class; the highly affluent have far more stocks and other financial assets. Homes represent barely 9 percent of the assets of the top 1 percent of Americans, notes the New York University economist Edward Wolff, 30 percent for the top 20 percent, and 66 percent for the middle 60 percent. One key reason for the disproportionate asset losses of the middle class after the Recession, and the relative gains of the very rich, lies with the decline of housing prices while stock and other asset prices soared.[5]

Over the past half-century, suburbs have been where most home purchases have taken place. And suburbs remain the locale for such aspirations, including for minorities, whose generally lower net worths reflect, more than anything, their relative lack of ownership. As a recent report by the liberal think tank Demos indicates, much of the "ethnic wealth gap"—white households with wealth more than ten times that of their Latino or African American counterparts—comes from differing homeownership rates. On average, some 71 percent of Anglo households in the major metropolitan areas own their own homes, compared to only 43 percent for Latinos and 38 percent for African Americans. At 59 percent, the Asian homeownership rate is much higher than it is for these other two minorities.[6]

Yet despite these lower rates of ownership, for most minority homeowners (compared to nonminority owners), houses make up a larger portion of assets. That's because minorities don't tend to own other assets, such as stocks, and also often lack significant inheritances. This made these owners more vulnerable to the collapse of the housing bubble, particularly in metropolitan areas where regulations tended to limit supply, driving house prices up beyond an affordable rate and, in too many cases, leaving minority households with mortgages beyond their means.[7]

In the aftermath of the 2007–8 housing bust, it has been widely suggested that the desire for homeownership has been undermined. Criticism of homeownership has included suggestions that it has become, in the words of the popular urbanist Richard Florida's "overrated." Others, including voices from Wall Street, have hailed the rise of a "rentership society."[8] The "end of single family housing" thesis is most strongly held in luxury cities

1   Robert Bruegmann, *Sprawl: A Compact History* (Chicago: University of Chicago, 2005), 23.
2   Fernand Braudel, *The Perspective of the World* (Berkeley and Los Angeles: University of California Press, 1992), 201.
3   Fernand Braudel, *The Structures of Everyday Life* (Berkeley and Los Angeles: University of California Press), 281.
4   Bruegmann, *Sprawl*, 111–12, 132.
5   Jordan Weissmann, "The Recession's Toll: How Middle Class Wealth Collapsed to a 40-Year Low," *Atlantic*, December 4, 2012, accessed November 17, 2015, http://www.the atlantic.com/business /archive/2012/12 /the-recessions-toll -how-middle-class -wealth-collapsed-to-a -40-year-low/265743/.
6   Laura Sullivan et al., "The Racial Wealth Gap: Why Policy Matters," *Institute for Assets and Social Policy, Brandeis University and Demos*, 2015, accessed November 17, 2015, http://www .demos.org/sites/default /files/publications /RacialWealthGap_1.pdf.
7   Sullivan et al., "The Racial Wealth Gap."
8   Richard Florida, "Homeownership Is Overrated," *Wall Street Journal*, June 7, 2010, accessed November 17, 2015, http://www.wsj .com/articles/SB100014 24052748703559004575 25670302198436; Donna Westlund, "Views Differ on Transition in US from Ownership to Rentership Society," *Guardian Liberty Voice*, May 3, 2014, accessed November 17, 2015, http://guardian lv.com/2014/05/views -differ-on-transition -in-u-s-from-ownership -to-rentership-society/.

where homeownership has become unaffordable for all but the wealthiest.

Despite these claims, the desire for homeownership has not ebbed. Research for the Woodrow Wilson Center has indicated a continuing aspirational preference for it. Homeownership was generally considered more important after the housing bubble than it was before—even after the damaging housing crisis, Americans still continued to sanctify homeownership. A survey by the *New York Times* found that nine out of ten Americans value homeownership as a critical part of the "American Dream."[9]

Perhaps no group will more significantly determine the future of housing than the foreign-born. Between 2000 and 2011, there was a net increase of 9.3 million in the foreign-born (immigrant) population, largely from Asia and Latin America. These newcomers have accounted for roughly two out of five in the growth of homeownership. In relatively slow-growing California, they are four out of five. In New York, the immigrant portion of housing growth is two-thirds. It is 30 percent in Georgia and 25 percent in North Carolina; neither of these states are traditional immigrant magnets.[10]

For both Hispanics and Asians, the preference has been for single-family detached homes, precisely what one finds in the suburbs. Approximately 67 percent of Hispanic household growth since 2000 has been in detached housing. Among Asians, the increase has been 60 percent, more than 20 percent above the 2000 share. Today nearly half of all Hispanics and Asians live in single-family homes.[11]

This may seem incongruent, given the experience of the housing crash and the recommendations of financial pundits, among others. Richard Florida, for example, takes aim not only at the "suburban myth" but at homeownership itself, and its "long-privileged place" at the center of the US economy. If anything, he suggests, the

government would be better off encouraging "renting, not buying."[12] Nobel Prize economist and New York Times columnist Paul Krugmann also agrees with this notion, suggesting that we already have "too many homeowners."[13]

So why do most Americans continue to aspire to homeownership? Because the benefits remain very real. A survey by Zogby International suggests many of the same factors that drive buyers to suburbs and lower-density cities: safety, security, and privacy are the prime motivators.[14]

Perhaps the largest social benefits relate to families. Because owners remain in their homes longer than renters do, they add a degree of stability to their neighborhoods, which is valuable for children. Research published by Habitat for Humanity identifies a number of other advantages for children associated with homeownership versus renting.

People who own their own homes also tend to volunteer more in their community, notes the National Association of Realtors. This applies to the owners of both expensive and modest properties.[15] One 2011 Georgetown study suggests that homeownership increases volunteering hours by 22 percent. Another study showed a higher incidence of church attendance among homeowners.[16]

Homeowners also, naturally, have a much greater financial stake in their neighborhoods than renters do. With the median national home price in 2010 at $166,000, even a 5 percent decline in home values will translate into a loss of more than $8,300 for a typical homeowner.[17] New owners also reap the financial gains of any appreciation in the value of their property, so they tend to spend more time and money maintaining their residences, which also contributes to the overall quality of the surrounding community. The right to pass property to an heir or to another person also provides motivation for proper maintenance.

9 Suzy Khimm, "Buying a Home: The American Dream That Won't Die," *MSNBC*, July 10, 2014, accessed November 17, 2015, http://www .msnbc.com/msnbc /homeownership-credit -access-minority-low -income-mortgages; David Streitfeld and Megan Thee-Brenan, "Despite Fears, Owning Home Retains Allure, Poll Shows," *New York Times*, June 29, 2011, accessed November 17, 2015. http://www.nytimes .com/2011/06/30 /business/30poll.html ?_r=0; Dave Sackett and Katie Handel, "Key Findings from National Survey of Voters," Tarrance Group, May 21, 2012, accessed November 17, 2015, http://www .wilsoncenter.org/sites /default/files/keyfind ingsfromsurvey_1.pdf.

10 Miriam Jordan, "Immigrants Buoy the Housing Market," *Wall Street Journal*, March 6, 2013, accessed November 17, 2015, http://online .wsj.com/article/SB1000 1424127887324034804578 344580600357570.html.

11 Calculated from American Community Survey data, 2007–11.

12 Florida, "Homeownership Is Overrated."

13 Paul Krugman, "Home Not-So-Sweet Home," *New York Times*, January 23, 2008, accessed November 17, 2015, http://www.nytimes.com /2008/06/23/opinion /23krugman.html.

14 "Home Ownership and Living: HOA Members and Homeowners Nationwide," Zogby International, 2005.

15 "Social Benefits of Homeownership and Stable Housing," *National Association of Realtors*, April 2012, accessed November 17, 2015, http://www.realtor .org/sites/default/files /social-benefits-of-sta ble-housing-2012-04.pdf.

16 Katherine Drew, "Homeownership and Its Effects on Volunteering: A Comparison across Communities" (master's

Given their stake in election outcomes, homeowners vote much more frequently than renters do. Renters have little or no incentive to protect the value of their landlords' property via the political process. One study found that 77 percent of homeowners had at some point voted in local elections, compared with 52 percent of renters. The study also found a greater awareness of the political process among homeowners. About 38 percent of homeowners knew the name of their local school board representative, compared with only 20 percent of renters.[18]

These often overlooked factors may help explain why, despite the real estate crash, sentiment for homeownership remains remarkably strong. A 2012 study by the Joint Center for Housing Studies at Harvard found "little evidence to suggest that individuals' preferences for owning versus renting a home have been fundamentally altered by their exposure to house price declines and loan delinquency rates, or by knowing others in their neighborhood who have defaulted on their mortgages."[19]

Suburbs as Aspirational Geography

Suburbia had emerged as the key aspirational geography for the working and middle class by the early part of the twentieth century, and came to full flower in the 1950s and 1960s.[20] Still, only one in four Americans lived in suburbs in 1950; in 1960, one in three. By 1990, suburbanites constituted an absolute majority of all Americans. A nation of farm dwellers, and then of city denizens, had become truly suburban. A conservative estimate indicates that today, more than 70 percent of metropolitan area residents are in suburban settings.[21]

For many, moving to suburbia provided the chance to own a house, with a touch of green in the back, and a taste of private paradise.[22] Renters make up a majority of residents in the cores of our eleven largest cities, while roughly two-thirds of all Americans own their own homes.[23] Landownership has become closely entwined with geography: whereas roughly a quarter of urban core residents own their own homes, over three-fifths of residents of older suburbs and more than seven in ten of those in newer suburbs and exurbs own theirs.[24]

This confluence of ownership and dispersion once had a distinctly social democratic tenor. "A nation of homeowners," President Franklin D. Roosevelt believed, "of people who own a real share in their land, is unconquerable."[25] New Dealers encouraged both the dispersion of population and an increase in home ownership through various legislative acts, including the creation of the Federal Housing Administration (FHA) and the Federal National Mortgage Association (Fannie Mae), and later through the GI Bill, which provided low-interest loans to returning veterans.[26] Almost half of suburban housing, notes the historian Alan Wolfe, depended on some form of federal financing.[27]

This diffusion of ownership occurred in an era marked by upward mobility. By the mid-1950s the percentage of households earning middle incomes had doubled to 60 percent, compared with the boom years of the 1920s. By 1962, over 60 percent of Americans owned their own homes; the increase in homeownership, notes the historian Stephanie Coontz, between 1946 and 1956 was greater than that achieved in the preceding century and a half.[28]

In the ensuing decades, this egalitarian trend weakened, but most Americans still continue to seek out single-family houses and suburban lifestyles. Roughly four in five American homebuyers, according to a 2011 study conducted by the National Association of Realtors and Smart Growth America, for example, prefer a single-family home.[29] This

thesis, Georgetown University, April 12, 2011), accessed November 17, 2015, http://repository .library.georgetown.edu /pdfpreview/bitstream /handle/10822/553710 /drewKatherine .pdf?sequence=1.

17 See, for example, Kim Manturuk, Mark Lindblad, and Roberto Quercia, "Friends and Neighbors: Homeownership and Social Capital Among Low- to Moderate-Income Families," *Journal of Urban Affairs* 32, no. 4 (October 2010): 471–88.

18 "Social Benefits of Homeownership and Stable Housing."

19 Rachel Bogardus Drew, "Post-Recession Drivers of Preferences for Homeownership," *Joint Center for Housing Studies Harvard University*, August 2012, accessed November 17, 2015, http://www.jchs .harvard.edu/sites/jchs .harvard.edu/files/w12-4 _drew_herbert.pdf.

20 Michael Lind, *Land of Promise* (New York: Harper Collins, 2012), 208–9.

21 Calculated from the US Census Bureau, American Housing Survey (AHS): 2011. These figures actually understate the case, because AHS classifies a number of suburban municipalities as central cities (such as Long Beach, California, and Tacoma, Washington), and, as noted elsewhere, many of the central cities (historical core municipalities) include large areas of post–World War II suburban employment.

22 Kevin M. Kruse and Thomas J. Sugre, "Introduction: A New Suburban History," in *The New Suburban History*, ed. Kevin M. Kruse and Thomas J. Sugrue (Chicago: University of Chicago Press, 2006), 1; Robert Fishman, *Bourgeois Utopias* (New York: Basic Books, 1988), 192–93; Dawn Wotapka and S.

extends to the vast majority of millennials, a generation that sees homeownership as a critical life goal.[30] Another survey of millennials, published by the National Association of Homebuilders in 2014, found that 75 percent favor settling in a single-family house, 90 percent in the suburbs or an even more rural area, but only 10 percent in the urban core.[31]

Similar patterns can be seen in other high-income countries. Nearly two-thirds of Canadians live in the outskirts of cities.[32] About 50 percent of Australia's population is currently living in middle and outer suburbs. Australians also overwhelmingly prefer single-family houses.[33] In Europe, immigration has slightly boosted the population in urban cores, but the flow of domestic migration still heads toward the periphery. In the United Kingdom, roughly two-thirds of the population lives in suburban settings. The preference for suburban living in Britain has remained fairly constant throughout the last half-century.[34]

The Assault on the Suburban Dream

For the participants, the move to suburbia often represented a quest for "simple happiness," as Juliet Gardiner observed.[35] But many social critics found much about suburbanization objectionable. In a 1905 book, *The Suburbans*, the poet T. W. H. Crossland launched a vitriolic attack on the "low and inferior species," the "soulless" class of "clerks" who were spreading into the new, comfortable houses in the suburbs, mucking up the aesthetics of the British countryside.[36]

Writers and pundits on this side of the Atlantic expressed similar sentiments. In Los Angeles, in the words of the journalist Mildred Adams, migrants came to town "like a swarm of locusts" over the expanding roads of the rapidly expanding region.[37] The urban historian Becky Nicolaides suggests that whatever their other differences, intellectuals generally

Mitra Kalita, "Owning One's Home Loses Some Appeal," *Wall Street Journal*, October 7, 2011, accessed November 17, 2015, http://online.wsj.com/article/SB100014240529702042945045766153602340568 34.html.

23 Laura Kusisto and Kris Hudson, "Renters Are Majority in Big US Cities," *Wall Street Journal*, February 8, 2015, accessed November 17, 2015, http://www.wsj.com/articles/renters-are-majority-in-big-u-s-cities-1423432009?ref=/home-page&cb=logged0.8001066217238658&cb=logged0.262065261025769.

24 Calculated by Wendell Cox from 2010 Census Bureau data.

25 Crystal Galyean, "Levittown: The Imperfect Rise of the American Suburbs," *US History Scene*, August 13, 2012, accessed November 17, 2015, http://www.ushistoryscene.com/uncategorized/levittown/.

26 Eric John Abrahamson, *Building Home: Howard F. Ahmanson and the Politics of the American Dream* (Berkeley: University of California Press, 2013), 5.

27 Stephanie Coontz, *The Way We Never Were* (New York: Basic Books, 1991), 77.

28 Coontz, *The Way We Never Were*, 29, 61.

29 Ed Braddy, "Smart Growth and the New Newspeak," *New Geography*, April 4, 2012, accessed November 17, 2015, http://www.newgeography.com/content/002740-smart-growth-and-the-new-newspeak.

30 Morley Winograd and Michael D. Hais, "The Millennial Metropolis," *New Geography*, April 19, 2010, accessed November 17, 2015, http://www.newgeography.com/content/001511-the-millennial-metropolis.

31 Rose Quint, "Most Millennial Buyers Want Single-Family Home in the Suburbs," *National Association of Home Builders*, January 28, 2015, accessed November

17, 2015, http://eyeonhousing.org/2015/01/most-millennial-buyers-want-single-family-home-in-the-suburbs/; Joe Pinsker, "Young Americans: Yearning for the Suburbs, Stuck in the City," *Atlantic*, January 27, 2015, accessed November 17, 2015, http://www.theatlantic.com/business/archive/2015/01/young-americans-yearning-for-the-suburbs-stuck-in-the-city/384752/; Kris Hudson, "Generation Y Prefers Suburban Home over City Condo," *Wall Street Journal*, January 21, 2015, accessed November 17, 2015, http://www.wsj.com/articles/millennials-prefer-single-family-homes-in-the-suburbs-1421896797.

32 Jennifer Keesmaat, "Here's How to Change Canada from a Suburban to an Urban Nation," *Global and Mail*, May 16, 2014, accessed November 17, 2015, http://www.theglobeandmail.com/globe-debate/heres-how-to-change-canada-from-a-suburban-to-an-urban-nation/article18606842/.

33 Kevin O'Connor and Ernest Healy, "Rethinking Suburban Development in Australia: A Melbourne Case Study," *European Planning Studies* 12, no. 1 (January 2004); Maryann Wulff, Ernest Healy, and Margaret Reynolds, "Why Don't Small Households Live in Small Dwellings? Disentangling a Planning Dilemma," *People and Place* 12 (2004): 57–70, accessed November 17, 2015, http://arrow.monash.edu.au/vital/access/manager/Repository/monash:64024; António F. Tavares and Jered B. Carr, "So Close, Yet So Far Away? The Effects of City Size, Density and Growth on Local Civic Participation," *Journal of Urban Affairs* 35, no. 3 (2013): 283–30, accessed November 17, 2015, http://onlinelibrary.wiley.com/doi/10.1111/j.1467-9906

.2012.00638.x/abstract.

34 Karl Sharro, "Density versus Sprawl," in *The Future of Community: Reports of a Death Greatly Exaggerated*, ed. Dave Clemens et al (London: Pluto Press, 2008), 67. Mark Clapson gathered surveys of people's living aspirations, in *Suburban Century* (New York: Berg, 2003), 55–57. Ben Kochan, in research for the *Town and Country Planning Association* and the *Joseph Rowntree Foundation*, collected more resent research on people's living aspirations and satisfaction, published in *Achieving a Suburban Renaissance: The Policy Challenges* (London: Town and Country Planning Association, 2007), 4, 23.

35 Juliet Gardiner, "How Britain Built Arcadia: The Growth of the Suburbs in the Thirties Brought a Better Life to Millions," *Daily Mail UK*, January 29, 2010, accessed November 17, 2015, http://www.dailymail.co.uk/femail/article-1247156/How-Britain-built-Arcadia-The-growth-suburbs-Thirties-brought-better-life-millions.html.

36 Martin Durkin, "Three Cheers for Urban Sprawl," *New Geography*, January 13, 2012, http://www.newgeography.com/content/002622-three-cheers-urban-sprawl.

37 Carey McWilliams, *Southern California: An Island on the Land* (Salt Lake City: Gibbs Smith, 1975), 127–38.

38 Becky Nicolaides, "How Hell Moved from the Cities to the Suburbs," in *The New Suburban History*, ed. Kevin Kruse and Tom Sugrue (Chicago: University of Chicago Press, 2006), 98.

39 Jane Jacobs, *The Death and Life of Great American Cities* (New York: Random House, 1961), 233.

40 Ibid., 91–97.

41 Quoted in Karl Sharro, "Density versus Sprawl," in Clemens et al., *The Future of Community*, 68–77.

agreed about suburbia: "The common denominator was hell."[38] Other critics often saw suburbs as largely homogeneous and spiritually stultifying. Jane Jacobs, who famously detested suburban Los Angeles, also considered the bedroom communities of Queens and Staten Island "the Great Blight of Dullness."[39] The 1960s social critic William Whyte predicted in *Fortune* that people would tire of such dull places and move back to the city core.[40]

Some present-day critics of suburbanization openly embrace a return to an earlier form of class-based urban development. Britain's Richard Rogers speaks directly to the ideal of "medieval" cities and towns. This archaic, backward-looking vision has little room for the development of suburbs; Rogers regards suburbia's often ungainly structures and lack of aesthetic character as having "no community." He also views suburban communities as socially destructive. "Do you really want to be living in the suburbs with five cats, four dogs, a cabbage patch and five rooms?" he asks blithely.[41]

Yet many critics of the suburbs—including Rogers himself—occupy large blocks of expensive space.[42] Al Gore's gargantuan carbon imprint is another example of this kind of double standard.[43] And in yet another notable case, an examination of where high-profile "smart growth" advocates in Los Angeles live found that almost all lived in large houses, on suburban or even exurban-sized lots. A few were even in gated communities, and none were located anywhere near the public transit lines these advocates want everyone else to use.[44]

Suburbs: The Last Egalitarian Geography

In the past, core cities were the places where people sought to improve their lives and those of their families. A great city, wrote René Descartes in the seventeenth century, represented "an inventory of

the possible," a place where people could create their own futures and lift up their families.[45] In early nineteenth-century New York, artisans and small shopkeepers provided the "reservoir of people" who had joined the landowning class and could afford spacious places to live.[46] But increasingly, our most successful cities now follow the scenario laid out by the author Alan Ehrenhalt in *The Great Inversion*.[47] This represents a return to an earlier kind of urbanism, with the rich clustered in the center and the hoi polloi—who can't afford to live decently in the city—serving them from the dull, dreary periphery.[48]

This shift has transformed places into geographies of unmatched inequality. New York's wealthiest 1 percent earn an income roughly twice as much of the local GDP than is earned in the rest of country.[49] Manhattan's Gini index—a measurement of income distribution—now stands higher than that of South Africa before the apartheid-ending 1994 election. If Manhattan were a country, it would rank sixth-highest in income inequality in the world, out of more than 130 nations for which the World Bank reports data.[50]

The same patterns can be seen, albeit to a lesser extent, in other major cities, notes a recent analysis of 2010 Census data by the Brookings Institution. In many of these core cities, the percentage of middle-income families has been in a precipitous decline for the last thirty years.[51]

In most cases, this phenomenon of increasing inequality in large metropolitan areas has not led to an eradication of poverty. In fact, neighborhoods with entrenched urban poverty actually grew in the first ten years of the new millennium, increasing in numbers from 1,100 to 3,100, and in population from two to four million. "This growing concentration of poverty," note the urban researchers Joe Cortright and Dillon Mahmoudi, "is the biggest problem confronting American cities."[52]

42　Robert Mendick, "Architect Richard Rogers Falls Foul of Planning over Renovation of His £12m House," *Telegraph*, September 5, 2010, accessed November 17, 2015, http://www .telegraph.co.uk /finance/property /news/7981664/Architect -Richard-Rogers-falls -foul-of-planning-over -renovation-of-his-12m -house.html.

43　Bruce Nussbaum, "Al Gore's Carbon Footprint Is Big," *Bloomberg Business*, February 27, 2007, accessed November 17, 2015, http://www.busi nessweek.com/innovate /NussbaumOnDesign /archives/2007/02 /gores_carbon_fo.html.

44　David Zahniser, "Do as We Say, Not as We Do," *LA Weekly*, May 30, 2007, accessed November 17, 2015, http://www.laweekly .com/2007-05-31/news /do-as-we-say-not-as -we-do/.

45　Braudel, *The Perspective of the World*, 30.

46　Sven Beckert, *The Monied Metropolis: New York City and the Consolidation of the American Bourgeoisie* (Cambridge: Cambridge University Press, 2001), 7.

47　Marcus Gee, "Cities Seeing a Reversal of Flight to the Suburbs," *Globe and Mail*, October 6, 2012, accessed November 17, 2015, http://www.theglobeand mail.com/news/toronto /marcus-gee-cities-see ing-a-reversal-of-the -flight-to-the-suburbs /article4593585/.

48　Derek Thompson, "Why Middle-Class Americans Can't Afford to Live in Liberal Cities," *Atlantic*, October 29, 2014, accessed November 17, 2015, http://www .theatlantic.com/busi ness/archive/2014 /10/why-are-liberal -cities-so-unaffordable /382045/; Alan Ehrenhalt, "Cities of the Future May Soon Look Like Those of the Past," *Governing*, April 2012, accessed November 17, 2015, http://www

The New Suburban Population

Often attacked as racist and even elitist, suburbs are now far less unequal than dense cities.[53] The shameful discrimination that occurred in developments such as Levittown largely has come to an end.[54] Yet, as the Urban League has pointed out, the very cities most praised as exemplars of urban revival—San Francisco, Chicago, and Minneapolis—also suffer the largest gaps between black and white incomes.[55] Notwithstanding rhetoric to the contrary, much of the "hip cool" world increasingly consists of monotonic "white cities" with relatively low, and falling, minority populations.[56] San Francisco, Portland, and Seattle, for instance, while achingly politically correct in theory, are actually becoming whiter and less ethnically diverse as the rest of the country diversifies.[57]

Instead of clustering in cities, all three large racial minorities—African Americans, Asians, and Latinos—are steadily moving into the suburbs and, whenever possible, into single-family homes. Between 1970 and 1995, the number of African Americans in suburbia grew from 3.6 million to over 10 million. The 2010 Census indicated that 56 percent of African Americans in major metropolitan areas live in the suburbs.[58] Black America, like the rest of the country, is suburbanizing.

The results are more marked among the country's fastest-growing minority groups, Asians and Latinos. Roughly 60 percent of Hispanics and Asians, notes Brookings, already live in suburbs.[59] Many immigrants no longer wait for greater legal status before moving from the city; more than 40 percent of noncitizen immigrants now move directly to suburbs.[60] The choice of suburbia as a destination can also be seen among Asians. Between 2000 and 2012, the Asian population in suburban areas of the nation's fifty-two biggest metro areas grew 66.2 percent,

.governing.com/topics/economic-dev/gov-cities-of-future-may-soon-look-like-past.html.

49 Patrick McGeehan, "More Earners at Extremes in New York than in US," *New York Times*, May 20, 2012, accessed November 17, 2015, http://www.nytimes.com/2012/05/21/nyregion/middle-class-smaller-in-new-york-city-than-nationally-study-finds.html; Sam Roberts, "Income Data Shows Widening Gap Between New York City's Richest and Poorest," *New York Times*, September 20, 2012, accessed November 17, 2015, http://www.nytimes.com/2012/09/20/nyregion/rich-got-richer-and-poor-poorer-in-nyc-2011-data-shows.html?_r=0; C. Zawadi Morris, "New York City Council Study Shows NYC's Middle Class Shrinking Fast," *Patch Network*, February 11, 2013, accessed November 17, 2015, http://bed-stuy.patch.com/articles/new-city-council-study-shows-nyc-s-middle-class-shrinking-fast.

50 According to the American Community Survey (2008–2012), Manhattan's Gini index is 0.599. According to World Bank figures, pre-Mandela South Africa was 59.3 in 1993.

51 Alan Berube, "All Cities Are Not Created Unequal," *Brookings*, February 20, 2014, accessed November 17, 2015, http://www.brookings.edu/research/papers/2014/02/cities-unequal-berube.

52 Joe Cortright and Dillon Mahmoudi, "Lost in Place: Why the Persistence and Spread of Concentrated Poverty—Not Gentrification—Is Our Biggest Urban Challenge," *City Observatory*, December 2014, accessed November 17, 2015, http://cityobservatory.org/wp-content/uploads/2014/12/LostinPlace_12.4.pdf.

53 "HUD Targets Zoning in Suburbs as Racist,"

Yahoo! Finance, April 3, 2015, accessed November 17, 2015, http://finance.yahoo.com/news/hud-targets-zoning-suburbs-racist-230000213.html; Galyean, "Levittown: The Imperfect Rise of the American Suburbs."

54 Robert Beuka, *SuburbiaNation: Reading Suburban Landscape in Twentieth-Century American Fiction and Film* (New York: Palgrave Macmillan, 2004), 24.

55 Francis Wilkinson, "Why Are Liberal Cities Bad for Blacks?," *Bloomberg View*, April 9, 2014, accessed November 17, 2015, http://www.bloombergview.com/articles/2014-04-09/why-are-liberal-cities-bad-for-blacks.

56 Aaron M. Renn, "The White City," *New Geography*, October 18, 2009, accessed November 17, 2015, http://www.newgeography.com/content/001110-the-white-city; Stu Kantor, "How Do the Top 100 Metro Areas Rank on Racial and Ethnic Equity?," *Urban Institute*, February 2, 2012, accessed November 17, 2015, http://www.urban.org/publications/901478.html.

57 Heather Knight, "Families' Exodus Leaves S.F. Whiter, Less Diverse," *SF Gate*, June 10, 2013, accessed November 17, 2015, http://www.sfgate.com/bayarea/article/Families-exodus-leaves-S-F-whiter-less-diverse-3393637.php; Nikole Hannah-Jones, "In Portland's Heart, 2010 Census Shows Diversity Dwindling," *Oregonian*, May 6, 2011, accessed November 17, 2015, http://www.oregonlive.com/pacific-northwest-news/index.ssf/2011/04/in_portlands_heart_diversity_dwindles.html; Dick Morrill, "Seattle Is Shedding Diversity: The State's Minority Populations Grow," *Crosscut*, April 29, 2011, accessed November

17, 2015, http://crosscut.com/2011/04/29/seattle/20804/Seattle-is-shedding-diversity-states-minority-popu/.

58 William H. Frey, "Melting Pot Cities and Suburbs: Racial and Ethnic Change in Metro America in the 2000s," *Metropolitan Policy Program at Brookings*, May 2011, accessed November 17, 2015, http://www.brookings.edu/~/media/research/files/papers/2011/5/04%20census%20ethnicity%20frey/0504_census_ethnicity_frey.pdf.

59 Ibid.

60 Census Bureau Current Population Survey for 2013 to 2014. The number is actually higher, because this report uses the "principal cities" to identify non-suburban immigration. Principal cities include the core cities as well as municipalities that are suburban employment centers and which are overwhelmingly suburban in their built form. Wendell Cox, "Urban Cores, Core Cities and Principal Cities," *New Geography*, August 1, 2014, accessed November 17, 2015, http://www.newgeography.com/content/004453-urban-cores-core-cities-and-principal-cities.

61 Joel Kotkin, "The Changing Geography of Asian America: To the South and the Suburbs," *New Geography*, September 13, 2012, accessed November 17, 2015, http://www.newgeography.com/content/003080-the-changing-geography-asian-america-to-the-south-and-the-suburbs.

62 Stephanie Czekalinski, "Suburbs Diversify but Many Areas Still Segregated, Report Says," *National Journal*, July 19, 2012, accessed November 17, 2015, http://www.nationaljournal.com/thenextamerica/demographics/suburbs-diversify-but-many-areas-still-segregated-report-says-20120719.

while in the core cities it expanded by 34.9 percent.[61]

In the process, "white suburbia" has become less emblematic of life on the periphery. Indeed, in the decade ending in 2010, the percentage of suburbanites living in "traditional" largely white suburbs fell from just more than half (51 percent) to 39 percent. Over the same period, the number of people who lived in diverse suburbs—areas where the non-white population made up between 20 and 60 percent of the total population—increased from 42 million to 53 million.[62]

To some observers, the movement of minorities into suburbs, once rightly derided for being exclusionary, is now seen as indicative of their decline.[63] Chris Leinberger, a scholar at the Brookings Institution, suggests that the only people likely to head for exurbia will be poor families—many of them minorities—crowding into dilapidated former McMansions in the "suburban wastelands."[64]

Although the suburbs' share of poverty may have increased, this rise also reflects the massive growth of suburbs over the past decade. In 2010 the average poverty rate in the historical core municipalities of the fifty-two largest US metro areas was 24.1 percent, more than double the 11.7 percent rate in suburban areas. The majority of poor people, like the largest chunk of the overall metropolitan population, now do live in the suburbs, but on a percentage basis the concentration of poverty remains far greater in the central cities.[65]

In contrast, the University of Washington's Richard Morrill American Community Survey Data for 2012 indicates that the less dense suburban dominated areas tend to have "generally less inequality" than denser core cities. For example, Riverside–San Bernardino is far less unequal than Los Angeles, and Sacramento is less unequal than San Francisco.[66] Within the fifty-one metropolitan areas with populations of more than 1 million, notes the demographer Wendell Cox, suburban areas were less unequal (measured by the Gini coefficient) than the core cities in forty-six cases.[67]

Preserving an Aspirational Geography

The future of suburbia hinges largely on the entwined futures of homeownership and the fate of the middle class. A house is the largest asset of most households, usually about two-thirds of a family's wealth.[68] But in the aftermath of the Great Recession, first-time buyers, critical to the health of the housing market, have declined well below the historical average of 40 percent.[69]

Some celebrate, and others hope to profit from this tragic situation, embracing the idea of a "rentership society" as a potential vehicle for pocketing revenues from would-be owners turned renters.[70] But arguably the primary losers from a decline of homeownership and suburbia would be ethnic minorities, immigrants, and the next generation—all those who will be reshaping suburbia in the decades ahead.[71]

Ultimately, the prospect of being able to buy or rent an affordable residence may well be the key to future social justice in America. A recent MIT report by the researcher Matthew Rognile suggests that much of the reason for growing inequality has been the rise of housing prices. Without access to affordable, usually suburban homes, working- and middle-class families face a somewhat dismal future. Draconian attempts to limit or even eliminate suburban growth would guarantee that people without wealth will be hard-pressed to achieve upward mobility.[72]

For all their faults, suburbs still represent the promise of upward mobility. They are the prime theater for upward mobility in our evolving, metropolitan America. The abandonment of the

63 Leigh Gallagher, "The End of the Suburbs," *Time*, July 31, 2013, accessed November 17, 2015, http://ideas.time.com/2013/07/31/the-end-of-the-suburbs/; William H. Whyte, "The Anti-City," in *Metropolis: Values in Conflict*, ed. Claude E. Elias, James Gillies, and Svend Riemer (Belmont, CA: Wadsworth, 1965), 69.

64 Lara Farrar, "Is America's Suburban Dream Collapsing into a Nightmare?," *CNN*, June 21, 2008, accessed November 17, 2015, http://www.cnn.com/2008/TECH/06/16/suburb.city/index.html?eref=rss_us.

65 Wendell Cox, "Suburban and Urban Core Poverty: 2012: Special Report," *New Geography*, October 23, 2013, accessed November 17, 2015, http://www.newgeography.com"/content/004006-suburban-urban-core-poverty-2012-special-report.

66 Richard Morrill, "Inequality of the Largest US Metropolitan Areas," *New Geography*, September 1, 2013, accessed November 17, 2015, http://www.newgeography.com/content/003921-inequality-largest-us-metropolitan-areas.

67 Joel Kotkin, "Where Inequality Is Worst in the United States," *New Geography*, March 21, 2014, accessed November 17, 2015, http://www.newgeography.com/content/004229-where-inequality-is-worst-in-the-united-states.

68 Edward N. Wolff, "The Asset Price Meltdown and the Wealth of the Middle Class," *National Bureau of Economic Research*, Working Paper No. 18559 (November 2012), accessed November 17, 2015, http://www.nber.org/papers/w18559.pdf?new_window=1.

69 Julie Schmit, "First-time Buyers Losing Out as Home Sales Rise," *USA Today*, June 29, 2013, accessed November 17, 2015,

suburban ideal raises the prospect that more Americans would become renters and live largely in apartments. It represents nothing less than an attempt to reverse the class gains of the post–World War II era and a return to a more stratified society, a lethal affront to the interests, preferences, and aspirations of the majority. This should be of concern to anyone who cares about the future and most especially to the next generation. Young people are being asked to give up the traditional American Dream and to live instead in a less permeable class structure as suggested by some of their more "enlightened," and often far more affluent, superiors.

As we consider the future of cities, suburbanites need to be seen not as outsiders but as an essential part—even the dominant part—of the metropolitan continuum. Buildings, even the most arresting sort, do not make cities, nor do the centers of tourism, arts, and culture that we frequently enjoy while traveling on business or holiday trips. Instead, a city's heart exists where its people choose to settle. "After all is said and done, he—the *citizen*—is really the city," Frank Lloyd Wright suggested: "The city is going wherever he goes."[73]

Parts of this essay appeared earlier in The New Class Conflict *(Telos, 2015) and also in* The Human City *(Agate, 2016), as well as in numerous articles for* Forbes.com, *the* Daily Beast, City Journal, *the* Washington Post, *the* Orange County Register, *and* Real Clear Politics. *Some of this also appeared in the essay "Retrofitting the Dream" for the Fieldstead Foundation.*

http://www.usatoday.com/story/money/business/2013/06/29/first-time-home-buyers/2472925/; Jason Gold, "Why the Housing Market Can't Move On without More First-Time Homebuyers," *US News*, January 2, 2013, accessed November 17, 2015, http://www.usnews.com/news/blogs/home-front/2013/01/02/why-the-housing-market-cant-move-on-without-more-first-time-homebuyers.

70 John Gittelsom, "US Moves toward Home 'Rentership Society,'" Morgan Stanley Says," *Bloomberg Business*, July 20, 2011, accessed November 17, 2015, http://www.bloomberg.com/news/2011-07-20/u-s-moves-to-rentership-society-as-owning-tumbles-morgan-stanley-says.html.

71 Amy Traub, "The Racial Wealth Gap: Why Policy Matters," *Demos*, March 10, 2015, accessed November 17, 2015, http://www.demos.org/publication/racial-wealth-gap-why-policy-matters.

72 Matthew Rognile, "A Note on Piketty and Diminishing Returns on Capital," June 15, 2014, accessed November 17, 2015, http://www.mit.edu/~mrognlie/piketty_diminishing_returns.pdf.

73 Frank Lloyd Wright, *The Living City* (New York: New American Library, 1958), 87.

1.4
MILLENNIALS' HEARTS ARE IN THE SUBURBS

Morley Winograd and Michael D. Hais

HOUSING
AFFORDABILITY

SOCIAL
DIVERSITY

Even William Fulton, the president of policy and research at Smart Growth America, a nonprofit national coalition dedicated to fighting "suburban sprawl," argues that in order for cities to retain their recent influx of young residents they will have to supply all the amenities of suburban life—such as "schools, recreational activities, safety, housing, child care and outdoor space."[1] While such an urban planning strategy might help central cities, millennials, most of whom were raised in the suburbs, are more likely to return as they age to the setting they grew fond of in their childhood, no matter what cities do to attract them. When they do, millennials will remake America's suburbs in ways that will reflect the generation's unique beliefs and behaviors.

The millennial generation (born 1982–2003) is the largest generation in US history, one with remarkably uniform attitudes for a cohort whose ethnic diversity is exceeded only by the generation born after theirs. In the years ahead, the sheer size of the generation (ninety-five million) and the broad consensus among millennials on where and how to live will make the generation the driving force in determining the future of American suburbs. Their imprint on suburban life in America will prove every bit as powerful and transformative as the one caused by the exodus of families to the suburbs in the last half of the twentieth century.

Suburbs Change with the Generations

From 1940 to 1960, the percentage of Americans living in the suburbs doubled, from 15 to 30 percent. Over the next two decades, when most members of the generation that preceded millennials—Generation X—were born, that percentage rose again as much to 45 percent.[2]

In his autobiographical film *Avalon*, the director Barry Levinson captured what he thought was the impact of this exodus on his large, fractious-but-loving Baltimore family. He suggested that the weakening of his family's ties was caused by its dispersal to the suburbs, rather than to the social upheavals of the 1960s. In the 1996 film *Suburbia*, teens grapple with the angst of their seemingly meaningless lives as residents of the suburbs. But the weakening of families, as measured by such social indicators as rising teenage crime and pregnancy rates, had more to do with changes in generational attitudes and behaviors than with Americans chose to raise their families.

Movies were not the only entertainment medium to take aim at suburban life. Dysfunctional families portrayed with snarky humor in television shows, such as *Married…with Children* or *The Simpsons*, became cultural icons for the cynical, slacker attitude of Generation X children as well as the suburban environment in which those kids increasingly lived.

Some of these portrayals had the ring of truth. During the 1970s, suburban homes were often inhabited by the nation's first "latchkey kids," children who came back from school to an empty house because both parents found it necessary to go to work to keep up with double-digit inflation.[3] Under this economic pressure, as well as the liberating power of the pill, which freed many wives from what they considered to be the stultifying mores of their day, the amount of time Generation X children spent with a "significant adult role model" dropped to an all-time low, averaging just over an hour per day even for children lucky enough to have two parents living at home.

Now in their thirties and forties, members of Generation X, who tend to be the parents of the youngest millennials, are determined not to rear their children in that way. Their zealous focus on what is best for their offspring has earned them the sobriquet "stealth fighter parents"— determined to defend and protect their children from all threats, even as they seek

1   Haya El Nasser, "American Cities to Millennials: Don't Leave," *USA Today*, December 4, 2012, accessed November 17, 2015, http://www.usa today.com/story/news /nation/2012/12/03 /american-cities-to -millennials-dont-leave -us/1744357/.

2   Morley Winograd and Michael D. Hais, *Millennial Momentum: How a New Generation Is Remaking America* (New Brunswick, NJ: Rutgers University Press, 2011).

3   Mark Donald, "Latchkey Kids: Every Day after School Thousands of Children Come Home to Boredom, Loneliness, Even Fear. Other Cities Are Reaching Out to Help Them. Why Aren't We?," *D Magazine*, July 1985.

the safety and comfort of suburban living to raise their millennial children.[4]

As a result, the millennial experience in suburbia has been much better than that experienced by X'ers, or boomers, for that matter, even as media portrayals frequently failed to keep up with this contemporary reality. Millennials were loved, nurtured, indeed revered, by both their parents. The millennial generation became the first one ever to fully experience the concept of coparenting, with both fathers and mothers playing an equal role in their children's upbringing. The amount of time parents spent interacting with their children rose on average to almost three hours per day by 1995, with the largest gains occurring among fathers.

The goal of most parents of millennials, whether they were members of the baby boom generation or Generation X, was to maximize the feelings of self-esteem of their children.[5] The rationale for this parenting style was to give millennial children an emotional fortress so strong that life's hard knocks and disappointments could not penetrate it. To accomplish this, the parents of millennials sought to become friends with their children, forswearing physical discipline while imposing a regime of rules and consequences (called "time-outs") for breaking them. As a result, unlike many boomers or X'ers, millennials enjoy being with their parents. Ninety-one percent of millennials are satisfied with their relationship with their parents.[6]

Nor do they harbor any resentment toward the suburban lifestyle they experienced as children. In a 2010 survey by Frank N. Magid Associates, 43 percent of millennials described suburbs as their ideal place to live. Only 17 percent of those surveyed said they wanted to live in a big city, the same percentage that preferred small-town or country living. By comparison, only 36 percent of Generation X'ers and just 28 percent of

boomers expressed a predilection for suburban living.[7]

These attitudes will become more evident as boomer pundits, many of whom have pushed an antisuburban, pro-downtown density point of view, fade from the scene. By the end of this decade, approximately 36 percent of all adult Americans will be millennials, and their beliefs will become the dominant motif of American life.

Millennials Want a Suburban Home of Their Own

America's suburbs will be completely reshaped—and reinvigorated—as greater numbers of millennials decide to buy a home there. Millennials rank owning their own home as one of their top three priorities in life, second only to being a good parent.[8] A full 82 percent of adult millennials and 90 percent of married millennials say owning their own home is important, percentages that are higher than for the two preceding generations (X'ers, 80 percent; boomers, 76 percent).[9]

These earlier survey results have been confirmed by more recent studies. For instance, Zillow's 2014 Housing Confidence Index found that two-thirds of eighteen- to thirty-four-year-olds said owning their own home was necessary to live "the good life" and achieve "the American Dream." Contrary to media stories written about millennials turning the country into a nation of big city–dwelling renters, these percentages were actually higher than for older generations.[10]

Most of this growth in homeownership will take place in the suburbs. A Nielsen survey done for the Demand Institute found that 48 percent of the eighteen- to twenty-nine-year-olds they interviewed planned on moving to the suburbs, while only 38 percent said they would be moving into large urban areas. A scant 14 percent

4 Neil Howe, "Meet Mr. and Mrs. Gen X: A New Parent Generation," *School Administrator* 67, no. 1 (January 2010): 18–23.

5 Jean M. Twenge, *Generation Me: Why Today's Young Americans Are More Confident, Assertive, Entitled—and More Miserable Than Ever Before* (New York: Free Press, 2006).

6 Pew Research Center, "A Portrait of Generation Next: How Young People View Their Lives, Future, and Politics," January 9, 2007, accessed November 17, 2014, http://pewresearch.org/pubs/278/a-portrait-of-generation-next.

7 Morley Winograd and Michael D. Hais, "Twenty-First-Century Political Coalitions: Two Parties Headed in Opposite Directions: A Twenty-First-Century America Report," NDN, March 4, 2010, accessed November 17, 2014, http://ndn.org/sites/default/files/paper/21st%20Century%20America%20Project%20March%202010%20PPT%20Presentation.pdf.

8 Pew Research Center, "Millennials: A Portrait of Generation Next," February 2010, accessed November 17, 2015, http://pewsocialtrends.org/file/2010/10/millennials-confident-connected-open-to-change.pdf.

9 Morley Winograd and Michael D. Hais, "A Return to Avalon," *New Geography*, July 27, 2008, accessed November 17, 2015, http://www.newgeography.com/content/00119-a-return-avalon.

10 Aaron Terrazas, "Zillow's Housing Confidence Index: Will Youthful Exuberance Today Mean More Sales Tomorrow?," Zillow Real Estate Research, September 22, 2014, accessed November 17, 2015, http://www.zillow.com/research/housing-confidence-index-sept-2014-7698/.

planned to move to rural environments.[11] In a 2012 study, 70 percent of millennials said they would prefer to own a home in the suburbs if they can "afford it and maintain their lifestyle."[12]

These preferences are reflected in the decisions millennials are already making on where to live and raise a family. Between 2000 and 2010, the nation's fifty-one largest urban areas lost 15 percent of adults ages twenty-five to thirty-four; by contrast, during that decade suburbs saw an average 14 percent gain within that age group.[13]

Nor were rural areas likely to stop their steady decline in population by attracting more millennials with back-to-nature beliefs. From 2007 to 2013, the ten counties with the most millennial residents had an average population of 587,522.[14] The National Association of Realtors list of the top ten metropolitan areas for millennial home buying included college towns like Raleigh, North Carolina; Austin, Texas; and Madison, Wisconsin; but, in addition, medium-sized cities and/or the suburbs of places such as Des Moines, Iowa; Grand Rapids, Michigan; Ogden, Utah; Nashville, Tennessee; and Omaha, Nebraska.[15]

In recent years, this underlying demand for a single-tract home in the suburbs has been obscured by the slow pace of the nation's housing recovery. It has also been missed by forecasters who extrapolate from the current revival of downtowns in cities such as Washington, DC, and New York to a prediction of a similarly configured future. These media memes fail to take into account the differences between those just starting out in life and those entering into the years of family formation when most people make their first home purchases. Trulia's chief economist Jed Kolko points out that the likelihood of living in urban neighborhoods rather than the suburbs peaks when people are in their mid- to late twenties,

as many millennials are today, but steadily drops off as thirty-somethings move out of the city.[16]

The tendency of millennials to settle down later in life than earlier generations further clouds the crystal balls of those attempting to see America's suburban future. According to Census data, from 1960 to 2011, the median age for first marriages increased by six years, from twenty-three to twenty-nine for men and twenty to twenty-six for women. The share of eighteen- to thirty-four-year-olds who were married fell from 47 percent in 1983 to only 30 percent today. Moreover, just 29 percent of those who are married have children, compared to 39 percent three decades ago. One analysis found that if millennials were marrying at the same pace as previous generations, their rate of homeownership would be 33 percent, four percentage points higher than now, and roughly the same as in the 1990s.[17]

Among millennials who are married with both spouses working, homeownership rates are actually above the rates of eighteen- to thirty-four-year-olds in the 1980s and 1990s. Even single, employed millennials own homes at a greater rate than similarly situated young people did twenty or thirty years ago.

Millennial unemployment rates have been above historical ranges for their age group ever since the Great Recession began in 2008. Even though the employment rate among twenty-five to thirty-four-year-olds grew about 29 percent faster in 2014 than the overall employment rate did, the unemployment level for this age cohort is just beginning to return to levels considered normal before 2008.

Stories about adult millennials living with their parents, such as in the movie *Failure to Launch*, were validated by Pew survey data showing that about 34 percent of the generation was still staying at their family houses as a means of coping

11 Jeremy Burbank and Louise Keely, "Millennials and Their Homes: Still Seeking the American Dream," Demand Institute, September 16, 2014, accessed November 17, 2015, http://demandinstitute.org/blog/millennials-and-their-homes.

12 Morley Winograd and Michael D. Hais, "Millennial Lifestyles Will Remake American Homes," *New Geography*, May 6, 2013, accessed November 17, 2015, http://www.newgeography.com/content/003685-millennial-lifestyles-will-remake-american-homes.

13 Jacob Davidson, "What Everyone Gets Wrong about Millennials and Home Buying," *Time.com*, November 12, 2014, accessed November 17, 2015, http://time.com/money/3551773/millennials-home-buying-marriage/.

14 Beau Dure, "Millennials Continue Urbanization of America, Leaving Small Towns," *NPR*, October 21, 2014, accessed November 17, 2015, http://www.npr.org/2014/10/21/357723069/millennials-continue-urbanization-of-america-leaving-small-towns.

15 Joel Cone, "10 US Real Estate Markets Investors Should Watch," *US News and World Report*, December 1, 2014, accessed November 17, 2015, http://money.usnews.com/money/blogs/the-smarter-mutual-fund-investor/2014/12/01/10-us-real-estate-markets-investors-should-watch.

16 Shane Ferro and Andy Kiersz, "The Era of City-Dwelling Millennials Is Coming to an End," *Business Insider*, January 28, 2015, accessed November 17, 2015, http://www.businessinsider.com/we-have-reached-peak-urban-millennials-2015-1#ixzz3Rr9XqjcP.

17 Davidson, "What Everyone Gets Wrong about Millennials and Home Buying."

with economic hardship. Only 43.7 percent of college-educated millennials owned a home in 2014. More than two-thirds of those who didn't own a home said they needed a higher salary or income before they could afford to buy one.[18]

The problem for the housing market is not millennials' rejection of home-ownership; rather, it is that too few millennials are currently married and working full time. These are the obstacles that have hindered the housing market's recovery. But over time the sheer size and inevitable maturation of the millennial generation is destined to produce a suburban boom in this next decade as more and more millennials enter their mid-thirties, start families, and make progress in their careers.

While only 30 percent of eighteen- to twenty-nine-year-olds are married, seven of ten say they expect to be within the next five years. Fifty-five percent also anticipate becoming parents during this period.[19] Data from the National Center for Health Statistics suggest this is already happening. There were over four million births in 2014, making it one of the top twenty-five years for births since 1909. Since the median age of millennials is twenty-four, the United States can expect at least ten more years with large numbers of births.

This will inevitably lead to increased numbers deciding to buy a home in order to provide space for their growing families. Indeed, nearly three-fourths of the eighteen- to twenty-nine-year-olds interviewed by Nielsen planned on buying a new home within the next five years. Although half said that their plan to purchase a home was motivated by a desire to establish their own household, an even greater number (59 percent) wanted more privacy or space.[20]

These future aspirations reflect the underlying optimism of the millennial generation. Since 1998, Americans between the ages of eighteen and thirty-four have consistently been more optimistic about their economic future than those between thirty-five and sixty-five years old. This gap has only widened as millennials came to comprise a greater portion of the eighteen-to-thirty-four cohort.

By 2043, the Mortgage Bankers Association predicts that millennials will have formed twenty-four million new households.[21] The Demand Institute estimated the number of households headed by millennials would increase by 8.3 million in just the next five years, growing from 13.3 million in 2013 to 21.6 million in 2018. They estimate that these home purchases will be worth 1.6 trillion dollars and make millennials the largest segment of the US housing market when taking into account both owners and renters.[22] The chief economist for the real estate site Zillow.com predicted that by the end of 2015, "Millennial buyers will represent the largest group of homebuyers, taking over from Generation X."[23]

Three-fourths of current millennial homebuyers are purchasing their first one; more than two-thirds are single-family, detached homes of less than 2,000 square feet (186 square meters).[24] To continue to be successful in selling such homes to millennials, realtors will have to adjust their offerings to accommodate the way millennials want to live.

Millennials Will Remake America's Suburbs

Reflecting their cautious attitudes about spending their hard-to-come-by money, millennials look more for value than "pizzazz" in a new home. Seventy-seven percent of millennials say they prefer an "essential" home over a "luxury" model.[25]

Befitting of the generation that started the social media craze with teenage posts on MySpace, most millennials want a house that can be customized to their individual preferences. Forty-three

18 Sam Ruiz, "What Stands between Millennials and Homeownership," Lending Tree, November 24, 2014, accessed November 17, 2015, http://www.lendingtree.com/blog/millennials-and-home ownership/.

19 Burbank and Keely, "Millennials and Their Homes: Still Seeking the American Dream."

20 Ibid.

21 Scott K. Stucky, "Changing of the Guard: Are You Prepared for Millennials to Become the Future of Mortgage Lending?," *National Mortgage Professional*, November 14, 2014, accessed November 17, 2015, http://national mortgageprofessional.com/news/51753/changing-guard-are-you-prepared-millen nials-become-future-mortgage-lending.

22 Burbank and Keely, "Millennials and Their Homes: Still Seeking the American Dream."

23 Susan Johnston, "What Real Estate Trends to Expect in 2015," *US News and World Report*, December 9, 2014, accessed November 17, 2015, http://money.usnews.com/money/personal-finance/articles/2014/12/09/what-real-estate-trends-to-expect-in-2015.

24 Natalia Siniavskaia, "What Homes Do Millennials Buy?," NAHB, *Eye on Housing*, December 8, 2014, accessed November 17, 2015, http://eyeon housing.org/2014/12/what-homes-do-millennials-buy/.

25 Winograd and Hais, "Millennial Lifestyles Will Remake American Homes."

percent want their home to be less a "cookie cutter" offering and more capable of allowing them to put their own finishing touches on it. Almost one-third prefer a "fixer upper" to a "move-in-ready" home.

The millennial generation's love affair with technology is reflected in its housing preferences. A majority believes the technological capabilities of a house are more important than its "curb appeal"; almost two-thirds want to live in a home that is "tech-friendly." Nearly half focus on the technological sophistication of the family room rather than other rooms in making that determination. In fact, about as many would rather turn their living room into a home theater with a big screen TV than use it in more traditional ways. Even in the kitchen, a solid majority said they would rather have a television screen than a second oven. Almost half of millennials say a security system is one of the technological essentials in a home and about a quarter want to control such a system from their smart phone.[26]

The generation's belief in protecting the future of the planet—as well as their desire for cost savings—is also reflected in its housing preferences. Almost half don't want a home that wastes energy, with an energy-efficient washer and dryer topping its essential technology wish list. A smart thermostat was also considered important, placing it third on the list of millennials' technological housing essentials.

These preferences aren't the only reasons that millennials' homes will reduce the nation's carbon footprint in coming years. Millennials see their home as a place to "do work," not just a place to return to "after work." Already one in five millennials say that "home office" is the best way to describe how they use what has been traditionally called a dining room. The generation's blurring of gender roles as well as its facility in using digital technologies means that millennials will likely work as much from home as "at

work," as both parents share child-rearing responsibilities. All of these beliefs suggest that telecommuting will become a common characteristic of suburban millennial life.[27]

The millennial penchant for community service and sharing will also bring benefits to those communities that find ways to better connect their new residents.[28] An analysis by the National Conference on Citizenship (NCoC) found that municipalities having the greatest amount of "social cohesion," defined as interacting frequently with friends, family members, and neighbors, had a greater ability to ameliorate job losses during the Great Recession. Places with high social cohesion had unemployment rates two percentage points lower than their less connected counterparts.[29]

Millennials will be attracted to suburbs that build opportunities for such interactions into the design of the community. One way to accomplish this is by placing major amenities within walking distance of homes or just a short drive away in town centers. Another is to encourage the type of nonprofit activity and community volunteerism that appeal to many millennials. The challenge for suburban planners will be to build this type of social cohesion into their designs while offering the single-tract homes millennials prefer.

Unleashing the Millennial Transformation of America's Suburbs

The single biggest barrier to the country enjoying a new wave of spending on suburban housing from the rising rate of millennial family formation remains the generation's unique burden of student debt. Almost one in three (28.7 percent) of nonhomeowning, college-educated millennials said they wanted to pay off their student loans before becoming homeowners.[30]

26 Ibid.
27 Ibid.
28 Tom Spengler, "Civic Engagement: Why Millennials Have Outpaced Seniors," *Huffington Post*, June 2014.
29 Morley Winograd and Michael D. Hais, "Communities Need to Build Better Millennial Connections," *MikeandMorley.com*, March 6, 2013, accessed November 17, 2015, http://www.mikeandmorley.com/communities_need_to_build_better_millennial_connections.
30 Ruiz, "What Stands between Millennials and Home Ownership."

One study estimated that the burden of student debt cost the US housing market 414,000 sales in 2014, worth about $83 billion in sales. The study found that households paying more than $750 per month in student debt were effectively priced out of the market altogether, with every $250 in monthly payments reducing their home purchasing power by $44,000. Since 2005, the number of households headed by someone under the age of forty with student debt payments of at least $250 per month nearly tripled to just under six million. This means that about one-third of young adults have student debt burdens that limit their ability to buy a home, even as it remains their fondest dream to do so.[31]

One way to address this issue would be to minimize the down payment requirements for a new home for millennial, first-time buyers. The decision of Fannie Mae and Freddie Mac to securitize mortgages with only a 3 percent down payment is a good step in that direction. Another would be to offer a lease-to-purchase option, which would be attractive to 69 percent of millennials.[32] As multigenerational homes become more popular, older members of the family may well decide to cosign a mortgage for the whole house, in the expectation that their millennial children or grandchildren will eventually take on the responsibility of paying it off. Some or all of these solutions to the problem of millennials' student debt burden will need to be pursued if the full force of millennials' suburban preferences is to be felt in the economy in the near future.

Whether it happens sooner or later, the overwhelming desire of millennials to own a piece of the American Dream will inevitably reshape the nation's suburbs. Those communities, which offer millennials the type of lifestyle and housing they desire, will be rewarded with growth. Those that cling to outdated notions of what constitutes suburban living will find it difficult to compete for the millennial generation's housing dollar and the vibrant economic activity that will flow from their decisions. The choice of which path to pursue is best made with a clear understanding of the values and beliefs of America's next great generation.

Thank you to Justin Chapman, Project Fellow, University of Southern California Annenberg Center on Communication Leadership & Policy.

31 Tim Logan, "Student Loan Debt Curbs Housing Market by $83 Billion, Study Says," *Los Angeles Times*, September 22, 2014, accessed November 17, 2015, http://www.latimes.com/business/realestate/la-fi-student-loan-debt-housing-market-20140922-story.html.

32 Burbank and Keely, "Millennials and Their Homes: Still Seeking the American Dream."

Fontana, California, United States

Greenacres, Palm Beach County, Florida, United States

1.5
SUBURBAN
HOLY LAND

D. J. Waldie

I live in a tract house on a street of more tract houses in a neighborhood hardly distinguishable from any other in Southern California. The rows of houses extend as far as the street grid allows. My exact place on the grid is at the extreme southeast corner of Los Angeles County in a midcentury suburb called Lakewood, but that's just an accident of family history. While I live in Lakewood, my home might as well be anywhere in what some call suburbia.

Lakewood is an ordinary suburb, but its backstory includes Spain's seventeenth-century Laws of the Indies, the United States occupation of Mexican Los Angeles in 1847, upper-class anxieties about race and hygiene in early twentieth-century America, and the assumptions and compromises of planners and politicians who have imposed their imagination on an indifferent landscape for more than a hundred years.

Lakewood was developed in 1950 as an experiment in placemaking on an almost unimaginable scale. There were failures of placemaking in Lakewood and elsewhere in Southern California, but the suburban experiment ultimately succeeded for my family and for millions of others. Lakewood's 9.5 square miles (24.6 square kilometers) of small houses on small lots reflect a durable idea about the way working-class people ought to be housed, beginning with Progressive Era beliefs about the power of a "house in its garden" to improve the morals of mill hands and ending with mass-produced, "minimal traditional" housing in neighborhoods that I, like some of my neighbors, regard as a kind of holy land.

There are plenty of toxic places to reside—in McMansion wastelands or behind the gates of bunker suburbs—but that's not the sort of place where I live. Where I've lived for my entire life is a 957-square-foot (89-square-meter) wood-frame house, set back 20 feet (6 meters) from the sidewalk on a 5,000-square-foot (465-square-meter) lot. There's a strip of lawn along the curb that has just enough room for a tree the city trims every four or five years. Where I live, shops and services were clustered at intersections every half-mile (0.8 kilometers) along arterial streets in the 1950s, so that anyone today who wants to can walk to a convenience store, a bar, a drug store, or a fast-food place. Where I live, there are ten neighborhood parks, so that everyone is no more than a mile from city-maintained playgrounds, ball diamonds, picnic tables, and barbecue grills. There are no walls around my neighborhood, and very few around any neighborhood in Lakewood. We live with the anxieties and promises of a grid that opens outward, the antithesis of a ghetto.

There's a persistent belief that places like this must be awful, monstrous, and soul-destroying. In 1957 the writer John Keats saw newly made tract house neighborhoods and lamented:

> For literally nothing down—other than a simple two percent and a promise to pay—you too can find a box of your own in one of the fresh-air slums we're building around the edges of American cities… inhabited by people whose age, income, number of children, problems, habits, conversations, dress, possessions, and perhaps even blood type are also precisely like yours. [They are] developments conceived in error, nurtured by greed, corroding everything they touch.[1]

In 1969 Nathaniel Owings damned the planning that produced neighborhoods like mine with an image of nuclear apocalypse. "Regard suburbia," Owings rhetorically commanded in *The American Aesthetic*: "The land is being chopped into temporarily usable fragments, stripped of its natural contours, and covered by the suburban population fallout."[2] In a chilling

1   John Keats, *The Crack in the Picture Window* (New York: Houghton Mifflin, 1957), xi–xii.

2   Nathaniel Alexander Owings, *The American Aesthetic* (New York: Harper & Row, 1969), 17.

speech by the suburban critic James Howard Kunstler at the 1999 Congress for the New Urbanism, the kind of place where I live was described as an "anti-place," a perversion of a place. "It is the dwelling place of untruth," Kunstler warned his audience. The title of Kunstler's speech was "Where Evil Dwells."[3]

And yet, despite the opprobrium expressed by their cultural betters, most working-class Americans live in that kind of neighborhood. Fortunately, most of them are not much aware of the criticism or the historical significance of suburbanization, even though, for the sociologists Rosalyn Baxandall and Elizabeth Ewen, "the history of suburbia is at the heart of twentieth-century American history."[4]

At every critical juncture, suburban history collides with the history of housing and its pivotal role in the evolution of American society. The idea of suburbia was central to visionaries, planners, and socially conscious architects who began to imagine a new America where ordinary people, not just the elite, would have access to attractive, modern housing in communities with parks, gardens, recreation, stores, and cooperative town-meeting places.

It's now sixty-six years since the last harvesters left the lima bean fields of not-yet-Lakewood while an idling road grader waited. It was among the first in a very long line of graders and bulldozers that scraped the rest of Los Angeles County into the suburbs. When my parents bought their home, the idea of a house like that in that kind of neighborhood was new. No one knew what would happen next, when tens of thousands of working-class husbands and wives—so young and inexperienced—were thrown together and expected to make a fit place to live.

It was a rough demand that was roughly answered, despite the careless *Ozzie and Harriett / Leave It to Beaver /*

Brady Bunch mythology that continues to obscure actual suburban places. What happened next in Lakewood was the usual redemptive mix of joy and tragedy, for which the laments of the country western music coming out of Bakersfield were some consolation for my neighbors, most of whom had come from Oklahoma, Texas, Arkansas, and other places on the borders of the Dust Bowl.

There are Californians today who don't regard their suburb as a place of pilgrimage, but my parents and their friends did. At least their home wasn't in an oil camp outside Taft, or rented rooms in a clapboard tenement in Los Angeles, or a farmworker's shack somewhere west of Fresno. My parents' friends, who in 1950 had recently lived in those places, were grateful for the comforts of their not quite middle-class life. For those who came (and still come) to Lakewood, the aspiration wasn't for more, but only for enough.

My parents and their neighbors understood, more generously than Owings or Keats did, what was to be found and lost in owning a small house on a small lot in a neighborhood connected to square miles of just the same. Despite everything that was ignored or squandered in Lakewood's making, I believe a kind of dignity was gained. The fathers of my friends—and my own father—later told me that living here allowed them habits that did not make them feel ashamed, and a life they felt was whole.

As far as I could tell by their lives together, my parents did not escape to their mass-produced suburb. Nor have I. But I'm not unusual in living in Lakewood for all the years I have. According to the 2012 American Community Survey, 22 percent of Lakewood's residents have lived here thirty years or more.[5] Perhaps, like me, they've found a place that permits restless people to be still.

By 1954, nearly forty thousand families had joined mine in Lakewood on

3 James Howard Kunstler, "Where Evil Dwells" (paper presented at the 1999 Congress for the New Urbanism, Milwaukee, June 6, 1999).

4 Rosalyn Baxandall and Elizabeth Ewen, *Picture Windows: How The Suburbs Happened* (New York: Basic Books, 2001), 39.

5 Data provided by the City of Lakewood Department of Community Development.

the dead-level floodplain between the Los Angeles and San Gabriel Rivers north of Long Beach. The men made their living riveting jets together at the Douglas Aircraft plant in Long Beach or cracking crude oil into gasoline at refineries in Carson and Wilmington across the Los Angeles River. Their wives made homes. Their children thrived more or less carelessly in the smoggy sunshine.

The parceling out of their postwar dreams into rows of tract houses had been made possible in the previous decade by enormous changes in the way affordable housing was created, sold, and financed. But the redefinition of *home* had been the subject of a national conversation long before then. Since the 1890s, utopians, socialists, architects, writers for women's magazines, union leaders, city planners, and businessmen like the Boston department store owner Edward Filene had argued that working-class housing was the overriding issue of the modern age. To make houses affordable, make them like Fords, Filene insisted in his influential book *The Way Out* in 1925.[6] By the mid-1940s, as New Deal planning shaded into postwar prosperity, houses were finally mass-produced just like Fords and sold with mortgages from banks and savings institutions working under New Deal regulations, backed by New Deal–created federal agencies.

Suburban stories like Lakewood's were mass-produced for millions of Americans who sought escape from memories of the agricultural depression of the 1920s, the industrial depression of the 1930s, the years of World War II, and the months of the Korean War. They were stories for displaced Okies and Arkies, Jews who knew the pain of exclusion, Catholics who thought they did, and anyone white with a steady job. Left out of this spectacle of democracy were people of color. Their exclusion was not only a Lakewood transgression but also a

general one, found in both elite suburbs and places more modest, including Levittown.

In Lakewood, this sad legacy is now past. Today the residents of Lakewood—and most working-class suburbs in California—are becoming as mixed in their colors and ethnicities as all of maximally diverse Los Angeles County. (In 2002 the Public Policy Institute of California reported that Lakewood had one of the highest rates of ethnic diversification of any California city.)[7] I still live in Lakewood with anticipation, because I want to find out what happens next to these new narrators of suburban stories who happen to be my African American, Latino, Filipino, Chinese, Korean, Lao, and Vietnamese neighbors. They're stories I already know.

The Commonplace Community
City planners have told me that my neighborhood should have been bulldozed by now to make room for something they insist would be less suburban and therefore better, and yet Lakewood's small houses stubbornly resist, just as loyal to their idea of how a community can be made as I try to be. That idea in Lakewood can still bring out four hundred park league coaches in the spring and six hundred volunteers to clean up the weedy yards of their elderly and disabled neighbors on Volunteer Day, and over two thousand on Wednesday evenings to listen to summer concerts in the park. Loyalty to the commonplace is the last habit that anyone would impute to those of us who live here; we're supposed to be so dissatisfied (or numbed) in the suburbs.

"Exceptionalist" claims—both negative and positive—have flattened our understanding of suburban history into doom-laden darkness or vapid sunniness (the latter, always wreathed with irony). As a result, the everyday, which ought to be a source of wholeness, is experienced

6   Edward Filene, *The Way Out: A Forecast of Coming Changes in American Business and Industry* (Garden City, NY: Page & Co., 1924).

7   Juan Onésimo Sandoval, Hans P. Johnson, and Sonya M. Tafoya, "Who's Your Neighbor? Residential Segregation and Diversity in California," *California Counts: Population Trends and Profiles* 4, no. 1 (August 2002): 14.

1.5.1 William A. Garnett, *Framing, Lakewood, California*, 1950. Gelatin silver print, 7 ¼ × 9 ½ in. (18.4 × 24.1 cm).

as unsatisfying or alienating. And because much of the everyday in America is suburban, some Americans see suburban places as aesthetically, politically, and morally perverse as well.

When I walk out the door of my house on Graywood Avenue, I see the human-scale, specific landscape that has sheltered the habits that shape my work, my convictions, and my aspirations. Even nature is present there, necessarily complicit and implicated in the landscape. The vista in front of my house hasn't been emptied of possibilities by its familiarity. The everyday never lacks trajectories into and out of the sensuous matter of what is being lived. The everyday at my doorstep is expectant, arrives laden with a burden of history, and sometimes unfolds into moments of beauty.

There's an education in streets when they're bordered by sidewalks and lawn in front of unassuming houses set close enough together that their density is about 8 units per acre (20 units per hectare). With neighbors just 15 feet (5 meters)

apart, we're easily in each other's lives across fences, in front yards, and even through our thin, stucco-over-chicken-wire house walls. You don't have to love all of the possibilities for civility handed to us in my suburb, but you have to love enough of them, specifically enough of the play between life in public and life in private that I see choreographed by the design of Lakewood.

The builders of postwar suburbs depended on the reciprocal embrace of people and place. It meant developers could build their minimal houses so cheaply that anyone who wasn't African American, Asian, or Latino was welcome to buy one. That kind of house was an astonishing gift to grateful men and women like my parents.

Suburbia Photographed: The Shock of the New

The gift was immediately branded a swindle, in part because William A. Garnett, a brilliant young photographer working for the Lakewood Park Corporation

1.5.2 William A. Garnett, *Finished Housing, Lakewood, California*, 1950. Gelatin silver print, 7 3/8 × 9 7/16 in. (18.7 × 24 cm).

between 1950 and 1953, shot a series of aerial photographs that looked down on the houses the company was putting up at the rate of five hundred a week.[8] Garnett's iconic photographs—marked by raking light that casts impenetrable shadows over the flat landscape—depend for their aesthetic effect on what's missing from the image of suburbia: no internal scale of reference, no organizing line of the horizon, and no identifiable human figures. (fig. **1.5.1**) Seen from above in Garnett's photographs, suburbia has no history and no human dimensions, not even a blade of grass. The photographs resemble "abstract expressionist paintings or views through a microscope," wrote the Getty Museum in 2004 about its collection of Garnett's aerial photographs, including six of Lakewood.[9] After Garnett, ominous patterns in the landscape were confirmed as emblems of suburban lives.

In Ansel Adams and Nancy Newhall's *This Is the American Earth*, and Peter Blake's *God's Own Junkyard: The Planned Deterioration of America's Landscape*, Garnett's photographs of Lakewood became, as the architectural historian Kazys Varnelis argues, "symbols of environmental devastation…meant to be understood as political avant-garde: both aesthetic and critical."[10] The rows of uninhabited houses, treeless streets angling into the frame, and interminable workings on featureless ground in Garnett's Lakewood photographs lingered in the midcentury imagination and merged with newsreel footage of atomic bomb test buildings in the equally featureless Nevada desert.

Always, in Garnett's Lakewood photographs, the sun pours tarry shadows across the barren backyards of not yet homes. Their stucco walls are blisteringly white in contrast. You can't see the intersection of character and place from an altitude of 1,000 feet (305 meters), and Garnett never came back to photograph daily life on the ground. (fig. **1.5.2**)

The developers of Lakewood—S. Mark Taper, Ben Weingart, and Louis Boyar— saw Garnett's photographs unironically, as records to be filed with work logs and

8   The Getty Museum's collection of Garnett's aerial photographs of Lakewood includes those that were reprinted in the decades after 1950. All the examples can be found at http://www.getty.edu/art/collection/artists/1545/william-a-garnett-american-1916-2006/.

9   The J. Paul Getty Trust, "William A. Garnett," J. Paul Getty Museum, accessed January 4, 2015, http://www.getty.edu/art/gettyguide/artMakerDetails?maker=1580.

10 Ansel Adams and Nancy Newhall, *This Is the American Earth* (San Francisco: Sierra Club, 1960); Peter Blake, *God's Own Junkyard: The Planned Deterioration of America's Landscape* (New York: Holt, Rinehart and Winston, 1964); Kazys Varnelis, "Psychogeography and the End of Planning: Reyner Banham's Los Angeles: The Architecture of Four Ecologies," Varnelis.net, accessed January 4, 2015, http://varnelis.net/articles/banham_psychogeography_and_the_end_of_planning.

construction accounts. But in some of Garnett's photos, which they proudly displayed, they read a grander vision, a collective heroism of the sort that still clings to the charismatic infrastructure projects of the Great Depression. Taper, Weingart, and Boyar knew that the Progressive Era model of affordable housing they adapted to postwar mass production would necessarily result in a new idea of home for a new class of homeowners. For many disappointed observers, then as now, Garnett's photographs of geometric forms on a grid that extends beyond the edge of the frame—apparently forever—permanently contaminated the suburban idea with dread.

Progressive architects and planners, who had presumed to mold working-class houses for the improvement they would give working-class lives, were appalled by the houses that working people bought. Although Garnett's photographs were factually out-of-date as soon as the prints were dry, the image of suburbia they served became perfectly timeless. Writing about the persistence of these anachronistic images, Robert Beuka noted, "The oddly trans-historical look at suburbia… underscores how firmly the vexed cultural perception of the suburbs remains tied to visions of suburbia in post[–]World War II America."[11] The fixed myth of suburbia is sustained in part by the continuing shock of seeing long-ago Lakewood from the air.

Garnett's aesthetic was essential in creating a "no place" where suburbia is simultaneously imagined into being and rejected. Doctrinaire modernists and nascent environmentalists constructed a fearsome image of suburbia from (among other things) a few photographs of a few days in the construction of Lakewood—beautifully realized photographs in which height, a bombardier's appraising exactness, and uncertainty of scale evoke the mechanical replication of enigmas.

Suburbia's Imperfections through a Humble Lens

Former advocates of the suburban idea—like Lewis Mumford—believed, on mostly aesthetic grounds, that the tract house suburb was inevitably a place of dehumanizing conformity and aching regret. Suburban places were ugly, photographs of uninhabited Lakewood in 1950 seemed to show, and the ugliness would leach into the people who lived there. But what was scorned even before the moving vans left the driveways of Lakewood soon became commonplace. Built-out Lakewood after 1953 settled into the fabric of everyday life without much regard to the reductive view that rescripted the tract house suburb as the place "where evil dwells."

I once thought my suburban education was a lesson in how to get along with other people. Now, I think the lesson isn't neighborliness; it's humility. I can remember that the only sign of a man's success in Lakewood was the frequency with which a new car appeared in his driveway. Even today, it's hard to claim status through personal display because Lakewood is a suburb where life is still pretty much the same for everybody, no matter how much you think you're worth.

I still live there because my suburban habits have been adequate to the demands of my desire, although I know there's a price to pay to fit all kinds of people—working people, elderly people, immigrant people, and people who never feel they have enough—into my modest neighborhood. Places like Lakewood are places of presumed exile, and the "hunger of memory" (to use the memoirist Richard Rodriguez's troubling phrase) is acute there, but it's only a localization of the lasting problem of American places, which is "How do we make our home there?" We long for a home, but doubt its worth when we have it. We depend on the communitarian gifts of a place, but

11 Robert A. Beuka, *SuburbiaNation: Reading Suburban Landscape in Twentieth-Century American Fiction and Film* (New York: Palgrave Macmillan, 2004), 229.

dislike its claims on us. We're certain that our own preferences for a home are correct, but we're eager to question our neighbor's choice. And no American place is immune from the certainty, bred into our literature, that something more adequate to meet our desires—an even better "city upon a hill"—is just beyond the next bend in the road.

That road in Southern California has a newly posted "no exit" sign. There's hardly anywhere left to build another Lakewood or Irvine or Santa Clarita. Twenty-first-century Southern California continues to be what it has been since the mid-1990s: uniformly dense, urban in fact but suburban in appearance, and characterized by single-family homes in neighborhoods adjacent to (but not always dependent on) dispersed urban nodes that, in some instances, include a historic downtown. This is one design for living and working. It's imperfect, as are all designs and abstract plans. It's neither "incoherent" nor "mindless sprawl." And it's my home.

We often find it difficult to talk about home in California. Waves of newcomers who bought into the exuberant California sales pitch of health and happiness in the sunshine found, instead, a place often marked by discontinuity, estrangement, and willful amnesia. Because of those disorders, the philosopher Josiah Royce (1855–1916) believed that the Californians he grew up among in the 1860s were "sojourners with a dwelling place, but with no home."[12] Home, Royce thought, could be found in an "intentional community," a gathering of shared memories opening outward to shared hopes, none of which Royce thought impossible in the sudden California town he knew as a boy. The suddenness—the overnight appearance of new communities—of mid-nineteenth-century California is an analogue of the sudden emergence of our suburbanized nation.

1.5.3 Hersholt Avenue, Lakewood, California

12 Josiah Royce, "Provincialism Based on a Study of Early Conditions in California," *Putnam's Magazine* VII, October 1909–April 1910 (November 1909), 234.
13 Quoted in *Joan Didion, Where I Was From* (New York: Vintage, 2004), 35.

Royce's raw material for home was even less appealing than Lakewood in 1950. He remembered Grass Valley as "a community of irresponsible strangers" and "a blind and stupid and homeless generation of selfish wanderers."[13] Yet he saw the possibility of loyalties arising even among such strangers, and even the possibility of their loyalty to the idea of loyalty to each other, out of which a genuine community—he called it a "beloved community"—might be made in the confluence of memories and in the projection of common desires into a shared future. (fig. **1.5.3**)

Royce's experience propelled him to believe that "loyalty to the idea of loyalty" is possible, even if the object of our loyalty is uncertain, our application of the virtue is conflicted, and the outcomes of our efforts are distant, if not wholly unknowable. Patience, deference, and compassion have always been promises among strangers in suburbia's strange land (as they were and still are in Lakewood). There are no perfect places, Royce argued, but there can be places where longings will be assuaged. I live in an ordinary suburb, hardly distinguishable from others, and I actually imagine the place where I live is, in Royce's striking phrase, "a community of grace."

One revelation of grace is a sense of place, not to be confused with merely my idiosyncratic sensibility for gridded streets, blue-collar lives, and boxy houses.

A sense of place is an aspect of a "moral imagination," the imagination by which I write myself into the story of my place, inhabit it as my home, and negotiate a way from the purely personal there to the public.

The environmental writer Barry Lopez asked a question some years ago about suburban San Fernando Valley, his boyhood home and, like Lakewood, formerly a sudden place on terms comparable to Royce's Grass Valley. For Lopez, a genuine community doesn't begin solely with its social institutions, political processes, or the assertions of a tradition, all of which were Royce's concerns. Lopez asked a question tangential to Royce's "How do we make a home here?" Lopez's question was, "How can we become vulnerable to a place?" His answer was that vulnerability comes with the deepening and widening of a moral imagination:

> Over time I have come to think of…three qualities—paying intimate attention; a storied relationship to a place rather than a solely sensory awareness of it; and living in some sort of ethical unity with a place—as a fundamental human defense against loneliness. If you're intimate with a place, a place with whose history you're familiar, and you establish an ethical conversation with it, the implication that follows is this: the place knows you're there. It feels you. You will not be forgotten, cut off, abandoned. As a writer I want to ask on behalf of the reader: How can a person obtain this? How can you occupy a place and also have it occupy you? How can you find such a reciprocity?[14]

In questioning his boyhood suburb's distance from transformative encounter, Lopez found something more than a sense of place. "Always when I return," he wrote, "I have found again the ground that propels me past the great temptation of our time to put one's faith in despair."[15]

From suburbia had welled up something like redemption. You never know what might come from making some ordinary place your home and falling in love with it.[16]

"Suburban Holy Land" revisits "An Ordinary Place," an essay originally published in My California *(Sacramento: California Arts Council, 2004).*

14 Barry Lopez, "A Literature of Place," accessed January 4, 2015, http://arts.envirolink.org/literary_arts/BarryLopez_LitofPlace.html.

15 Barry Lopez, "A Scary Abundance of Water," *LA Weekly*, January 9, 2002.

16 Portions of this essay, in a significantly different form, originally appeared in *Where We Are Now: Notes from Los Angeles* (Los Angeles: Angel City Press, 2004). A further examination of the significance of William A. Garnett's Lakewood photographs, summarized here, can be found in "Beautiful and Terrible: Aeriality and the Image of Suburbia," *Places Journal*, February 2013, https://placesjournal.org/article/beautiful-and-terrible-aeriality-and-the-image-of-suburbia.

1.6 MEXICO'S SUBURBAN DREAM

Guénola Capron and Martha de Alba

DESIGN
MODELS

SOCIAL
INEQUALITIES

The elements of the American suburban model are well known: the single-family house, the car, the shopping center, and more recently, the gated community. The influence of the American suburban model in other countries seems to be an undeniable fact. For example, the French geographer Jean-François Staszak states:

> The future of the cities of the world is partly based on the American urban experience. Naturally, this is because it is very important but, above all, it is because it is observed attentively and copied with greater or lesser resolve and critical detachment…[1]

But it is not the actual American model that travels from the United States to the rest of the planet, of course, but rather an "imaginary" based on it.[2] The American model reaches other countries only after social actors have disseminated and filtered its meaning and symbols. These social actors have varying influence and include the media, businesspeople, architects, urbanists, developers, manufacturers, tourists, immigrants, and so forth. They reinterpret the model in their local social, political, and economic context, blending it with images that belong to their culture. This reinterpretation produces a shift whereby the original symbols of the model are clothed anew with other meanings, in addition to their original meanings. Analyzing the discourse of social actors reveals how these cross-cultural processes and the shift of meanings arise.[3]

We analyze the discourses surrounding two of the first middle-class suburban developments in Mexico City to gain a better understanding of the extent of the Americanization of Mexico City. In the 1940s and 1950s the Jardines del Pedregal de San Angel and Ciudad Satélite developments (designed by the famous Mexican architects Luis Barragán and Mario Pani)

played key roles in the production of ways of life and residential and urban imaginary, each development with its own differentiated social identities.

Jardines del Pedregal was planned by Barragán as an exclusive suburb located near the new educational campus Ciudad Universitaria (designed by a large team directed by Mario Pani and inaugurated in 1952) in the south of Mexico City. Large modern houses were built following the capricious volcanic landscape of the region. Various well-known architects, Barragán included, designed some of the houses with extensive areas for gardens and swimming pools.

Ciudad Satélite, planned by Pani, was conceived originally as a solution to the increasing development of Mexico City in the fifties. Pani first designed multifamily blocks for working-class employees at the center of the development, next to schools, administrative offices, and local services. This central sector was surrounded by green areas and lots for individual houses with private gardens and garages. The development also included a big shopping center with a large parking lot and monumental sculptures, the Torres de Satélite, designed by Barragán and Goeritz as a symbol of the new city at the northwest of the budding metropolitan area. (fig. **1.6.1**)

In Mexico, until the 1960s, the concept of the suburb referred to a neighborhood outside the city where poor people lived. During the sixties, the concept of the suburb underwent a process by which it became more bourgeois. As a result, the term began to be applied more specifically to upper- and middle-class neighborhoods distanced from the city center and associated with modernization.[4] This process coincided with a proliferation of residential developments, nicely exemplified by the cases of Ciudad Satélite and Jardines del Pedregal.

The suburbs receiving these migrants seemed, at the same time, to undergo

1   Jean-François Staszak, "Présentation: La ville américaine comme miroir," *Espaces et societies*, no. 107 (2001): 9–13, translation by authors.

2   We take the concept of imaginary from Cornelius Castoriadis's theory of social imaginary, as a set of symbolic systems created by societies (institutions, groups, individuals) according to their historic context. Social imaginaries are the basis of construction of meaning, representations, and actions. Cornelius Castoriadis, *L'institution imaginaire de la société* (Paris: Seuil, 1975).

3   Cynthia Ghorra-Gobin, *Le mythe américain inachevé* (Paris: CNRS Editions, 2002).

4   Claudia Zamorano Villareal, "La palabra periferia en México, sus vecinas y sus falsas amigas," *Ordinaire Latino-américain*, no. 207 (2007): 13–30.

1.6.1 View of Torres de Satélite and Periférico highway

5   Alfonso Pérez-Méndez and Alejandro Aptilon, *Las casas del Pedregal, 1947–1968* (Barcelona: Gustavo Gilli, 2007).

6   Castoriadis, *L'institution imaginaire*.

7   Martha de Alba and Guénola Capron, "Utopías residenciales en la Ciudad de México de los años cincuenta y sesenta: El anuncio publicitario como vehículo de modelos urbanos," *Ordinaire Latino-américain*, no. 207 (2007): 91–116.

a process of Americanization, in the sense of the influences on modes of production and consumption. What happened to make these "cities within cities," neither of which was particularly inspired by the American model, come to embody American suburban ways of life and the imaginary of American suburbia? The insertion of the American residential imaginary in a society that is culturally distant from the United States (albeit geographically close) became possible through the implementation of diverse discursive strategies, in particular urbanistic and marketing ones.[5] We analyze these discourses using the philosopher Cornelius Castoriadis's theory of the social "imaginary."

Within the theory, Castoriadis distinguishes between the instituted imaginary and the radical one.[6] The former refers to an instituted symbolic system, already existing in society—for instance, ways of living and using urban spaces that are recognized and common to Mexican society. Meanwhile, the latter refers to an original creation of the imagination that becomes a novel form of thinking. If we take this distinction between the dominant, instituted imaginary and the radical, creative imaginary, then the urbanistic utopia—the concept for a new, changed urban model—might correspond to the radical imaginary as it proposes novel ideas. We suggest that the new ways of living and using urban spaces proposed by modern urbanistic developments, such as Jardines del Pedregal and Ciudad Satélite, are examples of a radical imaginary introduced in Mexico under the influence of American and European architectural and urban models.

Such modern residential projects have been diffused into Mexican society through real estate marketing. Meanwhile, publicity—while having a heavy utopian payload—is not detached from reality (institutionalized society) but rather reflects and transforms it.[7] Thus, the marketing image would be a symbolic instrument that combines instituted imaginary (traditional society) and new patterns. This is an example of the process by which American-European urban

1.6.2 House advertisements of Jardines del Pedregal de San Angel neighborhood

8   Castoriadis, *L'institution imaginaire*.
9   The ways of life promoted by residential publicity in the suburbs were not completely new in Mexico City, since other urbanistic projects, such as the highly elitist development of Lomas de Chapultepec, designed by José Luis Cuevas in the thirties, were based on similar concepts (the edge of the city, the garden city, use of the car, the curvilinear design that broke up the traditional plan, etc.).
10 Keith Eggener, *Luis Barragán's Gardens of El Pedregal* (New York: Princeton Architectural Press, 2001).
11 Pécassou, 1973, quoted in Claude Bataillon and Louis Panabière, *Mexico aujourd'hui: La plus grande ville du monde* (Paris: Publisud, 1988), 175.

models are transformed to adapt to local culture. Marketing transforms the publicity images into stereotyped prescriptions of what constitutes good living, based on the morals of the family and its class aspirations. In this way, the property market becomes the field in which social and urban models are propagated, and where the function of the propagation is, like all publicity, "to define for the subject both reality and desire for it."[8] Property advertising sells products, styles, and ways of life as if they are "new"; it sensitizes consumers to adopt new patterns of consumption, and it exploits the latent aspirations of homes and families.[9] The advertisement doesn't refer directly to a concrete reality but creates imaginary and mythical realities that correspond with desires, dreams, and fantasies that seek to awaken pleasant emotions in the consuming public.

Barragán, also a skilled businessman, turned to the services of a famous photographer, Armando Salas Portugal, to dramatize the projects and houses that he built. These highly stylized pictures often served as supporting images for the promotional materials for Jardines del Pedregal and Arboledas.[10] A study of the language used in Mexican publicity points out, "Publicity lives on assumptions and myths that help to forge happiness, progress, youth, abundance. It is a powerful instrument for psychological standardization that stipulates the promotion of a common ideal and generally accepted human stereotypes."[11] In the case of Pedregal, the images were clearly directed at a political and economic elite, both Mexican and foreign. (fig. **1.6.2**) In the case of Ciudad Satélite, the first receptors of these new tastes and patterns of consumption were the upper-middle classes. (fig. **1.6.3**)

The influence of international urbanistic models, mainly American, is quite clear in some advertisements: "Today, for the first time in Mexico…House and land for only $74,500 (3 bedrooms, 2 bathrooms, 200 m² plot)…Built using the most modern American designs…." In another example, the "Inmobiliaria Comerical Bustamante SA de CV congratulates the

12 *El Universal*, Agosto 1958.
13 Néstor García Canclini, *Culturas híbridas: Estrategias para entrar y salir de la modernidad* (Mexico City: Grijalbo, 1989); Alicia Lindón, "El imaginario suburbano americano y la colonización de la subjetividad espacial en las periferias pauperizadas de la Ciudad de México," *Ordinaire Latinoaméricain*, no. 207 (2007): 117–38.
14 Eggener, *Luis Barragán's Gardens*; Pérez-Méndez and Aptilon, *Las casas del Pedregal*.
15 Lindón, "El maginario suburbano americano."

1.6.3 Advertisements of Ciudad Satélite neighborhood

construction company California Homes de México S.A. for choosing Jardines de Santa Mónica y Jardines de Atizapán developments to carry out its attractive plan of house construction following the latest modern American techniques."[12]

As several authors mention, from the forties onward, the media played an important role in the transmission of images and messages, whether via radio, cinema, or television.[13] Property was publicized in all these media. There was publicity for Jardines del Pedregal on television in the 1950s; a television advertisement for Ciudad Satélite in the early 1960s showed some Martians discovering a "beautiful city in sight" from their flying saucers.[14] As the Mexican Argentinian sociologist and geographer Alicia Lindón points out, the creation of narratives in the media, in particular in cinema, was one of the strategies used to publicize and secure the suburban imaginary outside the United States, without mentioning that country explicitly in the messages.[15]

It is through these and other tricks of the symbolic world that the utopian residential imaginary proposed by modernism

and functionalism, sifted through the ideas of Mexican urbanists, becomes a more concrete and effective imaginary that lays down fashions and ways of life for Mexican society. The ideal of the home becomes the functionalist style house, or the bungalow in a garden city. The ideal of the city becomes a space that is rationally compartmentalized by functions. The ideal for mobility becomes the car and fast roads. (figs. **1.6.4–6**)

The International Movement

Modernist urbanistic and functionalist discourse, related to the International Movement, constitutes a fundamental link in the construction of the imaginary of the suburb. The International Movement was a dominant discourse in the sense that it exercised a relative dominance in academe and in architectural and official urbanistic projects. However, in practice, the social and political context into which this discourse was inserted modified the original "pure" modernist project and radically transformed it.

Starting in the 1920s, various channels made worldwide circulation of

1.6.4 Maid and chauffeurs in front of a residence at Jardines del Pedregal, mid-1970s

16 Peter Krieger, "Hermann Zweigenthal–Hermann Herrey: Memoria y actualidad de un arquitecto Austriaco-Alemán Exiliado," *Anales del Instituto de Investigaciones Estéticas*, no. 85 (2004).

17 Ibid.; Eggener, *Luis Barragán's Gardens*; Graciela de Garay, *Modernidad habitada: Multifamiliar Miguel Alemán, Ciudad de México, 1949–1999* (Mexico City: Instituto Mora, 2004).

18 Stephen V. Ward, *Planning the Twentieth-Century City: The Advanced Capitalist World* (Chichester, UK: Wiley, 2002); Jeffrey W. Cody, *Exporting American Architecture, 1870–2000* (London: Routledge, 2002); Ward and Cody, quoted by Robert Freestone, "The Americanization of Australian Planning," *Journal of Planning History* 187, no. 3 (2004): 187–214.

19 Freestone, "The Americanization of Australian Planning."

architectural and urbanistic concepts of modernism possible. For Mexico, a rich exchange of ideas came about thanks to travel, visits, publications in the press, conferences—in short, all the means of communication. One example would be the revolving traffic system concept of Hermann Herrey, a German who emigrated to the United States, that inspired the urbanists Mario Pani and Domingo García Ramos in the design of Mexico's Ciudad Universitaria and Ciudad Satélite.[16] Others might be articles on Jardines del Pedregal published in several American and European magazines.[17] Mexican projects were more than mere imitations of what was done in the United States or in Europe. Even the developers of shopping centers understood that their products needed at least a minimum of adaptation to local societies. In regard to urban planning, authors such as Stephen V. Ward or J. W. Cody preferred to speak of "cross-national learning" and "points of contact between the urban planning repertoires of different countries," rather than imitation or adaptation.[18] Robert Freestone, an Australian professor of

planning, reflecting on the influence of the American model in the Australian context, ended up reversing the title of his article, "The Americanization of Australian Planning," with a provocative "Australization of American Planning." In doing so, he suggests a remake of the model, a kind of "culturalizing" appropriation by applying it in another context.[19]

In Mexico, we could say that rather than a mere transplant or diffusion of American models, there was a triangulation of ideas between Europe, Latin America, and the United States. It is undeniable that the ideas of Le Corbusier (Radiant City and Plan Voisin) and Frank Lloyd Wright (Broadacre City), among other architects and urbanists, played an important role in Mexican urban design works. The modernist utopia exalted in both Europe and the United States was enriched and applied on a large scale in Latin America. The most obvious example of this is perhaps Brasília, although in Mexico it can be clearly seen in projects such as those by Pani or Barragán, who designed Ciudad Satélite and Jardines del Pedregal, respectively,

1.6.5 A prototype house at Ciudad Satélite

1.6.6 Urban landscape at Ciudad Satélite

and also designed a great variety of internationally well-known architectural works. The Mexican historian Graciela de Garay and the Swiss historian of urban design Vittorio Magnago Lampugnani mention a kind of Mexicanization process of international architecture through its reinterpretation in a Mexican context, where "the technical, material and financial resources" were different; a "Mexican synthesis," according to de Garay.[20] Moreover, the immense scale on which progressive, urbanistic ideas were applied in Latin America stands out. Note the case of Brasília, but also Ciudad Satélite, planned for around thirty thousand inhabitants, or Lomas Verdes, also in the municipality of Naucalpan (a project by Barragán and Juan Sordo Madaleno). These last two had similar plans; neither was finished as planned initially.

The Ciudad Satélite and Jardines del Pedregal projects were initially a reinterpretation and hybridization of the modernist and functionalist ideas applied in the context of Mexico City in the mid-twentieth century.[21] The concepts of internationalist modernism that were introduced in such projects included, for example, the very notion of a satellite city, the superblock, the purification and functionalism of architectural forms, the integration of architecture on rocky ground, and Wright's organic architecture. Such ideas were hybridized when Barragán and Pani were faced by the necessity of carrying out proposals to control the powerful expansion of the city, or by the desire to promote local architecture.

The modern and functionalist utopia, however, tends to become diluted in a context like the Mexico City of that day. This was due not only to hybridization, or a shift of meaning from the original model, but also to the conditions in which it was created, as we will see in the next section.

From Satellite City to Suburb

Such urbanistic and architectural projects emerge in a city characterized by accelerated urban expansion, robust industrial development, deep-seated nationalism and presidential centralism. These characteristics, particularly the last one, gave rise to a close association of interests among industrialists, property developers, politicians, architects, and urbanists during the presidency of Lázaro Cárdenas (1934–1940). These characteristics continued with the subsequent presidencies of Manuel Avila Camacho (1940–1946), described as "urbanization-led industrial development" by the American professor of planning Diane Davis, and Miguel Alemán (1946–1952), noted as a "pro-business presidential administration" by the historian Keith Eggener.[22] The conjunction of economic, political, and urban interests that favor the modernization of the city is a matter that has already been sufficiently documented, particularly when referring to the presidency of Alemán.[23] It is well known that Alemán was the owner of the land where Ciudad Satélite was built, and this project might have been unimaginable without his initiative. For their part, Pani and Barragán were involved in the promotion of both of these developments; Barragán was the main partner of the investors and property developers, the Bustamante brothers.[24]

Through the ideas of efficiency and productivity, the industrialization of the production of the city is contained in Le Corbusier's idea of urbanism. According to the architectural and urban historian and theorist Françoise Choay, it is "the progressive model that inspires the new development of the suburbs and the remodeling of the majority of big cities within American capitalism." She also adds: "It is a truncated and degenerate system that motivated and continues to inspire the majority of large French

20 Graciela de Garay, "La historia oral en la arquitectura urbana (1940–1990)," *Secuencia*, no. 28 (1994); Vittorio Magnago Lampugnani, "Luis Barragán: Diseño urbano y especulación," in *Luis Barragán, La Revolución Callada*, ed. Federica Zanco (Zurich: Barragán Foundation, with Vitra Design Museum, 2001), 146–77. The "Mexican synthesis" or "hybridation" refers to certain modifications in the application of modernist and functional architectural or urban models to Mexican cultural, economic, and political reality, for instance, the use of local materials, like volcanic rock, in functional constructions, or the use of Mexican muralism on buildings facades, as in some of the Ciudad Universitaria buildings. The original project of Ciudad Satélite was modified by economic interests, and supported by the political class that followed Miguel Alemán's administration. Economic speculation transformed exclusive Jardines del Pedregal into a middle-class neighborhood, losing its original architecture.

21 Mario Pani, "México: un problema, Una solución," *Arquitectura*, no. 60 (1958): 199–226; Eggener, *Luis Barragán's Gardens*.

22 Diane Davis, *El leviatán urbano: La Ciudad de México en el siglo XX* (Mexico City: Fondo de Cultura Económica, col. Sociología, 1999); Eggener, *Luis Barragán's Gardens*.

23 Anahí Ballent, "El arte de saber vivir: Modernización del habitar doméstico y cambio urbano, 1940–1970," in *Cultura y comunicación en la Ciudad de México*, ed. Néstor García Canclini (Mexico City: UAM-Grijalbo, 1998), 65–131; Armando Cisneros, *La ciudad que construimos* (Mexico City: UAM-I, 1993).

24 Eggener, *Luis Barragán's Gardens*.

developments, such as the unfortunately well-known Sarcelles."[25]

Both Barragán and Pani, years after the curtailed execution of their works, declared that they were disappointed.[26] Their projects had been transformed: the concepts of the satellite city, of a city within the city, had generated huge developments and gigantic middle-class suburbs that did not resemble the original projects.[27] In Pedregal, little by little the gigantic lots that had initially been planned were split up, transforming the original architecture and urban planning. In Ciudad Satélite, the lots sold also became smaller and smaller, as did the houses. The urban scheme that Pani had initially proposed was never respected, in particular the construction of multifamily blocks at the heart of the superblocks. The mechanisms of land valuation, subject to severe speculation, as well as the mixture of political and economic interests, put an end to the utopian dreams of Pani's Ciudad Satélite as a socially heterogeneous satellite city, and of Barragan's Jardines del Pedregal as an exclusive landscaped city. Gradually, Ciudad Satélite's green belt was absorbed by property speculation.

At the same time that the modified concept of Ciudad Satélite was being built, the so-called NZT area— Naucalpan-Atizapán de Zaragoza-Tlalnepantla—was being urbanized at high speed. Faced by the limits on subdividing plots for new developments imposed by Mayor of Mexico City Ernesto Uruchurtu in 1954, property companies turned toward neighboring territory in the State of Mexico, with the support of that government. As Pani himself says ironically, the urban landscape rising from the land became "Tinacolandia" in a few decades.[28] Tinacolandia is the Mexican version of Levittown in United States or Sarcelles in France. The name

refers to the typically Latin American landscape of *tinacos*, the water tanks on the roofs of houses.

The imposition of zoning by the state and its consequences for developers played an important role in industrializing the means of production of the city at its edges. The suburb was born from this encounter. For example, the original urban plan of Ciudad Satélite, Jardines del Pedregal, and Arboledas was curvilinear.[29] But the new projects inspired by these curvilinear plans returned to the grid, which is a more economical urban form. Houses were sold from catalogs by developers such as Austroplan in Ciudad Satélite, and by Bustamante in Jardines del Pedregal. Most of the houses or plots were aimed at median sectors and sold on credit after buyers had put down an initial deposit.

It is important to question commonly accepted suppositions about the American mold for the middle-class suburb. Ciudad Satélite is seen, in general and by its own inhabitants, as an American suburb with American ways of life. Yet it is clear that the initial urban models were not completely suburban, nor were they solely American. The arrival of this imaginary in Mexico started with the hybridization of progressive urbanism as it came into contact with a society with a different political context.

The Evolution of Identity and Mexico City Today
It is a remarkable fact that, even when urban practices changed and these areas of the city were functionally integrated into the central city, this illusion is still alive as a creator of social and territorial identities. There can be no doubt that there are significant differences in the evolution of developments such as Ciudad Satélite and Jardines del Pedregal: the former continues to have a profoundly ingrained suburban imaginary, which

25 Authors' translation, Françoise Choay, *L'Urbanisme, utopies et réalités: Une anthologie* (Paris: Seuil, 1965), 62–63.
26 Graciela de Garay, *Mario Pani: Investigaciones y entrevistas* (México DF: Instituto Mora, CONACULTA, 2000); Eggener, *Luis Barragán's Gardens.*
27 Upper-middle class in Naucalpan, upper class in Atizapan (Arboledas) and Jardines del Pedregal, lower-middle class in Tlalnepantla.
28 Garay, *Mario Pani.*
29 Arboledas was another of Barragán's unfinished projects.

doesn't seem to be the case for the latter. Jardines del Pedregal is now perceived as an upper-middle-class neighborhood integrated to the urban area, as any other. On the contrary, Ciudad Satélite continues to reinforce its suburban identity. It is striking that *Travesías DF*, a magazine published in Mexico City, published in 2005 an issue titled "We Are All Ciudad Satélite Suburbanites," dealing with this type of suburbanization.[30] Their competitor, the magazine *Chilango*, gave space to the topic a few months later. In both magazines it is possible to note the existence of a territorial identity with Ciudad Satélite as the main reference point. The cultural counterpart of this identity is, as is to be expected, the American way of life.

Are these stereotyped representations of the area shared by the inhabitants themselves? To what extent did the residents of these areas adopt the lifestyles proposed by the dominant discourses in the publicity? How did the American suburban imaginary filter the practices of the city? These questions about the experiences of the subjects require a different analysis from the one undertaken here; however, they provide guidelines for continuing deliberations on the Americanization of Mexico City.

Will house buyers be the mere receptors of this advertising discourse? The very paradigmatic case of Ciudad Satélite seems to suggest that for the pioneers who began the residents' association, these discourses and the suburban identities thus created were instrumental in their pursuit of political autonomy, even when faced by the property company itself, which was both the vendor of the land and administrator of the development.[31] It is striking that Pani's plan, in spite of the transformation of the original ideas, continues to be the inspiration for the territorial imaginary of the Ciudad Satélite residents, even though it has disappeared from the architects' and planners' memories.[32]

Ciudad Satélite was an urban reference for further developments in the area. In fact, the large zone surrounding Ciudad Satélite, at the northwest of Mexico City, is known as Zona Satélite. As these neighborhoods declined in fashion, people from the area moved to Zona Esmeralda, a large agglomeration of gated communities located in the municipality of Atizapan some six miles (ten kilometers) away from the neighborhood imagined by Pani at the end of the 1950s. Developments like Zona Esmeralda can be considered a new modality for the Americanization of the gated suburb: hypersecured and -controlled, in response to Mexican middle- and upper-class cravings for exclusivity, tranquility, and security.

Gated communities have spread all over Mexico City (Federal District [DF] and State of Mexico municipalities located next to DF) as a comfortable and secure way of life.[33] Nevertheless, it is not the predominant residential typology in Mexico City. New trends have emerged since the 1990s, which can be seen in three examples: the Santa Fe business district, the repopulation of central areas at Federal District, and suburban in the State of Mexico.

Santa Fe (located at extreme west of Federal District) can be considered a business district that congregates other functions: malls and commercial areas, private schools, private hospitals, and residential buildings and gated communities. It is a zone that benefits wealthy residents who can pay for expensive apartments or houses sold preferentially in US dollars. Most of the employees travel at least one hour to get to their jobs at Santa Fe.[34]

Since the beginning of the twenty-first century, the government of Mexico City promoted the repopulation of Mexico City's central districts by facilitating

30 *DF por travesías: La revista de la Ciudad de México*, no. 41 (August 2005).

31 See María Luisa Tarrés, "Del abstencionismo electoral a la oposición política: Las clases medias en Ciudad Satélite," *Estudios sociológicos* IV, no. 12 (1986): 361–89.

32 See Martha de Alba et al., *Satélite el libro* (Mexico City: UAM, 2011).

33 See Guénola Capron, "Autoségrégation résidentielle et ordre urbain chez les classes moyenne et supérieure à Mexico: Une question d'échelle?," *L'espace politique* 17, no. 2 (2012), http//espacepolitique .revues.org/2346.

34 Margarita Pérez Negrete, *Santa Fe: Ciudad, espacio y globalización* (Puebla: Universidad Iberoamericana, 2010).

construction licenses for apartment buildings to reverse the loss of population from these central neighborhoods and attract new residents.[35] Seemingly overnight, residents in central areas experienced a transformation of their streets: the traditional old houses characteristic of the historic city center were transformed into six-floor, new, minimalist-style buildings.[36] The western and southern areas of the historical center and part of Downtown (Reforma, the biggest avenue of the core of Mexico City) are home to new developments such as "New Polanco," a formerly industrial area now changing to capture middle-upper and upper classes.

While upper classes are settling in the west and northwest Mexico City, and middle classes in the central areas, huge suburban projects were designed for low-income classes at the edge of the metropolitan agglomeration by 1990. Each project is composed of thousands of identical little houses (about 540 square feet or 50 square meters). The owners of these cheap houses have to do expensive and long journeys of about four hours to get to their jobs during the week. Housewives and children stay in the dormitory suburb the whole week.[37]

As we can see, the imaginary of modern urban utopias, like Ciudad Satélite and Jardines del Pedregal, are no longer models for the new developers. Compared with the 1960s, suburban life lost its charms for newcomers and urban dwellers: traffic jams and urban saturation overcame it. The green factor doesn't seem to be as seducing to move to the suburbs, as in the past decades; security and "all services included" partly replaced it. Mexico City became a metropolis of more than twenty million inhabitants, suffering of all vices of "monster" cities: overpopulation, traffic congestions, rush hours, transportation problems, pollution, urban stress, and so forth. Residents

from Satélite Zone complain about spending hours in traffic jams to move from their homes to Mexico City's downtown.

Under these conditions, the concept of suburbia for upper and middle classes has been replaced by smaller gated communities integrated in to the urban area, or by minimalist constructions in central areas near cultural and commercial centers.

35 Autoridad del Centro Histórico, Gobierno del Distrito Federal, *Plan integral de manejo del centro histórico de la Ciudad de México (2011–2016)* (Mexico City: Gobierno del Distrito Federal, 2011).

36 Sergio Tamayo, ed., *Los desafíos del Bando 2* (Mexico City: GDF-UACM, 2007).

37 Céline Jacquin, "Producir y habitar la periferia: Los nuevos conjuntos urbanos de vivienda de bajo costo en México (ZMVM)," *Bulletin de l'Institut Français d'Études Andines* 41, no. 3 (2012): 389–415.

Waterval, Midrand, Gauteng, South Africa

Qingheyingcun, Beijing, China

1.7 AUSTRALIA'S MISPLACED WAR ON THE SUBURBAN DREAM

Ross Elliott

ANTISUBURBAN CRUSADES

GOVERNANCE & POLICY CHALLENGES

HOUSING AFFORDABILITY

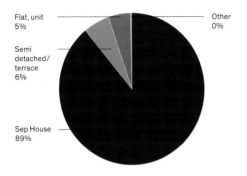

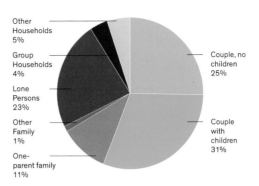

1.7.1 Dwelling type chosen by families with children, Australia, 2011

1.7.2 Household types, Australia, 2011

Relative to income, housing costs in Australia's capital cities have become some of the most expensive in the world.[1] This is a relatively recent phenomenon—certainly, a problem that emerged only since the late 1990s, as a mixture of tax and land use regulations led to rapid policy-induced land price escalation. For most of the country's twentieth-century history, housing and the land on which it was built were readily affordable to working- and middle-class families. During that period, Australia enjoyed some of the highest rates of homeownership in the developed world.[2] Homeownership and the growth of the suburbs became a feature of the democratization of wealth, and a measure of the egalitarian nature of Australian society.[3]

In a country that continues to boast an embarrassing abundance of land, housing affordability is now a cause of national concern and daily media discussion. The "Australian Dream" of a house in the suburbs is now widely regarded as beyond the reach of young families. Young people are deferring homeownership: the median age of a first-time homeowner with a mortgage in 1981 was twenty-seven, which rose to thirty-two years by the year 2000, and by 2013 had risen to thirty-four. One in five first-time buyers is now aged over forty.[4] If entering the market early, many are taking on high-debt burdens that cripple their lifestyles and leave them exposed to minor fluctuations in loan costs or unexpected changes in the economy.

This essay identifies the factors that were largely responsible for increasing the cost of basic suburban housing in Australia and reveals that the imposition of inappropriate urban planning policies combined with tax policy have not only needlessly increased the cost of housing but also reduced choice for new homebuyers. The evidence shows that despite the rhetoric and ideological agenda of various planning authorities, experts, and official agencies, the suburban home remains the preferred choice of families. In 2011 89 percent of all couples with children at home lived in a detached dwelling. Only 4.8 percent of families with children lived in a flat, unit, or apartment, and 5.8 percent lived in a townhouse or semidetached dwelling. Family households continue to make up 68 percent of all household types in Australia, and families with children (couples and single parents) are the largest of the family groups, representing 42 percent of all household types. Families without children, which can include pre- or postchildren families, constitute the next largest groups with 25 percent of all household types.[5] (figs. **1.7.1–2**)

This essay argues that it has been an erosion of affordability (rather than any alleged erosion of interest in suburban housing due to fundamental social or demographic change) that poses the greatest challenge to Australian society. Australian capital city home prices are now higher than those in

1   The escalation of prices relative to incomes has been amply demonstrated by Wendell Cox and Hugh Pavletich's various Demographia reports, and by many other similar measures that look at average or median incomes relative to average housing prices or to loan repayment ratios. See "Eleventh Annual Demographia International Housing Affordability Survey: 2015 Ratings for Metropolitan Markets," Demographia, last modified January 19, 2015, accessed November 6, 2015, http://www.demographia.com/dhi.pdf.

2   See, e.g., Tony Kryger, "Home ownership in Australia—Data and Trends," Parliament of Australia, February 11, 2009, accessed November 6, 2015, http://www.aph.gov.au/binaries/library/pubs/rp/2008-09/09rp21.pdf; Dan Andrews and Aida Caldera Sánchez, "The Evolution of Homeownership Rates in Selected OECD Countries: Demographic and Public Policy Influences," *OECD Journal: Economic Studies 2011*, no. 1 (2011).

3   Egalitarianism in Australia is a cultural value widely regarded as having its roots in the nation's experiences in World War I under British Command. Australian troops were considered by the British ill-disciplined and disrespectful of authority. They were also regarded as excellent combatants, and the concept of mateship and equality were said to be given meaning by the Australian experience of WWI. Attempts to define egalitarianism today are no less shrouded in popular culture, but the Australian Bureau of Statistics has commenced a data series that explores elements of egalitarianism and the Australian sense of "a fair go." See Australian Bureau of Statistics, "1370.0—Measures of

most major markets. According to Demographia's 2015 report, with the exception of Hong Kong, Australia's major housing markets are among the most unaffordable in the world.[6]

A Short History of Housing in Australia

Australia's major cities developed rapidly in the late 1800s and early 1900s ascenters of trade and commerce, with industrial activity concentrated in the inner city and port areas. The ports of Sydney, Brisbane, and Melbourne were on the doorstep of what we know now as the central business districts (CBDs). Housing for workers was created in close proximity to factories and other work centers, given the limitations of transport at the time. Worker housing was typically small, low cost, and built with any readily available materials. In these cramped conditions, working-class families raised generations of children.

After World War II, a housing shortage occured, due to returning servicemen and an influx of immigration from Europe. As a result, local governments actively encouraged the supply of new suburban housing. The high cost of materials—due to postwar shortages—did not prove to be much of an obstacle: unrestrained by complex building regulations or planning laws, estimates are that up to a third of new homes constructed during this period were owner-built.[7] A growing middle class emerged, and the great Australian dream of a quarter-acre lot in a suburban location was born. Housing in Australia was transformed as families left cramped inner-city housing and relocated on the outskirts of established urban areas.

The merits of homeownership and the importance of the suburban development that had created the opportunity for broader homeownership found support across the political spectrum. Australian prime minister Robert (Bob) Menzies, in a landmark speech in 1942, set the tone for decades to follow:

The material home represents the concrete expression of the habits of frugality and saving "for a home of our own." Your advanced socialist may rage against private property even while he acquires it; but one of the best instincts in us is that which induces us to have one little piece of earth with a house and a garden which is ours: to which we can withdraw, in which we can be among our friends, into which no stranger may come against our will…National patriotism, in other words, inevitably springs from the instinct to defend and preserve our own homes.[8]

From the 1950s through the 1990s, homeownership and growth of the suburban lifestyle became more than an aspirational goal: it was a social norm and a cornerstone of economic and social life in Australia, undisputed by either end of the political spectrum. Land for further suburban development was abundant and available at low cost with few conditions. Housing prices in most cities rarely exceeded a multiple of four times incomes.[9] Australia enjoyed some of the highest rates of home ownership in the world with 70 percent of households either owning their homes outright or holding a mortgage.[10]

The Brawl over Sprawl

By the 1990s, the outward growth of low-cost suburban housing had become a topic of increasing concern within some policy circles. At the time, state governments were overwhelmingly from the Labor Party, and their electoral fortunes relied heavily on preference votes from the Green movement. This was fertile ground in which antigrowth, anti-sprawl, and generally negative attitudes toward suburban living could take root. Larger suburban homes and their estates were derided by planning academics and urban commentators as soulless "McMansions."[11] Suburban expansion and

Australia's Progress, 2013," May 9, 2014, accessed November 6, 2015, http://www.abs.gov .au/ausstats/abs@.nsf /mf/1370.0.

4 Australian Bureau of Statistics, "6541.0.30.001—Microdata: Income and Housing, Australia, 2013–14," accessed November 6, 2015, http://www.abs.gov.au /AUSSTATS/abs@.nsf /Lookup/6541.0.30.001 Main+Features12013 -14?OpenDocument; see also "2012 Mortgage Choice Future First Homebuyer Survey," Mortgage Choice, November 14, 2012, accessed November 7, 2015, www.mortgage choice.com.au.

5 Australian Bureau of Statistics, "2011 Census of Population and Housing, Australia," Dwelling Structure by Household Composition and Family Composition Table 14, 2011, accessed November 7, 2015, http:// stat.abs.gov.au/Index .aspx?DataSetCode= ABS_CENSUS2011_T14 _LGA.

6 "Eleventh Annual Demographia International Housing Affordability Survey: 2015 Ratings for Metropolitan Markets."

7 See exhibit notes for "Suburbia," National Museum of Australia, accessed June 22, 2015, http://www.nma.gov .au/exhibitions/nation /suburbia.

8 Sir Robert G. Menzies, "The Forgotten People," radio broadcast, transcript, Menzies Virtual Museum, May 22, 1942, accessed June 22, 2015, http://menziesvirtualmu seum.org.au/transcripts /the-forgotten-people.

9 "Eleventh Annual Demographia International Housing Affordability Survey: 2015 Ratings for Metropolitan Markets."

10 See Kryger, "Home Ownership in Australia—Data and Trends"; and Australian Bureau of Statistics, "1301.0—Year Book Australia, 2012: Home Owners and

gated communities were linked to everything from obesity to environmentally irresponsible living and social decay.[12]

A fast-popularizing environmental agenda also helped fan concerns about further suburban growth. Fears for the loss of bush land and loss of farmland mixed with habitat protection, population control, private automobile use, long commutes, and global warming to create a policy cocktail that viewed suburban expansion as a public enemy. In a break with long-held tradition, antigrowth and antisuburban sentiments began to find political support and expression. Bob Carr, premier of New South Wales from 1995 to 2000, famously declared in 2000 that "Sydney was full."[13] He wanted population controls and a halt to Sydney's outward expansion. Its population then was just four million people—small by global city standards. Today it is roughly 4.6 million.

A "solution" to outward suburban expansion was needed. Smart growth was one that found widespread support in policy circles at the time. The concept, broadly imported from the United States, quickly became a cause célèbre in planning circles. Australia's town planning systems had been heavily influenced by the British Town and Country Planning Act (mainly by the 1954 later versions), but it was smart growth and its North American exponents that captured the attention and imaginations of planners, architects, and policy makers in politics and industry.

By the early 2000s, every major city and urban area had adopted regional planning guidelines based closely on the precepts of smart growth: imposition of urban growth boundaries to prevent further outer suburban development and encouragement of high-density development in inner-city areas and around major transit nodes. According to Rod Fehring, residential executive general manager of a leading housing developer, Australand:

> There is clear evidence that all Australia's major cities are pursuing almost identical strategic planning policies. Just read them. The stated objective in all of them is to encourage more compact urban form and gain greater efficiencies in the use of existing infrastructure and future infrastructure investment.[14]

These schemes became increasingly driven by the promise of great things. For example, the 2013 Draft Metropolitan Strategy for Sydney to 2031 promised: "A home I can afford. Great transport connections. More jobs closer to where I live. Shorter commutes. The right type of home for my family. A park for the kids. Local schools, shops and hospitals. Livable neighborhoods."[15]

Not everyone was convinced. The highly respected urban planner Tony Powell, a former commissioner of the National Capital Development Commission (NCDC), described in 2007 the various regional plans as "a sad parade of failing capital city strategic plans" more concerned with public relations than planning:

> The most obvious methodological shortcoming in all of the capital city strategic plans is the paucity of urban research… in terms of development land, housing, employment, transport, health and welfare services, regional open space (and) water and communications infrastructure.[16]

The long-term strategic plan for Melbourne—Melbourne 2030—was singled out as "superficial to the point of ridiculousness."[17]

Powell was right to be critical. Few of the urban plans at the time, for example, identified or even mentioned housing choice or affordability as legitimate

Renters," May 24, 2012, accessed June 22, 2015, http://www.abs.gov.au/ausstats/abs@.nsf/mf/1301.0.

11 See "New Rules Will Curb Energy-Guzzling McMansions," *Sydney Morning Herald*, June 2, 2005, in which the views of the then New South Wales premier Bob Carr are made clear; or the feature article by Larissa Dubecki titled "Swimming against the Tide," *Age* (Melbourne), May 6, 2006 in which suburbia is referenced as "the opiate of the middle classes" and McMansions referenced as "crass over class."

12 Alan Davis, "Is Obesity Really Caused by Suburban Sprawl?," June 11, 2010, accessed June 22, 2015, http://blogs.crikey.com.au/theurbanist/2010/06/11/is-obesity-really-caused-by-suburban-sprawl/.

13 The then NSW Labor Premier made the comment at a press conference in 2001, in response to news that the national immigration intake numbers would be lifted. For an analysis of Carr's career, including the point at which he declared Sydney to be full, see Tom Dusevic's article "The Second Coming of Bob Carr," *Australian*, April 21, 2012.

14 Rod Fehring (executive general manager, Residential, Australand Property Group), interview by Ross Elliott, January 15, 2015.

15 NSW Department of Planning and Environment, "Draft Metropolitan Strategy for Sydney to 2031," March 2013.

16 Anthony Powell, "Illusions and Realities in Contemporary Metropolitan Planning Practice—Notes for a Lecture to Town Planning Students in the Faculty of Architecture, Building and Planning," (University of Melbourne, Melbourne, Victoria, Australia, July 27, 2007).

1.7.3 Yarrabilba

17 Anthony Powell,
    "Illusions and Realities
    in Contemporary
    Metropolitan Planning
    Practice—Notes for
    a Lecture to Town
    Planning Students in the
    Faculty of Architecture,
    Building and Planning,"
    (University of
    Melbourne, Melbourne,
    Victoria, Australia, July
    30, 2007).
18 Ibid.
19 Fran Metcalf, "Diverse
    Family Units, High
    Density Housing in
    Store," *Courier Mail*,
    August 24, 2009.

planning objectives. They generally demonstrated a lack of sympathy for consumer choice, were silent on development or market economics, and were largely devoid of basic math. Many included heroic and untested assumptions about the capacity of increased urban density to provide for future population growth. Powell was one of many who were critical:

> The proposition in the latest crop of metropolitan strategy plans that 50 percent or more of future housing development can be accommodated in existing suburban areas of the major cities is patently ridiculous. These are simply unexamined and unreliable hypotheses, not strategies.[18]

Undeterred by a lack of basic arithmetic, proponents of the high-density "solution" continued to promote the promised merits of density and the implied evils of sprawl by referencing numerous supposed social and demographic drivers. The Australian demographer Bernard Salt got caught up in the tide of enthusiasm for the high-density housing solution when responding to a news media article dealing with the "new face" of residents moving into high-density inner-city areas, focusing on a young lesbian couple as an example. "No longer will a typical Australian family comprise mum, dad and two children," the article claimed. "In the middle of the twentieth-century, you got married and moved to the suburbs," Salt was reported as saying. He added:

Today, there's about 10 variations on that theme. There's gay couples, divorcees, married couples who don't have kids, singles, ex-pats, de facto couples and we can't forget that we have an ageing population. Those groups didn't exist thirty or forty years ago, so there's different kinds of families now who have different housing requirements. There's less need for basic three-bedroom brick veneer homes in the suburbs.[19]

This type of argument flew in the face of the evidence. According to the Australian Census, in 2001 family households accounted for 68.8 percent of all household types. By 2011, this proportion was little changed at 67.8 percent. The proportion of lone-person households rose from 22.8 percent to 23.1 percent in the same period—hardly evidence of any demise in the family unit or of any need to radically change the development industry's response to housing choice. (fig. **1.7.3**)

While smart growth planning schemes had their origins mostly when State Labor governments were in power, these same ideologies have transferred almost seamlessly to Conservative governments as the political landscape shifted. By 2012, Labor lost power in all three of Australia's largest states: Victoria, New South Wales, and Queensland. Yet the dominant principles of smart growth in various regional planning schemes were adopted with minimal challenge or alteration. Despite ongoing industry calls for reform, urban growth

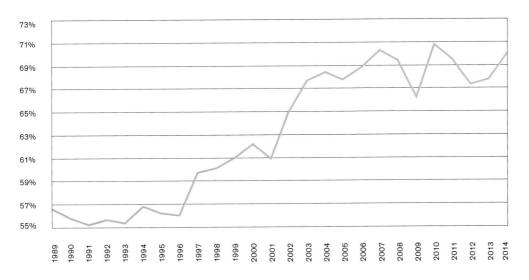

1.7.4 Australian residential land as a percentage of dwelling values

20 David Keir (managing director, Devine Limited), interview by Ross Elliott, January 12, 2015.

21 The governmental habit of blaming "greedy developers" for escalating land costs was endemic. The development industry called for more land releases and lower taxes to alleviate affordability, but authorities resisted, pointing the finger instead at developers. For an illustration, see Kathy Sundrom, "Mayors Attack 'Greedy' Developers," *Sunshine Coast Daily*, April 23, 2008, accessed November 8, 2015, http://www.sunshinecoastdaily.com.au/news/mayors-attack-greedy-developers/338680/. The attitude of a group of mayors and the response by industry could have been repeated—and was—right across the country.

22 See Property Council of Australia, "Reasons to Be Fearful: Government Taxes, Charges, and Compliance Costs and Their Impact on Housing Affordability," Residential Development Council, March 2006.

boundaries and unrealistically ambitious targets for infill and high-density housing growth remain key planning features of Australia's major cities.

Affordability Worsens

As urban growth boundaries (UGBs) were introduced from the late 1990s to early 2000s, the impact of reduced land supply was almost immediate. Developers quickly sought to acquire developable parcels within UGBs, and competition for available sites was intense. Prices for development parcels rose rapidly due to the policy-induced scarcity. According to David Keir, managing director of the developer Devine Limited in Australia, "The imposition of growth boundaries—or, more so, growth constraints—during the 1990s limited the ability of new suburbs to evolve, and subsequently limited supply. [There were] rapid increases in both the cost of undeveloped land and subsequently the cost of new product."[20] (fig. **1.7.4**)

Many economists have argued that the rapid escalation in housing prices from roughly the late 1990s onward was due to a strong domestic economy, population growth, and readily available mortgage finance. This demand-side analysis rarely considers the costs of bringing new supply into the market. As Keir identifies, the price paid for limited developable (namely,

permissible) land within the artificially imposed growth boundaries was a key factor driving costs up for developers and hence prices for homebuyers.

Other factors also affected supply. At almost the same time as urban growth boundaries appeared, local and state governments began to adopt a new "user pays" system of charging for community infrastructure. Whereas local infrastructure had traditionally been funded from community-wide sources (local council rates, land taxes, stamp duties, and other forms of revenue), the move to "upfront" development taxes was enthusiastically and rapidly embraced. The method by which these charges were calculated was rarely disclosed. For governments, it became a simple proposition to charge land developers a per-lot infrastructure charge, however exorbitant, in order to fund community-wide policy commitments, whether arising from new development or not. Complaints about lack of equity or transparency were batted away as the complaints of "greedy developers" and the consequential impact on land pricing ignored.[21]

Per-lot levies of upward of $50,000 Australian dollars ($37,000 US dollars) had by 2007 become commonplace in the urban growth areas of major markets across the country.[22] While the market

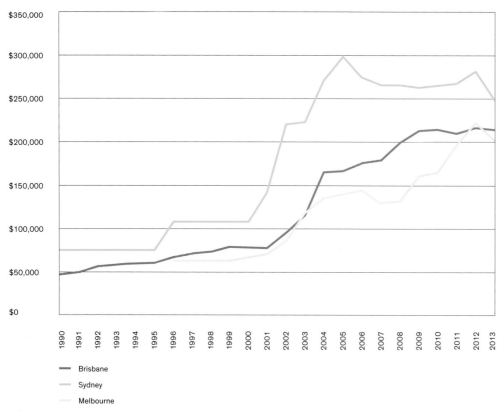

23 Guy Gibson (General
   Manager Queensland,
   Communities, Lend
   Lease), interview by Ross
   Elliott, January 9, 2015.
24 Allen Consulting Group,
   "Taxes and Charges
   and New Homes,"
   *Residential Developer
   Magazine*, April 12, 2012,
   accessed June 26, 2015,
   http://www.residential
   developer.com.au
   /Article/NewsDetail
   .aspx?p=129&id=208.

Brisbane
Sydney
Melbourne

1.7.5 Median residential land costs, major markets, Australia, 1990 to 2013

remained strong and the economy healthy, these charges were absorbed by developers and passed on to their purchasing public.

Completing the assault on new housing in Australia was federal tax reform. The introduction of a 10 percent Goods and Services Tax (GST) in 2000 created a more progressive tax base for the nation. The state governments, which were to be the recipients of GST revenues, promised to abolish a variety of state taxes in exchange, including stamp duty on sales of assets. But the states reneged on their promise to reform stamp duties, while keeping the GST revenues. Because the GST only applied to the final end price of new supply, it was not levied on existing (or secondhand) housing, but it did add 10 percent to the cost of new housing, paid for by the purchaser. This exemption of established housing, combined with the retention of stamp duties, meant that the new housing supply was more punitively taxed than ever before. According to Guy

Gibson, Communities general manager in Queensland for the global developer Lend Lease, "Overnight, the industry went from paying very little wholesale sales tax, to 8 to 10 percent GST…which made new homes less competitive against the established house market."[23]

A 2011 report revealed the extent to which this combination of policy factors had affected new housing. Overall, taxes, charges, and compliance expenditures on new housing amounted to 30.4 percent of housing costs in Sydney and 25.9 percent in Brisbane.[24] The result was that everywhere, except in Perth, these policy-induced charges make up a larger part of the cost of new housing than the cost of the land itself. Given that land prices were already inflated due to supply constraints imposed under UGBs, this approach to taxing land added further direct pressure to the cost of new housing supply.

Research by the Urban Development Institute of Australia (UDIA) into land

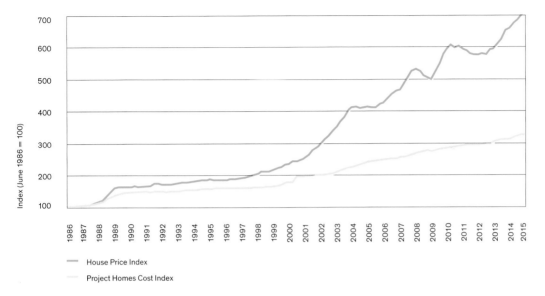

House Price Index

Project Homes Cost Index

1.7.6 Australian house prices versus construction costs

supply and pricing further illustrates the impact on land prices.[25] The situation was worse than figures show because developers quickly shrank typical lot sizes to meet market price points. Thus, homebuyers were paying more for smaller lots, with the rate per square meter accelerating even faster than indicated by the per-lot price. (fig. **1.7.5**)

"The traditional suburban quarter-acre block is nothing but a distant memory," the UDIA lamented in 2014, noting that the average size of a new residential lot was now one-tenth of an acre, after falling 29 percent in size over the previous decade.[26]

Suggestions that escalating expectations of new homebuyers and McMansion-style homes were to blame for worsening affordability did not stand up to the evidence. The cost of actually building the structure on the land, apart from the GST, had remained largely in line with inflation over time. It has been the cost of land that has escalated, leading to higher new housing prices.[27] (fig. **1.7.6**)

Detractors of suburban living choices also point to rapidly rising housing starts for apartment projects in inner-city areas in their search for evidence to prove that Australians are now choosing high-density housing over the suburban

alternative.[28] Nothing could be further from the truth. The rapid escalation in apartment construction in Australia's capital cities is little more than a frenzy of speculative investment by purchasers who have no intention of actually living in the apartment they have bought, many of which at only one or two bedrooms are entirely unsuited to family accommodation anyway.[29] One recent study of the Brisbane apartment market revealed that across a large number of recently completed projects, as few as 3 percent of units were sold to owner-occupiers. The balance was sold to (mainly) interstate and overseas investors.[30]

The absence of owner-occupiers is a market signal that what is occurring in apartment construction is a development industry response to investor appetite, not to housing preference by families. Rising rental vacancies in newer apartment projects is a further market signal that what is being built, contrary to the booster mythology, is not meeting with the expected depth of demand. A recent Melbourne study concluded that as many as one in five apartments was vacant, leading to the description of new projects as "ghost towers."[31]

To the chagrin of density advocates, official data reinforce the preference

25 "The 2014 UDIA State of the Land Report," Urban Development Institute of Australia, November 1, 2013, accessed June 22, 2015, http://www.udia.com.au/reports-and-submissions/reports-submissions-2014.

26 Ibid.

27 See also Leith van Onselen (writing as "the Unconventional Economist") in "Australian Land Prices Go Vertical," *Macrobusiness*, April 23, 2015, accessed November 8, 2015, http://www.macrobusiness.com.au/2015/04/australian-land-prices-go-vertical/.

28 For a good summary of how approvals have shifted from detached housing to attached housing, see Leith van Onselen, "A Land of Sweeping Plains and Shoebox Apartments," *Macrobusiness*, March 3, 2015, accessed November 8, 2015, http://www.macrobusiness.com.au/2015/03/land-sweeping-plains-shoebox-apartments/. The story includes evidence that capital city apartment starts have overtaken house starts for the first time in Australia's history.

29 I wrote about this as a topic in "High Density Housing's Biggest Myth," published via my blog *The Pulse*, February 25, 2015, accessed November 8, 2015, http://thefingeronthepulse.blogspot.com.au/.

30 See Michael Matusik, "Investors Dominate: Inner Brisbane Apartment Update," Matusik Property Insights, May 19, 2015. In none of the larger projects studied in this report was the proportion of owner-occupiers much above 20 percent.

31 See Aisha Dow, "'Ghost tower' warning for Docklands after data reveals high Melbourne home vacancies," *Age* (Melbourne), November 12, 2014.

1.7.7 Greater Springfield, exurban master-planned community

32 Australia's Census shows little change in the composition of housing form despite nearly twenty years of pro-density policy. See for example Liz Allen, Anna Reimondos, and Edith Gray, "Fewer Occupants, More Bedrooms: Census Shows Australians Prefer Bigger Houses," *The Conversation*, June 29, 2012, http://thecon versation.com/fewer -occupants-more-bed rooms-census-shows -australians-prefer -bigger-houses-7871.

33 Australian Bureau of Statistics, "2011 Census of Population and Housing, Australia."

34 Raynuha Sinnathamby (managing director, Springfield Land Corporation), interview by Ross Elliott, January 13, 2015.

of Australian households—especially families—for suburban housing.[32] Those who suggest that suburban housing is no longer in demand are disregarding market evidence to the contrary. The most reliable and accurate measure is provided by the official Census, which shows that nine out of ten families with children at home lived in a detached house in 2011, despite the rapid increase in the supply of alternatives. And families with children—as couples or single parents—remain the largest of all household groups, making up 41 percent of Australian households: a figure that has remained largely unchanged in more than twenty years.[33]

According to Raynuha Sinnathamby, managing director of Springfield Land Corporation, the developer of Australia's largest master-planned residential community:

> There is plenty of market feedback that indicates that young couples move away from the dense inner city environments to ensure that, as they start a family, they will have more space for their household to grow, i.e., a bigger house, more access to a backyard or parks close to the home, access to quality schools, a safe environment for children and preferably jobs close to home. There is feedback to indicate that when moving from inner city

environments, couples would achieve these aspirations by owning a detached house rather than an apartment product and generally in suburban areas.[34] (fig. **1.7.7**)

The Springfield development in southeast Queensland is proof of ongoing community-wide interest in the detached housing model. The 7,000-acre (2,800-hectare) site commenced development in 1992, and by the late 1990s, growth was accelerating despite widespread antipathy from a cross-section of urban elites. Its exurban location—some 12 miles (20 kilometers) from the city center and in a region not previously regarded as a preferred residential address—led many to question the vision of its founders, Maha Sinnathamby and Bob Sharpless. But Springfield today is home to some twenty-eight thousand residents, countless businesses, schools, shopping centers, a new hospital, a railway station and new rail line, parklands, a golf course, and a growing commercial hub. By 2030, it's projected that more than one hundred thousand people will live here. Detached housing was the primary driver of its growth because Springfield at the time offered abundant detached land supply at reasonable prices. It was also subject to its own development legislation, which meant it was not caught by the changes in land regulation that affected other developers.

Being able to offer the market an afford-able opportunity to buy the suburban dream of a house and land proved a win-ning business formula for the company.[35]

Conclusion

In the relatively short space of a decade—from around the mid-1990s to the mid-2000s—Australia's efficient, broadly accessible, and highly affordable new housing market, through a series of quite deliberate policy decisions, became one of the least affordable markets in the world. It now takes many new homebuyers an average of four years just to save for a down payment, let alone contemplate the challenge of paying off a home, which is up to eight times their combined house-hold income.[36] Housing investors are increasingly dominating purchases, lever-aging the equity in existing homes that have benefited from house price inflation. But while this is creating an even wealth-ier property-owner class, it is pricing out younger people and families who retain a strong preference for the suburban hous-ing model but are increasingly finding it cost prohibitive. There is little evidence yet to suggest that this market has embraced apartment living as an alternative, but it is reasonable to speculate that a number are renting this form of housing as they save for the preferred but deferred option of a suburban detached dwelling. The consequences of lower levels of homeown-ership, financial duress for families paying excessive mortgages during their working lives, or unfunded future retire-ment plans are all a question of debate and speculation. But it is almost cer-tain that the radically different housing fundamentals now in place will lead to significant changes in what Australia has considered social and economic "norms" for generations.

The policy settings that drove this fundamental change are now deeply ingrained in land use regulation and public policy. There is little evidence to suggest that policy makers from both sides of the political spectrum have much interest in reversing these decisions in order to restore affordability and improve access to housing for future generations.

Australia is a country with a long history of placing a high value on equal access to homeownership and on raising families in generous suburban locations. The new ideological framework for land use, housing, and urban planning is having profound repercussions across the spectrum of social and economic life in Australia. A full and dispassionate reap-praisal of the policy settings that have led to this outcome might offer some hope of substantial policy change. What's required is a much-reduced emphasis on urban growth boundaries, an elimination—or at least significant reduction—of up-front and discriminatory taxation on new housing supply, and a relaxation of overly prescriptive regulatory controls and conditions. However, given the prevailing new orthodoxy, these reforms are unlikely to find much support, meaning that the suburban housing dream in Australia will fade even further from view.

35 Raynuha Sinnathamby (managing director, Springfield Land Corporation), interview by Ross Elliott, January 13, 2015.

36 "Bankwest First Time Buyer Deposit Report 2014," Bankwest, December 18, 2014, accessed June 22, 2015, https://www.bankwest .com.au/media-centre /financial-indicator -series/bankwest-first -time-buyer-deposit -report-1292518533842.

1.8
HOW BRITAIN'S GREENBELTS CHOKE SUBURBS AND FORCE UP PRICES

James Heartfield

The preservation of open land has long been a key component of British planning. But the effects on middle-income households, and on suburban residents, are rarely discussed—namely, that restrictions on building are forcing up prices. One good example can be found in Oxford, to the west of London, best known as an ancient university town. The local authorities have tried to keep its traditional character and protect the centrality of its colleges, some of which date back to medieval times. The colleges own much of the land around Oxford, but it cannot be built on because of the greenbelt established around it under the Town and Country Planning Act of 1947.

This restraint on development has had a predictable effect: Oxford is Britain's "least affordable" city, and the average property now sells for more than eleven times local salaries, $507,035 (£340,864), or twice the national average.[1] The results have been devastating on many middle- and working-class families. Early in 2015, the city authorities used a light airplane fitted with infrared cameras, and found 2,300 suspicious heat patterns and have so far discovered three hundred people living illegally in garden sheds. People live in sheds because they cannot afford a home.

To the east of London is England's other major ancient university town, Cambridge. Though historically it had less industry and a smaller population than Oxford, the city fathers decided in the 1980s to attract new technologies in order to grow. Like Oxford, Cambridge has a greenbelt around it, but the local plan, drawn up with advice from the architect Marcial Echenique, cleared the way for expansion at its suburban fringes and in the smaller surrounding towns. Unlike Oxford, it is building new homes in Trumpington and in the North West between Madingley Road and Huntingdon Road on former greenbelt land. To be sure, even Cambridge suffers from the English

disease of unaffordability, with houses costing seven times average salaries, but nothing on the scale of Oxford.

These differing attitudes toward suburban growth constitute a major issue in the future of Britain. According to government's breakdown of where people live, 9 percent are in urban cores, 23 percent are in areas that are suburban/urban, 43 percent in suburbs proper, and 20 percent in what they call suburban/rural, with 5 percent in wholly rural areas.[2] Overwhelmingly, then, Britain is a suburban country.

What is more, despite assertions to the contrary by urban pundits, people like living in suburbs. Sociological surveys from the 1940s right up to the present day consistently find that people prefer the idea of living in suburbs, with detached or semi-detached homes. In addition, people who live in the suburbs are generally happier than those who live in inner cities. Research for the Joseph Rowntree Foundation found that "residents in suburbs, both deprived and affluent, were far less dissatisfied than similar groups in urban areas." Another Joseph Rowntree survey found that "dramatically increased density is not favored as the answer to the perceived housing shortage," adding, "the clear message is that the majority of people aspire to live in detached or semi-detached homes with gardens."[3]

All the more remarkable, then, that the British government's housing plans since 1947, and even more so over the last twenty years, have been designed to restrict suburban sprawl and to concentrate populations more densely in urban areas. Though Britain is an overwhelmingly suburban country, most of its suburbs, like Willesden or Basildon, were first developed between the wars, before the creation of the greenbelt under the Town and Country Planning Act of 1947. Indeed, current plans aim to fill in suburban areas, presently at a density of

1   Patrick Collinson, "Oxford the Least Affordable City to Live in as Houses Sell for Eleven Times Local Salaries," *Guardian*, March 9, 2014, accessed November 13, 2015, http://www .theguardian.com /money/2014/mar/10 /oxford-least-affordable -city-house-prices -lloyds; Matt Oliver, "Beds in sheds: Almost Three Hundred Illegal Dwellings across Oxford," *Oxford Times*, January 29, 2015, accessed November 14, 2015, http://www .oxfordtimes.co.uk /news/11755998.Beds _in_sheds__Almost_300 _illegal_dwellings_across _Oxford/?ref=mr.

2   Jane Todorovic, *Living in Urban England: Attitudes and Aspirations* (London: Department of the Environment, Transport and the Regions, 2000).

3   A survey in 1943 by the Society of Women Housing Managers, and another by Mass Observation, found that people overwhelmingly wanted to live in suburbs, reported in Mark Clapson, *Invincible Green Suburbs* (Manchester: Manchester University Press, 1998), 69–72. In 1960 and 1961 there were two social surveys on suburbanization that also found marked satisfaction with suburban life, written up as J. Barry Cullingworth, "Social Implications of Overspill: The Worsley Social Survey," *Sociological Review* 8, no. 1 (July 1960): 77–89; J. Barry Cullingworth, "Swindon Social Survey: A Second Report on the Social Implications of Overspill," *Sociological Review* 9, no. 2 (July 1961): 151–66. A 1998 Joseph Rowntree Foundation survey was published as Roger Burrows and David Rhodes, *Patterns of Neighbourhood Dissatisfaction in England* (London: Joseph Rowntree Foundation, 1998), which again found greater satisfaction among suburban

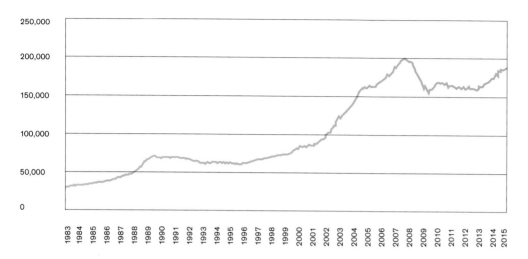

250,000

200,000

150,000

100,000

50,000

0

1983 1984 1985 1986 1987 1988 1989 1990 1991 1992 1993 1994 1995 1996 1997 1998 1999 2000 2001 2002 2003 2004 2005 2006 2007 2008 2009 2010 2011 2012 2013 2014 2015

1.8.1 UK House Prices

between six and sixteen dwellings per acre (15 to 40 per hectare), up to twenty-six dwellings per acre (65 per hectare) around London, and twelve dwellings per acre (30 per hectare) elsewhere.[4] Right now, numerous suburban areas are earmarked for densification.

In 2002 the government's Urban Task Force under Lord Richard Rogers set out the goal of dissuading greenfield development in the suburbs, in favor of increasing the building of new homes on existing brownfield sites in major cities by 60 percent over the next ten years.[5] His task force's goal was to achieve much higher densities—to "build up, not out"— through smart growth, using the ingenuity of architects to fit more people into less space. The policy has, at least in that sense, been a great success; the housing charity Shelter reports that overcrowding doubled between the censuses of 2001 and 2011.[6]

Across the country, a shortage of affordable homes has led people to desperate solutions. Many younger people and immigrants, unable to buy or rent a room, have taken places in garden sheds and other converted buildings. In East London, Newham Council had to create a special unit to evict the mostly immigrant tenants illegally renting converted garden sheds. The sheds have been broken up to prevent reoccupation, and immigration officers are on hand to harass the evicted tenants. The number of people aged between twenty and thirty-four living in their parents' homes has increased from 2.4 million in 2002 to 3.3 million in 2013.[7]

The unplanned outcome of the preference for building on brownfield sites was that overall construction slumped to a level insufficient to meet housing need or replace the existing housing stock. The falling off of home building can be seen in the number of dwellings since the high point of the late 1960s. (fig. **1.8.1**) Between the 2001 and the 2011 censuses, the population of the United Kingdom living in households grew from 57.7 million to 62 million, or 7.5 percent, while the number of households grew from 24.5 million to 26.4 million, or 8 percent. The number of households grows for different reasons. Some of it is due to immigration, though less than most people think. Some of it is natural population growth. Up until 2001, when the trend stopped, some of the growth in the number of households is because of the proclivity for smaller households, with more households containing the same total number.[8]

We can see that the trend is that new home construction is falling off while the number of households is increasing. Is a growth in the housing stock of two

dwellers than urban. In 2005 the Commission for Architecture and the Built Environment published its survey *What Home Buyers Want: Attitudes and Decision Making among Consumers* (London: CABE, 2005), which again found that people preferred the idea of suburban to urban homes. Mark Clapson gathered surveys of people's living aspirations, in *Suburban Century* (Oxford: Berg, 2003), 55–57, and see footnotes; Ben Kochan, in research for the Town and Country Planning Association and the Joseph Rowntree Foundation, collected more resent research on people's living aspirations and satisfaction, published in *Achieving a Suburban Renaissance: The Policy Challenge* (London: TCPA, July 2007).

4 Kochan, *Achieving a Suburban Renaissance*, 4, 23.

5 Urban Task Force, *Towards an Urban Renaissance* (London: Taylor and Francis, 1999), 173.

6 Randeep Ramesh, "Quarter of Households in Parts of UK Overcrowded, says Shelter," *Guardian*, December 23, 2012, accessed November 14, 2015, http://www .theguardian.com /society/2012/dec/23 /households-uk-over crowded-shelter.

7 Emily Knipe, "Young Adults Living with Parents," Office for National Statistics, 2013, accessed May 6, 2015, http://www .ons.gov.uk/ons/rel /family-demography /young-adults-living -with-parents/2013 /sty-young-adults.html.

8 "Households and Household Composition in England and Wales, 2001–11," Office for National Statistics, May 29, 2014, accessed May 6, 2015, http:// www.ons.gov.uk/ons /dcp171776_361923 .pdf. Household size decreased from 3.1 per household to 2.4 per

hundred thousand a year enough to meet the additional households? To accept that premise would be to imagine that houses once built stand forever and do not need to be replaced. In the 1960s, when slum clearance was a policy, and more new homes were being built, demolition rates stood at about eighty thousand a year. Today's demolition rates are much lower, but with the sorry outcome that Britain's housing stock is now the oldest in Europe: 55 percent of UK homes were built before 1960. Not surprisingly about a tenth of those are decrepit houses and flats, with leaking roofs or rotten windows. The Home Builder's Federation estimates that, at the current rate of building, each house in Britain would have to stand 1,200 years before it was replaced, or about as long as the Tower of London.[9]

The Planning System

Britain's laws on land and land use are distinctive, though in recent years many countries have borrowed smart growth ideas from them. For many long years—since the Norman Conquest of 1066—Britain has managed its population by creating monopolies in land ownership. Today, those in the Campaign to Preserve Rural England (CPRE) demand that green and pleasant land be kept pristine. "Surely you would not let people build houses on the New Forest," one CPRE spokesman, Shaun Spiers, challenged me.

The New Forest that Spiers referenced was once thickly populated with Anglo-Saxon homes before it was cleared to make way for the Norman lord William Rufus's deer park. In the fifteenth century, peasants were cleared from the land and made into dependent wage laborers. Right up to the late nineteenth century, the law enforced an aristocratic monopoly over the land, which could be sold only once in each generation. That system broke down because the aristocracy had impoverished themselves and lobbied for the right to

sell their land. After the Settled Land Act of 1882 liberalized the sale of estates, land quickly passed into the hands of farmers. After World War I, when food prices were low and the demand for "homes for heroes" was high, people took advantage of the free market to buy up thousands of plots to build their own homes.[10]

These spontaneous settlements between the wars, called "plot lands," "ribbon development," or "sprawl," provoked howls of protest from the old gentry. Demands were made to re-create the restrictions on landownership, and to re-create feudalism without lords, with the presumable result of keeping the poor in the cities. Indebted country houses could be passed on to the National Trust, but large landed estates could not easily become national property.

The answer was a unique reform that separated rights to own land from the right to develop the land. Under the 1947 Town and Country Planning Act, a new restriction was created: development from that point on could only be done with planning permission from the authorities. Ownership no longer entailed a right to develop land for habitation. Under local and regional authority plans, building was restricted to areas between greenbelts that were set at the outskirts of towns and cities to prevent the imagined scourge of ribbon development.

A whole new planning system was created, with a new caste of planning officials to operate it. The pent-up demand for new homes after World War II was reconciled with the hostility of the home counties by creating what were called "new towns" outside major cities to siphon off the pressure. Planning was in keeping with the postwar idea of a welfare society with a planned economy. In the 1960s the planning law was even used by Housing Minister Richard Crossmann to accelerate building plans and meet the additional housing need.

household between 1961 and 2001, or around two people fewer for every three households, making a total of around 17 million additional persons needing housing; net migration to the UK between 1961 and 2011 was 2,149,000. Ian Macrory, "Measuring National Well-Being—Households and Families," Office for National Statistics, April 26, 2012, 4; Jen Beaumont, *Population* (London: Office for National Statistics, 2011), 6.

9 John Stewart, "Building a Crisis; Housing Under-Supply in England," Home Builders Federation, June 2002, accessed May 6, 2015, http://www.hbf.co.uk /policy-activities/news /view/building-a-crisis -housing-under-supply -in-england-by-john -stewart-june-2002/; Oliver Rapf, *Europe's Buildings under the Microscope* (Brussels: Buildings Performance Institute Europe, 2011), 35; James Heartfield, *Let's Build!* (London: Audacity, 2006), 17.

10 Settled Land Act in Dominic Hobson, *The National Wealth* (London: Harper Collins, 1999), 78–79; land buying in W. Robertson Scott, *England's Green and Pleasant Land* (Harmondsworth: Penguin, 1947), 38; plotlands in Dennis Hardy and Colin Ward, *Arcadia for All: The Legacy of a Makeshift Landscape* (London: Mansell, 1984).

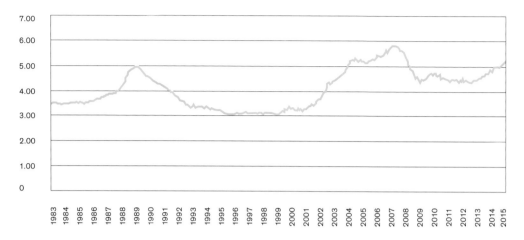

1.8.2 Price earnings ratio

11 Urban Task Force,
*Towards an Urban
Renaissance*, 50; Peter
Hetherington, "Rogers
Laments Failing
Vision," *Guardian*,
January 6, 2002,
accessed November 14,
2015, http://www
.theguardian.com
/society/2002/jan/26
/regeneration
.urbanregeneration.

12 Urban Task Force,
*Towards an Urban
Renaissance*, 26.

13 Kate Barker, *Barker
Review of Land Use
Planning* (London:
HMSO, 2006), 44; and
see Mark Urban, "The
Great Myth of Urban
Britain," BBC, June
28, 2012, accessed
May 6, 2015, http://
www.bbc.co.uk/news
/uk-18623096, for a
breakdown of the land
use statistics.

Later, in the 1970s, antidevelopment forces had a much greater impact on the planning system than those who were in favor of growth. The movement started with protests against the Covent Garden development in London and against the widening of the A1, the major thoroughfare the goes from London into Scotland. These well-meaning conservationists had an inordinate impact, and the authorities introduced clauses into the planning regulations that gave local communities rights to object to new developments. "Not in my back yard" attitudes were empowered, but the future generations had no say. The planning system was like a car with brakes, but no accelerator. Always dreaming about its bucolic past, Britain by the 1980s was fiercely conservative. Not only did it have a Conservative government that was beholden to the county shires that dreaded urban sprawl, it also had a growing green movement committed to protecting the countryside. All of the firepower was on the side against development, with the Campaign to Protect Rural England, the National Trust, Heritage England, the Tory shires, the anti-road protestors and the Green Party. To top it off, the new Labour government in 1998 appointed the Urban Task Force under the architect Sir Richard Rogers. Rogers, along with his adviser Anne Powers, was committed to the inner-city

renaissance, meaning higher urban densities. In particular, he warned against the "extreme forms of social isolation of many American suburbs," and the danger of "segregation."[11] In London, Sir Richard had the ear of the radical mayor Ken Livingstone, who was opposed to any sprawl that would dilute the city's tax base.

One of the strongest arguments against new building has been the fear that Britain's countryside would be put under too much pressure, the Urban Task Force arguing that "large tracts of our countryside have been eroded."[12] But this is largely built on a misunderstanding. When surveyed as to their opinion of what percentage of the country is built up, Britons settled on an average of 40 percent developed, 60 percent countryside. The true figure is less than 10 percent developed and fully 90 percent countryside.[13] The reasons for the misunderstanding are twofold. First, people do not spend much time in the countryside, so experientially the cities loom much larger. Second, the countryside has a symbolic meaning for people as a respite from the kind of pressures that they feel in the city, which they project by imagining the countryside being eaten away. Environmental and conservation movements of course have drawn on that romantic attachment to rural England. In itself that is no bad thing, but it does lead to a thoroughly

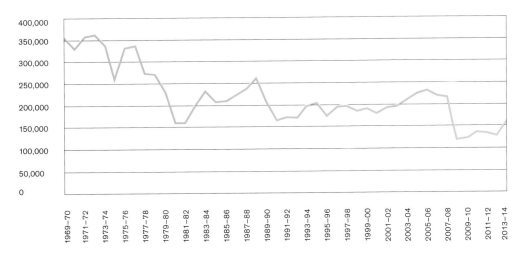

1.8.3 Dwellings started, UK

14 "Where to Build?,"
    Audacity, accessed
    November 14, 2015,
    http://www.audacity.org
    /downloads/audacity
    -Where-to-build-01.pdf.

15 Patrick Collinson, "UK
    House Price Growth
    Slows in Last Three
    Months as Property
    Market Cools," *Guardian*,
    December 30, 2014,
    accessed November 13,
    2015, http://www
    .theguardian.com
    /money/2014/dec
    /30/uk-house-price
    -growth-slows-last
    -three-months-property
    -market-cools.

16 Halifax House Price
    Index, "Historical
    House Price Data,"
    July 2015, accessed
    November 14, 2015,
    http://www.lloydsbank
    inggroup.com/media
    /economic-insight/hali
    fax-house-price-index/.

17 Ibid.

exaggerated belief in the danger to the countryside from new developments. Put simply, if one were to increase developed Britain by fully one-tenth, it would reduce undeveloped Britain by one-ninetieth.

The conservationist lobby has responded to every proposal for development with a warning that the greenbelts in Britain were being encroached on. But the greenbelts that the planning authorities sketched around their urban centers just kept growing, more than doubling in size since 1993, until today they cover 13 percent of England, or 6,327 square miles (16,386 square kilometers). But the greenbelt is just one of the legislative limitations on development. The thirteen national parks of England and Wales together cover one-tenth of the land. All other significant categories of managed land (e.g., Areas of Outstanding Natural Beauty, Ramsar Wetland Sites, Heritage Coast, or Sites of Special Scientific Interest) restrict development in nine-tenths of England.[14] (figs. **1.8.2**–**3**)

The effect of all these regulations is to strangle development in Britain. The greenbelt has turned out to be a noose around our necks. The impact of the planning system is easy to sum up: In the United Kingdom as a whole, the value of a plot of land with planning permission is about a hundred times greater than one without it. All of that additional value is an artificial creation of the planning regime, forcing up the cost of houses, and restricting new developments.

Spiraling Housing Costs

An average house in the United Kingdom was changing hands at $288,130 (£189,002) at the end of 2014, and in London for $620,053 (£406,730). Property prices in London rose by 17 percent over 2014.[15] House prices have been rising precipitately since the turn of this century. They fell back in 2008 with the credit crunch, only to climb right up again.[16]

In Britain in 1983 the average price of a house was three and a half times the average earnings; in 2007 it peaked at a ratio of 5.82 to earnings, before falling back sharply in the mortgage crisis; it then climbed again to just over five times average earnings today.[17] In some places, such as Oxford and much of London, the figures are still higher. Not surprisingly, the call today is for "affordable housing."

Some commentators thought that the overheated housing market showed that Britons are hung up on homeownership. "There's a lot to be said for renting," said the British writer and commentator Owen Hatherley. But the rents are up, too, averaging $1148 (£753) a month UK-wide, and $1880 (£1233) in London. Broadly speaking, rents rise in line with prices, so renting offered no escape from the housing problem.[18] In fact, rising house prices have reversed Britain's long-term preference for homeownership. Home-ownership had been rising since 1918, while renting as a share of tenures had been falling, right up until 2001 when ownership reached 69 percent. Today ownership is down to 64 percent, with young people finding it impossible to get their first foothold on the ladder. They have been called "generation rent."[19]

Britons have $8.69 trillion (£5.7 trillion) tied up in their houses, a substantial proportion of the country's estimated $11.13 trillion (£7.3 trillion) of all wealth; 11.1 million have borrowed $1.97 trillion (£1.292 trillion) to buy their homes, and each year feed their debts with $62.5 (£41 billion) in interest payments.[20]

With the remarkable rise in house prices, any normal market would respond to those price signals by increasing output, but with homebuilding, the opposite has happened. As prices have increased, sales have stagnated and even fallen. Increased demand has not increased supply. The cost of building a house in Britain is $137, 200 (£90,000).[21] But homes sell for twice as much—more than four times as much on average in London. The markup is so great because the restrictions on new building under the Town and Country Planning Act limit supply, forcing prices up.

Britain's onerous planning regime is a system out of control. Nobody who set out to create a plan in 1947 would have planned a system that would push house prices up to five times national income today.

Social Inequality

The impact of the house price ramp on social inequality is profound. More and more city centers are becoming gentrified. "Inner city" used to be a euphemism for social problems, when, in the early 1980s, city centers had largely been abandoned by the upwardly mobile. The rise in house prices came at the same time that many better-off people had second thoughts about living in the countryside, and helped to launch what Lord Rogers called an "Urban Renaissance." Over the last twenty years, areas whose names evoked poverty, like Hoxton, Notting Hill, Brixton, Hackney, and Camden, have become gentrified, or at least their prices have climbed, so that today they stand for wealth. Those with modest or just average incomes are finding it impossible to buy in city centers and move instead to the suburbs and outer suburbs. Others who need to be in town to be close to work suffer overcrowding and rent poverty.

Long-term, the unrealistic price levels have an impact, too. With house prices so high, inherited wealth plays a much greater role in social positioning. Social mobility in Britain had already slowed in the 1980s. The education system today is much more geared to passing on credentials to those who can afford to go to college, than it is to training or to disinterested reflection. Now that home ownership is coming to be beyond the reach of working-class people, while the better off can help their children onto the property ladder, life chances are being set at birth for many.

The Solution

There have been many "quick fix" solutions to the housing problem, but it will take some time to build the homes that people need. There is one solution, proposed by the architect and commentator Ian Abley of the 250 New Towns Club, which would help not just immediately but in the medium and the long term as well.

Abley proposes that we abolish the division between the rights of land ownership and rights of development by repealing the 1947 Town and Country Planning Act. Without the artificial legislative constraint, the price of a home

18 Owen Hatherley, "Is Home Ownership Really So Desirable?," *Guardian*, May 31, 2011, accessed November 14, 2015, http://www.theguardian.com/commentisfree/2011/may/31/home-owner ship-debt-renting; Amy Loddington, "Rent Rises Creep above Inflation for First Time in over a Year," *financial-report*, August 15, 2014, accessed November 14, 2015, http://www.financialreporter.co.uk/specialist-lending/rents-rises-creep-above-inflation-for-first-time-in-over-a-year.html; London Councils, "London Key Facts," accessed May 6, 2015, http://www.londoncouncils.gov.uk/londonfacts/default.tm?category=10.

19 Lisa Batchelor, "UK House Prices Rose Almost Eight Per Cent, in 2014," *Guardian*, January 8, 2014, accessed November 13, 2015, http://www.theguardian.com/money/2015/jan/08/uk-house-prices-rose-almost-8-percent-2014.

20 "UK Homes Now Worth a Total of over £5.7 Trillion, Up 10 percent Year on Year," *Savills*, January 12, 2015, accessed May 6, 2015, http://www.savills.co.uk/_news/article/72418/185344-0/01/2015/uk-homes-now-worth-a-total-of-over-%C2%A35.7-trillion—up-10—year-on-year; The Money Charity, "Money Statistics," January 2015, accessed May 6, 2015, http://themoneycharity.org.uk/money-statistics/january-2015/.

21 James Heartfield, "Give Us the Freedom to Build Our Own Homes," *Spiked*, March 30, 2015, accessed November 14, 2015, http://www.spiked-online.com/newsite/article/give-us-the-freedom-to-build-our-own-homes/16828#.Vdezx_lViko.

could come down to an affordable $137,200 (£90,000). Land in Britain is not overly expensive, and the possibility of self-build solutions on the part of individuals and housing cooperatives would open up. The impact of repealing the Town and Country Planning Act would be to favor greenfield development. In particular, the opening of land that was formerly without planning permission, outside developed areas, to development would reduce land costs— by a hundred times in principle (though market rates would of course alter with demand).

This is far from unrealistic. Between 1919 and 1939, much of Britain was developed without any need of an overarching planning law. The specter of sprawl was just a bogey that disguised a snobbish loathing for the working class.

The sociologist Paul Barker notes that the Housing Corporation Commission demands more planning to deal with the problem of a housing shortage, but says, "the long-lived, plan-less model of suburbia was a much better bet…Could a preference for non-plan be any worse that the failures of almighty plan? It hardly seems so."[22]

Britain's madly overgrown officialdom has led not to a greater rationalization of housing but to an irrational chaos that leaves people at the mercy of slum landlords in overcrowded buildings, or rent poor. Was the 1947 Act intended to impoverish our children and exacerbate social inequality? If so, it is working. The best plan is to leave people to make their own decisions about how they will address the need for new homes in the twenty-first century. That would open the way for a much more expansive and attractive suburban growth.

[22] Paul Barker, *Freedoms of the Suburbs* (London: Francis Lincoln, 2009), 210.

Dainfern, Midrand, Gauteng, South Africa

Mulund, Mumbai, Maharashtra, India

1.9
THE MYTH OF HOMOGENEOUS SUBURBIA

Jon C. Teaford

ECONOMIC
DIVERSITY

TRANSPORT
INFRASTRUCTURE

SOCIAL
DIVERSITY

SOCIAL
INEQUALITIES

In the English-speaking world, the word *suburb* has long conjured stereo-typical images of middle-class family residences removed from the social and environmental pollution of the city. The oft-proclaimed suburban dream of Britain, North America, and Australia has been to escape from the density and diversity of the city to a home of one's own along the metropolitan periphery. Whereas some sylvan suburban refuges approximate this dream, the suburbia of yesterday and today is a more complex and varied world.

There is no "one" suburbia, and there never has been. That is a myth. The nineteenth and early twentieth centuries witnessed the rise of industrial suburbs, as well as residential enclaves for the wealthy. Some suburbs became known for their illicit roadhouses and gangster presence; others were sanctuaries for God-fearing teetotalers. Late twentieth-century suburbs were the site of mammoth shopping malls and soaring skyscrapers, as well as tract houses and mansions. They were home to millions of immigrants and to persons of every social status. Suburbia has not been a world apart from the metropolitan norm. Instead, it has been, and is, a diverse reflection of the heterogeneous world of the modern metropolis.

Transportation Expands Suburbia

Suburbs have existed since antiquity, accommodating those people and func-tions not welcome within the city walls. Driven by transport technology in the nineteenth-century English-speaking world, however, suburbanization acceler-ated and diversified the outward flow of residents and enterprises. Especially significant was the development of steam railroads that carried commuters from outlying communities to the urban center. For example, by the close of the 1840s, fifty-nine commuter trains offered

1.9.1 Nineteenth-century real estate office serving Chicago suburbanites

daily service for Boston businessmen with homes in such emerging suburbs as Cambridge, Newton, and Brookline.[1] Chicago's commuter rail lines likewise afforded "business men an excellent opportunity to avail themselves of the beautiful quiet of a country residence without shortening the number of hours usually devoted to their daily avocations."[2] In 1873 an account of Chicago's suburbs reported on the thousands of household heads who "do business in the city, and form a large percent of the passenger list of the 100 or more trains that enter and leave the city daily."[3] (fig. **1.9.1**) Chicago's North Shore communities from Evanston to Lake Forest were already acquiring a reputation as suburban refuges for upper-middle-class families seeking a quiet retreat from the vicissi-tudes of the city. Similarly, commuter rail lines were opening outlying areas to Londoners seeking to escape each evening from the heart of Britain's capital. At each station suburbs arose, attracting an increasing corps of commuters.

As London rail lines gradually began to offer inexpensive fares to workers, the option of an outlying home opened to a broadening segment of the metropolitan population. At the beginning of the twentieth century, the *Times* of London reported that the population of the sub-urban ring beyond the limits of the County of London had risen by six hundred thousand between 1891 and 1901, or twice the increase within the county limits. The *Times* observed that, previously,

1   Kenneth Jackson, *Crabgrass Frontier: The Suburbanization of the United States* (New York: Oxford University Press, 1985), 37.
2   Michael H. Ebner, "In the Suburbs of Toun: Chicago's North Shore to 1871," *Chicago History* 40 (1982): 70.
3   Carl Abbott, "Necessary Adjuncts to Its Growth: The Railroad Suburbs of Chicago, 1854–1875," *Journal of the Illinois State Historical Society* 73 (1980): 117.

"the manner of suburban extension seemed to affect mainly the middle classes." But this was no longer true.

> The habit of living at a distance from the scene of work has spread from the merchant and the clerk to the artisan, and one has only to observe the substitution of small houses for large in the older suburbs, and the streets of cottages in new extensions, to realize that the suburb is now mainly the residence of the family of small means.[4]

In Australia, families of small means, as well as the more affluent, also established themselves in emerging suburbs. Boosters sold Australia as a land where newcomers could enjoy a home of their own on a generous plot of land. In 1871 one promoter promised that working-class immigrants to Victoria "will be able, whether by economy of saving, or through the help of one of the numerous building societies, to secure a comfortable freehold for himself and thus possess what every Englishman glories in—a house which will be his castle."[5] The result was a sprawling suburban hodgepodge of social diversity. In the late 1880s a newcomer to Melbourne noted that "a poor house stands side by side with a good house, a cottage, one might almost say a hovel, in close proximity to a palace."[6]

Beginning in the 1890s in the United States, the electrification of rail and tramlines hastened the heterogeneous outward flow. England's metropolitan areas, too, experienced a sharp increase in population along the newly electrified lines during the first four decades of the twentieth century. Between the two world wars, the construction of 4.2 million primarily detached or semidetached dwellings in England and Wales resulted in a nearly 50 percent increase in the extent of urbanized land.[7] London's rapidly expanding suburbs accommodated the range of economic classes within English society. Detached houses with ample garden space attracted the upper-middle class; miles of semidetached dwellings with popular Tudor-style trimmings were the domain of the middle and lower-middle classes, and council housing estates constructed by the County of London and other local public authorities offered a suburban home to those unable to afford the privately built semis. Critics of suburbia complained of the sprawling monotony and stultifying uniformity. But the expanse of new housing was, in fact, home to a diverse social mix. Middle-class suburbanites expressed the tensions provoked by this heterogeneity when they dubbed nearby council estates as Little Moscows—dangerously socialistic settlements located all too close to the refuges of the capitalist class.[8]

Electric streetcars and interurban lines, as well as the increasingly popular automobile, transported the diverse ranks of suburbanites in America. The far-flung suburbs of Southern California developed along the hundreds of miles of interurban lines of the Pacific Electric Railway. By the 1920s, Beverly Hills was becoming synonymous with wealth and glamor, while east of the Los Angeles city limits, the subdivision of Belvedere was the home of Mexican workers. Nearby Maywood, Huntington Park, and Bell were working-class communities, and Signal Hill was an oil town with 1,200 derricks. Reporting on Southern California's oil field towns in 1925, the sociologist Harlan Douglass noted, "Suburbs of this sort present many of the aspects of the frontier mining-camp."[9] Even from its early history, suburbia was home to diverse social classes and people.

Self-Built Suburbs

At the bottom of the lengthy suburban social ladder were the self-built communities, where workers purchased

4   "The Formation of London Suburbs," *Times* (London), June 25, 1904, 8.

5   Graeme Davison, "Australia: The First Suburban Nation?," *Journal of Urban History* 22 (1995): 54.

6   Graeme Davison, "The Past and Future of the Australian Suburb," *Urban Research Program Working Paper*, no. 33 (1993): 10.

7   Mark Swenarton, "Tudor Walters and Tudorbethan: Reassessing Britain's Inter-war Suburbs," *Planning Perspectives* 17 (2003): 267.

8   Trevor Rowley, *The English Landscape in the Twentieth Century* (London: Hambledon Continuum, 2006), 205; Alan A. Jackson, *Semi-Detached London: Suburban Development, Life and Transport* (London: Allen & Unwin, 1973), 305.

9   Harlan Paul Douglass, *The Suburban Trend* (New York: Century Company, 1925), 96.

inexpensive lots and constructed their own modest dwellings with whatever materials they could afford. In Britain, such settlements were dubbed "plotlands." For example, in South Essex east of London, makeshift communities arose that consisted largely of owner-built shacks and old railway cars, retrieved by plot owners and transformed into crude bungalows. Without paved streets, sewerage, gas, or electricity, the plotlands were suburbia on the cheap. Australia had a long tradition of suburban self-construction, and in Canada, immigrants from the British Isles, like their cousins down under, created makeshift castles of their own in the expansive communities of self-built housing on the periphery of Toronto.

In the United States, South Gate, southeast of Los Angeles, was advertised as "a town of, by and for workingmen."[10] Buying a lot for twenty dollars down and ten dollars a month, workers created a do-it-yourself suburbia with modest owner-constructed frame structures. A 1930s sociologist described the landscape of nearby, self-built Bell Gardens: "Here is a perfectly cubical building about half the size of a one-car garage and covered with tar paper. It is not a chicken coop or a rabbit pen but the home of a family."[11] Meanwhile, African Americans in Chagrin Falls Park, east of Cleveland, were likewise creating their own suburban places through the sweat of their labor. "The neighbors dug the basement by hand, and my father and another man that lived down the street built the house," reported one resident. "We paid for the stuff as we went along."[12]

Industrial Suburbs

The development of industrial suburbs in the United States also ensured that the periphery was not uniformly middle class, wholesome, or residential. Noxious, sprawling stockyards and slaughterhouses were consigned to the periphery. The giant Union Stock Yards located in the town of Lake, immediately south of Chicago, attracted both meatpacking plants and blocks of workers' cottages, as did expansive stockyards and packing plants in Nebraska's working-class suburb of South Omaha. In 1886 residents complained of the ills all too common in the industrial suburbs: "We are exposed without any protection against tramps and murderers—having no jail, no church, one school house (and that falling to decay), one saloon for every twenty inhabitants, one gambling house [and] two houses of ill fame."[13] Andrew Carnegie built his giant steel mills in Braddock and outside Homestead, beyond the city limits of nearby Pittsburgh, and by 1899, suburbia was the place of employment for 55 percent of the metropolitan district's production workers. At the same time, east of St. Louis, Granite City, Illinois, employed 8,500; the population included a large settlement of Macedonian and Bulgarian immigrants in the wretched suburban slum known as Hungary Hollow.[14]

In the Detroit area, Henry Ford had embarked on the mass manufacture of the Model T in an elephantine factory on an 80-acre tract in suburban Highland Park. Then, in the 1920s, he moved his base to the suburb of Dearborn, constructing his sprawling River Rouge industrial complex. Mass production required massive spaces, and suburbia offered the open land Ford and many of his fellow manufacturers needed.

In the Toronto region, Kodak chose the far northwestern suburbs for its plant; Goodyear located along the western periphery and Ford opened its expansive factory east of the city. Similarly, along the new highways stretching out from London, British manufacturers built their plants to make the new appliances intended for the recently constructed suburban homes. In suburban Dagenham, Ford constructed

10 Becky M. Nicolaides, *My Blue Heaven: Life and Politics in the Working-Class Suburbs of Los Angeles, 1920–1965* (Chicago: University of Chicago Press, 2002), 26.

11 Ibid.

12 Andrew Wiese, *Places of Their Own: African American Suburbanization in the Twentieth Century* (Chicago: University of Chicago Press, 2004), 74.

13 James W. Savage, John T. Bell, and Consul W. Butterfield, *History of the City of Omaha, Nebraska and South Omaha* (New York: Munsell & Company, 1894), 645.

14 Robert Lewis, "Running Rings around the City: North American Industrial Suburbs, 1850–1950," in *Changing Suburbs: Foundation, Form and Function*, ed. Richard Harris and Peter J. Larkham (London: E&F Spon, 1999), 149; Graham Romeyn Taylor, *Satellite Cities: A Study of Industrial Suburbs* (New York: D. Appleton and Company, 1915), 137, 151–60.

the British version of its Dearborn facility, a gigantic plant that would become Europe's largest manufacturing facility. These mammoth plants, the economic and industrial engine of nations, could only have been built in the suburbs because of land availability and nearby housing opportunities for their workers.

By the onset of World War II, the suburbia of the English-speaking world was not the stereotypical semirural retreat, a protected and homogeneous residential space reserved for the middle class and above. Instead, it was the site of the world's largest factories, great workshops that exploited the new technologies of electricity and the internal combustion engine. It comprised everything from shacks to mansions. Both socially and functionally diverse, it already had become the center of home life for millions living in the metropolises of Britain, North America, and Australia, and it represented a major source of employment.

Postwar Growth

During the six decades following World War II, the pace of outward residential migration accelerated. Automobile ownership increased, and prosperity enabled more people to become homeowners. In the late 1940s in suburban Long Island, Levitt and Sons built new houses at the rate of one every fifteen minutes in their sprawling, 17,447-house Levittown development. Such suburban tract projects helped satisfy the growing desire for home ownership, as the American rate of owner-occupied dwellings rose from 43.6 percent in 1940 to 61.9 percent in 1960.[15] In Australia, a shortage of building materials prevented construction of Levittown-scale developments in the immediate wake of World War II. Undeterred, Australians perpetuated their tradition of self-built suburbs by constructing modest homes with whatever scraps they could obtain. By the late

1950s, large-scale professional developers were exploiting the Australian suburban dream, boosting the rate of home ownership in the Sydney metropolis from 40 percent in 1947 to 70 percent in 1966.[16] The story was much the same in Canada, leading one authority to proclaim: "The most sacred belief in Canadian public policy has been the idea that everyone ought to own a suburban home."[17]

Yet not only was suburbia perpetuating its role as a place of residence, it was also assuming a new position as the principal metropolitan shopping district. Smaller family-run businesses, largely accessed by pedestrian and nonmotorized customers on main streets, had catered to the local population during the nineteenth and early twentieth centuries. Following World War II, the advent of shopping malls, designed for automobile access with nearby parking, served a regional customer base, transforming suburbia into the dominant retailing zone. In the mid-1950s, Northland Center opened in the Detroit suburb of Southfield, boasting one hundred retailers and a three-story branch of the Motor City's leading department store. In the Minneapolis suburb of Edina, Southdale shopping center pioneered the enclosed mall, offering a climate-controlled space for customers seeking a comfortable alternative to retailers in the central city core. Enclosed malls grew ever larger, culminating in Mall of America in suburban Bloomington, Minnesota. Its 520 stores drew over forty-two million visitors each year; the Bloomington Convention and Visitors Bureau labeled it "the nation's #1 visited attraction."[18]

In 1976 Britain's first major suburban mall, Brent Cross, opened north of London, and the phenomenon quickly spread across the nation, and throughout Australia and Canada. When big box stores began to challenge the retailing supremacy of the mall in the late twentieth

15 United States Census, "Historical Census of Housing Table—Homeownership," accessed February 7, 2015, https://www.census.gov/hhes/www/housing/census/historic/owner.html.

16 For home ownership figures for Sydney and Melbourne, see Lionel Frost and Tony Dingle, "Sustaining Suburbia: An Historical Perspective on Australia's Urban Growth," in *Australian Cities: Issues, Strategies, and Policies for Urban Australia in the 1990s*, ed. Patrick Troy (Cambridge: Cambridge University Press, 1995).

17 Larry McCann, "Suburbs of Desire: The Suburban Landscape of Canadian Cities, 1900–1950," in *Changing Suburbs: Foundation, Form and Function*, ed. Richard Harris and Peter J. Larkham (London: E & F Spon, 1999), 129.

18 Bloomington Convention and Visitors Bureau, "Mall of America," accessed June 13, 2003, http://www.bloomington.mn.org/mallofamerica.html.

1.9.2 Largest Hindu temple outside India, in suburban London

19 Westminster Chamber
    of Commerce, "Little
    Saigon," accessed
    January 3, 2006, http://
    www.westminster
    chamber.org/tourist
    /index.php.
20 Rupa Huq, "Flight of the
    Minorities: London's
    Soul Is in the Suburbs,"
    accessed November 21,
    2014, http://www
    .theguardian.com/com
    mentisfree/2013/feb
    /21/flight-minorities
    -london-suburb.

century, suburbia's grip on the shopping sector only increased. Massive Walmarts, Targets, and Tescos became supreme, drawing cash from the remaining central-city outlets as well as the aging malls.

Cosmopolitanism and Class Diversity in Suburbia

A cosmopolitan mix is not unusual in the suburbia of the early twenty-first century. The northern Toronto suburb of Markham is a predominantly Asian city, with more than 115,000 residents of Chinese ancestry and 57,000 South Asians out of a total population of over 300,000. It is home to the Pacific Mall, which together with nearby Market Village Mall and Splendid China Mall is North America's second-largest Chinese shopping complex (surpassed only by Golden Village in the Vancouver suburb of Richmond).

In Southern California, suburban Monterey Park has earned the title of Little Taipei, owing to its predominantly Asian population and its array of Chinese restaurants, mini-malls, and super-markets. A district of Westminster in suburban Orange County has won the nickname of Little Saigon; the local chamber of commerce proclaimed it "a major tourist attraction representing the largest concentration of shopping and Vietnamese cultural amenities in the world outside of Vietnam."[19]

Meanwhile, the semidetached Tudor-style homes of suburban London have filled with Asian immigrants. The largest concentration of South Asians in the London area is in suburban Southall, eleven miles west of the metropolitan core. By 2011, the Southall parliamentary district was 51 percent Asian, and the combined population of Sikhs and Hindus out-numbered professed Christians. Boasting the largest South Asian shopping dis-trict in metropolitan London, Southall is replete with South Asian restaurants, bazaars, and street vendors. Moreover, South Asians form a strong presence in a number of other London suburbs, most notably Harrow, Hounslow, and Brent, rendering the more posh districts of cen-tral London ethnically dull by comparison. (fig. **1.9.2**) "The urban gentrifiers who patronizingly deride the same suburbs they grew up in as featureless, bland zones of mediocrity miss the point," wrote one Briton of Asian ancestry in 2013. "In reality, contemporary suburbia is the opposite… Take a trip to Dagenham, Hounslow or Brent because…it's in the suburbs where you'll find London's true soul."[20]

Hispanics have likewise diversified the suburban soul of America. In the

Miami metropolitan area, the suburbs of Hialeah and Hialeah Gardens were overwhelmingly Hispanic by the dawn of the twenty-first century. In wealthy Coral Gables, where the per capita income is nearly twice that of the nation as a whole, approximately half the privileged suburbanites are Latino.

In contrast, the traditionally working-class suburbs of southeastern Los Angeles County have attracted the poorest of the Latino immigrants. Twenty-eight thousand Latinos crowd into the 1.2 square miles of Maywood, making it the most densely populated city in California; it has a higher population density than such aged hubs as Boston, Philadelphia, and Chicago. These Maywood Hispanics share living spaces in order to save money; their per capita income is less than half that of the median figure for the nation.

Such suburban poverty is not a historic anomaly. Nationwide, deindustrialization decimated many of the manufacturing suburbs that had developed in the late nineteenth and early twentieth centuries. In the Pittsburgh area, with the closing of the steel mills in the late twentieth century, outlying communities descended from the working class into the welfare class. The closing of auto plants left once prosperous communities, such as Michigan's Highland Park, destitute. Though a suburban municipality, East Cleveland shared the characteristics of a central-city ghetto, with a higher poverty rate than the troubled city of Cleveland itself. With a high crime rate and underperforming schools, the impoverished suburb defied the stereotypical image of suburbia.

Yet African American suburbia was not, and is not, uniformly destitute or underprivileged. Even today, Prince George's County, Maryland, outside Washington, DC, is the most populous predominantly African American suburban area in the United States. Some of

its older districts resembled the poor neighborhoods of the adjacent District of Columbia, but the outlying areas of the county offered the stereotypical suburban dream to more affluent African Americans. The *New York Times* described one upper-middle-class subdivision as "a predominantly African American gated community…with private security, town houses, sprawling estates and a golf course."[21] In the mid-1950s, African Americans began finding homes in upper-middle-class Shaker Heights outside Cleveland, and over the following half-century the community remained both integrated and affluent. Likewise, African American migration to the Chicago suburb of Oak Park did not incite a rapid departure of the white population or a notable decline in the social standing of the community.

Over the past two hundred years, suburbia has not conformed to the mythical ethnic and class attributes attributed to it. Suburbs have housed people of all races and national origins as well as the full range of economic classes. There were predominantly Asian suburbs, majority African American suburbs, overwhelmingly Hispanic suburbs, and suburbs with a cosmopolitan mix matched by few central cities. Moreover, suburbia has included a broad range of economic endeavors. Manufacturing and retailing have been located predominantly in the suburbs, and office employment has been a growing presence along the metropolitan fringe. Skyscrapers accent the landscape of suburbia in bold defiance to once prevalent stereotypes.

Suburbia had never been an uninterrupted sprawl of residences. In the present, as in the past, it has been a zone of varied endeavors with an equally diverse social composition. Today, this fascinatingly heterogeneous periphery reflects the rich variety of the metropolis.

21 Wiese, *Places of Their Own*, 269.

1.10
REEXAMINING RACE AND ETHNICITY IN THE SUBURBS

Ali Modarres

POLYCENTRIC
EXPANSION

SOCIAL
DIVERSITY

By the year 2000, America was a suburban nation. Yet in many circles, notably within planning and academe, this news was hardly celebrated. After all, suburbanization has been stigmatized with a long list of social, racial, political, and cultural problems. Specifically, the social ecology of suburbs was seen as white, middle class, and unfriendly to the environment. The stigma was partially created by initial portrayals of the suburbs in 1960s television shows like *Ozzie and Harriet*, with their monotonic development and social structure.[1] But today, the cultural diversity and social structure of suburbs defy the established stereotype.[2] During the last three decades, American suburbs have attracted an increasing number of minorities, including immigrants, a trend that has been discussed in academic and popular publications.[3]

In his 2001 report, the sociologist John Logan wrote that among all 330 US metropolitan areas, the proportion of suburban minority population had increased from 18 percent in 1990 to 25 percent in 2000.[4] Furthermore, during the same decade, the suburban white population grew by 5 percent while the African American, Latino, and Asian suburban populations grew by 38 percent, 72 percent, and 84 percent, respectively. Clearly, by 2000, when half of the entire population lived in the suburbs, the more recent growth had been fueled by the arrival of minorities.[5] In fact, by 2010, more than half of all minorities lived in American suburbs.[6]

Simultaneously, various authors have documented a higher concentration of suburban poverty.[7] The scholars Scott Allard and Benjamin Roth report that while in "1999, large US cities and their suburbs had roughly equal numbers of poor residents…by 2008 the number of suburban poor exceeded the poor in central cities by 1.5 million."[8] In fact, it appears that during this time period, poverty rates increased at a faster pace in suburban areas. This pattern has not ceased over the last few years. A January 2015 article in the *Atlantic* reports that "between 2000 and 2011, Atlanta's suburban poor population grew by 159 percent."[9] However, the rise in suburban poverty does not affect all suburbs equally. The poor typically concentrate where housing is more affordable. High-income suburbs are able to use various exclusionary mechanisms, particularly the real estate market, to prevent the poor from entering.[10] However, under such a spatial logic, it appears that minorities have followed the more well-to-do population, once into the central city at the dawn of suburbanization, and again when inner-ring suburbs aged. In every turn, however, minorities have inherited older housing stocks, left behind by those who can either gentrify the older inner-city neighborhoods or move to wealthier suburbs farther out.

By all indications, some of the all-white, middle-class suburbs have changed. As I show in this essay, diversity or cohabitation of various racial and ethnic groups has increased in some suburban settings as well. Yet the long-held image of suburbs as predominately white continues. As heterogeneous spaces, suburbs not only differ by their socioeconomic status and poverty concentration patterns, they also vary by their geographic attributes (e.g., inner-ring suburbs, outer suburbs). The diversity of suburban settings, by age and demographic composition, suggests that a singular definition of suburbs could lead to either confusing results or conclusions that are not easily verifiable. Perhaps a more reasonable approach to studying suburbs would focus on what data reveals at finer geographies, that is, census tracts or block groups. This would move away from a priori assumptions regarding density, social status, or demographic composition. Using these finer geographies will also help us examine

1 For detailed discussion of this antisuburban narrative, see Ali Modarres and Andrew Kirby, "The Suburban Question: Notes for a Research Program," *Cities* 27 (2010): 114–21.

2 Ibid.

3 William H. Frey, *Melting Pot Cities and Suburbs: Racial and Ethnic Change in Metro America in the 2000s* (Washington, DC: Brookings Institution, 2011); Thomas J. Vicino, *Transforming Race and Class in Suburbia: Decline in Metropolitan Baltimore* (New York: Palgrave Macmillan, 2008); John R. Logan, *The New Ethnic Enclaves in America's Suburbs*, Lewis Mumford Center for Comparative Urban and Regional Research, 2001, accessed January 26, 2015, http://mumford.albany.edu/census/report.html.

4 Logan, *New Ethnic Enclaves*, 1.

5 Frank Hobbs and Nicole Stoops, *Demographic Trends in the Twentieth Century*, US Census Bureau, November 2002, accessed November 14, 2015, https://www.census.gov/prod/2002pubs/censr-4.pdf.

6 Frey, *Melting Pot Cities and Suburbs*.

7 Steven Raphael and Michael Stoll, *Job Sprawl and the Suburbanization of Poverty* (Washington, DC: Brookings Institution, March 2010), accessed November 14, 2015, http://www.brookings.edu/research/reports/2010/03/30-job-sprawl-stoll-raphael; Emily Garr and Elizabeth Kneebone, *The Suburbanization of Poverty: Trends in Metropolitan America, 2000 to 2008* (Washington, DC: Brookings Institution, January 2010), accessed November 14, 2015, http://www.brookings.edu/research/papers/2010/01/20-poverty-kneebone.

8 Scott W. Allard and Benjamin Roth, *Strained Suburbs: The Social Service Challenges of Rising Suburban Poverty*

longitudinal growth patterns across multiple decades, and ultimately lead to a better understanding of the changing nature of suburbs, within a more nuanced and plural context.

Furthermore, locality does matter. The suburbs of Des Moines, Iowa, are not the same as the suburbs of New York or Los Angeles, given their differences in scale, ethnic populations, and economic structure. Even New York and Los Angeles differ significantly in their sub/urban trajectories. To illustrate this point and add complexity to the suburban discourse, we examine the changing social geography of New York and Los Angeles metropolitan areas across multiple decades. This analysis extends the geographic focus beyond assumed jurisdictional boundaries and includes neighboring counties to illustrate the changing nature of sociospatial patterns in New York, Los Angeles, and their suburbs. This wide geographic lens also allows us to examine how the demographic composition of central cities has changed and what that may mean for our understanding of the urban/suburban continuum.

Two Metros in Different Regions

The metropolitan areas of New York and Los Angeles have been subjected to a number of comparative analyses."[11] While New York is often seen as the quintessential city, Los Angeles has long been portrayed as an agglomeration of suburbs. However, New York and Los Angeles have some similarities. In both cities, Latinos have suburbanized significantly and African Americans continue to maintain a strong presence in the city center but are also expanding in the periphery.[12] Given the opposing urban images in New York and Los Angeles, the comparison is intended to illustrate how the suburbanization of minorities in both localities may be following the same patterns.

Using the Neighborhood Change Database (NCDB) from Geolytics, Inc., information at the census tract level on population and demographic composition was created. As mentioned earlier, the geographic scope of this database extended beyond the major urban core to include some of the neighboring counties. This analysis allowed a detailed assessment of sociospatial shifts from 1970 to 2010. It also visually exposed the nature of urban change without the use of arbitrary boundaries, such as county lines or census definitions of cities, suburbs, and rural areas. Having the flexibility to analyze across administrative boundaries is important because suburban areas are not necessarily well captured by census definition of urban and suburban areas. Plus, people in Los Angeles and New York do not always work and live within the same county.

The assembled database was then used to examine the tract-level population growth, including that of the minority population, from 1980 to 2010.[13] Population density was also included in the analysis to examine the relationship between growth and geography as it relates to race and ethnicity. Finally, while the suburbanization of the Asian population is significant, longitudinal data limitations at finer geographies prevent me from including that discussion here.

New York Metropolitan Area

The highest rate of census tract level population growth between 1970 and 2010 for the non-Hispanic white population has occurred primarily within the boundaries of New York City, in Brooklyn and Upper Manhattan. But the fastest growth for African Americans has taken place in the largely suburban Long Island counties of Nassau and Suffolk.[14] For Latinos, the fastest growth rates have also been found in Nassau and Suffolk, and in areas north of the Bronx. (figs. **1.10.1–4**)

(Washington, DC: Brookings Institution, October 2010), 2.

9 Alan Semuels, "Suburbs and the New American Poverty: More People with Low Incomes Now Live Outside of Cities, and Some Areas Are Ill-Equipped to Deal with the Influx of the Poor," *Atlantic*, accessed January 26, 2015, http://www.theatlantic .com/business/archive /2015/01/suburbs-and -the-new-american -poverty/384259/.

10 Kenya L. Covington, "Poverty Suburbanization: Theoretical Insights and Empirical Analyses," *Social Inclusion* 3, no. 2 (2015): 71–90.

11 See David Halle, ed., *New York and Los Angeles: Politics, Society, and Culture: A Comparative View* (Chicago: University of Chicago Press, 2003).

12 Frey, *Melting Pot Cities and Suburbs*. The longitudinal data used for this analysis do not include the Asian population. Data on the Asian community, particularly at census tract level, was not available in 1970.

13 From a methodological perspective, it should be noted that the 1970 data do not distinguish between non-Hispanic and Hispanic racial categories. For that reason, analyses focusing on exclusive racial and ethnic categories (e.g., non-Hispanic white) span the period of 1980 to 2010.

14 For all racial and ethnic groups, I have computed the ratio between the proportion of a group in 2010 and 1980. By using proportions, magnitude of growth is more accurately captured. However, growth in the actual number of people within each category is used for additional analyses.

When the data are examined at the census tract level, it becomes clear that between 1980 and 2010 the rate of population growth for the non-Hispanic white population is positively correlated with homeownership across all decades, especially the last two decades.[15] At the same time, the non-Hispanic white population has grown in areas that are negatively correlated with the growth of African Americans and Latinos, which has been the case across the 1980s, 1990s, and 2000s. Thus, there continued to be a spatial divergence between where the non-Hispanic white population lived and where others did, with the Latino population gradually increasing its copresence in non-Hispanic white neighborhoods. For African Americans and Latinos together, there appeared to be a spatial convergence in the New York metropolitan area: they gradually came to occupy the same neighborhoods. Correlations between tracts where non-Hispanic African American and Latino populations grew increased between the 1980s and the 2000s.

Homeownership, poverty, and the presence of children also affect particular spatial outcomes in American cities. Analyses of growth across the decades, and homeownership data for 1970 to 2010, provides a complicated result in the New York metropolitan area. For example, there appears to be a weak relationship between homeownership rates and non-Hispanic white population growth. However, there is a statistically significant relationship between the growth of the non-Hispanic white population and the proportion of children under the age of five, which has declined over time. This suggests that the non-Hispanic white's population growth in the past was more a function of housing for their families and children than it is today, which is also reflected in falling fertility rates. In the 1960s, fertility rates for the entire population in the United States were well above the replacement rate of 2.1. However, by 2010, fertility had declined to 1.9. This decline translates to a smaller number of children and a different household composition than when some of the original suburbs were built.

For African Americans, the scenario appears to have been different. In the 1990s and 2000s, areas where this population grew are associated with higher homeownership rates and less poverty. However, only in the 1980s can a statistically noticeable association with children under five be seen in the New York metropolitan area. This means that neighborhood population growth and presence of families are correlated.

In the 1980s there was a negative relationship between emerging Latino neighborhoods and homeownership, and Latinos were more likely to live in areas with higher rates of poverty in the New York metropolitan area. Yet by the 2000s, this relationship had reversed. Latino growth in neighborhoods was associated with homeownership and less poverty. Between 1980 and 2000, the relationship between Latino population growth and the presence of children was positive. Thus, the suburbanization of Latinos is perhaps driven by their desire for homeownership at affordable costs, and in places where they can raise their children. This focus on families could be a function of differing fertility rates between ethnic groups. While the fertility rate for the non-Hispanic white population was estimated to be about 1.8 in 2010, for Latinos that figure stood at 2.4 and African Americans at 2.[16]

We have observed over the last decade that as the number of children declines, particularly among non-Hispanic whites, the need for larger homes and larger suburban dwellings also declines. This spatial redistribution can be seen in the context of population density. The geography of changing densities suggests that between

15 Census tracts in the following counties were chosen for this analysis: Dutchess, Westchester, Bronx, New York, Richmond, King, Queens, Nassau, and Suffolk.

16 See Mark Mather, "Fact Sheet: The Decline in U.S. Fertility," Population Reference Bureau, July 2012, accessed June 2, 2015, http://www.prb.org/publications/datasheets/2012/world-population-data-sheet/fact-sheet-us-population.aspx.

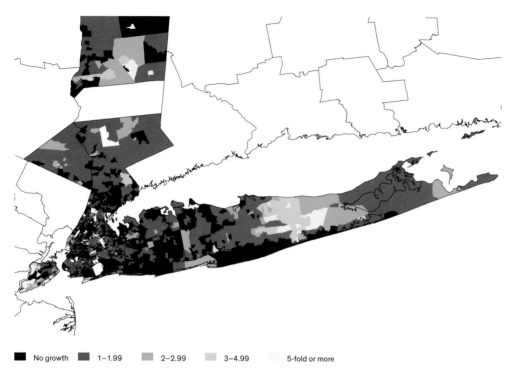

No growth █   1–1.99 █   2–2.99 █   3–4.99 █   5-fold or more

1.10.1 Rate of population growth from 1970 to 2010

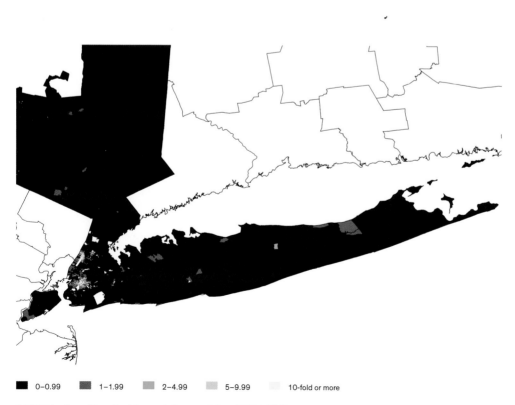

0–0.99 █   1–1.99 █   2–4.99 █   5–9.99 █   10-fold or more

1.10.2 Rate of non-Hispanic white population growth from 1980 to 2010

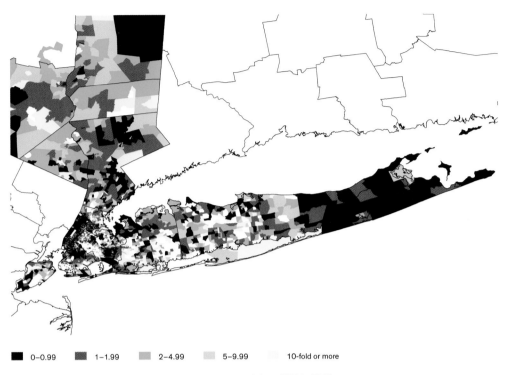

0–0.99　　1–1.99　　2–4.99　　5–9.99　　10-fold or more

1.10.3 Rate of non-Hispanic African American population growth from 1980 to 2010

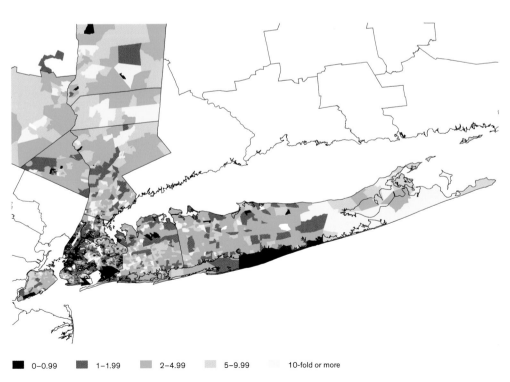

0–0.99　　1–1.99　　2–4.99　　5–9.99　　10-fold or more

1.10.4 Rate of Latino population growth from 1980 to 2010

1970 and 2010, the metropolitan region grew almost contiguously toward Suffolk and Staten Island. Statistical analysis, however, points to an interesting divergence between growth in the non-Hispanic white population and growth in other populations.

In general, population growth between 1970 and 1980 was negatively correlated with population density, suggesting that the people were moving into lower-density areas. However, by 2010, non-Hispanic whites were more likely to move to higher-density areas. In New York, this would mean that non-Hispanic whites have been moving into the more urban areas in the metropolitan area, as well as the higher-density areas in neighboring counties.[17] Yet this change has not been experienced universally. Between 2000 and 2010, non-Hispanic African American and Latino growth was negatively correlated with population density. Their population grew in lower-density areas. In fact, Latinos had the opposite of the non-Hispanic white trend; they shifted from an earlier positive correlation with density to a negative one by 2010.

The typical picture of suburbia in American history is based on the idea that the white population moved to the suburbs and segregated itself from minorities and poverty. The data show that now the reverse is occurring. As the middle-class, non-Hispanic white population's urban presence shifts to cities and higher-density areas, minorities inherit their older, inner-ring suburbs. The irony is that earlier antiurban narratives were directed at cities, where minorities had grown in numbers. Now the antisuburban narratives, if unabated, may appear to be doing the same, continuing to criticize places that include a growing number of minorities. It appears that at every turn, minorities are inheritors of the older housing left behind by their non-Hispanic

white counterparts. In the emerging reverse process of racial and ethnic urbanization patterns, one group gentrifies to increase its total assets; the other keeps paying for the maintenance of older houses.

Los Angeles Metropolitan Area
Population growth in the Los Angeles metropolitan area between 1970 and 2010 occurred everywhere from its center to its farthest edge, yet the latter showed the largest increases in population (tenfold or more). (fig. **1.10.5**) Los Angeles in this time period is perhaps the closest picture to what people imagine as sprawl and mass suburbanization.

When looking at the rate of growth in the proportion of racial and ethnic groups, something noteworthy appears. (fig. **1.10.6**) Between 1970 and 2010, the non-Hispanic white population grew, proportionally speaking, more rapidly in the central part of the metropolitan area (from downtown through the Wilshire corridor and Santa Monica), as well as in areas around Pasadena and Glendale. (The movement of non-Hispanic white population to outer-ring suburbs in some of the neighboring counties [Orange and Ventura] can be observed; however, there is a visible absence of majority non-Hispanic white neighborhoods in the region, including the suburbs.) The diminishing share of non-Hispanic white population in suburbs and increasing share in the center are likely due to the changing proportions of minorities that have increased faster in the suburbs and declined in the central area.

This pattern is evident in the non-Hispanic African American population, whose proportion grew faster outside the city core. (fig. **1.10.7**) Given the higher levels of segregation and more restricted access to the housing market (by practice and by price) in 1970, the changing geography of the African American population

17 As literature on this topic has shown, a significant portion of this sociospatial shift has been fueled by the younger population, who are in many cases childless. For an early example, see Donald Bogue et al., *The Population of the United States*, 3rd ed. (New York: Free Press, 1997), 285.

could be viewed as a movement toward job centers and more affordable housing opportunities outside the central area.

For Latinos, the growth is widespread throughout the metropolitan area, in both central and suburban areas. (fig. **1.10.8**) And there is a growing proportion of Latinos in neighborhoods where African Americans were once a majority. The widespread nature of Latino growth points to the socioeconomic diversity within the community in Los Angeles specifically. (The same is true for the foreign-born population in the metro area as a whole, including Asians, whose presence has grown in both low-income, central areas and low-income and middle-class suburban areas.)

Like New York, Los Angeles appears to have experienced a divergent geography for its non-Hispanic white population and a convergence between Latinos and African Americans. However, the separation between the latter groups is perhaps more pronounced in Los Angeles than in New York.

The changing geographic presence of various racial and ethnic groups can be put within the context of homeownership. In that regard, Los Angeles offers a more complicated history. Homeownership rates were significantly higher in 1970, compared to New York. In fact, contrary to the East Coast and older industrial cities, Los Angeles homeownership rates have historically been higher throughout the metropolitan area, including in minority neighborhoods. By 2010, homeownership rates were even higher and covered more neighborhoods than in 1970.

High levels of homeownership distributed throughout the metropolitan area are not the only striking characteristics of Los Angeles. Its changing population densities are equally noteworthy. In 1970 the majority of census tracts with densities exceeding ten thousand persons per square mile (3,860 people per square

kilometer) were in the central part of the city. (Some suburban areas in the San Fernando and San Gabriel Valleys, as well as in the northern sections of Orange County, also had noticeably high densities.) By 2010, however, high-density tracts can be seen throughout the region. This flies in the face of all the myths about Los Angeles as an endless, low-density suburb. In fact, LA is considered one of the densest American cities.

It appears that in the Los Angeles metropolitan area, minorities have grown on the edges, contributing to higher population densities and expanded homeownership there, although this pattern is also accompanied by the geographic expansion of poverty.[18] What seems to have been lost in the urban/suburban narrative is the degree to which density and poverty have converged in the entire Los Angeles basin. Using analyses similar to the study of New York, we can examine the visually observed patterns of sociodemographic relationships. The results allow us to understand some of the more nuanced aspects of population growth patterns in the Los Angeles metropolitan area and neighboring counties.

In the 1980s the overall rate of population growth closely mirrored the proportional growth of the non-Hispanic white population. Yet by the 1990s and 2000s, this relationship had diminished. In the 2000s the overall population growth more closely tracked Latino population growth. Furthermore, as in the case of New York, while population growth was negatively correlated with population density in 1970 (and at levels higher than those in the New York metropolitan area), the relationship with density declined in the successive decades.

In terms of geography, starting in the 1990s, the non-Hispanic white population grew more rapidly where Latinos were not present. In other words, as the Latino population grew and the non-Hispanic

18 Ali Modarres, "Persistent Poverty and the Failure of Area-Based Initiatives in the United States," *Local Economy* 37, no. 4 (2002): 289–302.

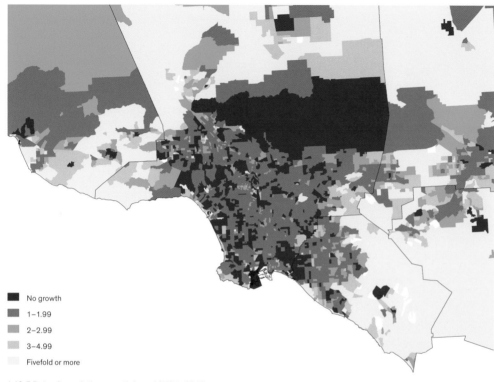

No growth
1–1.99
2–2.99
3–4.99
Fivefold or more

1.10.5 Rate of population growth from 1970 to 2010

Less than half
More than half but less than 1
1–1.99
2–2.99
Threefold or more

1.10.6 Rate of non-Hispanic white population growth from 1980 to 2010

1.10.7 Rate of non-Hispanic white population growth from 1980 to 2010

1.10.8 Rate of Latino population growth from 1980 to 2010

white population declined, the probability for cohabitation of these groups declined. This phenomenon is likely due to the economic sorting that tends to occur in American metropolitan areas, whereby neighborhoods (especially middle-class and wealthy areas) tend to be inhabited by people of the same socioeconomic backgrounds. On average, non-Hispanic whites have had higher incomes than Latinos in Los Angeles.

The correlation between non-Hispanic white populations and population density shifted from highly negative in 1980 to negligible in 2010, meaning this population was predominately suburbanizing in 1980 but not moving in any one major direction by 2010. Given the extensive geography of homeownership, while there is a positive relationship between the growth of this population and the proportion of homeowners, the correlation is statistically negligible at the census tract level. This means that we can no longer associate rising homeownership with the growth of non-Hispanic white population in an area.

African Americans' growing presence is negatively associated with density, meaning African Americans are moving toward lower population densities. However, as some suburbs have increased their density over time, the correlation between African American population and density has grown. Homeownership for African Americans is also showing a growing positive, albeit weak, relationship with population density. This suggests African Americans' move to suburbs is associated with higher homeownership. In terms of cohabitation, the relationship between the presence of African Americans and Latinos is weakly positive, but increasing.

For Latinos, homeownership began with negative figures in the 1970s and 1980s (indicating their higher association with renting) but was turning positive by 2010. The correlation between population

density and the growing presence of Latinos shifted from positive in 1980 to negative in 2010, suggesting that Latinos are moving to areas with lower densities. Compared with New York, there appears to be a significant similarity between Latinos' emergent neighborhood patterns. The shift to suburbs coincides with a desire to achieve nothing short of the American dream, albeit delayed. Latinos seek family-oriented neighborhoods and larger houses, in less crowded neighborhoods, in inner-ring, older suburbs and beyond.[19]

Putting Suburbs into Perspective

While visually one can see distinct differences between New York and Los Angeles, statistically there appear to be a number of similarities. In both places, the non-Hispanic white population moved to low-density areas for decades, but recently a portion of that population, mostly younger urban professionals, began to grow in the central areas. The emerging sociospatial shifts portray a more complicated but dynamic picture of American urban geography. For most of the twentieth century, minorities inherited the infrastructure left behind by the majority non-Hispanic white population in the central cities. However, over the last two decades, the direction of movement has somewhat changed. As the wealthier non-Hispanic white population moves to outer suburbs and a portion returns to the center, a growing number of racial and minorities are moving to inner-ring suburbs once inhabited by non-Hispanic whites. While once again minorities are inheriting the infrastructure left behind by others, it also means that the suburban promise of homeownership, single-family homes, larger parks, playgrounds, and amenities for families are enticements that cut across socioeconomic classes. As shifting non-Hispanic white populations have created exclusive gated communities

19 Other research has had similar findings: The Conference Board, "New Report Finds Significant Hispanic Home Ownership Gap," accessed September 10, 2015, https://www.conference-board.org/press/pressdetail.cfm?pressid=5470.

in outer suburbs or gentrified zones of expensive housing in city centers, working-class populations seek out the emerging in-between places, some of which are inner-ring suburbs.

If the case of New York and Los Angeles illustrates anything, it is that Americans—native, foreign, majority, and minority—continue to search for a better quality of life for themselves and their families according to their own ideals of comfort and of what they have come to understand as the urban experience. While commuting long distances to achieve such goals was a hallmark of the early postwar suburbs, more jobs have moved to the suburbs over the last two decades. Research has illustrated that with a growing presence of jobs, commute distances are declining in some suburbs.[20] Today, some suburbs are hardly bedroom communities. These factors complicate our understanding of suburbs as places of low density. It also puts into question what we mean by *suburban* and *urban*.

The case of Los Angeles is an opportunity for reflection on the meaning of suburbia as well. Los Angeles, with its vast landscape of high homeownership and increasing number of minority suburbs, whose population includes both the impoverished and the middle class, can be seen as the quintessential twenty-first-century urban form. With a mix of multiple centers of high density and employment, the metropolitan region blurs the boundary between *urban* and *suburban*, painting a picture of future American metropolitan areas. As cities continue their metamorphosis from a particular definition of *urbanness* and come to include a diversity of neighborhoods from the center to the edge, the use of the word *suburb* needs to express a more nuanced concept or lose any relevance at all.

20 Ali Modarres, "Polycentricity, Commuting Pattern, Urban Form: The Case of Southern California," *International Journal of Urban and Regional Research* 35, no. 6 (August 2010): 1193–211.

1.11
THE GRORUD VALLEY
BORDERLINE SUBURBIA

Espen Aukrust Hauglin and
Janike Kampevold Larsen

ECOLOGICAL
FUNCTION

SOCIAL
DIVERSITY

For those who want to live comfortably, in style, and amidst the green.

—May 2015 ad for housing in the Grorud Valley

The term *suburbia* is not specific. Suburban forms, both within countries and around the world, are highly divergent due to cultural planning norms, ideal ways of living, and especially topographical specificities. Norway's suburban areas are remarkably distinct. In Norway, the city and suburbia are clearly separated. Generally, cities are nestled between hills and mountains on one side and the sea on the other. As a result, areas for city expansion are limited. Thus, Norwegian suburbia involves a spatial leap, unfolding in pockets of farmland. As a result, suburbs in Norway often function as satellite towns. In fact, some claim that the satellite town was introduced as a conscious rejection of the existing development of private houses and cottage-like settlements found many places in Oslo before World War II. They were designed to provide an efficient solution to the housing shortage after the war and also to nurture communitarian qualities.[1] Norwegian suburbs are also distinct in how their design reflects traditional Norwegian housing and living ideals involving space, nature, recreation, and privacy.

The Grorud Valley is an important case study showing the distinctive features of Norwegian suburbia and the relationship between development and nature. The Grorud Valley is the general name for Oslo's northeastern area and comprises four parts that include housing, industrial areas, and remnants of old farms. About one-fifth of Oslo's total population lives in this valley, 138,224 people.[2] It is the largest suburban area in Norway at almost 14 square miles (36 square kilometers), a quarter of Oslo's total area. It is nestled in a wide valley, bounded by the publicly owned forest surrounding Oslo, called the "Marka" (meaning "the field" in Norwegian). The boundary of the Oslo Marka was drawn in 1934 following the datum line 220, which marked the limit for how high one could bring water without introducing any artificial mains pressure.

The distinct suburban form of the Grorud Valley is the result of the geological forming of the land, ancient farmland ambits, and planning and housing policies and ideals. First, we review some of the forces that have physically and culturally shaped the valley. We then discuss to what degree the valley's shaping forces are still in operation and what role they play as the valley faces radically different conditions for growth. The valley is not only an area for growth but also a specific geographical site faced with a growing global population, on the one hand, and increasing market interests, on the other hand. Its physical form, molded by geography and external forces, has a unique texture and grain, unlike any other suburban place in the country or even the world.

Geomorphology

Geological features and the shaping forces of the Ice Ages have determined the topography and land resources of Norway. In turn, these features have influenced the location of suburbs. The expanse of mountainous areas is vast, while the valleys, inlets, and fjords were carved out by ice erosion. (fig. **1.11.1**) The narrow strips of inhabitable seashore emerged only after the ice started to withdraw twenty thousand years ago and the land rose subsequently. It is in these areas that cities were founded. Meanwhile, the areas available for farming have been small and scattered, except in a few wider valleys. Wider agricultural valleys are largely made up of fertile till and silt from moraines and rivers. It is in these valleys (like the Grorud Valley, shaped by the

1 Hilde Haslum, *Reading Socio-Spatial Interplay* 37 (Oslo: Arkitektur- og designhøgskolen i Oslo, 2008), 163.
2 Statistics Norway, population January 1, 2015.

oldest landslide known in Norway eight thousand years ago) that we usually find suburban development. They occupy small areas of flat terrain and the forested foothills surrounding them, never far from expanses of mountain and larger forest areas.

In the Grorud Valley, the shaping forces are evident; some of the eighteenth- and nineteenth-century granite quarries are still operating, but more important, property lines still follow the ancient divisions of former farmland, some of it cleared between 1050 and 1350.[3] (There are even traces of Stone Age clearings, dating back to 3000 BCE.) The very names of the different "farms" in the valley, which are also the names of the twelve present satellite towns, testify to the centuries-old origins of some properties in the valley.[4] When urbanization started in the 1950s, some forty farms were still in operation in an area then easily characterized as countryside.

As a consequence of geomorphology, the Grorud Valley is marked by spatial fragmentation, creating a mosaic of land use: the subdivision of earlier farmland and older mining infrastructure, green areas, and lastly an urban fabric comprising satellite town models, housing in-fills, and pieces of new residential districts. Moraines, rivers, and transportation lines—all of which contribute to a surprising juxtaposition of different land use typologies within a quite limited area—also cut through it. Yet due to the valley's relative narrowness, it allows for an extreme closeness to the surrounding preserved forests, which play an important role in Norwegian culture.

Nature and Recreation in Norwegian Culture

Traditionally, Norwegians take peculiar interest in their proximity to natural areas. We appreciate the possibility of easy access to mountain and forest areas,

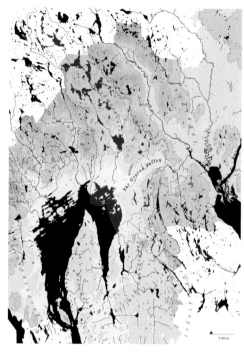

1.11.1 The Grorud Valley as part of a larger geomorphology and valley system

and skiing is a priority for a large percentage of the population. Sundays have historically been the day that families spent trekking, berry picking, hunting, and fishing in forests, mountains, lakes, and rivers. The development of satellite towns represented a welcome opportunity to accommodate access to nature and to connect with the postwar effort to build an extensive network of walking and skiing paths in the Marka. The appreciation of access to nature, natural views, and privacy in a home is inherent to Norwegian ideals for the residential environment.

Built in the 1950s, the layout of Lambertseter—the first satellite town in the south of Oslo—demonstrates some of the trademarks of satellite towns around Oslo; an effort to provide direct access to nature and the healthy attributes of air, light, and greenery (luxuries that the 1930 and 1940s city of Oslo could not provide). This new development (not strictly part of the Grorud Valley) was placed adjacent to and partly weaving into existing villas and older private housing associations, which resulted in its

3   *Store norske leksikon,* s.v. "Groruddalen," by Svein Askheim, accessed February 3, 2015, https:// snl.no/Groruddalen.

4   Thirty-nine of the old properties, now turned urban, have names ending in -rud (from *rydde*: to clear), and -vin (meadow), both of which have ancient roots. Twenty-three of these can be dated based on names—fourteen are medieval, seven from the Viking period, and two date back to before 800 BCE. See Eivind Heide, *Groruddalen* (Oslo: Tiden, 1980), 27–33.

particular performance as a composite of wooden houses, row houses, different-sized apartment buildings, church, schools, sports fields—and paths leading out to the surrounding woods. (fig. **1.11.2**)

In spite of attempts, the developments that followed in the Grorud Valley itself never achieved the same degree of integration with the older settlement.

Most sizable Norwegian cities have a park (inspired by the English landscape tradition) that was typically built around 1880 or later. However, priority was given to path systems at the edges of cities rather than inner-city parks, given the small expanse of most cities and their closeness to surrounding hills and mountains. Thus, a finely tuned relationship between parks and city has never strongly developed in the valley, although attempts were made but never fully realized. However, recent development demonstrates that this is about to change, and parks are finally becoming an integrated part of the valley's urban structure.

History of Park Planning in the Grorud Valley

Harald Hals, chief planner in Oslo from 1926 to 1947, had work experience as a planner in Chicago, Spokane, and Omaha, Nebraska, where he was strongly influenced by the City Beautiful movement and the garden city movement. Both Hals and his contemporary Sverre Pedersen were concerned with the city-nature relationship, although with some interesting differences. While Pedersen was concerned with formal layout, Hals's concern was primarily social—to provide "those who do not have garden of their own" with access to green areas and collective garden space.[5]

Hals's ideas and visions were recorded in the 1934 master plan for Oslo and pursued further in the 1950 master plan for the Grorud Valley. Enabled by the merging of the municipalities of Aker and Oslo in 1948, this master plan shows

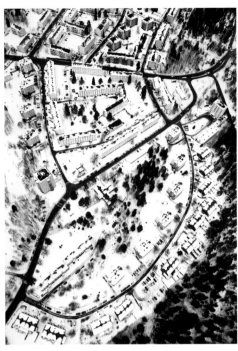

1.11.2 Housing cooperative from 1952, drawn by the Norwegian architect Erling Viksjø

the middle of the valley designated as an industrial area, while scattered housing districts dot the hillsides. Importantly, the master plan also shows an extensive park system. In the plan, continuous park areas connect the valley to the center of Oslo, as well as to the Marka to the east and west. In this context, the 1950 plan testifies to the fact that if North American landscape ideals ever influenced the valley, it is not as a model for horizontal sprawl but as a much older City Beautiful landscape model for landscape distribution and beauty. (fig. **1.11.3**)

The development of the Grorud Valley relied on government purchase of land for the city to expand after World War II, due to a tremendous demand for housing. The municipality of Oslo gained land from wherever it was available, with a desire to create decentralized urban communities as a respite from concentric urban growth.[6] A collective effort to provide housing for a growing population merged with the valley's peasant culture and property structure. In opposition to traditional notions of suburban

5 Mikkelsen Ingvar, "Hals' Og Pedersens Ideologier," *Plan* 45, nos. 4–5 (2013): 24–33.
6 Guro Voss Gabrielsen, *Groruddalen—Oslos Vakreste Verkebyll? Problemrepresentasjoner Og Stedsforståelser I Groruddalssatsingen* 70 (Oslo: Arkitektur- og designhøgskolen i Oslo, 2014), 89.

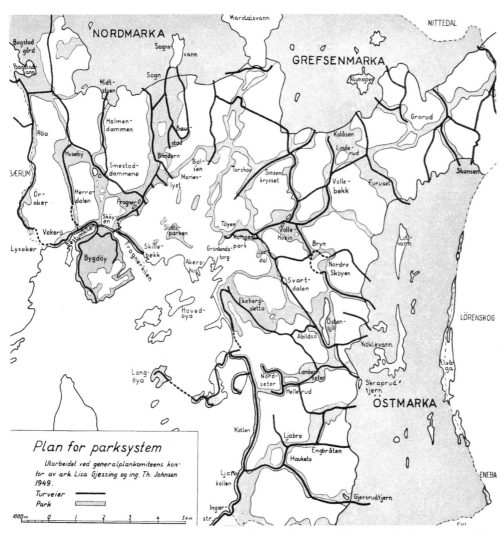

Plan for parksystem

Utarbeidet ved generalplankomiteens kontor av ark. Lisa Gjessing og ing. Th. Johnsen 1949.

Turveier
Park

1.11.3 1949 projective map of park system and pathways in the Oslo area. The proposed interconnection of green zones and the Oslo forest commons, Marka, is striking.

development based on cars, the public transport lines were laid down before a massive road and highway development. By 1950, of all peripheral development in Norway, the Grorud Valley was probably the most public transportation oriented from the very beginning, a situation not so common in suburban areas.

The new urban centers in the Grorud Valley are neatly tucked between the Marka boundary and the lower Valley infrastructure and industrial landscapes. (fig. **1.11.4**) This is due to climate zones; valleys in Norway tend to be colder, gustier, and more humid than the valley flanks. Also, the slight increase in altitude allows

for better views, a sense of loftiness and, not the least—the possibility of accommodating the specifically Norwegian desire to put on your skis right outside your door and take off.

The development of the valley relied heavily on prewar modernistic city planning ideals. The contemporary architect Karl Otto Ellefsen explains that the modernistic ideal in Norway consisted of strong planning, demand for scientific legibility, lifestyle ideals, and architectural ideals.[7] The valley as it appears today must be considered a partial expression of planning ideals where "urban technicians" demonstrate an ability to control

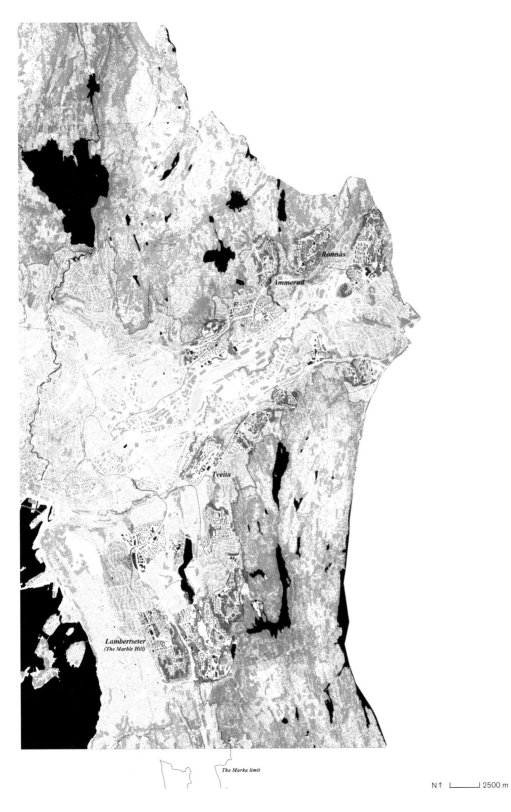

1.11.4 Foothills and ridges strewn with satellite towns from the 1950s, 1960s, and 1970s

mass production of buildings and have sufficient knowledge to be at the center of urban development. The role model was the German 1920 city planner, and also the Soviet Union's collective sharing of property.[8] An important condition for the present-day fragmentation of the valley is its former character of being an agricultural area with intermingled and small scale–mining industry and housing areas. When planning commenced, suburban thinking was laid on top of an existing structure of variegated land use—in act, this allowed the new satellite towns (except Romsås) to be weaved into existing property structure and infrastructural systems, mainly older farms, mines, and transportation arteries.

At each successive point in time, the development in the valley reflected different trends in the relationship to landscape, planning ideals, and social policies. The first "wave" from the 1950s, which was inaugurated by the development of Lambertseter, is characterized "by the carefully preserved landscape qualities of the natural forest areas."[9] Land use planning carefully considered access to landscape as a recreational resource, as well as the aesthetic pleasures entailed in the spacing of buildings, composition of buildings, and views from buildings. When the first satellite towns in the valley were planned, there was a strong emphasis on sheltered outdoor playgrounds and the need to prioritize pedestrians and their access to Marka over vehicular pathways.[10]

In the 1960s the second wave featured high-rises that were heavily criticized for their alienation of landscape and neglect of their inhabitants, "for not providing the inhabitants with a sense of belonging, identification and sense of community."[11] This second wave of satellite towns in the Grorud Valley may be characterized as "ultramodernistic" in a European context, especially Ammerud (with its fourteen-story buildings) and Tveita.[12]

(fig. **1.11.5**) Although like all Grorud towns, they are "gentler" than most Swedish, Polish, or Belgian ultramodernistic satellite towns, they are relatively low, close to Oslo, and connected to a good public transportation network. In fact, the height of the apartment complexes (130 feet, or 40 meters) harmonizes with the surrounding hills, and the long, low slab rests beautifully in the landscape.[13]

In response to the criticism of ultramodernistic developments, in the 1970s "residential environment" became a buzzword in satellite town planning. It reverts back to the ideals of smaller populated communities and adjustments to the local landscape, aiming to create more people-friendly spaces than the high-rise and Le Corbusier–inspired residential towers erected a decade earlier. Developments built at this time were also planned to be car-free, with roads on the outside connecting to parking garages. All traffic to kindergartens, schools, subway stations, and the forest was to be handled by walking, bicycle, or even skiing.[14] (fig. **1.11.6**)

The 1980s marked a turn toward extensive market liberalization and, at the same time, the end of a long period of political consensus and stability.[15] It reversed the three-decade trend of satellite town planning, and most leftover space in the valley was deregulated for housing infill and new residential districts. The spatial layout of satellite towns survived, however, even though houses and blocks were modified over the decades, with oriels and glassed-in balconies, recultivation and transformation of green areas. (fig. **1.11.7**) Property boundaries have more or less remained untouched, in contrast to the widespread subdivision of single-family housing properties occurring in other parts of the city to make space for more buildings.

Despite the relative density of developments in the valley today—a composite of satellite towns, newer urban infill,

7   Karl Otto Ellefsen, "Arkitekt Og Planlegger, Arkitekturidealer I Norsk Byplanlegging 1950–2000," *Plan*, nos. 5–6 (1999): 77.
8   Ibid.
9   Haslum, *Reading Socio-Spatial Interplay*, 37, 170.
10 "Byggekunst" (Oslo: Norske arkitekters landsforbund, 1952), 105.
11 Haslum, *Reading Socio-Spatial Interplay*, 37, 178.
12 Ellefsen, "Arkitekt Og Planlegger, Arkitekturidealer I Norsk Byplanlegging 1950–2000," 79.
13 Bjørn Bjørnsen, *Hele Folket I Hus: Obos 1929–1970* (Oslo: Boksenteret, 2007), 157.
14 Gabrielsen, *Groruddalen—Oslos Vakreste Verkebyll? Problemrepresentasjoner Og Stedsforståelser I Groruddalssatsingen* 70, 90.
15 Marius Grønning, "What Is the Fjord City?," *Territorio* 56, no. 4 (2011): 142.

1.11.5 The urban blocks at Tveita, representative of the second wave of satellite towns in the 1960s

1.11.6 View toward the satellite town of Romsås

industrial areas, and infrastructure—it is surprisingly green and in places even bucolic in character. It is not so difficult to see that the first plan for the valley advocated a strong park system, although it was not completed.

The park system in the 1950 master plan for Oslo was strongly influenced by the City Beautiful movement and bourgeois ideals of collective space and shared resources. It sought, however, to find ways for the different housing districts to be both autonomous urban centers and embedded in the natural environment. They were separated from the larger urbanity of Oslo, but still aspired to provide an urban setting. At the same time, they had easy access to the surrounding nature and leisure environments of the Marka. Hence, the valley expresses ambiguity; all centers are infiltrated by or located very close to nature, in concurrence with the original intention for the valley, but lacking the critical mass that would sustain urban life. As a result, these autonomous urban centers perform as merely imitators of urbanity. Now they often perform as empty shopping and management centers in the satellite towns. (fig. **1.11.8**) In fact, the spatial qualities around the centers prove more important than the centers themselves; green space, squares, and transit corridors for pedestrians and bikers are qualities still highly sought-after by inhabitants.

The Grorud Valley is a limited geographical space. This limitation may in fact prove incompatible to the imported ideals of large-scale sociospatial organization that have informed its planning. The Valley has served as a laboratory for ideas ranging from the garden city and the City Beautiful to Le Corbusier's *unité d'habitation* and the grandeur of socialist commonwealth planning. Yet while the tensions are still unresolved, the spatial dynamics in the valley are open enough to encourage productive future experiments.

1.11.7 A modified building with glassed-in balconies and cultivation of green areas

Future Grorud: Global Satellite Town
The Marka limit forms a political (although originally natural) urban growth boundary. Having been contested over the last years due to the growing need for buildable land, it seems to be withstanding development pressure. Landscape presence is as important in the valley today as in those first years of development and will continue to be the case. As a result, urban development in Oslo is no longer about expansion; instead, it is about the reuse and transformation of urban fragments. In this way, the valley itself is changing, gradually becoming a large urban district.

Yet the most significant change in the valley is demography. Over the last three decades, the valley has become a melting pot of diverse immigrant groups. Playing on the philosopher Marshall McLuhan's "global village" concept, the Norwegian scholars Thomas Hylland Eriksen and Elisabeth Eide introduced the concept "global satellite town" to describe its present character. It is global, not only

in the sense of being tied to a global technology network as described by McLuhan,
but also by migration and physical mobility.[16] Its demographic composition is an
expression of the ethnic variation in present-day European and Norwegian society.

The Valley's new inhabitants have
called into question the traditional
Norwegian relationship of nature and
housing. The new inhabitants in the valley
do not necessarily embrace the culture
of cross-country skiing, berry picking,
and general wilderness appreciation. In
fact, new immigrant groups have different
preferences and expectations of a suburban environment than the population it
was originally built for. Immigrants from
the Middle East and Asia prefer more
neighborhood meeting places and outdoor
activity areas. Few portions of the inner
landscape of the valley accommodate
these needs and desires.

Plus, the valley is now on the verge of
a major postindustrial economic transformation involving partial obliteration of its
industrial areas. This conversion of large
industrial areas into other land uses and
new neighborhoods offers the opportunity
to focus on developing the inner landscape
of the valley, which is in need of revival
and extension of both its social infrastructure and its physical spaces. In 2007
the municipality of Oslo launched a comprehensive plan for the Grorud Valley, a
project aimed at improving environmental
and living conditions in the Grorud Valley
at large.[17] Central to the plan is a scheme
for four larger parks, one for each part
of the valley. The "Groruddalen Project"
thus features a strong park policy, one
in which blue-green infrastructure and
recreational commons are at the forefront.

The plan extends the park system idea
from the 1950 master plan, where landscape structure was conceived of as the
backbone in urban development. However,
as the Norwegian landscape architect Ola
Bettum points out, the 2007 strategy is the

1.11.8 An empty shopping and management center in the
satellite town of Romsås

inverse of the 1950 plan; instead of closely
linking to the Marka surrounding the valley, the new park strategy aims to develop
recreational spaces within the valley.
The change in focus will bring new
attention to the geological layout of this
typically Norwegian moraine valley.

In the end, the new Grorud Valley
project is less about the visual aesthetics emphasized by the City Beautiful
movement than about socially and environmentally efficient landscapes. The
project includes daylighting of rivers,
revival of wildlife habitats, and an
increase in park space similar in scope
to the 1950 plan, although interrupted by
industrial and infrastructural systems.

In the history of the valley since World
War II, the strong presence of landscape
and nature created a unique suburban
condition. What the municipality of Oslo
seems to have learned from the successive
stages of suburbanization in this former
farming valley is that when a suburban
area densifies, changes, and develops into
a multicultural region, the status of nature
changes. The recent landscape projects
in the valley demonstrate that "there is
a major political profit to be made from
emphasizing parks as part of urban development."[18] The Bjerkedalen Park creates
new meeting places in a district with few
parks and plazas. (fig. **1.11.9**) New pedestrian paths wind through it, and sections
of the creek Hovinbekken have been daylighted. It will be opened throughout the
building zone and all the way down to the

16 Sharam Alghasi,
    Elisabeth Eide, and
    Thomas Hylland Eriksen,
    *Den Globale Drabantbyen:
    Groruddalen Og Det
    Nye Norge* (Oslo:
    Cappelen Damm akademisk, 2012), 8.
17 Guro Voss Gabrielsen's
    PhD dissertation deals
    with this project.
18 *Parkpolitikk*, vol. 06-2014,
    Parker I Groruddalen;
    Geilo Sentrum; Asker
    Rådhus; Konsept? (Oslo:
    Norske arkitekters
    landsforbund, 2014), 51.

19 Karl Otto Ellefsen,
    "Idealer I Norsk Bolig-
    Og Byplanlegging I De
    Siste Tiårene," *Plan* 35
    ER, no. 1 (2003): 6.

1.11.9 The new valley demography demands a need for meeting places and outdoor activity arenas that offer something to people from all culture groups.

historical parts of Oslo. This new development proves to partly realize the extensive park system plan from 1950.

Today there is indeed hope that the valley's inner landscape could be the mechanism that ties up its fragmented housing districts and will also be adapted to address the new social and cultural changes in the area.[19] The present challenge entails adapting the City Beautiful ideals that first created the valley's landscape in order to solve the needs and desires of a global village.

Spanish Springs, Reno, Nevada, United States

Georgetown, Texas, United States

2

POLYCENTRIC METROPOLITAN FORM

2.1
ENGAGING WITH THE PLANET'S URBAN EXPANSION

Shlomo Angel and Alejandro M. Blei, with Daniel L. Civco, Nicolas Galarza Sanchez, Patrick Lamson-Hall, Manuel Madrid, Jason Parent, and Kevin Thom

GOVERNANCE & POLICY CHALLENGES

NEOLIBERAL PROPERTY MARKETS

POLYCENTRIC EXPANSION

SOCIAL INEQUALITIES

TRANSPORT INFRASTRUCTURE

Urbanization—the movement of people from villages to cities and towns—began in earnest in 1800, when less than 10 percent of the planet's population lived in cities, and reached a peak in 2000, when half the world's population lived in cities. The world's urban-growth rate is slowing down and is likely to come to an end by 2100, when world population growth is expected to halt and as many as three-quarters of the world's population will live in cities. Short as it may be, the coming decades offer a critical window of opportunity to make minimal preparations for coming urban-population growth and its concomitant, mostly suburban, physical expansion. When cities grow in population and wealth, they expand. As they expand, cities need to prepare lands for urban use, ensuring that they are properly serviced yet affordable so that they may be of optimal use to their inhabitants.

Romantic as the notion may be, orderly, efficient, equitable, and sustainable cities are not self-organizing. They do not emerge from spontaneous actions by the multitudes of individuals, groups, or firms. Rather, they come about when these multitudes act in unison as a public to lay out areas of expansion in an orderly, efficient, and equitable manner before they are occupied, by reserving adequate lands for public works, public open spaces, and public facilities.

We cannot hope to slow down the urbanization process or to shift populations among cities. People are free to move within their own countries, and their right to move is enshrined in the Universal Declaration of Human Rights.[1] Population growth in cities cannot be effectively guided by policy. But the conversion of land to urban use is very much guided and influenced by policy. Defining future patterns of urban development is where planners, designers, and decision makers can intervene to precede and guide the operations of the free market on the urban fringe. Without this concerted public action in advance of development, land and housing markets, efficient as they may be in theory, will fail to perform properly in practice.

And yet, there is reluctance to engage with the prospects of urban expansion, perhaps for perfectly understandable reasons. Many people have come to believe that cities consume enough land as it is and that all future construction should take place within existing urban extents. Others oppose expansion so as to conserve municipal infrastructure budgets, ameliorate traffic congestion, help decaying central cities thrive again, conserve energy, reduce air pollution, or protect precious cultivated lands at the urban fringe. This reluctance, reasonable as it may seem, keeps the prospects of urban expansion rather obscure and prevents us from addressing them in a clear, forthright manner.

Part of this reluctance may also be ignorance, as our knowledge of the quantity and the quality of global urban expansion is meager and unsatisfactory. To tackle this lack of knowledge, the New York University Urban Expansion Program has initiated a multiphase research effort to monitor the quantitative and qualitative aspects of global urban expansion.[2]

Our empirical data on actual urban expansion and its key attributes—in many cities around the world over long periods of time—provides a much-needed basis for understanding the global and historical contexts of urban expansion. Our research focuses on studying a stratified global sample of 200 cities, strategically chosen from the 4,245 cities in the world with a population above one hundred thousand in 2010. This sample allows us to make powerful generalizations about cities worldwide.[3] (fig. **2.1.1**) Our data, coupled with theories that could explain the

1   UN General Assembly, *Universal Declaration of Human Rights*, Article 13, December 10, 1948, 217 A (III), accessed August 13, 2015, http://www.un.org/en/documents/udhr/.

2   The NYU Urban Expansion Program is supported by the NYU Stern Urbanization Project and the NYU Marron Institute of Urban Management, in partnership with the United Nations Human Settlements Programme (UN-Habitat) and the Lincoln Institute of Land Policy. The NYU Urban Expansion Program is described in a recent article in the *Economist* at http://www.economist.com/news/international/21604576-cities-are-bound-grow-they-need-planning-be-liveable-roads-redemption. A short video can be found at http://urbanizationproject.org/blog/urban-expansion. A primer describing it can be found at http://urbanizationproject.org/uploads/blog/UEPrimer2014.pdf. Animation of the expansion of thirty cities can be seen at https://www.youtube.com/playlist?list=PLzYZm159uzQNc7H5UCCXHx4c4TKdCeaNt. The intellectual foundation of the program is a ten-year research project on urban expansion, culminating in the publication of two books: Shlomo Angel, *Planet of Cities* (Cambridge, MA: Lincoln Institute of Land Policy, 2012); Shlomo Angel et al., *Atlas of Urban Expansion* (Cambridge, MA: Lincoln Institute of Land Policy, 2012).

3   The sample is roughly 5 percent of the 4,245 cities with one hundred thousand people or more in 2010. The sample was selected with three criteria in mind: (1) having cities from eight world regions in proportion to the urban population in each region; (2) having one-fourth of the cities drawn from each of the four population-size categories, each category

Regions	Number of Cities	% of total	Total Urban Population	% of total	Number of Cities	% of total	Population in Sample	% of total
			Universe					Sample
East Asia and the Pacific (EAP)	1,089	26%	645,356,592	26%	42	21%	154,459,839	21%
Southeast Asia (SEA)	232	5%	128,492,546	5%	15	8%	37,995,438	5%
South and Central Asia (SCA)	693	16%	392,876,899	16%	32	16%	121,380,230	17%
Western Asia and North Africa (WANA)	300	7%	180,525,762	7%	15	8%	62,177,236	9%
Sub-Saharan Africa (SSA)	331	8%	186,626,671	7%	18	9%	50,018,112	7%
Europe and Japan (E&J)	781	18%	396,157,559	16%	34	17%	127,216,190	18%
Land-Rich Developed Countries (LRDC)	334	8%	240,725,842	10%	18	9%	68,421,847	9%
Latin America and the Caribbean (LAC)	485	11%	320,102,523	13%	26	13%	98,805,345	14%
Grand Total	4,245	100%	2,490,864,393	100%	200	100%	720,474,237	100%

City Population Groups	Number of Cities	% of total	Total Urban Population	% of total	Number of Cities	% of total	Population in Sample	% of total
			Universe					Sample
100,000–425,677	3,150	74%	622,400,949	25%	56	28%	12,585,331	2%
425,678–1,559,789	814	19%	622,296,461	25%	50	25%	41,719,128	6%
1,561,742–5,556,200	227	5%	619,845,757	25%	54	27%	171,482,632	24%
5,718,232 +	54	1%	626,321,226	25%	40	20%	494,687,146	69%
Grand Total	4,245	100%	2,490,864,393	100%	200	100%	720,474,237	100%

Number of Cities per Country Categories	Number of Cities	% of total	Total Urban Population	% of total	Number of Cities	% of total	Population in Sample	% of total
			Universe					Sample
1–9	370	9%	184,155,422	7%	23	12%	39,166,655	5%
10–19	307	7%	154,896,704	6%	18	9%	35,382,060	5%
20+	3,568	84%	2,151,812,267	86%	159	80%	645,925,523	90%
Grand Total	4,245	100%	2,490,864,393	100%	200	100%	720,474,238	100%

2.1.1 A comparison of the universe of cities and the sample of cities, stratified according to the categories of region, city population group, and number of cities per country

underlying forces that are propelling and shaping this urban expansion, could provide the evidence needed to assess and address our various concerns: that it would be very difficult, if not futile, to resist urban expansion; that ignoring it or denying it in the hope that it will not occur will simply allow it to take place unhindered and in a more costly and destructive way; that acquiring a better understanding of it will make it less formidable and more manageable; and that making minimal yet effective preparations for it is the right way, and certainly the only responsible way, to proceed.

This essay presents some important findings from our ongoing research on the finite dimensions and the measurable attributes of our planet's increasingly infinite suburbia.[4] We focus on two simple questions. First, what is the physical extent of our planet's urban areas today, and how are they expanding over time? Second, how well laid out are recently built suburban peripheries, and how are layouts changing over time? With both of these questions, the aim is to reveal the containing one-quarter of the total population of the cities in the universe; and (3) selecting cities from three country categories—those with 1 to 9 cities, those with 10 to 19 cities, and those with 20 or more cities, with a slight bias toward the first two categories. It is also important to note that the second criterion—dividing the cities into four population-size groups, each containing the same total population—biases the sample toward larger cities: The four population size groups contain the same total population,

reasons for change and to expose the ways in which change matters.

We believe that provisional answers to these questions can make us less fearful of the rapid expansion of the suburban peripheries of our cities. Better knowledge will help us confront this expansion in a meaningful way, one that will allow us to engage with suburban peripheries pragmatically and realistically in the years to come.

Urban Expansion Is Greatest in Developing Countries

Our research into urban expansion adds some important information to the widely known fact that urban expansion is greatest in developing countries. There is near universal agreement that a settlement of 100,000 people or more constitutes a city.[5] We have now identified 4,245 cities (not single municipalities, but entire metropolitan areas) on our planet that were home to 100,000 people or more in 2010. The total 2010 population of this universe of cities amounted to 2.5 billion, or 70 percent of the world's 2010 urban population of 3.6 billion.[6]

Three-quarters of these cities are in developing countries. More precisely, 3,130 cities out of the total 4,245 (74 percent), housing 1.85 billion people out of a total 2.5 billion (also 74 percent), are in developing countries. Moreover, the share of projected urban-population growth in coming decades in the developing countries is much greater. Between 2015 and 2050, the world's urban population is now expected to increase by 2.38 billion people.[7] Only 5 percent of that increase (130 million) will be in developed countries. The rest, 95 percent (or 2.25 billion), will be in the developing countries. In other words, the increase in the city populations in developing countries will be eighteen times that of the increase in the city populations of developed countries.

The challenge of urban expansion in the coming decades is therefore largely a challenge facing cities in developing countries. Compared to the developed world, these cities, on the whole, have fewer fiscal resources, weaker rules of law, higher levels of corruption, and less experienced public servants, but also higher built-up area densities, more reliance on public transport, and lower levels of energy use. It may well be that the suburbanization agenda for cities in developing countries is quite different than the suburbanization agenda of those in developed countries. Nonetheless, from the point of view of monitoring suburbanization, we believe that it is important to study both developed-country cities and developing-country cities using the same conceptual framework and the same methods for data collection and analysis.

The Urban Extent

Our mapping and measuring of global urban expansion since 2003 has exposed important relationships between the spatial extent of an urban area and specific factors.[8] The findings from our early modeling of the urban extent of ninety cities were consistent with classical models of the city—for example, the economic geographer William Alonso's *Location and Land Use*.[9] Specifically, we found that the following parameters positively correlate with a greater spatial extent in a statistically significant way: city population, per capita income, availability of buildable land on the urban periphery, amount of arable land per capita in the country, and cheaper cost of transport. In other words, the greater the magnitude of these parameters (and the cheaper the cost of transport), the larger the urban extent.[10]

Moreover, we have found that urban extents grew at a faster annual rate between 1990 and 2000 than the population of cities did. Cities in our sample expanded at an average annual rate of

but there are as many as 3,150 cities in the first group (cities of 100,000 to 425,000 people), and 56 of them are in the sample, and there are only 54 cities in the fourth population size group (5.6 million and more) and 40 of them are in the sample. As a result, the 200 sample cities have a population of 720 million, 29 percent of the total population of the universe. We tested the representativeness of the sample in the following manner: We know the 2000–2010 population growth rates of all cities in the universe and in the sample. We compared their averages—both weighted and unweighted—and found that they were not statistically different from each other at the 95 percent confidence level.

4   Complete results for the first three phases of the program were presented at the Habitat III conference in Quito, Ecuador, on October 2016, and are available at http://atlas ofurbanexpansion.org/.

5   With the important exception of China where there were only 657 officially designated cities in 2015, we identified hundreds of additional settlements of one hundred thousand people or more that we have counted as cities.

6   United Nations, Department of Social and Economic Affairs, Population Division 2014, File 3: Urban Population at Mid-Year by Major Area, Region and Country, 1950–2050 (thousands), accessed August 13, 2015, http:// esa.un.org/unpd/wup /CD-ROM/.

7   Ibid.

8   Shlomo Angel et al., *The Dynamics of Global Urban Expansion* (Washington, DC: World Bank, Transport and Urban Development Department, 2005); Shlomo Angel et al., *Atlas of Urban Expansion: The 2016 Edition*, 2 vols. (New York; Nairobi; Cambridge, MA: NYU Urban Expansion

3.6 percent, while their populations grew at an average rate of 1.6 percent per year.[11] The consumption of urban land per person increased at an annual rate of 2.1 percent, and the inverse metric, the average residential density in the built-up areas of cities, declined at the same average rate of 2.1 percent per year.[12] This is largely explained by increases in income, the availability of land for expansion, and inexpensive transport.

We also found that average built-up area densities were significantly different among the three world regions: land-rich developed countries (the United States, Canada, and Australia); Europe and Japan; and developing countries. Average built-up area densities in developing countries, 428 people per acre (173 people per hectare) circa 1990 and 334 people per acre (135 people per hectare) circa 2000, were found to be double those of Europe and Japan, 205 people per acre (83 people per hectare) circa 1990 and 163 people per acre (66 people per hectare) circa 2000. Yet those in Europe and Japan were found to be triple those of land-rich developed countries, sixty-seven people per acre (27 people per hectare) circa 1990 and fifty-four people per acre (22 people per hectare) circa 2000.

Our analysis of thirty cities for the period 1800 to 2000 revealed that the decline in average urban density was in motion for a majority of cities during most of the twentieth century, after a period of increases during the nineteenth century. In 1800, during the time of Napoleon, Paris had a population of 0.5 million people and covered an area of some 4 square miles (11 square kilometers). By 2000, it had a population of some ten million people and an area of some 770 square miles (2,000 square kilometers). In other words, its population grew twentyfold, while its area grew two hundredfold. The average density in Paris declined ninefold during this

period—from 180 people per acre (450 people per hectare) to 20 people per acre (50 people per hectare)—at an average annual rate of 1.1 percent. Similar rates of decline from peak density to that observed in Paris were observed in the other cities in the group as well. (fig. **2.1.2**)

Preliminary results for one-third of the cities in our stratified sample of two hundred global cities, results that still need to be checked, suggest that the average densities of the built-up areas of cities continued to decline in the period 2000–2014.[13] (fig. **2.1.3**) For example, Accra's expansion during this period was quite extraordinary. Results yet to be confirmed suggest that its population grew from 1.32 million in 1991 to 2.54 million in 2000, and to 4.5 million in 2014, at an average annual growth rate of 5.3 percent. Its built-up area grew from about 24,700 acres (10,000 hectares) in 1991 to 79,600 acres (32,200 hectares) in 2000, and to 152,700 acres (61,800 hectares) in 2014, at an average annual growth rate of 7.8 percent, a rate one and a half times that of its population growth rate. As a result, the average built-up area density in Accra declined from 336 people per acre (136 people per hectare) in 1991 to 222 people per acre (90 people per hectare) in 2000, increasing to 247 people per acre (100 people per hectare) in 2014. Its population density fell by slightly more than one-quarter during the 1991 to 2014 period, declining at an average annual rate of 1.3 percent.

What can we say now about the prospects of the urban/suburban explosion in the coming decades? Between 2010 and 2050, the developing world's urban population is expected to double, from 2.6 billion to 5.2 billion. Economic development and cheap transportation are likely to increase land consumption per person, meaning they will hasten a decrease in average urban densities. If the consumption of land per capita

Program at New York University, UN-Habitat, and the Lincoln Institute of Land Policy, 2016), http://atlasofurban expansion.org/data.

9 William Alonso, *Location and Land Use* (Cambridge, MA: Harvard University Press, 1964).

10 These variables were all significant at the 95 percent confidence level, and together they explained more than 80 percent of the variation in urban extent in the ninety cities studied.

11 These average rates were significantly different from one another at the 95 percent confidence level.

12 These average rates were significantly different from zero at the 95 percent confidence level.

13 At a rate significantly different from zero at the 95 percent confidence level.

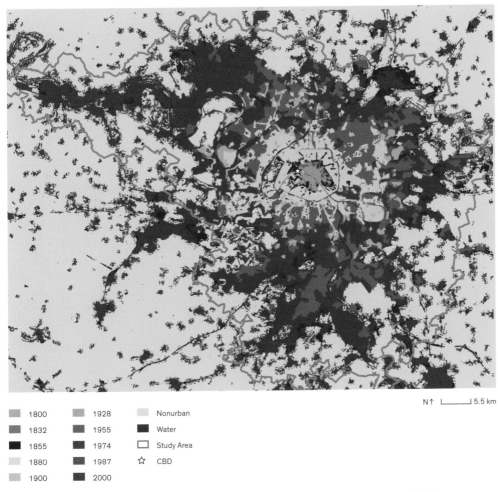

	1800		1928		Nonurban
	1832		1955		Water
	1855		1974		Study Area
	1880		1987	☆	CBD
	1900		2000		

N↑ ⌞_____⌟ 5.5 km

2.1.2 The expansion of Paris, France, from 11 square kilometers in 1800 (gray) to 2,000 square kilometers in 2000

increases at 1 percent per annum—the rate at which it increased in Paris, on average, during the last two centuries—the land area of cities in developing countries is likely to triple. If it increases at 2 percent per annum—the average rate of increase in our earlier sample of 120 cities between 1990 and 2000—the land area of cities in developing countries is likely to more than quadruple.

The prospects of urban expansion in sub-Saharan Africa will be much more extreme than in the rest of the developing world. Between 2010 and 2050, the urban population in sub-Saharan Africa is expected to quadruple, from 295 million to 1.15 billion. If densities remain the same, urban areas will increase fourfold as well. If the consumption of land per capita

increases at 1 percent per annum, the land area of cities in sub-Saharan Africa is likely to increase almost sixfold. If it increases at 2 percent per annum, land area of cities in sub-Saharan Africa is likely to increase more than eightfold.

Lower, more modest, increases can be expected in developed countries: a 75 percent increase in area if land consumption increases at 1 percent per annum, and a 160 percent increase if land consumption per capita increases at 2 percent per annum. These are indeed explosive increases in the expansion of cities.

Policy makers at the local, national, and international levels, as well as activists and interested citizens, should be aware of the dimensions of the coming

Study area

Urban extent

Urban built-up area

Suburban built-up area

Rural built-up area

Urbanized open space

Rural open space

Exurban built-up area

Exurban open space

Water

No data

☆ CBD

N↑ └─────┘ 5 km

2.1.3 The expansion of Accra, Ghana, 1985–2014

urban expansion, so that adequate lands can be prepared for that expansion, and so that it is orderly, efficient, equitable, and sustainable. Turning a blind eye to urban expansion will likely result in just the opposite: disorderly, inefficient, inequitable, and unsustainable expansion. Limiting it forcefully, in the name of rural land conservation, for example, will likely choke the residential land supply and place housing out of reach of the majority of households. Whether observed urban expansion now is orderly and whether land and housing are affordable are empirical questions being explored in subsequent phases of our monitoring effort.

Urban Layouts at the Periphery

We know very little about the peripheries of our cities, where urban expansion is now taking place. Radical and irreversible transformations are taking place in these vast areas, as lands that may have been in cultivation for centuries are converted to urban use, never to convert back to rural use. The owners of rural land may sell it to urbanites—speculators, developers, or ordinary city folk—who may have much better information about its market price, the laws governing it, and its potential use and value. The urban periphery, being far from the center of the city, may also be less regulated and less familiar to public officials. Land documents may be incomplete or nonexistent, while property rights and property lines, possibly enshrined for generations through continuous use, may be quite resistant to abrupt change.

Land-use change on the urban fringe is subject to this asymmetry of information and is not well understood. Nonetheless, land is being transferred and put to urban use one way or another at a rapid rate, a rate commensurate with the pace of population growth and economic development in the city. Once land is transferred to urban use and to

urban users, its character changes. It can join the city in two quite different ways: it can become a marginalized part of the city, never making a full transformation from rural to urban use, retaining the old property lines and rural lanes; or it can be integrated properly into the city, with appropriate urban layouts that include new property lines, new street grids, and new arterial roads. The unfettered actions of the land market cannot and will not ensure that urban peripheries are properly laid out. If they are not properly laid out at first, they are likely to remain in that condition in the future. Strictly speaking, barring clearance and redevelopment—a highly unlikely outcome anywhere that people have a voice—rural or semirural layouts cannot be transformed into urban ones once they are fully occupied. Street layouts and property lines in built-up areas are, for all intents and purposes, irreversible.

The rebuilding of London after the Great London Fire of 1666 epitomizes the power of old, often invisible, property lines over urban form. Sir Christopher Wren, the architect of London's St. Paul's Cathedral, quickly presented King Charles II a plan for rebuilding the city with modern street grids, wide avenues with open vistas, and public squares. (fig. **2.1.4**) Others, notably the writer John Evelyn and the architect Robert Hooke, presented competing plans as well. But the king, fearful of an uprising, was reluctant to assume the power to confiscate the lands needed to implement the plans. In the resulting confusion, it was impossible to identify landowners for purposes of compensation, and the city was quickly rebuilt along the old property lines.

Modern-day suburban Bangkok, Thailand, and suburban Lima, Peru, offer a striking contrast in their street layouts. The hands-off, laissez-faire approach to urban development that characterizes Bangkok illustrates how

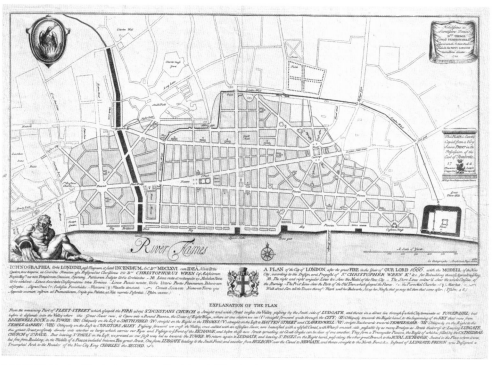

2.1.4 Sir Christopher Wren's plan, never realized, for rebuilding London after the Great Fire of 1666

the absence of arterial roads creates large efficiency losses and stymies organized urban expansion. (fig. **2.1.5**) As a result, in a large northeastern inner suburb of Bangkok there are networks of narrow lanes that were developed during the 1960s, 1970s, and early 1980s, leaving rural property lines largely intact. This example underscores one of the drawbacks of quick, laissez-faire, market-driven urban expansion: it ignores the substantial land needs of public works. The result in Bangkok is that many arterial roads are spaced no less than 5 miles (8 kilometers) apart, and the local roads, while connecting each plot to the outside world, are not connected to each other to facilitate through traffic. Congestion is high because long intracity trips are crowded into a small number of arterial roads, resulting in elevated levels of air pollution and energy use and low labor productivity.

The absence of an arterial road grid in Bangkok makes it very difficult to extend the primary grid of key infrastructure services: water supply, sewerage, and storm drainage. This absence also makes it much more difficult for the city to collect and treat its stormwater and sewer water before pumping it out or recycling it. Indeed, Bangkok does not have a piped water system, a piped drainage system, or a piped sewerage system. Finally, in the absence of any public pressure or appropriate and binding legislation, the newly developed areas outside Bangkok's traditional center have little public open space.

For Bangkok, one of the world's largest and fastest-growing cities, the absence of adequate land for public works has been devastating. It is expanding rapidly without an arterial road network or a primary infrastructure network that can carry water, sewerage, or stormwater; without a system of dikes to manage its stormwater; and without a hierarchy of public open spaces. The solutions to this self-inflicted environmental crisis require massive investments in public works. But in the absence of rights-of-way for an arterial road network, a dike system, and the lands for a hierarchy of public parks and playgrounds protected from development, such investments are now exorbitant and quite possibly unaffordable. Necessary as they may be, the destruction of private property that building these facilities would entail makes the likelihood of their creation next to impossible.

Planning and acquiring the land for public works requires organization. While Bangkok illustrates hardly any organization to speak of—a virtual state of anarchy—the creation of Pampa de Comas, a large squatter settlement on the desert outskirts of Lima, demonstrates what can be achieved through planning and coordination. Located on public land, Comas was formed by a series of organized invasions that were carefully thought out and far from spontaneous. People came together in the city, often organized by zealous priests, to plan and prepare the settlement. Each invading family occupied one building site that had been properly surveyed and selected in advance. The sites were relatively large, measuring about 33 by 66 feet (10 by 20 meters). There were twenty sites to a block, and roads between the blocks that were 33 feet (10 meters) wide. Some blocks were intentionally left open for markets, schools, and public open spaces. Comas is now a fully built urban neighborhood, indistinguishable from any other neighborhood in the city. Squatters were eventually awarded title documents, and the houses in the district are now part of Lima's formal housing market. With its small blocks and wide streets, no less than 27 percent of the land area in Comas was devoted to local streets, and an additional 3 percent to public open spaces. (fig. **2.1.6**)

The planning and the reservation of rights-of-way for street grids at the block level are essential. In his book, *La grilla y el parque*, Adrián Gorelik equates the 1898 street grid in Buenos Aires— the street grid shown in its 1904 plan as covering the entire territory of the Federal Capital—with the homogenization of its

2.1.5 The absence of arterial roads in a 60-square-kilometer section of northwest Bangkok, Thailand, 1984

territory. In the spirit of social reform, the differentiation between rich and poor, between the formal and the informal, was obliterated, and the distribution of public services, including streets and public open spaces, was equalized.[14] Indeed, it stands to reason that the Comas street grid and its open spaces accelerated its incorporation into metropolitan Lima as a district among equals. By making all plots similar to each other and having each face a broad street, the Comas plan also reduced the difference in real estate values among the houses in the neighborhood, and increased the value of real estate in the metropolitan area as a whole.

The lessons from Bangkok and Lima are quite clear. To facilitate the provision of infrastructure services, arterial roads and streets must to be laid out *before* plots revert from a rural to an urban use. New street layouts must not discriminate between rich and poor. An adequate share of the land needs to be dedicated to streets, and streets have to be wide enough. Blocks must be small enough to make neighborhoods walkable. To serve low-income households, plot sizes in

14 Adrián Gorelik, *La grilla y el parque: Espacio publico y cultura urbana en Buenos Aires* (Buenos Aires: Universidad Nacional de Quilmes, 2001).

residential subdivisions must be small enough to be affordable.

Block Sizes and Road Density

In a global sample of two hundred cities, we measure block sizes and road density in a randomly chosen set of 25-acre (10-hectare) locales in each city's urban periphery.[15] We also identify and measure access to arterial roads in the expansion area as a whole. Our initial findings reveal inefficient patterns of urbanization that are now common in the developing world's urban peripheries. (fig. **2.1.7**)

Using high-resolution satellite images of each locale, trained analysts digitized street boundaries as well as the boundaries of residential and nonresidential areas.[16] Residential areas were classified into four types, depending on their stage of evolution: (1) Atomistic Housing, laid out in succession, one house after the other; (2) Informal Land Subdivisions, where land is subdivided into plots and narrow lanes, typically ignoring land subdivision regulations; (3) Formal Land Subdivisions with proper street layouts; and (4) Housing Projects, with identical houses or apartment buildings arranged in a regular pattern on the site. In addition, wherever possible, analysts identified plots in land subdivisions and measured their widths and lengths. Finally, in addition to the digitization and labeling of land uses in locales, analysts digitized the medians of all blocks that intersect the locale, as well as the medians of all arterial roads—roads 59 feet wide (18 meters) or greater that are connected to other 59 foot-wide roads—within 0.6 miles (one kilometer) of the expansion area. (fig. **2.1.8**)

Initial results from thirty-eight cities reveal some important regularities in the urban layouts on the peripheries of cities in 2015. On average, the share of the built-up area devoted to streets and boulevards is 21 percent, with Kolkata, India,

2.1.6 The El Carmen squatter settlement in the Comas district of Lima, Peru, in 2009

as a low outlier at 8 percent, and Palmas, Brazil, as a high outlier at 35 percent. Block sizes on the urban periphery of cities were found to be quite large, compared to, say, blocks in Manhattan, New York, a highly walkable urban area. Blocks in Manhattan average 5.4 acres (2.2 hectares) in area, compared to the average of 14.8 acres (6 hectares) in thirty-eight out of two hundred cities for which we can report preliminary results. It is quite clear that in most urban peripheries, relatively large block sizes compromise their walkability. In Manhattan, average intersection density is 236 per square mile (91 per square kilometer). The average intersection density in the urban peripheries of the thirty-eight cities was much lower, 54 per square mile (21 per square kilometer). (fig. **2.1.9**)

Preliminary results for the thirty-eight of two hundred cites also reveal a maximum density of arterial roads of 2.0 miles per square mile (1.25 kilometers per square kilometer), in Karachi, Pakistan. The minimum was observed in Springfield, Massachusetts, in the United States, which had no arterial roads in its expansion area at all. The average distance to an arterial road in this subset of thirty-eight cities was 1.6 miles (2.6 kilometers), beyond convenient walking distance; the average share of the area in the urban peripheries of these cities that was within walking distance of an arterial road was 37 percent. These values confirm that most of the area of present-day urban

15 In early 2016 we plan to report on all two hundred cities as well as on the change of urban layouts over time. Locales were chosen from those areas of cities that were new between 1990 and 2014. In these expansion areas, we picked an initial set of 40 points, using a halton sequence to generate the points. The halton sequence generates a quasi-random number sequence, in our case a set of quasi-random coordinates of points the expansion area. The points are not truly random in the sense that, given the same origin, the halton sequence will always generate the same sequence of coordinates for points. Around each point, we drew a circle with an area of about 25 acres (10 hectares or 0.1 square kilometers), and we focused our analysis on that circle, referred to as a *locale*. The extent of the sampling in a particular city's expansion area is not predetermined. We start out with forty locales in each city, but the decision of when to stop analyzing locales depends on results of a test designed to tell us whether we have captured the average expansion area value for a particular metric with a high degree of statistical confidence. Until this criterion is met, we continue the sequential sampling of locales within the expansion area.

16 The digitized results for forty locales in the expansion area of each city in the global sample are processed in an automated Python Script in ArcGIS to result in a set of up to eighteen metrics—some more useful than others—that characterize urban layouts in a given expansion area. Selected average metric results—including their 95 percent confidence limits—for forty locales in a subset of thirty-eight selected cities from the global sample of two hundred

peripheries is not accessible to arterial roads and is therefore quite unlikely to be served by public transport in an efficient and equitable manner.

We look at one specific example: a typical residential area in the expansion zone on the northern periphery of Kolkata, India. Most of the housing is atomistic housing, built over land that was not subdivided into regular plots with street access to each plot before it was occupied. There are very few roads in the area, and only one wide paved road a considerable distance away from most houses.

New statistical findings for the expansion zone of Kolkata confirm these observations. The share of the residential area occupied by atomistic housing in the expansion area of Kolkata is 92 percent. The share of the built-up area devoted to roads and boulevards is 8 percent. Arterial roads are practically nonexistent. Given the density of arterial roads, 0.18 miles per square mile (0.11 kilometers per square kilometer), we can estimate that, on average, arterial roads are spaced some 11 miles (18 kilometers) apart.

Our superficial examination of the data suggests that urban peripheries the world over are not being developed in an efficient, equitable, and sustainable manner. That said, we need the full data set, soon to be completed, for all two hundred cities in the sample if we are to begin to understand the scope of the problem and chart effective paths for solving it, or at the very least ameliorating it, in the coming years.

The Implications of an Infinite Suburbia
It is clear that cities in the developing countries will see the most dramatic expansions of their built-up areas over the next decades. It is not clear that these rapidly growing cities are making or will make the necessary preparations for their inevitable expansion. How can we

2.1.7 The expansion area of Addis Ababa, Ethiopia, in 1990–2014, and the set of quasi-random, 24.7-acre (10-hectare) locales used to analyze the quality of urban layouts there

ensure that residential land on the urban fringe remains affordable to all of those in need and accessible to jobs by efficient and sustainable transport? What can be done to see to it that neighborhoods are laid out before they are occupied, to ensure the orderly and efficient provision of infrastructure services?

The authors and their colleagues at the New York University (NYU) Urban Expansion Program are working toward providing a pragmatic answer to this question. The primary mission of the program is to train, assist, and empower municipalities of rapidly growing cities so that they can make room, in a set of four practical steps, for their inevitable expansion:

— Making realistic thirty-year projections of land needs for urban expansion to 2045
— Extending official city limits to encompass the projected expansion
— Securing the rights-of-way for an arterial infrastructure grid in expansion areas
— Creating the institutional framework for protecting areas of high environmental risk from development

Making room is seen as critical in ensuring that residential land on the urban fringe remains affordable by all those in need as well as readily accessible by efficient public transport. Making room is also seen as critical in ensuring that new

cities—for which preliminary data are already available—are presented, for illustrative purposes, together with data on arterial roads in the expansion areas of these cities. It was not possible to include data on housing characteristics or on the share of roads in different road-width categories in the expansion areas of these cities at the time of writing, as these were still being tested for accuracy.

17 The NYU Urban
   Expansion Program is
   described in a recent
   article in the *Economist*,
   online at http://www
   .economist.com/news
   /international/21604576
   -cities-are-bound-grow
   -they-need-planning-be
   -liveable-roads-redemp
   tion.

2.1.8 Atomistic housing (left) and housing projects (right) in two 24.7-acre (10 hectare) locales in the expansion area of Addis Ababa

urban neighborhoods are laid out before they are occupied to ensure the orderly and efficient provision of infrastructure services.[17] To date, there are two urban expansion initiatives—one focused on four intermediate cities in Ethiopia and one focused on five intermediate cities in Colombia—in advanced stages of completion. In both countries, a number of cities have finalized their infrastructure grid plans and are now actively securing the rights-of way for an arterial 98.4-foot-wide (30-meter-wide) road grid, spaced 0.6 miles (1 kilometer) apart. The national governments of both countries are now actively transforming these initiatives into national programs. Exploratory work on new urban expansion initiatives in several other countries—Mexico, China, India, Myanmar, Indonesia, and Rwanda—is now underway.

The key message of this work for confronting Infinite Suburbia is that the remaining decades of the present century offer a window of opportunity for taking action that will shape the suburban peripheries of cities—peripheries that will be vastly larger than the cities of today—for centuries to come. These actions must now move away from the offices of academics and bureaucrats to putting stakes in the ground. To succeed, they must be done at scale.

To be done at scale, they must engage thousands of municipalities. To engage thousands of municipalities—the great majority of them in developing countries—they must be simple and inexpensive, and the time for undertaking them is now.

City, Country	Share of built-up area occupied by roads & boulevards	Average block size (hectares)	4-Way intersection density (no. per km2)	Density of arterial roads (km per km2)	Average beeline distance to arterial road (meters)	Share of area within walking distance (625 m beeline) of arterial road
Accra, Ghana	18 ± 3%	3.9 ± 1%	12 ± 8	0.09	2,915	14%
Addis Ababa, Ethiopia	25 ± 4%	3.5 ± 1.4%	34 ± 11	0.66	618	69%
Ahmedabad, India	23 ± 4%	8.3 ± 2.7%	15 ± 6	1.04	637	71%
Arusha, Tanzania	13 ± 3%	4.4 ± 0.9%	15 ± 6	0.55	624	60%
Astrakhan, Russia	22 ± 4%	2.7 ± 0.7%	27 ± 12	0.49	945	53%
Auckland, New Zealand	22 ± 4%	7.8 ± 2.9%	6 ± 5	0.19	1,481	52%
Baghdad, Iraq	32 ± 6%	5.1 ± 1.2%	18 ± 11	0.23	2,127	23%
Baku, Azerbaijan	15 ± 2%	5.4 ± 1.1%	9 ± 5	0.27	1,468	35%
Bangkok, Thailand	19 ± 5%	5.3 ± 2.3%	9 ± 9	0.01	8,990	4%
Belgrade, Serbia	14 ± 2%	7.7 ± 3.4%	9 ± 8	0.17	1,279	37%
Berlin, Germany	18 ± 4%	8.1 ± 2.2%	6 ± 4	0.19	1,693	29%
Bishan, China	20 ± 4%	14.5 ± 4.2%	4 ± 6	0.29	1,397	54%
Bogotá, Colombia	20 ± 7%	8.5 ± 2.7%	28 ± 17	0.47	663	57%
Buenos Aires, Argentina	15 ± 2%	3.3 ± 0.9%	42 ± 10	0.09	4,387	11%
Cabimas, Venezuela	22 ± 4%	7.6 ± 2.7%	19 ± 9	0.02	1,568	27%
Caracas, Venezuela	19 ± 3%	8.1 ± 4.7%	3 ± 4	0.11	1,787	25%
Curitiba, Brazil	17 ± 2%	5.9 ± 2.5%	19 ± 11	0.07	2,811	16%
Haikou, China	21 ± 4%	3.6 ± 1.2%	16 ± 13	1.11	473	77%
Johannesburg, South Africa	18 ± 3%	7.5 ± 3.1%	17 ± 8	0.01	10,132	3%
Karachi, Pakistan	26 ± 5%	1.9 ± 0.8%	72 ± 34	1.25	409	80%
Kayseri, Turkey	27 ± 4%	4.2 ± 2.6%	48 ± 20	1.14	443	79%
Kolkata, India	8 ± 2%	8 ± 5%	3 ± 3	0.11	2,929	24%
Lagos, Nigeria	16 ± 2%	4.4 ± 0.9%	4 ± 3	0.15	1,954	26%
Luanda, Angola	15 ± 2%	2.4 ± 0.8%	44 ± 18	0.23	1,740	27%
Mexico City, Mexico	23 ± 3%	2.8 ± 0.6%	28 ± 11	0.02	11,546	3%
Montreal, Canada	17 ± 3%	6.6 ± 2%	6 ± 6	0.04	2,850	14%
Mumbai, India	26 ± 7%	5.7 ± 2.2%	12 ± 9	0.36	1,477	46%
Palmas, Brazil	35 ± 4%	3.1 ± 1.1%	44 ± 19	0.72	465	74%
Paris, France	15 ± 2%	7.4 ± 2.2%	6 ± 5	0.05	4,685	12%
Pingxiang, China	12 ± 3%	6.5 ± 2.6%	28 ± 27	0.17	1,261	51%
Riyadh, Saudi Arabia	33 ± 4%	6.0 ± 2.5%	4 ± 5	0.13	5,828	6%
Rovno, Ukraine	11 ± 2%	8.9 ± 2.3%	9 ± 9	0.26	879	48%
Shenzhen, China	25 ± 4%	3.9 ± 1.8%	16 ± 7	0.11	4,497	12%
Sialkot, Pakistan	16 ± 3%	4.7 ± 1.4%	17 ± 11	0.68	685	59%
Springfield, MA, United States	22 ± 4%	13 ± 4.5%	4 ± 6	0.00	4,759	3%
St. Petersburg, Russia	19 ± 3%	5.3 ± 1.5%	11 ± 10	0.19	2,929	25%
Tokyo, Japan	22 ± 4%	3.5 ± 0.8%	39 ± 14	0.29	1,021	42%
Valledupar, Colombia	26 ± 2%	2.3 ± 1.2%	92 ± 23	0.15	638	52%
Average	**20 ± 2%**	**6.0 ± 0.9%**	**21 ± 6**	**0.32 ± 0.11**	**2,553 ± 882**	**37 ± 8%**

2.1.9 Preliminary values for selected characteristics of urban layouts in a subset of thirty-eight cities from the global sample of two hundred cities, 2015

2.2
SPRAWL OF THE CENTURY
CONTEMPORARY CHINESE SUBURBIA

Thomas J. Campanella

GOVERNANCE & POLICY CHALLENGES

TRANSPORT INFRASTRUCTURE

2.2.1 Sales brochure rendering, Country Garden Estates, Guangdong Province, 1999

1 Kam Wing Chan, "China: Internal Migration," in *The Encyclopedia of Global Human Migration*, ed. Immanuel Ness (Oxford: Wiley-Blackwell, 2013).

2 See Leo Marx, *The Machine in the Garden: Technology and the Pastoral Ideal in America* (New York: Oxford University Press, 1964).

China is urbanizing faster than any nation on earth, and the lightspeed growth of its cities is one of the great epics of our time. Since the economic reforms of the late 1970s, China's urban population has increased by some 440 million people—nearly the combined population of the United States, Italy, and the United Kingdom.[1] The tremendous metropolitan growth surge is occurring simultaneously along two axes: cities rising rapidly upward at the core while sprawling outward on the edges at a pace and scale not seen since the wholesale suburbanization of the United States. But unlike the postwar American experience, suburban growth in China is hardly a function of urban decline and comes despite a strong preference for cities and urban life among both workers and elites. There is also little historical antipathy toward cities in China of the sort that rationalized suburbanization in the United States—that mythology of the pastoral "middle landscape," as the American studies scholar Leo Marx termed it, that has long asserted the moral superiority of *rus* over *urbe*.[2] Even Mao's proletarian revolution, which championed agrarian life and the rural peasantry, was organized in Shanghai and declared victory at the center of Beijing in 1949. Cities have always been the polestars of Chinese civilization. Suburbs there evolved out of necessity, not lifestyle choice or ideology. And where Americans created suburbs to get away from the city, the Chinese do so to get as close to the city as possible. (fig. **2.2.1**)

The drivers of Chinese sprawl are many and complex. Ironically, it was Maoist development policy during the Cultural Revolution that primed the pump. In the 1960s and early 1970s, China's major cities—especially coastal giants like Shanghai, Guangzhou, and Tianjin—were purposely undernourished in terms of population and development in order to limit their power. They were—and still are—administratively vast, with large areas of rural land technically within city limits. Shanghai overlaid on a map of the New York metropolitan area fills a great triangle from Lake Ronkonkoma on Long Island, west to Denville, New Jersey, and north to West Point. If you include Chongming Island at the mouth of the Yangtze River—also administratively part of the Shanghai municipality—the area would reach Poughkeepsie and extend as far east as Danbury, Connecticut.

But the physical footprint of the Maoist city, its actual built-up area, remained compressed and compact right up to the Deng Xiaoping reform era, with a sharp urban-rural boundary and—consequently—an abundance of rural land close to the center. Maoist cities also developed a unique spatial structure based on the *danwei* work-unit model. Rooted in Soviet planning practice and the paternalistic utopianism of the West (which created industrial new towns like Port Sunlight and Bourneville in the United Kingdom and Pullman in the United States), the danwei was a socialist live-work production machine designed to encourage social cohesion among workers. The model was applied to not only mills and factories but nearly every institution of modern Chinese life, including universities, hospitals, schools, research centers, and government bureaus and ministries. By the 1960s, some 90 percent of China's urban population belonged to a danwei. It became the basic unit of social and economic life in the People's Republic.

The typical danwei included both workplace and residential facilities, with buildings and spaces arranged campus-like within a walled compound. In terms of physical layout, the danwei compounds recalled traditional or "ancestral" Chinese spatial forms, especially that of the courtyard house, itself a distillation of classical Chinese urban design principles. As the sinologist David Bray has argued, familiar forms were thus called on "to secure the boundaries of new modes of social life."[3] Each danwei was a realm unto itself; collectively, these formed an urban fabric reminiscent of a patchwork quilt. But there was little communication between or across work units, nor much functional engagement with the larger city. The result was a uniquely cellular kind of urbanism, one that yielded "cities that

were collections of independent workplace-based communities, rather than integrated urban environments."[4] Because the danwei was designed to accommodate nearly all of a resident's needs in situ, it internalized a host of functions, services, and amenities previously scattered around the city. The traditional Chinese city was thus turned inside out, its teeming streets and lively markets now largely desolate. Indeed, the Mao-era metropolis was "planned on the assumption," writes the urban geographer Piper Gaubatz, "that most residents would rarely need to travel beyond their compounds."[5] The vast Soviet-style avenues laid out in Beijing and other cities in the 1950s came to life only during military parades and other state spectacles. The philosopher Walter Benjamin's *flâneur*, connoisseur of the churning, kaleidoscopic streets of Paris, would have found the Maoist city very dull indeed.

With the economic reforms of the 1980s, people in China's cities began moving around again like atoms in a heated flask. Many center-city enterprises and institutions were shut down or forced to the fringe by urban redevelopment. The danwei model was gradually abandoned, and state-supplied housing phased out in favor of direct subsidies to enable workers to purchase or rent housing on the open market. The demise of the danwei led to a growing spatial separation between workplace and residence. No longer could people just roll out of bed to their place of work; now many had to commute, and often long distances. The law of supply and demand quickly priced housing in the urban core beyond the reach of many families. Not surprisingly, the most affordable housing was erected on all the farmland within city limits that had been spared development during the Mao years. Improvement of this rural-urban land was itself newly possible due to changes in the structure of Chinese municipal

3   David Bray, *Social Space and Governance in Urban China: The* Danwei *System from Origins to Reform* (Stanford, CA: Stanford University Press, 2005), 94, 199–200.

4   David Bray, "Urban Design and Community Governance in China: A Study of Space and Power," in *Comment vivre ensemble*, ed. Paola Pellegrini and Paola Viganó (Venice: Universitá Iuav di Venezia, 2006), 83–84.

5   Piper R. Gaubatz, "Changing Beijing," *Geographical Review* 85, no. 1 (January 1995): 2.

governance. While all urban land in the People's Republic is held by the central government, responsibility for its management and administration, including the authority to sell or lease development rights, was decentralized in the reform era. Land Conversion, as it is known, soon became a lucrative—and much-abused—source of revenue wealth, yielding billions of yuan annually to local municipalities.

As dictated by the bid-rent curve, land-use rights on the urban fringe sold to developers for far less than in the sought-after city core. Farmers had to be compensated for their land, of course; but this was mere peanuts next to the immense cost of clearing a heavily built urban site, where there might be several thousand families to negotiate with and resettle. Farmers were "cheap" because compensation was pegged to the crop value of the land, not its value as real estate. Municipalities and their development partners literally had a field day, carpeting millions of acres of productive agricultural land with residential estates, shopping malls, and office parks. Additional cropland was sacrificed for ill-considered economic and technological development zones called *kaifa qu*. Designed to attract domestic and foreign direct investment, the zones were modeled on the successful Special Economic Zones of the early 1980s, and inspired by American precedents like the Stanford Industrial Park and Research Triangle Park. By 2003, there were some four thousand economic development zones on the outskirts of China's cities, spanning some 14,000 square miles (36,260 square kilometers) of land, more than New Jersey and Connecticut combined.[6] The siting of these zones was often arbitrary and extraneous to regional transport networks, thus contributing to a particularly egregious form of leapfrog sprawl. Creating the zones led to the eviction of many thousands of peasants, prompting

parallels between Chinese "zone fever" and the land enclosure movement that transformed rural England before the Industrial Revolution. Like the jungle runways built by South Pacific "cargo-cult" devotees to lure bounty from the heavens (having witnessed cargo-laden transport planes land on just such fields during World War II), many of the development zones failed to attract any investment at all.

There is a homey popular expression in China, *tan da bing*, that likens sprawl to a cook pouring pancake batter on a hot skillet. To truly appreciate these mighty pancakes, however, requires a truly elevated vantage point. It was long claimed (erroneously) that the Great Wall of China was the only humanmade object visible from space; today it is Chinese metropolitan expansion that dazzles orbiting eyes. Over the last thirty years, Landsat and other remote-sensing satellites have been quietly documenting the surging tide of Chinese metropolitan expansion. Satellite data have revealed that China's collective urban footprint—the actual built extent of its cities within their administrative districts—grew by some 3,177 square miles (8,228 square kilometers) in the 1990s alone, an increase ten times the land area of New York City.[7] The geographer Karen C. Seto's Landsat studies of the Pearl River Delta revealed a 364 percent increase in urbanized land there between 1988 and 1996.[8] An equally compelling snapshot of Chinese sprawl was compiled using night imagery from the Defense Department Meteorological Satellite Program (DMSP). Its satellites circle the globe closely in a sun-synchronous, low-altitude orbit, detecting cloud luminescence as well as artificial light from the earth's surface. Using DMSP radiance data captured in 1996, the University of Georgia geographer C. P. Lo created three-dimensional "illuminated urban area domes" of China's metropolitan areas. Though the brightest

6   F. Frederic Deng and Youqin Huang, "Uneven Land Reform and Urban Sprawl: The Case of Beijing," *Progress in Planning* 61 (2004): 214–19, 227.

7   Jiyuan Liu et al., "China's Changing Landscape during the 1990s: Large-Scale Land Transformations Estimated with Satellite Data," *Geophysical Research Letters* 32 (January 2005): 1–5.

8   See Karen C. Seto et al., "Monitoring Land-Use Change in the Pearl River Delta Using Landsat TM," *International Journal of Remote Sensing* 23, no. 10 (2002): 2001–2.

9   Chor Pang Lo, "Urban
     Indicators of China from
     Radiance-Calibrated
     Digital DMSP-OLS
     Nighttime Images,"
     *Annals of the Association
     of American Geographers*
     92, no. 2 (2002): 225–40.

2.2.2 The great pancake spreads to the setting sun; high-density sprawl on the outskirts of Beijing, 2014

jewels were the cores of major cities, the data also revealed extensive sprawl around Beijing, Tianjin, and Shanghai, and throughout the Pearl River Delta.[9] (fig. **2.2.2**)

Americans were the pioneers of modern sprawl, and so it's tempting to read manifestations in other lands as a form of mimicry or emulation. But suburbanization in China differs in profound ways from the North American variety. In the United States, suburbanization began in earnest after World War II, when a booming economy, plentiful jobs, federally subsidized mortgages, and an expanding highway infrastructure put the American Dream of homeownership within the reach of millions. Between the war's end and 1960, millions of middle- and working-class Americans left the aging cities of the rustbelt for the suburbs. American suburban communities in the postwar period were surprisingly affordable, mass-produced by pioneers like the Levitt brothers. They were low in density, served by an extensive automobile infrastructure and typically segregated along ethnic and racial lines. They were also autonomous

political entities, fiscally independent of the cities they orbited. They could tax themselves to pay for a level of municipal service and infrastructure that yielded a higher quality of life for residents than most cities could offer at the time—better schools, better-staffed agencies, better-equipped police and fire departments. Suburbs in the United States thus evolved in antithesis and opposition to the city, especially in the postwar era, when many Americans rejected outright cities and urban life. As noted earlier, doing so was leavened by a long tradition of antiurbanism in US culture. In its archetypal form, the space of the American dream was not the city but that gentle pastoral realm just beyond city limits. It was a contagious ideology; many immigrants, even those from Old World urban cultures, also yearned for the suburbs (Italians and Jews in New York proved to be enthusiastic suburbanites, as have many more recent immigrants from Korea, India, and China). But there were also real and compelling reasons for the "white flight" of the 1960s. American cities at the time were increasingly bedeviled by an array of seemingly intractable problems. Crime and vandalism were out of control, and racial tensions soared despite the many gains of the civil rights movement. Maintenance on key infrastructure was deferred, while ill-considered urban renewal and highway projects destroyed entire communities.

Except for times of war, there has been no comparable era of urban decline in China, nor any deep-rooted philosophy of antiurbanism to stoke it. The city has never been stigmatized in China the way it was for much of American history. Moreover, because suburban development occurs well within the vast administrative limits of Chinese cities, suburbs there are really just far outlying urban neighborhoods. *Suburban* development in China is technically still *urban* development, for city and suburb are one, part and parcel of a single administrative unit. This is the most critical difference between China and the United States in terms of suburbanization. In the United States, suburban coffers swelled with the tax dollars of urban refugees. City businesses followed the money out of town, abandoning downtown for the suburban mall. Suburbs in postwar America grew at the city's expense. Not so in China. As the geographers Yixing Zhou and Laurence J. C. Ma point out, "No such devastating impact on the central city's tax revenues has resulted from suburbanization in China because suburbanization has taken place entirely within areas that are under the administrative jurisdiction of the cities themselves." Indeed, Chinese suburbanization "has occurred while the city center is undergoing dramatic positive spatial and economic transformations…Instead of urban environmental decline, social conflict, and the shift of fiscal resources to the suburbs that American cities have experienced, cities and suburbs in China have been flourishing at the same time."[10]

Nonetheless, Chinese suburban districts are far from the center of things.

Amenities are few, and services—especially public transit infrastructure—are poor in quality or nonexistent. Suburban housing estates are advertised and understood as oases of order, tranquility, and privilege in the churning transitional space between city and countryside. Ironically, they are just as isolated from their surroundings—and from each other—as the old danwei compounds. While not formally affiliated with a workplace, housing estates are just as inwardly focused as the danwei, guarded by a formidable perimeter fence or wall with gated entrances staffed around the clock. Within, a wide range of on-site amenities and services are provided—fitness centers, spas, banquet halls, playgrounds, computer rooms, karaoke parlors, billiard rooms, pools, tennis courts, and so forth—all "under the control of a professional property management company." The typical Chinese suburban residential estate is a full-function, privatized realm where money not only "buys a bigger apartment in a better-serviced compound," writes David Bray, but "peace of mind and a greater sense of security."[11] This is very different from the typical American suburban development, which is little more than a collection of private homes on a public street. Except for the occasional high-end gated community (which might have a community center or common pool or playground), all such services, amenities, and attractions are found in the larger community beyond the subdivision. (fig. **2.2.3**)

If American suburban homebuyers study community quality-of-life benchmarks like school quality, crime rate, or proximity to parks, and houses of worship, their Chinese peers focus instead on the residential estate itself. Services and amenities nearby—ready access to the regional highway network, shopping malls in the vicinity—certainly add appeal. But what really sells places is the quality and

10 Yixing Zhou and Laurence J. C. Ma, "Economic Restructuring and Suburbanization in China," *Urban Geography* 21, no. 3 (2000): 226.

11 Bray, "Urban Design and Community Governance in China," 88–89.

12 Ian Buruma, "Asia World," *New York Review of Books*, June 12, 2003, 55.

2.2.3 Gated housing estate, suburban Jiangsu Province, 2006

range of services provided by the property management company on-site and within the gates. This makes marketing suburban residential property in China as much about selling lifestyle as a roof, floor, and walls. Developers have been very creative in crafting appealing identities for projects, or at least in copying ideas and motifs from elsewhere. Driven by fierce competition, they have scoured the globe for memorable place-themes and imagery that could be used to put an alluring spin on a project, drawing literally from a global grab bag of markers that convey status prestige and "arrival" to potential buyers. Such plays of fantasy and illusion also serve another end— they help distance homebuyers from a too-real present, from a metropolitan landscape in a constant state of creative destruction. Enter the suburban gates and you are in Cambridge, Tuscany, or the foothills of Southern California, far from the rush and tumult of history's greatest building boom. As the journalist Ian Buruma has written, "Every theme park is a controlled utopia, a miniature world where everything can be made to look perfect."[12] Themed residential estates offer kindred residents a respite from reality; a chance to control and shape their imagined place in a changeful world. (figs. **2.2.4–5**)

So too do the many shopping malls on the urban fringe. The behemoth South China Mall was built in 2001 on a former sugarcane and banana plantation in suburban Dongguan. Its developer, the foodstuffs billionaire Hu Guirong, described it as China's "First Super-Mega Themed Shopping Park." A global smorgasbord of place-culture selections, the mall was anchored by a half-scale Arc de Triomphe and looped by a mile-long canal plied by Venetian gondolas. There was a "Caribbean District" complete with salsa club; an "Amsterdam" full of colorful Dutch canal houses; and an Egyptian plaza guarded by sphinxes. South China Mall so overshot its market that it still sits largely vacant, just off the busy Guangzhou-Shenzhen Expressway (itself modeled on the New Jersey Turnpike). It was briefly the world's largest mall, but the crown moved west in 2013 to another half-empty colossus: New Century

2.2.4 Billboard advertisement for luxury villa development, Nanjing, 2006

2.2.5 Billboard advertisement for neo-Mediterranean Ai Hua Zhe Villas, Nanjing, 2006

2.2.6 Sales office model, Vanke Fifth Garden Villas, Shenzhen, 2007

13 J. Matthew Roney, "Bicycles Pedaling into the Spotlight," *Earth Policy Institute*, May 12, 2008, accessed September 19, 2015, http://www.earth -policy.org/index.php ?/indicators/C48/.

14 Philip P. Pan, "Bicycle No Longer King of the Road in China," *Washington Post*, March 12, 2001.

Global Centre in the suburbs south of Chengdu, by the city's fourth ring road. With more than 18 million square feet (1,672,250 square meters) of floor space, it is the largest building ever constructed, so capacious that three Pentagons could fit under its roof. Inside, shoppers can visit a Mediterranean town or bask in an artificial sun on an ersatz beach, complete with lapping waves and a LED-panel "horizon" the size of an American football field. Across the way, a complementary project, Zaha Hadid's 500,000-square-foot (46,450-square-meter) Chengdu Contemporary Arts Center, is still under construction.

Just as China's suburban shopping malls dwarf those in America, the density of the typical Chinese suburban residential development is far greater than anything found in the United States. While large-lot, single-family, McMansion-style complexes (*bie shu qü*) certainly exist in the People's Republic, they are relatively uncommon and very expensive. Far more numerous are gated residential estates composed of ganged mid- to high-rise apartment buildings, called *zhu zhai xiao*

qü. Regardless of their density, however, Chinese suburbs are nearly as dependent on the automobile as those in the United States. China is in the middle of a titanic motoring revolution, where rising incomes and an aggressive national highway-building campaign have minted millions of new motorists. It is easily the fastest-growing automobile market in the world, with more Buicks now than the United States. It is China—not Dallas or Los Angeles—that boasts the world's biggest automobile showrooms. Bicycles may still be the vehicles of choice for millions of city folk, but they are increasingly shunted aside in favor of cars. Nationwide, the number of bicycles dropped by 235 million between 1995 and 2005 (a 35 percent decrease), while automobile ownership doubled in the same period.[13] Even as the bicycle becomes a symbol of sustainability and fitness in the West, it is increasingly considered a relic of poverty in China. As one Beijing cabbie put it, "What kind of country would we be if we were all still riding bicycles?"[14] There are hopeful signs, however, that this attitude is changing—especially among the young.

The world's largest bike share systems today are not in London, Copenhagen, or New York, but in Wuhan and Hangzhou.[15] (figs. **2.2.6**–**7**)

For Chinese suburbanites with limited public transit options, too far from their workplaces to bike, a car is a great convenience indeed. A 2005 post-occupancy survey of one of the Vanke company's popular housing estates in suburban Shanghai, Holiday Town, revealed that nearly 70 percent of responding households owned a car, with 100 percent of adult residents under age sixty reporting in the affirmative.[16] They not only drive to work—the Vanke interviewees reported a commute length of forty-nine to sixty minutes—but they also drive their children to school and shop at suburban supermarkets and big-box stores with plentiful parking. (fig. **2.2.8**)

To an even greater degree than in the United States, car ownership in China fundamentally alters one's relationship to the city. For example, Chinese suburban dwellers will often avoid the city center because of traffic congestion and the scarcity of parking. Of course, many suburban Americans avoid downtown for the same reasons, but American cities have grown with the automobile for decades now and are much more accommodating of motorists. Chinese cities, on the other hand, have only recently been inundated with cars and are terribly ill equipped to handle their soaring numbers. You quite literally bump into this everywhere in town, for motorists often park right on the sidewalk, creating a hazard and inconvenience for pedestrians. Such incursions are tolerated—for now, at least—because there remains a strong element of class entitlement and privilege associated with automobile ownership in China. (fig. **2.2.9**)

More so than even the suburban landscapes it has authored, motoring in the People's Republic has a very strong

2.2.7 Perspective rendering, Renshan Zhishui Estate, Shenzhen, a typical residential complex incorporating a range of housing types—from single-family homes to mid-rise towers. Courtesy Chengjian Development Company.

American pedigree. Detroit started swooning over the potential of the Chinese market more than a century ago. Americans stole the show at China's first automobile exhibition in Shanghai in 1921 and soon had a 95 percent grip on the north China motor vehicle market.[17] By the 1930s, American-made vehicles were outselling British models by a factor of ten, despite a major British advantage: the English custom of driving on the left side of the road had been introduced in China via the treaty ports, forcing Americans to make costly retrofits to the steering systems on their models.

Sun Yat-sen, the founding father of modern China, considered the development of a domestic automobile industry crucial to the growth of the Republic. In 1924 he wrote to Henry Ford, commending the Michigan industrialist on his "remarkable work" putting Americans on the road. "I think you can do similar work in China," wrote Sun, "on a much vaster and more significant scale."[18] Indeed, Ford was well aware of China's colossal motoring potential. That year he hosted a visit by China's trade commissioner, Chang Chien Jr., who gave a speech—in Chinese—to a large group of Chinese service trainees then in residence at Ford's Highland Park plant. Chien foresaw an extraordinary future for the motor car in China: "More than 100,000,000 automobiles, or five times the present world total," he pointed

15 Sherley Wetherhold, "The Bicycle as Symbol of China's Transformation," *Atlantic*, June 30, 2012.

16 Tunney F. Lee and Liang Zhao, eds., *Vanke Vision: Sustainable Residential Development in Shanghai Urban Planning and Design Handbook*, vol. 1, Research Seminar and Field Survey (Cambridge, MA: MIT Department of Urban Studies and Planning, February 2006), 127.

17 William I. Irvine, *Automotive Markets in China, British Malaya, and Chosen*, Department of Commerce, Bureau of Foreign and Domestic Commerce Special Agents Series, no. 221 (Washington, DC: Government Printing Office, 1923), 32.

18 Mira Wilkins and Frank Ernest Hill, *American Business Abroad: Ford on Six Continents* (Detroit: Wayne State University Press, 1964), 149–50.

2.2.8 B&Q home improvement superstore, Nanjing, 2006

2.2.9 Parking anarchy, Xi'an, 2013

2.2.10 "Motordom" section in bookstore, Nanjing, 2006

19 "Chinese Ready for Autos Says Commission Head," *Ford News* 3, no. 16 (March 22, 1924).

20 Hewlett Johnson, "The Civilizing Road," *Times of London*, July 26, 1932, reprinted in Oliver J. Todd, *Two Decades in China* (Peking: Association of Chinese and American Engineers, 1938), 263.

21 Jonathan Spence, *To Change China: Western Advisors in China, 1620–1960* (Boston: Little, Brown, 1969), 210–12.

22 Oliver J. Todd, "Motor Roads for South China," *Oriental Engineer* (May 1927), 223–28.

out, "would be required to provide China's 400,000,000 people with the same ratio of cars as Iowa."[19] Yankee automakers were as creative as they were aggressive in marketing their wares. Salesmen drove cars up the ramps of Beijing's city walls and sent motor convoys to China's most remote corners. Even in ancient Xi'an, American auto dealers were "straining every nerve to gain a footing," reported an English visitor, who later crossed paths with an "expedition of adventurous young men" drumming up sales for the Dodge Motor Company on the Tibetan plateau.[20] (fig. **2.2.10**)

Americans were also at the forefront of the Good Roads movement in China. Industry analysts well understood that the key to conquering China's nascent motoring market was a network of modern roads. But there were also altruistic reasons why the United States helped China build its first highways. Good roads were seen as agents of political and economic reform, opening remote rural areas to trade and better governance. Along such roads, "trucks would roar," writes Jonathan Spence, "carrying grain and rice to stricken areas, while the private cars of officials and merchants would speed by with the promises of fairer administration and wider trade."[21] Indeed, China's first modern highways were built by engineers of the American Red Cross to bring food and supplies to famine-stricken Shandong, Henan, Hebei, and Shanxi provinces in the 1920s. The Red Cross constructed nearly 1,000 miles (1,610 kilometers) of simple, tamped-earth motor roads, the first strands of China's vast modern highway grid. Appropriately enough, it was a Michigan engineer named Oliver J. Todd who led this campaign. Todd helped build Hetch Hetchy Dam and San Francisco's Twin Peaks Tunnel before moving to China. He spent nearly twenty years there, directing the construction of some 3,000 miles (4,800 kilometers) of highways in fourteen provinces, including China's first urban ring road, an eight-mile loop around Guiyang.[22] The new motorways were cheered by the Good Roads Association of China, which also argued that old walls around cities "be demolished to construct loop highways."

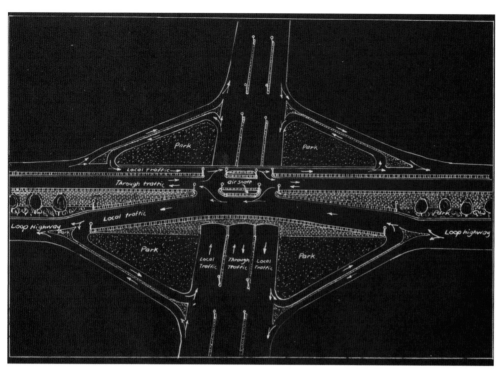

23 J. Morgan Clements,
*China: Automotive
Conditions and the Good
Roads Movement*, Trade
Information Bulletin,
no. 2, Automotive
Division (Washington,
DC: Department of
Commerce, 1922), 3–19.

2.2.11 City wall as highway infrastructure

Ironically, the idea was implemented by Mao in Beijing in the late 1950s, where the six-hundred-year old defensive ramparts were torn down for the first of many ring roads.[23] (fig. **2.2.11**)

That all traffic flows to the right in China today is itself an American legacy. In 1944 President Franklin D. Roosevelt appointed Albert C. Wedemeyer to replace General Joseph Stilwell as commander of the United States Army in China. Wedemeyer and Chiang Kai-shek planned an offensive code-named "Carbonado" to liberate Hong Kong and the south China coast from Japanese hands. The vast campaign required airlifting two divisions of American-trained Chinese troops from Burma. Men and material had to be moved 700 miles (1,130 kilometers) south from Sichuan Province to the Pearl River Delta, in a convoy made up largely of American vehicles. But because traffic in China at the time followed the British model, these vehicles were effectively being driven on the "wrong" side of the road; scores of accidents ensued, many fatal. Wedemeyer's solution was to shift all traffic in China to the right side of the road, just like in the United States. Chiang Kai-shek concurred. A publicity campaign was launched in early 1945, "showing diagrammatically how traffic would move and giving instructions to pedestrians in order to minimize accidents." Articles in the local press, scornful of the idea and urging the Generalissimo "to reconsider and uphold the old and the tried method of moving traffic," were promptly traced to the British embassy, which suspected—with good reason—that Wedemeyer was acting on behalf of Detroit, surreptitiously paving the way for a postwar invasion of American cars. The new law went ahead regardless—and despite the Japanese surrender. In Shanghai on New Year's Eve, 1945, Wedemeyer saw—in an extraordinary display of American power—his traffic order implemented. Stealing away for a moment from the New Year's revelry, he went up to the hotel roof and peered down at the Bund below to see "the traffic at midnight change over to move along the right side of the road." When Mao and the Communists took control of China four years later, they kept the American pattern.[24]

In the United States today, suburban sprawl is increasingly recognized as a major cause of environmental degradation and fossil fuel dependence. Popular books like Jeff Speck's *Walkable City* and Vishaan Chakrabarti's *A Country of Cities* make compelling new cases against sprawl and for the necessity of living in compact, walkable, pedestrian-friendly communities.[25] At the same time, a great rediscovery of urban life is underway across America; cities are once again the polestars of dreams. Older city centers are being revalorized as elites at both ends of the life spectrum flock there— creative-class millennials seeking local grit and cultural authenticity to counter globalized mass culture; aging Boomers seeking amenity-rich communities in which to retire and age in place. The very slums abandoned by the middle class a generation ago are now coveted places to live. Strong demand for walkable urbanism, a scarce commodity in our sprawled-out nation, will continue to drive property values through the roof in places like Brooklyn, Durham, Pittsburgh, and San Francisco, and eventually extend to cities and neighborhoods currently off the radar of urban chic. The poor will be forced outward to declining first-ring suburbs, turning on its head the century-old pattern of suburban affluence and inner-city blight. Ferguson, Missouri, may well be the new South Bronx.

In China, there is yet relatively little appreciation of the environmental and social hazards of sprawl. Only recently has the central government begun to take action to reverse the horrific air pollution that bedevils most of its major cities today, much of it caused by motor vehicles. But China is so vast in scale and scope that it seems to be doing all things wrong and all things right in equal measure. Even as China wraps its cities in asphalt and opens another coal-fired power plant every month, it has created transit infrastructure that is the envy of the world. China has built more miles of both light and heavy rail—above ground and below—than all other nations combined.

What will the future bring for China's vast suburban supernovas? The nation's vast urbanization epic is hardly over yet. An estimated 250 million more rural dwellers will move to cities in coming years, and accommodating such huge numbers may well require infilling much of the sprawled urban borderlands. Add to this China's breathtaking ability to build infrastructure, and it seems almost certain that today's distant outlying metropolitan districts will eventually be drawn into the urban fold, served by rail and bus, and no longer largely dependent on the automobile. Suburbia in China, already more dense than most American cities, may well be just a station-stop on the way to a hyperurban future.

This essay draws substantially from Thomas J. Campanella, The Concrete Dragon: China's Urban Revolution and What It Means for the World *(New York: Princeton Architectural Press, 2008).*

24 Albert C. Wedemeyer, *Wedemeyer Reports!* (New York: Henry Holt, 1958), 221, 328–56.

25 Jeff Speck, *Walkable City: How Downtown Can Save America, One Step at a Time* (New York: Farrar, Straus and Giroux, 2012); Vishaan Chakrabarti, *A Country of Cities: A Manifesto for an Urban America* (New York: Metropolis Books, 2013).

Pudong, Shanghai, China

2.3 MEASURING URBAN CORES AND SUBURBS IN THE UNITED STATES

Wendell Cox

POLYCENTRIC
EXPANSION

SOCIAL
DIVERSITY

TRANSPORT
MODES

Since World War II, many core municipalities have experienced substantial suburban expansion within their borders. Los Angeles, Milwaukee, Portland, and Denver are just a few examples. In some cases, new suburban areas were annexed, while in others, such as Los Angeles, there was ample agricultural land within the city limits for broad, postwar suburban greenfield expansion. Other core municipalities that were largely developed after World War II, such as Phoenix and San Jose, are virtually all low-density and automobile-oriented suburbs. All of these places contrast with the higher densities and more transit-oriented development typical of core municipalities such as New York and Boston, which were largely developed before World War II.

Many analysts have treated "core municipalities "as if they were the same thing as urban cores, with suburbs being the rest of the metropolitan area. That was a rough approximation of reality before World War II. However, since that time, thousands of suburban municipalities have been established, virtually all of which are low-density and automobile-oriented. Some core municipalities have annexed suburban areas; others have not. In short, urban versus suburban analysis based on municipal jurisdictions produces only the crudest results. There is a need for more fine-grained analysis based on function, whether urban core or suburban.[1]

The need is made more pressing by the currently influential strain of urban theory that seeks to restore urban forms and travel behavior to prewar—or resembling prewar—conditions.[2] At its most extreme, there is an interest in reconfiguring even the built form of present neighborhoods. Data that exaggerate the extent of the urban core, which is inevitable in conventional analysis, could lead to underestimating the complexity of such an endeavor.

Homeowners and Automobile Owners

The United States experienced a sea change in urban form and travel patterns after World War II. The suburbs came to dominate urban growth, and automobile ownership rose substantially. This was an acceleration of trends that began in the nineteenth century and intensified in the first three decades of the twentieth century as the automobile became available.[3] Between 1900 and 1930, automobile ownership rose from virtually zero to approximately 0.79 per household. Continuation of this trend was postponed for a decade and a half by the Great Depression and World War II. In 1945 automobiles had declined to 0.68 per household.[4]

However, things changed radically as soon as the war ended. The next five years were transformational, as automobile ownership increased at a 6 percent rate annually, reaching 0.93 by 1950. By 2013, the number of light vehicles (cars, light trucks, and sport utility vehicles) per household had reached 2.00.[5] The automobile now accounts for 98 percent of passenger transport within US cities (metropolitan areas or urban areas).[6]

At the same time, urbanization expanded substantially. Since 1940, 95 percent of the population growth has occurred in metropolitan areas, rather than nonmetropolitan areas, and has been mostly in suburbs.[7] Homeownership rose from 41 percent in 1940 to 65 percent in 1970. It has largely remained at this point, except for during the peak real estate bubble years between 2000 and 2010. Since the war, most owner-occupied housing has consisted of detached homes in suburban settings with larger yards. As a result, the average population density of urban areas has decreased. Between 1950 and 2010, the total population density of the largest urban areas within major metropolitan areas declined at least 48 percent.[8]

1 The term *functional urban core* is used to distinguish from the term *urban core*, which often refers to a municipal jurisdiction. Many urban core jurisdictions are not all functionally urban core, and some have no functional urban core as defined in the model.

2 Labeled variously, such as urban containment, compact city policy, smart growth, growth management, etc.

3 See, for e.g., Kenneth T. Jackson, "Urban Deconcentration in the Nineteenth Century: A Statistical Inquiry," in *The New Urban History: Quantitative Explorations by American Historians*, ed. Leo F. Schnore (Princeton, NJ: Princeton University Press, 1975); Dana Ferric Weber, *The Growth of Cities in the Nineteenth Century: A Study in Statistics* (New York: Macmillan, 1899).

4 Data from US Census Bureau, "Historical Statistics of the United States: Colonial Times to 1970" (Washington, DC: US Department of Commerce, 1975).

5 Calculated from the "2013 American Community Survey," US Census Bureau, accessed December 15, 2015, https://www.census.gov/programs-surveys/acs/; and "Highway Statistics 2013," US Department of Transportation, accessed December 15, 2015, https://www.fhwa.dot.gov/policyinformation/statistics/2013/.

6 Cities as referred to in this essay are either urban areas (areas of continuous urban development, as generally defined by the US Census Bureau, also called the physical city) or metropolitan areas (urban areas with peripheral commuting sheds, also called the functional city). This is to be contrasted with cities as municipalities or local authority areas, which in the United States and Canada (and most of the world) are subcomponents of urban areas or metropolitan

Virtually all population growth in major US metropolitan areas (defined as those with a population of one million or higher) has been suburban or exurban since before World War II. Nearly all of the core municipalities that have not been annexed and which were largely developed by 1940 have lost population (these municipalities are referred to as "constant border municipalities").[9] Further, among all other core municipalities, virtually all of the population growth has occurred in annexed areas or greenfield areas that were undeveloped in 1940. These expansions have been more suburban than urban core in nature or function.

Conventional Analysis

Analyses that contrast prewar US urban form with postwar automobile-oriented suburbs have been hampered by the lack of conveniently available data. Typically, to denote the urban core, data for core municipality (or for *central city*, an Office of Management and Budget long-time term) have been used. The remainder of |the metropolitan area has been considered suburban (although some of it may be considered exurban).[10] Core municipalities usually contain the entire historic center, characterized by areas of high-density housing (usually multi-unit buildings) and high percentages of transit use. Alternatively, suburbs tend to be dominated by automobile travel, and much of the housing is detached.

Yet this jurisdictional bifurcation is not a reliable way to differentiate the suburbs from the urban core. While core municipalities vary considerably in their urban form and travel patterns, most contain large areas that have the suburban characteristics of low-density detached housing and high automobile use. In fact, the majority of core municipality residents can be classified as living in suburban areas, rather than in urban cores. There are also a few cases of high-density urban cores that stretch across the boundaries of core municipalities into jurisdictional suburbs: New York, into southern Westchester County and into Hudson and Essex counties in New Jersey; Boston into its inner suburbs, such as Cambridge, Somerville, and Brookline; and Washington, DC, into Arlington and Alexandria Counties in Virginia and into Montgomery County, Maryland. And there are other instances of urban core characteristics outside the centers of metropolitan areas, such as Gary, Indiana (outside Chicago), Fall River (Providence), and Tacoma (Seattle). These are not suburban expansions of urban areas but smaller urban cores that have been engulfed by larger urban areas.

Principal Cities

Analysis has become further complicated since the Office of Management and Budget (OMB), which defines US metropolitan area criteria, has replaced the term *central city* with *principal city*. OMB sought to acknowledge that metropolitan areas were no longer monocentric but had become polycentric.[11] The polycentrism had become evident in employment centers, as large suburban employment districts had proliferated around metropolitan areas (termed *edge cities* in Joel Garreau's book of the same name).[12] Virtually without exception, these new centers have been much lower in employment density than the historic downtown areas (central business districts, or CBDs).

Yet in some popular usage (even sometimes by federal agencies such as the Census Bureau, the Department of Education, and the Federal Bureau of Investigation), any area that is not a principal city is considered to be suburban.[13] The result of this usage is that postwar suburban municipalities such as Arlington (in the Dallas–Fort Worth metropolitan area), Mesa (in Phoenix),

areas; Wendell Cox, "US Urban Personal Vehicle & Public Transport Market Share from 1900," in *United States Urban Transport Statistics: A Compendium*, Demographia report, December 2008, accessed November 6, 2015, http://www.publicpurpose.com/ut-usptshare45.pdf.

7 Derived from US Census Bureau data. Urban and rural definitions have changed over the period. This estimate combines the 1940 to 1950 change under the previous definition with the 1950 to 2010 change under the current definition. A simple subtraction of the 1940 data from 2010 yields a 99 percent urban growth figure, though it does not account for the change in urban definition.

8 The actual decline was greater because of a significant change in the "building blocks" of urban areas. In 1950 the smallest building block was the municipality. In 2010 the smallest building block was the census block. In both cases, population densities were the principal criteria. As a result, in 1950 municipalities with large rural areas (such as the city of Los Angeles) were completely included in urban areas, forcing densities down. Census blocks have little or no rural area, making them more reflective of built-up urbanization. The Census Bureau estimated that the change in criteria (made for the 2000 census) increased urban densities at that time by about 7 percent. The percentage increase from 1950 would have been greater, because much of the rural area within municipal boundaries had become urban. See Wendell Cox, "Urban Areas in the United States: 1950 to 2010 Principal Urban Areas in Metropolitan Areas over 1,000,000 Population in 2010," *Demographia*, March 31, 2012, accessed November 6, 2015, http://

CITY SECTOR & Relationship to City	Criteria 1	Criteria 2
Pre-WW2 Urban Core (URBAN CORE) (in physical and functional city)	In principal urban area (AND) Population density > 7,499 density per square mile (AND) Transit, Walk & Bike Share > 19.9%	(OR) In pr. Urban area (&) Median year house Built before 1946
Post-WW2 Suburban: Earlier (EARLIER SUBURB) (in physical and functional city)	Not Urban Core (AND) Not EXURB (AND) Median year house built before 1980	
Post-WW2 Suburban: Later (LATER SUBURB) (in physical and functional city)	Not URBAN CORE (AND) Not EXURB (AND) Median year house built 1980 & Later	
Exurban (EXURB) (Not in physical city, in functional city)	Outside 2010 principal urban area	(OR) Under 250 density per square mile

2.3.1 City-sector model criteria. The city sector model classifies zip codes by urban characteristics rather than jurisdictions.

Hillsboro (in Portland, Oregon), and Irvine (in Los Angeles) are classified as nonsuburban. Their average population density, at 3,200 people per square mile (about 1,200 per square kilometer), is well below the average density of the fifty-four core municipalities, even with the large share of functional suburban population in those cores.[14]

The City Sector Model

A more ideal and accurate method of analysis would be based on function, specifically urban form and household behavior, both of which vary substantially between the urban core and the suburbs. Due to the pitfalls of jurisdiction-based analysis, we have developed what we labeled the city sector model, which uses neighborhood-scale analysis (zip code tabulation areas) to classify segments of metropolitan areas by the way that they function at a smaller scale.[15]

The city sector model is similar in approach to previous research on Canadian metropolitan areas by the urban planning professor David Gordon and colleagues at Queens University, Canada.[16] In a recent analysis, Gordon and the urban planner Isaac Shirokoff found that Canada's largest metropolitan areas are more than 80 percent suburban.[17]

Gordon's method of categorizing small areas by urban core versus suburban indicators can also be applied in the United States to avoid the problems of jurisdictional analysis. We used this approach to develop the city sector model, which provides a small-grained approach to classifying today's urban form. Development of the small area analysis in the city sector model has been made feasible with the greater availability of the necessary data. This has encouraged others to perform similar analyses using the smaller areas.[18]

The criteria used in the city sector model for the United States were similar, but differed from those used by Gordon. We defined four city sectors that categorize neighborhoods by age of development and density: (1) Pre–World War II Urban Core, (2) Post–World War II Earlier Suburbs (generally inner suburbs), (3) Post–World War II Later Suburbs (generally outer suburbs), and (4) Exurbs (generally outside the urban areas). (fig. **2.3.1**) The city sector model classifies each of the neighborhoods (zip code tabulation areas) in all of the fifty-two major metropolitan areas of the United States.

The urban core includes any zip code tabulation area in the principal urban areas within metropolitan areas that has a 2010 population density of at least

www.demographia.com/db-uza2000.htm.

9 For the purposes of this essay, there are fifty-four core municipalities, which are defined as the largest municipalities in the fifty-two major metropolitan areas (more than one million in population in 2013), with the following exceptions. Norfolk is the core municipality of Virginia Beach (suburban Virginia Beach has become the largest city in the metropolitan area). In addition, Oakland, in the San Francisco metropolitan area, and St. Paul, in the Minneapolis–St. Paul metropolitan area, are also core municipalities. See Wendell Cox, "Major Metropolitan Area and Core Municipality Population: 1950 and 2010 (Metropolitan Areas over 1,000,000 in 2013)," Demographia, accessed January 10, 2015, http://www.demographia.com/db-19502010mmsa.pdf.

10 The Office of Management and Budget (OMB) defines metropolitan area criteria in the United States. As used in this essay, *exurban* means generally outside the continuously built-up urban area.

11 Office of Management and Budget of the United States, "Final Report and Recommendations from the Metropolitan Area Standards Review Committee to the Office of Management and Budget Concerning Changes to the Standards for Defining Metropolitan Areas," *Federal Register*, 2000.

12 Joel Garreau, *Edge City: Life on the New Frontier* (New York: Doubleday, 1991).

13 Wendell Cox, "Urban Cores, Core Cities and Principal Cities," *New Geography*, accessed January 9, 2015, http://www.newgeography.com/content/004453-urban-cores-core-cities-and-principal-cities.

14 Historical core municipalities, which include the largest municipalities in fifty-one

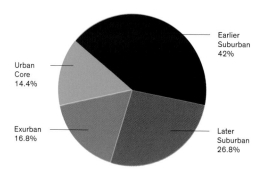

2.3.2 Population in 2010: City sectors major metropolitan areas. More than 85 percent of major metropolitan area population is in lower-density automobile-oriented neighborhoods.

7,500 people per square mile (about 2,900 people per square kilometer), and when at least 20 percent of travel by mass transit, walking, and cycling is devoted to work commutes.[19] In addition, any neighborhood in the principal urban area with a median house construction date before 1946 is included in the urban core.[20]

Exurban areas include small areas outside the principal urban area and small areas with a population density under 250 per square mile (about one hundred people per square kilometer). Suburban areas make up the rest of the metropolitan area (outside the urban core and exurbs) and are divided into earlier suburbs, which have a median house construction age before 1980, and later suburbs, aged 1980 or later.

These city sectors, representing all zip code tabulation areas, in all fifty-two major metropolitan areas reflect the lower density, automobile-oriented suburbanization that occurred after World War II. While urban core population densities average 11,000 per square mile (about 4,200 per square kilometer), earlier suburban density is a much lower 2,500 per square mile (about 1,000 per square kilometer), and later suburban density is even lower, at 1,300 per square mile (about 500 per square kilometer). A similar contrast is evident in travel patterns. The combination of mass transit, walking, and bicycling make up 44.9 percent of trips in the urban core, much higher than the 8.7 percent in the earlier suburbs and the 3.9 percent in the later suburbs.

Population Trends in Twenty-First-Century Cities
The results that follow are for the fifty-two major metropolitan areas and are all based on the City Sector model. The results show that urban cores—the densest, innermost portion of metropolitan areas—represented 14.4 percent of the major metropolitan area population in the

2010 US Census. Earlier and later suburbs together contained 68.8 percent of the population, while the exurbs had 16.8 percent. (fig. **2.3.2**)

In the years leading up to the 2010 Census, some analysts suggested that population growth had begun to increase more rapidly in the urban cores than in the suburbs and exurbs. Yet the 2010 census indicated that population growth in the suburbs actually continued to remain stronger than growth in the cores.[21] In other words, growth in the entire metropolitan area was understood, by some, to reflect a preference for "city living." But metropolitan areas include large swaths of what we generally think of as "suburban living," with automobiles playing a central role. And it has been these functionally suburban (and exurban) areas that have attracted nearly all metropolitan area growth since World War II.

Between 2000 and 2010, the share of the metropolitan population that resided in the urban cores declined from 16.1 percent to 14.4 percent. (fig. **2.3.3**) Urban cores lost approximately 160,000 residents in the fifty-two metropolitan areas, despite gains in what might be called the "micro-cores"—areas in or adjacent to the CBDs. Census data indicate that there was a total gain of two hundred thousand residents within two miles of major metropolitan area cores. However, the same data indicate that the gain was more than offset by losses in the ring that falls between two and five miles from the city halls.[22]

metropolitan areas, plus Norfolk (instead of Virginia Beach), and second municipalities in San Francisco (Oakland) and Minneapolis–St. Paul (St. Paul). See *Major Urban Areas: 2010 (Largest Urban Areas in Metropolitan Areas over 1,000,000) Classified by Historical Core Municipality and Suburban Jurisdictions.*

15 A number of articles have been published at newgeography.com. There is an index at "City Sector Model" at http://www.newgeography.com/category/story-topics/city-sector-model. Maps are available at *Demographia City Sector Model Metropolitan Area Maps,* at http://www.demographia.com/csm-maps.pdf. Wendell Cox, "From Jurisdictional to Functional Analysis of Urban Cores and Suburbs," *New Geography,* accessed January 9, 2015, http://www.newgeography.com/content/004349-from-jurisdictional-functional-analysis-urban-cores-suburbs.

16 David L. A. Gordon and Mark Janzen, "Suburban Nation? Estimating the Size of Canada's Suburban Population," *Journal of Architectural and Planning Research* 30, no. 3 (2013): 197–220.

17 David L. A. Gordon and Isaac Shirokoff, "Suburban Nation? Population Growth in Canadian Suburbs, 2006–2011," Council for Canadian Urbanism, School of Regional and Urban Planning, Queen's University, 2013, accessed November 6, 2015, http://www.canadianurbanism.ca/wp-content/uploads/2014/07/CanU%20WP1%20Suburban%20Nation%202006-2011%20Text%20and%20Atlas%20comp.pdf.

18 See, for e.g., Jed Kolko, "No, Suburbs Aren't All the Same. The Suburbiest Ones Are Growing Fastest," *City Lab,* February 15, 2015, accessed April 26, 2015, http://www.citylab

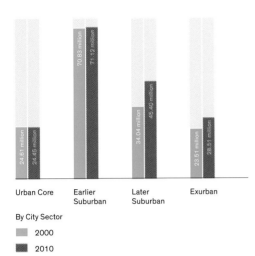

2.3.3 Population by functional sectors. Major metropolitan areas: 2000–2010. All 2000–2010 population growth was in lower density, automobile-oriented neighborhoods.

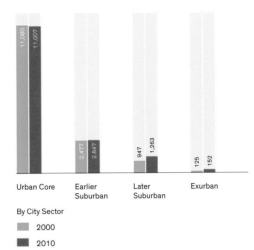

2.3.4 Population density by functional sectors. Major metropolitan areas: 2000–2010. Population densities are much lower outside the urban cores.

Urban cores had the highest population density in 2010, at eleven thousand people per square mile (about 4,250 people per square kilometer). The earlier suburban areas were less than a quarter as dense, while the later suburbs were about one-half as dense as the earlier suburbs. Densities were little changed between 2000 and 2010 in the urban cores and earlier suburbs, but rose in the later suburbs and the exurbs, where more vacant land was available for greenfield development. (fig. **2.3.4**)

Interestingly, the shares of population in urban cores ranged substantially. In only two metropolitan areas did the urban core account for more than one-third of the population: New York at 52 percent and Boston at 33 percent. Some metropolitan areas had little or no urban core population. Some of the newer and fastest-growing metropolitan areas were too small, too sparsely settled, or insufficiently dense to have strong urban cores.

Our analysis reveals three general metropolitan typologies of growth, based on the time period, which result in large, small, or almost nonexistent urban cores. Chicago is an example of an older metropolitan area that experienced strong growth in the nineteenth century. It has a large, prewar urban core, which accounts

for 26 percent of the population. Seattle experienced strong growth in the first half of the twentieth century, yielding a smaller urban core, containing 8 percent of the population. (fig. **2.3.5**) Phoenix may be the most typical example of a postwar metropolitan area, with virtually no urban core. Since 1940, the Phoenix metropolitan area has grown from 120,000 residents to more than 4 million, with virtually all growth being suburban. In each of these metropolitan areas, most of the land and population are in suburban areas. And in 2010 virtually all of the population growth in municipal cores was in their suburban (and exurban) sectors. (fig. **2.3.6**)

Employment and Employment Trends
According to Census Bureau County Business Patterns data, there was a reduction of 1.7 percent in major metropolitan area employment between 2000 and 2010.[23] (fig. **2.3.7**) The entire decline of 3.74 million jobs was in the urban core and the older suburbs. Despite the overall employment reduction, jobs increased by 2.67 million in both the newer suburbs and the exurbs. (fig. **2.3.8**)

The net effect on employment shares was to transfer 4.8 percentage points of total employment from the urban cores and older suburbs to the newer suburbs

.com/housing/2015/02 /no-suburbs-arent-all -the-same-the-suburbi est-ones-are-growing -fastest/385183/.

19 The principal urban area is the largest continuously built-up urban area in the metropolitan area. In two cases, adjacent urban areas were added to the largest urban area, resulting in a larger principal urban area. Mission Viejo was added to Los Angeles and Concord was added to San Francisco.

20 The median house age specification is an additional criterion and, as a result, does not interfere with the possibility of a ZCTA becoming urban core if its densities and transit, walking, and cycling commute shares rise sufficiently.

21 Joel Kotkin and Wendell Cox, "Cities and the Census," *City Journal*, accessed January 9, 2015, http://www.city-journal .org/2011/eon0406jkwc .html.

22 Wendell Cox, "Flocking Elsewhere: The Downtown Growth Story," *New Geography*, accessed January 9, 2015, http://www.new geography.com/con tent/003108-flocking -elsewhere-the-down town-growth-story.

23 US Census Bureau. County Business Patterns provides data principally for private-sector employment.

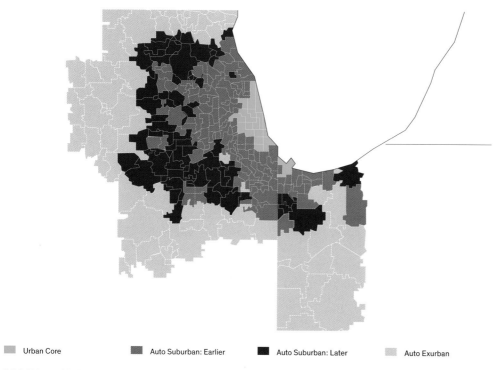

Urban Core — Auto Suburban: Earlier — Auto Suburban: Later — Auto Exurban

2.3.5 Chicago: 2010. City with large pre-auto urban core. Most of the Chicago metropolitan area is post–World War II suburban and automobile oriented.

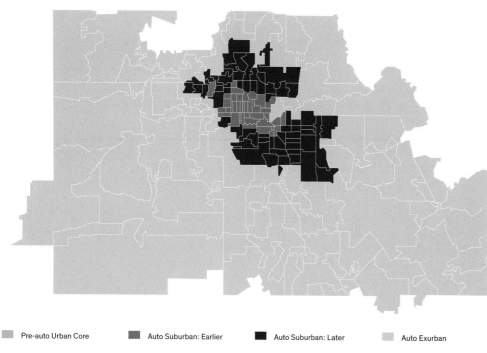

Pre-auto Urban Core — Auto Suburban: Earlier — Auto Suburban: Later — Auto Exurban

2.3.6 Phoenix: 2010. City without a pre-auto urban core. All of the Phoenix metropolitan area is post–World War II suburban and automobile oriented.

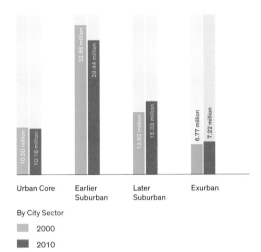

By City Sector

▨ 2000

▨ 2010

2.3.7 Employment by functional sectors. Major metropolitan areas: 2000–2010. All employment growth was in the newer suburbs and exurbs between 2000 and 2010.

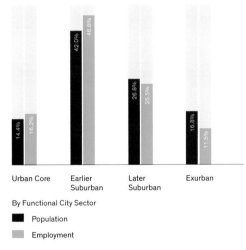

By Functional City Sector

■ Population

▨ Employment

2.3.8 Population and employment locations: 2010. City sectors: Major metropolitan areas. Resident worker population and jobs are relatively well balanced in the city sectors.

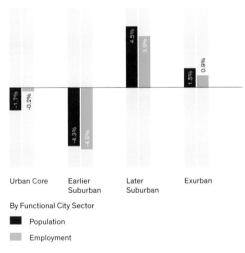

By Functional City Sector

■ Population

▨ Employment

2.3.9 Population and employment: 2000–2010. Percentage point change by city sector. Resident worker population and job trends were similar by city sector from 2000 to 2010.

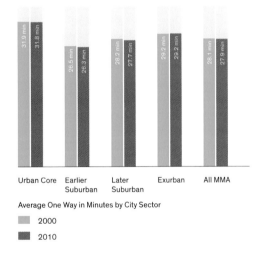

Average One Way in Minutes by City Sector

▨ 2000

▨ 2010

2.3.10 Work trip travel time 2000 and 2010. Major metropolitan areas. Work trip travel times are the least for residents in earlier suburban areas and the most in the urban core.

and exurbs. The urban core share of employment dropped from 16.4 percent to 16.2 percent, while the share in older suburbs dropped from 51.4 percent to 46.8 percent. The share of jobs in the newer suburbs and exurbs combined rose from 32.2 percent to 37.0 percent.

Employment dispersion is following that of the population, especially in the older and newer suburbs. Employment growth has been tracking population growth for decades, as cities have evolved from being monocentric to polycentric.

Thus, employment patterns have dispersed accordingly. (figs. **2.3.9–10**)

Average Commute Times

There is a perception that commuters living farthest from the urban core spend the most time traveling to work. However, the data indicate that the longest average travel times are experienced by residents who are closest to the urban core.

Since the largest share of both population and employment is in the older suburbs, rather than the urban core, it's

not surprising that resident workers in
the newer suburbs have the shortest work
trip travel times, at 26.3 minutes, and
commute times of 27.7 minutes. Urban
core residents have average one-way work
trip travel times of 31.8 minutes. Those
living the farthest from the urban core, in
the exurbs, have one-way work trip travel
times of 29.2 minutes. (fig. **2.3.11**)

More than a quarter century ago,
at the University of Southern California,
Peter Gordon and Harry Richardson
concluded that "the co-location of firms
and households at decentralized locations
has reduced, not lengthened commuting
times and distances."[24] Decentralization
reduces pressures on the CBD, relieves
congestion, and diminishes gridlock. The
dispersed and well-coordinated location
of jobs and residences may be a reason
why commute times and traffic congestion
are lower in US metropolitan areas than in
those of Europe, Australia, and Canada.[25]

At the same time, government transportation spending has not reflected the
realities of where people live and work.
Expenditures on transit are proportionally higher on transit than on roads.
Transitcarries 1 percent of personal travel
and virtually no freight.[26] Roads carry 98
percent of travel and all surface freight
that is not moved by rail or waterway. Yet,
at all levels of government, expenditures
on transit are 22 percent of total road and
transit expenditures.[27]

Work Access between 2000 and 2010
Despite the often-expressed perception
that Americans are giving up their cars,
driving alone dominates commuting
numbers with a metropolitan share of
73.5 percent of commuters as of 2010.
Among urban core residents, the share of
those who drove alone was down slightly,
as was the case in the newer suburbs.
However, the older suburbs and exurbs
had slightly increased drive alone shares.
Yet, in absolute terms, the overall number

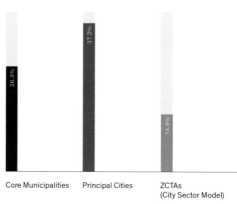

Core Municipalities   Principal Cities   ZCTAs
(City Sector Model)

Share of Population in Urban Cores

■ Functional
■ Jurisdictional

2.3.11 Urban core population share. Major metropolitan
areas: 2010. Functionally urban populations are much less
than core and principal city populations.

of commuters driving alone increased
by 6.1 million and rose in all city sectors.
Most notably, this increase is nearly equal
to the total number of major metropolitan
area residents commuting by transit
(6.2 million).

Transit's share of work trips by urban
core residents rose a full 10 percent,
to 32.7 percent. There were also small
transit commuting gains in the suburbs
and exurbs. Transit commuting has
always been strongest in urban cores
(especially commutes into CBDs) because
of a strong concentration of destinations.
The lack of such concentrations outside
CBDs, even in suburban centers, explains
the small transit shares to such locations.
Approximately 55 percent of transit
commuting in the United States is to
destinations within the six "transit legacy
cities" of New York, Chicago, Philadelphia,
San Francisco, Boston, and Washington,
DC. In each of these municipalities, more
than 40 percent of commuters to CBDs
use transit, with a high of more than 75
percent in New York's Manhattan south of
Fifty-Ninth Street.[28]

Between 2000 and 2010, transit
commuting trips increased by approximately 975,000 overall, 61 percent of
which was in the urban core. Like transit,
the increase in commuting trips by

24 Peter Gordon and
Harry W. Richardson,
"Gasoline Consumption
and Cities: A Reply,"
*Journal of the American
Planning Association* 55,
no. 3 (Summer 1989):
342–46.
25 Wendell Cox, "Urban
Travel and Urban
Population Density,"
Journeys, accessed
January 9, 2015,
http://www.lta.gov
.sg/ltaacademy/doc
/J12%20Nov-p19Cox
_Urban%20Travel%20
and%20Urban%20
Population%20
Density.pdf.
26 This is all surface
travel, urban and rural.
In urban areas, mass
transit carries 2 percent
of travel.
27 Calculated from
"Highway Statistics
2010," US Department of
Transportation, accessed
December 15, 2015,
https://www.fhwa.dot
.gov/policyinformation
/statistics/2010/; and the
US Census Bureau, 2010.
28 Wendell Cox,
"Demographia United
States Central Business
Districts," Demographia,
accessed January 9, 2015,
http://www.demographia
.com/db-cbd2000.pdf.

nonmotorized modes (walking and cycling) of 400,000 was concentrated among urban core residents (54 percent). By contrast, working at home increased by approximately 1.25 million, but this increase was more dispersed among city sectors. Only 14 percent of the increase in working at home was in the urban cores, nearly the same as the urban core share of the metropolitan area population. Each of these three modes of work access is an alternative to driving, a major goal of many regional transportation plans. Yet the gains in two of these modes are concentrated in the urban core of metropolitan areas, where population is declining. The exception in gains is in working at home, where suburban increases are similar to the share of population.

Housing Preferences
The preference for detached housing was evident across the city sectors between 2000 and 2010. Overall, there was a 14 percent increase in detached housing in the major metropolitan areas, where detached housing rose the most (35 percent) in the newer and exurban areas (24 percent). The number of detached houses increased 2.8 million in the newer suburbs, and 1.5 million in the exurban areas. A smaller 50,000 increase in detached houses was registered in the older suburbs.

The increase of 4.4 million detached housing units is six times that of multifamily housing (owned and rented apartments), at 700,000. There were slight decreases in the number of multifamily houses in both the urban cores and the older suburbs. At the same time, multifamily housing increased by 800,000 units in the newer suburbs and 17,000 in the exurbs.[29]

Demographic Trends
Families with children are moving farther out in metropolitan areas. The proportion of primary and secondary school–age children (ages five to fourteen) has dropped in the urban cores. Between 2000 and 2010, the share of this age group living in the urban cores dropped from 15 percent to 12 percent.

There have been recent anecdotal reports claiming that a large share of younger adults aged twenty to twenty-nine (millennials) has been moving to urban cores. Between 2000 and 2010, there was an increase of 310,000 younger adults in urban cores. Yet only 12 percent of the younger adult population increase was in the urban core, with the 88 percent balance in the suburbs and exurbs. Overall, the percentage of major metropolitan area younger adults living in the urban cores declined between 2000 and 2010. The young-adult increase was more than four times as great in the newer suburbs, and twice as high in the exurbs in comparison to the urban core. Further, approximately 40 percent of the national increase in the younger adult population was outside the major metropolitan areas.

Similarly, there have been frequent press reports that baby boomers, those born between 1945 and 1964, are abandoning the suburbs and moving to the urban cores. The trend has been the opposite. Contrary to some reports, between 2000 and 2010, the population of baby boomers dropped 1.15 million in the urban cores, a reduction of 17 percent. A decline was also registered in the older suburbs, while increases occurred in the newer suburbs and exurbs. Overall, the major metropolitan areas lost 2.2 million boomer generation residents, while areas outside the major metropolitan areas added approximately 350,000.

It has also been anecdotally reported that older adults have been moving into the urban cores and away from suburban and exurban areas. The data show otherwise. Between 2000 and 2010, urban-core older populations declined by more than 100,000 residents. In contrast,

29 There was a reduction in single-family homes as a share of total residential building permits from 2010 to 2014 to 62.7 percent. This is below the 74.3 percentage in the 2000s and the 77.1 percentage in the 1990s. The new, lower single-family percentage is, however, above the decade rates of the 1980s, 1970s, and 1960s. Calculated from US Census Bureau data, "New Privately Owned Housing Units Authorized by Building Permits in Permit-Issuing Places," accessed July 15, 2015, https://www.census.gov/construction/nrc/xls/permits_cust.xls.

the suburbs and exurbs added 2.8 million seniors, with the largest share in
the newer suburbs (1.64 million). Senior
populations also rose strongly outside
the major metropolitan areas, with an
increase of 2.67 million.

What the City Sector Model Reveals
The 14.4 percent of the major metropolitan
area population classified as urban
core under the city sector model is considerably less than would be indicated by
conventional, jurisdiction-based analyses.
A core municipality analysis would yield
a nearly double 26 percent, and a principal city analysis would result in a 37
percent urban core share.

Further, the city sector model analysis
indicates a continuing dispersion of US
metropolitan areas into the suburbs and
exurbs between 2000 and 2010. Overall,
suburbs and exurbs accounted for all
of the population growth, employment
growth, senior growth, baby boomer generation growth, school-age children growth,
and nearly all of the millennial generation
growth. And there has been virtually no
shift away from driving during commutes
in the major metropolitan areas.

The smaller area analysis in the city
sector model provides a substantially
finer-grained and more reflective picture
of trends within the metropolitan area.
In some cases, this analysis has shown
anecdote-based conceptions of suburban
decline to be generally incorrect. This
need not be a concern for advocates of the
urban core. The metropolitan area, which
is the modern city, will perform best if
all its parts prosper. The prosperity of
the urban core does not require suburban
decline, nor does the prosperity of
the suburbs require urban-core decline.

2.4
THE CONTINUED SUBURBANIZATION OF AMERICA

Jed Kolko

HOUSING AFFORDABILITY

POLYCENTRIC EXPANSION

SOCIAL DIVERSITY

At the start of this decade, as America began to recover from the housing bust, possibilities of permanent change emerged. There was a widespread recognition that decades of pro-home-ownership policies went too far. New regulations were developed to prevent the worst lending practices of the housing bubble, and fundamental reform of the mortgage finance system seemed within reach.

There were also pronouncements and predictions about where and how Americans would live. Among these was that suburbanization had been reversed, possibly for good. America was witnessing, we were told, the death of the suburbs; cities were thriving while "suburbs were sputtering."[1] Urban areas were indeed seeing an acceleration of population growth, and apartment construction boomed while single-family home construction languished.

But the suburbanization of America is continuing. Although this century's housing bubble, bust, and recovery caused wild swings both in the housing market and in residential population growth patterns, there's little evidence of a fundamental or permanent change in where Americans live.

What Is a Suburb?

Any analysis of suburban and urban population trends needs to define these areas in a way that is both meaningful and consistent with the available data. It would seem natural to define urban and suburban areas by official city boundaries, identifying the largest city or several primary cities as the metropolitan area and referring to the remainder as the suburbs. The problem with this definition, however, is that many cities include low-density residential neighborhoods within their boundaries, and some high-density, walkable neighborhoods are outside big-city boundaries. For instance, Staten Island and parts of the western San Fernando Valley—which lie within the cities of New York and Los Angeles, respectively—are less urban than Hoboken, New Jersey, and Santa Monica, California, which are outside those big-city boundaries. It makes sense to analyze political, fiscal, and public services questions like crime, schools, and local taxes at the city level, but city boundaries are often a poor guide for distinguishing urban from suburban neighborhoods.

At the real-estate marketplace Trulia, our analytics were instead based on two different approaches, both of which relied on density measures to identify urban and suburban areas. The first divides all United States counties into four quartiles based on housing unit density, with cutoffs chosen so that each quartile contains approximately one-quarter of the population.[2] Roughly speaking, the top quartile of each county is urban; the second is higher-density suburban; the third is lower-density suburban; and the bottom quartile is rural. This approach is well suited for historical analysis, since Census Bureau population data are available over many decades for counties, whose boundaries change little over time; it is also well suited for demographic analysis, since county-level population changes by age and other categories are reported annually in Census reports. However, many counties are large and comprise a variety of neighborhoods: those containing downtown Chicago and Los Angeles, for example, also contain low-density suburban neighborhoods.

The second approach is to base the classification of urban or suburban on neighborhood density-related measures. In this approach, zip codes (or their Census approximation, ZIP Code Tabulation Areas [ZCTAs]) from the one hundred largest metros are used to categorize neighborhoods within metro areas. Neighborhoods are defined as suburban

1   Leigh Gallagher, *The End of the Suburbs: Where the American Dream Is Moving* (New York: Penguin, 2013); William H. Frey, "Demographic Reversal: Cities Thrive, Suburbs Sputter," *Brookings*, June 29, 2012, accessed October 1, 2015, http://www.brookings.edu/research/opinions/2012/06/29-cities-suburbs-frey.

2   The measure is the weighted average of Census-tract housing units per square mile, weighted by housing units in the tract, for the county.

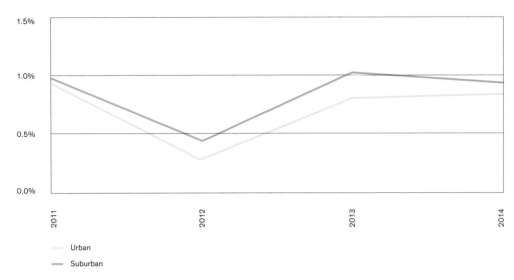

3   Jed Kolko, "How Suburban Are Big American Cities?" FiveThirtyEight, May 21, 2015, accessed October 1, 2015, http://fivethirtyeight.com/features/how-suburban-are-big-american-cities/.

2.4.1 Population growth, urban vs. suburban. Population growth in suburban neighborhoods is outpacing that of urban neighborhoods.

when the majority of the housing stock is detached, single-family homes, and as urban when the majority of the housing is townhouses, apartments, and condos. This definition can be further refined to create an urban-suburban continuum. The advantage of the neighborhood-based approach is greater geographic precision; however, relatively few sources of population (or other) data are available at the neighborhood level. The data source used here is monthly US Postal Service information on the number of residential addresses that receive mail in each zip code. These data are used to estimate population (technically, household) growth.

Together, these density-based measures capture the experience of "urbanness" and "suburbanness" better than a definition based on city boundaries. In late 2014 Trulia surveyed 2,008 American adults and asked whether they lived in an urban, suburban, or rural area, without providing further definition. Self-reported urban locations aligned better with density or housing stock definitions of urban versus suburban than with official city boundaries.[3]

Housing Recovery Favors the Suburbs
The most current detailed population data show that population growth in suburban neighborhoods is outpacing that of urban neighborhoods. In 2014 suburbs grew 0.96 percent and cities 0.85 percent, according to USPS occupied-homes data. (fig. **2.4.1**) Since mid-2011, cumulative household growth was 3.1 percent in suburban neighborhoods versus 2.5 percent in urban neighborhoods. These comparisons use the neighborhood-based urban-suburban definition: within the one hundred largest metros, suburbs are the ZCTAs where a majority of housing units are detached single-family houses.

When we split neighborhoods into two categories, urban and suburban, we can miss some of the action. Urban neighborhoods, by this definition, would include those that have wall-to-wall high-rises as well as quieter townhouse areas; suburban neighborhoods would be those where single-family homes are close together, as well as lower-density areas where homes are far apart. A finer-grained approach is to treat urban-to-suburban as a spectrum. Using several neighborhood measures, including the housing-stock measure, other density measures, and some diversity measures, we developed an urban-suburban score and divided ZCTAs into ten buckets of approximately equal numbers of households. The scale went from the most urban (the highest score; the first decile) to the most suburban (the lowest score, the tenth decile).[4] Tying this back to the two-category split between urban and suburban, the top three deciles are urban, while the other seven are suburban.

This finer division shows that the neighborhoods with the fastest population growth since mid-2011 were the lowest density, most suburban suburbs (the tenth decile). (fig. **2.4.2**) The more urban suburbs (deciles four to six) were among the slowest-growing neighborhoods, suggesting that there's little evidence of a recent shift to more walkable, higher-density suburbs. The top decile—the densest urban neighborhoods—also saw strong population growth, more so than other urban neighborhoods (deciles two and three). The clearest evidence for a shift toward higher-density living is this recent growth in hyperurban neighborhoods, not a shift within suburbia toward denser suburbs or a broader population shift from suburban to urban neighborhoods.

The Housing Cycle and the Longer-Term View
In one sense, urban America has had a tremendous recovery since the bubble burst. At the height of the housing bubble, in 2006, the densest quartile of counties actually lost population even though suburbs, exurbs, and rural areas were growing at their fastest rate of the decade. (fig. **2.4.3**) Then, urban growth recovered such that in 2011 the densest counties outpaced the other three quartiles of counties. More generally, comparing the bubble years (2000 to 2006) with the postbubble years (2006 to 2014), the rate of population growth accelerated in the densest quartile of counties but slowed in the suburbs, exurbs, and rural areas. If one extrapolates the trend between these two time periods, it looks like the start of a reversal of decades of suburbanization.

But that simple extrapolation is misleading. On closer examination, these

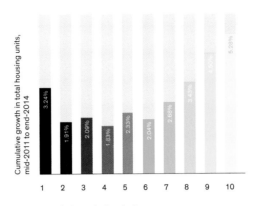

Cumulative growth in total housing units, mid-2011 to end-2014

3.24% 1.91% 2.09% 1.83% 2.33% 2.04% 2.68% 3.43% 4.50% 5.29%

1 2 3 4 5 6 7 8 9 10

Neighborhood urban-suburban decile
1= most urban; 10 =most suburban
Each decile has approximately equal number of households

2.4.2 Housing unit growth by neighborhood type. Population has grown most in the lowest-density suburban neighborhoods.

4   Jed Kolko, "No, Suburbs Aren't All the Same: The Suburbiest Ones Are Growing Fastest," *Atlantic CityLab,* February 5, 2015, accessed October 1, 2015, http://www.citylab .com/housing/2015/02 /no-suburbs-arent-all -the-same-the-suburbi est-ones-are-growing -fastest/385183/.

recent trends look more cyclical than structural. The bubble favored housing construction and population growth in exurban and rural areas, where there was land to build on and housing prices that remained somewhat affordable, even as prices ballooned nationally. The bust put an end to this low-density hypergrowth. In the recovery, rental apartments have led the construction rebound. But even with this cyclical boost, in 2014 population growth in the densest quartile of counties has once again fallen behind that in the second and third quartiles, the suburbs and exurbs.

To see if there has been a structural shift toward higher-density living, it's necessary to average across the entire cycle—bubble, bust, and recovery. Over the fifteen-year period 2000 to 2014, the densest quartile of counties had the slowest population growth, far behind growth in the second and third quartiles. This pattern is largely unchanged from the prior twenty years: in 1980 to 2000, the densest quartile had the slowest growth, too. The broad patterns of population change in this century look similar to those at the end of the last century.

Even at the individual metro level, there is surprising continuity in population growth patterns. Among the fifty-one metropolitan areas with one million

Density is households per square mile, tract-weighted

- **■** Big, dense cities (density > 2000)
- **━** Big-city suburbs and lower density cities (density 1000–2000)
- ━ Lower-density suburbs and smaller cities (density 1000-2000)
- ━ Small towns and rural areas (density < 500)

2.4.3 Annual county population growth by density quartile. The densest urban counties are once again growing more slowly than suburbs and exurbs.

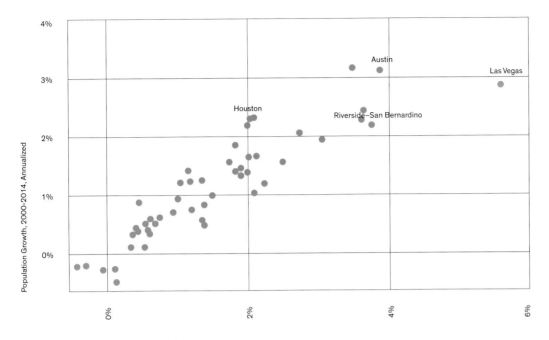

2.4.4 Metro population growth, 2000–2014 vs. 1980–2000. The fastest-growing metros since 2000 were among the fastest growing prior to 2000.

5   This analysis uses the 2013 five-year American Community Survey and the 2000 decennial Census, which are the most recent and comparable sources of detailed demographic characteristics for smaller geographic areas.

6   Jed Kolko, "Millennials Are Suburbanizing, While Big Cities Are Having a Baby Boom," *Trulia's Blog*, June 26, 2014, accessed October 1, 2015, http://www.trulia .com/trends/2014/06 /millennials-suburban izing/.

population in 2010, three of the five fastest growing in 2000 to 2014 were also among the five fastest growing in 1980 to 2000: Austin, Las Vegas, and Orlando. (The other two fastest growing were Raleigh and Charlotte in 2000 to 2014, and Riverside–San Bernardino and Phoenix in 1980 to 2000.) Among these fifty-one large metros, the correlation between 2000 to 2014 and 1980 to 2000 growth rates is 0.91. (fig. **2.4.4**) Among the nearly one thousand metropolitan and micropolitan areas in the United States, the same correlation (population weighted) is 0.85. In short, US population growth patterns have been surprisingly stable between this housing cycle overall and the prior two decades.

One of the oft-cited claims about urban growth in the housing recovery is that millennials are increasingly living in cities. The grain of truth is that millennials are a large group, with twenty-four being the most common age in the United States, and twenty-somethings are more likely than any other age group to live in urban neighborhoods (using the housing-stock definition explained above). But

these young adults were in fact slightly less likely to live in urban neighborhoods in 2009 to 2013 than they were in 2000.[5] The millennial population in 2012 to 2013 grew fastest in the second quartile of counties by density, followed by the third and top quartiles. Among the one hundred largest metros, Colorado Springs and San Antonio had the fastest population growth of millennials, ahead of the big-city, denser metros.[6]

There are two reasons young people might appear to be more urban today. First, certain millennials are more likely to live in certain urban neighborhoods: there's been a notable increase in the share of college-educated twenty-five- to thirty-four-year-olds living in the densest urban neighborhoods between 2000 and 2009 to 2013. Although the movement of these particular young adults into these particular neighborhoods has been well represented in the media and pop culture, it is not representative of a broader generational trend. Most twenty-five- to thirty-four-year-olds—two-thirds of them—lack a bachelor's degree,

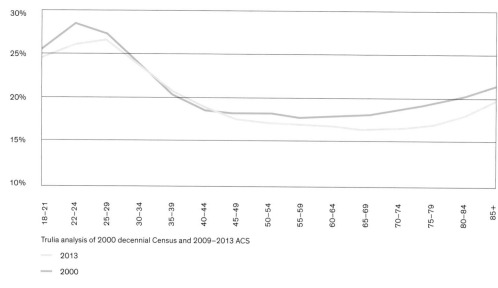

Trulia analysis of 2000 decennial Census and 2009–2013 ACS

— 2013

— 2000

2.4.5 Percentage living in urban neighborhoods by age group. Nearly all age groups—including millennials and especially seniors—have become more suburban since 2000.

7   Jed Kolko, "Why Millennials Are Less Urban Than You Think," FiveThirtyEight, April 7, 2015, accessed October 1, 2015, http://fivethirty eight.com/features/why -millennials-are-less -urban-than-you-think/.

8   Jed Kolko, "Urban Headwinds, Suburban Tailwinds," Trulia, January 22, 2015, http://www.trulia.com /trends/2015/01/cities -vs-suburbs-jan-2015/.

and this group's decreasing likelihood of living in urban neighborhoods more than offsets the increase among the one-third with bachelor's degrees.[7]

The changing US age distribution will be, if anything, a headwind for urban areas. Today, urban neighborhoods are getting a demographic jolt. The largest segment of the big millennial group—folks in their early twenties—are entering the peak age for urban living. Some 26 percent of twenty-two- to twenty-four- year-olds live in urban neighborhoods, rising to 27 percent for twenty-five- to twenty-nine-year-olds. Urban living starts to decline after ages twenty-five to twenty-nine.

There's a second reason that young people appear to be more urban than they were in the past: While young adults are a bit less likely to live in urban neigh-borhoods than in 2000, there's been a sharper decline in the share of older adults, especially seniors, living in urban neighborhoods. Therefore, the average age of urban residents has fallen, but that's because older adults have become less urban, not because young adults overall have become more so. (fig. **2.4.5**)

Will Suburbanization Reverse in the Future?
Properly extrapolating from the recent past, it does not appear that the trend toward suburbanization is on the verge of a reversal. The acceleration of popula-tion growth in urban counties after 2006 has already slowed, and averaging over the years of this housing cycle since 2000 points to little fundamental change from earlier decades.

Two other approaches show little evidence that suburbanization is ending. First, a recent online survey of 2,008 American adults by Trulia found greater interest in moving from urban to suburban and rural areas than in the other direction. While 26 percent of adults described where they live today as urban, just 22 percent said that they wanted to live in an urban area in five years. For every ten suburbanites who said that they wanted to live in an urban area in five years, sixteen urban dwell-ers said that they wished to live in the suburbs.[8]

Second, urban living drops to its lowest level among those aged sixty-five to sixty-nine. And just 17 percent of the largest segment of baby boomers—those in their early fifties—live in such

neighborhoods, a third lower than the
share of early twenty-somethings.

On the other hand, the baby boomer
leading edge is nudging seventy, when
urban living starts to rise again. Meanwhile, however, as millennials get older,
many will partner up, have kids, and move
to the suburbs. The return of older boomers to cities will less than fully offset the
pending millennial suburban migration.
If the propensity of each age group for
urban living remains at 2009–2013 levels,
the changing age distribution projected
by the Census Bureau would lead to a
slight decline in the share of adults living
in urban neighborhoods.

Of course, other harder-to-predict
factors could shift US population growth
away from the suburbs. Higher gas prices
could encourage people to reduce driving and move closer to jobs and transit;
drought could curtail housing development in unbuilt areas in the West.
Anything that affects the relative costs
of living in suburban versus urban areas
could change US population patterns,
including public policy changes. It's essential to understand both policy and prices
when analyzing past, current, and future
population patterns.

The Role of Housing Prices in Suburbanization

Interpreting the faster population growth
of the suburbs takes some care. Where
people live is not only a reflection of what
they want. Housing and migration decisions reflect a mix of those desires with
what is available and how much it costs. In
the language of economics, quantities and
prices are jointly determined by supply and
demand. Looking just at quantities—that
is, how many people live in different places
and how that changes—doesn't by itself tell
us about the demand for suburban living.
We need to add prices to the picture.

While suburban population has
been growing faster in recent years than

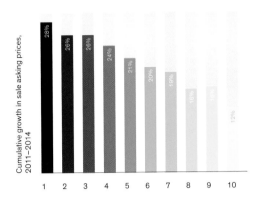

Cumulative growth in sale asking prices, 2011–2014

28% | 26% | 26% | 24% | 21% | 20% | 19% | 16% | 14% | 12%

Neighborhood urban-suburban decile
1 = most urban; 10 = most suburban
Each decile has approximately equal number of households

**2.4.6 Home price growth by neighborhood type. Home prices
have risen fastest in the densest urban neighborhoods.**

urban population, home prices are
rising more in urban areas, and most of
all in the densest urban neighborhoods.
(fig. **2.4.6**) It's ambiguous, therefore,
whether demand for urban living or for
suburban living has been growing more,
since strong demand can result in higher
prices or faster population growth,
depending on how much supply responds.

The fact that urban areas have both
faster price growth and slower population
growth than suburban areas points to
housing supply being more constrained
in urban areas than in suburban areas.
Most new construction takes place outside
urban neighborhoods. Cities have less
open land and often more onerous regulations limiting new construction. It's true
that in 2014 multiunit buildings—typically
located in urban neighborhoods—
accounted for the highest share of overall
construction since 1973. Still, in urban
neighborhoods, fewer new units are built
relative to the size of the housing stock.
Limited construction holds back urban
population growth and worsens urban
affordability, even when, as rising prices
show, housing demand in cities is strong.

For some purposes, it doesn't matter
whether the growth of the suburbs is due
to preferential demand or to looser supply
relative to urban areas. Where people
actually live determines demand for infrastructure and other local public services,

as well as the optimal location for employ-ers and retailers. But if the faster growth of suburbs is due, to a significant extent, to supply or other factors that affect relative housing prices in cities and suburbs, then it raises the question of whether policies are distorting (in the economist sense of the word) location choices.

The Role of Public Policy in Suburbanization

Public policies have the potential to affect the cost of living in different locations. Housing policies are significant, of course, but policies affecting transportation, energy, local public services, and local revenues can be, too. The effect of these policies on local costs of living might be intentional—that is, designed to affect where people live—or inadvertent.

A notable example of a policy intended to encourage higher-density living is Senate Bill (SB) 375, the California law that requires coordination between transportation and land-use planning, with the goal of reducing vehicle-miles traveled and, ultimately, greenhouse gas emissions. Among other mechanisms, it encourages residential development near public transit. Given that public transit is concentrated in higher-density areas, SB 375 is a direct attempt to shift popula-tion growth from suburban areas to more urban areas.

While it's difficult to come up with examples of policies where the explicit intention is to encourage suburban or exurban growth, the unintentional effect of some of America's most prominent housing and transportation policies is to favor suburban growth. Start with the mortgage interest deduction, a home-ownership subsidy with benefits that are concentrated among higher-income taxpayers in more expensive homes.[9] Because homeownership rates, incomes, and home sizes are all higher in subur-ban than in urban areas, the deduction in

effect subsidizes living in suburbs relative to cities.[10]

Transportation policies have also traditionally favored suburban growth. The massive public investment in the interstate highway system reduced com-muting time per mile, therefore shifting population growth toward the suburbs.[11] Low gas taxes relative to other rich coun-ties also likely encourage suburbanization by reducing commuting costs.

Local policies favor suburban growth more directly. Many of America's densest cities, like New York, Washington, DC, San Francisco, and Los Angeles restrict housing development through various regulations, pushing construction and therefore population growth to the suburbs. (Some dense or high-income suburbs also restrict housing supply, encouraging growth in the lower-density or lower-income suburbs.)

How would relative home prices and population growth in cities versus suburbs change if there was no mortgage interest deduction, no incentives for transit-ori-ented development, higher gas taxes, and fewer constraints on the urban hous-ing supply? On balance, neutralizing these policies would raise the relative cost of suburban living and would shift more population growth toward cities. Whether neutralizing these policies would actually reverse suburbanization is hard to say. And whether neutralizing these policies would be good from a public policy per-spective hinges on whether these policies can be justified by externalities or other "market failures," a question that's beyond the scope of this essay. Whether neutral-izing these policies is feasible is easier to answer: There's little political will to reform the mortgage interest deduction, raise the gas tax, or significantly increase housing construction in expensive cities. Furthermore, as the suburbanization of the United States continues, the consti-tuency for such changes weakens.

9   Eric Toder et al., "Reforming the Mortgage Interest Deduction," *Urban Institute*, April 2010, http://www.urban .org/sites/default/files /alfresco/publication -pdfs/412099-Reforming -the-Mortgage-Interest -Deduction.pdf.

10   Edward Glaeser, "Rethinking the Federal Bias toward Homeownership," *Cityscape* 13, no. 2 (July 2011), http://www .huduser.org/portal /periodicals/cityscpe /vol13num2/Cityscape _July2011_rethinking. pdf.

11   Nathaniel Baum-Snow, "Did Highways Cause Suburbanization," *Quarterly Journal of Economics* 122, no. 2 (2007), http://qje.oxford journals.org/content /122/2/775.short.

The suburbanization of America, therefore, is not necessarily only about the demand for or desirability of suburbia. The continued shift of population to lower-density counties and neighborhoods reflects both demand preferences and supply constraints: Suburbanization is also in part the result of public policies that tilt the playing field away from cities and toward the suburbs. Still, whatever the reasons, the reality is that the suburbanization of America continues. Despite much commentary to the contrary, the housing boom, bust, and recovery has probably done little to change that direction.

This essay draws heavily on posts that first appeared on Trulia's Blog *and on the* Atlantic's CityLab *blog, used with kind permission. See Jed Kolko, "Millennials Are Suburbanizing, While Big Cities Are Having a Baby Boom,"* Trulia's Blog, *June 26, 2014, accessed October 1, 2015, http://www.trulia.com/trends/2014/06/ millennials-suburbanizing/; Jed Kolko, "Urban Headwinds, Suburban Tailwinds,"* Trulia, *January 22, 2015, http://www .trulia.com/trends/2015/01/cities-vs-sub- urbs-jan-2015/; Jed Kolko, "No, Suburbs Aren't All the Same: The Suburbiest Ones Are Growing Fastest,"* Atlantic CityLab, *February 5, 2015, accessed October 1, 2015, http://www.citylab.com/housing/2015/02/ no-suburbs-arent-all-the-same-the-subur- biest-ones-are-growing-fastest/385183/.*

Spanish Springs, Reno, Nevada, United States

Damonte Ranch, Reno, Nevada, United States

2.5
TRANSPORT
DEFINES
SUBURBIA

David L. A. Gordon

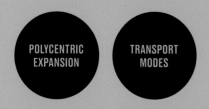

POLYCENTRIC
EXPANSION

TRANSPORT
MODES

We routinely hear that Canada is one of the most urbanized nations in the world, but that does not mean most Canadians live in inner-city apartments and travel by public transit.[1] Although it is estimated that approximately 80 percent of the Canadian population lives in an urban setting, this category includes downtown, inner-city, suburban, and exurban development.[2]

The existing urban-rural classification has genuine utility, since many demographic, environmental, housing, and economic policies need to be different for rural areas. However, if *urban* simply means nonrural, then it is too broad a category for community planning. Suburban planning techniques and problems, such as resource conservation, greyfield redevelopment of dead malls, and auto dependence, are significantly different from those related to inner-city intensification and brownfield redevelopment.[3]

We do not need an exact count of suburban households to create the rough estimate of the number and proportion of suburban residents needed for practical policy-making purposes.[4] However, an improved estimate of the proportion and the rate of growth of the Canadian suburban population may be useful, for example, for shaping an urban infrastructure program or for public-health research.[5] A secondary objective is to establish a definition of *suburb* that would be credible across Canada. Our research team's six-year struggle at Queen's University was partly to establish a definition that would produce a dependable classification of neighborhoods in all thirty-three Canadian census metropolitan areas (CMAs), rather than the handful of case studies usually covered in research studies. The policy implications of this work have led many observers to accept that Canada is a suburban nation.[6]

Our initial estimates indicate that perhaps two-thirds of the Canadian population lives in neighborhoods that most observers would consider suburban (i.e., using cars and living in often postwar single-family homes). We reached that conclusion through our long-term project of using innovative research methods and discarding outdated approaches.[7] The result was reported across Canada on newspaper front pages. The idea that "Canada is a suburban nation" is now a standard observation.[8]

Suburban Expansion in Canada

The 1931 Canadian census was the first in which the country's urban population exceeded the rural population.[9] This means Canada is likely to have been an urban nation for only about half a century, since our preliminary calculations indicate that many CMAs became majority suburban by the 1980s.

The pre–World War II urban areas had suburbs, of course, with pleasant neighborhoods of mainly single-family detached homes within walking distance of the central city in the nineteenth century and, later, streetcar suburbs in the early twentieth century.[10] Some superb historical scholarship by the McMaster University professor Richard Harris has demonstrated that there was considerable diversity in these prewar neighborhoods, including unplanned suburbs where working-class citizens built their own homes.[11]

In contrast, the scale of suburban development changed rapidly after 1945, as the federal government encouraged mass homeownership with long-term mortgages at the same time that automobile ownership soared. Large-scale land developers who were capable of building entire satellite communities emerged; Don Mills, a mixed-use neighborhood in Toronto, became an influential example of this large-scale development.[12] This new version of suburbia proved quite popular, and automobile-dependent

1　Alan Artibise, "Canada as an Urban Nation," *Daedalus* 117, no. 4 (1988): 237–64; Canadian Press, "Country Living Continues to Decline as Majority of Canadians Live in Big Cities," *Guelph Mercury*, February 8, 2012, accessed July 12, 2013, http://www .guelphmercury.com /news-story/ 2777855; Roy MacGregor, "City Slickers and the Legend of Canada as an Urban Nation," *Globe and Mail*, November 9, 2009, last modified September 6, 2012, accessed November 13, 2015, http://www.the globeandmail.com/news /national/city-slickers -and-the-legend-of-cana da-as-an-urban-nation /article4291877/, A1.

2　Laurent Martel and Éric Caron-Malenfant, *Portrait of the Canadian Population in 2006* (Ottawa: Statistics Canada Demography Division, 2007).

3　Lee S. Sobel and Steven Bodzin, Pricewaterhouse-Coopers, *Greyfields into Goldfields: Dead Malls Become Living Neighborhoods* (San Francisco: Congress for New Urbanism, 2002); Galina Tachieva, *The Sprawl Repair Manual* (Washington, DC: Island Press, 2010); Ellen Dunham-Jones and June Williamson, *Retrofitting Suburbia: Urban Design Solutions for Redesigning Suburbs* (New York: Wiley, 2011); Canada Mortgage and Housing Corporation, *Greyfield Redevelopment for Housing in Canada— Case Studies* (Ottawa: CMHC, 2011); Peter Newman and Jeffrey Kenworthy, *Sustainability and Cities: Overcoming Automobile Dependence* (Washington, DC: Island Press, 1999); Peter Newman and Jeffrey Kenworthy, *The End of Automobile Dependence: How Cities Are Moving beyond Car-Based Planning* (Washington, DC: Island Press, 2015).

4　Ann Forsyth, "Defining Suburbs," *Journal of Planning Literature* 27,

neighborhoods expanded to make up more than half of Canada's urban population in a remarkably short time—perhaps by as early as 1981.

Postwar suburban expansion was not unique to Canada. American analysts typically use political boundaries to distinguish between pre-1946 inner cities and more recent suburbs, although this tends to obscure the realities of how people live, as others have pointed out.[13]

Using political boundaries as a method to distinguish urban form is similarly unreliable. In Canada, annexations and amalgamations by local governments are more common.[14] For example, cities such as Calgary and Winnipeg make up a large proportion of their CMA's population, including all inner-city and most suburban areas. Some cities, such as Ottawa, have also included substantial exurban and rural areas following recent local government restructuring.

In addition, the classification of metropolitan areas as inner-city, suburban, or rural masks the growing polycentricity of North American cities.[15] This polycentricity has been strongly encouraged throughout many metropolitan areas by recent planning policies that attempt to cluster development around higher-access nodes in the transit system using mobility hubs and transit-oriented development (TOD).

There is a large literature on the geography of the suburban expansion of Canadian cities.[16] Similarly, there is a growing literature on the planning of Canadian suburbs.[17] Unfortunately, scholars of the history, geography, and planning of Canadian suburbs do not appear to have produced an estimate of the extent of this phenomenon that is as clear-cut as our estimates of urban, suburban, and rural populations.

University of Toronto professor Alan Walks and Statistics Canada analyst Martin Turcotte considered how the urban

no. 3 (2012): 270–81.

5 Lawrence Frank, Howard Frumkin, and Richard Jackson, *Urban Sprawl and Public Health: Designing, Planning, and Building for Healthy Communities* (Washington, DC: Island Press, 2004); Martin Turcotte, "Life in Metropolitan Areas: Are Suburban Residents Really Less Physically Active?," *Canadian Social Trends* 87 (Summer 2009): 32–41.

6 David L. A. Gordon and Isaac Shirokoff, "Suburban Nation? Population Growth in Canadian Suburbs, 2006–2011," Working Paper 1, Council for Canadian Urbanism, Toronto, Ontario, July 2014, http://www .canadianurbanism.ca /wp-content/uploads /2014/07/CanU%20 WP1%20Suburban%20 Nation%202006 -2011%20Text%20 and%20Atlas%20 comp.pdf. The media references, on page 21, include the *Vancouver Sun*, *Calgary Herald*, *Edmonton Journal*, *Saskatoon Star Phoenix*, *Hamilton Spectator*, *Toronto Star*, *Montreal Gazette*, and *Saint John Telegraph-Journal*.

7 David L. A. Gordon and Mark Janzen, "Suburban Nation? Estimating the Size of Canada's Suburban Population," *Journal of Architectural and Planning Research* 30, no. 3 (December 2013): 197–220.

8 Maria Cook, "Suburban Nation: An Ambitious New Study Says It's Time for Canadians to Dispel Our Urban Myth," *Ottawa Citizen*, September 6, 2013, B1–B3; Aaron Derfel, "Exurban Growth in Montreal Region Is Worst in Country," *Montreal Gazette*, September 7, 2013, A1, A3–A4; Kelly Sinoski, "Canada: A Suburban Nation," *Vancouver Sun*, September 7, 2013, accessed November 13, 2015, http://www .vancouversun.com /business/Canada +suburban+nation

9 The literature on how Canada became an urban nation was summarized by Larry McCann and Peter J. Smith, "Canada Becomes Urban: Cities and Urbanization in an Historical Perspective," in *Canadian Cities in Transition: Local through Global Perspectives*, ed. Trudi Bunting and Pierre Filion (Toronto: Oxford University Press, 1991), 69–99, while a precise method of measuring the urban population was described by Leroy Stone, *Urban Development in Canada* (Ottawa: Dominion Bureau of Statistics, 1967).

10 Larry McCann, "Planning and Building the Corporate Suburb of Mount Royal, 1910–1925," *Planning Perspectives* 11, no. 3 (1996): 259–301; "Suburbs of Desire: Shaping the Suburban Landscape of Canadian Cities, 1900–1950," in *Changing Suburbs: Foundation, Form, and Function*, ed. Richard Harris and Peter Larkham (London: Routledge, 1999), 111–45; Robert A. M. Stern, *Paradise Planned: The Garden Suburb and the Modern City* (New York: Monacelli Press, 2013).

11 Richard Harris, *Unplanned Suburbs: Toronto's American Tragedy, 1900 to 1950* (Baltimore: Johns Hopkins University Press, 1996); and Richard Harris, *Creeping Conformity: How Canada Became Suburban, 1900– 1960* (Toronto: University of Toronto Press, 2004); Richard Harris and Peter J. Larkham, *Changing Suburbs: Foundation, Form, and Function* (London: Routledge, 1999).

12 Macklin Hancock, "Don Mills: A Paradigm of Community Design," *Plan Canada* 34 (July 1994): 87–90; John Sewell, *The Shape of the City: Toronto Struggles with Modern Planning* (Toronto: University of Toronto Press, 1993).

13 Herbert J. Gans,

/8879988/story.html.

"Urbanism and Suburbanism as Ways of Life: A Re-evaluation of Definitions," in *People and Plans: Essays on Urban Problems and Solutions*, ed. H. J. Gans (New York: Basic Books, 1968), 41–64; Bruce Katz and Robert E. Lang, *Redefining Urban and Suburban America: Evidence from Census 2000* (Washington, DC: Brookings Institution Press, 2003); Alan Walks, "The Boundaries of Suburban Discontent? Urban Definitions and Neighbourhood Political Effects," *Canadian Geographer* 51, no. 2 (2007): 160–85; Wendell Cox, *Commentary: Mobility and Prosperity in the City of the Future* (Ottawa: Macdonald-Laurier Institute, May 2012), 1–2.

14 John B. Parr, "Spatial Definitions of the City: Four Perspectives," *Urban Studies* 44, no. 2 (2007): 381–92; Walks, "The Boundaries of Suburban Discontent?"

15 Trudi Bunting, Pierre Filion, and Heath Priston, "Density Gradients in Canadian Metropolitan Regions, 1971–96: Differential Patterns of Central Area and Suburban Growth and Change," *Urban Studies* 39, no. 13 (2002): 2531–52; Pierre Filion et al., "Canada-US Metropolitan Density Patterns: Zonal Convergence and Divergence," *Urban Geography* 25, no. 1 (2004): 42–65; Jiawen Yang et al., "Measuring the Structure of US Metropolitan Areas, 1970–2000," *Journal of the American Planning Association* 78, no. 2 (2012): 197–209.

16 Larry Bourne and David Ley, *The Changing Social Geography of Canadian Cities* (Montreal: McGill-Queen's University Press, 1993); Trudi Bunting and Pierre Filion, "Dispersed City Form in Canada: A Kitchener CMA Case Example," *Canadian Geographer* 43, no. 3 (1999): 268–87;

to rural spectrum might be analyzed for a limited set of metropolitan areas.[18] However, creating suburban definitions that produced credible results across Canada proved quite difficult. To our knowledge, ours is the first study to develop a classification of suburban areas that gives credible results across Canada, in cities large and small. This allows us to make nationwide estimates of the extent of suburbs and compare any or all of the thirty-three metropolitan areas on a standard basis.[19]

Built-Form Methods

Starting from these previous attempts to define the inner city and suburbs, the research team for this project developed simple models to classify and map definitions of suburbs at the census tract (CT) level using spreadsheets and GIS. The first step was a pilot study that tested many built-form variables for the Ottawa-Gatineau CMA.[20] Unfortunately, built-form definitions that produced reasonable results in our Ottawa pilot site often produced suburban classifications that made little sense in other cities. In contrast, a rural classification based on population density seemed to work reasonably well in most CMAs, although there were many anomalies associated with oversized CTs, water bodies, and small residential developments.

The most serious disadvantage of built-form definitions was the wide variation in building types deployed across Canadian metropolitan areas. A lower proportion of single-family detached homes did not work as an exclusion criterion because of the pockets of suburban townhouses and apartments that were identified in Ottawa-Gatineau, and found in almost every Canadian city. This phenomenon is not an accident. Standard land-use planning procedures have called for a mix of dwelling-unit types in

suburban communities since the 1960s.[21] For example, Don Mills, the iconic suburb built in the 1950s, contains many apartment buildings in the core of the community and clusters of townhouses in most neighborhood units.[22]

Similarly, the presence or absence of apartments may not signal an inner-city CT. Several of Montreal and Quebec's inner-city neighborhoods contain few apartments, but have large concentrations of town houses that are sometimes stacked. These building-type anomalies confounded all of the classification schemes we attempted to deploy across Canada. Local and regional variations in building types and densities broke all of our attempts at a standard definition. Another problem with the built-form methods was the almost purely empirical and iterative nature of the models. In our attempts to produce a classification model that would reproduce the results on the ground, we drifted further and further from the slender theoretical bases of the built-form literature. After eighteen months of experimentation with built-form methods, the research team switched to models based on transportation data, which immediately produced more credible results.

Transportation Methods

In its long-form census, Statistics Canada collects valuable information on the mode of transportation that people use to get to work.[23] These data were quite useful for classifying neighborhoods according to the transportation behavior of their residents.

Only 7 percent of the Canadian labor force uses active transportation (walking or cycling) to get to work.[24] This form of active transportation was heavily concentrated in the cores of the metropolitan areas and was the dominant transportation mode in some inner-city CTs. Active transportation was a better criterion for

Bunting et al., "Density Gradients"; Pierre Filion and Trudi Bunting, "Understanding Twenty-First-Century Urban Structure: Sustainability, Unevenness, and Uncertainty," in *Canadian Cities in Transition: Local through Global Perspectives* (Toronto: Oxford University Press, 2006), 1–23; Pierre Filion and Karen Hammond, "Neighbourhood Land Use and Performance: The Evolution of Neighbourhood Morphology over the Twentieth Century," *Environment and Planning B: Planning and Design* 30, no. 2 (2003): 271–96; Hugh Millward, "Evolution of Populati on Densities: Five Canadian Cities, 1971–2001," *Urban Geography* 29, no. 7 (2008): 616–38; Peter J. Smith, "Suburbs," in *Canadian Cities in Transition: Local through Global Perspectives*, ed. Trudi Bunting and Pierre Filion (Toronto: Oxford University Press, 2006), 211–33.

17 Pierre Filion, "Suburban Mixed-Use Centres and Urban Dispersion: What Difference Do They Make?," *Environment and Planning* 33, no. 1 (2001): 141–60; Pierre Filion and Kathleen McSpurren, "Smart Growth and Development Reality: The Difficult Co-ordination of Land Use and Transport," *Urban Studies* 44, no. 3 (2007): 501–23; Avi Friedman, *Planning the New Suburbia: Flexibility by Design* (Vancouver: UBC Press, 2002); David L. A. Gordon and Shayne Vipond, "Gross Density and New Urbanism: Comparing Conventional and New Urbanist Suburbs in Markham, Ontario," *Journal of the American Planning Association* 71, no. 2 (2005): 41–54; Jill Grant, "Can Planning Save the Suburbs?," *Plan Canada* 30, no. 4 (1999): 16–18; Jill Grant, *Planning the Good Community: New Urbanism in Theory and Practice* (New York: Routledge, 2006); Jill

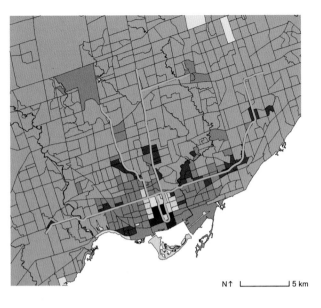

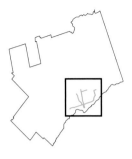

N↑ └────────┘ 5 km

— TTC subway

■ Active transportation

■ Public transit

▨ Automobile

■ Predominately automobile and public transit

▨ Predominately active transportation and public transportation

■ Predominately active transportation and automobile

▨ Unclassifiable

2.5.1 Toronto CMA, Toronto's 2006 journey to work by mode of transport

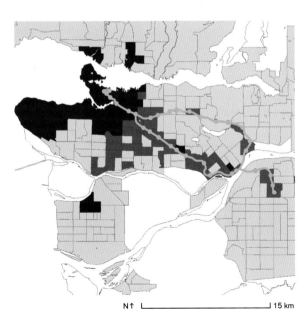

N↑ └────────┘ 15 km

● Sky Train stations

— Sky Train stations

■ Walkable core

■ Transit suburb

▨ Auto suburb

2.5.2 Vancouver transportation method T8, classification of suburbs for the Vancouver CMA in 2006

Grant, "An American Effect: Contextualizing Gated Communities in Canadian Planning Practice," *Canadian Journal of Urban Research* 16, no. 1 (2007): 1–19; Jill Grant, Katherine Greene, and Kristin Maxwell, "The Planning and Policy Implications of Gated Communities," *Canadian Journal of Urban Research* 13, no. 1 (2004): 70–88.

18 Alan Walks, "Place of Residence, Party Preferences, and Political Attitudes in Canadian Cities and Suburbs," *Journal of Urban Affairs* 26, no. 3 (2004): 269–95; Alan Walks, "The City-Suburban Cleavage in Canadian Federal Politics," *Canadian Journal of Political Science* 38, no. 2 (2005): 383–413; Martin Turcotte, "Life in Metropolitan Areas: The City/Suburb Contrast: How Can We Measure It?," *Canadian Social Trends* 85 (Summer 2008): 2–19.

19 Gordon and Janzen, "Suburban Nation?"; Gordon and Shirokoff, *Suburban Nation? Population Growth in Canadian Suburbs, 2006–2011.*

20 David Gordon and Chris Vandyk, "Suburban National Capital: A Pilot Study of Canada's Post-1945 Suburbs in Ottawa-Hull," (paper presented at the Fourteenth International Planning History Society Conference, Istanbul, July 12–15, 2010).

21 Gerald Hodge and David L. A. Gordon, *Planning Canadian Communities: An Introduction to the Principles, Practice, and Participants*, 6th ed. (Toronto: Nelson, 2014); Hok-Lin Leung, *Land-Use Planning Made Plain*, 2nd ed. (Toronto: University of Toronto Press, 2003).

22 Sewell, *The Shape of the City.*

23 Andrew Heisz and Sebastien Larochelle-Côté, *Work and Commuting in Census Metropolitan Areas, 1996–2001* (Ottawa: Statistics

	Population 2006	% 2006	Population 2011	% 2011	Population Growth 2006–2011	Population Growth Rate 2006–2011	Share of Population Growth (%) 2006–2011
Active Core	2,673,222	12.4%	2,762,618	12.0%	89,000	3.3%	5.6%
Transit Suburb	2,364,482	11.0%	2,433,320	10.5%	69,000	2.9%	4.3%
Auto Suburb	14,756,374	68.5%	16,033,565	69.3%	1,277,000	8.7%	80.1%
Exurban	1,717,229	8.0%	1,868,923	8.1%	152,000	8.9%	9.5%
TOTAL CMA	21,529,226	100.0%	23,123,441	100.0%	1,594,000	7.4%	100%

2.5.3 Canadian metropolitan neighborhood population distribution for 2006 and 2011

defining the core of a city than transit use, which should not be a surprise, since one of the principal advantages of downtown living is the ability to walk or cycle to a job in the central business district. Transit use was highest in inner suburbs with good transit service, especially in the larger metropolitan areas. These neighborhoods were too far removed from employment concentrations to walk or cycle to work, but a transit pass provided a convenient alternative to commuting by automobile in congested areas. (fig. **2.5.1**)

We defined an "active core" as a neighborhood that has a 50 percent higher rate of active transportation (walking or cycling) than the overall average for the CMA. These CTs are generally in central areas and the downtowns of cities. They also include the new infill neighborhoods not classified by the University of British Columbia professor David Ley's inner-city definition based on pre-1946 buildings.[25] Our definition was structured using local proportions of active transportation, which had the virtue of producing results that seemed credible across Canada in both large and small centers. We also tried many combinations of active transportation with other variables, such as the ratios of households without children, or the percentage of pre-1946 buildings, but these additional variables did not demonstrate more credible results and detracted from the simplicity of the model.

In some larger cities, active cores have begun to form in some secondary centers outside the downtown, such as

Burnaby's MetroTown and Langley within the Vancouver CMA. (fig. **2.5.2**) In larger metropolitan areas, multiple active cores were also observed in the downtowns of older communities that have been absorbed into larger CMAs, such as St. Jerome in Montreal; Oakville in Toronto; and the polycentric CMA containing the cities of Kitchener, Waterloo, and Cambridge. This is one reason for using the term *active core* as opposed to *inner city*. Based on our analysis, in 2011 approximately 2.6 million Canadians were living in active cores, making up about 12 percent of the population in metropolitan areas. (fig. **2.5.3**)

We defined *exurban* areas as CTs that have low gross population density and mostly depend on automobile use.[26] We prefer the term *exurban* to *rural* for these neighborhoods, because these areas define the edges of CMA's since over half of the labor force commutes to the central city for employment. Moreover, most of the people in these outer CTs are not engaged in rural or agrarian activities on a full-time basis.[27] Although exurban areas may not be entirely included in the suburban category, most residents live in single-family detached homes and commute by automobile into central city and suburban employment clusters.

In 2011 about 1.9 million Canadians were living in the exurban districts of CMAs, where they made up perhaps 8 percent of the total metropolitan population. The exurban lifestyle appears to be harder to achieve in the largest cities;

Canada Business and Labour Market Analysis Division, 2005); Martel and Caron-Malenfant, *Portrait of the Canadian Population in 2006*; Martin Turcotte, "Life in Metropolitan Areas: Dependence on Cars in Urban Neighbourhoods," *Canadian Social Trends* 85 (Summer 2008): 20–30.

24 Martin Turcotte and Jimmy Ruel, *Commuting Patterns and Places of Work of Canadians, 2006 Census* (Ottawa: Statistics Canada, 2008).

25 David Ley and Heather Frost, "The Inner City," in *Canadian Cities in Transition: Local through Global Perspectives*, ed. Bunting and Filion (Toronto: Oxford University Press, 2006), 192–210.

26 "Low gensity" is defined as less than or equal to 150 people/km², from the Organisation for Economic Co-operation and Development's "rural communities" definition, one of the rural lands analysis methods recommended by Statistics Canada; Valerie du Plessis et al., "Definitions of Rural: Rural and Small Town Canada," *Analysis Bulletin* 3, no. 3 (2001): 1–17.

27 Ray Bollman, *The Demographic Overlap of Agriculture and Rural* (Ottawa: Statistics Canada Agriculture Division, 2007).

the exurban populations in Toronto, Montreal, and Vancouver were between 3 and 4 percent, perhaps because of the difficulty of long-distance commuting into metropolitan traffic congestion. In contrast, most of the smaller CMAs have exurban populations of 15 to 37 percent, making up a substantial proportion of their metropolitan populations. Commuting from rural areas to employment in the central city appears to be substantially easier in areas like Thunder Bay and Saguenay.

Once the active cores and exurban areas are excluded, the remainder of the metropolitan population is some form of suburb. Suburbs are areas that have low rates of active transportation and generally high rates of automobile use. We considered two main methods for classifying the suburbs: *auto suburbs* and *transit suburbs*. In the density family of definitions, CTs are classified by their potential for transit use based on population density. In the transportation family of definitions, CTs are classified based on people's actual behavior in using transit or automobiles to get to work. We tested four density definitions and eight transportation definitions for over five thousand CTs in thirty-three CMAs.[28] The transportation behavior models produced the most consistent and credible results. While the density models may be useful for some purposes, we decided to use the transportation models to classify suburbs for the remaining analysis because they are based on residents' actual behavior—taking transit to work—rather than a more abstract measure of potential for transit use.

In the transportation behavior models, CTs are classified by the residents' level of transit or automobile use to get to work. Auto suburbs exhibit very low transit-use rates, and the automobile is the dominant mode of transportation. Transit suburbs are CTs that have a higher rate of transit use than the overall average for the CMA. The most credible and consistent results emerged from a definition of transit suburbs based on a transit-use rate threshold of 150 percent of the 2006 CMA average transit modal split.

Using this classification, in 2011, approximately 69 percent of Canada's metropolitan population lived in auto suburbs and 11 percent lived in transit suburbs.[29]

Suburbs in Smaller Cities—Census Agglomerations

CMAs accounted for 23.1 million people in 2011, or 68 percent of Canada's population. However, another 4.3 million Canadians live in smaller cities classified as census agglomerations (CAs). The populations of these settlements range from ten thousand to one hundred thousand people, but only the larger CAs have the CTs needed for our analysis. We took a sample of ten CAs to estimate the proportion of suburbs in this category using the transportation behavior model. The sample was not random; to control for regional variations, we deliberately selected CAs from each region of the country.

The CAs we analyzed displayed characteristics similar to the smaller CMAs: a higher exurban population (23 percent), very little transit use, and a high proportion of auto suburbs. Extrapolating the sample forward, we estimate that another roughly 2.6 million Canadians live in the suburbs of smaller cities.[30]

A Suburban Nation

Whether we like it or not, Canada is a suburban nation. As of 2011, approximately 80 percent of Canadian metropolitan residents lived in suburbs, while only 12 percent lived in active core areas. Moreover, this result probably underestimates the proportion of suburban residents, since at least half of the exurban residents commute to central city jobs by automobile and live in single-family detached houses.

28 Gordon and Janzen, "Suburban Nation?," Table 3.

29 A similar study for Australian metropolitan areas also found that the transportation behavior model produced the most credible results across the country, with approximately 86 percent of 2011 metropolitan population in suburbs (Auto Suburbs, Transit Suburbs and Exurbs) vs. 88 percent in Canadian CMAs. David Gordon, "Is Australia a Suburban Nation?" (paper presented to the Planning Institute of Australia Urban Forum, Perth, June 29, 2015).

30 Gordon and Janzen, "Suburban Nation?," Table 5.

Despite the well-reported downtown booms in condominium apartment life in the largest cities, low-density automobile suburbs and exurbs absorbed the vast majority of the population growth in Canada's metropolitan areas from 2006 to 2011. The net effect of this trend is that 90 percent of the CMA population growth from 2006 to 2011 was in auto suburbs and exurbs.[31] Only 10 percent of the population growth was in the active cores and transit suburbs that many analysts, including this author, consider more sustainable.[32]

The results show that the characteristics of an active core may not be confined to the geographic center of metropolitan areas. By detaching the concept of the active core from the spatial classification of the inner city, we allow for the possibility of other cores embedded in a polynuclear metropolitan structure. This flexibility fits more modern models of urban geography and recent planning movements to create suburban town centers and transit-oriented developments.[33]

The calculation for the total suburban population across Canada summarized here is based on detailed estimates published elsewhere.[34] To estimate the proportion of Canadians who lived in suburbs in 2011, we combined the suburban populations of the CMAs and CAs, and added half the exurban population.

We suggest that at least half of the exurban population is essentially very low-density suburban, since the periphery of the metropolitan area is defined by the areas where more than 50 percent of the labor force commutes inward to central city and suburban employment clusters.[35] These trips are overwhelmingly taken by automobile, and housing in the exurban CTs mostly consists of single-family detached dwellings. Thus, it seems reasonable to allocate at least half of the exurban population of the CMAs and CAs to the total suburban population.

CMA Transit & Auto Suburbs	18.46	million
CA Transit & Auto Suburbs	2.59	million
Subtotal CMA & CA Suburbs	21.05	million
50% CMA Exurban	0.94	million
50% CA Exurban	0.50	million
Total 2011 suburbs	22.49	million
2011 total population:	33.48	million
Suburban population %	67%	

2.5.4 Estimating the total suburban population as a proportion of the Canadian population

The total national population in 2011 was 33.5 million.[36] Therefore, suburbs were home to approximately 67 percent of the total national Canadian population in 2011. Even if we assume that the remaining Canadian population is rural, Canada's suburban population must be approximately 22.5 million people. This is a conservative estimate, because many residents of small towns (less than ten thousand people) also live in suburban areas with extensive automobile use and low-density, single-family detached dwellings. (fig. 2.5.4)

If two-thirds of Canada's population currently lives in suburban neighborhoods, then plans for infrastructure programs, environmental sustainability, public health, land use, and community design must take this phenomenon into account.[37] Future researchers of these issues may wish to use a more refined understanding of the active core, suburban, and exurban components of metropolitan areas. But even if urban development trends were to become significantly more intense, the current suburban neighborhoods will make up the bulk of the nation's housing stock well into the twenty-first century. Thus, it appears that Canada is destined to remain a suburban nation in the decades ahead.

31 Dwelling unit growth could not be calculated reliably due to an unfortunate change in Statistics Canada's census. David Hulchanski et al., "Canada's Voluntary Census Is Worthless: Here's Why," *The Globe and Mail*, October 4, 2013.
32 Gordon and Shirokoff, *Suburban Nation?*, 5–7; Newman and Kenworthy, *Sustainability and Cities;* Newman and Kenworthy, *The End of Automobile Dependence.*
33 Bunting et al., "Density Gradients"; Yang et al., "Measuring the Structure of US Metropolitan Areas"; Filion and McSpurren, "Smart Growth and Development Reality"; Emily Talen, ed., *The Charter of the New Urbanism* (New York: McGraw Hill, 2013).
34 Gordon and Janzen, "Suburban Nation?," Tables 2, 4, 5; Gordon and Shirokoff, *Suburban Nation?*, Appendices A and B. See CanadianSuburbs.ca.
35 Bollman, *The Demographic Overlap of Agriculture and Rural.*
36 Statistics Canada, *2011 Census Highlight Tables* (Ottawa: Statistics Canada, January 2013).
37 Gordon and Shirokoff, *Suburban Nation?*, 14–15.

*Portions of this essay were previously
published as* "Suburban Nation? Estimating
the Size of Canada's Suburban Population,"
Journal of Architectural and Planning
Research *30, no. 3 (Fall 2013): 197–220,
coauthored by Mark Janzen, and as*
Suburban Nation? Population Growth
in Canadian Suburbs, 2006–2011
*(Toronto: Council for Canadian Urbanism,
2014). Reproduced from the* Journal of
Architecture and Planning Research *30,
no. 3 (Fall 2013), used with the permission
of the publisher Locke Science Publishing
Company, Inc.*

    *Maps and data tables for all Canadian
metropolitan areas from this project
are available at CanadianSuburbs.ca.
The research for this essay was funded
by the Social Sciences and Humanities
Research Council of Canada and the
Institute for Advanced Studies at the
University of Western Australia. Research
assistants included Angus Beaty, Mehdi
Bouhadi, Mathieu Cordary, Anthony
Hommik, Benjamin Jean, Devon Miller,
Andrew Morton, Michelle Nicholson,
Tyler Nightingale, Thierry Pereira,
Krystal Perepeluk, Julien Sabourault,
Jennifer Sandham, Isaac Shirokoff,
Amanda Slaunwhite, and Chris Vandyk.
Peer reviewers included Ajay Agarwal,
Pierre Filion, Jill Grant, Richard Harris,
Paul Hess, Nik Luka, Martin Turcotte,
and Andrejs Skaburskis, but the author is
responsible for any errors or omissions.*

2.6
INTERBURBIA
GROUND TRUTHING US METROPOLITAN URBANIZATION

Kenneth P. Laberteaux, Casey Lance Brown, and Alan M. Berger

COMMUTING PATTERNS

POLYCENTRIC EXPANSION

REGIONAL GOVERNANCE

TRANSPORT INFRASTRUCTURE

Debate and polarization have surrounded the topic of suburban expansion since its inception. Each new wave of horizontal growth promulgates a series of derisive condemnations of the suburbs as a kind of urban cancer and counternotions of suburbs as the ultimate expression of the free market. In order to look past these polemical valuations, the Toyota Research Institute of North America and the Project for Reclamation Excellence (P-REX) lab at the Massachusetts Institute of Technology launched a project to map urban expansion in its actual state and evaluate how dynamic suburbanization and urbanization forces may require altered forms of mobility.

Our investigation began by evaluating the overarching growth trends in the top one hundred populated metropolitan areas in the United States. The top one hundred yielded a regional reading of metro growth differences (i.e., Sun Belt versus Rust Belt) that we could select from to compare and contrast. For the purposes of this essay, we focus on two major US metropolitan areas with expanding suburban territories: Denver, Colorado, and Atlanta, Georgia. Denver was chosen as a medium-growth, medium-sized metro in the west, and Atlanta as a high-growth, large metro with a mostly unrestricted geography in the east. First, current and future urbanized territory was mapped based on projections from the relevant regional data-collecting agency (or entity) overseeing metro growth activity. Second, population and employment density projections were examined, considering both the level and location of density. Finally, we looked at transportation trend projections in terms of infrastructure (location and type of roads) and travel behavior. Collectively, the simultaneous trends of population and employment decentralization, growth in multiple nodes, and commuting flows from one suburb to another have produced a

distinct condition of metropolitan urbanization that we have termed *Interburbia*. By documenting the actual quantities of population, jobs, and transportation movements, we reveal that a planning focus on the developing suburban nodes and their infrastructural linkages (rather than suburb to city core) would more closely match the urbanizing processes we confirm on the ground. A renewed infrastructural focus on intersuburban commuting along with parallel policy and design solutions could help create a better interface between the flexible, service-based economy of suburban environments and the majority of the US population who live and work there.

The Rise of the MSA

The United States has urbanized slowly over the years, with its population overwhelmingly concentrated in and around metropolitan areas. The Census Bureau defines metropolitan statistical areas (MSAs) as urban areas containing a densely populated core of at least fifty thousand people and surrounding counties with strong economic and commuting links to the core. In 1950, 56.1 percent of the total US population lived in metropolitan areas. In 2010 this figure was 83.6 percent. More than 90 percent of the nation's entire population growth in the last decade occurred within MSAs.[1] Economically, the ports and airports located in the one hundred largest MSAs handle 75 percent of all foreign seaport tonnage and 79 percent of all US air cargo weight. In 2005, these MSAs also produced 78 percent of all patents, attracted 80 percent of National Institutes of Health and National Science Foundation research funding, and received 94 percent of all venture capital funding. As the Brookings scholars Bruce Katz, Mark Muro, and Jennifer Bradley note in their survey of metropolitan areas, "America is quite literally a 'MetroNation,' utterly

1 John Rennie Short, "Metropolitan USA: Evidence from the 2010 Census," *International Journal of Population Research* (2012), accessed January 30, 2015, http://www .hindawi.com/journals /ijpr/2012/207532/.

dependent on the success of its metropolitan hubs."[2] Attempting to describe these newer, larger urban entities, the sociologist Robert Lang and the geographer Paul Knox identify economic restructuring, improved telecommunications technologies, demographic shifts, and neoliberal policies as forces shaping new urban, suburban, and exurban landscapes.[3]

These collective forces forge metropolitan areas, which share five primary characteristics. First, their structure is polycentric: it exhibits multiple clusters of both population and employment density. These areas do not follow the traditional monocentric pattern of high density in the center that declines toward the edges. Instead, they demonstrate multiple scattered nodes of high and medium density, with clusters of housing, employment, and commercial development. The US Census Bureau has acknowledged this change by replacing the old term *central city* with the new term *principal city*, recognizing that metro areas may no longer have a single focus.[4]

Second, metropolitan areas exhibit development that is less constrained horizontally than vertically. Third, metropolitan areas represent a breakdown of the urban-rural dichotomy. They often contain locations that look rural, but are functionally metropolitan. Each decennial Census shifts several counties from the nonmetro (or rural) category to metro status as they grow economic connections to areas nearby, representing absorption of previously rural populations by the metropolitan area. Fourth, metropolitan areas are linked by transportation and communications infrastructure, sometimes imperfectly. For example, transportation infrastructure tends to focus on connections between metropolitan areas, rather than within individual metropolitan areas. However, Lang and Knox also emphasize "the

counter-intuitive notion that urban expansiveness…produces new types of connectivity."[5] It is also important to note that some of the most basic commodity exchanges and movements occur in more remote areas, such as rail yards, highway interchanges, and in small satellite towns.[6] Fifth, metropolitan areas demonstrate multiple, nonoverlapping jurisdictions, reflecting their complex economic and social links. For example, the New York and Chicago metro areas cross state boundaries, encompassing New York, New Jersey, and Pennsylvania, and Illinois, Indiana, and Wisconsin, respectively.

In some locations, metropolitan areas have grown so much that they have become megapolitan areas. The megapolitan phenomenon, first described by the geographer Jean Gottman as the Boston-to-Washington corridor, is a condition where clusters of metropolitan areas have populations greater than ten million people.[7] As of 2004, ten megapolitan areas contained about one-fifth of all land area in the lower forty-eight states, but almost 70 percent of the total US population, with over two hundred million people.[8] By 2040, megapolitan regions are expected to gain over eighty-three million residents, representing the majority of total US growth.[9]

An Enduring Role for the Automobile
There are several structural characteristics that suggest an enduring role for the automobile in US metro areas. Due to persistent housing and employment decentralization, access to home and work will likely require the flexibility of the automobile. Functionally, automobile use both accompanies edge growth and enables it. Service industries do not require the same infrastructural access that tended to cause manufacturing industries to cluster around central urban cores. Economically, the switch from

2 Bruce Katz, Mark Muro, and Jennifer Bradley, "Miracle Mets: Our Fifty States Matter a Lot Less Than Our One Hundred Largest Metro Areas," *Democracy: A Journal of Ideas* 12 (2009): 23.

3 Robert Lang and Paul K. Knox, "The New Metropolis: Rethinking Megalopolis," *Regional Studies* 43, no. 6 (2009): 789–802.

4 Ibid., 795.

5 Ibid., 790.

6 Alan Berger, *Drosscape: Wasting Land in Urban America* (New York: Princeton Architectural Press, 2006).

7 Jean Gottmann, *Megalopolis: The Urbanized Northeastern Seaboard of the United States* (New York: Twentieth Century Fund, 1961).

8 Robert Lang and Dawn Dhavale, *Beyond Megalopolis: Exploring America's New "Megapolitan" Geography*, Census Report Series (Washington, DC: Metropolitan Institute at Virginia Tech, 2005), 13–19.

9 Ibid., 20.

manufacturing to service-based economies also reduces the costs involved in opening new employment hubs and increases the benefits of being near housing locations where employee pools are already located.[10]

By 2001, 93 percent of all US households owned at least one vehicle.[11] In 2009, only about 5 percent of the US employed population used public transit to get to work, and this percentage had changed little since 2005. While automobile ownership does drop as population density increases, it does not do so significantly until densities are very high. In cities with densities of ten thousand or more people per square mile (about 3,860 people per kilometer) like Chicago or Philadelphia, almost 30 percent of households did not have a vehicle in 2009. However, in cities with densities of four thousand to ten thousand people per square mile (about 1,540 to 3,860 people per kilometer) like Seattle or Las Vegas, only slightly over 8 percent did not own a vehicle in 2009.[12] Only two MSAs in the United States register significant levels of public transit usage: the New York MSA at 31 percent and the San Francisco MSA at 15 percent.[13] Both of these MSAs have densely concentrated downtown districts accessible by transit. This prototypical urban structure is partly due to the island geography of Manhattan and the peninsular geography of San Francisco forcing the concentration and limited transportation access. Very few urbanized areas in the United States approach the densities of these restrictive geographies, making them the exception rather than the rule. For this reason alone, these two MSAs should not serve as transportation models for polynodal areas where very high densities are likely impossible to achieve and where land tenure, development codes, and property rights make radical changes to urban fabric prohibitive. Therefore, as our research for two metro areas (Denver

and Atlanta) reveals, new conceptualization of the American urban condition is critical to resolve future funding, policy, and design of mobility infrastructure for polynodal America.

Metro Area Case Study 1: Denver Metropolitan Area

Denver has experienced strong metropolitan growth, especially north–south along the Front Range of the Rocky Mountains, as well as eastward toward its bustling international airport. The Denver MSA includes one exploding suburban edge county, Douglas, which doubled in population from 1990 to 2000, and by 2010, added another 110,000 people (growing by 62 percent).[14] Like many metropolitan areas, Denver is characterized by overlapping jurisdictions. The territory overseen by the Denver Regional Council of Governments (DRCOG) covers not only a significant part of the MSA but also northern suburbs like Boulder, which are not included in the MSA. (figs. **2.6.1–2**)

In terms of both population and employment density, the Denver MSA exhibits a pattern of multiple, spatially distinct nodes of development. Instead of high density in the center, declining gradually toward the edges, there are multiple areas of high and medium density, creating a complex patchwork. Above-mean population density exists in the core urban area (the central business district [CBD] and surrounding dense area), the southeastern suburbs outside the tech center, and the northern suburbs toward Broomfield. (figs. **2.6.3–4**) Nodal development has reinforced existing employment centers like the Tech Center (15 miles or 24 kilometers south of the center city), as well as produced new urbanization in the distant suburbs north toward Boulder and Longmont, south toward Castle Rock, and east around Denver International Airport. (fig. **2.6.5**) These new nodes of suburbanization are typified by low-density,

10 Edward L. Glaeser and Matthew E. Kahn, "Sprawl and Urban Growth," in *Handbook of Regional and Urban Economics*, ed. J. Vernon Henderson and Jacques-François Thisse (Elsevier, 2004), 2497.

11 National Research Council, *Driving and the Built Environment: The Effects of Compact Development on Motorized Travel, Energy Use, and CO2 Emissions* (Washington, DC: Transportation Research Board, 2009), 20.

12 Federal Highway Administration, *Summary of Travel Trends: 2009 National Household Travel Survey*, by Adelia Santos et al., FHWA-PL-11-022, 20, accessed January 31, 2015. http://trid.trb.org /view.aspx?id=1107370.

13 US Census Bureau, *Public Transportation Usage among US Workers: 2008 and 2009*, by Brian S. McKenzie, ACSBR/09-5, 4–6, accessed January 20, 2015, http://www .census.gov/prod/2010 pubs/acsbr09-5.pdf.

14 Douglas County Community Planning and Sustainable Development Department, *Douglas County 2010 Census Profile*, accessed January 31, 2015, http:// www.douglas.co.us documents/douglas -county-2010-census -profile.pdf.

2.6.1 Urbanizing area near Brighton along the 85 corridor

2.6.2 Foreground: E-470 serves as the beltline conveyer around Denver, but much intersuburban traffic uses this to travel to work, shop, etc.

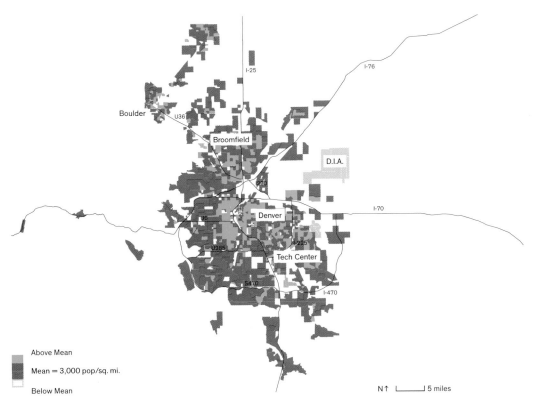

2.6.3 Population density per square mile around the Denver metropolitan area

2.6.4 Tech Center at Lincoln Ave/I-25 (19 miles from Denver)

2.6.5 Tech Center Arapahoe Rd/I-25 (12 miles from Denver)

2.6.6 Boulder Turnpike US 36 (between Broomfield and Superior, 12–15 miles from Denver)

horizontal urbanization with office park campuses and upgraded retail clusters. (fig. **2.6.6**)

Based on demographic data from DRCOG, our research reveals that urban growth will likely add another 190 square miles (492 square kilometers) of urbanized land—or land with at least one thousand people per square mile (about 390 people per square kilometer)—to the Denver metropolitan area from 2010 to 2035. This conservative prediction generally matches DRCOG's own estimate of urbanization increase at 260.5 square miles (674.7 square kilometers), or a 36 percent increase in urbanized area.[15] Significant urbanization will occur all around the south, east, and northern edges of Denver, both reinforcing existing peripheral nodes and creating new ones near attractors like the Denver International Airport. (fig. **2.6.7**) Employment projections show concentrations that relate to the population pattern but more clustered along major roadways (highways and interstates) and infrastructure (the airport). (fig. **2.6.8**) Most significantly, from 2010 to 2035, the core urban area is expected to add fewer jobs (164,000) than the suburbs (728,000). Thus, while the core urban area will remain a strong employment center, a substantially larger change will likely occur in suburban areas, as mutually reinforcing nodes of employment and housing nodes grow.

Denver Transportation Trends

Currently, Denver's transportation system is auto-dominated. Based on household travel surveys conducted by the DRCOG (as part of a Travel Behavior Inventory [TBI] project) only 2 to 4 percent of trips in the Denver metro area use mass transit, while vehicles make up about 88 percent of all trips.[16] The average private vehicle is driven 28.2 miles (45.4 kilometers) per day with each household taking an average of nine trips daily. The DRCOG

surveys found that 65 percent of all trips had origin and destination in the suburbs. DRCOG mapped daily trips within subregions, and found that intersuburban trips were particularly dominant in the northern quadrants and southeast quadrants of the metro area (both of which are relatively fast growing in population), with many travel connections not linked to the urban core at all.[17] There is no significant, dedicated infrastructure for intersuburban travel despite this being the supermajority of daily round trips. (fig. **2.6.9**) While beltways around urban areas perform some of this function, they are becoming congested due to heavy through-traffic.

In addition, the urban area is expanding past the beltways. Based on a transportation model developed by DRCOG to track functional roadway usage, in terms of vehicle miles traveled (VMT) and vehicle hours traveled (VHT), freeways and principal arterials will remain dominant. Freeways constitute 38 percent of VMT and 24 percent of VHT, and principal arterials make up 31 percent of VMT and 34 percent of VHT. The fact that principal arterials are almost as important as freeways, in terms of VMT and VHT, serves as another likely indicator that suburban travel is dependent on subordinate transportation infrastructure. Population density interacts differently with freeways than it does with principal arterials. Dense areas tend to be located away from freeways because of incompatible land uses. In contrast, principal arterials tend to funnel major traffic through density. Thus, a third alternative is needed to journey between density nodes within the metro area.

Denver's projected urban expansion, and its population and employment densities, suggests continued horizontal urbanization with multiple nodes of growth, which is likely to reinforce auto dependence. In order to support mass

15 Denver Regional Council of Governments, Metro Vision 2035 Plan, Denver Regional Council of Governments, 2011, accessed January 30, 2015, https://drcog.org/planning-great-region/metro-vision-2040.

16 Denver Regional Council of Governments, *Denver Regional Travel Behavior Inventory: Household Survey Report*, Denver Regional Council of Governments and Parsons Transportation Group, Inc., April 2000, 4, accessed January 31, 2015, http://drcog.org/documents/HHS_rpt_cov-chp1_gls.pdf.

17 Denver Regional Council of Governments, *Travel in the Denver Region: Results from the 1997 Household Travel Survey and 1998 Roadside Survey*, May 2000, accessed January 30, 2015, https://drcog.org/sites/drcog/files/resources/DRCOG%20TDR%20Report.pdf.

Polycentric Metropolitan Form
    2.6
    240

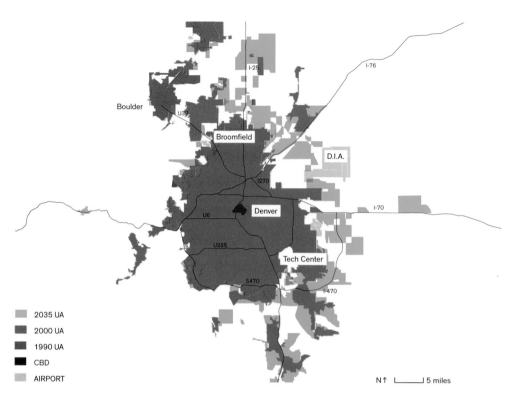

2035 UA
2000 UA
1990 UA
CBD
AIRPORT

N↑ └─────┘ 5 miles

2.6.7 2035 Urbanization footprint of the Denver metropolitan area

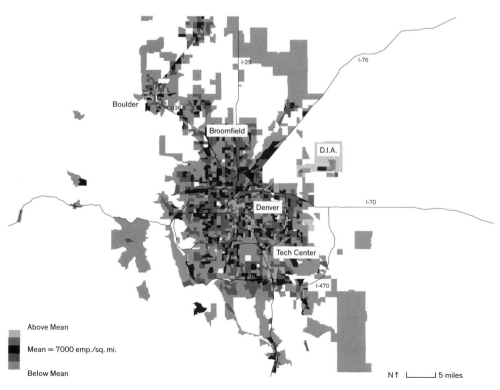

Above Mean

Mean = 7000 emp./sq. mi.

Below Mean

N↑ └─────┘ 5 miles

2.6.8 Expected employment densities for the Denver metropolitan area

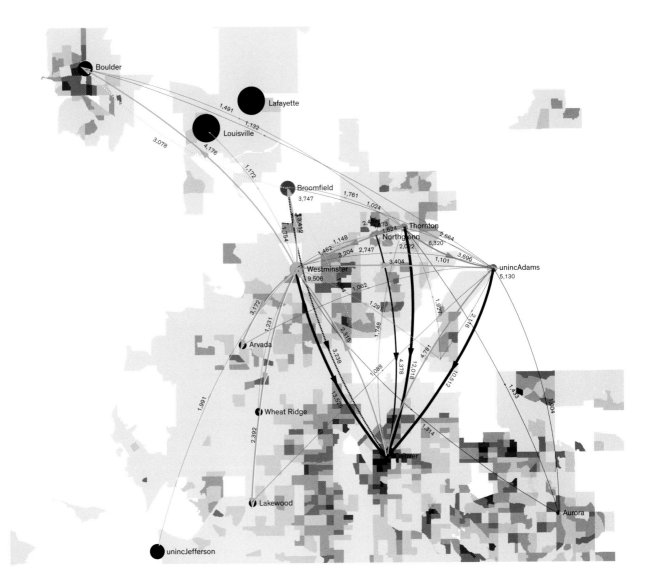

Pop/sq. mi. (2003)

■ 23620 – 38390
■ 14400 – 23620
■ 9630 – 14400
■ 7075 – 9630
■ 5168 – 7075
■ 500 – 5168

No. of Commuters > 1000

▬ 12K – 14K
▬ 10K – 12K
▬ 8K – 10K
▬ 6K – 8K
▬ 4K – 6K
▬ 2K – 4K
▬ 1K – 2K

— Denver
····· Broomfield
— Thornton
— Northglenn
— Westminster
— Unincorporated Adams

Suburban to City of Denver
Commuter Ratio

● 8.1 – 16.0
● 4.1 – 8.0
● 2.1 – 4.0
● 1.1 – 2.0
• 0 – 1.0

2.6.9 Suburban Denver commuter network

transit and reduced automotive VMT, housing, employment centers, and retail would need to be mutually concentrated. Even with intensive focus on transit planning and congestion concerns, DRCOG projects no significant increase in the share of trips that use transit.[18]

Our Denver research indicates that there is a wide gap in transportation planning for polynodal suburban trips. The traditional models of highway planning designed largely for downtown core destinations do not match the real mobility patterns of polynodal drivers, who avoid downtown destinations as they move between suburbs for their daily needs. A new dedicated intersuburban mobility infrastructure for automobiles would better serve the Denver MSA under its current build-out plans to 2035.

Metro Area Case Study 2:
Atlanta Metropolitan Area
Atlanta has experienced vast urbanization and horizontal growth. From 2000 to 2010, it was the MSA with the third-highest raw population growth, with over 1 million people added, behind only Houston and Dallas (each added about 1.2 million people). In addition, the Atlanta MSA included three out of the top ten fastest-growing counties in the United States from 2000 to 2010: Forsyth, Henry, and Paulding.[19] All three are suburban counties. Since 2010, suburban Gwinnett and Cobb County have continued to post the highest population increases in the MSA (8,000 to 9,000 people added per year), although Fulton County, which contains the city center, recently matched these levels.[20] This expansive condition, whereby the suburban and central counties both experience large growth over short amounts of time, is becoming more common.[21]

In terms of both population and employment density, the Atlanta metropolitan area exhibits a pattern of multiple nodes, with numerous areas of higher

density dispersed among low-density development. Above-mean population density exists around the CBD, in the historic city center, and northeast along the I-85 corridor. (fig. **2.6.10**) The Georgia 400 corridor runs north to Sandy Springs, a large employment center, with other business districts along the way. Sandy Springs and Dunwoody, just outside the beltline highway, to the north, and the I-85 corridor, to the northwest, function as major suburban employment nodes. The northern nexus of major beltways, suburban highways, and developable land form the paradoxically named Perimeter Center, which hosts extensive corporate headquarters, office parks, and retail and medical employment clusters entirely outside the Atlanta beltway. These agglomerations of infrastructure and commercial activity are the modern economic engine of newer metropolitan areas.

Based on data from the Atlanta Regional Commission (ARC), our research conservatively projects that urban growth will add 275 square miles (712 square kilometers) of urbanized land to the edges of the Atlanta metro area from 2010 to 2030. Population projections indicate the majority of population growth will occur in the suburbs (73 percent, adding 1,773,500 people), with the rest split between the exurbs (14 percent, 332,600) and the central county of Fulton (13 percent, 324,000). Growth will take place around the entire periphery, especially to the northeast and northwest. (fig. **2.6.11**)

In terms of employment, ARC data projects that suburbs will add twenty times as many jobs as the CBD from 2010 to 2030. By 2030, jobs located 10 to 35 miles (16 to 56 kilometers) from the CBD will make up almost 48 percent of total jobs in the metro area. Employment growth will cluster along the interstate system, marking a similar importance of mobility infrastructure to the Denver projections. (fig. **2.6.12**)

18 Denver Regional Council of Governments, *2035 Metro Vision Regional Transportation Plan*, February 2011, accessed January 30, 2015, https://drcog .org/programs/trans portation-planning /regional-transporta tion-plan.
19 US Census Bureau, *Population Distribution and Change: 2000 to 2010*, by Paul Mackun and Steven Wilson, C2010BR-01, 9, accessed January 30, 2015, http:// www.census.gov /prod/cen2010/briefs /c2010br-01.pdf.
20 Atlanta Regional Commission, *Regional Snapshot: 2013 Population Estimates*, accessed January 30, 2015, http:// documents.atlanta regional.com/enews letters/reg_snapshot /0813/pop_estimates _main.pdf.
21 Short, "Metropolitan USA: Evidence from the 2010 Census."

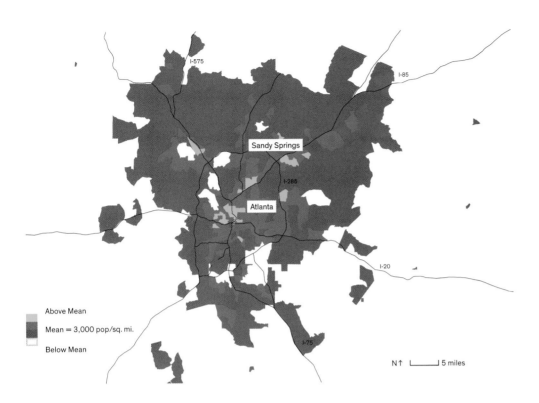

2.6.10 Population density per square mile around the Atlanta metropolitan area

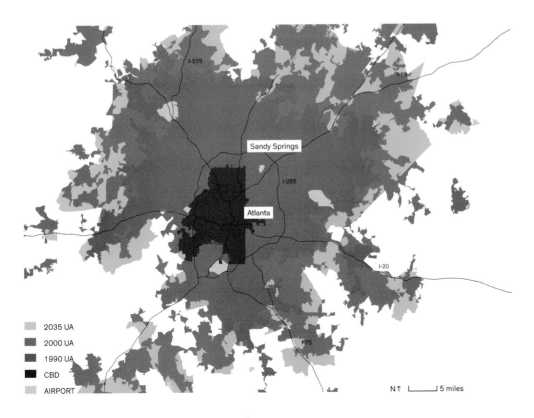

2.6.11 2030 Urbanization footprint of the Atlanta metropolitan area

Above Mean

Mean = 2,900 emp./sq.mi.

Below Mean

N↑ ⌞_____⌟ 5 miles

22 Atlanta Regional
    Commission and PTV
    NuStats, *Travel Survey
    Final Report: November
    2011*, accessed January
    20, 2015, http://www
    .atlantaregional.com
    /File%20Library
    /Transportation
    /Travel%20Demand%20
    Model/tp_2011regional
    travelsurvey_030712.pdf.
23 Texas Transportation
    Institute, *2012 Urban
    Mobility Report*, accessed
    January 15, 2015, http://
    tti.tamu.edu/documents
    /mobility-report-2012.
    pdf.

2.6.12 Expected employment densities for the Atlanta metropolitan area

Atlanta Transportation Trends

As with all American metropolitan areas, Atlanta's transportation system is auto-dominated. In 2011, 92.2 percent of workers drove to work, while only 5.1 percent used mass transit.[22] Of those who used mass transit, over 85 percent lived in the central counties and 64 percent did not have a vehicle to use. Thus, mass transit primarily aids individuals who live near the CBD and do not own a car, which is the vast minority of people in the metro area.

As in Denver, intersuburban commuting is a major component of travel in the Atlanta region. The major difference in travel patterns between Denver and Atlanta is the relative amount of time, in percentage of vehicle hours traveled (VHT), spent on arterials. It is significantly higher in Atlanta (44 percent) than in Denver (34 percent). This elevated VHT likely reflects the overloaded capacity on arterials in Atlanta's suburban matrix, many of which are the only conduits between different suburbs. Atlanta perennially ranks in the top ten worst metropolitan areas on congestion indexes in the United States.[23] Until significant capacity is added to these connections, congestion is likely to worsen, especially with continued suburban employment and population growth. This is likely the primary motivating factor behind the Northwest Corridor Project, the most expensive highway project in Georgia's history. It seeks to alleviate congestion and commute times through dedicated express lanes and connectors along the northwest suburban corridor of I-75 and I-575, far outside Atlanta proper. The construction of these billion-dollar, intersuburban connectors demonstrates the infrastructural mismatch of a center city–focused highway system and the emergent suburban employment nodes.

Toward Interburbia

The simultaneous trends of population and employment decentralization, growth of multiple nodes, and intersuburban commuting flows have produced a distinct form of metropolitan urbanization, the one we have termed *Interburbia*. Though geographically diverse, both Denver and Atlanta demonstrate this pattern. In terms of population and employment density, each is projected to have much stronger suburban than central city growth. Each metro has only a minority of trips occurring by modes other than car.

These case studies highlight two aspects of the emerging interurban condition in its present form: the need for new conceptualization and funding of transportation infrastructure to match intersuburban travel; and the necessity of better coordination for metropolitan-wide transportation solutions, and respective regional governance, that do not focus solely on the downtown core as a primary destination.

Congestion creates significant inefficiencies and costs. For example, the Texas Transportation Institute found that traffic jams resulted in approximately $121 billion in wasted gas and time in 2011. From 1982 to 2011, drivers in metropolitan areas with over three million people increased the amount of time delayed by congestion from about nineteen hours per year to fifty-two hours per year.[24] Currently, interurban areas demonstrate congestion and less efficient driving patterns due to a road system primarily built for driving in and out of the center city. Historically, the Interstate Highway System (IHS) was organized to create efficient conduits between dense population centers. It has not evolved fast enough to keep pace with widespread housing growth and employment opportunities in suburban and exurban territories. Barring unforeseeable, simultaneous shifts in housing, employment, and retail/service geography, the metro population will need flexible, energy- and time-efficient transportation modes for the majority of travel. While beltways have assumed some capacity for connecting suburban

locations, a connector system better aligned to such widespread polynodal urbanism deserves consideration.

The ubiquity and strength of interurban commuting flows demonstrates the need for new metropolitan forms of governance. While the United States is becoming more metropolitan, it lacks a comprehensive national surface transportation plan, which could guide investments across jurisdictions, metro areas, and states. Metro governments need federal support, because they do not have the authority or resources to act completely independently, especially in terms of cross-jurisdictional infrastructure upgrades.[25] One example is described in "Megapolitan America" by Robert Lang and the academic Arthur C. Nelson, who argue that the twenty-three US megapolitan regions, which dominate the country both economically and demographically (400 million residents by 2040), should become the basis for future planning and policy.[26]

Other prime examples of interurban-style developments are the leading tech industry nodes: Silicon Valley outside San Francisco, the Route 128 corridor outside Boston, and the Research Triangle Park scattered across the woodlands near Raleigh-Durham in North Carolina. Each of these tech agglomerations occupies a dispersed, horizontal landscape connected by congested highways. They sporadically cluster around private, leafy campuses and office parks that dot the interstitial spaces between major suburbs and are outside major cities. As major new employment centers, they possess enormous attraction for retail development, medical offices, housing, and recreational facilities. But the infrastructure that accesses them was built for bedroom communities and intercity travel half a century ago. It comes as no surprise that Apple, LinkedIn, Facebook, and Google have resorted to private bus lines

24 Ibid., 24.
25 Katz, Muro, and Bradley, "Miracle Mets," 31–32.
26 Robert Lang and Arthur C. Nelson, "Megapolitan America," *Places Journal*, November 2011, accessed January 30, 2015, https://places journal.org/article /megapolitan-america/.

and private car fleets to shuttle employees between far-flung campuses and housing locales.[27] Amazingly, these private mobility networks have pushed the drive-alone rate down to dense San Francisco levels in the dispersed transit desert of North Bayshore, a neighborhood in northern Mountain View, California.[28]

Summary

The idea of interburbia emerges out of the new live-work-leisure economy of the twenty-first century, which has more to do with global networking than static placemaking. In other words, where you physically are located does not inhibit your ability to participate in the global economy while still enjoying high quality of life based on economic choices and location preferences.[29]

Conceptualizing the metropolitan area in its interburban condition forces one to consider growth and economic opportunities well beyond the conceptual and physical trappings of single CBDs and the downtown core as sole destination. Our metropolitan areas will most likely be stunted, unable to reach their peak productivity until we recognize the rapid ascent of polynodal growth and the accompanying intersuburban mobility needs.

This research was conducted with P-REX lab at MIT, including Alan M. Berger, Casey L. Brown, and Sara Brown, and was supported by the MIT Norman B. Leventhal Center for Advanced Urbanism and Toyota Research Institute of North America.

27 Eric Rodenbeck, "Mapping Silicon Valley's Gentrification Problem through Corporate Shuttle Routes," *WIRED*, September 13, 2013, accessed May 13, 2015, http://www.wired.com /2013/09/mapping -silicon-valleys-corpo rate-shuttle-problem/.

28 John Markoff and Conor Dougherty, "Options for Simplifying the Commute," *Bits Blog*, accessed June 11, 2015, http://bits.blogs.nytimes .com/2015/06/10 /options-for-simplifying -the-commute/.

29 Alan M. Berger et al., "Where Americans Live: An Environmental and Geographical Tally," *Harvard Journal of Real Estate: Navigating Investments with Ethical Risk* (June 2013): 39–50.

Georgetown, Texas, United States

McKinney, Texas, United States

2.7
DRIVING WHILE SUBURBAN

Alan E. Pisarski

COMMUTING
PATTERNS

POLYCENTRIC
EXPANSION

TRANSPORT
MODES

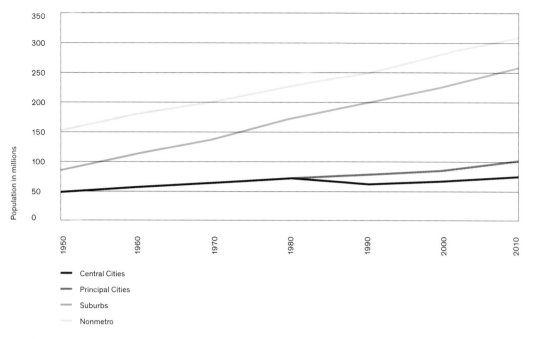

2.7.1 Long-term national population growth trend by census geography, 1950–2010

Although many urbanists may find it distasteful, it is the suburbs—not core cities—that will most likely determine the country's future transportation patterns. Much of what is missed in such thinking is that America's suburbs are now the dominant work destination in almost all metro areas. Today, work origin–destination patterns are predominantly circumferential movements from suburb to suburb, around the rim of a wheel and no longer, like the spokes of a wheel, focused on some central hub.

In 1950, with the nation's population roughly half of what it is today, America was already a majority metro population, according to the Office of Management and Budget (OMB). The population was roughly split 60/40 percent between cities and suburbs, as then defined.[1] By 2010, the shares shifted dramatically, with the split now 70/30 in favor of suburbs. In this period, suburbs gained more than 85 percent of national growth. (fig. **2.7.1**)

These figures are based on the research produced in a National Cooperative Highway Research Program (NCHRP) study conducted as part of the "Commuting in America" project, which distinguishes between the historical central cities and the new Census Bureau concept of a "principal city."[2] This new concept often leads some to cast essentially suburban, auto-dominated areas such as Frederick, Maryland; White Plains, New York; or Long Beach, California, as part of central cities.[3] Differentiating between principal cities that are central cities (as formerly defined) from those principal cities that are suburban, we find that 25 percent of principal cities are in fact suburban. (fig. **2.7.2**)

The impact on trends is a relatively small one. If historic central cities are subtracted from all principal cities, the remaining suburban principal cities account for only about a six-million-person difference in growth allocated to suburbs rather than center cities in the period from 2000 to 2010. Even if all of the principal cities were assumed to be part of historical central cities, the suburban share would still be 61 percent of metro population.

This suburban growth is a product of multiple trends, most particularly the accretion of formerly rural areas into the

1 The Office of Management and Budget (OMB), formerly the Bureau of the Budget (BOB), has responsibility for defining and identifying metro areas. The criteria employed are keyed fundamentally to the extent of commuting flow patterns and are thus central to the material presented here.

2 The Commuting in America series has been conducted for four decades as a product of the National Academy of Sciences, Transportation Research Board, and the American Association of State Highway and Transportation Officials. The most recent is *Commuting in America 2013: The National Report on Commuting Patterns and Trends* (Washington, DC: American Association of State Highway and Transportation Officials, 2013).

3 Bruce Spear, "US Commuting and Travel Patterns: Data Development and Analysis," National Cooperative Highway Research Program, NCHRP-8–36 Task 111, accessed November 15, 2015, http://apps .trb.org/cmsfeed /TRBNetProjectDisplay .asp?ProjectID=3298. A special study performed by the Transportation Research Board of the National Academies, to support the Commuting in America series update, which, among other activities, separated the traditional central cities from the concept of principal cities. Principal cities were developed, in part, to recognize the fact that many suburban communities and small cities had been incorporated into metropolitan areas as the metropolitan areas expanded outward and small towns evolved into cities that were destinations of workers in their own right. Some statistical treatments inappropriately assume that principal cities, as

	1990	2000	2010	% Change
	Count Millions	Count Millions	Count Millions	2000–2010
Total US Population	248.7	281.4	308.7	9.70%
Living in Metro Areas	198.2	232.6	262.5	12.85%
Living in Central Cities	65.8	70.3	75.3	7.11%
Living in Other Principal Cities	12.9	23.6	24.1	2.12%
Living Outside Principal Cities (Suburbs)	119.5	138.7	163.1	17.59%
Living Outside Metro Areas	50.5	48.8	46.2	-5.33%

2.7.2 National population trends by geographic elements

suburbs as the commuting shed to central areas expanded, as well as the designation of new metropolitan areas. In just the twenty years between 1990 and 2010, the number of MSAs (metropolitan statistical areas) grew from 323 to 381 areas, and the number of counties in MSAs went from 839 to 1,167—a third of the nation's counties. Given that the OMB determines such additions largely on the basis of work-commute statistics, this is a valid metric of suburban growth. In many ways, the decline in the size of the nonmetro population in America has been the product of successful growth, rather than failure, as rural areas gained population and became associated with a nearby metropolitan area or became the center of a new area.

The key idea for transportation planning is that the vast majority of the job and population growth occurred outside the core cities, and even outside the principal cities. Research reveals that US population growth has now dropped below 1 percent a year and that metro areas have gained the great majority of the growth. Within metros, the growth has been predominantly in suburbs.

Population Growth Varies Widely

These trends are more evident if we look at population growth at the county level, which shows a startling picture of a nation sharply divided by growth characteristics. Of the 3,143 counties in America, over a thousand (a bit more than a third of the counties), consisting of both metro and nonmetro areas, lost about 2 million people between 2000 and 2010. Roughly another third, all in metro areas, gained over 27 million. The remaining third, consisting of nonmetro areas, gained slightly above 2 million. Overall, the nation is almost equally separated into three parts: a third losing population, a third with 93 percent of national growth, and a third just muddling through.

Among the almost two thousand nonmetro counties, about half lost 700,000 in population and the other half gained over 2 million, suggesting that travel behavior and demand will vary sharply around the nation depending on growth patterns.

Labor Force Moves

Beyond population change, the Census Bureau and the Bureau of Labor Statistics' Current Population Survey is a major source for tracking the crucial data on flows of the labor force within and between metro and nonmetro areas. Between 2012 and 2013, about 19 million labor force members moved residences in the nation. As can be expected, the majority of flows are local and remain within a given area. Principal cities, in the Census Bureau definition, generated a six million shift of workers within their own areas, while suburbs accounted for about 5.5 million, and nonmetro areas accounted for about 1.8 million intra-area moves. The principal city labor force tends to move more frequently than suburban workers, given the greater tendency for rentals in cities. The

now defined, are the natural continuation of the original central city concepts. Principal cities include, for example, Frederick, Maryland, 50 miles from the District of Columbia; Lakewood, New Jersey, 80 miles from Manhattan; Framingham, 24 miles from Boston; or Marietta, 20 miles from Atlanta. An estimate provided by the NCHRP study indicates that about 75 percent of the principal cities population is attributable to central cities.

	All movers	To suburbs	To central city and other pc	To nonmetro
Total	19242	8837	8018	2386
From subs	7368	5513	1600	255
From cc and oth pc	8831	2637	5905	289
From nonmetro	2584	492	279	1813
From abroad	458	195	234	29
Net gain/loss	458	1469	-813	-198

2.7.3 Labor force mobility trends

following are brief notes of other revealing shifts between areas:

The almost six million intra–principal city moves consisted of several components: about 0.8 million worker moves occurred between principal cities in different metro areas; and 0.5 million shifted between different principal cities in the same metro area; and the large remainder, roughly 4.6 million, shifted within the same principal city.

Among the 5.5 million suburban labor force shifts, 4.7 million labor force members shifted within the same metropolitan area suburbs and the remainder shifted between suburbs in different metro areas.

The key outcome to understand is that within metro areas, suburbs gained about 0.7 million workers from principal cities as the suburbs received about 1.8 million workers from cities and sent 1.1 million to cities.

In intermetro moves, the suburbs also realized strong gains in workers, with a net gain of almost 0.4 million. At the same time, suburbs lost about 0.5 million to a principal city in a new metro area but received almost 0.9 million from principal cities in other metros. Suburb to suburb and principal city to principal city shifts between metros were almost exactly the same amount.

Again, the overall effect was that of the 1.3 million who left a suburb for another metro, 62 percent went to a suburb; and of the 1.7 million that left a principal city for another metro, only 47 percent went to a principal city in that new metro.

Of the limited nonmetro flows to metro areas, about 0.5 million went to suburbs and under 0.3 million went to principal cities. In net terms, nonmetros lost about 0.25 million to suburbs and showed a small positive gain from principal cities.

In contrast to historical patterns of a heavy focus on center cities, labor forces arriving from abroad divided about evenly between principal cities and all other areas.

Overall, the effect of all of these worker flows in just one year was the following: suburbs gained about 0.7 million workers from central cities in intrametropolitan moves; suburbs gained about 0.4 million workers from central cities in intermetropolitan moves; suburbs gained about 0.25 million from rural areas; and central cities lost slightly to rural areas. (fig. **2.7.3**)

Transportation Modes
The variation in modes of transportation employed by commuters nationwide has been relatively stable over long periods. Between 1990 and 2010, the overall share of private vehicle use registered at above 86 percent over the two decades, but with driving alone adding twenty million users. This represents a gain in national share from 73.2 percent to 76.6 percent for driving alone, amid continued sharp declines in carpooling. Carpooling declined by two million workers, with its share dropping from 13.4 percent to 9.7 percent. Transit use gained almost a million users, raising its share slightly

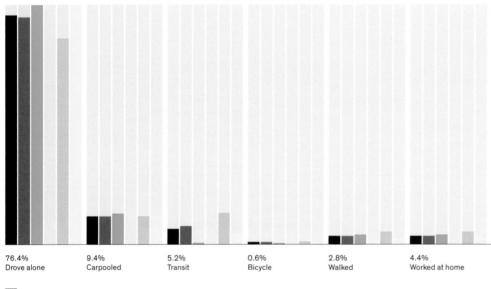

76.4%   9.4%   5.2%   0.6%   2.8%   4.4%
Drove alone   Carpooled   Transit   Bicycle   Walked   Worked at home

■ US total

■ In metropolitan statistical areas

■ Not in metropolitan statistical areas

■ In principal cities of metropolitan statistical areas

Area within metropolitan statistical areas but outside a principal city

2.7.4 Mode shares by metropolitan geography, 2013

4   The term *jobs*, as used
here, is an estimate
based on counts of
workers at their work-
place, as observed in the
American Community
Survey. Consequently,
it excludes second jobs
held by some workers
and is therefore a slight
undercount of all jobs.

from 4.6 percent to 4.9 percent. Walking continued its decline, with a loss of seven hundred thousand and a drop in share from 3.9 percent to 2.8 percent. Working at home continues to mushroom, with a gain of 2.5 million and a share increase from 3 percent to over 4.3 percent. In all but the largest metro areas in America, working at home exceeds transit usage.

Similar to these national trends, the dominance of driving alone persists when we examine travel modes by more detailed geography. (fig. **2.7.4**) For 2013, we analyzed the travel mode shares for commuters for the Census designations of principal cities and metro statistical areas (MSA). Driving alone is about 70 percent in all principal cities nationally. In all parts of MSAs that are not principal cities—in other words, in metro area suburbs—over 80 percent of commuters drive alone. Transit use was much higher in principal cities (10.6 percent) than in suburbs (3 percent). Walking had similar but not as marked differences at 4.3 percent and 1.8 percent, respectively.

The levels of working at home and carpooling exhibit strong similarity across all metro size classes, whereas transit is extremely affected by metro size and the age of the urban core.

The Case of Fairfax County, Virginia

We can see the emerging national transportation patterns by examining the trends in Fairfax County, Virginia, an affluent, large suburb outside Washington, DC. The Commuting in America series has tracked Fairfax County's relationships between workers and jobs for several decades.[4] In the 1980s Fairfax County looked like a stereotypical bedroom suburb with many more workers than jobs (the jobs to worker ratio was 0.70). As a result, the county had to "export" many of its workers every day to job-rich inner-core areas, particularly Washington, DC. (fig. **2.7.5**)

This changed dramatically in the 1990s and first decade of the new millennium. By 2010, the ratio of workers to jobs was just about equal, making the county ideal for study. In other words,

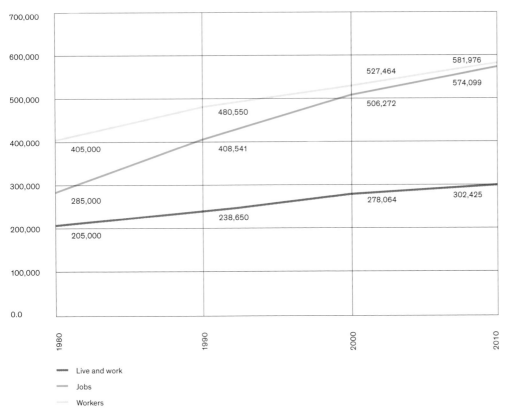

2.7.5 Long-term worker trend for Fairfax County, Virginia

if all the resident workers worked in the county, then no workers would have had to be imported each day to work; and only about 8,000 workers would have had to be exported each day to jobs elsewhere, in a county with over a million in population. In fact, only some 300,000 resident workers actually worked in the county, amounting to 52 percent of the worker population. This level is rather good for most suburban counties. For example, Prince Georges County (just across the Potomac) has only 39 percent of the population working within the county. Thus, in Fairfax, some 550,000 workers flowed across the county's borders each day commuting out to jobs elsewhere while others flowed into the county to work. The difference between a potential 8,000 and an actual 550,000 flow across the county's borders each day is the real story and challenge of American commuting.

By 2013, the balance in the county had already changed, indicating the transmutation of Fairfax County to a city-like destination; it was no longer a bedroom suburb. Most notably, the jobs to worker ratio had reached 1.04, as jobs increased far faster than workers in the period from 2010 to 2013. Another pertinent factor is that the share of those resident workers who remained in the county to work had increased from 52 percent to 54 percent. Despite that, the total number of those flowing across the county border each day had risen by 20,000, as the total number crossing the county's borders rose from 552,000 to 572,000. As a result, worker inflow to the county has exceeded outflow for the first time. (fig. **2.7.6**)

This labor export/import story is key to understanding commuting flows in America, illustrated so effectively by Fairfax County. What Fairfax demonstrated in 2010 is that it is more the skills mix that governs whether workers remain in a given county to work or must go elsewhere to locate a congenial job, rather than the simple ratio between the supply of jobs and workers available. Seen from the point of view of the employer, the commuter market-shed of skills needed within, say, a half hour's commute time will be critical to their effective acquisition of the staff levels and skills they require.[5]

2010 updated	2010	2013
Resident workers	582,000	605,584
Jobs	574,000	630,614
Jobs/worker ratio	0.99	1.04
Workers who live and work in county	302,000	332,086
Percent who live and work in county	52%	55%
Workers exported each day	280,000	273,498
Workers imported each day	272,000	298,528

2.7.6 Current Worker Patterns, Fairfax County, Virginia

5 *Commuting in America 2013: The National Report on Commuting Patterns and Trends.*

National Commuting

The story of cross-county flows is a dramatic one and exemplifies the massive role that the additions of new counties to suburbs of metro areas and their growth have had on the nation's work-travel patterns. Over a fifty-year period, the number and share of workers who leave their residence county to work each day has been tracked by the Commuting in America series. (fig. **2.7.7**) America's counties vary in size substantially, thus, a snapshot of work travel could be misleading. However, they do retain constant borders over time, so their trend patterns are significant. In the 1960–2010 period, in which the number of workers roughly doubled, those leaving their home counties to work quadrupled from 9.4 million to over 37 million. The flatter trend line from 2000 to 2010 is a result of the more limited growth in workers in the period due to demographic and economic trends. Virginia leads all states with over 51 percent leaving their residence county to work, and Maryland is just behind it at 47 percent (attesting to the power of the federal establishment), followed by New Jersey at 46 percent and Georgia at 41 percent, compared to the national average of 27.4 percent.

Commuting across state lines is also growing, providing an indicator of the enormous scale of our major metro areas. Interstate commuting has increased from 3.6 percent of all commutes in 2000 to 3.8 percent in 2010, reaching a level of over 5 million workers. There are twenty states with more than 100,000 workers crossing state lines, and sixteen where that flow exceeds over 5 percent of the workforce, despite the fact that the sharp reductions in employment growth during the 2000 to 2010 period were largely felt in those occupations that tend to be longer distance activities (e.g., example, construction and factory work). The states with more than 10 percent of workers leaving their home state are, after the District of Columbia at 23 percent, Maryland, New Hampshire, Delaware, Rhode Island, New Jersey, and West Virginia. At 9.1 percent, Virginia is just below that threshold. This attests to the economic strength of New York City, Boston, and Washington, DC.

West Virginia is of particular interest because of its bimodal trip length distribution. Although many workers have short local trips within rural areas or small metros, at the same time, there is a large segment (just short of 12 percent) commuting across state lines to the Pittsburgh, Washington, DC, and Ohio areas. As jobs move farther out into suburban areas, they become increasingly accessible to rural workers.

The male-female distinctions in out-of-county commuting indicate that men are more likely to work out of state than women, as well as in a different county within state. (fig. **2.7.8**) This is linked to a series of patterns involving occupational choices, that is, men are more likely to work in those occupations that are generally at greater distances, such as construction. Other factors, such as greater household responsibilities, often act to keep female workers closer to home.[6] These factors are further reflected in that women have overall shorter work trip lengths and later work start times. Yet these differences have been diminishing over time.[7]

The use of the various modes of transportation varies significantly with travel destinations. (fig. **2.7.9**) Walking would typically be considered a close-to-home mode, but about 4 percent of those who walk to work as their sole means of transportation indicate that they do cross a county line, and another 2 percent cross state lines in their walk-to-work travel. Such walk trips rarely exceed two miles.

In 2010 driving alone shows substantial increases for those leaving their home county. Driving alone constitutes 76.6 percent of all trips nationally; however, driving alone constitutes 81.5 percent of trips crossing a county line within a state. But it then drops down to just above 71 percent for trips crossing a state line. In part, this is due to the greater role of the short distance modes, which are all largely intracounty in character, such as walking, biking and working at home. Carpooling also shows some limited increase in out-of-county commutes, ranging from a national average below 10 percent to almost 11 percent. Transit use, too, exhibits a substantial increase in interstate commuting, in significant part due to the large commuter rail usage around New York City from neighboring New Jersey and Connecticut. More than 12 percent of work trips crossing state lines are transit based.

The Commuting in America series has mapped county changes in flows beyond county boundaries based on those counties exporting more than 25 percent of their workers over several decades. (fig. **2.7.10**) The research shows that much of the country—from mid-Texas eastward—exports above 25 percent of workers each day from their residence county. The

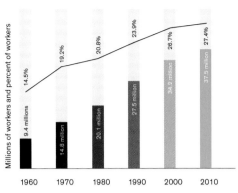

2.7.7 National trend in cross-county flows

6   National Household
    Travel Survey
    series 1969–2009,
    US Department of
    Transportation, http://
    nhts.ornl.gov/.
7   *Commuting in America
    2013: The National Report
    on Commuting Patterns
    and Trends.*

accretion of new areas is likely the product of metro fringe counties increasingly sending workers to metro area jobs and the attraction of high paying jobs in new rural auto plants and energy sites bringing workers from greater and greater distances. In total, there are 2,177 counties that are net exporters of workers each day heading toward 964 net importing counties.

Flow Patterns and Trends

Depicting work trip flow patterns and volumes at the metro level is a complex task given current Census categories of geographic delineation. (fig. **2.7.11**) Previous Census delineations made clear the difference between central cities and their surrounding metro area (suburbs). Current Census geographic delineations suffer from a significant spatial weakness. They have created the concept of the principal city, which does not differentiate central cities from suburban centers that have grown up over the years. Those suburban centers may lie at considerable distance from the center. As a result, much meaningful geographic context is lost. As noted earlier, it is estimated that roughly 75 percent of the populations identified as living in principal cities fit the original concept of central cities, as previously understood, and the remaining 25 percent are geographically suburban in nature. This has had the effect of distorting some of the statistics displayed.

The central reality is that principal cities have no explicit geographic location

	All		Male		Female	
Total workers	136,941,010	100.0%	71,948,651	100.0%	64,992,359	100.0%
Worked in state of residence	131,726,663	96.2%	68,712,557	95.5%	63,014,106	97.0%
Worked in county of residence	99,361,852	72.6%	50,380,850	70.0%	48,981,002	75.4%
Worked outside county of residence	32,364,811	23.6%	18,331,707	25.5%	14,033,104	21.6%
Worked outside state of residence	5,214,347	3.8%	3,236,094	4.5%	1,978,253	3.0%
Total working outside county	37,579,158	27.4%	21,567,801	30.0%	16,011,357	24.6%

2.7.8 Workers leaving their residence county to work by gender, 2010

in a metro area, weakening efforts to compare to the past. Statistically, it means that the intra–principal city flows can include the internal flows within both the central city and within suburban principal cities, but also can include flows between them. In 2011 within-suburb or suburb-to-suburb commute trips remained the largest category, capturing 42.4 million commuters—more than 30 percent of metro-commute trips. Recognizing that approximately 25 percent of principal cities are in fact suburban would shift approximately at least that much to the suburb-to-suburb flows, putting that category in the range of 50 million commuters, far more than the traditional suburb-to-city commute.

The second-largest share of commuting occurs within or between principal cities, at nearly 25 percent, which, again, would be reduced by the transfer of population and workers to the suburban category in a more geographically rigorous depiction. Third in significance is suburb-to-principal-city commuting, at more than 16 percent of commuting, much of which is, in fact, intra-suburban as well as the traditional downtown commute. Fourth is nonmetro-to-nonmetro commuting, at more than 12 percent; this category is basically unaffected by the shifts among principal cities and suburbs. Principal city–to-suburb commuting (reverse commuting) is more than 6 percent.

Remaining flows to and from other metro and nonmetro areas are modest. The largest of these is suburb to a suburb in another metro, at 2 percent; it should be

recognized that, although low in volume, these flows affect two metro areas—the one they leave and the one they enter. Historically, these intermetro flows were the fastest growing trip patterns, but the recession, which disproportionately affected construction and factory jobs, reduced such trips from about 7.5 million in 2000 to 7.3 million in 2010.

Nonmetro flows, both within nonmetro areas and to metro areas, also declined appreciably, largely as a result of the recent incorporation of nonmetro counties into metro areas. Overall, these flows amounted to below 23 million in 2010, dropping down from over 31 million commuters in 2000.

In summary, these figures firmly establish the point that today, commuting patterns are increasingly complex. They interact across immense metro areas spanning thousands of square miles, including exchanges between rural and urban areas and across state lines. These patterns are the product of a dynamic economy with highly specialized job skills requirements. Employers need to locate in very large metros with massive agglomerations of workers in order to have reasonable access to the highly specialized workers they need.

The *Leave It to Beaver* model of a sole male worker living in the suburbs and commuting to downtown is far less relevant than in the past. So, too, is the idyllic notion that people can optimize their work travel by living near their workplace and walking to work. Where people choose to live is an even more complex choice today

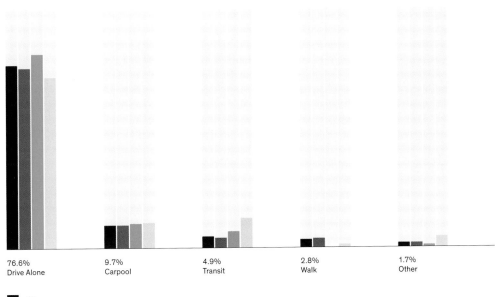

■	All
■	Worked in county of residence
■	Worked outside county of residence
■	Worked outside state of residence

76.6%
Drive Alone

9.7%
Carpool

4.9%
Transit

2.8%
Walk

1.7%
Other

2.7.9 Mode shares by county flow, 2010

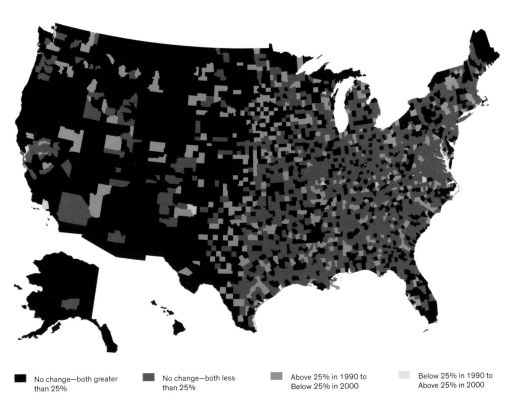

■ No change—both greater than 25%   ■ No change—both less than 25%   ■ Above 25% in 1990 to Below 25% in 2000   ■ Below 25% in 1990 to Above 25% in 2000

2.7.10 Rate of population growth from 1970 to 2010

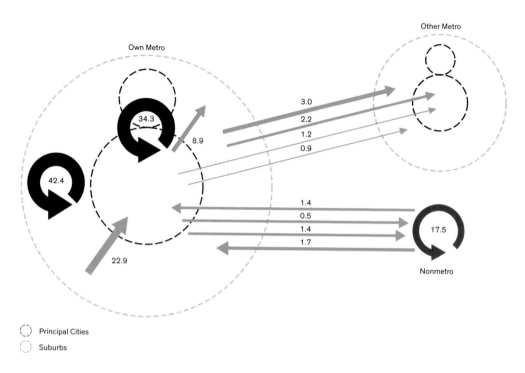

8   US Census Bureau, *2014 Projections of the Population for the United States: 2015 to 2060*, accessed November 15, 2015, http://www .census.gov/population /projections/data /national/2014.html.

Principal Cities

Suburbs

2.7.11 Commuting flows, 2011, in millions

than in the past. With approximately two-thirds of workers living in a household with other workers, whose job will one live close to? With the velocity of job change, will people move each time they change jobs, incurring costs, disrupting lifestyles, school plans, and the like?

As the nation's job picture brightens, it will become clearer that the key issue for the nation will be a lack of workers, particularly skilled workers to serve the nation's economic development needs. The latest census projections indicate a gain of fewer than fourteen million men and women of the traditional working age, eighteen to sixty-five, over the next twenty years.[8] Finding the workers to replace the baby boomer workforce will be a national challenge. Employers and employees will need to be able to access job opportunities over immense distances to meet those needs.

Given the declining skilled workforce supply in the coming decade, future productivity will depend in large part on the the ability of employers to reach out over longer distances to obtain the skills they require. It will be a period driven by worker supply rather than employer

demand. This implies that large metro areas with their bigger pools of workers will be even more important. Further, it implies the need for transportation investments providing the ability to access distant workers with even more flexible work arrangements and schedules. So many work activities are increasingly around-the-clock, seven-days-a-week activities, at the same time that employees demand more flexible schedules and the ability to work at off-site locations. Freight movements, access to suppliers, and access to employers/employees will be central to the nation's economic success.

Employers, increasingly footloose in terms of location, will go where the skilled workers are or where they want to be. Perhaps the central consideration for the future is that America's major metro areas must be recognized as large multicounty, often multistate, economic engines.

This research is based on the Commuting in America series published each decade since 1986. The most recent version, Commuting in America 2013, is published as a series of

*sixteen briefs and an executive summary
by AASHTO, the American Association of
State Highway and Transportation Officials,
supported by its Census Transportation
Planning Products program and the
National Cooperative Highway Research
Program of the Transportation Research
Board of the National Academies. The
data are all the product of the American
Community Survey of the United States
Census Bureau or as otherwise noted. The
author is solely responsible for its content.*

2.8
MEGAREGIONAL AUSTRALIA IN THE TWENTY-FIRST CENTURY

Richard Weller and Julian Bolleter

DESIGN MODELS

HOUSING AFFORDABILITY

PRODUCTIVE SUBURBS

TRANSPORT INFRASTRUCTURE

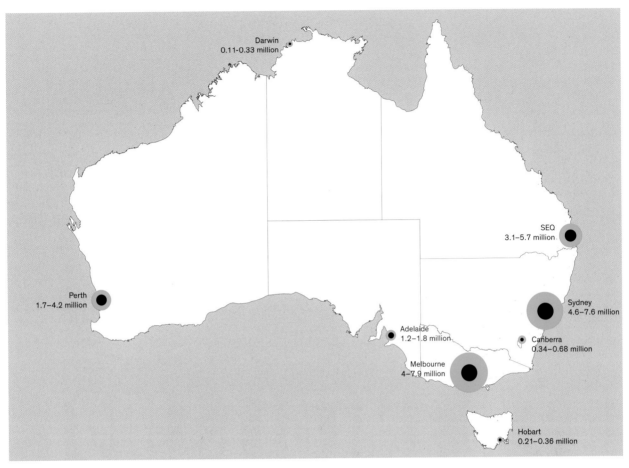

Darwin
0.11–0.33 million

SEQ
3.1–5.7 million

Perth
1.7–4.2 million

Sydney
4.6–7.6 million

Adelaide
1.2–1.8 million

Canberra
0.34–0.68 million

Melbourne
4–7.9 million

Hobart
0.21–0.36 million

2.8.1 Projected population increase to 2056

Australia is a nation of just over twenty-three million people, occupying a landmass more or less the size of the United States. The Australian Bureau of Statistics (ABS) forecasts that by 2101, the population of Australia could reach 62.2 million.[1] (fig. **2.8.1**) Translating this into the nation's preferred urban form of low-density suburbia means that eight Sydneys will need to be constructed in the next eight decades. As the Council of Australian Governments (COAG) explains it:

> Australia is at a watershed point for its capital cities and their strategic planning. Population growth, demographic change, increasing energy costs and the shift to a knowledge economy have changed the assumptions underpinning the shape and development of Australian cities…

this must also include reconsideration of Australia's settlement patterns.[2]

Despite opposition from some prominent Australians and the Stable Population Party, most commentators recognize that Australia needs growth to supply the nation's labor market and bolster its economy against an aging population. However, the antigrowth lobby argues that such economic rationalism overlooks environmental, social, and infrastructural pressures associated with population growth. Despite population growth being the historical norm for Australia, it is now couched in terms of crisis.

Instead of population growth and immigration being cast as a creative opportunity for nation building (as it was for the United States in the early twentieth century), it is generally portrayed as a

1   Australian Bureau of Statistics, "Population Projections, Australia, 2006 to 2101," November 26, 2013, accessed April 28, 2015, http://www.abs .gov.au/ausstats/abs@ .nsf/Lookup/3222.0main +features52012%20 (base)%20to%202101.

2   Council of Australian Governments, *Council Review of Capital City Strategic Planning Systems* (Canberra: Council of Australian Governments, 2010), 2.

threat to both the great Australian dream of owning a detached suburban house and Australia's natural environment. On a visit to Australia, the eminent population biologist Paul Ehrlich of Stanford University claimed, "What's crystal clear is Australia should have a shrinking population. Australia's already in deep trouble, way beyond its carrying capacity and I'm afraid that not only are we not going to see forty million or one hundred million Australians, we are likely to see many fewer than twenty million and many may have to evacuate."[3]

In contrast, the prominent developer Harry "High-Rise" Triguboff has urged that Australia should become a nation of one hundred million and its wayward rivers should be reengineered to ensure food supplies.[4] And so it goes: both views are inflammatory. The fact is that Australia is growing rapidly. It is also a fact that, to date, suburbia has been both a prominent cause and effect of Australia's exceptionally high quality of life.

The intertwined issues of population growth and urban planning periodically flare up in the Australian media, but debate is superficial, and state and federal governments have largely swept the issues under the carpet. Notable exceptions include a 1994 report from the House of Representatives Standing Committee for Long Term Strategies, which concluded that a high growth rate of between thirty and fifty million by 2045 was "reasonable."[5] The committee stressed that "the single most important management decision associated with that growth relates to settlement patterns." In 2002 the Commonwealth Scientific Industrial Research Organization (CSIRO), in a study regarding growth forecasts, found that there is enough land, water, and energy in Australia to provide for what it referred to as a "moderate" lifestyle for fifty million people up to 2100.[6] By 2010, in a famous speech, the then prime minister

of Australia Kevin Rudd declared his enthusiasm for a "big Australia":

Australia's rapid population growth will have profound implications for our destiny as a nation. The century ahead stands to be the greatest century of economic growth and nation-building in Australian history. I have said before that I believe in a big Australia. This is good for our national security. Good for our long-term prosperity. Good in enhancing our role in the region and the world. The time to prepare for this big Australia is now.[7]

In response, Treasury Secretary Dr. Ken Henry asked, "Where will these people live—in our current major cities and regional centers, or in cities we haven't even started to build?"[8] The answer is: all of the above. We do not argue for either low-density suburbia or high-density infill development as exclusive solutions. Rather, we find that Australia has opportunities and can derive benefits from increasing the production of both. However, as opposed to laissez-faire growth, we argue that Australia's existing cities will reach capacity by circa mid-century, and that thereafter they should not continue to grow into megacities (cities of ten million or more citizens). Alternatively, further urban development should be decentralized so as to intentionally form east and west coast "megaregions," comprising networks of smaller cities connected by effective public and private transport infrastructure. These new cities offer the opportunity to develop a form of urbanism responsive to pressing issues of resource depletion, climate change, and changing demographics—rather than trying to retrofit nineteenth- and twentieth-century cities that were predicated on cheap oil, a stable climate and a fairly homogeneous demographic.[9]

3 "Today Tonight, News Article," *Yahoo*, accessed December 15, 2014, http://au.news.yahoo .com/today-tonight /latest/article/-/6076863 /population-explosion/.

4 "Population to Hit 55m by 2050," *Sydney Morning Herald*, January 25, 2010, accessed December 15, 2014, http://www.smh .com.au//breaking-news -national/population -to-hit-55m-by-2050 -triguboff-20100125 -mt45.html.

5 House of Representatives Standing Committee for Long Term Strategies, *Australia's Population Carrying Capacity: One Nation—Two Ecologies*, (Canberra: Australian Government Publishing Service, 1994).

6 Barney Foran and Franzi Poldy, "Dilemmas Distilled: A Summary Guide to the Csiro Technical Report 'Future Dilemmas: Options to 2050 for Australia's Population, Technology, Resources and Environment'" (Canberra: Department of Immigration & Multicultural & Indigenous Affairs, 2002).

7 Kevin Rudd, "Building a Big Australia: Future Planning Needs of Our Major Cities," prime minister address to the Business Council of Australia, Canberra, 2009.

8 Ken Henry, "The Shape of Things to Come: Long Run Forces Affecting the Australian Economy in Coming Decades," *Queensland University of Technology Business Leaders' Forum* (Brisbane: Queensland University of Technology, 2009).

9 Peter Newman, Timothy Beatley, and Heather Boyer, *Resilient Cities* (Washington, DC: Island Press, 2009).

Planning Shortcomings

Australia needs innovative proposals for the future. An analysis of the various current plans for Australia's state and territory capital cities reveals that their planning policies do not adequately deal with population growth, either statistically or spatially. First, despite the availability of long-term population projections, the plans typically reach out only as far as 2031, and collectively only account for an additional 5.5 million people. Second, the plans all have the same basic approach to growth: apart from Sydney and Adelaide, they all fix on (more or less) a 50:50 infill to greenfield development ratio. Even though the policy settings reflect a balance, the polemic of the reports is heavily skewed toward infill development, which is assumed to align with greater sustainability. Yet there is research literature that indicates that infill development is not necessarily more sustainable, particularly with respect to supporting biodiversity, mitigating urban heat island effects, maintaining natural drainage patterns, and sequestering carbon and other pollutants.[10] Regardless of this evidence, the collective rejection of suburbia is unprecedented in Australia.

According to both its apologists and its critics, the infrastructure costs for greenfield development, which are typically borne by the community at large and not developers, are becoming prohibitive in comparison to infill development.[11] The result of this situation is suburban infrastructure deficits, which can include a lack of public transport systems, suitable roads, schools, community centers, cultural facilities, hospitals, and sometimes essential services (water, power, and telecommunications).[12] Paradoxically, a recent National Housing Supply Council "State of Supply" report notes that in all major cities, except Sydney, it costs more to build a two-bedroom apartment as infill development than a comparable three-bedroom house with a backyard in greenfield development.[13] (figs. **2.8.2–3**) Either way, the cost of housing in Australia is such that a generation is being jettisoned into extreme debt or precluded from homeownership entirely. The average first home house price in Australia is now well above $400,000.[14] These costs are directly linked to lack of land supply on the edges of Australia's cities, in conjunction with an increase in taxes and infrastructure charges, and a trend toward the construction of larger houses.[15]

If the ABS midcentury projections for Australia's major cities are met, then by 2056, Brisbane will be made up of 5.7 million people; Sydney, 7.6 million; Melbourne, 7.9 million; Adelaide, 1.8 million; and Perth, 4.2 million. To grow these cities in a way that does not compromise livability is the central challenge facing Australian planning and urban design in the first half of this century. As these cities reach their midcentury forecasts, they also reach their infrastructural capacities. By way of example, it is estimated that as early as 2020, Australia will incur $20.4 billion's worth of avoidable social costs of congestion.[16] By extension, any further growth will then significantly compromise productivity and livability, unless infrastructural improvement occurs, too.

The challenge of the second half of the twenty-first century, then, will be to answer the question of where to build entirely new cities, and how to string them together along efficient public and private transport, and digital communication networks. We argue that through a concerted planning effort, Australia should avoid the development of stand-alone megacities and instead "cultivate" its emerging east and west coast megaregions. This cultivation could take inspiration from the United Kingdom's post–World War II decentralization efforts, which by 1980 saw the creation of thirty-three substantial "new towns" in a polycentric

10 Tony Hall, *The Life and Death of the Australian Backyard* (Collingwood, Victoria: CSIRO Publishing, 2010); Brendan Gleeson, "Waking from the Dream: Towards Urban Resilience in the Face of Sudden Threat," *Urban Studies* 45, no. 13 (2008): 2653–68.

11 Jason Dowling and Clay Lucas report that "for every 1000 new dwellings, the cost of infill development (in existing suburbs) is $309 million and the cost of fringe development is $653 million," due to the difference imposed by new infrastructure. See Jason Dowling and Clay Lucas, "$40bn: The Price Tag on Melbourne's Sprawl," *Age*, June 17, 2009.

12 Outer Suburban/ Interface Services and Development Committee, *Inquiry on Growing the Suburbs: Infrastructure and Business Development in Outer Suburban Melbourne* (Melbourne: Victorian Government Printer, 2013), 100.

13 Commonwealth of Australia, "National Housing Supply Council: 2nd State of Supply Report" (Canberra: National Housing Supply Council, 2010), http:// www.treasury.gov .au/~/media/Treasury /Publications%20 and%20Media /Publications/2010 /NHSC/Downloads /stateofsupplyreport _2010.ashx.

14 Toby Johnstone, "First Timers Make Comeback," *Domain*, accessed December 15, 2014, http://news.domain.com .au/domain/real-estate -news/first-timers-make -comeback-20140211 -32fga.html.

15 Urban Development Institute of Australia (National), *Housing Affordability in Australia* (Canberra: Urban Development Institute of Australia, 2008).

16 Bureau of Transport and Regional Economics, *Estimating Urban Traffic and Congestion Cost Trends for Australian*

2.8.2 Greenfield housing being erected on Melbourne's western fringe

2.8.3 The suburb of Dunlop sprawls into unconstrained land on Canberra's northwestern fringe

urban configuration. This situation was enabled by the regional provision of quality affordable housing, efficient road and rail networks, and jobs provided by the relocation of government departments and business to regional centers.[17]

Why should Australia attempt to decentralize its future population growth? If decentralization does not occur, Australia's cities will become megacities, which typically rate badly in livability indexes. These livability indexes are calculated in relation to the following categories: stability, healthcare provision, culture and environment, education, infrastructure, and spatial characteristics. The category spatial characteristics, which are of most relevance to urban design and planning, incorporates the amount of greenspace (parks, squares, and gardens), the degree of urban sprawl (with its generally inadequate public transport systems), and access to natural assets (seas, rivers, lakes, and mountains), cultural assets, connectivity to the rest of the world, and pollution.[18] According to the *Economist*'s Intelligence Unit, megacities tend to be more polluted and more congested, offer less greenspace and natural amenities, and are harder to get around without a car. For example, Los Angeles is a city that bears many similarities to Australian cities, albeit at a larger scale. It is currently ranked forty-third in the 2014 "Global Livable Cities Index" of the *Economist*. Similarly, cities such as London comes in as fifty-first.[19] In comparison, Melbourne is ranked first; Adelaide, fifth; Sydney, seventh; and Perth, ninth. The average population of the top ten most livable cities in the world is 1.8 million.[20] Size matters!

As Australia plans its future growth, it might look not to the great imperial centers of industry and culture but to cities that are small, dispersed, and networked. Referring to a McKinsey Global Institute study, Joel Kotkin notes that small cities (many under a million people) are responsible for more than half the world's growth and, in the case of the United States, some 70 percent of GDP.[21] Not only are small- to mid-sized cities economically effective, they also offer their citizens a high quality of life insofar as they are relatively free from the social and environmental problems that beset megacities.

A Model for the Future

We propose a "bioregional" take on megaregional planning that integrates regional-scale ecosystems, settlement patterns, and infrastructure.[22] The regional-scale ecosystem provides the lineaments of settlement: productive landscapes are responsibly cultivated and provide sources of renewable energy. This is not a platitude. Rather, this conception of the megaregion as a sophisticated, synthetic ecology marks an important departure from the historical image of nature as a mere backdrop to, or resource for, the city. As the New Urbanist Peter Calthorpe points out, "more than standalone 'sustainable communities' or even 'green cities' we now need 'sustainable regions'—places that carefully blend a range of technologies, settlement patterns and lifestyles."[23] This notion is evident in some current megaregional scale planning in the United States. For example, planning for the Great Lakes and Southern California megaregions attempts to weave together the challenges of protecting biodiversity habitat and farmland while providing the housing and infrastructure required for accommodating rapidly growing populations.[24] This interwoven conception also marks a departure from the twentieth-century landscape planning typified by Ian McHarg, who saw the city as a scourge on the landscape.

In order to model a scenario of decentralization to absorb Australia's forecasted twenty-first-century population growth, we first conducted a national landscape

Cities, Working Paper 71 (Canberra: Bureau of Transport and Regional Economics Department of Transport and Regional Services, 2007).

17 Peter Hall, *Cities of Tomorrow: An Intellectual History of Urban Planning and Design in the Twentieth Century*, 3rd ed. (Oxford: Blackwell Publishing, 2002), 104.

18 Economist Intelligence Unit, "Best Cities Ranking and Report: A Special Report from the Economist Intelligence Unit," 2012.

19 "Liveability Ranking: Australian Gold," *Economist*, August 14, 2012, accessed January 6, 2014, http://www.economist.com/blogs/gulliver/2012/08/liveability-ranking.

20 The top ten most livable cities according to the *Economist* and their population sizes are as follows: 1. Melbourne (4 million); 2. Vienna (1.7 million); 3. Vancouver (0.5 million); 4. Toronto (2.5 million); 5. Calgary (1.1 million); 5. Adelaide (1.2 million); 7. Sydney (4.6 million); 8. Helsinki (0.5 million); 9. Perth (1.7 million); and 10. Auckland (0.4 million).

21 Robert Dobbs et al., "Urban World: Mapping the Economic Power of Cities," McKinsey & Company, accessed November 17, 2015, http://www.mckinsey.com/Insights/MGI/Research/Urbanization/Urban_world.

22 Margaret Dewar and David Epstein, "Planning for 'Megaregions' in the United States," *Journal of Planning Literature* 22, no. 2 (2007): 109.

23 Peter Calthorpe, *Urbanism Climate Change, Sustainable Urbanism, and Beyond: Rethinking Cities for the Future* (New York: Rizzoli, 2012), 14.

24 Margaret Dewar and David Epstein, "Planning for 'Megaregions' in the United States," *Journal of Planning Literature* 22, no. 2 (2007): 112.

analysis and concluded that both the southeast and southwest coasts of Australia were most suited to megaregional expansion. Second, we subtracted the number of people likely to be accommodated in Australia's major cities and regional centers at midcentury (42.5 million) from the end-of-century total population projection of 62.2 million. This left 19.7 million people unaccounted for.[25] We then distributed this population along high-speed rail and high-speed broadband telecommunications corridors in towns of circa one million people each.

There are several rationales for encouraging these people to live in the east and west coast megaregions. These regions have productive agricultural landscapes, and they are centered on established cities approaching capacity. They also have substantial road, rail, port, and airport infrastructure in place and established regional settlement patterns that are conducive to spatial expansion and economic consolidation. Additionally, these two regions have high cultural and natural amenities, excellent global connectivity and, while the impact of climate change is uncertain, there is no evidence to suggest that these landscapes will be rendered uninhabitable.

The east coast megaregion (ECM) is a 1,050-mile (1,700-kilometer), predominantly coastal stretch of land east of the Great Dividing Range from southeast Queensland to southern Victoria. (fig. **2.8.4**) This potential megaregion incorporates four major cities (Brisbane/SEQ, Sydney, Canberra, and Melbourne) and numerous substantial towns, and has over 17 million hectares of cleared productive land. The combined ABS 2056 forecast for Brisbane/SEQ, Sydney, Canberra, and Melbourne is 23.1 million people. Accepting the principle that the high-speed rail (HSR) can stop every 40 to 60 miles (70 to 100 kilometers) without

compromising its overall viability, for the purpose of this scenario we work with a total of twenty-three stops. The selection of stops shown is indicative only; the final determination would be dependent on the results of the cost-benefit analysis of the various routes the HSR could take. If an HSR system was in place by midcentury, the numbers of inter–capital city riders could be substantial. The ridership from regional centers would be less, but what is of importance in regard to the nation's 2101 population projection is the potential for the regional stops to become population attractors. Of course, employment opportunities and lifestyle choices would render population distribution uneven, but to conceptually illustrate the development of the ECM, we have simply distributed 19.7 million people evenly across the HSR's seventeen regional stops. Each HSR station services a new city of approximately 1.2 million people. (fig. **2.8.5**) In this scenario, only three of the seventeen cities are brand-new. The majority are grafted onto existing regional townships.

It is hard to imagine many of the regional towns in this megaregion becoming a city of 1.2 million people, but this difficulty is largely related to the fact that we still think in terms of isolated towns set within regional agrarian economies instead of thinking in terms of networked megaregions. For example, it is 571 miles (919 kilometers) from Sydney to Brisbane, thus the greatest distance from either metropolis would be 286 miles (460 kilometers). A HSR clocking an average of 210 miles per hour (350 kilometers per hour) could therefore have the megaregion's most "isolated" citizen in either city in under two hours. While this distance is not quite within a comfortable daily commute, vast areas of the HSR corridor would fall within a reasonable commuting distance. Additionally, telecommuting will surely become an increasingly acceptable

25 Australian Bureau of Statistics, "Population Projections, Australia, 2006 to 2101," 1.

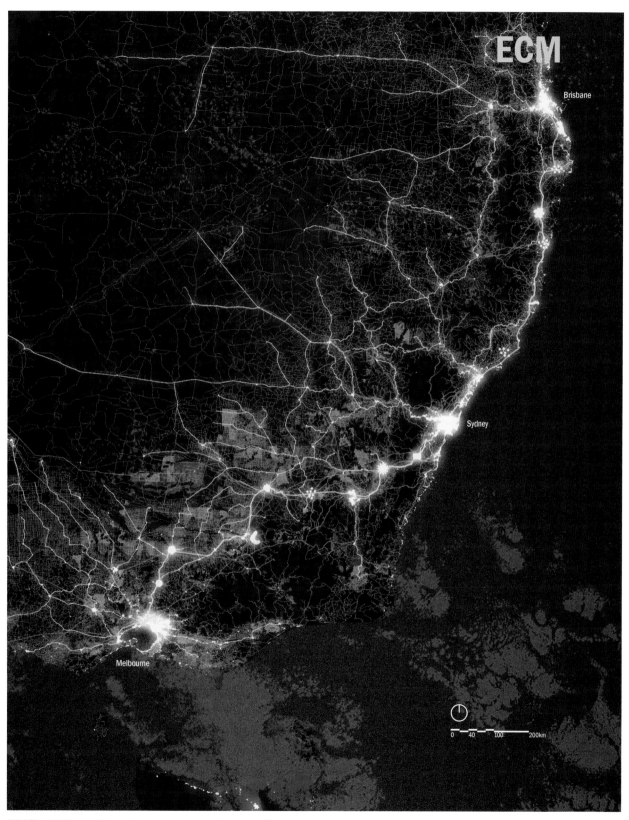

ECM

Brisbane

Sydney

Melbourne

0   40   100   200km

2.8.4 Proposed east coast megaregion extending from Brisbane to Melbourne

2.8.5 Hypothetical new city in the east coast megaregion

work arrangement for citizens spread throughout the region. This compression of space and time renders a megaregion viable: it unlocks vast new landscapes to human habitation just as it binds them together.

The west coast megaregion (WCM) is a 367-mile (590 kilometer) stretch of land along the Swan Coastal Plain from Geraldton in the north to Busselton in the south. (fig. **2.8.6**) With only one major city, Perth, as the predominant hub in a network of smaller regional centers, the emergence of a WCM is not imminent, but it has potential. Set in the Asian time zone, Perth is the epicenter of a mining boom state where 10 percent of the nation's population produces 45 percent of its exports and 15.5 percent of its GDP. If western Australia can use its wealth to diversify and "green" its economy this century, then its longevity can be secured. Although population growth is stereotypically associated with draining resources and damaging ecosystems, the concept of

the megaregion as described above sees more people and more intelligence being added to a region that is currently (apart from mining) underproductive. If western Australia were to construct an HSR service through the WCM from Geraldton to Busselton, then it would "unlock" extensive coastal environs and hinterlands, potentially attracting millions of people. With the connectivity that an HSR affords, population growth in the west could be focused tightly on the train's stops, expanding and also consolidating existing towns with careful regard for local landscape conditions. (fig. **2.8.7**)

New settlements throughout megaregional landscapes could breathe life into the Australian dream for yet another century. This is in contrast to the socioeconomic entrapment of the fringes of our major cities. And this dream needn't be a monoculture of placeless housing estates that erase the landscape. On the contrary, we could shape mosaics of new, innovative, and capacious development.

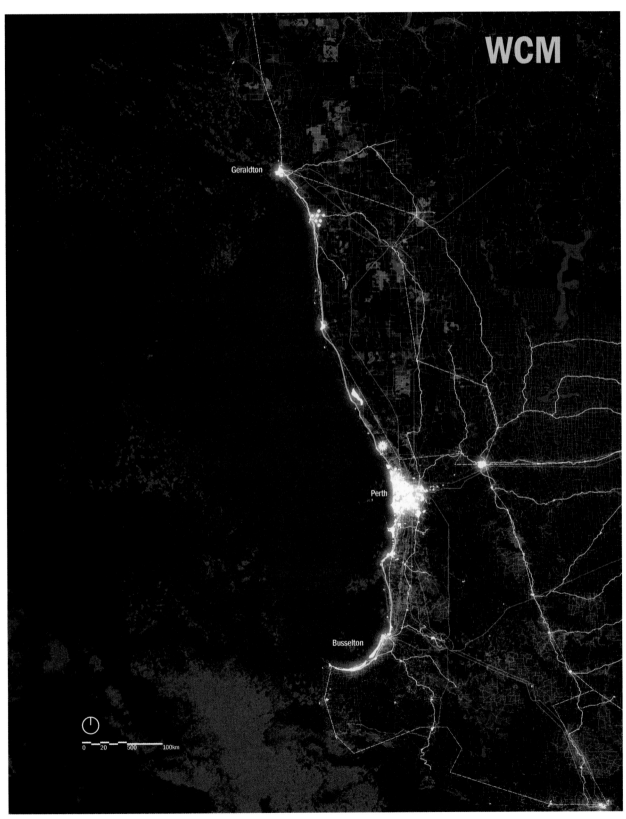

WCM

Geraldton

Perth

Busselton

0   20   500   100km

2.8.6 The proposed west coast megaregion extending from Geraldton in the north to Bussleton in the south

2.8.7 A hypothetical new city in the west coast megaregion

This essay is based on material adapted from Richard Weller and Julian Bolleter, Made in Australia: The Future of Australian Cities *(Crawley, Western Australia: UWA Publishing, 2012).*

McKinney, Texas, United States

Sunrise, Florida, United States

2.9
HEALTH, TRANSPORTATION, AND THE COMMUNITY-BUILT ENVIRONMENT

Michael Brauer

HEALTH

TECHNOLOGY

TRANSPORT INFRASTRUCTURE

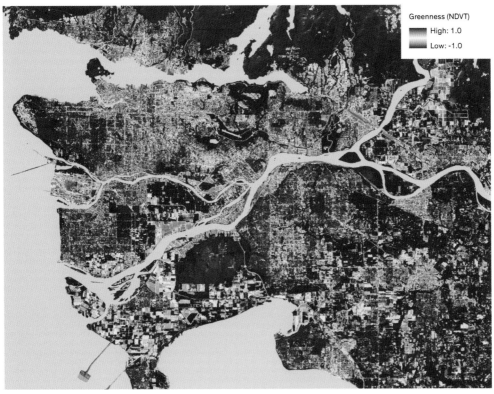

Greenness (NDVT)
High: 1.0
Low: -1.0

2.9.1 "Sweet-spot" areas in Vancouver   2.5 km

The design of communities and our interactions with the built environment can profoundly affect health. Perhaps the most important of these interactions are those related to mobility—the ways in which we move within our environment. Levels of traffic-related air pollution and noise display substantial variability related to road traffic density. Both air pollution and noise have been linked to a wide array of adverse health impacts, including birth outcomes and cardiovascular mortality. Physical inactivity, obesity, and the resulting burden of chronic diseases are among the leading public health challenges of our time. Evidence suggests that differences in the design of neighborhoods and community form can affect individual behaviors related to physical activity levels, with design modifications providing the potential to reduce these risks. Residential community design features may also lead to small-scale variations in temperature that can exacerbate heat-related mortality, a threat that is likely to increase with a warming planet.

Linked to these relationships between the built environment and health is a body of literature that associates improved health to proximity to the natural environment—water and green spaces—including spaces within urban areas. While the mechanisms of this association are not clear, natural spaces may be refuges from harmful exposures, such as air, noise, and heat. They may provide a place for healthy physical activity or social interactions, may harbor greater healthful microbial diversity, or may ameliorate stress through psychological mechanisms. Design of suburban communities that enhance interactions with the natural environment may therefore prove beneficial to health. (fig. **2.9.1**) Therefore, it is meaningful to examine the linkages through which community design and transportation infrastructure may affect health and discuss the implications for our communities.

Traffic-Related Air Pollution and Noise

Motor vehicle infrastructure has long been an important factor in community design, with many benefits associated with efficient infrastructure for mobility of the population and goods. Access to road networks largely shapes the form of most modern communities. However, along with this dependency come some challenges. Specifically, motor vehicles have long been known as a significant contributor to overall levels of air pollution, especially in urban areas. This contribution is responsible for substantial health impacts, including some 15,000 deaths per year in the United States and more than 180,000 per year worldwide.[1] More recent research has demonstrated that, beyond the contribution of motor vehicle emissions to the general level of air pollution in populated areas, traffic leads to within-community variation in air pollution, which dramatically increases the health impact of motor vehicle pollution within urban areas.[2]

Sharp gradients in levels of a number of pollutants emitted from motor vehicles have been measured downwind of highways and major arterial roads.[3] For example, pollutant levels within the first 980 to 1,640 feet (300 to 500 meters) of roads are elevated above surrounding levels, and increased health impacts have clearly been observed for those residing within 490 feet (150 meters) of highways and major arterial roads. Several analyses in North America and Asia suggest that approximately one-third of the population resides in such high exposure zones.[4] Similarly, within urban areas, one-third of schools are located in these areas.[5]

Among the health impacts associated with residence in areas of high exposure to traffic-related air pollution are low birth weights and preterm births; increased middle-ear infections (the leading reason that children under age two see a physician, and the leading reason

for prescription of antibiotics in this age group); respiratory infections (the leading cause of hospitalization for children in their first year of life); and development of childhood asthma.[6] Among adults, increased mortality, especially from cardiovascular disease, has been demonstrated to be linked to traffic-related air pollution, as well as accelerated progression of cardiovascular disease.[7]

Several studies have compared individuals who move from locations of high to low traffic versus moving from low to high traffic, and have demonstrated the health benefits of avoiding this exposure.[8] These findings, therefore, suggest that displacement of roads from residential locations by setbacks or via tunnels may mitigate health impacts.[9] In addition, a large number of communities in Europe have implemented congestion charges to reduce traffic within urban centers, as well as the implementation of low emission zones that more directly target air pollutant levels.[10] Health benefits related to air quality improvements have resulted in some cases. Such strategies to mitigate air pollution effects through changes in community design are relatively new and can accelerate mitigation efforts that are not spatially targeted, such as those focused on vehicle emissions and fuel quality.

Noise has long been linked to increased cardiovascular disease in occupational environments, and a strong body of research now suggests similar impacts from community noise exposure.[11] This exposure has also been linked to cognitive impairments; there have also been some suggestions of impacts on diabetes.[12] Although airports may be an especially important source in some locations, one of the major sources of noise within residential areas is motor vehicle traffic.

While traffic-related noise and air pollution share common sources, the

1 Kavi Bhalla et al., *Transport for Health: The Global Burden of Disease from Motorized Road Transport* (Washington, DC: World Bank Group, 2014), http://documents .worldbank.org/curated /en/2014/01/19308007 /transport-health-global -burden-disease-motor ized-road-transport.

2 Laura Perez et al., "Chronic Burden of Near-Roadway Traffic Pollution in Ten European Cities (APHEKOM Network)," *European Respiratory Journal* 42, no. 3 (2013): 594–605.

3 Alex A. Karner, Douglas S. Eisinger, and Deb A. Niemeier, "Near-Roadway Air Quality: Synthesizing the Findings from Real-World Data," *Environmental Science & Technology* 44, no. 14 (2010): 5334–44.

4 Michael Brauer, Conor Reynolds, and Perry Hystad, "Traffic-Related Air Pollution and Health in Canada," *Canadian Medical Association Journal* 185, no. 18 (2013): 1557–58; Michael Jerrett et al., *Estimates of Population Exposure to Traffic-Related Air Pollution in Beijing, China, and New Delhi, India: Extending Exposure Analyses Reported in HEI Special Report 17: Traffic-Related Air Pollution: Critical Review of the Literature on Emissions, Exposure, and Health Effects* (Boston: Health Effects Institute, 2010), http://www.healtheffects .org/International /Jerrett_Asia_Traffic _Exposure.pdf; H E I Panel on the Health Effects of Traffic-Related Air Pollution, *Traffic-Related Air Pollution: A Critical Review of the Literature on Emissions, Exposure, and Health Effects*, vol. HEI Specia (Boston: Health Effects Institute, 2010).

5 Ofer Amram et al., "Proximity of Public Elementary Schools to Major Roads in Canadian Urban Areas," *International Journal of*

factors that determine levels, and therefore spatial patterns, may differ.[13] For example, motor vehicle exhaust emissions are often high when a car is idling or traveling at low speeds under about 20 miles per hour (less than 30 kilometers per hour). Stop-and-go traffic flow has been specifically implicated in leading to respiratory health impacts.[14] In contrast, noise emissions are comparatively low from idling vehicles, or at speeds below 25 miles per hour (40 kilometers per hour), but increase with higher speeds. Further, traffic volume is more closely linked to air pollution levels than it is to noise. A doubling of traffic volume only increases noise levels by three decibels.[15] Wind speed and air direction are important determinants of air pollution impacts, while rain and wet road surfaces can substantially increase noise levels. A number of studies have evaluated traffic-related air pollution and noise together and demonstrated independent impacts: in other words, areas with both high traffic-related noise and air pollution experience the most severe effects.[16]

Future vehicle technologies, for example, hybrid and plug-in electric or fuel cell vehicles, show promise toward substantially reducing both vehicle-related air pollution and noise. However, it is worth noting that such changes may occur very slowly—for example, hybrid electric vehicles have been available to consumers for about fifteen years, with present market penetration less than 2 percent. Given the important contributions to noise and air pollution from trucks used for goods movement, reductions in these emissions sources will also be necessary to maximize potential benefits.

Several promising trials show the potential of reducing exposure to traffic-related air pollution and noise. For example, a study of births among women residing within 1.2 miles (2 kilometers) to the New Jersey turnpike demonstrated a 12 percent reduction in low birth weights and an 11 percent reduction in preterm births after the introduction of E-ZPass toll payment transponders to eliminate congestion around toll plazas.[17] Noise barriers are common alongside many highways in densely populated areas, and noise insulation has shown some ability to reduce the negative impacts of noise on blood pressure.[18] Reduced vehicle speeds can result in less traffic noise and more safety for pedestrians and cyclists.

Health and Neighborhood Design

One of the greatest public health challenges faced globally—and especially in high-income countries—are inadequate levels of physical activity and their wide array of consequent health impacts.[19] Given that a large proportion of the population (35.5 percent of US adults and 83 percent of US students in grades 9–12) does not obtain recommended levels of physical activity, there has been substantial interest in population-level strategies to facilitate shifts in behavior.[20] Specific interest has focused on the role of neighborhood design.

Areas of mixed land use, higher street connectivity, residential density, and neighborhood features such as pedestrian and cyclist infrastructure are associated with higher levels of physical activity. Similar associations exist with composite measures of neighborhood "walkability": a combination of commercial floor space, land use mix, residential density, and connectivity. Yet relationships between neighborhood walkability and measures of obesity or improved health have been less consistent, despite a strong relationship between active transportation with decreased obesity and improved health.[21] (fig. **2.9.2**)

The relationships described above and the potential importance of neighborhood design features for health have been popularized with tools such as Walkscore

Health Geographics 10, no. 1 (2011): 68.

6 Brauer, Reynolds, and Hystad, "Traffic-Related Air Pollution and Health in Canada," 1557–58; Jerrett et al., *Traffic-Related Air Pollution*; Nina Annika Clark et al., "Effect of Early Life Exposure to Air Pollution on Development of Childhood Asthma," *Environmental Health Perspectives* 118, no. 2 (2010): 284–90; Elaina A. MacIntyre et al., "Residential Air Pollution and Otitis Media during the First Two Years of Life," *Epidemiology* 22, no. 1 (2011): 81–89.

7 Sara D. Adar et al., "Fine Particulate Air Pollution and the Progression of Carotid Intima-Medial Thickness: A Prospective Cohort Study from the Multi-Ethnic Study of Atherosclerosis and Air Pollution," *Plos Medicine* 10, no. 4 (2013): e1001430–e1001430; Wen Qi Gan et al., "Association of Long-Term Exposure to Community Noise and Traffic-Related Air Pollution With Coronary Heart Disease Mortality," *American Journal of Epidemiology* 175, no. 9 (2012): 898–906.

8 Wen Qi Gan et al., "Changes in Residential Proximity to Road Traffic and the Risk of Death from Coronary Heart Disease," *Epidemiology* 21, no. 5 (2010): 642–49; Jaime E. Hart et al., "Changes in Traffic Exposure and the Risk of Incident Myocardial Infarction and All-Cause Mortality," *Epidemiology* 24, no. 5 (2013): 734–42.

9 Christine T. Cowie et al., "Redistribution of Traffic Related Air Pollution Associated with a New Road Tunnel," *Environmental Science & Technology* 46, no. 5 (2012): 2918–27.

10 Giulia Cesaroni et al., "Health Benefits of Traffic-Related Air Pollution Reduction in Different Socioeconomic Groups: The Effect of Low-Emission Zoning in Rome," *Occupational and*

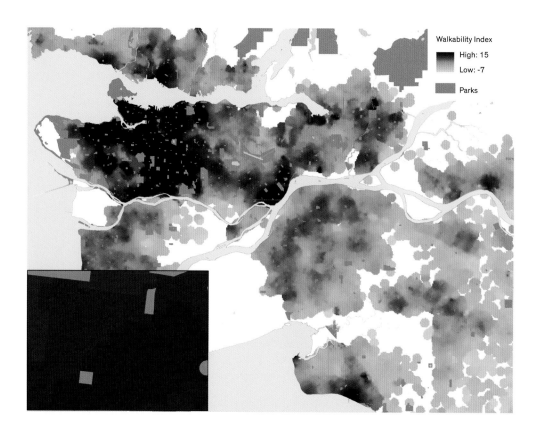

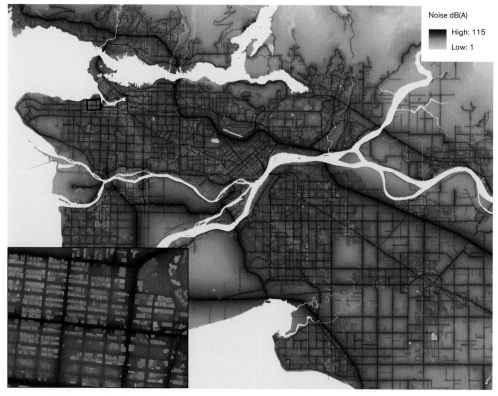

2.9.2 Maps of Vancouver, Canada, analyzing walkability, noise, population density, and air pollution

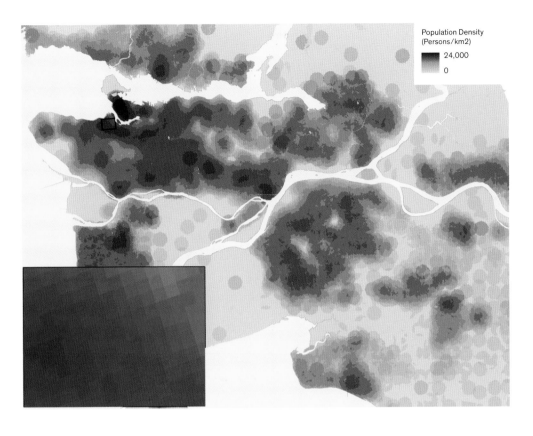

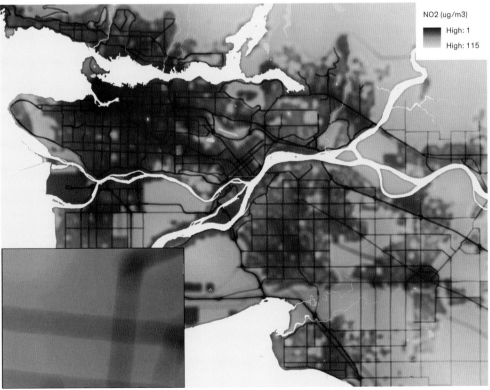

and Bikescore, which measure the "walk-ability" and "bikeability" of communities. The scores may serve to promote certain forms of the community design as attractive features and facilitate awareness among those seeking such areas. Although research increasingly supports a causal role of neighborhood design in promoting physical activity, the degree to which specific efforts can increase actual physical activity and lead to measurable health benefits is not yet clear. For example, many earlier studies relating community design with physical activity, on the one hand, or measures of obesity, on the other, did not account for self-selection. That is, people who engage in more physical activity may choose to live in neighborhoods that have supportive characteristics. A number of more recent quasi-experimental and longitudinal studies do indicate that specific modifications to neighborhood design to promote physical activity lead to the desired impacts.[22]

It is also important to note that some of the same attributes of neighborhood design that promote active transportation may also support other health-related beneficial attributes such as increased social capital and reductions in motor vehicle injuries to pedestrians. In contrast, given that residential density is a factor determining walkability, but one that also increases exposure to traffic-related air pollution, a study in Vancouver, Canada, identified very few areas of both low air pollution and high walkability. It found a larger number of areas with higher air pollution and low walkability, and many neighborhoods with high air pollution and high walkability.[23] An extension of this analysis to travel survey data in Los Angeles indicated that, in the context of ischemic heart disease, the population health benefits from increased physical activity in high-walkability neighborhoods may be offset by adverse effects of air pollution exposure.[24] This research

Environmental Medicine 69, no. 2 (2012): 133–39; Christer Johansson, Lars Burman, and Bertil Forsberg, "The Effects of Congestions Tax on Air Quality and Health," *Atmospheric Environment* 43, no. 31 (2009): 4843–54; Cathryn Tonne et al., "Air Pollution and Mortality Benefits of the London Congestion Charge: Spatial and Socioeconomic Inequalities," *Occupational and Environmental Medicine* 65, no. 9 (2008): 620–27.

11 Thomas Muenzel et al., "Cardiovascular Effects of Environmental Noise Exposure," *European Heart Journal* 35, no. 13 (2014): 829.

12 Mathias Basner et al., "Auditory and Non-Auditory Effects of Noise on Health," *Lancet* 383, no. 9925 (2014): 1325–32; Angel M. Dzhambov, "Long-Term Noise Exposure and the Risk for Type 2 Diabetes: A Meta-Analysis," *Noise & Health* 17, no. 74 (2015): 23–33.

13 Wen Qi Gan et al., "Modeling Population Exposure to Community Noise and Air Pollution in a Large Metropolitan Area," *Environmental Research* 116 (2012): 11–16.

14 Patrick H. Ryan et al., "Is It Traffic Type, Volume, or Distance? Wheezing in Infants Living near Truck and Bus Traffic," *Journal of Allergy and Clinical Immunology* 116, no. 2 (2005): 279–84.

15 Gan et al., "Modeling Population Exposure to Community Noise and Air Pollution in a Large Metropolitan Area."

16 Gan et al., "Association of Long-Term Exposure to Community Noise and Traffic-Related Air Pollution with Coronary Heart Disease Mortality," 898–906; Mette Sorensen et al., "Combined Effects of Road Traffic Noise and Ambient Air Pollution in Relation to Risk for Stroke?," *Environmental Research* 133 (August 2014): 49–55.

17 Janet Currie and Reed Walker, "Traffic Congestion and Infant

Health: Evidence from E-ZPass," *American Economic Journal: Applied Economics* 3, no. 1 (2011): 65–90.

18 Wolfgang Babisch et al., "Exposure Modifiers of the Relationships of Transportation Noise with High Blood Pressure and Noise Annoyance," *Journal of the Acoustical Society of America* 132, no. 6 (2012): 3788–808.

19 I-Min Lee et al., "Effect of Physical Inactivity on Major Non-Communicable Diseases Worldwide: An Analysis of Burden of Disease and Life Expectancy," *Lancet* 380, no. 9838 (2012): 219–29.

20 Centers for Disease Control and Prevention, "State Indicator Report on Physical Activity, 2010" (Atlanta, GA: US Department of Health and Human Services, 2010), http://www.cdc.gov/physical activity/downloads/PA_State_Indicator_Report_2010.pdf.

21 Gerlinde Grasser et al., "Objectively Measured Walkability and Active Transport and Weight-Related Outcomes in Adults: A Systematic Review," *International Journal of Public Health* 58, no. 4 (2013): 615–25; Alva O. Ferdinand et al., "The Relationship between Built Environments and Physical Activity: A Systematic Review," *American Journal of Public Health* 102, no. 10 (2012): e7–13; Jana A. Hirsch et al., "Changes in the Built Environment and Changes in the Amount of Walking over Time: Longitudinal Results from the Multi-Ethnic Study of Atherosclerosis," *American Journal of Epidemiology* 180, no. 8 (2014): 799–809; Mark Hamer and Yoichi Chida, "Active Commuting and Cardiovascular Risk: A Meta-Analytic Review," *Preventive Medicine* 46, no. 1 (2008): 9–13; Lars Ostergaard et al., "Cycling to School Is Associated with Lower

BMI and Lower Odds of Being Overweight or Obese in a Large Population-Based Study of Danish Adolescents," *Journal of Physical Activity & Health* 9, no. 5 (2012): 617–25; Kristina Sundquist et al., "Neighborhood Walkability, Deprivation, and Incidence of Type 2 Diabetes: A Population-Based Study on 512,061 Swedish Adults," *Health & Place* 31 (2015): 24–30.

22 Hirsch et al., "Changes in the Built Environment and Changes in the Amount of Walking over Time: Longitudinal Results from the Multi-Ethnic Study of Atherosclerosis," 799–809; Matthew W. Knuiman et al., "A Longitudinal Analysis of the Influence of the Neighborhood Built Environment on Walking for Transportation," *American Journal of Epidemiology* 180, no. 5 (2014): 453–61; Gavin R. McCormack and Alan Shiell, "In Search of Causality: A Systematic Review of the Relationship between the Built Environment and Physical Activity among Adults," *International Journal of Behavioral Nutrition and Physical Activity* 8 (2011): 125.

23 Julian D. Marshall, Michael Brauer, and Lawrence D. Frank, "Healthy Neighborhoods: Walkability and Air Pollution," *Environmental Health Perspectives* 117, no. 11 (2009): 1752–59.

24 Steve Hankey, Julian D. Marshall, and Michael Brauer, "Health Impacts of the Built Environment: Within-Urban Variability in Physical Inactivity, Air Pollution, and Ischemic Heart Disease Mortality," *Environmental Health Perspectives* 120, no. 2 (2012): 247–53.

25 Jereon Johan de Hartog et al., "Do the Health Benefits of Cycling Outweigh the Risks?," *Environmental Health Perspectives* 118, no. 8 (2010): 1109–16; David Rojas-Rueda et al., "The Health Risks and

was sensitive to the observation that only a small proportion of the population in general was sufficiently physically active and contrasts with a number of analyses that indicate that health benefits of active transportation among those who engage in it greatly outweigh any negative impacts associated with increased air pollution exposure (e.g., that experienced by cyclists in traffic or pedestrians walking alongside major roads).[25] More generally, these studies indicate a need to consider multiple pathways through which community design may affect health.

Green and Blue Spaces

One of the more intriguing aspects of community design that influences health is the presence of natural green or blue spaces. An increasing number of studies have shown that residents of neighborhoods with more green areas have lower rates of mortality and other negative health outcomes.[26] While these associations may suggest merely that healthier individuals choose to live in greener areas, the research is supported by focused environmental psychology studies that show lower levels of stress when people are in contact—even visual contact—with nature.

For example, in a classic study, the behavioral scientist Roger Ulrich and colleagues compared surgical recovery between hospital patients. Those patients with a view of a natural setting had shorter postoperative hospital stays, and took less pain medication, than twenty-three matched patients in similar rooms with windows facing a brick wall.[27] A recent observational study reported that improved survival following stroke was associated with surrounding greenness.[28]

These studies and others suggest the importance of psychological pathways that reduce stress.[29] Natural spaces may also be refuges from harmful exposures (air, noise, heat) either by direct removal of pollutants, by reduced perceived

exposures, or via the simple absence of emissions sources.[30] Natural spaces also provide a place for healthy physical activity and are especially important for active transportation as well.[31]

Natural spaces, especially green places, have also been associated with stronger social cohesion: shared neighborhood norms, friendly relationships, and a sense of neighborhood belonging, all attributes that are themselves associated with improved health.[32] A series of studies in Chicago evaluated an experiment in which public housing residents were randomly allocated to otherwise similar buildings with differing levels of outdoor greenery. The presence of more green space was associated with greater use of common spaces, more informal social contacts among residents, and lower rates of crime.[33] The quality and accessibility of natural space is also important. Dense forests within urban areas may be perceived as unsafe, while poorly maintained parks or vacant lots are unlikely to support social cohesion and may negatively affect health.

A still-unexplored mechanism may be the role of natural spaces within communities in harboring microbial diversity, which has been linked to immune system regulation and hypothesized to improve health.[34] For example, in an extension of the "hygiene hypothesis," research on the development of allergic disease suggests that early life exposure to natural environments, and the diverse microbiology that they harbor, leads to healthy immune system development. This contrasts with exposure to a more sterile environment with lower microbial diversity and the development of reduced immune tolerance and a greater likelihood for allergic responses.

Recently, the environmental epidemiologist Perry Hystad and colleagues showed that greenness had positive impacts on birth weight and preterm birth

Benefits of Cycling in Urban Environments Compared with Car Use: Health Impact Assessment Study," *British Medical Journal* 343 (2011): d4521.

26 Terry Hartig et al., "Nature and Health," *Annual Review of Public Health* 35 (2014): 207; Marcel F. Jonker et al., "The Effect of Urban Green on Small-Area (healthy) Life Expectancy," *Journal of Epidemiology and Community Health* 68, no. 10 (2014): 999–1002; Paul J. Villeneuve et al., "A Cohort Study Relating Urban Green Space with Mortality in Ontario, Canada," *Environmental Research* 115 (2012): 51–58.

27 Roger S. Ulrich, "View through a Window May Influence Recovery from Surgery," *Science* 224, no. 4647 (1984): 420–21.

28 Elissa H. Wilker et al., "Green Space and Mortality Following Ischemic Stroke," *Environmental Research* 133 (2014): 42–48.

29 Diana E. Bowler et al., "A Systematic Review of Evidence for the Added Benefits to Health of Exposure to Natural Environments," *Bmc Public Health* 10 (2010): 10.

30 Diana E. Bowler et al., "Urban Greening to Cool Towns and Cities: A Systematic Review of the Empirical Evidence," *Landscape and Urban Planning* 97, no. 3 (2010): 147–55; Angel M. Dzhambov and Donka Dimitrova Dimitrova, "Urban Green Spaces Effectiveness as a Psychological Buffer for the Negative Health Impact of Noise Pollution: A Systematic Review," *Noise & Health* 16, no. 70 (2014): 157–65, doi:10.4103/1463-1741.134916; Barbara A. Maher et al., "Impact of Roadside Tree Lines on Indoor Concentrations of Traffic-Derived Particulate Matter," *Environmental Science & Technology* 47, no. 23 (2013): 13737–44; David J. Nowak et al.,

rates that appeared to be independent of adverse impacts from air pollution and noise exposure, and not affected by neighborhood walkability levels or park distance, suggesting a role for psychological impacts or processes linked to increased social contacts.[35] Similarly, another study found that the association between surrounding green space and mortality was not mediated by walking, despite the fact that green space was itself strongly correlated with increased walking, again suggesting the potential role for psychosocial factors.[36] Vegetation too may have some negative impacts on health. For example, certain species of trees and grasses that are heavy pollen producers, and the male tree clones commonly used in nurseries, can lead to an increase in the severity of allergies among residents.[37]

The current state of understanding suggests that community design that incorporates and facilitates contact with natural spaces has potential to lead to improved health. It is also important to note that these benefits may be most pronounced among the more disadvantaged members of the population. Different mechanisms are likely to achieve different health impacts. But we do know that natural spaces with access to high- quality areas for social interactions and physical activity are likely to be beneficial, while larger natural spaces areas may provide cooling effects and lower levels of air pollution and noise. The important potential stress-reducing role of natural spaces may in fact be their most important aspect, but it is not yet known whether the mere presence of greenery (i.e., street trees) or active engagement with natural spaces is sufficient to provide these benefits. Understanding the specific mechanisms of action, which are relevant for different health benefits, will be important in identifying features of healthy community design. It is quite likely that different features, for example, park

access in relation to physical activity and visual green spaces for mental health, will be more important for different objectives. Suburban areas, which have a greater density of natural spaces, have great potential to provide many of the features believed to be desirable although ensuring access and facilitation of social contacts will likely also need consideration.

The Next Step: Health Impact Assessment in Community Planning
From the above examples, it is clear that community design can affect exposures that may be unhealthy or be health promoting. In some cases the same design features may affect multiple exposures, with potential (positive or negative) impacts on health possibly enhanced. There are also examples where beneficial and adverse impacts may partially or completely offset each other. Given this complexity, there is a need for multicriteria assessment of the potential health ramifications of design considerations.

Health impact assessment, a systematic process by which the health impacts of nonhealth decisions are evaluated, offers one possible approach. In impact assessment, design decisions are evaluated through a multistakeholder, multistage process with the following major components: (1) screening—determining whether a health impact assessment is required or will be useful for a specific project or decision; (2) scoping—determining which health effects to include in the assessment; (3) assessing risks and benefits—estimating which populations may be affected and the direction and magnitude of impacts; (4) developing recommendations—suggesting changes to proposed projects or policies to promote health benefits or to minimize adverse health impacts; (5) reporting—presentation of results to stakeholders; and (6) monitoring and evaluating—determining

Modeling the Effects of Urban Vegetation on Air Pollution, vol. 22, NATO Challenges of Modern Society, 1998; Marie-Pierre Parenteau and Michael Charles Sawada, "The Role of Spatial Representation in the Development of a LUR Model for Ottawa, Canada," *Air Quality Atmosphere and Health* 5, no. 3 (2012): 311–23.

31 Kate Lachowycz and Andy P. Jones, "Greenspace and Obesity: A Systematic Review of the Evidence," *Obesity Reviews* 12, no. 501 (2011): e183–89.

32 Takemi Sugiyama et al., "Associations of Neighbourhood Greenness with Physical and Mental Health: Do Walking, Social Coherence, and Local Social Interaction Explain the Relationships?," *Journal of Epidemiology and Community Health* 62, no. 5 (2008): e9; Sjerp de Vries et al., "Streetscape Greenery and Health: Stress, Social Cohesion, and Physical Activity as Mediators," *Social Science & Medicine* 94, (2013): 26–33.

33 Frances E. Kuo et al., "Fertile Ground for Community: Inner-City Neighborhood Common Spaces," *American Journal of Community Psychology* 26, no. 6 (1998): 823–51.

34 Graham A. Rook, "Regulation of the Immune System by Biodiversity from the Natural Environment: An Ecosystem Service Essential to Health," *Proceedings of the National Academy of Sciences of the United States of America* 110, no. 46 (2013): 18360–67.

35 Perry Hystad et al., "Residential Greenness and Birth Outcomes: Evaluating the Influence of Spatially Correlated Built-Environment Factors," *Environmental Health Perspectives* 122, no. 10 (2014): 1095–102.

36 Kate Lachowycz and Andy P. Jones, "Does Walking Explain

the effect of the health impact assessment process on the actual decision.[38]

The air pollution and transportation expert Audrey de Nazelle and colleagues provide an example framework for the application of health impact assessment in the context of policies that encourage active transportation.[39] Their assessments range from those that include a simple hypothetical scenario and a rather small number of benefits and risks, to those that include a more complete set of risks and benefits and numerous specific policies.[40]

Health impact assessments or other approaches are important tools for considering the health implications of community planning and design decisions and policies. These approaches should be viewed not as barriers to change or as necessarily requiring additional cost. Rather, they would more properly be viewed as a means by which maximum health benefits and minimal adverse health impacts can be achieved.

Associations between Access to Greenspace and Lower Mortality?," *Social Science & Medicine* 107 (2014): 9–17.

37 Brian Sawyers, "Regulating Pollen," *Minnesota Law Review Headnotes* 98 (April 2014): 96.

38 National Academy of Sciences, *Improving Health in the United States: The Role of Health Impact Assessment* (Washington, DC: National Academies Press, 2011).

39 Audrey de Nazelle et al., "Improving Health through Policies That Promote Active Travel: A Review of Evidence to Support Integrated Health Impact Assessment," *Environment International* 37, no. 4 (2011): 766–77.

40 Graeme Lindsay, Alexandra Macmillan, and Alistair Woodward, "Moving Urban Trips from Cars to Bicycles: Impact on Health and Emissions," *Australian and New Zealand Journal of Public Health* 35, no. 1 (2011): 54–60; Alexandra Macmillan et al., "The Societal Costs and Benefits of Commuter Bicycling: Simulating the Effects of Specific Policies Using System Dynamics Modeling," *Environmental Health Perspectives* 122, no. 4 (2014): 335–44.

2.10
HEALTH ADVANTAGES IN SUBURBS

Bridget Catlin

COMMUTING PATTERNS

HEALTH

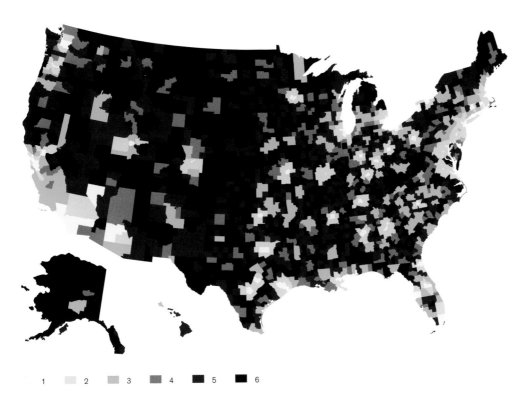

1   2   3   4   5   6

2.10.1 NCHS classification of counties, urban–rural classification

1   Melinda Beck, "City vs. Country: Who Is Healthier?," *Wall Street Journal*, July 12, 2011, accessed January 18, 2015, http://www.wsj .com/articles/SB1000142 405270230479350457643 4442652581806.

2   "County Health Rankings," University of Wisconsin Population Health Institute, accessed January 18, 2015, http://www.county healthrankings.org/.

3   Debora Ingram and Sheila J. Franco, "NCHS Urban-Rural Classification Scheme for Counties," *Vital Health Stat* 2 (2012): 1–65.

In 2011 the *Wall Street Journal* published an article with the headline "City vs. Country: Who Is Healthier?" It neglected to mention that it appears that suburbs are actually healthier than both urban and rural areas.[1] This is a finding from the County Health Rankings project, a collaboration between the University of Wisconsin Population Health Institute and the Robert Wood Johnson Foundation. Published annually since February 2010, the Rankings help counties understand the influences on residents' health and how long they will live.[2] The Rankings are targeted at policy makers, planners, and community leaders, and intended to spur policy development and efforts to improve the health of communities.

The Rankings measure a broad set of vital health factors, including high school graduation rates, obesity, smoking, unemployment, access to healthy foods, air and water quality, income, and teen births in nearly every county in America. We compile the Rankings using county-level measures from a variety of national data sources. We then provide two overall ranks: health outcomes (how healthy a county is now) and health factors (how healthy a county will be in the future). We rank counties within states, not on a national basis, but questions arose regarding the influence that county type and size might have on ranks. To answer these questions, we examined the Rankings in relation to level of urbanization, using the National Center for Health Statistics (NCHS) classification system to define urban to rural counties.[3]

The NCHS urban-rural classification scheme is based on the Office of Management and Budget's metropolitan statistical area (MSA) designations. We refer to the six NCHS categories as "Major Urban" (county within an MSA with more than 1 million people), "Suburban Metro" (non-central county within an MSA greater than 1 million), "Medium Metro" (county within an MSA between 250,000 and 1 million), "Small Metro" (county within an MSA between 50,000 and 250,000), "Micropolitan" (rural county with a city of 10,000 or more population), and "Non-Core" (rural county without a city of 10,000 or more population). (fig. **2.10.1**) We use the term *suburbs* to refer to the Suburban Metro category of counties, although clearly within any given county there may be urban, suburban, or rural areas. Thus, factors that rank high or low for Major Urban counties could be attributed to their dense centers or their suburbs. Meanwhile, Suburban Metro counties do not include large cities but may include rural areas. For example, in California, Los Angeles, Sacramento, San Diego, and San Francisco Counties are among those considered Major Urban counties, while Marin, San Bernardino, and San Mateo counties are among those considered Suburban Metro.

The Rankings are based on counties or county equivalents (e.g., parishes in Louisiana, independent cities in Virginia, and census districts in Alaska). Any entity that has its own Federal Information Processing Standard (FIPS) county code is included in the Rankings. Certain major cities, such as Baltimore and St. Louis, are considered county equivalents and have their own FIPS county code. Other cities, such as Milwaukee, do not have a FIPS code and are not individually ranked.

How do we define and measure county health? We select measures based on a framework for understanding that health is determined by a wide range of factors such as individual behaviors and the social, economic, and physical environment. (fig. **2.10.2**) How healthy a place is currently (referred to as health outcomes) is measured in terms of how long people live (length of life) and how healthy they feel (quality of life). Based on a value judgment that length and quality of life are both important, we weight these two categories equally. We use a composite score of one measure of length of life and four measures of quality of life to come up with overall rankings for the health of counties by state.[4]

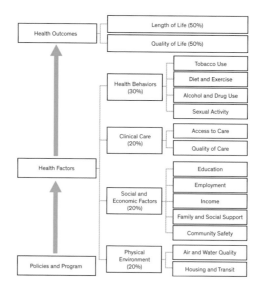

2.10.2 County health rankings model

We had enough data to rank 3,047 out of 3,143 counties. The health of counties is ranked within their respective states by urban-rural classification. (fig. **2.10.3**) In the chart, dark green denotes counties that rank in the first quartile, or the top 25 percent of healthiest counties. The lightest green denotes counties that rank in the bottom quartile (or bottom 25 percent). Noncore counties have the smallest percentage of counties in the healthiest group, and the largest percentage of counties in the least healthy group. Suburban Metro counties have the highest percentage in the healthiest category.

Specifically, residents in Suburban Metro counties have lower rates of premature death (years of potential life lost before age seventy-five) than those who live in other types of counties, and a better health-related quality of life; 15 percent of adults in Suburban Metro counties report being in fair or poor health compared to 18 percent of adults in Non-Core counties.[5] (fig. **2.10.4**)

To understand why suburban counties are healthier than their urban or rural counterparts requires looking at the multitude of factors that influence health. In the Rankings, we measure four types of health factors: health behaviors, clinical care, social and economic conditions, and

4 "County Health Rankings—Ranking Methods," University of Wisconsin Population Health Institute, accessed January 18, 2015, http://www.county healthrankings.org /ranking-methods.

5 "County Health Rankings—Data Sources and Measures," University of Wisconsin Population Health Institute, accessed January 18, 2015, http://www.county healthrankings.org /ranking-methods/data -sources-and-measures.

physical environment factors. In turn, each of these factors is based on several measures. A fifth set of factors that influence health (genetics and biology) is not included.

Health Behaviors

We look at four different types of health behaviors: smoking, diet and exercise, alcohol and drug use, and sexual activity. Tobacco use is the leading cause of preventable death in the United States. Each year, smoking kills 480,000 Americans, including about 42,000 who die from exposure to secondhand smoke. On average, smokers die ten years earlier than nonsmokers.[6] The highest rates of smoking among adults are found in rural (Micropolitan and Non-Core) counties, and the lowest rates are found in Major Urban areas. Suburban counties have smoking rates just below the median of all US counties of 21 percent.[7]

Sufficient nutrition and regular exercise are, of course, important to health, with inadequate physical activity contributing to an increased risk of coronary heart disease, diabetes, and some cancers. Yet, half of US adults and nearly 72 percent of high school students do not meet the Center for Disease Control's recommended physical activity levels, and American adults walk less than adults in any other industrialized country. As of 2013, 29 million Americans lived in a food desert, without access to affordable, healthy food. More than two-thirds of all American adults and approximately 32 percent of children and adolescents are overweight or obese. Obesity is one of the biggest drivers of preventable chronic diseases in the United States.[8] As with smoking, the highest rates of adult obesity (31 percent) and physical inactivity (29 percent) are currently seen in rural counties, and the lowest rates (27 percent and 23 percent) are in Major Urban centers. Suburban counties fall in between at

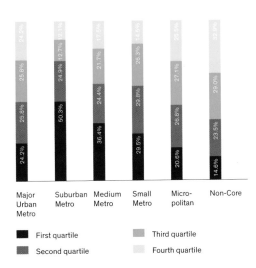

2.10.3 Percentage of quartile for the 2014 County Health Rankings by NCHS urban and rural classification

First quartile   Third quartile

Second quartile   Fourth quartile

29 percent for obesity and 26 percent for physical inactivity.

Two of the prerequisites for healthy eating and active living are opportunities to purchase healthy foods and opportunities for exercise. Suburban counties performed better on our index of factors that contribute to a healthy food environment than all other types of counties. This index, from 0 (worst) to 10 (best), reflects limited access to healthy foods, that is, the percentage of the population who are low income and do not live close to a grocery store, often referred to as "food deserts," and food insecurity, that is, the percentage of the population who did not have access to a reliable source of food during the past year. For example, the only county with an index of 10 is Loudon County, a suburban county in Virginia, where only 1 percent of the population has limited access to healthy food and 5 percent are food insecure. On average, Suburban counties have a food environment index of 8.1 with, on average, 5 percent of the population with limited access to healthy food and 13 percent experiencing food insecurity. Major Urban counties have a food environment index of 7.2 on average and have similar levels of limited access to healthy food (4 percent) but the highest levels of food insecurity (17 percent). Other types of counties ranged

6   "Smoking and Tobacco Use—Fast Facts," Centers for Disease Control and Prevention, accessed January 18, 2015, http://www.cdc.gov /tobacco/data_statistics /fact_sheets/fast_facts/.

7   "County Health Rankings—2014 National Statistics," University of Wisconsin Population Health Institute, March 12, 2014, accessed May 12, 2015, http://www .countyhealthrankings .org/resources/2014 -national-statistics.

8   "F as in Fat: How Obesity Threatens America's Future," Robert Wood Johnson Foundation, August 2013, accessed January 18, 2015, http:// healthyamericans.org /assets/files/TFAH2013 FasInFatReportFinal%20 9.9.pdf.

	All	Major Urban Metro	Suburban Metro	Medium Metro	Small Metro	Micro-politan	Non-Core
All	3,047	62	354	332	339	686	1,274
Health Outcomes							
Years of potential life lost before age 75 per 100,000 population (age-adjusted)	8,060	7,247	6,829	7,553	7,497	8,097	8,733
Percent of adults reporting fair or poor health (age-adjusted)	17.3%	15.6%	14.6%	16.5%	16.8%	18.0%	18.3%
Average number of physically unhealthy days reported in past 30 days (age-adjusted)	3.8	3.5	3.5	3.8	3.8	3.9	4.0
Average number of mentally unhealthy days reported in past 30 days (age-adjusted)	3.6	3.5	3.4	3.6	3.6	3.6	3.6
Percent of live births with low birthweight (< 2500 grams)	8.3%	8.9%	8.0%	8.4%	8.1%	8.3%	8.3%
Health Factors							
Health Behaviors							
Percent of adults that report smoking >= 100 cigarettes and currently smoking	21.3%	16.9%	19.7%	20.3%	20.7%	21.6%	22.4%
Percent of adults that report a BMI >= 30	30.6%	26.5%	29.2%	29.9%	30.6%	31.0%	31.2%
Index of factors that contribute to the food environment	7.4	7.2	8.1	7.6	7.5	7.3	7.2
Percent of adults aged 20 and over reporting no leisure-time physical activity	27.8%	22.9%	25.6%	26.3%	26.8%	28.0%	29.3%
Percent of the population with adequate access to locations for physical activity	52.7%	92.8%	65.1%	59.7%	57.0%	53.3%	44.0%
Binge plus heavy drinking	16.4%	17.3%	17.1%	15.8%	16.0%	15.5%	17.2%
Proportion of driving deaths with alcohol involvement	32.1%	30.8%	31.4%	33.4%	31.9%	30.4%	33.1%
Chlamydia rate per 100,000 population	354.6	697.9	314.8	379.1	402.7	376.1	315.2
Teen birth rate per 1,000 female population, ages 15–19	44.4	41.2	33.0	40.4	41.6	47.9	47.6
Clinical Care							
Percent of population under age 65 without health insurance	17.9%	17.9%	15.1%	16.7%	17.3%	18.0%	19.1%
Rate of population to primary care physicians per 100,000	56.1	86.3	57.8	60.4	60.4	57.5	50.9
Rate of population to dentists per 100,000	40.1	73.3	46.6	45.4	45.5	40.9	33.4
Rate of population to mental health providers per 100,000	88.6	181.4	86.0	103.0	103.1	94.3	70.9
Hospitalization rate for ambulatory-care sensitive conditions per 1,000 Medicare enrollees	76.5	59.7	69.7	65.6	69.3	74.3	85.8
Percent of diabetic Medicare enrollees that receive HbA1c screening	83.9%	83.3%	85.1%	84.7%	84.8%	84.1%	83.0%
Percent of female Medicare enrollees that receive mammography screening	60.7%	60.8%	61.8%	62.7%	63.2%	61.6%	58.7%
Social and Economic Factors							
Percent of ninth grade cohort that graduates in 4 years	81.5%	73.1%	83.7%	79.9%	81.1%	80.9%	82.4%
Percent of adults aged 25–44 years with some post-secondary education	54.9%	65.8%	61.7%	59.0%	57.7%	53.7%	51.3%
Percent of population age 16+ unemployed but seeking work	7.8%	8.3%	7.6%	7.9%	7.7%	8.0%	7.7%
Percent of children under age 18 in poverty	24.6%	25.9%	17.2%	22.8%	23.4%	25.8%	26.8%
Percent of adults without social/emotional support	19.4%	22.6%	18.1%	19.6%	18.8%	19.7%	19.5%
Percent of children that live in household headed by single parent	31.9%	39.9%	28.0%	31.9%	32.6%	33.5%	31.6%
Violent crime rate per 100,000 population	260.2	642.5	239.8	328.9	305.1	291.9	196.3
Injury mortality per 100,000	76.1	59.3	61.0	67.5	67.2	73.7	88.7

	All	Major Urban Metro	Suburban Metro	Medium Metro	Small Metro	Micro-politan	Non-Core
Physical Environment							
Average daily measure of fine particulate matter in micrograms per cubic meter (PM2.5) in a county	11.6	11.2	11.9	11.7	11.8	11.7	11.5
Percentage of population potentially exposed to water exceeding a violation limit during the past year	9.0%	5.2%	6.9%	8.4%	6.2%	7.8%	11.4%
Percentage of households with at least 1 of 4 housing problems: overcrowding, high housing costs, or lack of kitchen or plumbing facilities	14.2%	21.9%	14.8%	14.8%	14.6%	14.5%	13.2%
Percent of the workforce that drives alone to work	78.6%	69.5%	80.5%	80.9%	80.2%	79.7%	76.8%
Percentage of the workforce who drives their commute alone for more than 30 minutes	29.8%	34.7%	44.0%	32.6%	26.7%	25.0%	28.2%
Best Value Tally		14	14	0	1	4	2
Worst Value Tally		10	2	2	0	2	18

2.10.4 Mean values of measures in the 2014 County Health Rankings by NCHS urban and rural classification

from 7 to 10 percent with limited access to healthy foods and 15 percent experiencing food insecurity. However, having access to healthy foods is only the first step toward healthy eating. Healthy choices for food purchases and cooking techniques are also important, as is matching consumption with energy output.

Suburban counties performed better than all but Major Urban counties for opportunities for exercise (defined as the percentage of the population who live reasonably close to locations for physical activity, including parks or recreational facilities). Sixty-five percent of the population in Suburban counties lives reasonably close to a location for physical activity compared to 93 percent in Major Urban counties and 44 to 60 percent in other types of counties. As with the food environment, having access to parks and recreational facilities does not mean that people will use them. Residents have better access to these opportunities in Suburban counties than in rural counties, but strategies to increase exercise levels need to address more than just access, including factors such as motivation and time.

It's well-known that excessive alcohol consumption, prescription drug misuse, and illicit drug use have substantial health,

economic, and social consequences. Excessive alcohol use is the third leading cause of preventable death in the United States.[9] Drug poisoning is the leading cause of injury death, and the drug overdose death rate has more than doubled from 1999 through 2013.[10] Excessive drinking rates are similarly high in Major Urban, Suburban Metro, and Non-Core counties; Medium, Small Metro, and Micropolitan counties have the lowest rates.

Last but not least among the behaviors that influence our health is sexual activity. Sexually transmitted infections (STIs) and unplanned pregnancies, often the result of risky sexual behavior, have lasting effects on health and well-being, especially for adolescents, as well as the economic and social well-being of individuals and communities. Suburban counties have the lowest rates of chlamydia (the most prevalent STI) and teen birth rates. The highest rates of chlamydia are found in Major Urban counties and the highest teen birth rates are found in Micropolitan and Non-Core counties.

Ranking Suburban Clinical Care

What are the opportunities for maintaining good health in our nation's suburban counties? Access to affordable, quality

9   Centers for Disease Control and Prevention, National Center for Chronic Disease Prevention and Health Promotion, *Excessive Alcohol Use: Addressing a Leading Risk for Death, Chronic Disease, and Injury at a Glance* (Atlanta, GA: National Center for Chronic Disease Prevention and Health Promotion, Division of Population Health, 2011).

10   "Injury Prevention and Control—Prescription Drug Overdose," Centers for Disease Control and Prevention, accessed January 18, 2015, http://www.cdc.gov/drug overdose/index.html.

health care is clearly important to physical, social, and mental health. Health insurance helps residents access needed primary care, specialists, and emergency care, but does not ensure access on its own—it is also necessary for providers to offer affordable care, be available to treat patients, and be in relatively close proximity to patients. Together, health insurance, local care options, and a consistent source of care help ensure that individuals can enter the health care system, find care easily and locally, pay for care, and get their health needs met.

In 2013 over 41 million Americans younger than age sixty-five were uninsured.[11] The Affordable Care Act (ACA) extended coverage to some, but not all, of these people. Current estimates suggest that in the first six months of 2014, 14 percent of persons under sixty-five lacked health insurance coverage, down from 18 percent in 2010.[12] The uninsured are much less likely to have primary care providers than the insured; they also receive less preventive care, dental care, chronic disease management, and behavioral health counseling. Those without insurance are often diagnosed at later, less treatable disease stages than those with insurance and, overall, have worse health outcomes, lower quality of life, and higher mortality rates.[13]

Having health insurance is not enough to ensure access to care. Nationally, many geographic areas lack sufficient providers to meet patient needs; as of June 2014, there were about 6,100 primary care, 4,000 mental health, and 4,900 dental federally designated "Health Professional Shortage Areas" in the United States.[14]

Residents of Suburban counties are more likely to be insured than those in other types of locations, but they do not have the best access to providers. Non-Core areas have the highest rates of the uninsured, coupled with the most difficulty in finding primary care physicians,

dentists, and mental health providers. Major Urban areas have the best availability of these critical health care providers.

But not all health care is equal; there can be wide variations in the quality of care in different communities. High-quality health care is timely, safe, effective, and affordable—the right, personalized care at the right time. High-quality inpatient and outpatient care improves health and reduces the likelihood of receiving unnecessary or inappropriate care. Despite efforts toward higher quality care, an estimated 30 percent of patients do not receive recommended care or treatment.[15]

Suburban counties received mixed reviews for quality of care, while Non-Core counties consistently fare worst. We looked at preventable hospital stays, that is, hospitalization for selected conditions that can normally be treatable outside hospitals, and found that Major Urban counties had the lowest rates. Suburban counties fared better than Non-Core counties, but not as well as Major Urban counties. Higher rates of hospital stays for these conditions suggest that the quality of care provided in the outpatient setting was less than ideal.

Two other ways to measure the quality of care look at how often recommended services are received, such as mammograms for women and monitoring of glucose levels for diabetic patients. In general, there was little variation across the six types of counties for these services, but Suburban counties fared best and Non-Core rural residents fared worst for mammograms and monitoring of diabetics.

Social and Economic Factors in Suburban Health

The third set of health factors we examined included education, income, employment, family and social support, and community safety. Better-educated individuals live longer, healthier lives than those with less education, and their children are more

11 "Key Facts about the Uninsured Population," Henry J. Kaiser Family Foundation, Kaiser Commission on Medicaid and the Uninsured, October 5, 2015, accessed January 18, 2015, http://kff.org /uninsured/fact-sheet /key-facts-about-the -uninsured-population/.

12 Centers for Disease Control and Prevention, National Center for Health Statistics, *Health Insurance Coverage: Early Release of Estimates from the National Health Interview Survey, January–June 2014,* by Michael Martinez and Robin Cohen, NCHS 2014 (Atlanta, GA: National Center for Health Statistics, Division of Health Interview Statistics, 2014).

13 US Department of Health & Human Services, Agency for Healthcare Research and Quality, *National Healthcare Quality Report, 2013,* AHRQ 2014 (Rockville, MD: US Department of Health and Human Services, 2014).

14 "Shortage Designation: Health Professional Shortage Areas & Medically Underserved Areas/Populations," US Department of Health and Human Services, Health Resources and Services Administration, accessed January 18, 2015, http://www.hrsa .gov/shortage/.

15 *National Healthcare Quality Report, 2013.*

likely to thrive, even when factors like income are taken into account. More schooling is linked to higher incomes, better employment options, and increased social support that, together, support opportunities for healthier choices. Yet in 2013, about 12 percent of adults older than twenty-four had not graduated high school, and another 30 percent had no education beyond high school.[16] Higher levels of education are linked to better health, healthier lifestyle decisions, and fewer chronic conditions.[17] Education is also connected to lifespan. On average, college graduates live nine more years than high school dropouts.[18] Suburban counties have the best timely high school graduation rates (the percentage of ninth graders who graduate within four years) and are second only to Major Urban counties for adults ages twenty-five to forty-four with at least some college education.

Along with an individual's level of educational attainment, the economic condition of a community plays an important role in shaping employment opportunities. Working in a safe environment with fair compensation often provides not only income but also benefits such as health insurance, paid sick leave, and workplace wellness programs that, together, support opportunities for healthy choices. Those who are unemployed face great challenges to health and well-being, including lost income and, often, health insurance. Unemployed individuals are 54 percent more likely to be in poor or fair health than individuals who are employed, and are more likely to suffer from increased stress, high blood pressure, heart disease, and depression.[19] Historically, Major Urban counties have had the highest unemployment rates, but Suburban and rural counties are no longer that far behind, with unemployment rates at 8.3 percent for Major Urban counties, 7.6 percent in Suburban

counties, and rates from 7.7 to 8.0 percent in other counties.

Income provides economic resources that shape choices about housing, education, childcare, food, medical care, and more. Wealth—the accumulation of savings and assets—helps protect us in times of economic distress. As income and wealth increase or decrease, so does health; it allows medical care and options for healthy lifestyles. The poor are most likely to live in unsafe homes and neighborhoods, and to have limited access to healthy foods and good employment and schools.

While the starkest difference in health is between those with the highest and lowest incomes, this relationship persists throughout all income brackets. Adults in the highest income brackets are healthier than those in the middle class and will live, on average, more than six years longer than those with the lowest incomes. The ongoing stress and challenges associated with poverty can lead to cumulative health damage, both physical and mental. Chronic illness is more likely to affect those with the lowest incomes, and children in low-income families are sicker than their high-income counterparts.[20]

Although rates of poverty are increasing in the suburbs, Suburban counties still fare best in terms of having the smallest proportion of children living in poverty. Current estimates suggest that 17 percent of children in Suburban counties live in poverty, compared to 27 percent in Non-Core and 26 percent in Major Urban counties. We report specifically on children in poverty in the Rankings primarily because of bipartisan concerns around the needs of children. But data on income show a similar, but not identical, pattern. Suburban counties have the highest levels of median household income followed by Major Urban counties with lower household income levels in Medium and Small Metro counties and the

16 "Educational Attainment in the United States: 2013—Detailed Tables," US Department of Commerce, US Census Bureau, accessed January 18, 2015, http://www.census.gov/hhes/socdemo/education/data/cps/2013/tables.html.

17 "Exploring the Social Determinants of Health Issue Brief No. 5: Education and Health," Robert Wood Johnson Foundation, accessed January 18, 2015, http://www.rwjf.org/content/dam/farm/reports/issue_briefs/2011/rwjf70447.

18 "Education: It Matters More to Health Than Ever Before," Virginia Commonwealth University Center on Society and Health, January 2014, accessed January 18, 2015, http://www.rwjf.org/en/library/research/2014/01/education--it-matters-more-to-health-than-ever-before.html.

19 "Exploring the Social Determinants of Health Issue Brief No. 9: Work, Workplaces and Health," Robert Wood Johnson Foundation, May 2011, accessed January 18, 2015, http://www.rwjf.org/en/library/research/2011/05/work-and-health-.html.

20 "Exploring the Social Determinants of Health Issue Brief No. 4: How Social Factors Shape Health: Income, Wealth and Health," Robert Wood Johnson Foundation, April 2011, accessed January 18, 2015, http://www.rwjf.org/en/library/research/2011/04/how-social-factors-shape-health1.html.

lowest levels in Micropolitan and Non-Core counties.

People who have greater social support—including those who are less isolated and experience greater interpersonal trust—live longer and healthier lives than those who do not. Socially isolated individuals have an increased risk for poor health outcomes. Individuals who lack adequate social support are particularly vulnerable to the effects of stress, which has been linked to cardiovascular disease, overeating and smoking in adults, and obesity in children and adolescents.[21] Adults and children in single-parent households, often at-risk for social isolation, have an increased risk for illness, mental health problems, and mortality, and are more likely to engage in unhealthy behaviors than their counterparts.[22] Contrary to popular belief that labels the suburbs as socially isolating, Suburban counties fare better than all other types of counties for adults reporting insufficient emotional and social support, and for children living in households headed by a single parent. Major Urban counties have the highest reports of inadequate support, and the highest percent of children in single-parent households.

Community safety is among the social and economic factors we include in the Rankings. Injuries are the third-leading cause of death in the United States, and the leading cause for those between the ages of one and forty-four. Accidents and violence affect health and quality of life in the short and long term, for those directly and indirectly affected. Community safety reflects not only violent acts in neighborhoods and homes but also injuries caused unintentionally through accidents. Many injuries are predictable and preventable, yet about 50 million Americans receive medical treatment for injuries each year, and more than 180,000 die from these injuries.[23]

Rates of violent crime are highest in Major Urban counties and lowest in Non-Core rural communities, whereas the reverse is true for injuries. Suburban counties fare relatively well with violence rates and injury death rates. Suburban violence rates are closer to rural rates than to urban ones. For injury deaths, Suburban counties have rates very close to those of Major Urban areas and significantly lower than those of more rural counties. About 30 percent of injury deaths are considered intentional, that is, due to homicide or suicide, while 70 percent are unintentional deaths or accidents. Poisonings, motor vehicle accidents, and falls are the leading causes of unintentional death.

Suburbia's Physical Environment

Our final category of factors that influence health is the physical environment, including characteristics such as air and water quality, housing, and transit. Clean air and safe water are prerequisites for health; their absence is particularly detrimental to vulnerable populations such as the very young, the elderly, and those with chronic health conditions. Air quality data do not vary that much across the different types of counties, most likely due to location of air quality monitors, although Suburban counties do have the highest levels of fine particulate matter. In water quality, Non-Core counties fare worst, and Major Urban areas do best.

The choices we make about housing and transportation, and the opportunities underlying these choices, also affect our health. Housing protects residents from extreme weather and provides safe environments for people to live and form social bonds. But houses and apartments can also be unhealthy or unsafe: issues of concern include presence of lead-based paint, improper insulation, unsanitary conditions, and indoor allergens such as mold or dust. Housing is also a substantial expense, and people with lower incomes are more likely to live in unhealthy, overcrowded, or unsafe

21 "Exploring the Social Determinants of Health Issue Brief No. 3: Stress and Health," Robert Wood Johnson Foundation, accessed January 18, 2015, http://www.rwjf.org/content/dam/farm/reports/issue_briefs/2011/rwjf70441.

22 David M. Fergusson, Joseph M. Boden, and L. John Horwood, "Exposure to Single Parenthood in Childhood and Later Mental Health, Educational, Economic, and Criminal Behavior Outcomes," *Archives of General Psychiatry* 64, no. 9 (2007): 1089–95.

23 *The Facts Hurt: A State-by-State Injury Prevention Policy Report*, Robert Wood Johnson Foundation, January 2013, accessed January 18, 2015, http://www.rwjf.org/content/dam/farm/reports/reports/2013/rwjf72972.

housing. Suburban counties fare relatively well in terms of severe housing problems (high costs, overcrowding, lack of kitchen, or plumbing facilities), whereas Major Urban areas fare worst. Suburban areas do not fare as well for transit—81 percent of workers drive alone to work, and 44 percent of these workers commute for more than thirty minutes. The Rankings data show some correlation between driving alone to work and obesity levels, but other research has shown that each additional hour spent in a car per day is associated with a 6 percent increase in the likelihood of obesity.[24]

Suburbia's Final Scores

While the Rankings model is extensive, our results do not take into account all possible measures of health in a county, nor can it be assumed that the results are true for every urban, suburban, or rural county, given the use of averages. In addition, our findings demonstrate only associations between health and place, not causality. Another limitation relates to small population sizes in rural counties— rural county estimates based on these small values are less reliable. To address the issue, we did remove from the analysis the smallest of the small counties, and many of the measures are based on multiple years of data.

Notwithstanding these concerns, overall the findings are still useful and extend earlier work. Residents of suburban communities surrounding urban centers tend to have better health than those in the most rural areas and those in large urban centers. Suburban Metro counties fare the best for ten of twenty-nine factors that influence health, including rates of residents' chlamydia and teen births, health insurance coverage, diabetic monitoring, high school completion, children in poverty, unemployment, social support, and children living in single-parent households.

Planners, policy makers, and designers should acknowledge the ways that suburbs are healthier and work to reinforce these factors while helping to mitigate the bad ones. For example, since income is a major contributor to health, increasing rates of poverty in the suburbs may lead to worsening health, or at a minimum, less improvement in health in the suburbs. Yet the benefit of the Rankings is that they provide a hook to draw attention to the different factors at play so policy makers and other community leaders can be better informed about what to look at when they make decisions. In addition, the entire Rankings data set is available to other researchers interested in further study of the health of counties.

This research was supported by the County Health Rankings and Roadmaps Program, a joint program of the Robert Wood Johnson Foundation and the University of Wisconsin Population Health Institute (UWPHI). The author wishes to thank current and former County Health Rankings and Roadmaps staff at UWPHI for their assistance with the research.

24 "Health Policy Snapshot: Public Health and Prevention Issue Brief— How Does Transportation Impact Health?," Robert Wood Johnson Foundation, October 2012, accessed January 18, 2015, http://www .rwjf.org/content /dam/farm/reports /issue_briefs/2012 /rwjf402311.

Dainfern, Midrand, Gauteng, South Africa

Cyber City, Gurgaon, Haryana, India

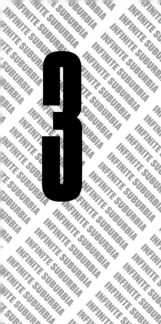

METROPOLITAN ECONOMIC INTER-RELATIONSHIPS

3.1
TRADING PLACES AMONG CITIES AND SUBURBS

William T. Bogart

LOCAL GOVERNANCE

SUBURB-CITY INTER-DEPENDENCIES

I use the phrase *trading places* to describe the metropolitan economy. It has layers of meaning: the locations where we trade, the switch in the roles of those places, and the act of trading are all suggested. The tools of international trade can help us understand the ways that different parts of the metropolitan area specialize and trade with each other. These interactions are vital for seeing how metropolitan structure evolves over time. If we neglect the economic nature of suburbs, we'll ultimately mischaracterize the evolution of metropolitan structure as a fall from the ideal monocentric model. Instead, we should recognize the monocentric city as a special case of decentralization and specialization.

The expression "trading places" is more evocative of the structure of urban areas than the usual terminology of central city and suburb for (at least) three reasons. First, municipalities, employment centers, neighborhoods, and the other components of metropolitan areas are small, open economies. Second, in the monocentric metropolitan structure of the early twentieth century, the central city was dominant, and the rest of the metropolitan area was a satellite. Now they have traded places in the economic hierarchy. Third, the phrase is dynamic rather than static, reflecting the reality that people and goods move daily throughout the metropolitan area and the existing structure continues to evolve.

If you are like most twenty-first-century Americans, you live in a metropolitan area. By definition, then, you live in or near a relatively large city. But to understand your location, it is not sufficient to look only at the city, even if that's where you live. Conversely, one cannot ignore the city and only study suburbs. What really matters are the relations among the commercial districts of the city and suburban employment centers, the manufacturing areas typically found along the

metropolitan fringes, and the large and small residential neighborhoods. This set of relationships is not stable; instead, it continues to evolve as businesses open and close, houses are bought and sold, and land is converted from one use to another.

Trading places include the central business district (CBD) of the monocentric city and the employment centers ("edge cities" and so on) that have become familiar in recent decades. But another example of a trading place is the bedroom suburb of a monocentric city: it locally produces and consumes housing and local government services. It exports labor services and imports everything else. Trading places also include the various diffused employment opportunities that make up the majority of jobs in the metropolitan area of the twenty-first century.

Gains from Trade

The lens of trade is useful for understanding the unfamiliar economic role of suburbs in metropolitan structure. One effect of trade is to reduce differences between places, especially the opportunities for consumption. In 1977 a popular movie, *Smoky and the Bandit*, was premised on the idea that someone in Georgia could drink Coors beer only if it had been smuggled in from Texas. Today, that notion is difficult to explain.

On the other hand, another effect of trade is to increase differences, especially in production, as areas specialize in producing those goods and services in which they have a comparative advantage. It is well known that metropolitan areas differ in their pattern of production; for example, no one would mistake the economy of Las Vegas for that of Baltimore. It is less well known but equally true that there is specialization among the parts of each metropolitan area.[1] It is possible to investigate whether a metropolitan area is unstructured sprawl or a recognizable pattern of activity. The data strongly

1   William T. Bogart, *Don't Call It Sprawl: Metropolitan Structure in the Twenty-First Century* (New York: Cambridge University Press, 2006), 71–74.

support the latter interpretation, with the best simple description of a modern metropolitan area being one composed of multiple centers of economic activity, each of which is surrounded by a region like a small monocentric city.[2]

The defining characteristic of metropolitan areas is population density. With that density comes congestion. Once we understand a metropolitan area as a trading zone, we clearly see that congestion, for example, is a tax on trade. Suppose that in the absence of congestion one can travel from home to office in twenty-three minutes. During rush hour, when the roads are full of other people, the trip might instead require thirty-two minutes. That is nine minutes added to the price of transporting labor to the office. This extra time must be compensated for somehow, whether in the form of higher wages to the worker, which in turn lead to higher prices for the consumer or lower profits to the shareholder, or, more simply, in the form of lower net benefits of holding the job. If an added nine minutes must be spent on the commute instead of leisure, and pay does not increase commensurately, then the wage has decreased, just as it would if a tax had been imposed.

Thinking of congestion as an additional cost to trade helps to better understand the alternative ways to address it. One way to reduce congestion is to help trade occur in different ways, such as walking instead of driving. Julius Caesar, in his Law on Municipalities, promulgated in 44 BCE, advocated reducing Rome's congestion by making it illegal to "drive a wagon along the streets of Rome or along those streets in the suburbs where there is continuous housing after sunrise or before the tenth hour of the day."[3] A modern Caesar might forbid trucks in the CBD during rush hour. Alternatively, manufacturers have moved themselves out of the CBD to avoid traffic congestion, which can be especially costly in terms of idle time for plants using a just-in-time inventory system.

There is a variety of other approaches. One is to reduce congestion by increasing road capacity, allowing a greater volume of trade to occur. Another is to reduce congestion when the benefit does not exceed the cost it imposes on others; this is the approach of congestion tolls. In every case, though, the emphasis is not on reducing congestion for its own sake but on maximizing the net benefits from trade. In particular, having some congestion might be efficient, just as it can be efficient for other forms of taxation to exist.

Homogeneity versus Heterogeneity
Trade, as already emphasized, both increases heterogeneity by increased specialization in production (Las Vegas versus Baltimore) and increases homogeneity by allowing consumption of products where they are not produced (Coors beer). To understand the impact of trade, one must keep in mind the simple but powerful truth that people differ from each other in many ways.

Economists define a person who is at the margin as someone who is on the boundary of undertaking an action or not. When circumstances change, the people on the margin take action; they are the crucial people for understanding the impact of any new policy. If a person is on the border between driving a car and riding the bus, then a congestion toll might lead him or her to ride, while a firmly committed person's modal choice would be unaffected. Regardless of the situation, this heterogeneity among individuals is important to remember. Not every person will be affected by changes in the same way, and not every person will react in the same way. The distribution of preferences among people implies that almost no one gets exactly what they want.

Heterogeneous individuals who voluntarily sort themselves into

2 Ibid., 80–88.
3 Julius Caesar, "Law of Caesar on Municipalities, 44 B.C.," The Avalon Project: Documents in Law, History and Diplomacy, Lillian Goldman Law Library, Yale Law School, accessed June 27, 2015, http://avalon.law.yale .edu/ancient/law_of _caesar.asp.

homogeneous communities constitute the essence of the Tiebout model, the workhorse starting point for most formal analysis of suburbs. While Charles Tiebout's original insight concerned only different tastes for local government taxes and services, the same force has played out in multiple dimensions. For example, the move to segregate by age, although prompted in part by different demands for public services (i.e., example, emergency medical assistance versus public schools), is not simply a matter of public finance.

Although the vestiges of legal segregation by race continue to fade, we nevertheless find voluntary ongoing segregation. On the one hand, segregation is antithetical to a dream of an integrated society. On the other hand, the opportunity to associate with a similar group creates a rich diversity for all to enjoy. This mixed legacy can be seen in many ways, but one familiar setting is in New York City. Several of its identifiable and popular areas, such as Chinatown, Little Italy, and Harlem, originally arose at least in part from involuntary segregation.

Voluntary segregation dates back to the founding of the American colonies. Religious dissenters from England founded a colony in Massachusetts. Dissenters from the orthodox beliefs in Massachusetts went to Connecticut and Rhode Island, while Quakers and Catholics started Pennsylvania and Maryland, respectively. Valuing diversity requires respecting differences, including the choice to live separately.

A college dormitory represents an extremely homogeneous population, typically consisting of people in a narrow age range who share many other similarities. The dormitory is typically gated or otherwise isolated from the surrounding neighborhood, whether for security reasons or to create a campus ambience.

Colleges are an export activity for towns, so decisions about how to house students are important for the local economy. There doesn't seem to be one single correct answer. If the dormitories are too isolated, the college is accused of being an ivory-tower institution not interested in the health of the town. If the dormitories are too integrated into the community, then negative externalities ranging from congestion to noise to litter dominate the conversation. These extremes are not unlike much of the discussion regarding gated communities or, more broadly, suburbs.

Zoning is often blamed for both cultural sterility and excessive driving because it separates commercial and residential land uses. While these criticisms have some validity, optimistic hopes regarding the impact of promoting a jobs-housing balance must be tempered. First, simple numerical balance does not solve the assignment problem of people to houses and jobs. Planned suburbs built in Sweden during the 1950s, designed to have one-half of the residents working locally, nevertheless experienced considerable cross commuting.[4] The United States in the twenty-first century is unlikely to be more amenable to this type of planning than Sweden of the mid-twentieth century. Second, the expectation that changing land use to require mixed commercial and residential areas will usher in a golden age free from cars is not supported by the experience of the past century. Indeed, Houston, which allows mixed uses to a greater extent than many other metropolitan areas, is not held up as a paragon by planners. And cars are not necessary to create homogeneous and differentiated residential settings, as studies of the "streetcar suburbs" of the late 1800s illustrate.

The market for loans is an important source of pressure toward homogeneity. To reduce the risk of a geographically

4   Peter Hall, *Cities in Civilization: Culture, Innovation, and Urban Order* (London: Weidenfeld and Nicolson, 1998), 867.

concentrated loan portfolio, it makes sense (and benefits homeowners) for lenders to resell their loans in a national market. However, this requires the ability to compare loans from many places quickly and easily. A common set of conditions on the loans facilitates those comparisons. The cost advantage of so-called conforming loans reduces the incentive of developers to experiment with financing structures that do not already enjoy the advantage of a national market suffused with liquidity. The widespread belief that nontraditional housing finance was a primary cause of the Great Recession of 2008 reinforces the advantage of familiar financial instruments.

The scale of activity in the twenty-first-century metropolitan area creates a challenge to those who will understand and shape it. In the spatial dimension, this challenge is sometimes met with brute force. Pennsylvania, for example, mandates that every municipality must make provision within its boundaries for every industrial, commercial, and institutional land use that is not "inherently objectionable."[5] While the impulse to reduce exclusion is no doubt well intended, it is not clear that the municipal level is the right area at which to take this approach, given the fragmented nature of Pennsylvania. This limitation has been recognized, and multimunicipal or regional planning is permitted but not required.[6] The urban-growth boundaries found in Oregon and elsewhere also represent a blunt instrument for creating categories to bring perceived order to the landscape.

A better way to address the issue of scale is to look at another dimension in addition to space. Too much attention is paid to land use and land-use regulation at a single point in time. In practice, even zoning can be changed as municipalities and metropolitan areas evolve, so there's no good reason to focus discussion on a static picture.[7]

Again, it's useful to think in terms of "trading places" and the elastic vision of a metropolitan area that it affords. A longer time horizon that explicitly allows for flexibility in development is more likely to lead to a good outcome. The use of transferable development rights illustrates how flexibility in specific cases can be linked successfully to an overall set of constraints, and how beneficial economic interactions can be maximized. Even in Houston, which is famous for its lack of zoning, developers must follow a set of city ordinances that are specifically aimed at preventing negative externalities.

The Evolution of Metropolitan Structure

Before Copernicus, the dominant view of the solar system was that the sun and the other planets orbited the earth. Increasingly ingenious explanations were proposed to justify this theoretical construct in the face of empirical observations. Finally, Copernicus demonstrated that there was a more sensible way of understanding the world.

A fundamental misunderstanding of how metropolitan areas work has hampered the current debate on the causes and consequences of urban sprawl. This misunderstanding is analogous to the pre-Copernican fallacy that the earth was the center of the universe. In the discussion of urban sprawl, the downtown or central city takes the place of the earth in the Ptolemaic cosmology, and the rest of the metropolitan area is defined only in relation to the downtown.

It is possible for the basic structure of a metropolitan area to change over time. Such a change has been occurring in US metropolitan areas for the last one hundred years, and the change came to fruition at the beginning of the new century. To plan for future urban growth, it is vital to recast our understanding of how urban areas operate. It is time for a Copernican revolution that puts the

5   Pennsylvania Local Government Commission, "Pennsylvania Legislators Municipal Deskbook," accessed June 27, 2015, http://www.lgc.state.pa.us/deskbook14/Land-Use-04-Exclusionary-Zoning.pdf.

6   Ibid.

7   Bogart, *Don't Call It Sprawl*, 58.

downtown and the central city in their appropriate place: not unique and solitary but rather one important part of a system.

Metropolitan structure over the last two hundred years has changed in ways that can be summarized in two words: *decentralization* and *specialization*. The urban historian Kenneth Jackson calls the period from 1815 to 1875 "the most fundamental realignment of urban structure in the 4,500 year past of cities on this planet."[8] The patterns observed in the second half of the twentieth century are continuations of ongoing trends, not dramatic breaks with the past. Even the stereotypical automobile city, Los Angeles, had achieved a familiar metropolitan form well before the advent of the freeway.[9]

The monocentric city of the late 1800s and early 1900s exemplified decentralization and specialization. Unlike in previous urban structures, residences were separated from businesses by the newly acquired ability of workers to live a streetcar ride away from the CBD. Thus, the boundaries of the city expanded, and the parts of the city became specialized. The downtown or CBD was the place where industrial, commercial, and retail activity occurred, while the residential areas were almost exclusively devoted to housing.

Mass transit was not invented until the 1800s. The first omnibus was instituted in Nantes to bring people to a hot bath warmed by mill-produced excess steam power. This initial role as an adjunct to private enterprise continued throughout the period during which mass transit flourished.

Real-estate developments in the early twentieth century were often initiated by a person who controlled a streetcar line. The houses, by increasing the traffic on the line, increased the line's value, while the direct access to the workplace provided by the streetcar made the houses more valuable. Even the famous Red Car trains of Los Angeles were not profitable in their own right but were supported by the land development operations of their owners.

By helping people move beyond walking distance of commercial and industrial activity, the streetcar was a tool of specialization. It was a tool of decentralization that moved people from downtown, "hyperdense" housing to the more spread-out suburbs. The communities built by such luminaries as J. C. Nichols in Kansas City and the Van Sweringens in Shaker Heights, Ohio, were the urban sprawl of their day, greatly expanding the scale of the city while instituting new policies, such as deed restrictions, that are still controversial today.

Explosive urban growth is not unique to the period after World War II. The Industrial Revolution enabled cities to grow beyond previous limits by providing rapid transportation and abundant food. New locations could change from wilderness to metropolis if the transport network and their industrial mix permitted.

The confluence of factors that made the monocentric city the template for US cities was powerful but short-lived. The heyday of the monocentric city was about 1890 to 1930, spanning the period between the widespread adoption of streetcars and the widespread use of trucks and cars. The distribution of economic activity in the monocentric city was extreme by modern standards. For example, in 1910 the one-half-square-mile Loop in downtown Chicago accounted for almost 40 percent of the assessed land value in the entire 211-square-mile (546-square-kilometer) city.[10] Perhaps the climax of the monocentric city was the competition between the Chrysler Building and the Empire State Building in the late 1920s to be the tallest skyscraper. Unfortunately, the incipient changes in urban structure, combined with the onset of the Great Depression, left the Empire State Building less than fully occupied, which changed its symbolism, at the time, from triumph to futility.

8 Kenneth Jackson, *Crabgrass Frontier: The Suburbanization of the United States* (New York: Oxford University Press, 1985), 20.
9 Ibid., 250.
10 Ibid., 114.

The widespread adoption of the truck in the 1920s allowed businesses to move away from the railheads and docks of the CBD. Firms that could do so fled the city, beginning with manufacturing businesses, which desired the lower land prices and the fewer neighbors afforded by a more rural setting. Automobiles allowed residential decentralization throughout the metropolitan area, continuing the trend that had begun along streetcar lines in the late 1800s. Because developments were no longer tied to streetcar lines, one impact of automobiles was to increase the density of development in areas not served by transit.

Urban structure has adapted to this new mobility by increasing spatial reach while keeping transport times roughly constant at levels found since the first cities were built. I wouldn't call it sprawl. A better approach would be to appreciate the advantages and work to reduce the disadvantages in this kind of trading place.

Implications for Policy

As children, we were told that "sticks and stones may break your bones but names will never hurt you." The world in which we live is often described as sprawl, a loosely defined or indefinable set of problems to be solved. This automatically creates pressure on public policy for a solution, in this case by changing the form of the city. If the world in which we live were to be defined instead as a city-state composed of trading places, then there would be different implications for policy. So, as adults, we find that sticks and stones may break our bones but names can lead to bad public policy.

Economists view people as active participants in decisions about work, housing, and public services. Planners tend to view people as passive inhabitants of an area, using whatever residential, commercial, and recreational possibilities are provided. This contrast is the underlying

reason that the professions tend to have different attitudes toward suburban development—benign neglect tinged with concern about externalities by economists, concern leading to wholesale design pronouncements by planners. The contrast between people as active participants and as passive inhabitants is fundamental to the creation of effective policy.

One important but often neglected component for effective policy design is humility. Cutting-edge regional planning in 1941 advocated for culs-de-sac and large private housing developments, admonishing that "nothing should be constructed unless it fits into the Plan."[11] The current state of the art in planning would agree that all construction and renovation should conform to the plan, although the specific admonitions have changed considerably. New construction will last for decades, and no one knows what the impact of ongoing technological progress and social change will be on the most desired allocation of land use. A greater emphasis on flexibility in land use can lead to better outcomes. The classic example is the research by Richard Peiser on the way that less restrictive zoning could lead to greater ending densities than more restrictive zoning due to infill development.[12]

Public policy is especially difficult in urban settings because of the weight of past decisions in shaping both the built environment and the culture. The built environment of the past continues to exist into the present, making current urban areas into anachronisms. The past plays an even stronger role, though, in the legal environment and culture of a region. Because the past is different for each state, and often for each metropolitan area, it is naive to expect a common template to be appropriate for planning their different futures.

One of the interesting features of most utopian urban plans is how divorced

11 Bogart, *Don't Call It Sprawl*, 24–25.
12 Richard Peiser, "Density and Urban Sprawl," *Land Economics* 65, no. 3 (August 1989): 193.

from space and time they are. They will typically depict a stylized city, one that seems to have no history and no constraints, rather than engaging with the more difficult reality that there is not a tabula rasa from which to begin but rather an evolutionary opportunity. The Platonic ideal of urban plans remains the garden city of Ebenezer Howard as reinterpreted by successive generations. Phoenix, Arizona, for example, explicitly patterned its future growth after the concept of self-sufficient urban villages.[13] This focus on self-sufficiency is the antithesis of the "trading-place" nature of metropolitan areas. Plans that fail to recognize the basic economic nature of their surroundings are unlikely to accomplish their goals.

Even planners who seem at first glance to be responsive to the idea that metropolitan areas evolve can advocate policies that don't necessarily help. Metropolitan revenue sharing is one suggested way to improve intrametropolitan equity. But even if it solves today's challenge, it is only a long-term solution if whatever problems arise in the future can be solved by that same policy. More broadly, metropolitan-area government is proposed. However, that flies in the face of the long-standing reluctance of suburban residents to take responsibility for the central city as well as the long-standing reluctance of central-city residents to trust in the goodwill of the suburban residents that would outnumber them in most places. Further, as of 2004, there were thirty-nine metropolitan areas that crossed state boundaries, with eight that included parts of three states and two (Philadelphia and Washington, DC) that included parts of four states. I am unaware of even the most adamant advocate of metropolitan government suggesting that state boundaries can be erased, so this approach is not compelling.[14]

If we were building cities from scratch today, we might not build them to be the same as those that currently exist. But given that costs prevent removing and replacing entire cities at once, we instead gradually modify what was there before. We must not mistake gradual change for stasis, however. The slow accumulation of changes over time can have quite dramatic effects, as anyone can attest after attending a high school reunion. Public policy that interferes with adaptive reuse of existing infrastructure is counterproductive.

Rapid metropolitan growth is not a new phenomenon. In the nineteenth century, the impact of the Industrial Revolution was reflected in speedy transition from rural to urban land use: "The visitor to Birmingham could expect to find a street of houses in the autumn where he saw his horse at grass in the spring."[15]

The long-run nature of real estate investments, combined with the rapidity of change, underscores the importance of flexibility. If a building, road system, or other infrastructure is too rigid, then it runs the risk of locking in mistakes for a long time. Granted, it would be ideal to lock in an ideal pattern, and allowing flexibility can undermine this happy occurrence. But even an ideal pattern at one time might not be ideal in the future. The "trading-place" structure of metropolitan areas will continue, even as the goods and services traded change and the patterns of specialization change. Balancing the need to plan the future with the need to maintain flexibility will continue to be the policy challenge in metropolitan areas.

This essay is adapted from William T. Bogart, Don't Call It Sprawl: Metropolitan Structure in the Twenty-First Century *(New York: Cambridge University Press, 2006). Reprinted with permission.*

13 City of Phoenix Planning Department, "Phoenix Urban Village Model: General Plan for Phoenix 1985–2000," accessed July 5, 2015, https://www.phoenix.gov/pddsite/Documents/pdd_pz_pdf_00330.pdf.
14 Bogart, *Don't Call It Sprawl*, 27–28.
15 Asa Briggs, *Victorian Cities* (New York: Harper and Row, 1965), 23.

3.2 SUBURBS IN THE METROPOLITAN ECONOMY

Nicholas A. Phelps

ECONOMIC
DIVERSITY

INNOVATION

SUBURB-CITY
INTER-
DEPENDENCIES

What the economist Edward Glaeser terms the "triumph of the city" is actually an economic triumph in which various settlements across metropolitan and even megapolitan regions participate.[1] It is the result of long-standing processes of suburbanization. What if we were to look at the triumph of the city from the outside in—if we were to read it from the perspective of a variety of suburban economies that surround historic city cores? Some argue that the city has been turned inside out and that terms such as city and suburb are now redundant or "zombie" categories.[2] But it may be more accurate to say that there is now a regional variety of specialized economic trading places, the majority of which are suburban.[3]

While there is an undoubted unity to the metropolitan urbanization process, there is also great variety in the economic dynamics of different settlement types in the metropolitan region.[4] The switching of capital in and out of various parts of the metropolis over time can render distinctions between different settlement types—such as cities, or inner and outer suburbs—arbitrary. Yet distinguishing between types of settlements, with their unique economic dynamics, can be an important first cut in the analysis not only of the suburban economy but also of the unity of the metropolitan urbanization process.

We can begin this account of suburbs in the metropolitan economy by defining a suburb. The scholars Richard Harris and Peter Larkham, drawing from a review of the literature, offer a composite definition of a suburb as a settlement with these characteristics:

1. in a peripheral location relative to a dominant urban center;
2. partly or wholly residential in character;
3. low density of development;
4. distinctive culture or way of life; and
5. having a separate community identity, often embodied in a local government.[5]

Clearly, with the outward physical expansion of metropolitan regions, item (1) alone admits to an ever-increasing variety of suburbs, to which the labels "inner" and "outer" suburbs and exurbs may not do full justice. The variety of the suburban landscape—including the economic composition of suburbs—is also a result of the fact that items (2) to (5) are subject to change over time. Notably, the historical employment contribution of (mostly industrial) inner suburbs has been obscured by the annexation of suburbs by established cities. Affluent, purely residential inner and outer suburbs have incorporated as separate communities, often motivated by a desire to exclude all but a narrow socioeconomic segment of the population. In other instances, as a sense of community and way of life has developed over time, the end product has been broadly inclusionary. The residential-employment balance and building density of suburbs of different vintages, and even individual suburbs, continue to change in ways that make it important to find labels that adequately capture the complexion of different suburbs, including their economies. After all, the potential for planning interventions to further effect change in the suburban economy reflects this suburban diversity in terms of their vintage and their scale and scope, for example.

Such diversity makes clear the value—at least as a first cut in analysis—of identifying a number of suburban economic scenarios. The scenarios were developed with differential land-development pressures and state involvement in mind and not the diversity of economic activities taken as a whole. (fig. **3.2.1**) They do not exhaust the possibilities of the variety in the suburban (and, indeed,

1 Edward Glaeser, *The Triumph of the City: How Our Greatest Invention Makes US Richer, Smarter, Greener, Healthier, and Happier* (New York: Penguin, 2011).

2 See Edward Soja, *Postmetropolis: Critical Studies of Cities and Regions* (Oxford: Blackwell, 2000); and Robert Lang and Paul K. Knox, "The New Metropolis: Rethinking Megalopolis," *Regional Studies* 43 (2009): 789–802.

3 William T. Bogart, *Don't Call It Sprawl: Metropolitan Structure in the Twenty-First Century* (Cambridge: Cambridge University Press, 2006).

4 Nicholas A. Phelps, *Sequel to Suburbia: Glimpses of America's Post-Suburban Future* (Cambridge, MA: MIT Press, 2015).

5 Richard Harris and Peter J. Larkham, "Suburban Foundation, Form, and Function," in *Changing Suburbs: Foundation, Form and Function*, ed. Richard Harris and Peter J. Larkham (London: E. & F. N. Spon, 1999), 1–31.

urban) economy that follows. But they provide a starting point for discussion.

I start with stories of the economic dynamism apparent at the outer suburban or exurban reaches of the metropolitan economy and move progressively inward toward the sometimes-less-robust economies of inner suburbs and historic city cores.

New Suburbs: Exurbia

The land-development imperative at the urban fringe is strong. This fringe can be extensive and typically occurs over primarily agricultural land. It is settled at very low density in the absence of historic settlements or new residential tracts of any size. In these locations, land is cheap, but sites have nonetheless often been highly accessible to the metropolitan region as a result of major road building since the 1950s. Population-growth rates in these outermost US suburbs or exurbs have typically been high. However, the economy has been strong, too. For example, in the case of Richmond, Virginia, the planning professors William Lucy and David Phillips note how most of the employment growth in the Richmond metropolitan area from 1970 to 1990 had been in the surrounding suburbs, and that 1990 out-commuting rates from Richmond were four times those in 1960.[6]

Today, rates of new firm formation and survival appear especially strong (though often from a low initial-base level) in the newest, outermost suburbs and exurbs. The "counterurbanization" represented by these suburbs and exurbs has been a selective one, mostly involving those social classes and occupations most likely to spawn new businesses. The professor of planning Henry Renski's study indicated how American suburban areas performed especially well with regard to new firm formation, growth, and longevity, including in relation to urban cores thought traditionally to be incubators of

MODERN CITY	
i.	City→suburb
LATE MODERN CITY REGION	
ii.	City→suburb→postsuburb
CITY REGION OF SECOND MODERNITY	
iii.	Postsuburb→city
iv.	Growing suburb→postsuburb→city
v.	Stable affluent suburb→stable affluent suburb
vi.	Declining suburb→sub-suburb?
vii.	Declining city→suburb

3.2.1 Urban development processes and past and possible future relationships among settlement types

new firms.[7] Renski found that the suburban share of new entrant firms in high-technology advanced services was 24 percent higher than expected, based on the suburban population.

In many metropolitan areas, as much as two-thirds of all office space is now concentrated in what the urban-policy expert Robert Lang describes as "edgeless cities," which includes sprawl from inner suburbs all the way out to the exurbs.[8] Lang is referring to the very scattered manufacturing, office, and retail spaces along the extensive new economic corridors of county parkways, interstate highways, tollways, and beltways, with the most accessible junctions producing what has been termed the "exit-ramp economy."

Boston's Route 128 might be one high-technology example of edgeless-city-style suburbanization of employment, although perhaps an atypical one. Between 1954 and 1967, 80 percent of Greater Boston's new industrial space was built in the periphery.[9] As the planner James O'Connell describes, Route 128

> created a geographical corridor that demarcated the boundary between the metropolitan Boston of the early twentieth century and the suburbia that developed after World War II.... Towns liked locating industrial and office uses along the highway because it maximized

6 William H. Lucy and David L. Phillips, "The Post-Suburban Era Comes to Richmond Virginia: City Decline, Suburban Transition, and Exurban Growth," *Landscape and Urban Planning* 36 (1997): 259–75.

7 Henry Renski, "New Firm Entry, Survival, and Growth in the United States: A Comparison of Urban, Suburban, and Rural Areas," *Journal of the American Planning Association* 75 (2008): 60–77.

8 Robert E. Lang, *Edgeless Cities: Exploring the Elusive Metropolis* (Washington, DC: Brookings Institution Press, 2003).

9 James C. O'Connell, *The Hub's Metropolis: Greater Boston's Development from Railroad Suburbs to Smart Growth* (Cambridge, MA: MIT Press, 2013), 152.

tax revenues and employment while not disrupting town centers.[10]

The term *boomburb* has subsequently been used to capture some of the same edgeless-city tendencies found in the many large (100,000 residents or more), fast-growing communities across the United States. The boomburb of Irvine in California contains around 30 million square feet (3 million square meters) of office space and is reported to have a jobs-to-resident population ratio of 1:2. It may be exceptional, but other such boomburbs are also nevertheless notable for their high ratios of employment to residents, even if this balance is struck at the subregional scale.[11]

Postsuburbs

Postsuburbs are settlements that, in most instances, began as purely residential tracts with provision of some of the associated services—such as schools, police, fire services, hospitals, and recreational amenities—often lagging behind. However, regardless of incorporation, they have since evolved into communities with far more jobs than existed at their founding. Postsuburb is the label that the historian Jon Teaford has given to what the scholar Joel Garreau earlier dubbed "edge cities."[12] For Teaford, these postsuburbs actually began to take shape as early as the 1950s, as the fiscal implications of new purely residential development became apparent to both newly incorporated communities and to existing, ostensibly rural county governments. The economic realities—the need for residents of suburbs to pay their own way—almost immediately rubbed up against the ideology of suburbia as a bourgeois retreat from the city and big government. Residential-only suburbs soon encountered a mounting property-tax bill to pay for basic services such as fire, police, and schooling, let alone amenities that might be desired. These

economic realities prompted county and suburban governments to recruit tax-generating manufacturing, office, and retail developments to help pay the costs of the local services demanded by new and rapidly expanding residential populations.

In the case of Fairfax County, outside Washington, DC, the "bargain" struck between residents and county government was explicit and has produced the edge city Tysons Corner as the price to be paid for low residential-property taxes. As an employment center, Tysons Corner is larger than many historic downtowns, but suburban in location and morphology. It contains two regional shopping malls and a diverse collection of office types, underlining the suggestion of the economic-development scholars Richard Bingham and Deborah Kimble that edge cities have a far more diverse economic base than is often appreciated.[13] A recent plan envisages employment doubling and residential population increasing by over five times during the next decades, as Tysons becomes a true downtown for suburban Fairfax County.[14]

Elsewhere, communities were born with a postsuburban aspiration in mind. The town of Schaumburg, outside Chicago, was incorporated with a population of just 132 as a reaction to a nearby housing-tract development in unincorporated Cook County. Shortly afterward, with further land annexations through an early plan and zoning ordinance, an enormous area of land was reserved for a regional employment center. The center was to enable Schaumburg to be the downtown for the outer northwest suburbs of Chicago. It lay largely undeveloped for another decade, until the development of the Woodfield Shopping Mall and a string of corporate campuses and speculative office developments eventually projected Schaumburg into the role foretold in the plan.

10 Ibid., 149, 152.
11 Robert E. Lang and Jennifer Le Furgy, *Boomburbs: The Rise of America's Accidental Cities* (Washington, DC: Brookings Institute, 2007).
12 Jon C. Teaford, *Post-Suburbia: Government and Politics in the Edge Cities* (Baltimore: John Hopkins University Press, 1997); Joel Garreau, *Edge City: Life on the New Frontier* (New York: Doubleday, 1991).
13 Richard D. Bingham and Deborah Kimble, "The Industrial Composition of Edge Cities and Downtowns: The New Urban Reality," *Economic Development Quarterly* 9 (1995): 259–72.
14 Nicholas A. Phelps, "The Growth Machine Stops? Urban Politics and the Making and Re-Making of an Edge City," *Urban Affairs Review* 84 (2012): 670–700.

15 International Council
of Shopping Centers,
"2013 Economic Impact
of Shopping Centers,"
New York, 2013, accessed
May 26, 2015, http://
www.icsc.org/uploads/
default/2013-Econom-
ic-Impact.pdf.

3.2.2 Urban development processes and past and possible future relationships among settlement types

The postsuburban landscape is littered with significant discrete and specialized employment sites. These regional shopping malls, airports, corporate-head-office and research-and-development campuses, and office parks are worth considering in their own right.

The Mall as an Economic Trading Place

Shopping malls have become a significant ingredient of postsuburbia, with a range of different types. The modest strip malls (averaging 13,000 square feet with a trade area of 1 mile or 1,200 square meters and 1.6 kilometer trade area) of earlier decades persist, though many are faltering with the rise of "neighborhood," "convenience," and "lifestyle" centers (each larger than a strip mall and with a larger trade area). Moreover, the large regional malls with which we are, by now, familiar (approximately half a million square feet with a trade area of 5 to 15 miles or about 465,000 square meters and 8 to 24 kilometers) have been joined by superregional malls (twice the size of regional malls with ancillary attractions and a trade area of

5 to 25 miles or 8 to 40 kilometers) and lifestyle centers.[15] The vision of the architect Victor Gruen—one of the pioneer suburban developers in the early post–World War II years—was that such malls would become downtown destinations for residential suburbs. However, malls have rarely performed such a role, languishing as part of a pattern of extreme land-use separations found in the outer suburbs.

After many years, there is some evidence to suggest that they may become suburban downtowns with dense commercial and residential development. The increased density has sometimes been made possible by extensions to mass-transit systems. In some cases, a greater mix of uses has been promoted, as in Kendall Dadeland's downtown in Miami-Dade County, Florida. (fig. **3.2.2**) The largest suburban mall in the United States by some distance is the Mall of America in Bloomington, Minneapolis, which opened in 1992. The mall operators' own figures show an area covering of 4.2 million square feet (390,000 square meters), and it has 11,000 permanent employees, although the number rises to 13,000 at peak season. Significantly, it is more than a shopping mall; it also includes nightclubs and an amusement park. Its role is set to expand further: a second phase of development will see mixed-use development (including offices) on 5.6 million square feet of space (520,000 square meters).[16]

Its wider economic development impact is likely to be significant. The Mall of America operators claim that it has more visitors than all of the state's other visitors' attractions combined; four out of ten of its current forty million annual visitors are tourists, and two billion dollars of economic impact are generated for the state.[17]

Shopping malls provide significant direct regional employment. While they attract significant nonlocal or export expenditures by shoppers from outside their suburban community, there are also some leakages, since commuting workers are likely to spend their salaries in other suburbs. The sum of their local economic impact is often rather less than the headline figures suggest, due to diversion and displacement effects. Even the most populous suburban reaches of metropolitan areas can sustain only so many malls. For those suburbs or postsuburbs that have been lucky enough to acquire one, or for those aggressive enough to have recruited one, the gains can be as significant as the impacts upon neighboring communities. For example, the presence of the Woodfield regional shopping mall in Schaumburg has been the major reason that the community has not had to levy a property tax. The Woodfield mall is something that neighboring communities are greatly envious of, and it has been the target of as-yet-unsuccessful political and policy efforts aimed at tax redistribution at the metropolitan scale.

The Airport as an Economic Trading Place

Airports are also a significant component of the suburban economy and have been touted by the academic John Kasarda and the journalist Greg Lindsay as the focal point for de facto or planned suburban "aerotropoli."[18] A measure of the sorts of potential economic impacts of airports is exemplified in the case of O'Hare Airport, which was annexed from the suburbs by the city of Chicago. O'Hare airport generated $203 million in nonairline revenues in 2010.[19] As the geographer Julie Cidell reports, with over 290,000 jobs within a 2.5-mile (4.0 kilometer) radius of the airport, O'Hare is large in comparison to suburban magnets such as regional shopping malls. It also proves to be the exception rather than the rule; in a study of twenty-five US airports, only half proved to be regionally significant employment centers of their own accord, while a quarter were unimportant.[20] While what the curator Paul Ceruzzi calls "Internet Alley" has grown to meet the Washington Dulles International Airport, this airport and its immediate vicinity still stand in comparative isolation and are not especially important compared to some of the nodes, like Tysons Corner, found along the way.[21] (fig. **3.2.3**)

Similar to retail malls, the suburban expanses of America can only sustain so many airports with genuinely significant regional economic impacts, though they appear in many other instances to form part of the economic diversity sought by those communities transitioning from suburbs to postsuburbs.

The Corporate Campus as an Economic Trading Place

As the landscape architect Louise Mozingo explains, the "pastoral capitalism" of corporate headquartersand research-and-development campuses also emerged as a distinct and important part of the

16 "Overview: Mall of America," Mall of America, accessed May 26, 2015, http://www.mallofamerica.com/about/moa/facts.

17 Ibid.

18 John D. Kasarda and Greg Lindsay, *Aerotropolis: The Way We'll Live Next* (New York: Penguin, 2011).

19 Chicago Department of Aviation, "Chicago Midway International Airport and Chicago O'Hare International Airport" (paper presented at Chicago Investors Conference, Chicago, Illinois, April 26, 2012), accessed June 1, 2015, http://www.cityofchicago.org/content/dam/city/depts/fin/supp_info/Bonds/CityofChicagoDepartmentofAviation.pdf.

20 Julie Cidell, "The Role of Major Infrastructure in Subregional Economic Development: An Empirical Study of Airports and Cities," *Journal of Economic Geography* (2014), accessed October 14, 2015, http://joeg.oxfordjournals.org/content/early/2014/07/30/jeg.lbu029.

21 Paul E. Ceruzzi, *Internet Alley: High Technology in Tysons Corner, 1945–2005* (Cambridge, MA: MIT Press, 2008).

3.2.3 Washington Dulles International Airport

22 Louise Mozingo, *Pastoral Capitalism: A History of Suburban Corporate Landscapes* (Cambridge, MA: MIT Press 2011).

23 Peter O. Muller, "The Suburban Transformation of the Globalizing American City," *Annals of the American Academy of Political and Social Science* 551 (1997): 44–57.

24 "Apple Campus 2," City of Cupertino, accessed May 26, 2015, http://www.cupertino.org/index.aspx?page=1107.

economic landscape of suburbs. It represented a spatial division of labor within giant corporations, with key management and conceptual-development activities secluded from the externalities of the city on suburban campuses.[22] As employment land uses, these campuses and parks represented an acceptable accommodation to the sensibilities of suburban residential communities. As a result, in the post–World War II era, the suburbs have acquired a national, if not international, significance as part of corporate organizations. The proportion of Fortune 500 companies that were headquartered in the suburbs increased from 11 percent in 1969 to 47 percent by 1994.[23]

The prospects of companies that developed and occupied such extensive suburban spaces have changed significantly, since many were created at the height of American industrial preeminence. An increasing number of such campuses have now become obsolete, though they represent prime sites for residential or other employment-related development, given their scale and single ownership. Even as some become obsolete, the suburban campus model nevertheless continues to have a life, illustrated by Apple's determination to house around fourteen thousand employees in a new four-story campus in Cupertino, California.[24]

Stable, Affluent Suburbs

Stable, affluent suburbs (such as Inverness, Illinois, in the northwest outer suburban expanses of Chicago) are composed of single-family detached houses on large lots with little prospect of greater density in residential development and very little employment. (fig. **3.2.4**) It might be convenient to dismiss the economies of stable, affluent, residential suburbs as insubstantial. These suburbs are able to stay almost exclusively residential by virtue of their populations' ability and willingness to pay high property taxes for local or imported services. Such communities frequently have extremely small and exclusive populations. They remain perhaps the purest modern incarnation of the classical ideal of the suburb as a

3.2.4 New large-lot detached homes in Inverness, Illinois, a stable, affluent residential suburb

25 Robert Fishman, *Bourgeois Utopia: The Rise and Fall of Suburbia* (New York: Basic Books, 1987).

26 Bertil Thorngren, "How Do Contact Systems Affect Regional Development?," *Environment and Planning A* 2 (1970): 409–27.

"bourgeois utopia," where the value placed on environmental and private residential amenity trumps any need for the recruitment of employment land uses.[25] Yet, as already implied, these suburbs are not without their consequences for the other suburban economies described here.

Historically, residential suburbs have played an important economic role within metropolitan economies—a role that has tended to be rather overlooked in terms of suburban dependence on central cities. Since these suburbs often exported high-skilled, high-productivity labor to cities, one might question whether city economies were not in fact dependent on the economic potential of suburbs. Today, such stable, affluent suburbs continue to export labor not only to cities but also to an expanding range of employment locations, including a variety of suburbs across the metropolitan economy.

In the past, suburban economic dependence on central cities could be depicted as lying outside the hierarchical spatial pattern of "corporate contact systems" discussed by the geographer Bertil Thorngren. The contact systems of major corporations encompassed what Thorngren distinguished as the "orientation" (essentially entrepreneurial) activities that are crucial to the long-term survival of major corporations and the "planning" and "programming" activities that sustained the existing expertise and capacities of corporate organizations on a regular basis.[26] The orientation and planning activities, in particular, were centered on very large workplaces in downtowns, even if programming work was decentralized and took place in suburban and interurban factory and office locations.

With the rise of the distributed workplace, affluent residential suburbs take on an increasing significance in at least three regards. First, distributed employment is frequently located in suburbs, underlining the likely export of labor from affluent residential suburbs to other suburbs or postsuburbs in the metropolitan economy.

Second, the home becomes much more of a focal point for corporate contact systems. Orientation, programming, and planning activities have become even more decentralized by the coupling of virtual mobility (enabled by devices such as laptop computers and mobile phones) with increasing personal mobility.

Third, the home, rather than the workplace, becomes the anchor for the worker, as work takes place ever more on the move and across a greater number of sites within and between metropolitan areas. The home is now integrated into corporate contact systems in a way that it was not in the past. Even in the absence of any real data in this regard, we can speculate that the home will continue to become much a more important node within increasingly distributed patterns of work.

A 2011 study by the workplace experts Kate Lister and Tom Harnish found working from home represented around 4 percent or less of total employment in those US metropolitan areas where it was most prevalent, with one-fifth of all home workers being self-employed.[27] Yet the potential for more working from home for the suburban economy in the future seems clear, given that the same study suggests that as many as 45 percent of jobs are compatible with part-time work at home.

Declining Suburbs and Historic Cities as Suburbs

The declining inner suburbs of many metropolitan areas are typically ones of modest single-family detached houses in a more densely packed formation, including row houses and multifamily apartments often in proximity to major sites of employment. The past economic dynamism of certain area districts has begun to decline, especially that of some historic cities, as well as inner, older and typically industrial, suburbs. Their plight stands in marked contrast to stable residential suburbs, postsuburbs, and exurbs elsewhere in the metropolitan economy. For some historic cities, the loss of industry means that they have, in a

sense, become suburbs, in that they export labor to surrounding suburbs.

This suburbanization process is often associated with the requirements of capital intensive and land-extensive factories seeking economies of scale. Yet, as the geographer Robert Lewis describes, historically smaller, labor-intensive factories also decentralized to suburbs to create a "highly differentiated and specialized industrial suburban landscape" in most metropolitan areas in the hundred years or so beginning in the late 1800s.[28] Indeed, Lewis goes on to identify four types of industrial suburbs alone: informally created industrial complexes often found at the fringe of existing cities; relatively self-contained satellite industrial towns that were nevertheless rapidly absorbed into the physical expansion of metropolitan areas; single-company suburban towns; and the organized industrial districts adjacent to major infrastructure, which are often purposely developed by infrastructure-providing companies such as railway and utility companies.

Given the manufacturing complexion of these suburbs, and given their reliance in some instances on a single company or a limited number of companies, these mostly industrial inner suburbs have experienced decline. In cities such as Cleveland, largely derelict former industrial suburbs continued to form a girdle around the downtown into the new millennium. Moreover, industrial suburbs tended to have an associated and distinct working-class residential development market, and a closer connection between the workplace and home than is typically associated with the generalized notion of residential suburbia as a bourgeois retreat from the city.

As the scholars Bernadette Hanlon, Thomas Vicino, and John Rennie Short describe, employment decline in suburban industries has translated more immediately into problems of joblessness

27   Kate Lister and Tom Harnish, "The State of Telework in the US: How Individuals, Business, and Government Benefit," Telework Research Network (June 2011), accessed May 26, 2015, http://www.workshifting.com/downloads/downloads/Telework-Trends-US.pdf.

28   Robert Lewis, "Running Rings around The City: North American Industrial Suburbs, 1850–1950," in *Changing Suburbs*, ed. Richard Harris and Peter Larkham (London: E. & F. N. Spon), 156.

and poverty. In as many as one in four of the suburbs in America's rust belt, there is a close correspondence between manufacturing employment and poverty.[29] The Dundalk suburb of Baltimore also serves as an example of suburban decline associated with restructuring in the steel industry.

Suburbia's Economic Wins and Losses

The suburban economy reveals a great variety of patterns of economic specialization and trajectories of change over time. The different suburban economic scenarios outlined here provide only a crude decomposition of these experiences. Some postsuburban economies now have the scale (in terms of the numbers of businesses involved) and scope (in the range of industries found there) that traditionally we have reserved for great cities. At the other extreme, some historic cities have shrunk sufficiently to the point of having lost a measure of their economic greatness.

Taken together, the different suburban economies outlined here also highlight the range of economic actors and activities found across suburban economies. We can also see the different suburban location factors that have proved attractive to different economic activities. These range from the availability of cheap land made accessible by major infrastructure to the subsidized recruitment of major factories and office campuses, to the exclusive private residential communities that attract and retain some of the highest-paid members of society, to the moderately dense edge-city collections of offices, retail, and manufacturing that are neither the most expensive nor the cheapest, nor the most or least accessible, nor the most or least attractive locations.

A measure of planning or collective action has been implicated in the growth of suburban economies in the past, and it will surely be needed in the future if those struggling inner suburbs and the most ordinary outer residential suburbs are to play a greater economic role in the triumph of their respective metropolitan regions. In this regard, American suburbs present a potentially immense laboratory in which to observe the remaking of the suburban economy, in which not only will suburbs become more urban in certain respects, but also, cities may acquire suburban attributes.[30] The fate of older, inner industrial suburbs reminds us of the potentially unsustainable recipes of cheap, accessible land and of reliance solely on single big employers for suburban economic success. In such suburbs, collective actions will be vital, given the scale of regeneration projects that so far has often only been practiced in historic city cores. Elsewhere the challenge may be to make creative use of opportunities to recover the extensive spaces devoted to suburban infrastructure, such as highways and their easements, but also parking lots and underoccupied office campuses. Finally, while the single-family detached suburban home might be seen as a significant barrier to the urbanization of the suburbs, including their taking on a greater economic complexion, increased personal, physical, and virtual mobility also suggests the yet-greater incorporation of suburbs of all sorts into the life of the national economy. This glimpse of a world of work centered ever more on the home finds its ultimate expression in the bourgeois utopia of stable, affluent residential suburbs. While these stable, affluent residential suburbs are likely to be the exception, they continue to project a message to the more-numerous but less-exclusive residential suburbs of the value of fine-grain planning efforts to fashion a higher degree of public and private amenity—albeit with an eye on the thought that amenity drives growth.

29 Bernadette Hanlon, Thomas Vicino, and John R. Short, "The New Metropolitan Reality in the US: Rethinking the Traditional Model," *Urban Studies* 43 (2006): 2129–43.

30 Judith K. De Jong, *New SubUrbanisms* (London: Routledge, 2013).

Leander, Texas, United States

Addison, Dallas, Texas, United States

3.3
WHY SHOULD SUBURBS CARE ABOUT CITIES?

Michael Hollar

REGIONAL GOVERNANCE

SUBURB-CITY INTER-DEPENDENCIES

Metropolitan areas throughout the United States are made up of many local governing bodies. With few exceptions, neighboring city and county governments set policies independently or with minimal coordination. In many cases, local areas compete against each other to attract businesses sometimes already located in the metropolitan area, but in a different jurisdiction. This type of competition most notably surfaces with the financing of sports stadiums but is prevalent in many lesser-known industries and takes various forms, from tax breaks to infrastructure improvements. In particular, this lack of coordinated metropolitan growth policies has fostered an image of rivalry between central cities and their suburbs, and started a debate about whether competition or coordination between local governments would be the most beneficial for regional growth. Over the latter decades of the twentieth century, as suburban jurisdictions thrived in the face of growing inner-city blight, it was no longer clear whether these suburbs relied economically on their central cities.

Knowing whether central cities and suburbs grow together or independently provides important guidance in urban planning. If policies of one area indirectly affect growth of the other, a regional framework offers the best opportunity for growth. In contrast, a lack of synergies between central cities and suburbs would suggest that the additional costs of coordinating regional policies, or even merging certain functions, are not offset by the benefits of additional growth and therefore need not be considered.

Economic models of urban growth, especially those examining submetropolitan effects, focus on the concept of economies of scale as the primary determinant in the central city-suburb relationship. As businesses expand, average production costs are lower because per-unit costs of supplies and materials decrease as firms purchase larger quantities. Expansion can also lead to firms learning or adopting more efficient aspects of production. Most important for urban planners, these economies of scale can also benefit production external to the firm. These external economies of scale, also called agglomeration economies, can exist in one of two forms—localization or urbanization—and determine whether expansion of an industry benefits the entire geographic area or simply imposes greater costs without the benefits of decreased production costs.

Localization economies increase the productivity of businesses in one particular industry. As an industry expands within a local area, competing firms in that industry benefit from an increase in labor specialized to that industry and from the expansion or location of supplier industries in the same area. With localization economies, however, the growth of a particular industry does not benefit firms in other industries. Instead, growth simply increases congestion costs, mostly notably related to transportation, which increase the production costs of other industries. An example of a localization economy is the clustering of firms that serve the automobile industry in Detroit. Competing firms in this industry greatly benefited from locating near one another, taking advantage of a common skilled labor pool and proximity to supplier industries that served all of the automobile companies.

In contrast, with urbanization economies, the productivity of all firms in an area increases when any industry expands. Economies of scale that benefit all industries arise when knowledge and technological innovation flow across industries. Otherwise unrelated industries also benefit from growth as the labor pool increases. The increase in the labor supply fosters the exchange of ideas between workers in different industries, and also increases occupational specialization. In urbanization economies, economic growth attracts firms that provide more specific goods and services. The medical, legal, and financial industries often expand and provide more specific services as a result of general urban growth. The largest cities, such as New York, have more specialized doctors, for example, than smaller cities.

The key to understanding the relationship between central city and suburban economies lies in the determination of whether industries exhibit localization or urbanization economies. The empirical literature, however, has produced conflicting results preventing clear guidance. Urban simulation models, notably those developed by the economist Arthur Sullivan, assume the existence of localization economies and therefore predict a rivalrous relationship as central city and suburban businesses compete for labor.[1] Empirical studies by the economists Stuart Rosenthal and William Strange as well as those by Vernon Henderson provide evidence in favor of localization economies over small distances, indicating that industrial growth may not even provide scale economies between cities and suburbs but instead only raise labor costs.[2]

A number of economic studies, however, find considerable support for the existence of urbanization economies and a nonrivalrous relationship between central cities and their suburbs. The economists Edward Glaeser, Hedi Kallal, Jose Scheinkman, and Andei Shleifer find that industrial diversity fosters city growth, indicating that urbanization economies dominate and cities grow best when knowledge spreads from one industry to another.[3] Applied to the central city–suburb relationship, these findings suggest that the exchange of ideas between industries ties together the economic fortunes of all parts of an urban area.[4]

Thus, even though clear theories for understanding and explaining the economic interdependence of central cities and their suburbs exist, namely, urbanization versus localization economies, empirical research has generally failed to provide a conclusive answer. Moreover, studies focusing specifically on the relationship between central cities and suburbs suffer from an empirical problem: endogeneity. The endogenous nature of the urban economy makes it difficult to isolate the effect of central city growth or decline on suburban economic performance, and vice versa. Shocks that affect one part of an urban area often also directly affect other parts of the area. Thus, much of the literature studying the economic relationship between central cities and suburbs has relied on noneconomic changes in its econometric models. For example, the economist Richard Voith relied on changes in central city boundaries through annexation of land to identify exogenous growth of central cities and suburbs.[5] While this solves the technical econometric problems, it does not provide an intuitive understanding that can be applied to urban planning. Despite the measurement difficulties, the literature generally finds support for a positive interdependence between central cities and suburbs. Unfortunately, however, the interactions are not grounded in urban economic theory and thus cannot provide planners with a clear understanding of metropolitan dynamics or the implications of coordinating central city and suburban policies.

Measuring Economic Shocks

As discussed above, measuring the interdependence of central cities and suburbs has been difficult. Empirical testing of urban economic models at the metropolitan level has been hampered by the lack of exogenous measures of growth, that is, the nonlocal factors stimulating

1 Arthur Sullivan, "A General Equilibrium Model with External Scale Economies in Production," *Journal of Urban Economics* 13 (1983): 235–25; Arthur Sullivan, "A General Equilibrium Model with Agglomerative Economies and Decentralized Employment," *Journal of Urban Economics* 20 (1986): 55–74.

2 Stuart Rosenthal and William Strange, "Evidence on the Nature and Sources of Agglomeration Economies," in *Handbook for Urban and Regional Economics* 4, ed. Vernon Henderson and Jacques Francois Thisse (New York: North-Holland, 2004); and Vernon Henderson, "Marshall's Scale Economies," *Journal of Urban Economics* 53 (2003): 1–28.

3 Edward Glaeser et al., "Growth in Cities," *Journal of Political Economy* 100 (1992): 1126–52.

4 This discussion, similar to Arthur Sullivan's models, assumes that suburbs contain different export industries than central cities, which, aside from a few smaller metropolitan areas, is true.

5 Richard Voith, "Do Suburbs Need Cities?," *Journal of Regional Science* 38 (1998): 445–64.

or inhibiting economic growth. The economist Anthony Pennington-Cross addressed this need by constructing a price index of goods and services produced by export industries located in 196 metropolitan areas.[6] This Export Price Index (EPI) provides a measure of demand shocks, or unexpected changes in demand, to the metropolitan economy. This provides an ideal measure of exogenous growth, since shocks to export industries are the primary driver of metropolitan growth in urban growth theory.

Theoretical models of urban growth, beginning with the cities model developed by Henderson, rest on the assumption that export industries (which drive local growth) produce a small fraction of total national output. Therefore, they don't affect national prices for their goods or services.[7] This means that changes in the national price of these goods are due not to changes in local conditions but to changes in national demand for those products. Thus, changes in the EPI reflect these exogenous demand shocks. The resulting data facilitate tests of urban economic theory.

The EPI is a weighted price index of goods and services produced in a metropolitan area for export outside the metropolitan area. Export industries are identified using a method popular in urban economics called "location quotients." Defined as the ratio of an industry's share of total metropolitan employment to the industry's share of national employment, location quotients indicate the extent of an industry's concentration in a local area relative to the industry's national presence. If the location quotient for an industry in a specific metropolitan area is greater than one, the industry has a larger presence than otherwise expected and produces more than needed to satisfy local consumption. Therefore, that industry exports a portion of its output to the national market.

One of the best examples of an export industry is automobile manufacturing in Detroit, Michigan. Despite recent declines in Detroit's automobile industry, and the industry's expansion in other areas of the United States, it remains Detroit's largest export industry. Based on the latest employment data from the Bureau of Labor Statistics (BLS), transportation equipment manufacturing represents 9.89 percent of Detroit's employment, but only 1.76 of total US employment. That means that the location quotient for automobile manufacturing in Detroit is approximately six. Given this magnitude, the industry clearly produces more than needed to satisfy local consumption. Repeating this calculation for all industries, and at a more detailed level, provides a picture of an area's economic base.

For our model at George Washington University, we constructed separate EPIs for central cities and suburbs, in order to test theories of central city–suburban interdependence.[8] Export industries were identified using metropolitan location quotients. We assumed that export employment—employment supported by the production of an industry's exported goods and services—equals total local industry employment minus that which is needed for local consumption, in other words, employment that increases the location quotient greater than one.

Then we allocated export employment between the central city and suburbs based on the share of an industry's employment in each area. The share of export employment for each industry in the central city and the suburbs, separately, serve as weights to output prices. Summing the weighted output prices produces separate EPI indexes for the central city and suburbs.

We used Bureau of Labor Statistics' (BLS) county employment and producer price data from 1981 to 2000, and Office of Management and Budget (OMB)

6   Anthony Pennington-Cross, "Measuring External Shocks to the City Economy: An Index of Export Prices and Terms of Trade," *Real Estate Economics* 25 (1997): 105–28.

7   Vernon Henderson, *Urban Development: Theory, Fact, and Illusion* (New York: Oxford University Press, 1988).

8   Michael Hollar, "Central Cities and Suburbs: Economic Rivals of Allies?," *Journal of Regional Science* 51 (2011): 231–52.

county-based, metropolitan area definitions. The county containing the central city represents the central city, and all other counties in the metropolitan area combine to represent the suburbs. Using these definitions excluded areas with multiple central cities in different counties, and metropolitan areas made up of only one county. However, the sample contained seventy-seven of the largest metropolitan areas.

We employed a simultaneous model of central city and suburban labor markets to empirically measure the economic interdependence of central cities and suburbs. Specifically, we estimated the response of central city and suburb export industries to exogenous demand shocks as measured by the EPI while holding constant intermediate input prices, wages, capital costs, and consumer prices. As an indication that the EPI correctly captures demand shocks, increases in the own-area (local) EPI had a positive effect on employment.

The change in a neighboring area's EPI in response to demand shocks identifies the nature of interdependence. The neighboring area's EPI (i.e., the suburb EPI in the central city equation, or the central city EPI in the suburb equation) represents the response of one area to cross-area demand shocks and determines the extent of interdependence. This specification also allowed us to look for asymmetric effects between the central city and suburbs, that is, shocks that directly affect the central city, for example, but not the suburbs. This asymmetry occurs when an industry is primarily located in only the central city or suburbs, such as aircraft and aircraft equipment manufacturing in Wichita, Kansas, which accounts for two-thirds of export employment in the central city but nearly none in the suburbs. The results would thus shed light on the nature of agglomeration economies, since localization economies

in the suburbs could reduce central city employment, while urbanization economies in the central city could yield positive changes in the suburbs.

Study Results

The results show a strong positive interdependence in both directions between the central city and suburbs of the seventy-seven metropolitan areas analyzed. This indicates that the suburbs have not grown independent of their central cities and that central cities also exhibit a reliance on thriving suburban economies.

The effect of a shock to the central city on suburban employment, however, is considerably larger than the effect in the opposite direction. Specifically, the cross elasticity of suburban employment with respect to center city employment is 1.18, while the cross elasticity of central city employment with respect to suburban employment is 0.24. Thus, a 1 percent increase in demand for goods and services produced in central cities increases suburban employment by 1.18 percent. An equivalent increase in the demand for goods and services produced in the suburbs, however, increases central city employment only 0.24 percent in response.

Overall, this implies that the spillover effects and labor pooling benefits stemming from urbanization economies bind the economic fortunes of central cities and their suburbs. Recalling from the discussion above, urbanization economies increase productivity in geographically close but otherwise unrelated industries due to the ability to easily adopt new technology and utilize the larger supply of labor. Our results support the theory that urbanization economies exist between central cities and suburbs. Given the empirical support of localization economies throughout the literature, we further investigated the conditions, which could support the possibility of localization economies between central cities and suburbs.

The Effect of Industrial Diversity

Urban economic theory explains that the presence of urbanization economies fosters an industrially diverse region, while the presence of localization economies promotes an industrially concentrated region. One would, then, expect a possibly more nuanced result with differences in the central city-suburb relationship depending on the industrial structure of each area. Empirical studies of external scale economies, that is, the existence of localization versus urbanization economies, provide some evidence relevant to the understanding of central city–suburb dynamics. One set of studies examines individual industries to determine whether they grow faster in an industrially diverse or an industrially concentrated environment. Although the results vary by industry, not unsurprisingly, the bulk of the literature supports the existence of localization economies. For example, the economist Vernon Henderson's examination of various manufacturing industries indicates that growth of export industries did benefit the urban area as a whole.[9] A second set of studies measures the persistence of agglomeration economies over distance. Studies of this effect, notably by the economists Stuart Rosenthal, William Strange, and Vernon Henderson, conclude that localization economies dominate but the external scale effects diminish rapidly and exist only across short distances.[10]

Taken together, this literature on industrial and geographic dimensions of agglomeration economies predicts a negative relationship between central cities and suburbs. These studies, however, tend to focus on a limited number of broadly defined manufacturing industries, whereas our direct test of central city–suburb interdependence includes all export industries in the metropolitan area. Our model and results are more industrially inclusive, and differences in results may simply reflect differences in the industries that were studied.

A third set of studies on agglomeration economies examines the effect of external scale economies over time. The results of this set of literature provide contrasting conclusions, again indicating that the effects may vary by industry. For example, the economists Edward Glaeser, Hedi Kallal, Jose Scheinkman, and Andei Shleifer examined the industrial structure of 170 metropolitan areas and found that industrially concentrated areas grew more slowly.[11] In contrast, the economists Henderson, Ari Kuncoro, and Matt Turner focused on a small set of manufacturing industries across 224 metropolitan areas and found that industrial concentration results in higher growth.[12] These results could imply that younger firms thrive in a more diverse area, such as a dense central city, while more established industries prosper in a more industrially concentrated suburban setting.

To determine the effect of industrial diversity on the relationship between central cities and their suburbs, our model was modified to account for the industrial structure of the central city and suburbs in each metropolitan area and then reestimated. A Hirschman-Herfindahl Index (HHI) of export employment provided the measure of industrial structure. The HHI quantifies industrial structure as the sum of the squared share of industry export employment in the central city or suburbs. A higher measure of HHI indicates a more concentrated area. For example, in Detroit, the three largest export industries, primarily related to automobile manufacturing, account for almost half of the central city's export employment; the HHI equals 0.10.

HHI analysis of many cities shows that the positive relationship previously

9   Vernon Henderson, "Efficiency of Resource Usage and City Size," *Journal of Urban Economics* 19 (1986): 47–70.

10 Stuart Rosenthal and William Strange, "Geography, Industrial Organization, and Agglomeration," *Review of Economics and Statistics* 85 (2003): 377–93; and Vernon Henderson, "Marshall's Scale Economies," *Journal of Urban Economics* 53 (2003): 1–28.

11 Glaeser et al., "Growth in Cities," 1126–52.

12 Vernon Henderson, Ari Kuncoro, and Matt Turner, "Industrial Development in Cities," *Journal of Political Economy* 103 (1995): 1067–90.

discovered decreases as industrial concentration increases, generally confirming
the previous finding that urbanization
economies dominate except in industrially
concentrated areas. (fig. **3.3.1**) The effect of
central city growth on the suburban economy, however, turns negative when the
largest three export industries in the suburb account for approximately 60 percent
of export employment. The suburbs of
Phoenix and Canton, Ohio, have this level
of concentration, and are nearly independent of their central cities. For these
areas, growth of the central city increases
population, which in turn increases traffic
and consumer prices as much as or more
than productivity.

A lower threshold exists for the central city, just above 40 percent, indicating
that congestion costs of more traffic and
higher prices outweigh productivity gains
faster in central cities than the suburbs.
The central cities of Fort Worth, Seattle,
and Wilmington, Delaware, each exhibit
this level of industrial concentration
and display little or no response to exogenous changes in the economies of their
suburbs. In these cases, regional planning
is less beneficial to the area as a whole,
since the benefits of coordinated planning
may not outweigh the costs.

The Bottom Line for Urban Planners
Urban economics literature provides
clear theories regarding the interaction
between central city and suburban economies, depending on whether localization
or urbanization external scale economies
exist. The results from our study indicate that central cities and suburbs grow
together, supporting the existence of
urbanization economies and therefore
regional cooperation. Positive demand
shocks to export industries in the central
city result in substantial growth in the
suburbs, and vice versa. The benefits of
spillover effects and labor market pooling
outweigh congestion costs, which tend to
increase wages and local production costs.
Coordinated regional planning could further offset costs related to congestion and
further enhance metropolitan growth.
This planning could include active policies
such as a coordinated transportation
network or passive policies such as local
jurisdictions agreeing not to compete
using tax subsidies for the relocation
of firms.

But there is a caveat: the positive
externalities diminish as industrial concentration increases. For central cities or
suburbs with only a few dominant export
industries, positive demand shocks to
the neighboring area's export industries
result in an increased cost of living, which
more than offsets the positive spillover
effects. This explains some of the empirical results that support the existence of
localization economies.

Developing local economic policy
clearly requires understanding the local
economy. To begin, planners should learn
the industrial structure of both central
cities and suburbs, paying particular
attention to the concentration of export
industries. In industrially diverse areas,
planners should work to coordinate
policies across the metropolitan area with
the goal of lowering costs of government-
provided services. Although there are
extreme examples of merging multiple
jurisdictions, such as the unification of the
city of Indianapolis and Marion County,
planners could urge for other forms of
cooperation through regional authorities
that, for example, administer transportation systems.

In addition to improving the efficiency
of locally provided government services,
planners should examine regulations
across jurisdictions that may affect the
local cost of living. Although regulations
are implemented to provide a basic
level of health, safety, or general welfare,
planners could work to eliminate discrep-
ancies between jurisdictions that increase

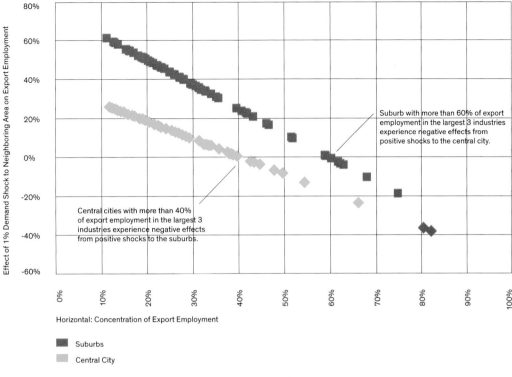

Horizontal: Concentration of Export Employment

■ Suburbs
□ Central City

Suburb with more than 60% of export employment in the largest 3 industries experience negative effects from positive shocks to the central city.

Central cities with more than 40% of export employment in the largest 3 industries experience negative effects from positive shocks to the suburbs.

3.3.1 How industrial concentration affects central city–suburb dynamics

costs. Land-use regulations may have the greatest impact on the local cost of living. Enforcing drastically different lot-size restrictions in neighboring jurisdictions would cause excessive development in the area with the lower standard and under-development in the other. This would lead to increased congestion costs in the lower-standard jurisdictions and higher house prices in the higher-standard jurisdiction. Raising local costs of living unnecessarily in this way slows growth and harms the entire area.

Theories of urban growth provide potentially competing outcomes for the relationship between central city and suburban economies. The evidence dis-cussed above, however, clearly indicates that central cities and suburbs have a strong, positive interdependence. Thus, in order to maximize growth for an entire metropolitan area, planners and policy makers for individual jurisdictions should work as allies rather than act as rivals.

3.4
SIX TYPES OF HIGH-TECHNOLOGY DISTRICTS

Ann Forsyth

The second half of the twentieth century brought a number of major world changes. Women's roles evolved; environmental damage increased; the world economy became increasingly linked through flows of money, goods, and information; and high-technology industries became major economic players.[1] High technology is a broad category of industries from software to hardware, from biotechnology to information technology, and from research and manufacturing to data processing. These emerging industries have produced a set of gadgets and modes of communication that have infiltrated most parts of the human environment. The places where people design and build these devices and programs have also become an important part of the urban landscape. Are these high-tech production environments fundamentally different places of employment?

The quest to foster high technology innovations has led to many ideas about how to create better environments for such innovative work. Perhaps the predominant set of such proposals or assessments have come from the field of economic development, where the environment being designed is the economic, business, organizational, or regulatory environment, often at the regional scale although also including subregional areas.[2] In these studies, the overall physical design is seen at most as a side effect of a set of economic, organizational, and governmental arrangements. Parallel work has analyzed broad social and educational features attractive to a "creative class" or fostering economic growth more generally such as universities and other lifestyle amenities.[3]

Looking though a different lens, that of physical place, this essay identifies six types of small- to medium-scale high technology districts in terms of their physical environments rather than their economic features: corridors, clumps, cores, comprehensive campuses, tech subdivisions, and scattered tech sites. As the high-technology industry grows, so too will the effect of such places on the future sustainability and livability of urban areas. (figs. **3.4.1–2**)

High-Technology District Types

In developing the typology, I focused on four key dimensions. First was the location in a metropolitan area, which is key to accessibility, and the development period of the surrounding area, and has implications for density. Second was the physical scale of the developments. Taking the region as the largest physical scale, the district types are either medium (thousands of hectares, sometimes tens of thousands of hectares), small (hundreds of hectares), or tiny (just a few hectares). Larger areas are likely to be more mixed use. Third was the level of overall physical planning and urban design—some types have little physical coordination, while others are designed in great detail. While there may certainly be planning and design activity to create the various less planned types, such planning may be for a building complex or basic transportation infrastructure rather than a comprehensive physical design at the scale of a district, corridor, or other segment of a city. Finally, I considered the level of economic planning, though this was not as important in defining physical types. The six types represent the scale that people experience daily as they move around in neighborhoods, employment districts, and similar areas. For brevity, I call these the "district" types. (fig. **3.4.3**)

Corridors

Corridors are linear features that grow up along a major road that may also support transit service. Economically, corridors are a concentration of activity within a metropolitan cluster, but physically, they are distinctive. The main road itself is

1   Manuel Castells, *The Power of Identity* (Malden: Blackwell, 1997); Manuel Castells, *The Rise of the Network Society*, 2nd ed. (Oxford: Blackwell, 2000).
2   Manuel Castells and Peter Hall, *Technopoles of the World* (London: Routledge, 1994); Ann Markusen, "Sticky Places in Slippery Place: A Typology of Industrial Districts," *Economic Geography* 72 (1996): 293–313; Martin Boddy, "Technology, Innovation, and Regional Economic Development in the State of Victoria," *Environment and Planning C* 18 (2000): 301–19; Francis Koh, Winston T. H. Koh, and Ted F. Tschang, "An Analytical Framework for Science Parks and Technology Districts with an Application to Singapore," *Journal of Business Venturing* 20 (2005): 217–39; Jennifer Clark, Hsin-I Huang, and John P. Walsh, "A Typology of Innovation Districts: What It Means for Regional Resilience" (paper presented at Industry Studies Association Conference, Chicago, 2009), accessed December 21, 2015, http://www.industry studies.pitt.edu /chicago09/docs /Clark%201.6.pdf.
3   See review in David W. Edgington, "The Kyoto Research Park and Innovation in Japanese Cities," *Urban Geography* 29 (2008): 411–54; Richard Florida, Charlotta Mellander, and Kevin Stolarick, "Inside the Black Box of Regional Development—Human Capital, the Creative Class, and Tolerance," *Journal of Economic Geography* 8 (2008): 615–50; Michael Storper and Allen J. Scott, "Rethinking Human Capital, Creativity, and Urban Growth," *Journal of Economic Geography* 9 (2009): 147–67.

Type (down); characteristics (across)	Location in metro	Typical scale[1]	Level of overall physical planning	Level of economic planning
Corridors	Radial or circumferential	Medium	Low to medium	Low to medium
Clumps	Typically middle to outer suburbs	Medium	Low to medium, may have highly planned components	Low to high
Cores	Central city	Small to medium	Low in terms of IT (the core city as a whole may be heavily regulated)	Low to medium
Campuses	Middle to outer suburbs	Small to Medium	High	Medium to high
Technology subdivisions	Typically middle to outer suburbs; may include core areas	Small	Medium to high	Low (an opportunistic private park) to high
Scattered sites	Anywhere—from core city to rural but many in suburban areas	Tiny	Varies	Varies

1 Medium environments are 1,000s or even 10,000s of hectares; small are 100s of hectares; tiny are a few hectares. A regional cluster would be large.

3.4.1 High-technology district types and characteristics

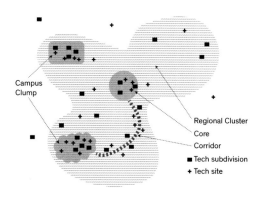

Campus
Clump

Regional Cluster
Core
Corridor
■ Tech subdivision
+ Tech site

3.4.2 Conceptual plan of district types within a metropolitan region

likely primarily for access, a major freeway or divided road. The IT Corridor (Rajiv Gandhi Salai) south of Chennai is a wide toll road, but like many Indian roads, the shoulders are unformed; thus, a shiny PayPal building is reached across a muddy verge. In this corridor, large IT facilities are typically walled. Much care is given to the facilities inside the boundaries, and the area outside is less cared for. However, these fairly unfinished roads are much used by people to get around. Even in areas where the physical infrastructure is more developed than Chennai, however, roads are likely to be primarily access-points, not designed public places. Limited access highways, such as Route 128 near Boston, are an example.

Visually, these developments demonstrate order through the continuity of the main road(s) and the similar boxy buildings set in landscaped parcels. But there is also a level of chaos or disorganization. Traveling along a street, or examining aerial photography of the corridor, it is apparent that high-tech businesses are spread out along the road and are not at all continuous. High-tech parcels or parks with a broadly international campus-garden-suburb appearance are interspersed with other developments from retail to housing.[4] This mixture of uses has great potential in the long term to create multifunctional places. However, in the present, different uses are often primarily linked by motorized modes with pedestrian and cycling infrastructure more discontinuous or informal. They typically lack continuous sidewalks or pedestrian-scaled street lighting, for example. While they may be used by pedestrians in locations such as India, this use is not intentionally designed. Similarly, housing may cater for some parts of the high-tech economy (the more affluent) and not others.

Clumps

Clumps are a nonlinear version of a corridor. Absent the transportation route as an organizing principle, they typically have some sort of overall physical and

4   Anne Forsyth and Katherine Crewe, "Suburban Technopoles as Places: The International Campus-Garden-Suburb Style," *Urban Design International* 15 (2010): 165–82.

Corridors

IT Corridor, Chennai

IT Corridor, Chennai

Route 128 area Burlington (Google Streetview)

Clumps

In Whitefield, Bangalore

Whitefield, a major node in the Bangalore cluster

One of the main facilities in Kansai Science City in Japan, a more heavily planned cluster

Cores

San Francisco, SoMa Area

MIT University Park Areas

Manhattan around Silicon Alley

Campuses

Kista, Sweden

Tsukuba, Japan

Irvine, USA

3.4.3 Larger district types illustrated: corridors, clumps, cores, and campuses

economic coordination. This coordination may be modest: a government puts in roads; buildings are likely regulated. A local government may provide economic incentives or contracts (e.g., for defense or telecommunications). They may even be created by higher-level (state or national) governments designating a special economic zone or a large industrial park (in the thousands of hectares). But overall most clumps, even ones developed with government incentives, are built incrementally, one parcel or technology subdivision at a time. They may be mixed in with housing and retail, but not developed according to a comprehensive vision.

Some are coordinated at a regional level in terms of their economic character. Kansai Science City in Japan is a public-private joint venture located in a 37,000-acre (15,000 hectare) triangle between Kyoto, Osaka, and Nara and with a network of technology parks or subdivisions coordinated by a public private partnership.[5] While the urban planners Ann Forsyth and Katherine Crewe propose it is a campus-garden suburb, and it has a network of manicured landscaped areas including paths and parks, it is a science economic zone more than a freestanding science city.[6]

Such developments can be identified visually. They often have a name and anchor buildings such as key firms, conference facilities, or shopping centers. They are not comprehensively designed in a physical sense, however, and like corridors are discontinuous. They include housing and retail, but uses are often sited opportunistically, and it may not be easy for people to get around. Transportation may be primarily based on motorized transportation. In countries where there is more overall planning, they will likely be better coordinated. Yet as the impetus comes from economic development, physical design and planning attention may be most focused on specific sites and on

the road network, but not on any overall idea of coordinated appearance, non-motorized transportation, or housing provision. Whitefield outside Bangalore is an example.[7]

Cores

Cores are small concentrations of high-tech development in the centers of bigger cities. One example is a private research park in the central district of Kyoto—the only one in Japan. Established in 1988, and developed by the Osaka Gas Corporation, twenty years later it was home to approximately 240 companies, many in new media and information technology.[8] In this case, as in the University Park in the Kendall Square area near MIT, or redeveloped areas in central San Francisco, many of the buildings are new.[9] However, in other cases, high-tech companies adapt existing buildings, renovating warehouse and older commercial buildings. Governments may also take a lead in coordinating redevelopment.[10]

Economically, core areas may be very similar to an outer clump or corridor. However, visually they have a distinctive identity defined by fitting into an existing street pattern. They may use new buildings, even groups of them, but typically on a smaller footprint, necessitating building vertically. They may be primarily visible through signage; building exteriors look much like other office or light industrial buildings. They will likely be mixed in with many other businesses. Transportation varies by city, but urban cores typically have better public transportation links than elsewhere in the metropolis. Housing, while often close, may be either expensive or run-down. Overall, cores have often already been redeveloped several times, contain a mixture of uses, and can be expected to be resilient. However, because high-tech companies and workers can frequently outbid local businesses and residences,

5 "Kansai Science City Portal Site," About Kansai Science City, last modified 2009, accessed February 7, 2017, http://www.kri-p.jp/english/keihanna.pdf.

6 Forsyth and Crewe, "Suburban Technopoles as Places," 177; see also Rosemary Wakeman, "Dreaming the New Atlantis: Science and the Planning of Technopolis, 1955–1985," *Osiris* 18 (2003): 255–90.

7 Dave Valler, Nick Phelps, and Andrew M. Wood, "Planning for Growth: The Implications of Localism for 'Science Vale,' Oxfordshire, UK," *Town Planning Review* 83 (2012): 457–87.

8 Edgington, "The Kyoto Research Park and Innovation in Japanese cities," 412.

9 Stephen Graham and Simon Guy, "Digital Space Meets Urban Place: Sociotechnologies of Urban Restructuring in Downtown San Francisco," *City* 6 (2002): 369–82.

10 Antònia Cassellas, "Collaborative Approaches to Innovation and Urban Regeneration: The Science Parks of Barcelona Metropolitan Region" (paper presented at Science and the City, Science and Technology Policy Institute, Seoul, Korea, October 2011).

there can be significant displacement of existing lower-income occupants.[11]

Campuses

Some purpose-built high-technology developments have adapted the campus and garden city or planned garden suburb model into what Forsyth and Crewe call the international campus-garden-suburb style.[12] True science cities, planned from the beginning for high-tech development, are comprehensively developed with housing and business areas. They vary in scale from the very large (e.g., Tsukuba, population planned for two hundred thousand) to the medium (e.g., Kista, planned for far fewer).[13] Some comprehensively planned mixed-use developments were not intended initially for high tech but attracted a great deal of businesses, for example, Izumi Park Town outside Sendai (benefiting from the Japanese Technopolis program) or Irvine in Southern California.[14] Some are less comprehensively designed, with an overall planning framework dealing with issues such as transportation, with key nodes being designed in the campus style. Kansai Science City, described above, in the clumps section, is one example of a hybrid of campus and clump.

Of course, a campus appearance is featured in many of the other types, in larger and smaller chunks. The comprehensive campus is distinctive, however, in several ways. Such environments are highly planned from the start for a variety of uses so people can live and work in an integrated environment. They draw on traditions of both self-contained garden cities and university campuses. They contain extensive open spaces. They are also large, meaning that their orderly and comfortable environments extend continuously over a large area, typically in a suburban setting.[15] This is a distinctively different type of environment to that of a corridor or clump; in those other cases

highly designed parcels and research parks are interspersed with more incremental developments.

Tech Subdivisions

Tech subdivisions are smaller campuses, less comprehensive than the prior group, mainly containing businesses and not explicitly coordinating with housing and transportation at a large scale. I use the term *subdivision* to designate areas of up to a few hundred hectares, not a few thousand. I avoided using the term *park* in the typology, as it often indicates a specific economic character; parks are frequently described in terms of numbers of firms and employees, not physical size.[16] Tech subdivisions are an important physical design worth distinguishing from these large economic zones.

One case is the Shenzhen Silicon Peak Software Ecological Park. This 336-acre (136-hectare) high-technology subdivision, developed in the 2000s, sported a design philosophy focused on people, resources, economy, environment, ecosystem, technology, and society. The designers hoped their landscape design could achieve aesthetic and ecological goals such as microclimate control, visual buffering, and protecting natural features. But their environmental goals also aimed to attract high-tech workers. [17]

While the example above demonstrates a high level of design attention, other tech subdivisions are more modest. They may be found as components of the prior four types but are dealt with separately here because they may also appear in areas without such larger concentrations of technology companies, both in urban and in rural settings. A number of science parks taking this character have been identified in semirural parts of South East England with a number of such subdivisions or "camps" in proximity forming Science Vale, United Kingdom.[18]

11 Graham and Guy, "Digital Space Meets Urban Place," 369–82.

12 Forsyth and Crewe, "Suburban Technopoles as Places: The International Campus-Garden-Suburb Style," 165–82; Blake Gumprecht, "The Campus as a Public Space in the American College Town," *Journal of Historical Geography* 33 (2005): 72–103; M. P. O'Mara, *Cities of Knowledge* (Princeton: Princeton University Press, 2005).

13 Forsyth and Crewe, "Suburban Technopoles as Places: The International Campus-Garden-Suburb Style," 165–82; Ann Forsyth and Katherine Crewe, "A Typology of Comprehensive Designed Communities since the Second World War," *Landscape Journal* 27 (2009): 56–78; Ester Baringa and Lena Ramfelt, "Kista: The Two Sides of the Network Society," *Networks and Communications Studies* 18 (2004): 225–44.

14 Ann Forsyth, "Who Built Irvine? Private Planning and the Federal Government," *Urban Studies* 39 (2002): 2507–30.

15 Forsyth and Crewe, "Suburban Technopoles as Places: The International Campus-Garden-Suburb Style," 165–82.

16 Koh, Koh, and Tschang, "An Analytical Framework for Science Parks and Technology Districts with an Application to Singapore," 217–39; Hsien-Che Lai and Jospeph Z. Shyu, "A Comparison of Innovation Capacity at Science Parks across the Taiwan Strait: The Case of Zhanjiang High-Tech Park and Hsinchu Science-Based Industrial Park," *Technovation* 25 (2005): 805–13.

17 Chuanglin Fang and Yichun Xie, "Site Planning and Guiding Principles of Hi-Tech Parks in China: Shenzhen as a Case

In general, because of their small size, they piggyback onto existing or incrementally developed infrastructure. They may be in well-serviced areas or quite isolated; housing may be close or at some distance. These are very flexible building blocks of a high-tech environment.

Scattered Sites

Scattered sites are individual technology buildings or smaller research parks of a few hectares that may be scattered throughout a metropolitan area or found in clumps and corridors. These meet the need for industrial and high-tech office space using existing or incrementally developed infrastructure. They are often the high tech equivalent of office sprawl, actually taking advantage of new communications and logistics capabilities to link to other parts of the high tech economy.[19]

Regional-Scale Clusters

The six types may all appear in a regional-scale cluster of high-tech industries—so one "cluster" may have all of them. I use the term *regional-scale cluster* because the literature is quite unclear about just how big a cluster needs to be, and they seem to come in sizes from part of a city upward.[20] Such clusters are at their base an economic category, related to a concentration in certain industries, although the concentration of industry does have physical effects. Clusters include suppliers, marketers, consumers of goods and services, companies in allied fields, and, potentially, related institutions such as think tanks, universities, and regulators. Regional clusters include Hollywood (Southern California) and the wine cluster in Northern California.[21]

Silicon Valley is the most well known of such technology clusters—and is unusual because of its strength in multiple industries. Many places around the world have tried to copy it in some way,

though at different scales and not always emphasizing multiple types of technology development.[22] Historical, case study, and insider accounts of high-tech innovation illustrate the extensive personnel mobility between firms in many high-tech areas and the need for varied funding sources.[23] Regional-scale clusters support those needs through both public- and private-sector activities.[24]

In terms of spatial character, clusters may include basically all the district-level types dealt with in this essay. Larger and denser clusters have a lot of high-tech activity, although such activities will not be visible everywhere. A cluster is an economic phenomenon with complicated physical outcomes. It may have many types of the districts dealt with here or just a few; clusters also evolve over time. In addition, even places without a high concentration of high technology may have some such high-tech district environments. An economic analysis of clusters may not say much at all about the physical places. However, physical places are important for people's daily experiences, for urban public finance (are they easy or difficult to service?), and for long-term sustainability of a region (do they foster social equity, energy efficiency, preservation of natural resources, and good long-term jobs?).

Future Evolution

This essay started with the question: does a high-tech economy create fundamentally different kinds of places? It argues that in urban design terms high-tech districts are not necessarily different from other employment areas that either employ knowledge workers or engage in precision manufacturing. There are many overlaps between such environments and generic urban industrial and office development, planned new towns, university campuses, and garden suburbs. However, high-tech areas do have a predictable character, at

Study," *Environment and Planning B* 35 (2008): 100–121.

18 Dave Valler and Nick Phelps, "Big Science and Small Villages: Understanding the Context and Constraints on High-Tech Growth in South East England" (paper presented at Science and the City, Science and Technology Policy Institute, Seoul, Korea, October 2011).

19 Randall Crane and Daniel G. Chatman, "As Jobs Sprawl, Whither the Commute?," *Access* 23 (2003): 14–19.

20 Ron Martin and Peter Sunley, "Deconstructing Clusters: Chaotic Concept or Policy Panacea?," *Economic Geography* 3 (2003): 5–35.

21 Michael E. Porter, "Clusters and the New Economics of Competition," *Harvard Business Review* November–December (1998): 77–90.

22 Boddy, "Technology, Innovation, and Regional Economic Development in the State of Victoria," 301–19; J. Cortright and Heike Mayer, *High Tech Specialization: A Comparison of High Technology Centers* (Washington, DC: Brookings Institution, 2001); Timothy Bresnahan and Alfonso Gambardella, introduction to *Building High-Tech Clusters: Silicon Valley and Beyond*, ed. Timothy Bresnahan and Alfonso Gambardella (Cambridge: Cambridge University Press, 2004).

23 Gordon Moore and Kevin Davis, "Learning the Silicon Valley Way," in *Building High-Tech Clusters: Silicon Valley and Beyond*, ed. Timothy Bresnahan and Alfonso Gambardella (Cambridge: Cambridge University Press, 2004); Porter, "Clusters and the New Economics of Competition," 77–90.

24 Steven J. Bass, "Japanese Research Parks: National Policy and Local Development," *Regional Studies* 32 (1998): 391–403; Sang-Chul Park, "Globalisation and

District type	Location in metro	Potential for positive evolution	Potential problems over time
Corridors	Radial or circumferential	Transportation spine orders landscape and can be redeveloped over time for multiple transportation modes, potentially with a series of vibrant mini-cores; the linear city is a model with a long tradition	Creating concentrated areas (activity centers) may be difficult given that the original street pattern and parcel layout is focused on large individual parcels, fairly homogeneous housing, and commercial enclaves
Clumps	Typically middle to outer suburbs	Have the ingredients of a comprehensive, sustainable design (mixed uses); economic activity provides local tax base for improvements	Lack of overall coordination may make it difficult to provide transit, housing, public spaces, and other infrastructure to fit sustainable city models
Cores	Central city	Typically have already evolved over time and can do so again; have a variety of building types and ages, as well as public spaces	Infrastructure may be aging and will require investment. Successful cores can be very expensive, limiting housing options
Campuses	Middle to outer suburbs	Campus mixed uses and coordinated transport allow intensification over time; typically provide ample, well-designed common spaces and a balance of housing opportunities	Designs may be highly regulated, making it difficult to adapt to changing circumstances. May not offer housing for the high or low end of the market
Technology subdivisions	Typically middle to outer suburbs; may include core areas	Small, adaptable for infill	Can be scattered and inaccessible. May be difficult to link to the rest of the metropolis by anything other than private vehicles
Scattered sites	Anywhere—from core city to rural but many in suburban areas	Building-scale renovation possible	Can be scattered and inaccessible, a contributor to sprawl

3.4.4 Potential evolution of high-tech districts over time

the site, technology subdivision, campus, core, clump, or corridor scale. Because many high-tech companies, and local governments and developers hoping to attract them, use a similar aesthetic, one might have an overall impression of low shiny buildings, large berms with monument signs, and tastefully designed security-guard shelters.[25] Many have at least some international companies, so one might see General Electric signage on a building in Bangalore or find an Adobe building in Noida (a suburb of Delhi). Even cores, while often featuring historic buildings, may also include new downtown tech subdivisions and scattered site developments that feature shiny buildings, obvious signage, and elegant landscaping. (fig. **3.4.4**)

Thinking about issues such as transportation, place making, social equity, and environmental effects, some of the types do better than others. In the short term, the older areas (such as cores) and the more coordinated developments (such as campuses) often do better in terms of providing alternatives to the car, creating a sense of place, and considering natural systems. Housing affordability

is not always so well treated, however. Others such as clumps and corridors may work well if part of a larger framework of transportation planning, placemaking, green-space design, and housing development. Absent this, however, they often suffer from congestion and monotony at least. The smaller subdivisions and sites depend very much on their contexts, whether placed in available parcels with little consideration of their connections or thoughtfully located as part of a larger system.

But what of the future design evolution of specifically high-tech developments? Governments seeking such development are often focused primarily on promoting economic development and companies focused on short-term profitability. What happens, however, when the needs of industry change or when a high-tech cluster fails to take hold in an area? This question is important because high technology is a growing industry and places will develop to accommodate it. It turns out that not all of these district types are equivalent in terms of how well they can be adapted over time. Some patterns are more or less

Local Innovation System: The Implementation of Government Policies to the Formation of Science Parks in Japan," *AI and Society* 15 (2001): 263–79; Vincente Mangematin and Khalid Errabi, "The Determinants of Science-Based Cluster Growth: The Case of Nanotechnology," *Environment and Planning C* 30 (2012): 128–46.

25 Forsyth and Crewe, "Suburban Technopoles as Places: The International Campus-Garden-Suburb Style," 165–82.

sustainable; leave more to chance in terms of coordinating jobs, transportation, and housing; or provide different qualities of public spaces.

Some aspects of the environment are relatively easy to change in the medium-term. For example, industrial and research buildings are typically designed to last for decades, rather than centuries, and can be replaced. However, once land is subdivided and sold, and roads put in, the overall street pattern is much harder to alter. Some developers hold on to large parcels and only lease buildings so they can redesign street patterns later; some governments are proactive about taking and consolidating land; but this is the exception rather than the rule. Houses are replaced less frequently than buildings used for business, so residential areas may be more complex to redevelop.[26] (fig. **3.4.5**)

There is not a single model for the sustainable future, of course, even looking at only one dimension such as natural systems.[27] Among planners, however, the idea of the compact city, or ecocity, has received great traction. This concentrates development and mixes uses together, enabling efficient use of urban infrastructure, making public transit service viable, allowing a diverse population to live in relatively close proximity, and saving land on the outskirts of cities.[28] The overall metropolitan area is focused on a series of walkable, transit-oriented centers. Some of the claims are disputed, but this is a widely held vision. An alternative is the low-density ecoburb that brings people close to nature, allows on-site infiltration of water, and may allow on-site energy production for buildings. Many consumers find this environment desirable and landscape architects have created important models. Low densities, however, mean that transportation is often via the automobile and energy use may be higher for transportation.[29]

Some of these high-tech districts may be able to conform to the compact city idea over time. Locations like Kista, a planned transit-oriented suburb (campus) in Stockholm and a high-tech center, already take this form. Many clumps and corridors have substantial medium and high-rise housing. In addition, urban cores are typically well serviced and have generally supported several waves of industrial evolution already. They are capable of evolving again as long as there are resources for such renewal given aging infrastructure and perhaps a lack of housing. But for other district types, it will be more of a challenge to evolve to an ecocity model due to being located away from infrastructure and existing development, as well as having initial designs that separate land uses. While there is often open space in high-tech districts, it is not always optimally located for intensifying activities. It may be difficult to add housing and shops to areas initially dominated by employment because there are no parcels of the right dimensions with adequate access, for example.

Alternatively, other areas may be able to be redeveloped as low-density ecoburbs bringing people in contact with nature in a decentralized vision of the good city. Redeveloped ecoburbs take advantage of the existing landscaping and open space to increase habitat, water infiltration, food production, and on-site energy generation. However, in both types of development—ecocities or ecoburbs— very successful high-tech districts may become so expensive that it is hard to provide housing for lower-income workers. Children may not be well accommodated. It is important that planning and design consider such longer-term redevelopment including effects on issues such as transportation options, housing balance, and sense of place.

While not unique as places, there is a predictability in the character of

26 Arthur C. Nelson, *Toward a New Metropolis* (Washington, DC: Brookings Institution, 2004), accessed November 21, 2015, http://www.brookings .edu/reports/2004 /12metropolitanpolicy _nelson.aspx.

27 Katherine Crewe and Ann Forsyth, "Compactness and Connection in Environmental Design: Insights from Ecoburbs and Ecocities for Design with Nature," *Environment and Planning B* 38 (2011): 267–88; Pere Vall-Casas, Julia Koschinsky, and Carmen Mendoza, "Retrofitting Suburbia through Pre-Urban Patterns: Introducing a European Perspective," *Urban Design International* 16 (2011): 171–87.

28 Yosef R. Jabareen, "Sustainable Urban Forms: Their Typologies, Models, and Concepts," *Journal of Planning Education and Research* 26 (2006): 38–52; Peter Calthorpe and William Fulton, *The Regional City: New Urbanism and the End of Sprawl* (Washington, DC: Island Press, 2001); Peter Newman and Jeffrey Kenworthy, *Sustainable Cities* (Washington, DC: Island Press, 2000); Ellen Dunham-Jones and June Williamson, *Retrofitting Suburbia* (New York: Wiley, 2009).

29 Philip R. Berke, "The Evolution of Green Community Planning, Scholarship, and Practice," *Journal of the American Planning Association* 74 (2008): 393–407; Judy Corbett and Michael Corbett, *Designing Sustainable Communities: Learning from Village Homes* (Washington, DC: Island Press, 2000).

Kista

Potential ecocity: Kista is a highly coordinated planned suburb of Stockholm already demonstrating high-density, transit-oriented, mixed-use designs favored by many planners as an option for redevelopment.

Kansai Science City

Potential ecoburb: Kansai Science City already has a low-rise environment with elements such as wide pedestrian bicycle paths, connected green spaces, green roofs, and low-rise homes and industrial buildings.

3.4.5 Examples of potential for evolution as ecocities and ecoburbs

environments for high-tech industry across the globe, reflecting the generic needs of research and manufacturing as well as the expectations and aspirations of a global workforce and businesses. While most attention has been placed on their economic character, the current experience and future evolution of urban areas depends at least in part on their physical form. Designing places that can be adaptable over time is a key challenge for the coming decades. Flexibility would be easiest where development is coordinated to evolve gracefully toward some form of ecoburb or ecocity models. In a world that prioritizes current economic activity over long-term efficiency and place making, this can be a difficult. The alternative will be a more complex and potentially wasteful process of rebuilding and reestablishing landscapes.

This essay is an adaptation of Ann Forsyth, "Alternative Forms of the High-Technology District: Corridors, Clumps, Cores, Campuses, Subdivisions, and Sites," Environment and Planning C: Government and Policy 32, no. 5 (October 1, 2014): 809–23. Copyright © 2014 by SAGE Publications, Ltd. Reprinted by permission of SAGE Publications, Ltd.

Diepkloof, Johannesburg, Gauteng, South Africa

Shanghai New International Expo Centre, Pudong, Shanghai, China

3.5
CREATIVE SUBURBIA
CULTURAL INNOVATION IN OUTER SUBURBAN AUSTRALIA

**Mark Gibson, Terry Flew,
Christy Collis, and Emma Felton**

FLEXIBLE
REGULATION

HOUSING
AFFORDABILITY

INNOVATION

SOCIAL
DIVERSITY

The past twenty years have seen a flourishing interest in the relationship between cities and creativity, and in particular between cities and the creative industries. For the most part, however, this interest has had a strongly urban bias, identifying how the clustering of creative industries workforces in densely populated city centers produces innovative cultural milieu, and how creative cities adapt to the bohemian cultural consumption preferences of a newly ascendant "creative class."[1] This interest has focused on the regeneration of the postindustrial cities of Europe and the "hipster" enclaves of North America, paying relatively little attention to low-density, peripheral, or nonmetropolitan forms.

At Queensland University of Technology and Monash University, our research project "Creative Suburbia" sought deliberately to question this bias, investigating the potential for the development of creative industries in outer suburban Australia.[2] Australia is a particularly appropriate case for such questioning, since suburbia has long been the dominant settlement pattern. In his classic 1964 book *The Lucky Country*, the journalist and essayist Donald Horne went so far as to describe Australia as "the first suburban nation."[3]

Historians such as Graeme Davison have suggested that suburbanization was "deeply rooted in Australia's colonial experience…[and] was consciously promoted by the country's founders," who "anticipated a sprawl of homes and gardens rather than a clumping of terraces and alleys."[4] From the earliest British settlements in the late eighteenth and early nineteenth centuries, urban design was enlisted to ensure that Australian cities avoided the crime, poverty, and ill-health of British industrial cities; the clustering of urban populations in close quarters was seen as a major source of those problems.

There have always been strong forces promoting suburbanization in Australia, with local, state, and federal governments all keen to promote home ownership on "the quarter acre block" as part of "the Australian Dream." In doing so, they have played to a diverse coalition of interests that includes property developers, real estate agents, the automobile industry, local chambers of commerce, and independent tradespeople. Australia is one of the most urbanized countries in the world, with 75 percent of the population living in seventeen major cities, and over 50 percent living in five cities with populations of over one million.[5] The contemporary face of Australian suburbanization is Master Planned Communities (MPCs), which have experienced rapid growth since the 1980s. These communities counter perceptions of unplanned suburban "sprawl" by developing mixed-use sites for fifty-thousand-plus residents on the urban fringe, combining housing, employment opportunities, leisure and recreation facilities, government service agencies, and university campuses, as well as shopping centers and golf courses.[6]

Suburbs on the Cultural Fault Line
To consider the creative potential of suburbia would strike many as counterintuitive. As the media studies scholar Sue Turnbull has remarked, attitudes toward the suburbs have constituted "a cultural fault-line in Australia over the last 100 years," with intellectuals and creative practitioners often strongly opposed to all that they have been taken to represent.[7] The Australian suburbs have been at various times associated with spiritual emptiness, the absence of community, the decline of working-class political consciousness, the promotion of consumerism and middle-class values, and the alienation and oppression of women in the domestic sphere.[8]

1 Graeme Evans, "Creative Cities, Creative Spaces, and Urban Policy," *Urban Studies* 46, nos. 5–6 (2009): 1003–40; Richard Florida, *Who's Your City? How the Creative Economy Is Making Where to Live the Most Important Decision of Your Life* (New York: Basic Books, 2008).

2 Publications from the project included Terry Flew and Mark Gibson, "Melbourne and Brisbane: The Claims of Suburbs," in *Cities, Cultural Policy, and Governance*, ed. H. Anheier and Y. R. Isar (London: Sage, 2012), 235–42; Mark Gibson, "The Schillers of the Suburbs: Creativity and Mediated Sociality," *International Journal of Cultural Policy* 17, no. 5 (2011): 523–27; Terry Flew, "Creative Suburbia: Rethinking Urban Cultural Policy—the Australian Case," *International Journal of Cultural Studies* 15, no. 3 (2012): 231–46; Terry Flew, Mark Gibson, Emma Felton, and Christy Collis, "Creative Suburbia: Cultural Research and Suburban Geographies," *International Journal of Cultural Studies* 15, no. 3 (2011): 199–203; Christy Collis, Emma Felton, and Philip Graham, "Beyond the Inner City: Real and Imagined Places in Creative Place Policy and Practice," *Information Society* 26, no. 2 (2010): 104–12; Emma Felton et al., "Resilient Creative Economies? Creative Industries on the Urban Fringe," *Continuum: Journal of Media and Cultural Studies* 24, no. 4 (2010): 131–37.

3 Donald Horne, *The Lucky Country* (Melbourne: Penguin, 1964).

4 Graeme Davison, "Australia: The First Suburban Nation?," *Journal of Urban History* 22, no. 1 (1995): 40–74.

5 Infrastructure Australia, *State of Australian Cities 2010* (Canberra: Commonwealth of Australia, 2010).

These associations, which have their strongest roots in the 1950s and 1960s, gained renewed potency during the long ascendency of the Howard government (1996–2007). The government's success rested significantly on a cultural divide: on one side, the tertiary-educated, inner-urban "elites" concerned with identity politics and ecological issues, and on the other, suburban "battlers" and "tradies" (self-employed tradespeople), more interested in jobs and the cost of living.[9] The conservative championing of suburban "common sense" has been met in kind by political progressives who lament the proliferation of what have been derisorily termed *McMansions*. These large, standardized houses, built in MPCs, are seen as prime symbols of environmentally unsustainable living, pursued by heavily indebted families chasing a false consumerist dream.[10] This cultural divide has long been a rich source of comedic material. The popular Australian television programs *Kath & Kim* and *Upper Middle Bogan*, for example, satirize the lives of outer-suburban "aspirationals" and the perceived lack of cultural capital commensurate with their economic prosperity.[11]

This context, in which art and culture have been routinely associated with urbanity, is not an immediately promising one for considering the possibilities of creativity and creative industries in the suburbs. And, indeed, creative industries development policy in Australia has largely been driven by an assumption that commercial creativity is a predominantly inner-urban phenomenon. For example, the Australian Local Government Association used Richard Florida's urban-centric "creative place" indexes to determine which places in Australia were the most creative and therefore most likely "to be successful in the modern globalized economy."[12] The winners were (in order): Sydney,

Inner Melbourne, the Australian Capital Territory, Central Perth, Central Adelaide, and Brisbane City. Not surprisingly, Australia's outer suburbs ranked poorly. When cultural and economic development policy is grounded in the assumption that creative industries are inevitably associated with dense urbanity and inner-urban amenities, it overlooks outer suburbia as a site of activity in creative industries.

Creative Workers in the Suburbs
Yet all studies of where cultural workers are actually located in Australia have suggested that they are as likely to be found in the suburbs of the major cities as in the urban centers, and that their movement to the urban fringes has accelerated in recent years.[13] This is consistent with wider tendencies. A marked development of suburban life since the urban consolidation of the 1980s is that suburbs are now places of service, retail, and light industries. More people now work in the middle and outer suburbs than they have during any other period. In Melbourne, for instance, 74 percent of the population work in the suburbs, and only 14 percent work in Melbourne's inner city and central business districts.[14] Nor is suburban employment confined to those working in the service industries: a significant number of professional jobs are also now located in the Australian suburbs.[15]

It is this disjuncture between perceptions and observed realities that prompted the three research questions that informed the "Creative Suburbia" project. First, we explored whether workers in the cultural and creative industries were more likely or less likely than other Australians to relocate to the outer suburbs. Was such movement primarily driven by "push" factors such as rising inner-city housing costs or by "pull" factors associated with the attractions of living in the less densely populated suburbs? Next, we asked how they felt about the development of their

6   Pauline McGuirk and Robyn Dowling, "Understanding Master-Planned Estates in Australian Cities: A Framework for Research," *Urban Policy and Research* 25, no. 1 (2007): 21–38.

7   Sue Turnbull, "Mapping the Vast Suburban Tundra: Australian Comedy from Dame Edna to Kath and Kim," *International Journal of Cultural Studies* 11, no. 1 (2008): 15–32.

8   Hugh Stretton, *Ideas for Australian Cities* (Melbourne: Penguin, 1970); Alan Gilbert, "The Roots of Australian Anti-Suburbanism," in *Australian Cultural History*, ed. S. Goldberg and F. B. Smith (Cambridge: Cambridge University Press, 1988), 33–49; Bill Randolph, "The Changing Australian City: New Patterns, New Policies and New Research Needs," *Urban Policy and Research* 22, no. 4 (2004): 481–93.

9   See, e.g., Allan Ashbolt, "Godzone—3) Myth and Reality," *Meanjin* 25, no. 4 (1966): 373–88.

10   Clive Hamilton and Richard Denniss, *Affluenza* (Sydney: Allen & Unwin, 2005).

11   Turnbull, "Mapping"; Barbara Pini and Josephine Previte, "Bourdieu, the Boom, and Cashed-Up Bogans," *Journal of Sociology* 49, nos. 2–3 (2013): 256–71.

12   National Economics, *The State of the Regions* (Melbourne: National Economics and the Australian Local Government Association, 2002), 1.

13   Chris Gibson and Chris Brennan-Horley, "Goodbye Pram City: Beyond Inner/Outer Zone Binaries in Creative City Research," *Urban Policy and Research* 24 (2006): 455–71.

14   Alan Davies, "The Structure of Suburban Employment in Melbourne" (PhD diss., University of Melbourne, 2000).

creative opportunities. Was being located in the suburbs and away from urban centers a disadvantage, or did it provide them with new affordances?

And, third, we wanted to know if there were there any policy implications from such findings. In particular, Australian governments, following the international trend of the 2000s, were investing in urban cultural amenities in order to attract the creative workforce.[16] Was the focus on inner cities misconceived? Might other forms of cultural investment, such as high-speed broadband infrastructure in the outer suburbs, be more beneficial than the standard "creative cities" policy menu of more bicycle paths, gay-friendly neighborhoods, and inner-city arts centers?

The concept of the creative industries goes back to the Blair government in the United Kingdom and the *Creative Industries Mapping Document* developed by the Department of Culture, Media and Sport (DCMS 1998) and has since seen significant developments and refinements. It is not possible here to discuss these here, but in broad terms our project adopted the Australian Culture and Leisure Classifications definition of creative enterprises, which includes: literature and print media; performing arts; visual arts; design; broadcasting; digital media; film and video and other arts.[17]

The study took place in six outer suburbs of Brisbane and Melbourne, two state capital cities situated on the east coast of Australia, separated by about 1,200 miles (2,000 kilometers). For the purpose of the study, an outer suburb was defined as being two-thirds or more of the distance from the center of the city to the urban periphery. Both Melbourne and Brisbane have experienced significant growth since the end of the twentieth century, with Melbourne's population now at approximately four million, and Brisbane at two million. (fig. **3.5.1**)

To explore the experience of working in an outer suburban location, we conducted over 150 in-depth interviews with creative industries practitioners and workers over a two-year period. The interviews consisted of open-ended questions and canvassed participants' decision-making processes regarding living and working in the suburbs. We also explored their experience of locality in relation to work, such as markets, audiences, and creative inspiration. Networking factors such as access to clients, markets, supplies, and the use of technology for overcoming distance were also investigated.

The study was focused on workers in creative industries who were able to support themselves primarily from their creative work, and interview data revealed that participants fell into one of two distinct categories. We termed these groups "commercial creatives" and "artisans." The "commercial creatives" worked predominantly in design-based industries: graphics, the web, architecture, interior design, and fashion. The "artisans" either worked in and/or ran a small to medium enterprise (SME), and were involved in generally individual creative endeavors, such as visual art, music, or writing. Participants from both commercial and artisan groups have different audiences and markets, which informed their relationship with their locality as a work environment. Thus, each group had a set of distinct responses to questions about the nature of their relationship with their outer suburb and what it meant for their creative work.

For example, a design-based commercial practitioner with an SME may have a complex business structure in comparison to an artisan; he or she is usually an employer with several staff members. Commercial creatives have a different set of networks than artisans. While many artisans operate among other artists in

15 Alan Davies, "Suburban Employment Trends: A Melbourne Case Study," *M/C Journal* 14, no. 4 (2011): http://journal .media-culture.org.au /index.php/mcjournal /article/viewArticle/358.

16 Michael Storper and Allen J. Scott, "Rethinking Human Capital, Creativity, and Urban Growth," *Journal of Economic Geography* 9, no. 1 (2009): 147–67.

17 Stuart Cunningham et al., *Brisbane's Creative Industries 2003*, Report prepared for Brisbane City Council, Community and Economic Development (Brisbane: CIRAC, 2003).

3.5.1 The outer suburbs of Australian cities are typically low-density, mixed-use zones such as Frankston—a research site for "Creative Suburbia"—on the outer edge of metropolitan Melbourne.

3.5.2 Creative industries often require space that can only be found at reasonable cost in the suburbs. Pictured here are industrial sheds in Redcliffe in Brisbane—a research sites for "Creative Suburbia"—housing a public art sculptor, a glass artist, advertising and web-design agencies, and other creative enterprises.

similar communities of practice, commercial creatives tend to tap into local business networks.

The vast majority of participants—94 percent—regarded their suburban place as significant to their creative work. Several key findings emerged from the interviews about lifestyle factors, space and serenity, and financial concerns.

The Creative Lifestyle

One of the main considerations in participants' decisions to live and work in an outer suburb was the quality of life it provides. This was common across both commercial and artisan groups, with affordability of the workplace and the home providing benefits that were articulated in terms of space and lifestyle. People value the space and tranquility of the outer suburbs, and the ability to buy a house with enough room for a studio or home office. Participants also liked the opportunity to buy or rent an outer suburban office or workplace at much lower cost than in the inner city. Many participants had families: outdoor space for children and for entertaining was important to them. (fig. **3.5.2**)

The "Creative Suburbia" interview data also point out that stage of life considerations are a key factor in attracting creative industries workers to outer suburbia. In their analysis of creative industries in rural areas of the United States, the economists David McGranahan and Timothy Wojan found that "the creative class is diffusing outward from central cities, growing most rapidly in sparsely settled suburbs," but that this shift is missed by studies that focus on a specific demographic: young and often childless.[18] The "Creative Suburbia" study produced corresponding findings: a significant number of interviewees had lived and worked in inner-city areas in their twenties, but had moved to the outer suburbs once they entered later stages of life,

and once they had children. This is not in itself a surprising finding, but it does mean that indexes of the types of places that attract creative industries' workers may need some recalibration to reflect stage-of-life considerations. An active music scene, for example, may attract some creative workers, but for many of those with children, amenities such as primary schools and sports fields may play a more important role.

Losses and Gains for Creative Work in the Suburbs

Participants with SMEs acknowledged that the attractions of a suburban lifestyle came with a trade-off: having a business in an outer suburb, rather than in the urban core (where they could most likely generate more business and earn a higher income) was a financial sacrifice.

Similarly, commercial creatives indicated that outer suburban business locations meant a loss of some professional networking opportunities. With many professional association functions held in inner cities, outer-suburban workers who did not want to, or could not, attend lost out on the types of interaction that stimulate cultural innovation and client base growth. Several outer-suburban commercial creatives observed that their local chamber of commerce business development infrastructure did not meet the specific needs of creative industries workers. Judy, a fashion designer, articulated the difference between her approach to business and that of a local business-networking group:

> They don't work the way I work basically… everybody had to stand up and say what their five year plan was and what they do… and how they got to this point. Very business focused. I'm not in the slightest like that so when I stood up and said well actually it grows depending on my clientele and depending on where I want to take

18　David McGranahan and Timothy Wojan, "Recasting the Creative Class to Examine Growth Processes in Rural and Urban Countries," *Regional Studies* 41, no. 2 (2007): 214.

it. So when I stood up and said that's how I work, I was shot down.[19]

Another commercial creative similarly noted that he had been unsuccessful with securing business development grants from the local, outer-suburban chamber of commerce because the grants programs were not designed to accommodate creative industries' business models. To some extent, creative workers' lack of networking opportunities and disconnect from outer-suburban business development organizations derive from the core assumption that creative industries are concentrated in inner-urban locales. A shift in outer-suburban business development policy and perspective could address these issues.

Suburban creatives who experience these difficulties are, at the same time, seeing benefits to the suburban environment, cultural and affective factors that they regard as conducive to their creative endeavors. Participants frequently invoked ambient and affective descriptors such as "tranquil," "serene," and "freedom" to describe their location. The natural environment (two of the suburbs are bayside localities) was also regarded as a resource for many people from the artisan group. One artist used bark and leaves to make paper and sculptural pieces. The findings of our project were similar to those in a study by the cultural studies scholars Chris Gibson and Susan Luckman of creative workers in Darwin, a small tropical city in Australia's far north, in which "the natural environment is without doubt seen as fundamental to local creativity."[20]

Questioning Inner-Urban Bias

Two findings from the project run directly counter to significant strands in the creative cities literature. The first concerns the importance of the cultural stimulation that is thought to be provided by an urban milieu. This is a major theme, for example, in Richard Florida's theorization of the "creative class": "Cities are cauldrons of creativity. They have long been the vehicles for mobilizing, concentrating and channeling human creative energy."[21]

The statement raises questions about what precisely is meant by *city*. Is it an urbanized region that includes the suburbs, or an inner-urban core? There is considerable slippage between the two. Florida's arguments gain much of their intuitive appeal from the visible energy and vibrancy of the inner city, while he is able at the same time to annex more "ordinary" suburban zones, such as Silicon Valley, by representing them as part of larger metropolitan regions. It is clear, nevertheless, that the primary emphasis in creativity theory is on the inner urban core, the idea that creative practitioners will always be drawn to the buzz of downtown zones with high bohemian and gay indexes.

Many of the interviewees for "Creative Suburbia" expressed skepticism about such assumptions. As a number pointed out, what might appear as the "stimulation" of the inner city could also be seen as distraction. Ready access to entertainment, cultural events, and social networks have their attractions, but also take time and energy that might otherwise be spent on developing one's own creative practice.

Another common view, particularly among musicians and artists, was that the inner city imposes pressures to conform, inhibiting creative freedom. As it was put by a visual artist from Frankston in outer suburban Melbourne, in the city "you have to wear the right clothes, have to go to the right exhibitions, have to go, you know."[22] This position reverses the charges of conformism that have been so widely laid against the suburbs, inscribing suburbia, not the city, as the site of creative independence and experimentation. It suggests that the polarity of such

19 Fashion designer, Redcliffe, interview with the authors, September 25, 2009.
20 Susan Luckman, "Creativity, the Environment, and the Future of Creative Lifestyles: Lessons from a Creative Tropical City," *International Journal of the Humanities* 7, no. 6 (2009): 7.
21 Richard Florida, *Cities and the Creative Class* (New York: Routledge, 2005), 1.
22 Visual artist, Frankston, interview with the authors, October 23, 2009.

charges is fluid and relative, reminding us of other times and places in which the bohemian and even the gay have been readily associated with the relative social sparseness and openness of suburbia.[23]

Suburban Diversity

The second finding that questions the inner-city bias relates to diversity.[24] It is probably true that there is a relation between diversity and creativity. However, at least in Australia, it is now questionable whether diversity is found in the inner city. The past thirty years have seen an extraordinary increase in the cost of inner urban property, so much so that it has become some of the most expensive in the world.[25] For any creative practitioner other than the most established, the inner city is now too expensive a place to work and live.

Apart from small pockets around inner-urban public housing, new migrants have also been driven to the suburban fringe. The inner city has become characterized by high-end consumption and retail outlets, and a predominantly professional population, making it relatively culturally homogeneous. By contrast, outer suburbs like Dandenong—one of the project's research sites in Melbourne— have become extraordinarily diverse, with 56 percent of the population born overseas in more than 156 different countries.[26] If diversity does indeed drive creativity, it is these suburbs that we might look for the next generation of cultural innovation.

To return to our opening questions, we found, in summary, that the decision by creative practitioners to locate in the suburbs was not informed only by "push" factors. The latter are obvious and widely cited: clearly, the cost of property and rents in the inner city is a significant driver. However, there are also a number of "pull" factors that lead creative practitioners to locate in the suburbs, including space, natural amenity, time to think

and reflect, freedom from the conformist pressures of inner-urban clique,s and, increasingly, cultural diversity. There is probably too much "exceptionalism" in relation to creative practitioners. Our research suggests that their decisions on location were similar in many respects to other areas of the population. There are significant differences among creative practitioners as there are within other groups. A certain, highly visible inner-urban sector should not be taken as representative of all.

Policies for Suburban Creative Industries

The suburbs are sites of creative businesses and workers. But this statistical fact runs up against a conceptual barrier: the deeply rooted cultural assumption that suburbs are geographies of consumption rather than production, conformity rather than creativity, and homogeneity rather than diversity. This assumption continues to inform creative industries policy and analysis in Australia and elsewhere.[27]

The most obvious recommendations flowing from this perspective are for greater investment in cultural venues and educational or training opportunities in the suburbs. "Creative Suburbia" found that there are compelling arguments in terms of industry development for such cultural provisions in the suburbs, beside better-known arguments in terms of equity.[28] But there are also less obvious actions that could be taken to stimulate creative industries in suburban locations. Examples here include attention to practical issues such as public transport, affordable housing, and building regulations, which often inhibit the adaptation of domestic dwellings to accommodate studios and other light-work spaces. Communication infrastructure is also important, particularly broadband internet. In Australia, arts and cultural policy have generally been developed without

23 Martin Dines, Gay *Suburban Narratives in American and British Culture* (New York: Palgrave, 2010); Wayne H. Brekhus, *Peacocks, Chameleons, Centaurs: Gay Suburbia and the Grammar of Social Identity* (Chicago: University of Chicago Press, 2003); Andrew McCann, "Decomposing Suburbia: Patrick White's Perversity," *Australian Literary Studies* 18, no. 4 (1998): 56–71.

24 Allen J. Scott, "The Cultural Economy: Geography and the Creative Field," *Media, Culture, and Society* 21 (1999): 807–17; Charles Landry, *The Creative City: A Toolkit for Urban Innovators* (London: Earthscan, 2000); Thomas Hutton, "Spatiality, Built Form, and Creative Industry Development in the Inner City," *Environment and Planning A* 38, no. 10 (2006): 1819–41.

25 Alain Bertaud, "Tenth Annual Demographia International Housing Affordability Survey 2014," Wendell Cox Consultancy, accessed January 12, 2015, http://www.demographia.com/dhi.pdf.

26 City of Greater Dandenong, "Summary of Social Conditions in Greater Dandenong 2007," City of Dandenong, accessed November 23, 2011, http://www.greaterdandenong.com/Documents.asp?ID=10768&Title=Summaries+of+social+information+CGD&Type=d.

27 Andrey Petrov, "Talent in the Cold? Creative Capital and the Economic Future of the Canadian North," *Arctic* 61, no. 2 (2008): 162–76; Nick A. Phelps, "Suburbs for Nations? Some Interdisciplinary Connections on the Suburban Economy," *Cities* 27 (2010): 68–76.

28 Mark Gibson, "*Bildung* in the 'Burbs: Education for the Suburban Nation," *International Journal of Cultural Studies* 15, no. 3 (2012): 247–57.

reference to media and communication policy. There is a strong case in the development of suburban creative industries for them to be brought closer together.[29]

Australia's outer-suburban creative industries do not look like the stereotypical images of the creative industries cluster and creative *milieu*. They feature few dense agglomerations of cafes, galleries, and businesses; few hipsters on single-speed bicycles; and few government-funded creative precincts and creative business incubators. Regarded through this perceptual lens, Australia's outer suburbs are indeed places of little interest to creative industries policy makers or analysts.

Despite this, research confirms that the suburbs are sites of significance for the Australian creative industries: the "Creative Suburbia" project, along with similar studies conducted by the cultural studies scholars Chris Gibson and Chris Brennan-Horley, and Susan Luckman.[30] Ensuring that our policy addresses this economic geography of creativity means adjusting deeply ingrained assumptions about what suburbs are, what creative industries look like, and how they work. As the scholar Nicholas Phelps states, "It seems inevitable that academic and policy interest will have to address the topic of suburban creativity if our economic well-being is to be better understood and supported."[31]

29 Flew, "Creative Suburbia."

30 Gibson and Brennan-Horley, "Goodbye Pram City"; Luckman, "Creativity, the Environment."

31 Nick A. Phelps, "The Sub-Creative Economy of the Suburbs in Question," *International Journal of Cultural Studies*, 15, no. 3 (2012): 269.

3.6
THE GLOBAL SUBURB

DIVESTING FROM THE WORLD'S WHITE PICKET FENCES

Roger Keil

NEOLIBERAL PROPERTY MARKETS

SOCIAL DIVERSITY

SOCIAL INEQUALITIES

3.6.1 North American suburbia, Toronto, Canada

The explosion of the historic city was precisely the occasion for finding a larger theory of the city, and not a pretext for abandoning the problem.

—Henri Lefebvre

It is time to argue for an intervention into urban theory on the basis of the suburban explosion. Today, we are facing new realities of globalized urbanization, where central city and fringe are remixed. In this period of the postsuburban planet, new forms on the periphery blend together; the result has been a different suburbia and a different city. In simple terms and following the definition of the historian Jon Teaford, global postsuburbanization refers to myriad forms of "suburbanization carried to the extreme, the end product of two centuries of continuous deconcentration of metropolitan population" (and one might add of economic activities).[1]

Often, suburbs have rightly been discussed as a phenomenon associated with the Anglo-Saxon societal model.[2] Private land ownership, consumerist capitalism, and the ideology of freedom prevalent in the United Kingdom and British settler societies have made Australia, Canada, the United States, and, to some degree, Britain itself ideal places for the prototypical single-family home residential suburb to thrive during the twentieth century.

But Anglo-Saxon suburbia needs to be reevaluated in a global context. To examine its origins and role in a global light, we start from the assumption that suburbanization precedes the modern period and capitalist property relations but attains particular significance as a form of the production of space in capitalist societies.[3] Suburbanization has been an aspect of what Henri Lefebvre refers to as the "explosion" of the city.[4] It is necessary to depart from the common wisdom on suburbanization as a chiefly American domain in two important ways. The Anglo-Saxon model, most often associated with the United States, is dominant in reality and in the literature and important to acknowledge. But it obscures historical parallels and alternatives in suburbanization. There have always been different pathways to peripheral urban development, even in the American century that

Epigraph: Henri Lefebvre and Kristin Ross, "Finding a Larger Theory of the City: Henri Lefebvre und die Situationistische Internationale," *Dérive* 58 (2015): 45–50.

1   Jon Teaford, "Suburbia and Post-Suburbia," in *International Perspectives on Suburbanization: A Post-Suburban World?*, ed. Nicholas A. Phelps and Fulong Wu (Basingstoke, UK; New York: Palgrave Macmillan, 2011), 15–34.

2   Anne Forsyth, "Defining Suburbs," *Journal of Planning Literature* 27, no. 3 (2012): 270–81; Richard Harris, "Meaningful Types in a World of Suburbs," in *Suburbanization in Global Society*, ed. Mark Clapson and Ray Hutchison, vol. 10 (Bingley, UK: Emerald, 2010), 15–47; Jussi S. Jauhiainen, "Suburbs," in *The Oxford Handbook of Cities in World History*, ed. Peter Clark (Oxford: Oxford University Press, 2013), 791–809; Roger Keil, ed., *Suburban Constellations: Governance, Land, and Infrastructure in the Twenty-First Century* (Berlin: Jovis Verlag, 2013).

3   Anthony D. King, *Spaces of Global Cultures: Architecture, Urbanism, Identity* (London; New York: Routledge, 2004), 98; Richard Walker, "A Theory of Suburbanization: Capitalism and the Construction of Urban Space in the United States," in *Urbanization and Urban Planning in Capitalist Society*, ed. Michael J. Dear and Allen John Scott (London; New York: Methuen, 1981), 383–430.

4   Henri Lefebvre, *The Urban Revolution* (Minneapolis: University of Minnesota Press, 2003).

just ended. More important, in recent years, newer forms of suburbanization that give rise to the need for rethinking urban theory overall have sprung up around the world. (fig. **3.6.1**)

The Anglo-Saxon Suburb Revisited
Jon Teaford reminds us that historically, it was predominantly the unwelcomed functions, people, and activities that were once pushed to the periphery and beyond.[5] And yet, suburbanization also has its roots in bourgeois society. Wealthy patricians historically spent at least some of their year in the countryside in order to escape the effects of dense urban life that were considered negative, while the countryside was idealized as a pure idyll.

The notion of an escape from the city has a particular significance in the historiography of suburbanization. It denotes a foundational tendency that is captured by the scholar P. D. Smith, writing about the United States: "The suburbs offered a safe haven, a bourgeois utopia whose semirural location made possible a relaxed, outdoor lifestyle…affirming values deemed central to American society, such as the sanctity of the family and property ownership."[6]

The Anglo-Saxon single-family home suburb is often taken as the benchmark against which all suburbs are measured. In fact, as the eminent cultural and architectural historian and global city theorist Anthony King has observed, suburbanization (suburbia "both as settlement form and lifestyle") is part of the more general narrative of modern urbanization that is written as the contrasting script to the "traditional city."[7] At the beginning of the twentieth century, suburbanization developed from a necessary expansion of the old city to planned invention of a novel urban form. This new urban form was articulated not with classical notions of privilege, as has been the case with the mansions of the landed gentry, or with

exclusion, as in the *bidonvilles* of the early modern city. Suburbanization was now part of the reproduction of capital at a scale previously unknown.

The production of suburban space and the accumulation of capital became one and the same during much of the twentieth century. A particular form of development in the United States set the pace and created the imagery for this push. Here, more than anywhere else, the construction of the suburbs was instrumental in the "suburban solution" of capitalist overproduction crises. The erection of single-family homes on a massive scale, along with their associated shopping centers, was an ideal platform for the shift of capital from the (glutted) production sector into societal consumption.[8] Suburbanization created the environment for the consumer society of the post–World War II period. Apart from producing living space itself, it offered a close to limitless opportunity to create consumer demand for household gadgets, automobiles, electronics, and other commodities during the Fordist era of mass production. (fig. **3.6.2**)

This historically specific form of suburbanization, which came to define it, is also present in non-Anglo societies, like Germany and France. It is central not just to the shape and the relationships of the suburb and its ways of life but also to how urban research has traditionally viewed these processes. This historical form of suburbanization is predominantly tied to three important dynamics: homeownership, industrialization, and displacement.

Homeownership
In Anglo-American societies, and more pronouncedly in settler democracies of the New World, landed property, and particularly the suburban home, became the symbol of successful arrival, liberation from European shackles of status and

5   Teaford, "Suburbia and Post-Suburbia," 15.
6   Peter D. Smith, *City: A Guidebook for the Urban Age* (New York: Bloomsbury, 2012), 145.
7   King, *Spaces of Global Cultures*, 97.
8   Walker, "A Theory of Suburbanization: Capitalism and the Construction of Urban Space in the United States," 383–430.

3.6.2 Los Angeles subdivision

3.6.3 Industrial suburbanization, Los Angeles, California

class, and self-determination and cultural autonomy of the individual. The cultural preference for homeownership, supported by state policy and market institutions, is an important marker in the way housing development (and ancillary commercial and industrial development) is structured in space.[9] Suburbia was made possible by cheap land and energy and by the financial institutions that supported the purchase of affordable mass-produced, single-family homes on green fields at the urban periphery. This was the birth of the "drive till you qualify" formula of affordable homeownership that is often considered the origin myth of sprawl.

Industrialization

Suburbanization included the relocation (or new siting) of certain industrial and commercial functions from the city. Antiurban tendencies did not just characterize the residential populations of the home countries of United States immigrants (more a produced than an innate preference for sure); they were also integral to the ideologies of industrial pioneers like Henry Ford, who deliberately ran his famous assembly lines in the suburbs of Detroit. For the geographers Richard Walker and Robert Lewis, the role played by industrialization in the formation of suburbia is central.[10] Submetropolitan industrial districts, metropolitan labor markets, capitalist strategies, the needs of different economic sectors, and all manner of other factors influence the specific locational mix of the overall suburbanizing region. Part and parcel of industrialization were the "massification" of housing production itself and the expansion of mobility networks.[11] (fig. **3.6.3**)

Displacement

Suburbanization has historically been tied to displacement.[12] The American case displays a historical specificity in this context

that overshadows the debate about suburbanization through the present time. The so-called flight to the suburbs has been strongly overlaid with racializing or even racist tones. Suburbia has often been discussed in connection with the deliberate and planned efforts of white people of all social classes to distance themselves from African Americans, who at the same time became increasingly concentrated (and segregated) in the inner city.[13] While this unfortunate application of the flight metaphor in the context of suburbanization is specific to the United States, suburbanization as a sociospatial distancing strategy is a universal phenomenon. Especially today, in the age of privatized suburban developments, forms of private authoritarianism such as gated communities are increasingly a general experience.[14]

That said, the Anglo-Saxon "picket-fence" tradition is neither insular nor the only game in town. The massive post-Levittown sprawl of single-family homes in North America—from New York to Lakewood, California, and up through the peripheries of Quebec City—has necessarily clouded our collective memory; we no longer keep in mind that modern suburbia was a hybrid product from the very start.[15] The suburbs of the British Empire themselves had global roots. The modern American (or Anglo-Saxon) suburb certainly thrived on the colonial grid with its shared, property-oriented logic. This is where "house lust," as the Canadian urbanist Humphrey Carver called it, could unfold and be realized for the aspiring European immigrants.[16] But it got all its constitutive and spare parts from elsewhere. The bungalow, next to the veranda-fronted house, the ranch house, and the single-story villa, was as an archetype of the single-family home not just in the suburbs of the United Kingdom, the Americas, and Australia but more generally around the world. A truly global

9   Louise C. Johnson, "Desire, Dryness, and Decadence," in *Suburban Constellations: Governance, Land, and Infrastructure in the Twenty-First Century*, ed. Roger Keil (Berlin: Jovis Verlag, 2013), 190–94; Louise C. Johnson, "Governing Suburban Australia," in *Suburban Governance: A Global View*, ed. Roger Keil and Pierre Hamel (Toronto: University of Toronto Press, 2015); Roger Keil et al., "Modalities of Suburban Governance in Canada," in *Suburban Governance: A Global View*, ed. Pierre Hamel and Roger Keil (Toronto: University of Toronto Press, 2015); Jan Nijman and Tom Clery, "The United States: Suburban Imaginaries and Metropolitan Realities," in *Suburban Governance: A Global View*, ed. Roger Keil and Pierre Hamel (Toronto: University of Toronto Press, 2015); Jamie Peck, "Neoliberal Suburbanism," in *Suburban Governance: A Global View*, ed. Pierre Hamel and Roger Keil (Toronto: University of Toronto Press, 2015).

10 Richard Walker and Robert D. Lewis, "Beyond the Crabgrass Frontier: Industry and the Spread of North American Cities, 1850–1950," *Journal of Historical Geography Journal of Historical Geography* 27, no. 1 (2001): 9.

11 Nathaniel Baum-Snow, "Did Highways Cause Suburbanization?," *Quarterly Journal of Economics* 122, no. 2 (May 2007): 776.

12 Lefebvre, *The Urban Revolution*, 109.

13 Leah P. Boustan and Robert A. Margo, "A Silver Lining to White Flight? White Suburbanization and African–American Homeownership, 1940–1980," *Journal of Urban Economics* 78 (November 1, 2013): 71–80.

14 Michael Ekers, Pierre Hamel, and Roger Keil, "Governing Suburbia: Modalities and Mechanisms of

3.6.4 California bungalow, foreclosed

phenomenon, the one-story house has its origins in the distinctive imperialist history of Britain's colonization of India.[17] The imperial connection was kept alive as American consumerism was subsequently projected into the world with iconic images of suburban bliss; that America was ready to follow up the image with deeds was made clear whenever its armies put "boots on the ground" to safeguard the empire's global interests in defense of the suburban dream at home.[18] (fig. **3.6.4**)

Still, the process of global suburbanization, even in the modern period, was never a mere extension of the North American model. Lefebvre reminds us of the explosive growth of the Paris suburbs after World War II: "You know that there were very few suburbs in Paris; there were some, but very few. And then suddenly the whole area was filled, covered with little houses, with new cities."[19] The conditions under which these postwar suburbs and their successors were produced (and consumed) differed greatly from the Anglo-Saxon prototype. For one, there was always more direct involvement by the state.[20] The building typologies were mixed as well. The "little houses,"

the *pavillons* that Lefebvre saw originally mushroom around Paris, grew in tandem with the *grands ensembles* (tower in the park, disparagingly called the "habitat" by Lefebvre). Both congealed into a specific postsuburban landscape with variable densities that now house much, if not most, of the metropolitan population in France's large urban centers.[21] Canada, in breaking with the tradition of its neighbor to the south, often saw the same kind of mix, the single-family home and the tower in the park, as the distinctive landscape of its suburbia.[22]

Moreover, we have the different national and regional processes through which those suburbs were produced, even in the classic post–World War II period. Perhaps the first most visible alternative to the picket fences of North America is the large housing estates that were built on the "green" periphery all over the large Fordist North Atlantic countries such as, Great Britain, France, West Germany, and Canada.[23] These estates arose on an even larger scale in the countries of what friends and foes of the Warsaw Pact states came to call "real existing socialism"–the actual societies of the former Soviet Union

Suburban Governance," *Regional Studies* 46, no. 3 (2012): 405–22.

15 Andrée Fortin, "The Suburbs and the Bungalow Heritage in the Making," *The Encyclopedia of French Cultural Heritage in North America*, accessed March 30, 2015, http://www.ameriquefrancaise.org/en/article-612/The_suburbs_and_the_bungalow_heritage_in_the_making.html.

16 I am indebted to Steven Logan's fine dissertation "In the Suburbs of History," for this insight (Steven Logan, "In the Suburbs of History" [PhD diss., York University, Communications and Culture, 2015]). Logan discusses the importance of the house and the debates around it in the modernist discourses on urbanism between European and North American suburbanization in the twentieth century. Logan's work also points to a larger and more diversified ecology of suburban form than the one schematically discussed in this present argument that focuses on the British-colonial angle predominantly. Morphological and design considerations as well as moral attributions were meshed with Fordist political economies in these mostly transatlantic conversations among architects and planners from Eastern Europe to California. Interestingly, the generalized and in Europe often preferred "other" of the single-family house was the large housing estate in a modernist "settlement."

17 King, *Spaces of Global Cultures*.

18 Roger Keil, "Empire and the Global City: Perspectives of Urbanism after 9/11," *Studies in Political Economy: A Socialist Review* 79 (Spring 2007): 167–92.

19 Lefebvre and Ross, "Finding a Larger Theory of the City," 50.

3.6.5 Mitchell's Plain, Cape Town

20 Mustafa Dikec, *Badlands of the Republic: Space, Politics, and Urban Policy* (Malden, MA; Oxford: Blackwell Publishers, 2007); Stefan Kipfer, "Démolition et contre-révolution: La rénovation urbaine dans la région parisienne," *Période*, October 5, 2015.

21 Eric Charmes and Roger Keil, "The Politics of Post-Suburban Densification in Canada and France," *International Journal of Urban and Regional Research* 39, no. 3 (May 1, 2015): 581–602.

22 Douglas Young and Roger Keil, "Locating the Urban In-Between: Tracking the Urban Politics of Infrastructure in Toronto," *International Journal of Urban and Regional Research* 38, no. 5 (September 2014): 1589–608.

23 Charmes and Keil, "The Politics of Post-Suburban Densification in Canada and France."

24 Ibid.

25 Viktória Szirmai, *Urban Sprawl in Europe: Similarities or Differences?* (Budapest: Aula Kiadó, 2011).

26 Anthony D. King, *Spaces of Global Cultures: Architecture, Urbanism, Identity* (London; New York: Routledge, 2004), 103.

and its former satellites—where hundreds of millions of housing units (and factories) mushroomed in peripheral urban extensions. The second most prominent alternative is the ever-expanding self-built and squatter settlements in urban areas of the Global South—that is, Africa, Latin America, and developing Asia, including the Middle East. (fig. **3.6.5**)

In contrast to the mostly privatized suburbanization in North America (albeit subsidized through tax and other incentives by the state), suburban housing during high Fordism in Europe was mostly produced by state-led or co-op development and management corporations. In both western and eastern Europe, these estates became the focal points of a new urban crisis at the beginning of the twenty-first century, as planners and developers started to cultivate buzzwords such as *density, compactness, reurbanization, New Urbanism,* and *the creative city.*[24] In Eastern Europe, liberalization and deregulation of urban planning is leading to sprawl beyond peripheral high-rise estates.[25] (fig. **3.6.6**)

Globalized Sub/Urbanization

King speaks of diversity in the age of the postcolonial "globurb," by which he means "forms and settlements on the outskirts of the city, the origins of which—economic, social, cultural, architectural—are generated less by developments inside the city, or even inside the country, and more by external forces beyond its boundaries," and adds importantly that,

> dependent on their location, many of such suprurbs or globurbs, as with previous historical experience, continue to be generated not just by "international" or "global" forces but, more particularly, by those of imperialism, colonialism, nationalism, as well as the diasporic migratory cultures and capital flows of global capitalism.[26]

In the Global South, urbanization exploded predominantly as a result of the country-to-city migration that began in the middle of the twentieth century, first in Latin America and more recently across Asia and Africa. The majority of the newcomers move to places on informal urban peripheries, often squatter settlements, resulting

3.6.6 Scarborough high-rise intersection, Toronto, Canada

27 Teresa Caldeira, "São Paulo: The City and Its Protest," *openDemocracy*, accessed March 30, 2015, https://www.open democracy.net/open-security/teresa-caldeira /s%C3%A3o-paulo-city -and-its-protest.

28 Doug Saunders, *Arrival City: The Final Migration and Our Next World* (Toronto: Vintage Canada, 2011).

29 Robin Bloch, "Africa's New Suburbs," in *Suburban Governance: A Global View*, ed. Pierre Hamel and Roger Keil (Toronto: University of Toronto Press, 2015); Shubhra Gururani and Burak Kose, "Shifting Terrain: Questions of Governance in India's Cities and Their Peripheries," in *Suburban Governance: A Global View*, ed. Roger Keil and Pierre Hamel (Toronto: University of Toronto Press, 2015); Alan Mabin, "Suburbanisms in Africa?," in *Suburban Constellations: Governance, Land and Infrastructure in the 21st Century*, ed. Roger Keil (Berlin: Jovis Verlag, 2013); Fulong Wu and Jie Shen, "Suburban Development and Governance in China," in *Suburban Governance: A Global View*, ed. Pierre Hamel and Roger Keil (Toronto: University of Toronto Press, 2015).

(as in São Paulo) in "a dispersed city in which long distances separate the center from the peripheries."[27] The destinations of this rural-to-urban migration have been called "arrival cities."[28] In the metropolitan centers of Turkey, China, and India, large-scale high-rise neighborhoods surround the urban centers, where many of the in-migrants and those expelled from the gentrifying inner cities live. A large part of this primary peri-urbanization—this creation of the urban fringe—occurs in the form of gated communities.[29]

What are the intertwined processes that enabled and furthered the increased suburbanization and made suburbia the global dreamscape of the current epoch? Post-Fordism, for one. In the 1950s and 1960s, the political economies of the large nation-states of the American zone of influence in the West were organized in ways that tied productivity gains to rising wage levels among the working class and hence created constant yet controlled stimulation of large-scale production, pushing out batch-normed commodities in huge assembly line operations. This regime of accumulation, safeguarded by Keynesian demand-side economics and

welfare state "safety-nets," was called "Fordism" in reference to Henry Ford, who, at the start of the twentieth century, first used large-scale mechanized production and who stabilized income for some of his core workers in his factories. Suburbanization was one of the processes through which Fordist mass production was linked to a self-generating system of mass consumption based on expectations of increasing levels of wealth among large segments of the population. This "virtuous cycle" experienced a first structural crisis in the mid-1970s. Immediately afterward, in a period that was widely referred to as "post-Fordist" at the time, much attention was paid to the rapid shift in sociospatial structures that could be observed universally. Spatial forms that were more flexible replaced the classical, functional segregations that had dominated urban development since the Charter of Athens in the 1930s. Mixed-use environments became the new normative ideal, as both urban centers and peripheries started to change. More important than the normative ideal were the tendencies among core post-Fordist industries to settle in business zones on the peripheries, where they did not have to face contaminated sites, where land was cheap, where there weren't any traditional labor union organizations, and where the relevant infrastructures for the new just-in-time economy existed.

Globalization was another key. While the globalization debate in critical urban research was concentrating primarily on global cities and their centers, the urban peripheries were becoming the actual stages for the performance of the global economy and its culture. The global city literally went out of town, away from the command centers of the financial industry and advanced producer services, but toward other important nodes of the internationalized global economies. In almost all metropolitan regions in that period, the exurban airports and their surrounding regions became centers of economic activity and relay stations of the globalized word. Frankfurt, for example, is Germany's global city. The city is distinct not just by its financial center and high-rise skyline but also by its sprawling suburban economies around the airport and peripheral office and technology exurbs that are tied into global marketplaces. These suburban economies support the global city economy but are also often without immediate connection to the core of the city. In Toronto, the city that articulates the Canadian economy into the world economy, the bustling creative and financial core could not exist without the regional economies and ecological metabolisms that sustain it. In many urban regions the suburbs have become magnets for immigration, so-called ethnoburbs. Toronto's suburbs have become a "majority minority" demographic phenomenon with its own "globurban" economies that tie into the countries from where immigrants and their networked cultures originate.[30]

Simultaneously, capitalism worldwide is undergoing processes of neoliberalization, and this, too, is furthering suburbanization. Neoliberalism values the privatization of economic decision making and responsibilities over collective solutions, and suburbanization has proved to be an ideal field for a comprehensive restructuring of social and spatial relationships. The product—suburbia—has been an especially "vulgar" form of urban development, with ostensibly displayed wealth that expresses itself in supersized homes and guarded security zones. This new landscape of neoliberal urbanism is characterized by more prominent socioeconomic polarization and segregation (which is often racialized) largely as a consequence of liberated land markets and receding welfare states. This has caused aggressive gentrification in central and suburban areas and the radical redrawing of boundaries between public and private spaces; an important aspect related to suburbanization are variants of neoliberal ecological modernization, which has subjected large swathes of land at the peripheries of cities to extensive programs of boundary redrawing, "New Urbanism," and "green development" through which ever more land is financialized, privatized, and commodified.[31]

Suburban cityscapes are now so ubiquitous that they have led to a reevaluation of urban form and process overall. To reevaluate urban form is to throw into sharp relief the multidissected, no-longer-central structure of suburbanized landscapes. We have entered a state of continuous "post-suburbanization"—a term mostly trying to denote that historical suburbs are now in a complex, politically contentious, renewal and urbanization process.[32] (fig. **3.6.7**)

Urban Theory after the Suburban Explosion

Just as the "worlding" of formerly peripheral areas in the Global South has been observed in recent analyses, the presence

30 Roger Keil, "Suburbanization and Global Cities," in *International Handbook of Globalization and World Cities*, ed. Ben Derudder (Cheltenham, UK; Northhampton, MA: Edward Elgar, 2012).

31 Paul L. Knox, *Metroburbia, USA* (New Brunswick, NJ: Rutgers University Press, 2008); Peck, "Neoliberal Suburbanism."

32 Thomas Sieverts, *Cities without Cities: An Interpretation of the Zwischenstadt* (London; New York: Spon Press, 2003); Nicholas A. Phelps and Fulong Wu, *International Perspectives on Suburbanization: A Post-Suburban World?* (Houndmills, Basingstoke, Hampshire; New York, NY: Palgrave Macmillan, 2011); Pierre Hamel and Roger Keil, eds., *Suburban Governance: A Global View* (Toronto: University of Toronto Press, 2015).

3.6.7 Postsuburban landscape in Toronto

of the global suburb in the intellectual domain of the global city can no longer be ignored.[33] Critical urban research has been traditionally skeptical toward suburbanization.[34] Inasmuch as "the essence of the modern suburb is physical, social and spatial separation," its analysis may not have revealed much in general terms about the city as a theoretical object.[35]

This may be entirely different today. The global suburb is—perhaps—less about dichotomous separation and more about multifarious connectivity, although often "the social relations of global suburbs reinforce many of the same inequalities as in the traditionally segregated city."[36] They just do so differently. Suburbanization used to be a process of distance making: classes, ethnicities, race, etc.[37] Now there is a partial reversal going on: Suburbanization turns into a process of adventurous mixing and reshuffling of the urban, while the city (as much as it still exists as a recognizable unit) becomes the rarefied monoculture of condominium-dwelling millennials who operate in safe, sterile, predictable environments.

This is the shift from the wild city to the "wild suburb," from the "habitat" to "the world's city."[38] Global suburbs, globurbs, and ethnoburbs are the new assemblages of the global that surround our cities and, as they beg for explanation, yield a host of new insights about urbanization overall.[39] The global suburb explodes and reassembles the very categories we used to associate with the single-family home behind the picket fence: home ownership, industrialization, and displacement. The global suburb is somewhat of a pendant to the global city, although it is not clear whether it carries the same cosmopolitan cache or if it is likely going to "generate anxieties about both physical and social boundaries."[40] In any case, there is evidence that global suburbs, with their immigrant-based service economies, will involve significant social stratification as well as elaborate and multiple social distinctions.[41]

Suburbia allows a view into novel property relationships between community and land, urbanization beyond industrialization, and enclaving beyond displacement. At one end of this new spectrum of suburban form and life, we find the opportunity to redefine suburban everyday life altogether.[42] In this context,

33 Ananya Roy and Aihwa Ong, *Worlding Cities: Asian Experiments and the Art of Being Global* (Chichester, UK; Malden, MA: Wiley-Blackwell, 2011); Ananya Roy, "The Twenty-First-Century Metropolis: New Geographies of Theory," *Regional Studies* 43, no. 6 (2009): 819–30; Ananya Roy, "Governing the Post-Colonial Suburbs," in *Suburban Governance: A Global View*, ed. Pierre Hamel and Roger Keil (Toronto: University of Toronto Press, 2015); Jennifer Robinson, *Ordinary Cities: Between Modernity and Development* (London; New York: Routledge, 2006); Mabin, "Suburbanisms in Africa?"; Terry McGee, "Suburbanization in a Twenty-First Century," in *Suburban Constellations: Governance, Land, and Infrastructure in the Twenty-First Century*, ed. Roger Keil (Berlin: Jovis Verlag, 2013); Shubhra Gururani, "On Capital's Edge: Gurgaon: India's Millennial City," in *Suburban Constellations: Governance, Land, and Infrastructure in the Twenty-First Century*, ed. Roger Keil (Berlin: Jovis Verlag, 2013), 182–89; Kristen Hill Maher, "Borders and Social Distinction in the Global Suburb," *American Quarterly* 56, no. 3 (2004): 781–806.
34 David Harvey, "New David Harvey Interview on Class Struggle in Urban Spaces," *Critical-Theory*, August 7, 2013, http://www.critical-theory.com/david-harvey-interview-class-struggle-urban-spaces/.
35 King, *Spaces of Global Cultures*, 99.
36 Maher, "Borders and Social Distinction in the Global Suburb," 804.
37 Ibid.
38 Manuel Castells, "The Wild City," *Kapitalistate*, nos. 4–5 (1975): 2–30; Henri Lefebvre, Eleonore Kofman, and Elizabeth Lebas, *Writings on Cities* (Cambridge, MA: Blackwell Publishers, 1996).

one would expect to find modes of organizing everyday life in ways that neither find themselves locked in an unchanging state of stasis (as the classical commuter suburbs of the twentieth century were often caricaturized) nor imagined to be catching up to a certain ideal of urbanity that draws its inspiration variably from the medieval Italian city and New York. Much of this development depends on new technologies and the rapidly evolving complexities of peripheral communities that seek their organization beyond the societal model of the Anglo-Saxon tradition. At the other, we find the dialectics of territorial control, the martial state, social neglect, and private authoritarianism; between new types of poverty and the wealth of gated communities. All across the global suburban multiverse, we find a horizontal landscape of consumption.[43]

Suburbanization is no longer a simple, concentric extension of existing urban morphologies. "Extended urbanization" presents a number of conundrums.[44] In the Global South, where up to two-thirds of regional populations live in suburban areas, the morphologies, composition, and even concepts of suburban development abound.[45] Roy detects "a patchwork of valorized and devalorized spaces that constitute a volatile frontier of accumulation, capitalist expansion, gentrification, and displacement."[46] And "peri-urban areas" are often high density and include a wide and dynamic variety of forms and land uses.[47] The new and existing dynamics of emerging and existing suburbanization in the Global South add to a kaleidoscopic global suburban landscape.[48] There is plenty of idiosyncrasy and endogenic activity in the myriad suburban forms that are now emerging; there is also much blurring among and between the morphologies, lifestyles, and infrastructural technologies in different world regions. In a postcolonial, postsuburban world, the forms, functions, relations, and so forth of

one suburban tradition get easily merged, refracted, and fully displaced in and by others elsewhere, near or far.

In a ubiquitously suburbanizing world, we can differentiate between extended urbanization—that which occurs in highly urbanized but demographically stagnating industrialized regions—and primary urbanization, a suburban formation that occurs in high-tech or resource areas (oilburbs, etc.). Primary urbanization forms include gated and otherwise accessrestricted enclaves of privilege; slums of the displaced and squatter settlements of the hopeful; sprawling single-family home subdivisions; hyperdense tower neighborhoods; new developments pushing into ecologically sensitive areas; and existing, though sometimes abandoned, undervalued inner suburbs that await renewal and regeneration. Add to that residential districts of variable density and industrial or commercial districts where service infrastructures and non-desirable land uses are concentrated. (fig. **3.6.8**)

In this process, historically bland and clear-cut segregation(s) in land use, socioeconomic makeup, and socionatural relationships associated with suburban form and life begin to break down into more complex variations. So-called in-between cities have emerged where the urban and the suburban cannot easily be distinguished.[49] This globalizing suburbia, then, presents itself as a historically evolving human geography: the predominant human habitat is less urban than most observers of the urban century assume, and much less rural than where people lived one hundred years ago. It is time to face the emergence of a postsuburban planet where existing and new forms of peripheral urbanization interlace in a complex pattern of urbanity.

What urban theory increasingly learns from suburbanization is how the making of peripheries contributes to the building of new centralities. A simplistic view that

39 King, *Spaces of Global Cultures.*

40 Maher, "Borders and Social Distinction in the Global Suburb," 782; Keil, "Suburbanization and Global Cities."

41 Maher, "Borders and Social Distinction in the Global Suburb," 804.

42 Lisa Drummond and Danielle Labbé, "We're a Long Way from Levittown, Dorothy: Everyday Suburbanism as a Global Way of Life," in *Suburban Constellations: Governance, Land and Infrastructure in the 21st Century,* ed. Roger Keil (Berlin: Jovis Verlag, 2013), 46–51.

43 Rohan Quinby, *Time and the Suburbs: The Politics of Built Environments and the Future of Dissent* (Winnipeg, Canada: Arbeiter Ring Publishing, 2011); King, *Spaces of Global Cultures.*

44 Lefebvre, *The Urban Revolution.*

45 McGee, "Suburbanization in a Twenty-First Century."

46 Roy, "Governing the Post-Colonial Suburbs."

47 Gururani, "On Capital's Edge: Gurgaon: India's Millennial City"; Mabin, "Suburbanisms in Africa?"

48 Hamel and Keil, *Suburban Governance: A Global View.*

49 Sieverts, *Cities without Cities.*

3.6.8 Amadora, Portugal—old and new suburbanization

50 Roger Keil and Jean-Paul Addie, "It's Not Going to Be Suburban, It's Going to Be All Urban': Assembling Post-Suburbia in the Toronto and Chicago Regions," *International Journal of Urban and Regional Research* 39 (published electronically January 8, 2016): 892–911, doi:10.1111/1468-2427.12303.

51 Lefebvre and Ross, "Finding a Larger Theory of the City," 50.

52 Mike Davis, *Planet of Slums* (London; New York: Verso, 2006).

sees one territorial center in contradistinction to undefined (and implicitly less important) peripheries now gives way to multiscaled center-periphery assemblages with multiple centralities and peripheralities that sustain urban regions.[50] Global suburbanization has now imposed on us the imperative of challenging the models from which it ostensibly emerged and has forced us to change the ways we study suburbs in a world of complete urbanization. "The explosion of the historic city was precisely the occasion for finding a larger theory of the city, and not a pretext for abandoning the problem," noted Lefebvre (recollected during an interview with Kristin Ross in the 1980s). He was responding defiantly to the abandonment, by Guy Debord and his associates among the situationists of the 1960s, of the city and urbanism as arenas and pathways of societal change.[51] Lefebvre's intellectual provocation of sticking to "the urban" as a source of theoretical insight, revolutionary potential, and societal transformation proved to be of lasting significance. (fig. **3.6.9**)

The call for a renewed urban theory is once again before us today. The "explosion" was merely the starting gun of a much more far-reaching process of complete urbanization that turns the categories of geographical center and periphery upside down and creates new relationships among various parts of urban regions. It points to a more profound problem of constellations than the original astrophysical metaphor of the explosion would suggest.

We have, for example, now lived for two generations with Lefebvre's "little houses" and the towers in the park on the urban periphery. We have seen libraries of writings on communities of tree-lined streets with white picket fences; work that is ostensibly filled with the small and large pathologies of modern life. The social critique, the political critiques and now the environmental critique have not been kind to the single-family home suburb. Yet it persists. We have been through waves of real and intellectual demolition of the modern dream of the high-rise periphery, while China, Singapore, Vietnam, and Turkey, as well as many other countries, continue to produce them at breakneck speed. And we have seen reams of publications on the future of a "planet of slums."[52]

3.6.9 New centralities: Mississauga City Hall

53 Lefebvre, *The Urban Revolution*.

Suburbanization today enables insight into the real, existing processes of urbanization in the twenty-first century and hence into the emergence of "urban society" in the sense of Henri Lefebvre.[53] In its diversity, suburbanization ultimately shows itself to be the prism through which we can glimpse the "urban century." In contrast, the monocultures of the gentrified, "creative" inner cities that have been celebrated of late are being viewed through tunnel vision. (fig. **3.6.10**)

The Incomparable Suburb

Global suburbanism, then, becomes a programmatic intervention into the theoretical and empirical investigation of the massive worldwide proliferation of suburbanization in the twenty-first century. Rather than focus only on (sub) urban form, this reevaluation of global suburbanization also takes into account the political economy of urbanization, the governance of peripheral space, and the infrastructures supporting suburbanization globally today.

There is no teleology of suburbanization. Not all suburbs grow up to be cities. There is no direct line to urban paradise from the periphery. Some suburbs go straight to postsuburban hell. Others continue to define the horizon of possibility for aspiring, urbanizing masses from the rural countryside and from other parts of the urban world. Today's suburban areas are born into a postsuburban world. It is inconceivable today that suburbia could be left in some timeless state of never-changing bliss (as some homeowner associations might want it to be). The opposing extreme is equally implausible: suburbia as a juvenile version of a future city (as some believers in the transformative powers of urbanism have it). We now know that either option is unlikely. We must also abandon the dichotomy of single-family home subdivision on one end of our imaginations and

3.6.10 Self-built suburbia, Belgrade, Serbia

54 Jan Nijman, "The Theo-
retical Imperative of
Comparative Urbanism:
A Commentary on 'Cities
beyond Compare?'
By Jamie Peck," *Regional
Studies* 49, no. 1
(2015): 183–86; Jamie
Peck, "Cities beyond
Compare?," *Regional
Studies* 49, no. 1 (January
2, 2015): 160–82.

the tower-dominated "badlands" on the other. The in-between cities we find in the postsuburban landscapes of our "glob-urban" reality will have traces of both, but rarely monocultures of either.

This ultimately means that urban theory that is prompted by global suburbanization is necessarily comparative in nature.[54] Only, now the comparison is increasingly losing North American suburbanization as its assumed yardstick. We are now in a field with fast-moving referents that belie many of the old assumptions on suburbs and urban theory. It is time to bid the (conceptual) white picket fence farewell.

Qingheyingcun, Beijing, China

Aldeia da Serra, São Paulo, Brazil

3.7
SPAIN'S SPECULATIVE URBANIZATION

Christopher Marcinkoski

GOVERNANCE & POLICY CHALLENGES

NEOLIBERAL PROPERTY MARKETS

TRANSPORT INFRASTRUCTURE

3.7.1 Overview of Ensanche de Vallecas, looking southwest

The last fifteen years have witnessed the spectacular collapse of city and state economies that became too reliant on physical urbanization as their primary driver of economic growth. From the ghost estates of Ireland to the artificial oases of Dubai, to the gated suburban compounds of the American Sunbelt, to unoccupied housing in second- and third-tier Chinese cities, the increasing frequency of these large-scale, speculative expansions of settlement has emerged as a topic in demand of critical examination. In this context, perhaps no political body instrumentalized urbanization activities over this period to a greater effect—and consequence—than Spain. Thus, it is worth taking the time to consider the particular circumstances that motivated events on the Iberian Peninsula as they relate to both the question of "suburbia" and the contemporary activities of the urban design disciplines. (fig. **3.7.1**)

Certainly, a great deal of very good, comprehensive work has been published on the implications of these speculative pursuits, primarily from the perspectives of economic policy, political governance, and social equity.[1] However, a consideration of the motivations and consequences of these events from the viewpoint of urban design and planning is absent, and thus long overdue given the central, albeit little-acknowledged role these disciplines play in these urbanization activities.

For the purposes of such a discussion, I define *speculative urbanization* as the construction of new urban infrastructure or settlement for primarily political or economic purposes, rather than to meet real (as opposed to artificially projected) demographic or market demand. If we expand this definition further, we can include activities related to the legislative redesignation and reparcelization of land for the specific purpose of increasing its monetary value. The definition refers primarily to activities at the periphery of established urban areas, or in entirely exurban contexts with these pursuits most

1   See, for example, Herman Schwartz and Leonard Seabrooke, eds., *The Politics of Housing Booms and Busts* (Basingstoke, UK: Palgrave Macmillan, 2009); and Robert M. Hardaway, *The Great American Housing Bubble: The Road to Collapse* (Santa Barbara, CA: Praeger, 2011).

often operating at the scale of a district or territory.

Reflecting on this definition, one could argue that over the last two decades, city building (as in physical urbanization) has become the ultimate form of twenty-first-century industrial production, appealing to both politicians and investors alike in nearly every kind of politico-economic context, from the most liberal to the autocratically controlled. The significance of this pursuit is noteworthy in that the role of new urban settlement and infrastructure has fundamentally shifted away from a provision of basic urban services toward a projection of economic potential and political status. As a result, the promiscuous deployment of these speculative endeavors is increasingly producing moments of substantial social, environmental, and economic disruption.

Given this intensification and the consequences that have resulted, it is imperative that urban design and planning become far more cognizant of—and conversant in—the political and economic motivations driving this production. Without such a reorientation, it will become even more difficult for these disciplines to have any agency in the speculative urbanization processes that will be a primary source of much of their future work.

The Spanish Story

As mentioned above, no recent case is more indicative of this use of urbanization activities for politico-economic ambitions than the events in Spain that transpired between 1998 and 2012. During this period, the country experienced an unprecedented expansion of both its urbanized territory and its economy. From 2000 to 2005, Spain was transforming land at a rate of 187.3 acres (75.8 hectares) per day.[2] The proportion of Spain's economy tied directly to construction was nearly three times that of the United States during its

contemporaneous real estate convulsion (about 13 percent versus 4.8 percent).[3] Per capita GDP increased from roughly US$15,000 to nearly $35,000.[4] And though other contemporaneous property booms emerged globally, none occurred with the same intensity or for as long as Spain's.

Over the course of this period, Spain built enough new homes to house approximately sixteen million people, yet population growth was just over six million, mostly from immigration.[5] And despite this profusion of housing, other urbanization activities were also pursued. In little more than a decade, Spain achieved one of the highest concentrations of transportation infrastructure per capita in the world, becoming the European leader in highway length, number of international airports, and length of high-speed rail lines. Museums, congress halls, parks, stadiums, cultural centers, markets, and libraries were initiated throughout the country as companions to the newly developed housing. Golf courses, amusement parks, beachfront resorts, and shopping malls rounded out the spatial products arrayed across Spain during this period. The effect, unsurprisingly, was the highest rate of rural to urban land conversion in the European Union.[6] Or to put it another way, roughly one-third of all urbanized land in Spain was created between 1998 and 2008 alone.[7] (fig. **3.7.2**)

This urbanization was seen as endeavoring to prevent what former prime minister José María Aznar characterized as Spain's "consignment to a corner of history." This monumental effort was an attempt to elevate the country to the apex of global economic status through city building.[8] The pursuit of urban growth was not limited to the major cities; it was the quest of municipalities large and small, from towns with two hundred residents to cities of two million.[9] Urbanization had become an intoxicant,

2   Oriol Nel·lo, "Herencias territoriales, exploraciones geográficas y designios politicos," in *Ruinas modernas: Una topografía del lucro*, ed. Julia Schulz-Dornburg (Barcelona: Ambit serveis editorials, 2012), 25.

3   Yan Sun, Pritha Mitra, and Alejandro Simone, "The Driving Force behind the Boom and Bust in Construction in Europe," IMF Working Paper, European Department, August 2013, https://www.imf.org/external/pubs/ft/wp/2013/wp13181.pdf.

4   See "GDP Per Capita (Current US$)," World Bank, accessed April 15, 2014, http://data.worldbank.org/indicator/NY.GDP.PCAP.CD?page=1.

5   Eugenio L. Burriel, "Subversion of Land-Use Plans and the Housing Bubble in Spain," *Urban Research and Practice* 4, no. 3 (2011): 232–37.

6   Celia Barbero-Sierra, Maria J. Marques, and Manuel Ruíz-Pérez, "The Case of Urban Sprawl in Spain as an Active and Irreversible Driving Force for Desertification," *Journal of Arid Environments* 90 (2013): 101.

7   Juan Romero, Fernando Jiménez, and Manuel Villoria, "(Un)sustainable Territories: Causes of the Speculative Bubble in Spain (1996–2010) and Its Territorial, Environmental, and Sociopolitical Consequences," *Environment and Planning C: Government and Policy* 30 (2012): 473.

8   Quoted in Borja Bergareche, "The Pain in Spain," *World Policy Journal* 28, no. 1 (Spring 2011): 55.

9   Nuria Benach and Andres Walliser, "Introduction to the Special Issue: Urban Problems and Issues in Contemporary Spanish and Portuguese Cities," *Urban Research and Practice* 4, no. 3 (2011): 230.

extraordinarily addictive—and worse yet—readily accessible.

The consequences of the bust are in many ways as dramatic and wide-ranging as the dimensions of what was built. Over two million jobs were lost after the collapse of the economy, constituting roughly 10 percent of Spain's labor force. As of 2010, roughly one in four unemployed Spaniards had come from construction-related industries. By 2012, the unemployment rate in Spain had reached 26 percent. For those under age thirty, this number was upward of 45 percent.[10] During this period, Spain's construction sector saw the largest bankruptcy in the county's history when the property developer Martinsa-Fadesa announced it was more than €5 billion in debt.[11]

Many portrayals of these events have chosen to focus on the Land Law (Ley de Suelo) of 1998 or ill-conceived attempts to replicate the successes of the 1992 Olympics as the primary catalysts of the construction boom. Yet the story of this most recent Spanish miracle-cum-crisis is rooted in a much deeper, more complex set of politico-economic machinations of fundamental interest to urban design and planning: land, housing, and infrastructure. (fig. **3.7.3**)

Urbanize Everything!

While surplus housing in Spain has been the focus of media headlines, the less deliberated but more consequential aspect to consider is the role land policy played in setting the stage for these events. The 1956 Law of Urban Planning and Land Use Management (Ley del Regimen del Suelo y Ordenación Urbana) established for the first time a classification system for Spanish land organized under three designations: developed land (*suelo urbano*); land not to be developed (*suelo no urbanizable*); and land suitable for development as part of a municipal expansion (*suelo urbanizable*).[12]

3.7.2 Incomplete urban development around Madrid

10 "Employment and Unemployment (Labour Force Survey)," Eurostat, accessed May 10, 2014, http://ec.europa.eu/eurostat/web/lfs/overview.

11 "Banks, Bricks, and Mortar," *Economist*, November 6, 2008, accessed October 10, 2015, http://www.economist.com/node/12501011.

12 Burriel, "Subversion of Land-Use Plans," 238.

Under this law, urban planning responsibilities were placed in the hands of a town council or mayor and were considered compulsory.

A unique aspect of the legislation was that once a piece of land was designated as able to be urbanized, any assessment of its value from that point forward was based on what the land would be worth fully developed—not on its current state. The purpose of this was to provide a mechanism by which poor rural landowners could use their future land value as collateral to finance development and infrastructure that the state could not afford to provide. This mechanism, coupled with other aspects of the 1956 law, served to both slow urbanization and encourage rampant land speculation.

The 1956 law remained in place for nearly two decades until Franco's death in 1975. Shortly thereafter, minor revisions were made to ensure that the benefits of development were shared not only among private landowners but also with

3.7.3 Ciudad Valdeluz

municipalities, through a required 10 percent concession to the public administration on all development.[13]

Fifteen years later, the Amended Land Use and Assessment System Act (Ley de Reforma del Régimen del Suelo y Valoraciónes de 1990) was passed by the center-left PSOE (Partido Socialista Obrero Español) with the intention of undoing what it considered to be expansionist policies of a "preconstitutional" planning system reliant on the parameters of the 1956 law. This legislation attempted to limit the rights of private landowners by expanding planning and land-use administration responsibilities among the municipal, regional, and now national governments. The legislation also expanded the levy on development projects to 15 percent, while jettisoning the parameter of land value being based on its future state rather than its existing condition.[14] Whether it was a consequenceof the subsequent economic downturn, or simply a failure of the legislation, a constitutional

tribunal struck down roughly 80 percent of the 1990 law in 1997.[15]

With the state's limited authority in mind, a new land law the following year reduced the three designations set out in the original 1956 law to simply "developable" or "not developable." And rather than the not-developable land being thought of as residual—that which was left out of a municipal plan—the new law actively defined not-developable land only as territories having some significant intrinsic value or considered as a risk on which to build.[16] Enacted by the center-right PP (Partido Popular), the 1998 law was based on a simple but often disputed economic principle: the overregulation of land artificially drives up the cost of housing by limiting the supply on which to build.[17]

Housing prices in Spain had been considered high relative to other economic indicators since the 1980s, but with the new legislation, the solution to this quandary for the PP became obvious.[18] By

13 Pere Riera, Ian Munt, and John Keyes, "The Practice of Land Use Planning in Spain," *Planning Practice and Research* 6, no. 2 (1991): 6.

14 Jesús M. González Pérez, "Urban Planning System in Contemporary Spain," *European Planning Studies* 15, no. 1 (2007): 33–35; and Burriel, "Subversion of Land-Use Plans," 238.

15 Josep Roca Cladera and Malcolm C. Burns, "The Liberalization of the Land Market in Spain: The 1998 Reform of Urban Planning Legislation," *European Planning Studies* 8, no. 5 (2000): 550.

16 Ana Maria De La Encarnación Valcárcel, "New Land Valuation Criteria after the Spanish 2011 Valuation of Land Regulation: The Objectivation of Building Expectations in Rural Land," *Territorio Italia— Land Administration, Cadastre, Real Estate*, no. 1 (2013): 76.

17 John M. Quigley and Larry A. Rosenthal, "The Effects of Land

opening up all unprotected land to development, an inelastic system would become more elastic, in turn lowering housing prices. It was no surprise when development in Spain took off, with more than 2,200 Spanish municipalities approving or revising their general plans between 1998 and 2006.[19]

Eventually, in 2001, another constitutional tribunal annulled significant portions of the 1998 law, reaffirming that all land-use designations must be established at the regional level. However, the immediate "successes" of the national legislation compelled nearly every autonomous community in Spain to pass regional variations of the law.[20]

As regional governments enacted their own versions of the 1998 law, the concessions required of private developers became a primary source of revenue for many town councils during the boom. Municipalities would acquire their allotted levy and quickly sell this duty back to the developer in order to fund other municipal endeavors. This inherent conflict of interest was exacerbated by the fact that the regional savings banks (*caja de ahorros*) that provided many of the loans required for approval of these developments remained under the direction of the same municipal authorities responsible for planning approval.[21] What resulted was a delirious cycle of development proposals, municipal approvals, and easy credit lubricating this radical transformation of Spanish land. (fig. **3.7.4**)

Another effect of the 1998 law was the relegation of legally binding municipal plans to little more than pictorials of urban possibilities. Land-use regulations became effortlessly modifiable. Using various administrative mechanisms that allowed municipalities to approve future projects in exchange for public works in the present, the system of checks and balances within planning regulation in Spain was frequently superseded or

ignored.[22] This ease of modification led to poor coordination within and across individual autonomous communities, producing huge redundancies throughout the country.[23]

Sardonically referred to as a policy of "urbanize everything" ("*todo urbanizable*"), the Land Law of 1998 has been widely cited as the primary root of Spain's recent boom and bust. However, despite more than three decades of continuous political instrumentalization of land policy, this real estate convulsion cannot be fully explained by a single source, even one as fundamentally transformative as the 1998 law and its subsequent regional variants.

Housing Bubbles and the Periphery

The common impression of what happened in Spain is that there was a housing bubble. And while true, that fact on its own does not make Spain an exceptional case to consider. For one, there were other contemporaneous bubbles that appeared in Europe and globally over the same period.[24] And Spain itself has seen at least two other housing-related bubbles in the last half-century.[25] So while the focus of design and planning discourse has been on the surplus housing produced between 1998 and 2008, there is more to this story in the context of the increasing political and economic role that urbanization is being asked to play globally.

It is worth recounting a few of the metrics related to what occurred. At the height of Spain's recent boom, the country was building more housing units per year than Germany, France, and the United Kingdom combined, despite having only 20 percent of the total population of those three countries.[26] The number of new housing starts annually nearly tripled between 1996 and 2006.[27] Yet despite the massive volume of housing constructed, at the end of the boom, it was roughly twice as expensive to buy a home in Spain

Use Regulation on the Price of Housing: What Do We Know? What Can We Learn?," *Cityscape: A Journal of Policy Development and Research* 8, no. 1 (2005): 69–75.

18 Juli Ponce, "Land Use Planning and Disaster: A European Perspective from Spain," Oñati Socio-Legal Series 3, no. 2 (2013): 210.

19 Jesús M. González Pérez, "The Real Estate and Economic Crisis: An Opportunity for Urban Return and Rehabilitation Policies in Spain," *Sustainability*, no. 2 (2010): 1591.

20 Burriel, "Subversion of Land-Use Plans," 239.

21 Duncan Maclennan and Anthony O'Sullivan, "The Global Financial Crisis: Challenges for Housing Research and Policies," *Journal of Housing and the Built Environment* 26 (2011): 377.

22 Burriel, "Subversion of Land-Use Plans," 242–45.

23 Romero, Jiménez, and Villoria, "(Un)sustainable Territories," 467–69.

24 "In Come the Waves," *Economist*, June 16, 2005, accessed October 10, 2015, http://www.economist.com/node/4079027.

25 These previous housing bubbles occurred between 1969 and 1974 and 1986 and 1992. See González Pérez, "Real Estate and Economic Crisis."

26 Barbero-Sierra, Marques, and Ruíz-Pérez, "Case of Urban Sprawl," 100.

27 Ministerio de Vivienda / Ministerio de Fomento, accessed March 25, 2014, http://www.fomento.gob.es/MFOM/LANG_CASTELLANO/DIRECCIONES_GENERALES/ARQ_VIVIENDA/.

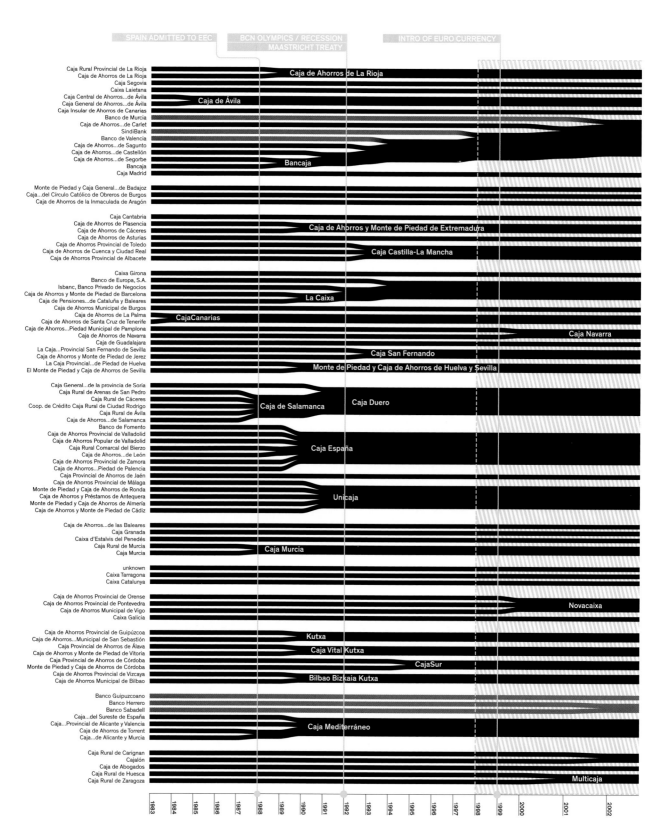

3.7.4 Radical consolidation of *cajas*

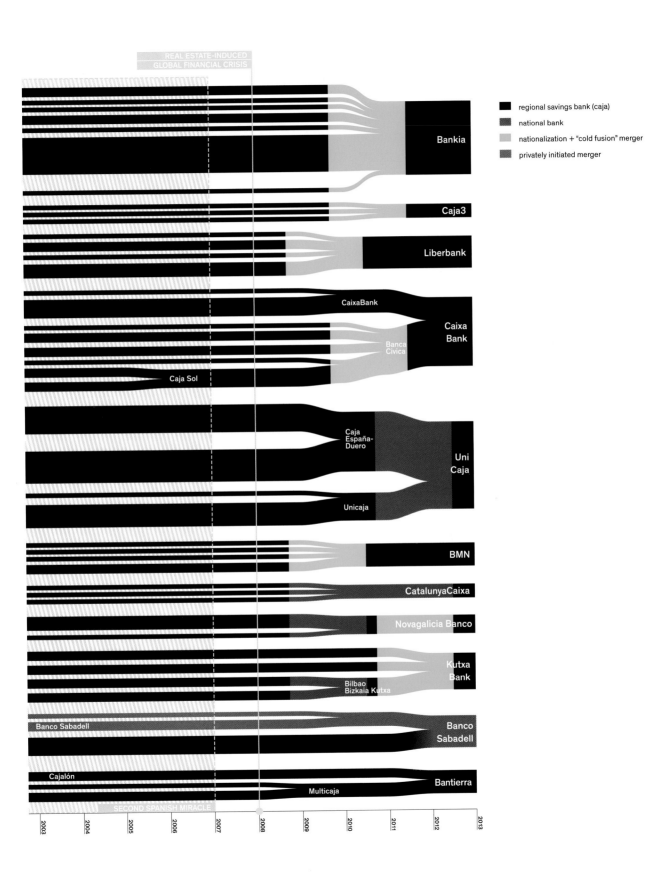

REAL ESTATE-INDUCED
GLOBAL FINANCIAL CRISIS

■ regional savings bank (caja)
▨ national bank
▨ nationalization + "cold fusion" merger
▨ privately initiated merger

Bankia

Caja3

Liberbank

CaixaBank

Caixa
Bank

Banca
Civica

Caja Sol

Caja
España-
Duero

Uni
Caja

Unicaja

BMN

CatalunyaCaixa

Novagalicia Banco

Kutxa
Bank

Bilbao
Bizkaia Kutxa

Banco Sabadell

Banco
Sabadell

Cajalón

Bantierra

Multicaja

SECOND SPANISH MIRACLE

2003 2004 2005 2006 2007 2008 2009 2010 2011 2012 2013

Ensanche de
Carabanchel
(350 ha / phase 1)

City of Madrid
Historic Core
(490 ha)

19th c. Expansion
Castro Plan
(1590 ha)

Valdecarros
(1,900 ha /
uninitiated)

Ensanche de
Vallecas
(700 ha / phase 1)

Los Berrocales
(830 ha / phase 2)

Los Ahijones
(570 ha / phase 2)

El Cañaveral
(530 ha / phase 2)

Los Cerros
(470 ha / uninitiated)

Arroyo del Fresno
(194 ha / phase 1)

Montcarmelo
(300 ha / phase 1)

Las Tablas
(361 ha / phase 1)

Sanchinarro
(401 ha / phase 1)

Valdebebas
(1,060 ha / phase 2)

Ensanche de
Barajas
(68 ha / phase 2)

3.7.5 1997 General Plan of Madrid

N→ └────┘ 2 km

28 González Pérez, "Real Estate and Economic Crisis," 1582.

29 Sharon Smyth, Neil Callanan, and Dara Doyle, "Spain Real Estate 'Madness' Continues despite Burst Housing Bubble," *Bloomberg News*, May 2, 2012, accessed October 10, 2015, http://www.bloomberg.com/news/2012-05-01/madness-in-spain-lingers-as-ireland-chases-recovery-mortgages.html.

30 Guillermo Abril, "Living Alone," *El Pais in English*, January 31, 2011, accessed October 10, 2015, http://elpais.com/elpais/2011/01/31/inenglish/1296454843_850210.html.

31 *Economist*, "Banks, Bricks, and Mortar."

32 Anna Cabré and Juan Antonio Módenes, "Homeownership and Social Inequality in Spain," in *Home Ownership and Social Inequality in Comparative Perspective*, ed. Karin Kurz and Hans-Peter Blossfeld (Stanford, CA: Stanford University Press), 233.

33 Ibid., 234.

than at the beginning, relative to inflation.[28] By the end of 2010, there were more than 1 million unsold homes on the market in Spain. By 2012, this number was closer to 2 million.[29] And in reality, it could have been as high as 3.6 million if all the homes that had been approved at the time of the collapse were actually built.[30] (fig. **3.7.5**)

In 1950 more than half of Spain's population was renters.[31] By 2012, upward of 80 percent of homes in the country were owner-occupied. Some have suggested that this high rate of homeownership is cultural and that the traditional role of housing in Spain is similar to other southern European countries. But as the demographers Anna Cabré and Juan Antonio Módenes argue, "High homeownership rates in Spain are not the result of tradition, [rather] they are the product of the rapid social and economic changes that took place during the second half of the twentieth century."[32]

Spain's 1959 National Stabilization Plan, catalyst of the original "Spanish miracle" or *desarrollismo*, drove much of this rapid change. The Franco regime—in consultation with the International Monetary Fund and Opus Dei—made homeownership a top priority of its newly liberalized economic policies. Notionally, the purpose of these regulations was to stave off the growth of communism by privileging homeownership over renters, whom it considered proletarian. Legislation enacted as part of this plan created a legal basis (and incentive) to develop multi-family housing structures in urban areas that could be sold unit by unit, something that up to that point was impossible under Spanish law.[33]

As Spain's economy shifted away from agriculture toward industry, hundreds of thousands of new residential units were built between 1960 and 1973 at the periphery of established cities like Madrid and

Bilbao. This new housing was often located near newly developed industrial estates that had the potential to offer employment to these migrants.[34] Since innovations in housing had been greatly repressed over the preceding decades, the bulk of these new units were poorly planned, poorly designed, and poorly constructed. Nonetheless, this new housing was rapidly filled, and the cultural shift from renting to ownership was set in motion.

Following the death of Franco, Spain's 1978 constitution revised national tax policy to further promote homeownership by allowing individuals to deduct from their tax burden the interest paid on their mortgages, as well as their mortgage principal up to a maximum of 15 percent. These provisions applied both to primary residences and to second homes, ostensibly encouraging the purchase of multiple dwellings as part of a family's long-term savings strategy.[35]

By the early 1990s, roughly 55 percent of the housing stock in Spain had been built between 1959 and 1974, meaning that more than half of all dwellings in the country were of questionable physical integrity.[36] This deficiency was interpreted as indicative of an urgent need to construct new housing throughout Spain and, in particular, in major cities where the bulk of housing from this prior boom period was located.

As early as 1997—before the passing of the 1998 Land Law—significant urban expansions were beginning in major metropolitan areas. But following the enactment of the 1998 law, these expansions began to proliferate in secondary municipalities throughout the country. The Catalan politician and geographer Oriol Nel·lo has described this as Spain's third stage of "metropolitanization," noting that by 2002 even the smallest rural villages were greatly expanding their urban footprint, despite not having seen population increases for the better part

of a century.[37] This widespread pursuit of urban expansions in even the most illogical of places was indicative of an increasing belief in Spain that urbanization was the ultimate recipe for economic prosperity.[38] (fig. **3.7.6**)

Spain's dramatically changing demographics fueled this perception of housing demand. Between 1998 and 2009, the country gained 2.67 million new residents from the European Union, two million immigrants from Latin America, and roughly one million immigrants from Africa.[39] Adding to this demographic pressure was the coming of age of Spain's baby boomers, born in the mid- to late 1970s shortly after the death of Franco. The demand created by these populations was aggravated by the dearth of rental properties available, as a result of the many laws put in place in the 1960s.

Further exacerbating the situation were the tax laws of the 1980s that implicitly encouraged the ownership of second and third homes as investment vehicles. The result was that about seven million middle-class Spanish households (35 percent of all home owners) owned two homes or more at the height of the bubble. This demand for second homes was not limited to residents of the country but also driven by foreign nationals who invested upward of €7 billion per year in property assets during the boom.[40]

What this suggests is that, in many ways, the paradox between the demand for second homes as investments and the need for affordable housing for immigrants and young workers is the real story of the most recent Spanish housing bubble. In this sense, the housing boom in Spain between 1998 and 2008 was not just the product of liberalized land policies, greedy developers, corrupt politicians, or naive investors. Rather, it was a consequence of a much longer shift in the cultural role of housing in Spain as an instrument of economic production.

34 González Pérez, "Real Estate and Economic Crisis," 1574.

35 Cabré and Módenes, "Homeownership and Social Inequality," 235–36.

36 Julie Pollard, "Political Framing in National Housing Systems: Lessons from Real Estate Developers in France and Spain," in *The Politics of Housing Booms and Busts*, ed. Herman M. Schwartz and Leonard Seabrooke (Basingstoke, UK: Palgrave Macmillan, 2009), 176.

37 Oriol Nel·lo, "La tercera fase del proceso de metropolitanización en España," in *Los procesos urbanos postfordistas*, ed. A. Artigues et al. (Palma de Mallorca: Universitat de les Illes Balears and Asociación de Geógrafos Españoles, 2007), 19–32.

38 Benach and Walliser, "Introduction," 230.

39 See Isidro López and Emmanuel Rodríguez, "The Spanish Model," *New Left Review* 69 (May–June 2011): 20; and Guillermo de la Dehesa, *La primera gran crisis financiera del siglo XXI: Orígenes, detonante, efectos, respuestas y remedies* (Madrid: Alianza Editorial, 2009), 443–44.

40 López and Rodríguez, "Spanish Model," 10–13.

3.7.6 The village of Yebes

3.7.7 Incomplete connection between MP-203 and R-3 south of Mejorada del Campo

How Infrastructure Fueled the Boom

Even beyond considerations of land and housing, the massive expansion of urban infrastructure seen throughout Spain leading up to and throughout the real estate boom should be understood as perhaps the most critical catalyst to what occurred. As recently as the early 1980s, Spain was an economic backwater characterized by poor infrastructure, limited competitiveness, and an economy dominated by tourism. Decades of isolation under Franco had left the country unequipped, while rapid population growth in metropolitan areas between 1960 and 1980 exacerbated deficiencies in intercity and urban infrastructures.[41] As a result, the country's economy remained reliant on poorly maintained rural roads and a rail system inefficiently centered on Madrid.

It was not until the mid-1980s that Spain saw the first significant state expansion of the highway system since the eighteenth century.[42] This renewed investment in national infrastructure was motivated not just by rising demand for intercity mobility connections and a growing economy but, more important, by an exceptional moment in Spain's history—the country's admission into the European Economic Community (EEC), the forerunner of the European Union, in 1986.[43] Membership in the EEC had a number of implications, but joining the EEC meant one very important thing for the urban form of Spain—access to massive amounts of capital via European Structural and Cohesion Funds.

Sebastián Royo, professor of government at Suffolk University, argues that the European Union benefits those who are best prepared to take advantage of the rights of membership.[44] Simply saying that Spain benefited from this program would be a gross understatement. Since the 1988 reform, the country has been one of the chief beneficiaries of the EU budget, receiving annually, on average, more than one-quarter of the total funds distributed between 1989 and 2006.[45] In fact, Spain has been the largest single beneficiary of this program in absolute terms, accepting a total of €186 billion in structural and cohesion funding.[46]

Roughly 20 percent of the monies received each year from 1994 through 2006 were used for infrastructure projects intended to improve economic productivity through advances in efficiency and access.[47] These investments included highways, bridges, conventional rail, high-speed rail, train stations, airports, seaports, desalination plants, sewage plants, and renewable energy facilities. Former Museum of Modern Art curator Terence Riley, in his opening essay of the catalog for the 2006 exhibition On-Site: New Architecture in Spain, described Spain's activities as "the most extensive building and rebuilding of…civil infrastructure since the Romans unified the Iberian Peninsula."[48] So, while the massive amount of housing built in Spain between 1998 and 2008 has received the majority of attention, in reality, the scale of infrastructural investment that underpinned this development should be understood as no less dramatic or consequential. (fig. **3.7.7**)

For example, by 2011, Spain had more miles of roadway per capita than any other European country; the length of its system quintupled from just over 1,860 miles (3,000 kilometers) in 1993 to more than 10,070 miles (16,200 kilometers) in 2011.[49] Highway expansion projects were initiated regionally and nationally, with roughly four out of every ten kilometers constructed in Spain between 1986 and 2007 financed by EU funds.[50] Metro systems in Madrid, Barcelona, Bilbao, Valencia, and Seville were also expanded. Madrid saw the most dramatic change, nearly tripling in total length between 1990 and 2012 from 70 miles (111 kilometers) to 183 miles

41 Ponce, "Land Use Planning and Disaster," 201.

42 Germà Bel, "Infrastructure and Nation Building: The Regulation and Financing of Network Transportation Infrastructures in Spain (1720–2010)," *Business History* 53, no. 5 (2011): 697.

43 Manuel Villoria, Gregg G. Van Ryzin, and Cecilia F. Lavena, "Social and Political Consequences of Administrative Corruption: A Study of Public Perceptions in Spain," *Public Administration Review* 73, no. 1 (2012): 87.

44 Sebastián Royo, "Lessons from the Integration of Spain and Portugal to the EU," *PS: Political Science and Politics* 40, no. 4 (2007): 692.

45 Ruiz, "New Methods and Results," 245.

46 *Economist*, "The Morning After."

47 Carmen Ruiz, "New Methods and Results in Measuring the Efficiency of EU Funds: The Spanish Case," *Society and Economy* 30, no. 2 (2008): 253.

48 Terence Riley, "Contemporary Architecture in Spain: Shaking Off the Dust," in *On-Site: New Architecture in Spain* (New York: Museum of Modern Art, 2005), 13.

49 Organisation for Economic Co-operation and Development, *OECD Factbook 2014: Economic, Environmental, and Social Statistics* (Paris: OECD Publishing, 2014).

50 Royo, "Lessons from the Integration of Spain and Portugal," 693.

(293 kilometers), and adding more than 150 new stations.

In addition to these terrestrial networks, the 1990s and early 2000s saw the construction of seven new airports and the expansion and renovation of numerous others across Spain. This represents an investment of over €16 billion by Spain's state airport authority, based primarily on projections that total passenger numbers would nearly double from 165 million to 311 million by 2020.[51] Spain now has fifty international airports, 2.5 times as many as in Germany, a country with twice the population. Predictably, not all these airports are sustainable. As of 2012, no fewer than twelve of these facilities qualify as "ghost airports" in economic terms because of low annual passenger numbers.[52]

The real star of Spain's infrastructural expansion, however, has been high-speed rail (HSR). Following the early 1990s recession and the economic recovery during the later part of the decade, the government declared its intention in 2000 to connect forty-seven of the country's fifty provincial capitals to Madrid in less than four hours via a vast new hub-and-spoke HSR system.[53] The result—though incomplete—is the second-longest HSR network in the world after China, currently measuring over 1,860 miles (3,000 kilometers). Like the highway expansion, the construction of high-speed rail in Spain has relied heavily on the EU, with roughly €38 out of every €100 spent coming from structural or cohesion funds.[54]

The importance of these metrics—beyond their sheer scale—is an understanding that without this massive investment in urban infrastructures, the housing boom in Spain would have been substantially less delirious, if it had occurred at all. These new lines of mobility became conduits along which real estate investment accumulated, fomenting the rapid, often unnecessary expansion

of urbanized lands throughout Spain. The redundancy, lack of coordination, overscaled structures, and general hubris of this building period catalyzed the construction and real estate industries in Spain to such an extent that they displaced tourism as the dominant sector of the country's economy. (fig. **3.7.8**)

Yet despite the events of the last half-decade, Spain is still seen as evidence of the true potential of the European Union as a politico-economic idea. Its utilization of EU funds produced strong increases in competitive economic metrics such as rate of growth and foreign direct investment.[55] The country is able to actively export its substantial construction expertise to other developing contexts. However, Spain has also been accused of using these infrastructural expansions for near-term "nation-building" purposes, rather than in support of longer-term economic growth and productivity.[56] Of course, Spain was neither the first nor will it be the last polity to employ such a model.

Doubling Down on Urbanization

Spain's response to its urbanization-induced crisis is as telling as the factors that led to it. Exacerbating the difficulty of absorbing the two-million-plus homes lying vacant was that by 2012, local governments throughout the country began to promote the building of even more housing. The city of Madrid announced in April of that year—as the country was struggling to avoid a bailout by the European Central Bank—that it would restart the tender process for twenty-two thousand new homes southeast of the city, despite the fact that an immediately adjacent area was less than 50 percent occupied.[57] Further complicating the absorption process was that many of the immigrants projected to occupy these new residences had simply packed up and left Spain for opportunities elsewhere.[58] (fig. **3.7.9**)

51 Luis Gómez, "Aeropuertos para todos," El País, May 1, 2011, accessed October 10, 2015, http://elpais.com/diario/2011/05/01/domingo/1304221962_850215.html.

52 According to Germà Bel, an economist at the University of Barcelona, Spain's commercial regional airports need a minimum of five hundred thousand passengers annually to break even. Any commercial airport handling less than one hundred thousand passengers a year is considered a ghost airport in economic terms.

53 Concha Martín del Pozo, "Aznar presenta por tercera vez su billonario plan de infraestructuras," El País, January 25, 2000, accessed October 10, 2015, http://elpais.com/diario/2000/01/25/espana/948754809_850215.html.

54 Royo, "Lessons from the Integration of Spain and Portugal," 693.

55 Ibid., 691.

56 Bel, "Infrastructure and Nation Building," 688.

57 José Marcos, "Las 22.000 casas de Los Berrocales se retomarán 'de forma inmediata,'" El País, April 24, 2012, accessed October 10, 2015, http://ccaa.elpais.com/ccaa/2012/04/24/madrid/1335249993_569936.html.

58 Suzanne Daley and Raphael Minder, "Newly Built Ghost Towns Haunt Banks in Spain," New York Times, December 17, 2010, accessed October 10, 2015, http://www.nytimes.com/2010/12/18/world/europe/18spain.html?pagewanted=all&module=Search&mabReward=relbias%3Ar.

3.7.8 Alcorcón South Extension

3.7.9 Overview of El Cañaveral, looking southwest

Despite growing social unrest and financial uncertainty, it was not only suspended building activities that were being resumed. Entirely new urban developments were being initiated as well, doubling down on the belief in urbanization-driven economic growth. In September 2011, Madrid announced its third consecutive bid for the Summer Olympics.[59] September 2012 saw the community of Madrid and the region of Catalonia engaged in the pursuit of an even larger urbanization initiative: a $30 billion casino development proposed by the Las Vegas Sands Corporation.

The project, "EuroVegas," was to include twelve hotel towers, six casinos, three golf courses, an arena, an international tennis center, a shopping mall, a convention center, leisure facilities, an outdoor amphitheater, a theme park, and "ample" areas of natural preserve and public open space. There were also demands for a new or an expanded airport adjacent to the development to serve the project's anticipated international clientele.[60] With little self-awareness, the "EuroVegas" project was being pitched as a massive new urban development district comprising many of the same spatial products already lying vacant or abandoned throughout Spain.

Potential sites were vetted. Tax breaks were offered. More new infrastructure was promised. And after roughly six months of negotiations, incentives, and backroom dealing, the Madrid dormitory town of Alcorcón was selected in February 2013 as the site of this next bit of urban panacea. Catalan officials, disappointed but not to be outdone, pivoted to a new project called BCN World to compete with the Madrid initiative. The 2,041-acre (826 hectare), $6.2 billion project was to include six theme parks, six hotels, multiple casinos, restaurants, theaters, and offices overlooking the Mediterranean coast in the town of Tarragona, 60 miles (100 kilometers) west of Barcelona.[61]

The implications are astonishing. Roughly two and a half years after the near collapse of the Spanish economy because of an unhealthy addiction to urbanization activities, Spain's two largest cities were in pursuit of three of the largest speculative building projects in the country's history, despite having thousands of acres of incompletely urbanized land in the country's hinterlands and unfinished projects throughout its urban cores. By December 2013, the "EuroVegas" project had been canceled because of an inability to resolve the developer's demands with broader EU laws.[62] The Barcelona project remains in development. And as of December 2014, Wang Jianlin, one of China's richest men, was proposing yet another entertainment megaproject for the Madrid periphery, looking to leverage the capital's seemingly insatiable appetite for new urban development.[63]

Global Speculative Urbanization

This response should be of little surprise to the keen observer of contemporary urbanization trends. The continued pursuit of these speculative initiatives is indicative of an increasingly common belief that mega-building projects offer the most expedient solutions to a polity's entrenched social and economic challenges. Even as severe urbanization-induced economic and social crises befell those places mentioned in the opening of this essay, numerous other polities have continued their speculative pursuits, showing limited inclination toward inflection or correction.

Dubai, like Spain, has doubled down on continued urbanization activities despite the International Monetary Fund having warned the Emirate of the emergence of yet another potential asset bubble as property prices increased more than 20 percent from 2012 to 2013. Nonetheless,

59 In early September 2013, Madrid was notified it fell short yet again, finishing a distant third to Tokyo (and Istanbul—itself a regular pursuant of "Olympic Glory").

60 "Place Your Bets on Euro Vegas," *Economist*, March 17, 2012, accessed October 10, 2015, http://www.economist.com/node/21550284.

61 Paola Del Vecchio, "Spain: Barcelona World, Catalonia's Challenge to Eurovegas," *ANSAmed*, September 7, 2012, accessed October 10, 2015, http://www.ansamed.info/ansamed/en/news/nations/spain/2012/09/07/Spain-Barcelona-World-Catalonia-challenge-Eurovegas_7440794.html.

62 Tobias Buck, "Sheldon Adelson Cancels $30bn Eurovegas Project in Spain," *Financial Times*, December 13, 2013, accessed October 10, 2015, http://www.ft.com/intl/cms/s/0/3783f5c8-63f7-11e3-98e2-00144feabdc0.html#axzz39TU8PKkv.

63 Marta Belver, "Primera jugada de Wang Jianlin en el tablero inmobiliario de Madrid," *El Mundo*, December 10, 2014, accessed October 10, 2015, http://www.elmundo.es/madrid/2014/12/10/5488a5aae2704e461c8b456c.html.

Dubai has continued to pursue new megaprojects like the Mohammed Bin Rashid City and the 2020 World Expo, a trade convention-cum-world's fair.[64]

Panama has chosen to emulate urbanization-driven economic growth models pursued elsewhere, looking to become, in the words of its president, the "Dubai of the Pacific."[65] Private development of high-end multiunit housing, and government spending on infrastructure has driven much of this economic expansion, with the country averaging over 8 percent annual GDP growth between 2006 and 2013, a rate closer to emerging Asian economies than its own Latin American neighbors.[66]

Turkey, like Panama, continues to rely on urbanization activities as a primary instrument in its economic modernization.[67] Government policies have included the reestablishment and empowerment of Turkey's housing development authority; an expansion of laws permitting foreign ownership of Turkish land; an "Urban Transformation" law intended replace poorly built neighborhoods throughout Istanbul; and the promotion of multibillion-dollar mega-infrastructure projects.[68]

And of course there is China, where the instrumentalization of urbanization activities for economic and political purposes has led to widespread accusations of corruption and wasteful development.[69] Municipal governments in China, as in Spain, have depended heavily on revenue from the sale of newly valuable rural lands. These locations, recently designated for urbanization, are being used as collateral against new debt to fund major infrastructure and cultural construction projects, as well as to provide operating revenue for a polity.[70] The result is that many second- and third-tier Chinese cities are growing faster than their populations, in turn depleting resources, denuding the environment, and

displacing rural populations that stand in the way of this transformation.[71]

Yet perhaps the most telling response to the recent urbanization induced financial crisis has been seen in Africa, where, shortly after the downturn, numerous proposals for speculative settlement began appearing in contexts as varied as Nigeria, Kenya, Ghana, the Democratic Republic of Congo, Angola, and Tanzania, to name just a few.[72] Population and economic growth projections for the continent, in combination with the shoddy state of its older cities, are said to be the motivation behind these initiatives. Yet these so-called African new towns are heavily reliant on exogenous models of urbanization-driven economic growth employed in places like China and the Middle East.[73]

What does this increasing proliferation of speculative urbanization have to do with suburbia? In short: everything. What is commonly categorized as "suburban" is nothing more than the inevitable horizontal expansion of settlement driven by a global capitalist economy. Postwar American housing policy and the US interstate system were deployed with similar intentions more than half a century ago, if over a much longer time threshold. The contemporary model is simply accelerated, intensified, and more urban, in that low-density formats of housing are being replaced with moderate to high-density configurations, and vehicular highways are being swapped for high-speed rail. The particular format of these contemporary expansions of settlement and infrastructure, then, is immaterial to our discussion here. The growth of the phenomenon is what must be engaged. (fig. **3.7.10**)

Operating Systems and Unintended Outcomes

Despite the widespread claims of rupture that followed our most recent economic crisis, the examples above clearly

64 "IMF Executive Board Concludes 2013 Article IV Consultation with United Arab Emirates," press release, International Monetary Fund, July 30, 2013, accessed October 10, 2015, https://www.imf.org/external/np/sec/pr/2013/pr13283.htm.

65 Randal C. Archibold, "Bursts of Economic Growth in Panama Have Yet to Banish Old Ghosts," New York Times, December 13, 2011, accessed October 10, 2015, http://www.nytimes.com/2011/12/14/world/americas/panamas-bursts-of-growth-have-yet-to-banish-old-ghosts.html?pagewanted=all&_r=0; and "A Singapore for Central America?," Economist, July 14, 2011, accessed October 10, 2015, http://www.economist.com/node/18959000.

66 "Panama Overview," World Bank, 2013, accessed February 15, 2015. http://www.worldbank.org/en/country/panama/overview.

67 Valentina Romei, "Chart of the Week: Turkey's Real Estate Boom Isn't Slowing Yet," Financial Times, beyondbrics (blog), August 5, 2013, accessed October 10, 2015, http://blogs.ft.com/beyond-brics/2013/08/05/chart-of-the-week-turkeys-real-estate-boom-isnt-slowing-yet/.

68 Pelin Turgut, "Turkey's Gold Rush: Is Istanbul's New Skyline a Boom or a Bubble?," Time, October 29, 2012, accessed October 10, 2015, http://content.time.com/time/magazine/article/0,9171,2127107,00.html; Romei, "Chart of the Week"; Çaglar Keyder, "Istanbul in a Global Context," London School of Economics Cities, Urban Age, November 2009, accessed October 10, 2015, http://lsecities.net/media/objects/articles/istanbul-in-a-global-context/en-gb/; and Peter Kenyon, "Istanbul's Mega-Projects: Bigger Is Better, or a 'Crazy

3.7.10 Overscaled and incomplete public realm throughout the Ensanche de Vallecas

demonstrate that the macroeconomic theories and mechanisms that motivated that particular moment in history remain firmly entrenched and minimally affected. In turn, design and planning must understand that the speculative expansions of settlement that were so central to that moment will continue in perpetuity, or at least as long as capitalism remains the dominant global economic system. As such, urbanization activities undertaken from these speculative motivations demand a new set of design and planning responses—responses that acknowledge the political and economic motivations behind these initiatives, but more critically, responses that anticipate the implicit volatility and wastefulness of these pursuits.

To understand the urgency of such a shift, one need only consider the myriad unintended consequences associated with these models of urbanization-induced economic growth. Artificially inflated land values, potentially massive capital waste, increased public and private debt, severe social disenfranchisement, environmental degradation, and potential political unrest are but a few. And while the incidence and severity of these consequences vary, we can presume that the increasing instrumentalization of urbanization as a primary driver of economic growth will result in a corresponding proliferation of these unintended outcomes. Thus, the ethical, social, economic, and environmental challenges that emerge from speculative urbanization practices present the biggest obstacle to and greatest motivation for retooling the practical and theoretical focus of contemporary urban design and planning.

Notably, the concern with these speculative activities is less a matter of the projects being pursued than it is of the social, environmental, political, and fiscal consequences that result. To be sure, this risk is inherent in all large-scale expansions of settlement, speculative

or otherwise. However, it becomes intensified as the scale of these expansions increases or as the frequency with which they occur accelerates.

Such circumstances suggest a revised approach to contemporary expansions of settlement, and the need to elaborate and deploy dynamic operating systems for urbanization that guide, but do not rigidly control, the implementation and occupation of these pursuits. This approach would shift the disciplinary products of this work away from solely defining the preferred outcome of proposals for new settlement plans, toward the anticipation of the myriad externalities and states of incompletion that may emerge over time. Such an attitude embraces the risk associated with these speculative pursuits as an attribute worth leveraging in the creation of new value centers and manifold contingencies, rather than something needing to be designed away.

While this may seem like a radical proposition, such a reorientation in no way precludes any of the myriad motivations that currently drive these speculative activities. Rather, it looks to harness these demands—defining new destinations for labor and capital, elevating land values, expanding tax revenue, creating the perception and image of growth, providing competitively distinct urban form, ensuring the capacity to accommodate population expansion, and more—all in the pursuit of approaches to the expansion of settlements that productively function in some capacity, even when they are interrupted or fail.

Such a reorientation relates specifically to what could be characterized as the "urban design" scale of practice. However, despite a retooled planning and design approach, the preceding legislative and financing processes that drive this urbanization remain unaddressed. And in truth, until these motivating protocols and procedures

Canal'?," *National Public Radio*, February 4, 2014, accessed October 10, 2015, http://www.npr .org/blogs/parallels /2014/02/04/267139656 /istanbuls-mega-projects -bigger-is-better-or-a -crazy-canal.

69 Paul Carsten, "China Unveils Anti-graft Rules for Urbanization Drive— State Media," *Reuters*, March 22, 2014, accessed October 10, 2015, http:// www.reuters.com /article/2014/03/29/us -china-realestate-idUS BREA2S0E920140329.

70 Kam Wing Chan, "Fundamentals of China's Urbanization and Policy," in "Urbanization in China: Processes and Policies," special issue, *China Review* 10, no. 1 (2010): 66–68.

71 Simon Cox, "Pedaling Prosperity," *Economist*, May 26, 2012, accessed October 10, 2015, http://www.economist .com/node/21555762.

72 Vanessa Watson, "African Urban Fantasies: Dreams or Nightmares?," *Environment and Urbanization* 26, no. 215 (2014): 229.

73 Jane Lumumba, "Why Africa Should Be Wary of Its 'New Cities,'" Informal City Dialogues, Rockefeller Foundation, May 2, 2013, accessed October 10, 2015, http:// nextcity.org/informal city/entry/why-africa -should-be-wary-of-its -new-cities.

are modified, planning and design's influence on speculative urbanization processes will remain measured at best.

Such a paradox poses an existential question for the disciplines involved in this work. On the one hand, despite adjustments to the means and methods employed, such a retooling does not change the fact that the work of these disciplines is more often than not rendered an instrument of capital and politics. On the other hand, we might optimistically infer that this instrumentalization suggests the possibility of an inherent, untapped agency in the work of planning and design. The challenge lies in enabling the logics and intelligence of a retooled approach to the physical articulation and deployment of speculative settlement to infiltrate the political and economic structures at the root of these endeavors. Achieving this is obviously easier said than done.

Whether this casts the urban designer in the role of negotiator, mediator, entrepreneur, manager, strategist, or tactician cannot be said with any degree of certainty. Perhaps it is all these things at different moments. What we can say with certainty is that the current disciplinary engagement by urban design and planning with the phenomenon of speculative urbanization is ominously inadequate, particularly given the seeming inevitability of its incidence and the increasing intensity of its consequence.

This essay is adapted from Christopher Marcinkoski, The City That Never Was *(New York: Princeton Architectural Press, 2015).*

3.8
NAVI MUMBAI
FROM NEW TOWN TO SUBURBIA

**Rahul Mehrotra and
Kanika Arora Sharma**

GOVERNANCE
& POLICY
CHALLENGES

NEOLIBERAL
PROPERTY
MARKETS

3.8.1 View of the CBD at the Belapur node in Navi Mumbai

The transformation of Navi Mumbai (formerly New Bombay) from idea to reality has significance for planners across the globe. It began as one of the most ambitious ideas for a new town in independent India, and became the bedroom suburb of Mumbai that we know today. The evolution occurred for multiple reasons; however, it was not by design. Today, in spite of being a suburb, Navi Mumbai's urban form of high-rise towers is denser than even the historic urban core of Mumbai. (fig. **3.8.1**)

This unexpected pattern has come to characterize the edges of most urban centers and metropolitan areas in India and South Asia, where expansion in the postindependence era was dealt with through the creation of new satellite towns.[1] The new town idea was fashionable in India in the 1950s and 1960s, when Chandigarh, New Bhubaneswar, and Gandhinagar emerged. With these developments as precedents, building new towns became a politically easy way

to acquire land and to gain acceptance within the political system for such investments. And, while new towns such as Chandigarh and Gandhinagar have retained their identities because they are also centers of political power, most new towns are eventually engulfed by their respective metropolitan regions. Initiated in the 1970s, Navi Mumbai is a case in point of how this loss of identity takes place. (fig. **3.8.2**)

The trajectory of Navi Mumbai starts with the establishment of unclear governance structures at its inception. The City and Industrial Development Corporation (CIDCO) was created to implement and manage Navi Mumbai, yet its relationship to Mumbai was not only never outlined or clearly understood, there was no connection at all between the two entities. Consequently, the new town was planned in complete isolation from the authorities managing "Old" Mumbai, which meant there were no shared visions for the region. Moreover, from the very

1   Satellite towns are smaller planned municipalities built in the vicinity of a major metropolitan city. Satellite towns generally depend on the core metropolitan city for employment and other services. Consumer-satellite towns are those that are designated as dormitory suburbs with few facilities, while producer-satellite towns have capacity for commercial, industrial, and other production distinct from that of the core metropolitan city.

beginning, CIDCO's objectives included contradictions that were never resolved.[2] On the one hand, Navi Mumbai was to be built from scratch and was to be geographically located at a very short distance from one of the world's largest cities. On the other hand, it was to become an independent new city, generating jobs and services from within. But encouraging the creation of Navi Mumbai just east of Mumbai, across the harbor, only created greater concentration in the metropolitan region and perpetuated Navi Mumbai's dependency and status as a dormitory suburb. (fig. **3.8.3**)

Ironically, this situation is far removed from the original vision of Navi Mumbai, which was intended to fundamentally alter the structure of Mumbai, its spirit, and its relationship to the hinterland. That ambitious vision carried all the optimism that symbolized independent India: a city on the water, people working and living in proximity, a new government center symbolizing the progressive nature of the state of Maharashtra, and, along with all of that, saving Mumbai from massive in-migration and uncontrolled growth. Most important, at least in the minds of the designers, there was a political agenda: creating a landscape of equity where the poor would have access to affordable land and be serviced by public transportation. (figs. **3.8.4**–**5**)

In 1964 the architects Charles Correa and the late Pravina Mehta, along with the civil engineer Shirish Patel, proposed the idea of urban development that would strike out onto the eastern mainland, instead of perpetuating growth in the northern direction. By building to the east, across the harbor, less pressure would be put on the north-south infrastructure that by the 1960s was already stretched to its limits. This idea was a response to the development plan of the Municipal Corporation of Greater Mumbai (MCGM), which continued to reinforce growth to

the north. For Correa, Patel, and Mehta, the starting point for this idea of a new city was the already planned extension of Mumbai's port at Nhava Sheva. There were also two industrial zones in the eastern mainland, Thane-Belapur and Taloja, for which housing and ancillary services would in any case have to be provided. Plus, the Thane Creek Bridge, a critical link to the mainland, was already under construction. (figs. **3.8.6**–**7**)

The idea of dispersing development away from Mumbai did not gain traction until 1969, when businessmen, leading architects and planners, and prominent public persons got behind a proposal to build a countermagnet across the Mumbai harbor. This proposal hinged on moving the state government to Navi Mumbai, which would help to divert pressure from the city's overburdened north-south infrastructure. The government offices would provide a clear purpose and core functions for the new town. But despite an initial, tacit agreement, the state government offices were never moved to Navi Mumbai, depriving the new town of its core function and the much-needed catalyst that would have generated independent growth. In the end, it was not plausible for a government institution, entrenched and thriving in an economically buoyant city, to uproot itself to a political tabula rasa and build a new constituency.

Governance, Policy, and Land Markets

The proposal for Navi Mumbai covered an area of about 133 square miles (344 square kilometers), integrating ninety-five villages spread over the districts of Thane and Raigad. The proposal for the new town included two million people; the population sources would be the old city, those already in the new town, and additional migration. Road, bridge, and waterway connections to the mainland from south Mumbai were proposed.

2   Almost as a checklist exercise, New Bombay Municipal Corporation (NBMC) was created in January 1992, some twenty years after CIDCO was formed. The councillors were elected after another three years and were given a part—almost less than one-third of the area falling under CIDCO's jurisdiction—to govern and manage. This hierarchal dilution of the government's authority in Navi Mumbai, at least theoretically, gave local population in the municipal area an easier access to the management of that part of Navi Mumbai. However, since the officials were elected for a very short duration of time, they never had the inclination to develop a concept of the city's future or take a long-term view of the city's condition. Instead, as the experience in Greater Mumbai has shown, the elected officials tend to resent direct citizen approaches to the civic officials, as in some cases the opportunity for extortion, graft, and blackmail are curtailed by such approaches.

Furthermore, in 1970 the state government established CIDCO as a corporate subsidiary—fully controlled and owned by the state—specifically to plan and manage Navi Mumbai.

This choice of organizational form was an ideological requirement for the business class, which had pushed through the Navi Mumbai idea and was anxious to ensure protection of its interests and a flow of favorable decisions from CIDCO Ltd. Had Navi Mumbai been planned by a conventional development authority, or by the Urban Planning Department of the state government, the business class would not have been able to influence day-to-day planning decisions as effectively as they were able to do with the establishment of CIDCO Ltd. Since the state government was the largest land shareholder in Mumbai, it voted quite favorably for this particular organizational structure, which gave it the best opportunity for control over the land. In retrospect, the arrangement could also be read as a way to perpetuate the corruption-related land management practices that were becoming the norm in early 1970s Mumbai. In fact, this massive infusion of developable urban land coincided with the beginnings of collusion between politicians and developers to control the supply—and thus the price—of this crucial urban commodity.

CIDCO's agenda was to plan and develop the new town, and give major relief to the existing city of Mumbai from pressures of population growth, overcrowding, and the intensification of both commercial and manufacturing activity. The 1973 charter declared as its main objectives: to avoid the spectacular and architectural grandeur of the city, to provide minimally for the affluent few, and to promote convenience for the greatest number of people. Thus, there was strong sentiment from the planners to make Navi Mumbai a city of the working class.

The original plan suggested that through its public ownership of land (CIDCO had acquired about 54,400 acres, or 22,000 hectares), a cash flow could be created to fund infrastructure, public transportation, and housing for the poor.[3] The planners chose, for instance, to emphasize public transport, giving less importance to private car traffic. For the business class, the approach of the proposal meant a diminishment of areas where it could intervene and make a profit.

As a result of their strengthened ties with the state government in Mumbai, many developments continued to flourish. For example, the development of the southern tip of Mumbai as a new commercial district added an enormous amount of office space, further congesting the city of Mumbai and increasing land prices. More important, this development sent two signals about the future of Navi Mumbai. First, that there was a lack of political will to cap the supply of land in south Mumbai in order to encourage and almost force growth into Navi Mumbai.[4] Second, because the market was saturated as a result of this new development, there would be diminishing demand for commercial space in Navi Mumbai. Limiting demand for commercial space in Navi Mumbai was critical, because the government needed to sell land in the new city in order to obtain funds for infrastructure investments there.

Moreover, in 1976 the Maharashtrian state government enacted the Urban Land Ceiling and Regulation Act (ULCAR), which limited the amount of urban land a person or a company could own to 5,382 square feet (500 square meters), in order to prevent land concentration in the hands of a few and improper land use. Any surplus land had to be surrendered to the state government at a minimal price. The act gave unlimited powers—or a near monopoly control—over land to the state

3 This situation raised another conflict in CIDCO's objectives for the new city. Navi Mumbai's land was intended to be used as a resource to generate "revolving funds" in order to finance projects in the city, whereas it also aimed at becoming "a city for all," where the basic urban and housing services would be provided both cheaply and sufficiently.

4 The Municipal Corporation of Greater Bombay (MCGB) submitted a development plan in 1964 that proposed a full-scale restructuring of the greater Bombay region by more stringent zoning laws, developing suburbs to absorb population growth, decentralizing industry, and developing the urban infrastructure. The business class was unhappy with the plan, as it would have caused increased taxation in terms of development taxes and burdened businesses with the heavy cost of relocating because of the large-scale restructuring of the city. Thus, the business class initially supported the planning of Navi Mumbai over MCGB's original development plan. However, CIDCO's objectives of planning a city for the common person were proving to be a deterrent in the business class's ambitions of making a profit in real estate, and thus it sought to monopolize land in Mumbai.

3.8.2 A typical water's edge condition in Navi Mumbai, where a buffer zone of mangroves is often left somewhat intact

3.8.3 A typical commuter train station in Navi Mumbai, where the air rights over the stations have been developed as commercial space to catalyze growth

3.8.4 Existing fishing villages, set in a landscape of mangroves, are often in a physically unresolved interface with the built environment of Navi Mumbai

3.8.5 Together with the fragile mangrove landscapes, existing *gaothans*, or villages, have been incorporated into the city as special zones to ensure their preservation

government, which already was by far the largest landholder in Mumbai.

The possibilities offered by ULCAR were fully exploited by big builders and developers, with the help of the state.[5] These firms developed many large tracts of land in suburban Mumbai as sprawling, composite housing complexes during the decades that followed the enactment of the ULCAR. Whenever there was no readily available land due to the constraints of the act, the state government created land by reclaiming it from the sea. This activity led to acute fluctuations in real estate prices. Land had become the single most important source for the funding of political parties in India and Mumbai—a golden goose for the party in power. Unfortunately, these construction and industrialization activities in Mumbai and Greater Mumbai were rapidly weakening the original intent of Navi Mumbai.[6] Its identity as a new town was compromised as the metropolitan region expanded to include more adjacent territory, reducing Navi Mumbai to merely one component in a larger urban conglomerate.[7]

For business interests, the bedroom suburb was a preferable scenario, in terms of control of land markets. Saturating the commercial land in South Mumbai ensured high real estate prices, and by limiting the supply of commercial land to be created at Navi Mumbai, it also ensured inflated values.

Competition from other nearby areas further diluted the purpose of Navi Mumbai. Vasai-Virar, covering 148 square miles (383 square kilometers), is the fifth-largest city in Maharashtra and located to the north of Mumbai. With a growing population of more than 1.2 million people, the area has emerged as a preferred location for affordable housing.[8] The city, by virtue of its relatively speedy development approval process, has attracted big real estate players and numerous massive construction plans for the near future.

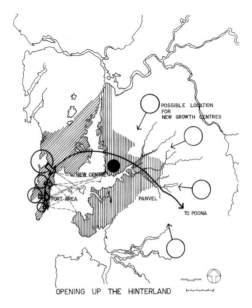

3.8.6 A schematic sketch by Charles Correa explaining the essential ideas for Navi Mumbai

This movement toward the north robs Navi Mumbai of land value, leaving it to the fate of being treated as a relatively inexpensive suburb, while Vasai-Virar is seen more as a natural extension of the city of Mumbai. The rapid influx of population has led to social and physical infrastructural capacity challenges while pushing the city beyond its limits and, inadvertently, fueling a rise in slums. In a sense, the urbanization of Vasai-Virar has pushed the clock back to the 1960s, when Navi Mumbai's original intention was specifically to avoid such a scenario of northward expansion.

Hence, what started out as a plan brimming with optimism and clarity was very quickly reduced to a blur of intentions. This outcome is particularly amazing given that, at its inception, the idea of Navi Mumbai was accepted by the state, which wanted to prove that effective action was possible. By supplying a critical resource—land—the government and planners hoped to increase housing construction (especially of affordable housing) in a dramatic way. Furthermore, by pooling the land under a single authority (through acquisition), the planners ensured that strategic planning at a macro

5 In fact this epitomized a larger structural problem in urban governance in India wherein while the central or federal government does construct national policy, and it is up to the state governments to implement these through local municipalities. Thus the disjuncture between the intent of the policy and the instruments to implement them on the ground sometimes is so great that these are susceptible to distortions. And often distorted subversively to facilitate corruption and to enrich the coffers of political parties.

6 When initially enacted, ULCAR was expected to act as a successful instrument in the hands of the state government to prevent the private sector from monopolizing the urban land. On the contrary, in practice, the state government largely took over that role and was playing the role of a developer or land speculator at the metropolitan scale.

7 Encouraging the creation of Navi Mumbai—or a new town in such proximity to the old—only created greater concentration in the Mumbai metropolitan region area and perpetuated dependency, forcing the new center to assume the role of a dormitory town.

8 Dilip Kumar Jha, "Vasai-Virar Emerging out of Mumbai's Shadows," *Business Standard*, April 11, 2015, accessed March 1, 2015, http://www.business-standard.com/article/pf/vasai-virar-region-114041101025_1.html.

level was possible. In spite of these advantages, Navi Mumbai failed to take off in any impactful way or measure up to its original intents of orchestrating growth in an equitable manner in the larger metropolitan region of Mumbai. In spite of a single authority owning the land, the development of Navi Mumbai continued to be sluggish up to 1985. It was only when India's economy liberalized, and the influx of capital increased speculation, that growth began to speed up tremendously.

Navi Mumbai in the Twenty-First Century

In the last decade, both economic and physical development has greatly accelerated. Much of the increase can be attributed to the physical linking by rail of Navi Mumbai with the major job centers of Mumbai, and the spurt in the liberalization of India's economy since 1991, which created a demand for commercial and residential space. It has been estimated that Navi Mumbai grew at 119 percent during 1991 to 2001, and that the population in 2011 was 1,119,477. However, Navi Mumbai still looks toward Mumbai for its success. A recent survey showed that 40 percent of the workforce is still dependent on the old city for jobs.[9] Furthermore, the rapidly increasing property rates in the old city are pushing middle-class households out to the periphery, including Navi Mumbai.

The fact still remains that this increased growth has been possible only because Navi Mumbai is so closely located to Mumbai proper. If Navi Mumbai had been located at a significant distance, as has been the case with most newly developed towns in the developing world, it would never have developed in the same way, and perhaps never have developed at all.

Today, Navi Mumbai is seen primarily as a landscape of four-story, reinforced-cement concrete structures that plod

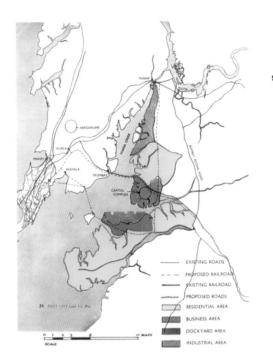

3.8.7 Plan showing the broad land-use and infrastructure components for Navi Mumbai

9   "Studies and Surveys," CIDCO, 2015, accessed March 5, 2015, http://www.cidco.maharashtra.gov.in/MD_Studies _Surveys.aspx#middel.

relentlessly through the landscape. The rail link, two decades too late, has brought a new gush of energy to the urban system. Oversized railway stations dwarf the surrounding built environment, waiting anxiously for the city to sprout around them. The central business district at Belapur is a ghost town (barring some government offices) under the ownership of Non-Resident Indians and Indian speculators who wait patiently for the emerging city to cause an appreciation in the prices of the property they own. The government and CIDCO now also speculate on this land to finance the development of physical and social infrastructure. Unfortunately, this speculation is limited by political decisions that dictate who can be allocated or sold land, which in turn constrains how these holdings could be leveraged through more dynamic investments in diverse global markets.

Nowadays, the idea of the state government moving to Navi Mumbai—the original idea that Navi Mumbai hinged on—is as distant a possibility as it was two decades ago.

However, growth is anticipated from a major infrastructural investment to construct a second airport for the region in Navi Mumbai, given the increasing contestation of land around the existing airport in Mumbai and the need for better hinterland connections. The proposal is for nothing less than the world's largest greenfield airport, spreading over 2,866 acres (1,160 hectares), and is expected to annually handle ten million passengers in 2017 (its first operational year) and, ultimately, sixty million by 2030.[10] It will be situated near Panvel in the geographical center of Navi Mumbai, and approximately 22 miles (35 kilometers) away from the existing Chhatrapati Shivaji International Airport in Mumbai.[11] The site chosen for the airport is in proximity to the central business district of Navi Mumbai, which is projected, in the imagination of the state government authorities, to cater to the future growth in population and in business and commercial activities in the Mumbai Metropolitan Region.

In February 2015 the current chief minister of Maharashtra set an ambitious deadline of four years for the airport project completion. The airport is expected to play the vital role of a catalyst that will accelerate the economy of Navi Mumbai. To make connectivity to the airport fast and reliable, multimodal transport linkages via road and rail/metro have also been proposed. These linkages are expected to both help manage the increased traffic the airport will generate and to significantly improve the quality of infrastructure in Navi Mumbai.

The Importance of an Urban Design Vision

How could the planners of Navi Mumbai really have expected to create, next door to a vital, capitalist, market-driven city that grew piecemeal, its exact opposite: a preconceived urban system based on true social justice? The last six decades of independent India have clearly demonstrated that the myopic view of Indian politicians leads them to "find and claim," cities rather than to "make" them. Or perhaps Navi Mumbai's initial failure stems from the tendency by planners to conceive of growth in ideal terms, creating a bridge too wide for the implementers of the plans to grapple with.

Similarly, perceived failures at the physical planning level also deserve critical attention. Planning policies and priorities for Navi Mumbai have been strangely misplaced, raising questions that range from the appropriateness of the housing and building typologies to those on macro-level issues such as the connections via bridge to Mumbai. In its original intent, Navi Mumbai was to be the "self-help city," where serviced, affordable land could allow both low-income and rich families to build incrementally.

The planning authority shift, as land prices increased, to encourage highrise buildings priced out a large segment of the low- and middle-income families for whom incremental investments in a home were the only way to afford and grow that home. Furthermore, in spite of CIDCO's majority ownership of the land, Navi Mumbai failed to break loose from replicating the building bylaws of Mumbai, which instituted a high floorarea ratio (FAR)—in other words, a requirement for high density—over the entire city, with no sensitivity to geográphy or terrain. In the case of Navi Mumbai, where the geography or terrain offered so many urban design possibilities, a blanket FAR ravaged the natural terrain, resulting in similar building forms whether the site was at the edge of the sea or on a hill. Couldn't policies have been more sympathetic to the natural landscape, as well as to issues of affordability, in terms of the building typologies they encouraged?

10 "Navi Mumbai International Airport (NMIA): About the Project," CIDCO, accessed March 2, 2015, http://www.cidco.maharashtra.gov.in/NMIA_AbouttheProjects.aspx.

11 "Navi Mumbai International Airport," NMIA, 2015, accessed March 2, 2015, http://cidconmia.com/website/nmia-2/nmia/about-navi-mumbai-international-airport/.

Given the fact that all the land is under single ownership, new bylaws that would allow innovative built forms were more than possible. In that sense, urban design visions were totally absent in the conception of Navi Mumbai. There were no pictures or images to work toward. A clear, compelling urban design vision might have more strongly motivated the multifaceted set of players—ranging from politicians to industrialists to technicians and citizens—to fulfill the new town concept.

The only physical image that the planners consistently referred to was the notion of the "city on the water." But this image is restricted to the experience of crossing the bay, and only once the water transport systems with bridges were put in place. Aside from the landing points, the remaining potential waterfront strips are definitively buffered from the waterfront by healthy mangrove forests or mud flats. One might argue that a city like Mumbai started in the same fashion; as the city swelled out, it became economical to reclaim land, as in the Apollo Bunder or the Marine Drive developments in Mumbai. To focus physical imagery on a relationship with the water's edge—without the water transportation systems—limited the idea to merely an evocative illusion. If planners had interrogated and negotiated the constraints of dealing with the mangroves on the water's edge, and imagined landing points for the ferries that would connect old Bombay, it would have perhaps resulted in specific imagery.

India's Suburban Imagination

Navi Mumbai would have truly been an idea ahead of its time had it more precisely linked the planning decisions of Navi Mumbai with that of Mumbai. Questions of renewal, conservation, and economic policies and of demographic projections would have perhaps more

precisely indicated a program for Navi Mumbai with clearer multiple strategies aimed at end results, rather than an open-ended, flexible planning strategy waiting to be fine-tuned as it went along. In that sense, the planning exercise can be perceived as a "flight into Utopia," the creation of a preferred reality far removed from the complexities of urban planning for an existing city.[12]

But even the most complex planning strategies for new towns often have not produced ideal results or made accurate projections about the future. The Navi Mumbai exercise has to be viewed strictly in the context of the available planning data and understanding of the future at the time. What the plan most importantly did was bring to the fore the importance of creating macro-level strategies for the orchestration of urban growth. Whether one likes the form of Navi Mumbai or not, it is a planned development with infrastructure and built form working in tandem.

The case of Navi Mumbai also resonates broadly across India. Especially in Indian megacities, similar developments—for example, Dwarka, Noida, and Gurgaon in Delhi, and Salt Lake City in Calcutta—built close to urban cores are in effect a new form of Indian suburbanism. Their proximity to urban cores limited their ability to flourish as centers in and of themselves. Furthermore, their governance structures, with the state government having ownership as well as legislative control, sealed their fate as dependent suburbs and not new towns, as they were politically presented. Perhaps the political argument for a new town was that it was the easiest mechanism by which governments could acquire land for development.

The idea of new towns in India became, by default, the trigger for the Indian suburban imagination. Landscapes that started off as settlements emulated

12 In the case of Navi Mumbai, CIDCO had to let go of many of its original objectives, indulging in the type of planning that involves overlooking and ignoring the problems, which affected the common man while finding justifications, real and imaginary, to push through solutions in the name of the poor to benefit the rich.

the low-rise, low-density patterns of the Colonial Cantonment, the ideal townscape for the middle-class, contemporary Indian urban dweller. These places were attempts to create self-sufficient job locations and opportunities within a matrix of adequate infrastructure. But they quickly morphed into suburban conditions. At the outset, they were epitomes of a new vision and of a preferred reality symbolizing the idealism and belief of being able to structure society through the design of the built environment. However, because they were often in proximity to large, existing urban centers, they became mere extensions of these urban conglomerates. The DNA of places like Navi Mumbai was not suburbia as imagined in North America but an urban imagination that aspired to create new towns. This was asynchronous with the urban Indian reality, resulting in a particular suburban condition for India.

This essay borrows a few short excerpts from Rahul Mehrotra, "From New Bombay to Navi Mumbai," Architecture + Design *XIV, no. 2 (March–April 1997).*

Kharghar, Navi Mumbai, Maharashtra, India

Airoli, Navi Mumbai, Maharashtra, India

3.9
POSTSUBURBAN JOHANNESBURG

Martin J. Murray

Like other rapidly expanding metropolitan agglomerations, the greater Johannesburg metropolitan region has become a vast, distended megalopolis without obvious or fixed boundaries. In a reversal of the conventional concentric model of urban expansion, the spatial configuration of the greater Johannesburg metropolitan region combines a high-density concentration of nodal points within an extended, low-density fabric.[1] This is the kind of place urban theorists have called the extended metropolis, polycentric metropolis, sprawl city, exopolis, postmetropolis, the dispersed metropolis, the limitless city, the one-hundred-mile city, or the city turned inside out.[2]

From the start, the Johannesburg central city was *primus inter pares*—"first among equals"—in a far-flung, rapidly urbanizing mining empire. The historic downtown core was supplemented by a number of satellite cities and small towns that stretched in an east-west line for sixty miles or so along the gold-bearing reef.[3] The sometimes gradual (and sometimes abrupt) unfolding of complex processes of spatial restructuring have reinforced the continuing mutation of Johannesburg. The city has changed from what was originally a dominant central nucleus and dependent residential suburbs into a polycentric, postindustrial metropolis. Today, it resembles a heterogeneous assemblage of highly differentiated and relatively autonomous edge cities, commercial clusters, gated residential estates, and corporate business nodes that have blossomed along the exurban fringe. Moreover, the coexistence of fragments from different historical periods has produced a mixed urban landscape of the "new" interwoven with the "old."[4] In this sense, Johannesburg is not really a single place but a makeshift patchwork of different places, each with its own particular sociospatial characteristics.[5] The declining significance of a singular

and once vibrant historic downtown core as the primary locus for corporate office complexes and upscale commercial activities—coupled with the accelerated pace of peripheral urbanization (or the urbanization of suburbia)—have produced a highly uneven, heterogeneous, and incongruous spatial landscape that consists of a largely unplanned hodgepodge of distinctive building typologies, design motifs, and architectural styles.[6] The postsuburban landscapes of the Greater Johannesburg metropolitan region are the outcome of the conjoined processes of spatial fragmentation, decentralization, and unregulated horizontal sprawl. The power of real estate capitalism, combined with lax regulatory frameworks governing land-use policies and spatial planning, has led to a highly fragmented, unequal, polycentric metropolis.[7]

Real Estate Capitalism

Simply put, real estate capitalism rests on private ownership of urban properties (land and buildings) where profit-seeking investments depend on competitive market exchange. Wherever the logic of market competition operates as the principal mechanism governing the organization and use of urban space, real estate capitalism is the driving force behind city building. The rule of real estate constantly transforms the built environment, reconfiguring land uses and building typologies in accordance with their relative value as marketable commodities (i.e., assets to be bought and sold). However, what gives real estate capitalism its historical specificity (i.e., its meaning in a particular time and place) as a form of commodity production and circulation is that capital invested in the built environment is immobilized for long periods of time in material embodiments of various kinds that are fixed in place. This "spatial fix" has the effect of tying up whole areas of real estate

1   See also Martin J. Murray, *The City of Extremes: Spatial Politics in Johannesburg* (Durham, NC: Duke University Press, 2011), 4, 32.
2   Peter Hall and Kathy Pain, "From Metropolis to Polyopolis," in *The Polycentric Metropolis: Learning from Mega-City Regions in Europe*, ed. Peter Hall and Kathy Pain (New York: Earthscan, 2006), 3–18; Oliver Gillham, *The Limitless City: A Primer on the Urban Sprawl Debate* (Washington, DC: Island Press, 2002); Edward Soja, "Inside Exopolis: Scenes from Orange County," in *Variations on a Theme Park*, ed. Michael Sorkin (New York: Hill & Wang, 1992), 94–122; and Edward Soja, *Postmetropolis: Critical Studies of Cities and Regions* (Oxford: Wiley-Blackwell, 2000); and Deyan Sudjic, *The 100-Mile City* (San Diego: Harcourt Brace & Company, 1993).
3   Gerhard-Mark Van der Waal, *From Mining Camp to Metropolis* (Pretoria: Chris van Rensburg for the Human Sciences Research Council, 1987).
4   Clive Chipkin, *Johannesburg Transition: Architecture & Society from 1950* (Johannesburg: STE Publishers, 2008), 375–400.
5   Murray, *City of Extremes*, 29.
6   David Dewar, "Settlements, Change and Planning in South Africa since 1994," in *Blank_____ Architecture, Apartheid and After*, ed. Hilton Judin and Ivan Vladislović (Rotterdam: NAi, 1999), 365–75; Murray, *City of Extremes*, 32; and Chipkin, *Johannesburg Transition*.
7   Clive Chipkin, "The Great Apartheid Building Boom: The Transformation of Johannesburg in the 1960s," in *Blank_____ Architecture, Apartheid and After*, ed. Hilton Judin and Ivan Vladislović (Rotterdam: NAi, 1999), 248–67.

3.9.1 Bunker architecture is ubiquitous in the northern suburbs

8 Murray, *City of Extremes*, 16.
9 Murray, *Taming the Disorderly City*, 125–27.
10 Robert Beauregard, "The Textures of Property Markets: Downtown Housing and Office Conversions in New York City," *Urban Studies* 43, no. 13 (2005): 2431–45.
11 Murray, *City of Extremes*, 16–17. These ideas are originally derived from David Scobey, *Empire City: The Making and Meaning of the New York City Landscape* (Philadelphia: Temple University Press, 2002), 7, 59, 87, 132–33, 173.

over long periods of time in one specific land use, thereby creating significant barriers to capital mobility and to new development elsewhere.[8] An example of a "spatial fix" would be investments in shopping malls or sports stadiums that are constructed to last a long time, despite the possibilities of declining revenues and outdated design.

The spatial dynamics of real estate capitalism embed their own dysfunctionalities, irrationalities, and incongruities into the built environment. The expansive cycle of entrepreneurial investment in land and property tends to break down over time, leading to abandonment and withdrawal. Real estate capitalism depends on functional interdependence of property investments (what real estate agents refer to as "location, location, location") for its continued success. Yet the achievement of this functional interdependence does not automatically take place through the operation of the frictionless market logic of supply and demand.[9] Because investments in different building typologies and land uses conform to different micrologics (with

dissimilar temporal rhythms and time horizons) that are often not synchronized with each other, real estate capitalism is notoriously fickle and unpredictable. Put simply, profit-seeking investments in buildings and land uses typically vary from the search for quick returns in a short time versus steady profits over a long time span. The social, institutional, and place-specific qualities of real estate investments—or what Robert Beauregard has called "the thickness" of property markets—impede the smooth functioning of marketplace competition in land and property.[10] (fig. **3.9.1**)

In theoretical terms, real estate capitalism responds to an erratic rhythm where investment decisions careen back and forth between the obsessive calculation of profit and loss in immobile assets ("sunk capital," which is fixed in place) versus speculative excess in anticipated yet untested profitability elsewhere.[11] Put in another way, the transformation of urban space into alienable commodified parcels "traps real estate capitalism between the unstable imperatives of alternating spatial logics." On the one side,

3.9.2 Fortified suburbs have proliferated

12 Murray, *City of Extremes*, 17.
13 Keith S. O. Beavon, "Johannesburg: A City and Metropolitan Area in Transformation," in *The Urban Challenge in Africa: Growth and Management in Large Cities*, ed. Carole Rakodi (Tokyo: United Nations University Press, 1997), 150–91; Keith S. O. Beavon, "Johannesburg: Getting to Grips with Globalisation from an Abnormal Base," in *Globalisation and the World of Large Cities*, ed. Fu-Chen Lo and Yue-Man Yeung (Tokyo: United Nations University, 1998), 352–88; Keith Beavon, *Johannesburg: The Making and Shaping of the City* (Pretoria: University of South Africa Press, 2004); and Murray, *City of Extremes*, 103–8.
14 Martin J. Murray, *Taming the Disorderly City: The Spatial Landscape of Johannesburg after Apartheid* (Ithaca, NY: Cornell University Press, 2008), 13; and Lindsay Bremner, "Remaking Johannesburg," in *Future City*, ed. Stephen Read, Jürgen Rosemann, and Job van Eldijk (London and New York: Spon Press, 2005), 32–47.
15 Keller Easterling, *Enduring Innocence: Global Architecture and Its Political Masquerades* (Cambridge, MA: MIT Press, 1995); and Murray, *City of Extremes*, 285.
16 Alan Lipman and Howard Harris, "Fortress Johannesburg," *Environment and Planning B* 26, no. 5 (1999): 727–40.
17 Lindsay Bremner, "Crime and the Emerging Landscape of Post-Apartheid Johannesburg," in *Blank_____ Architecture, Apartheid and After*, ed. Hilton Judin and Ivan Vladislović (Rotterdam: NAi, 1999), 48–63; Lindsay Bremner, "Closure, Simulation, and "Making Do" in the Contemporary Johannesburg Landscape," in *Under*

capital fixed-in-place gives property owners no other option but to squeeze profits out of existing investments (sometimes overvalued and underperforming) in the built environment. On the other hand, the lure of higher profit rates encourages real estate capitalists to undertake speculative investments in new locations.[12]

Real estate capitalism—with its stress on locational advantage, market-based competition over land and property, and the principle of "highest-and-best use" as an efficiency strategy for optimal allocation resources—has always been the dominant driving force behind city building in Greater Johannesburg.[13] In other words, private profit-seeking investments in landed property have transformed the built environment in ways that privilege private interests over the common good. Despite the concerted efforts of urban planners and public-policy makers to shape urban growth, Greater Johannesburg has developed more or less opportunistically in line with competitive property markets rather than as a result of the deliberate design of a centralized planning authority.[14] Large

commercial banks have collaborated with developers, building contractors, architectural and design firms, and real estate agents to carefully plan and aggressively market a wide range of commercialized "spatial products" (to borrow a term from Keller Easterling). These "spatial products" cater to the affluent middle classes seeking safe and secure environments to insulate them from the uncertain vagaries of metropolitan life, including the fear of crime, discomfort with overcrowded public spaces, and anxiety about the racialized "Other."[15] Without exception, these building typologies for the affluent are inward-looking, fortified enclaves that have turned their backs on the surrounding cityscape.[16] The long-term consequence is urbanism that is divided along class and race lines.[17] (fig. **3.9.2**)

Suburban sprawl is often thought of as the (unwelcome) outcome of cultural preferences (and the insatiable appetite) for single-family homes and automobile use. But real estate capitalism has its own logic for making cities and suburbs. Buying vast swaths of land cheaply on the exurban fringe and converting it

Siege: Four African Cities. Freetown, Johannesburg, Kinshasa, Lagos. Documenta 11_Platform 4, ed. Okwui Enwezor et al. (Ostfildern-Ruit, Germany: Hatje Cantz Publishers, 2002), 153–72; Lindsay Bremner, *Writing the City into Being: Essays on Johannesburg* (Johannesburg: Fourthwall Books, 2010, 140–48.

18   For the source of some of these ideas, see Richard Walker and Alex Schafran, "The Strange Case of the Bay Area," *Environment and Planning A* 77, no. 1 (2015): 10–29 (esp. 17–18).

19   Murray, *Taming the Disorderly City*, 189–224.

3.9.3 Fortifying homes typically consists of a range of security measures

into look-alike tract housing and mono-chromatic strip malls has long enabled large-scale property developers and land speculators alike to realize huge profits, where the mass production of everything from single-family detached suburban homes to cluster townhouse developments was made into a popular stylistic virtue.[18] Besides purchasing vast tracts of land on the exurban fringe, large-scale "merchant builders" were able to keep down costs through simplicity of building construc-tion and repetition of physical forms while increasing unit revenues through appeals to suburban tranquility and escape from "crime and grime" in areas closer to the central city. In deciding what to build and where to build it, real estate devel-opers have been aided by lax planning regulations governing land use. Starting in the 1990s and continuing for at least a decade, the combination of weak planning frameworks, lax regulatory mechanisms, and inconsistent code enforcement provided real estate devel-opers with a great deal of discretionary power to build without much public oversight.[19]

As a result, large-scale real estate developers were able to erect new shop-ping centers, office complexes, and other commercial establishments along the main arterial roadways that cut through the residential suburban neigh-borhoods of northern Johannesburg. At the same time, so-called merchant builders—in search of quick returns on investments—were able construct one cloned residential suburban subdivision after another on the exurban fringe, pushing the metropolitan boundaries farther afield from the historic downtown core. (fig. **3.9.3**)

In addition, competition between rival municipalities (particularly Sandton, Rosebank, and Randburg) seeking to lure private real estate investment meant that holistic and comprehensive spatial planning was very difficult to manage. In Johannesburg, as elsewhere, city-building processes have created a layered tapes-try of different building typologies that largely reflect the power of real estate capital to shape the built environment. The conjoined processes of in-fill high-rise development, plot subdivision, and land-use rezoning have contributed to high densities in distinct pockets spread unevenly across the metropolitan region.[20]

Building Postsuburbia

The transition from a mining-industrial city to a post-mining-industrial metropolis traces its origins to the 1950s and 1960s when the first wave of residential suburbs, small business nodes, and clusters of decentralized shopping that bulged to the north began to break free of the gravitational pull of the historic downtown core.[21] The suburbanizing pressures that gripped Johannesburg in the 1950s and 1960s produced, for the most part, a low-density city that extended horizontally rather than vertically.

The combined forces of centrifugal urbanism proved to be quite formidable. As the pace of suburbanization to the north of the downtown urban core accelerated, the influx of office-based businesses and retail shopping quickly followed. The establishment of Randburg (1959) and Sandton (1969)—both with their own central business districts—signaled the emergence of a polycentric metropolitan region. Their coming into being as independent municipalities marked the onset of a protracted phase of spatial restructuring. (fig. **3.9.4**)

Beginning in the 1970s, real estate developers began to systematically build spacious office parks, expansive shopping malls, and small-scale hypermarket retail complexes at key nodal points in the affluent residential suburbs that had spread north of the city center. By offering new employment opportunities, luxury housing, upscale shopping, and other services (which in the past had only been available closer to the city center), these business nodal points (like Sandton, Randburg, Hyde Park, Rosebank, Midrand, Sunninghill, Bryanston, Illovo, and Fourways) are paradigmatic

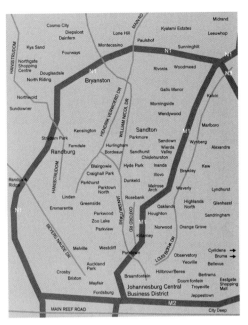

3.9.4 Northern suburbs

exemplars of what urban theorists have called edge cities, boomburbs, stealth cities, exurbs, edgeless cities, or technoburbs.[22] These emergent satellite cities have attracted significant capital investment, particularly in the areas of office headquarters, enclosed shopping centers, high-end residential compounds, light industries and small-scale manufacturing operations, and upscale leisure and entertainment sites.[23]

Starting in the 1980s (if not earlier), entirely new outer rings of concentrated business-commercial centers proliferated along the northern perimeter of the sprawling metropolis. Located much further afield than the original satellite cities (notably, Sandton, Randburg, and Rosebank), these new nodal growth points include Weltevreden Park, Randpark Ridge, Honeydew, Fourways, and Sunninghill, and—even farther afield—Lanseria, Midrand, and Kempton Park. Corporate headquarters, financial institutions (including the Johannesburg Stock Exchange), and upscale commercial establishments abandoned the central city for emergent business locations to the north. In doing so, they left behind a hollowed-out downtown core, with vacant

20 Alan Mabin, "Reconstruction and the Making of Urban Planning in Twentieth Century South Africa," in *Blank_____ Architecture, Apartheid and After*, ed. Hilton Judin and Ivan Vladislović (Rotterdam: NAi, 1999), 269–77; Alan Mabin and David Smit, "Reconstructing South Africa's Cities? The Making of Urban Planning 1900–2000," *Planning Perspectives* 12, no. 2 (1997): 193–223.

21 Beavon, *Johannesburg*, 147–96; and Murray, *City of Extremes*, 103–8; Chipkin, "The Great Apartheid Building Boom," 248–67.

22 Joel Garreau, *Edge City: Life on the New Frontier* (New York: Doubleday, 1991); Paul Knox, "Suburbia by Stealth," *Geographical Magazine* 64, no. 8 (1992): 26–29; Robert Lang and Jennifer LeFurgy, *Boomburgs: The Rise of America's Accidental Cities* (Washington, DC: Brookings Institution Press, 2007); Robert Lang, *Edgeless Cities: Exploring the Elusive Metropolis* (Washington, DC: Brookings Institution Press, 2003); Robert Lang and Paul Knox, "The New Metropolis: Rethinking Megalopolis," *Regional Studies* 43, no. 6 (2009): 789–802; and Robert Fishman, *Bourgeois Utopias: The Rise and Fall of Suburbia* (New York: Basic Books, 1987).

23 Soraya Goga, "Property Investors and Decentralization: A Case of False Competition?," in *Emerging Johannesburg: Perspectives on the Post-Apartheid City*, ed. Richard Tomlinson, Robert Beauregard, Lindsay Bremner, and Xolela Mangcu (New York: Routledge, 2003), 71–82.

3.9.5 Residential Associations have unilaterally and illegally closed off roads in their suburbs

24 Murray, *City of Extremes,*
    87–135; Beavon,
    *Johannesburg: The
    Making and Shaping of
    the City,* 287–34.
25 Murray, "City of Layers,"
    183–84.
26 Lindsay Bremner,
    *Johannesburg: One
    City, Colliding Worlds*
    (Johannesburg: STE
    Publishers, 2004), 30–61;
    Murray, *City of Extremes,*
    119–20; Alan Mabin,
    "Johannesburg: (South)
    Africa's Aspirant Global
    City," in *The Making
    of Global City Regions:
    Johannesburg, Mumbai/
    Bombay, São Paulo,
    and Shanghai,* ed. Klaus
    Segbers (Baltimore:
    Johns Hopkins
    University Press, 2007),
    32–63; and Mfaniseni
    Sihlongonyane, "The
    Rhetoric of Africanism
    in Johannesburg as a
    World African City,"
    Africa Insight 34, no. 2
    (2005): 22–30.

buildings, blighted residential neighborhoods, less-than-optimal land uses.[24]

While the original satellite cities have evolved into central components of the metropolitan region, the latest round of peripheral development has now spilled well beyond the metropolitan boundaries. New developments in Centurion and Pretoria South have emerged as major business-residential-entertainment nodes in their own right. They are connected to one another by almost uninterrupted ribbons of development: winding corridors of low-rise office buildings, warehousing and distribution facilities, industrial parks, manufacturing sites, and nondescript strip malls, interspersed with multiuse casino complexes (Montecasino, Emperors Palace), upscale shopping malls (Hyde Park Mall, Fourways Mall, and Pine Slopes), gated residential estates (Dainfern), luxury golf courses (Kyalami, Lone Hill, Blue Valley, Jackal Creek, and Leeukop), luxurious getaway conference facilities located in tranquil country settings, and completely new master-planned and holistically designed cities built entirely from scratch (Waterfall City and Steyn City).[25] (fig. **3.9.5**)

While still overshadowed by Sandton (universally acknowledged as the premier financial and corporate showcase destination in the Greater Johannesburg metropolitan region), these emergent development nodes are real-life laboratories for new experiments in urbanity. They are works in progress that give new substance and meaning to evolving patterns of peripheral urbanization. Their poorly planned landscapes—driven primarily by real estate developers with little outside interference by public authorities—provide visible clues for understanding the long-term implications of city building in the "new South Africa," and how the emergent glamor and luxury zones are linked to global flows of capital, information, commodities, and people. In the headlong rush to become recognized as an African world-class city, real estate developers have concentrated on building upscale enclaves that are in line with global standards of stylized luxury and convenience.[26]

Like other aspiring world-class cities around the world, Johannesburg at the start of the twenty-first century has

27 Murray, *City of Extremes*, 122, 127–28.

3.9.6 Street barricades have appeared everywhere

become an experimental site for improvisational engagements with modernity, cosmopolitanism, and globalization. City boosters have hailed such new additions to the built environment as high-speed rail (the Gautrain), the hosting of internationally acclaimed sporting events (the 2010 World Cup), and the construction of world-class hotels (the Michelangelo Towers in Sandton) as key catalysts in the branding effort to promote the roseate image of Johannesburg in the rank order of aspiring world-class cities. Since the end of apartheid and the transition to parliamentary democracy, the steady accretion of large-scale, mixed-use urban enclaves—inserted wherever they can fit in the existing metropolitan fabric—has become a standardized city-building strategy for real estate developers in Johannesburg seeking to produce a world-class city.

One example of a Greater Johannesburg satellite city is Midrand, located between Johannesburg and Pretoria. Midrand has all the ingredients of a bustling, energetic magnet within the polynuclear metropolis: corporate office parks, warehousing and distribution facilities, high-tech manufacturing sites, retail and commercial outlets, entertainment extravaganzas, and luxury residential developments, as well as its easy access to the main highways and its own distinctive identity. The combination of a business-friendly municipal government, amendments to existing zoning regulations, and land available for property development have fueled its rapid economic growth. In the minds of urban planners, corporate executives, and real estate developers, its central location about halfway along the growth corridor linking central Johannesburg with Pretoria makes Midrand the ideal site: an imaginary future city around which to "re-center" the sprawling metropolitan region. Despite the efforts of public authorities to control growth, the last remaining tracts of vacant land in and around Midrand have become vulnerable to poorly planned real estate development and to speculative leapfrog patterns of growth.[27] (fig. **3.9.6**)

3.9.7 Unauthorized street closures have carved up the suburban streetscape

The Uneven Topographies of Postsuburbia

Johannesburg after apartheid has entered a new era of distinctly postsuburban growth, which represents a paradigmatic shift in the shape and structure of cities.[28] To a certain extent, urban transformation in the greater Johannesburg metropolitan region has mimicked patterns (and followed similar pathways) that have occurred elsewhere in aspiring world-class cities.[29] Monochromatic residential suburbs, once dependent on the central city, have metamorphosed into semiautonomous "outer cities that rival and often surpass the traditional big-city downtowns as vibrant centers of socioeconomic power and commercial vitality."[30]

In a sense, these satellite cities are not really subordinate appendages of the historic downtown core anymore, rather they are evolving urban entities in their own right: metastasizing landscapes of high-rise skyscrapers, office parks, and upscale retail palaces, arranged in formidable clusters that create place-specific identities of their own. The kind of post-suburban development that has

taken place in Johannesburg does not represent a temporary deviation that can be expected to eventually return to the gravitational pull of the historic downtown core. Instead, this pattern of spatial restructuring signals a massive relocation of material and political power toward new centers of wealth on the exurban fringe. At the fringe, the affluent middle classes have recongregated and regrouped in their long march to escape the alleged "crime and grime" of the historic downtown and the impoverished inner-city residential zones (particularly Hillbrow, Berea, Joubert Park, Yeoville, Bertrams, and Doornfontein).[31] (fig. **3.9.7**)

The layering of various building typologies on top of what were once monofunctional residential suburban neighborhoods has fundamentally reshaped the social fabric of the city. These building types include gigantic shopping malls and "shoppertainment" extravaganzas, gated residential estates, strip malls and commercial clusters (along all major arterial roads), securitized office parks, townhouse cluster developments, entertainment enclaves, and,

28 Mark Gottdiener and George Kephart, "The Multinucleated Region: A Comparative Analysis," in *Post-suburban California: The Transformation of Orange County since World War Two*, ed. Rob Kling, Spencer Olin, and Mark Poster (Berkeley: University of California Press, 1995), 31–54; Nicholas Phelps, Andrew Wood, and David Valler, "A Postsuburban World? An Outline of a Research Agenda," *Environment and Planning A* 42, no. 2 (2010): 366–83; Paul Knox, *Metroburbia, USA* (New Brunswick, NJ: Rutgers University Press, 2008); and Jon Teaford, *Post-suburbia: Government and Politics in the Edge Cities* (Baltimore: Johns Hopkins University Press, 1997). See also Nicholas Phelps and Wulong Wu, eds., *International Perspectives on Suburbanization: A Post-Suburban World?* (New York: Palgrave Macmillan, 2011).

29 Catherine Coquery-Vidrovich, "Review Essay: Is L.A. a Model or a Mess?," *American Historical Review* 105, no. 5 (2000): 1683–91.

30 See David Kolb, "Many Centers: Suburban Habitus," *City* 15, no. 2 (2011): 155–66.

31 Murray, *Taming the Disorderly City*, 84–89; Martin Murray, "The City in Fragments: Kaleidoscopic Johannesburg after Apartheid," in *The Spaces of the Modern City: Imaginaries, Politics, and Everyday Life*, ed. Gyan Prakash and Kevin Kruse (Princeton, NJ: Princeton University Press, 2008), 144–78.

3.9.8 Private residences are walled off from the streets

most recently, entirely new satellite cities built entirely from scratch.[32] The steady accretion of these spatial products—sometimes replacing older building typologies, sometimes juxtaposed alongside them—has resulted in a highly irregular, "lumpy" metropolitan landscape that has come to resemble an assemblage of fragmented enclaves.[33]

With the prospects for a significant reduction in crime or improved public policing at best a remote possibility, real estate developers and marketing agencies have actively promoted these hybrid types of self-contained enclaves in the heart of suburbia as the wave of the future for urban South Africa.[34] Security-conscious business tenants and middle-class homeowners have embraced this type of sequestered urbanism, which combines a truncated version of New Urbanist principles (human-scale, pedestrian-friendly) with the fortress-like features of gated security estates. For relatively affluent South Africans, unsettled by many years of exposure to high levels of crime, mixed-use developments that combine a variety of activities in one location offer

opportunities for residents to work, shop, and play without venturing outside the confines of their secure urban village.[35] By projecting a new identity for affluent urban residents seeking to attach themselves to the image of cosmopolitan, global citizens, these showcase business and entertainment precincts represent the archetype of privately owned and privately managed postpublic space.[36] (fig. **3.9.8**)

Their serial replication of such bubble-like enclosures has transformed the urban landscape into an assemblage of sequestered business parks, gated residential estates, and upscale entertainment sites set apart from the dystopian realities of derelict buildings, declining municipal services, shrinking public spaces, deteriorating urban infrastructure, litter-strewn streets, homeless encampments, sidewalk hawkers, youthful runaways, abandoned children, jobless vagabonds, petty thieves, and criminal gangs.[37]

Inadequacy of Land-Use Planning
Up until the late 1990s, because of the existence of multiple municipalities

32 Teresa Dirsuweit and Florian Schattauer, "Fortresses of Desire: Melrose Arch and the Emergence of Urban Tourist Spectacles," *GeoJournal* 60, no. 3 (2004): 239–47; Andre Czegledy, "Villas of the Highveld: a Cultural Perspective on Johannesburg and Its "Northern Suburbs," in *Emerging Johannesburg: Perspectives on the Post-Apartheid City*, ed. Richard Tomlinson et al. (New York: Routledge, 2003), 21–42; Alan Mabin, "Suburbanisation, Segregation, and Government of Territorial Transformations," *Transformation* 57 (2005): 41–63; and Martin J. Murray, "The Quandary of Post-Public Space: New Urbanism, Melrose Arch, and the Rebuilding of Johannesburg after Apartheid," *Journal of Urban Design* 18, no. 1 (2013): 119–44.

33 Bremner, *Johannesburg: One City, Colliding Worlds*, 252–58; Bremner, "Remaking Johannesburg," 32–47; and Chipkin, *Johannesburg Transition*, 375–400.

34 Philip Harrison and Alan Mabin, "Security and Space: Managing the Contradictions of Access Restriction in Johannesburg," *Environment and Planning B* 33, no. 1 (2006): 3–20.

35 Derek Hook and Michelle Vrdoljak, "Gated Communities, Heterotopia and a 'Rights' of Privilege: A 'Heterotopology' of the South African Security-Park," *Geoforum* 33, no. 2 (2002): 195–219; and Murray, *City of Extremes*, 137.

36 Postpublic spaces are sequestered places of social congregation (like shopping malls, private clubs, and the like) that are privately owned and managed, and hence can exclude unwanted and undesirable persons.

37 Murray, "The City in Fragments," 144–78; and

Murray, *City of Extremes*, 137.

38 Murray, *City of Extremes*, 178.

39 Murray, *Taming the Disorderly City*, 189–244.

40 See Martin J. Murray, "Waterfall City (Johannesburg): Privatized Urbanism in Extremis," *Environment & Planning A* 47, no. 3 (2015): 503–20.

3.9.9 Private security guards provide static protection for suburban properties

with their separate administrative jurisdictions, there was no single municipal planning department and no unified spatial plan for the greater Johannesburg metropolitan region. For these two reasons, from at least the mid-1970s, the decentralized nodes that blossomed on the exurban fringe competed with one another for capital investments, rather than having their growth and expansion controlled by a central authority. This kind of unfettered development has resulted in a game of musical chairs, where newer office nodes have pushed the urbanizing frontier inexorably northward. Lured by discounted rental buildings, companies have migrated to these new developments, leaving behind acceptable office accommodation, which then degenerates due to a lower-quality tenant base and a lack of maintenance.[38] Thus, in the inner city, poor enforcement of building codes and health and safety regulations enabled property owners to exploit low-income tenants while neglecting to provide even rudimentary maintenance and repair.[39] (fig. **3.9.9**)

Despite the goal of rectifying the racial and class imbalances that occurred during the apartheid years, spatial planning in Johannesburg has moved away from holistic master planning (something that existed under apartheid rule) toward strategic spatial planning, where municipal agencies have emphasized broad directional guidelines rather than hard-and-fast regulations. The municipality has had limited success in restricting real estate development on the urban edge. On balance, real estate developers after the transition to parliamentary democracy appear to be one step ahead of municipal planning agencies and the efforts of public authorities to impose a strict spatial planning framework for the greater Johannesburg metropolitan region. What has emerged at the macrolevel in the construction of huge megaprojects (Melrose Arch, Montecasino, Waterfall City, and Steyn City, for example) are informal kinds of public-private partnerships, where municipal authorities seem willing to allow developers a free hand in building what they want in exchange for the private supply of basic infrastructure, like upgraded roadways, sewer lines, and storm drainage.[40] At a microlevel, the shift

41 Murray, *City of Extremes*, 245, 249.

3.9.10 Residential suburban neighborhoods resemble walled-off transportation corridors

from conventional managerial approaches to the public administration to more flexible modes of urban governance has meant the expanded participation of elite business coalitions in local decision making, the turn toward market-based solutions to service delivery, and introduction of administrative policies that privilege private enterprise. The adoption of these entrepreneurial modes of urban governance has gone hand in hand with a significant hollowing out and reduction of municipal functions and responsibilities, including the transfer of the mandate for regulating urban space to a mixture of quasi-autonomous, nongovernmental agencies and other nonstate, business-oriented stakeholder coalitions. An array of in-between administrative agencies—such as public-private partnerships, semiautonomous entities, and incorporated property-owner associations (like city improvement districts)—have replaced branches of city government, assuming the functions that municipalities once monopolized as their exclusive preserve.[41] (fig. **3.9.10**)

Conclusion

Patterns of postsuburban growth in Greater Johannesburg have fundamentally undermined stereotypical distinctions between the (business-commercial) city and its (residential) suburbs. But perhaps the most important aspect about the emergent contours of postsuburban development is not simply that the "lumpy" built environment has spread over such vast territory but that these have concealed a dramatically altered social geography sharply divided between upscale sites of luxury and impoverished spaces of confinement. Thus, the spatial restructuring of the greater Johannesburg metropolitan region has produced a hybrid metropolitan landscape that conforms to patterns of growth that are neither genuinely urban nor suburban. Rather, city-building processes have inventively recombined urbanizing and suburbanizing modes of development, folding one into the other to spawn a galaxy of relatively independent edge cities, business nodal points, and securitized office parks sandwiched in between upscale gated residential estates,

3.9.11 Walls line suburban streets

42 See, e.g., Jamie Peck, Elliot Siemiatycki, and Elvin Wyly, "Vancouver's Suburban Involution," *City* 18, nos. 4–5 (2014): 386–415 (esp. 390).

43 Ignasi de Solà-Morales, "Terrain vague," in *Anyplace*, ed. Cynthia Davidson (Cambridge, MA: MIT Press 1996), 118–23.

look-alike tract housing, and densely packed townhouse clusters scattered across the exurban fringe—or what was once an uninhabited grassland frontier. (fig. **3.9.11**)

In the utopian imaginary of the best of all possible worlds, a phalanx of city builders, architects, designers, real estate developers, and boosters have promoted a distinctive brand of urbanism that combines dense, vibrant, amenity-filled urban-like settings juxtaposed alongside an auto-oriented suburban landscape filled with a variety of residential building typologies catering for a range of income groups. In this sense, Johannesburg has become a rather variegated metropolitan landscape, where pockets of mixed-use, urban-like enclaves are mixed haphazardly with long-standing suburban residential subdivisions. These variegated building typologies juxtaposed in proximity to each other have resulted in a polycentric but nevertheless broadly postsuburban pattern of metropolitan-regional development. This model of postsuburbia (where the once regnant pattern of high-density

downtown core surrounded by low-density residential suburbs no longer holds true) has reinforced the dominance of certain values—such as class exclusivity, individualism, personal consumption, aesthetic predictability, and status conformity.[42] The seeds for the future city of Johannesburg exist in the present. While the downward spiral of neglect and decay has stabilized, the historic downtown core of Johannesburg—built to serve the gold-mining industry—is at best a shadow of what it once was. The evolving postsuburban realm no longer responds to the gravitational pull of a single center but instead has come to resemble an archipelago of island-like enclosed luxury spaces connected more to each other than to the *terra vague* (literally, the anywhere "in-between" space, the antithesis of desirable space) that surrounds them.[43] As a normative ideal, the idea of urban citizenship revolves around the capacity to stake a claim to what the city has to offer. But by carving the metropolitan landscape into an assemblage of spatial enclosures with their own rules of inclusion and exclusion, the right to assert a sense of belonging

to the mainstream of urban life increasingly rests in the hands of those who can
assert this "right to claim rights" through
the market, that is, through their ability
as "entitled private citizens" to purchase
what they want and need.[44]

*This essay borrows (with permission
from the publishers) from Martin J.
Murray, "City of Layers: The Making and
Shaping of Affluent Johannesburg after
Apartheid," in* Urban Governance in Post-
Apartheid Cities, *ed. Marie Huchzermeyer
and Christoph Haferburg (Stuttgart:
Schweizerbart, 2014), 179–96. See also
Martin J. Murray,* The City of Extremes:
Spatial Politics in Johannesburg *(Durham,
NC: Duke University Press, 2011), 4, 32.*

44　See Leslie Kern,
"Reshaping the
Boundaries of Public
and Private Life:
Gender, Condominium
Development, and
the Neoliberalization
of Urban Living," *Urban
Geography* 28, no. 7
(2007): 657–81 (esp.
675–76).

3.10 SUBTRACTING THE SUBURBS

Keller Easterling

DESIGN MODELS

FLEXIBLE REGULATION

NEOLIBERAL PROPERTY MARKETS

SUBURB-CITY INTER-DEPENDENCIES

Large swaths of suburbia were destroyed or demolished in the wake of the financial crisis of 2008 and in the aftermath of natural disasters like Katrina and Sandy, and many Rust Belt cities have long been shrinking because of population shifts. Values for buildings rapidly inflate and deflate in volatile financial markets. Deteriorating or troubled buildings depress the real estate values of neighboring buildings. Distended suburban growth is abandoned. The repeatable spatial products of suburbia—formulaic homes, malls, golf courses, retail, and so forth—have rapid cycles of obsolescence. Changes in sea level erase coastline properties, as invasive development destroys sensitive landscapes. Ruin and decay have their own set of arresting visuals, which have been compared to pornography. Disassembly and teardown are now popular art forms. Demolition companies have their own TV shows. Perhaps more than ever, it is easy to see with half-closed eyes an economy of subtraction that is the flip side of building.

But rather than being the accidental by-products of crisis, what if these subtractions were deliberately managed or designed? What if we could relieve exhausted fields of development or retreat from sensitive landscapes? Different from the modernist love of tabula rasa, the goal of a subtraction playbook might be to arrange an interplay of spatial variables that generates interdependencies rather than violent deletions. Architects and other design professionals—trained to make the building machine lurch forward—may know something about how to put it into reverse.

The Single Family Home as a Financial Instrument

In the United States, there is a long tradition of shaping suburbia with financial instruments. In 1934 the Federal Housing Administration (FHA) legally transformed houses into a kind of currency. Depression-era housing was linked to two areas of distress: banking and jobs. The FHA positioned the single-family house as a commercial multiplier. It would stabilize banks with a streamlined financial organ—the long-term, low-interest loan that provided mortgage insurance for banks. And since the construction industry employed a large number of workers, the house would not only stimulate banking but also create jobs.[1]

In the postwar period, the FHA further streamlined the process by granting insurance approvals for entire populations of houses to merchant builders like William Levitt.[2] An aerial view of thousands of these nearly identical houses—in Levittown or other similar sites—clearly portrays a repeatable product, or a currency cultivated for new mortgages in the financial industry and for jobs in the construction industry. (fig. **3.10.1**) New houses are still treated as a sign of economic confidence, despite the fact that a surplus of the same houses devalues them in a market flooded with foreclosures. For this very reason, after 2008, economists and financiers often regarded the new house as both a positive and a negative economic indicator, an object that simultaneously exacerbated and relieved financial crisis.

Before 2008, this precarious home building currency and the cultural, environmental effects of producing crops of houses was primarily an American issue. But the recent failure of the financial industry left behind more than dead malls, empty big-box stores, and foreclosed suburbs. Bundled mortgages and other complexities invented by financial industry quants made these otherwise banal objects into global contagions of financial disaster.

The financial industry that is now attached to global stakeholders stares at the suburban house—a mascot of the disaster—and demands that it behave like

1 Keller Easterling, *Organization Space: Landscapes, Highways, and Houses in America* (Cambridge, MA: MIT Press, 1995).

2 Edward P. Eichler, *The Merchant Builders* (Cambridge, MA: MIT Press, 1982).

3.10.1 Aerial photograph of Levittown on Long Island, New York, in 1954

money again. As long as it behaved like money, everything was fine. But in the event of failure, banks have developed an arsenal of tools like equities, currencies, or hedge funds for manipulation of and protection from the market. Currencies can be bought and sold in milliseconds, and global speculators can get in the game. The financial crisis has yielded millions of failed homes; multitudes have been sold for a few thousand dollars and then flipped on the Internet to be resold at an only slightly higher price to buyers halfway around the world.

Economic science tells us that the financial industry may have a portfolio that controls "the house," but that the home itself does not have a portfolio with comparable tools for protection. The durable object does not represent a number of shares that can have multiple interests. It may have fixtures, appliances, and furnishings that are in a gray area, but in general, the value of all of its component parts is not traded because the house is supposed to remain intact. Mortgages fix the house as a marker for debt, and its auxiliary economic instruments are limited. The homeowner cannot divide the home into smaller pieces and speculate on them in the market, even if it would provide alternative revenue streams or sources of stability. The house, intact, can only serve as collateral for more banking instruments.

But what if buildings—the heavy, physical bulk of urban space—constitute a portfolio of spatial attributes and qualities, and what if trading in this parallel market of spatial components offers more tangible risks and rewards? This is the first page of a subtraction playbook, and

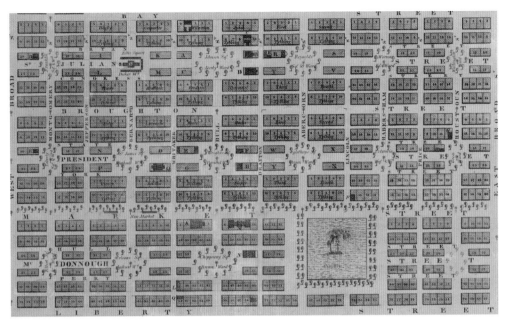

3.10.2 Savannah Ward

it relies on an ability to design not only things but an interplay between things in urban space—not only object forms but also active forms.

Interplay: Hacking the Suburban Operating System

Return to the aerial view of Levittown or any similar suburb. In this field of nearly identical suburban houses we see object forms like houses, but we also know that there is an operating system running in the background that is making some things possible and some things impossible. There is a simple rule set—an active form with a disposition to multiply. Most architects consider buildings to be inert objects that can be fixed and named as things, events, or values. They often assume that their training only qualifies them to address a building like a house as a static object with shape and outline. Architects can redesign the single house with object forms, but it extends their power to also design an active form— another multiplier or contagion that uses the organization as a carrier.

Or consider the deceptively simple formula for an eighteenth-century settlement like Savannah, Georgia, as planned by its founder James Oglethorpe. (fig. **3.10.2**) Different from a master plan, Savannah was a growth protocol designed to curb rampant speculation. The town was designed to grow by wards, each of which contained a quotient of public, private, and green space. The individual lot was not an independent absolute value but was often abstractly linked to other values and physical spaces in other portions of the settlement. The lots and central space were also collectively linked to remote reserves of land outside the town. While the shape of the town's extent was indeterminate, the formula was explicit. It was an active form—an interplay that operated like a self-regulating governor.

An active form can hack into the suburban operating system in ways that affect populations of buildings. Active forms are multipliers, switches, remote controls, deltas, or governors; time-released protocols that generate or manage a stream of objects and spaces. A remote control may activate a distant event to affect a local condition. Extending the reach of object forms, an active form is an updating platform that remains in place to condition, divert, or enhance the process. The designer of active forms may find other artistic satisfactions in altering a population of buildings or initiating network effects across a broader spatial field.

The making of object form usually results in the addition of building. But active forms can result in either the creation of buildings or their gradual removal. Managing an entire ecology, designing subtraction is less about removal than about exchange and reabsorption; about establishing interdependencies between properties— about inaugurating and relieving, or replacing and recasting buildings. Different from the trigger-happy architect of the *tabula rasa*, the architect of subtraction designs relationships between properties so that their value is never wholly negative.

Playbook 1: The Distended Suburb

In a turnabout, what if the physical house was to become a more prominent and palpable asset than its attending financial constructs? If the era of architecture as a currency is over, then perhaps it is now possible for homeowners to trade in other values related to their home and neighborhood. A home could become a portfolio of assets that a homeowner or groups of homeowners control. These assets include its presence, capacity, and location—measured in real estate transactions—as well as all its materials when disassembled: its energy-producing capacity (wind, sun, geothermal), its biodiversity value, its carbon value, its cultural value, and the shares it holds in related properties. In areas prone to erasure from floods or earthquakes, insurance risk is also part of that portfolio.

Consider the Savannah formula in reverse—where the thing created is not building but clearing. A governing interplay of spatial variables can be used to curb speculation and hedge against risk. In a twist on the usual notion of the home as autonomous entity, interdependencies would make the house both more stable and more financially independent. Also, while the wealthiest markets have well-rehearsed techniques for deleting the constructions of the disenfranchised, here the tables are turned, and distended populations of McMansions are the subject of deletion.

In an elementary ecology of properties, the game might play out through a number of simple moves. Densifying properties are linked to properties in places where development is being deleted. The increased tax revenues from one or the other sustain both, and relieve sites that are toxic or without value. Not only relieved of a toxic property, these owners now also have some share in their new partner space—a hedge space that may be remote or nearby.

As a reserve of value, the remote lots help overcome the normal obstacles to land acquisition. They ease the city's start-up costs for innovations like solar, wind, or rail that can be located on peripheral or even polluted sites. The owners of the densified lots that produce the increased tax revenues also become automatic shareholders in the new enterprises located on the remote sites. They too have an offset or a hedge against further real estate perils, since they own not only interests in their own lot. Like a diversified portfolio, the game is filled with offsets and interdependencies. For banks, the protocol generates business and stabilizes loans previously in default. Revenues from the cleared space act as micro-dividends, strengthening densified areas while still remaining a safe percentage of the total worth of the property. (fig. **3.10.3**)

Not only in the overbuilt suburbs of the affluent, the protocol might be used in any location where development would be wise to retreat from exhausted land, flood plains, or special land preserves. It might even be used in areas that are the

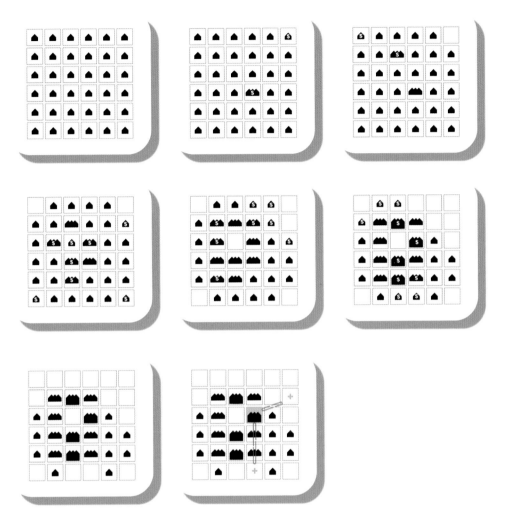

3.10.3 Subtraction Playbook 1

target of slum clearance. A subtraction economy offers developers and land-owners somewhat less violent tools of acquisition with safeguards against disenfranchisement.

Playbook 2: Rethinking Flood Plains
Although climate change causes changes in sea levels that are measured in fractions of an inch, hurricanes and other extreme weather events can cause the sea to quickly erase the planet's major settlements. In the United States, hurricanes Katrina and Sandy have rewritten the rules about property and insurance. Many along the coast are asking how to retreat, relo-cate, or concentrate development. Those

homeowners who can afford to spend $100,000 to elevate their homes avoid nearly the same amount in increased insurance over a period of years. But in New Orleans, poverty, poor documen-tation, and a host of other problems have often paralyzed the city's recovery, leaving a checkerboard of vacant lots and an inability to leverage investment without the help of philanthropy or dwindling federal subsidies. Planners are forced to admit that "the financials don't work."

But maybe this failure of the financial industry is good news. Banks, insurance companies, and real estate operators manage property as a generic

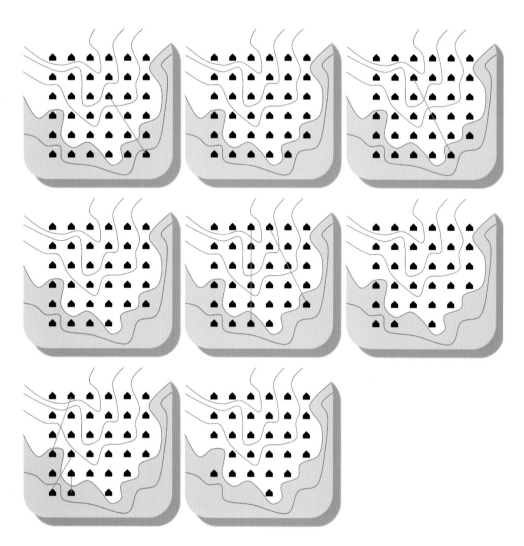

3.10.4 Subtraction Playbook

product, whether it is in a desert or on a mountaintop or coastline. Financiers quantify differences between assets with technical indicators that mark things like mineral resources, wind, or underground aquifers. These terms are added to the already thick layers of bureaucratic jargon—from mortgage points to actuarial tables—that are used in the game of buying, selling, and insuring a property.

But again, what if, rather than relying solely on generic econometrics, a market of spatial variables, parallel to financial market considerations, could offer a way to avoid or recover from natural disaster? An information-rich index with the benefit of intelligence from urbanists, landscape architects, and regional environmentalists could target and rate properties for their complementary risks and benefits, or their counterbalancing attributes. In other words, like a matchmaking website, the exchange would rate not only properties themselves but the benefits of changing use or swapping positions in the urban/regional landscape. It could rate or certify mortgage transactions that result in an advantageous relocation or consolidation of property with reduced collective risk for all. The more advantageous the swap, the higher the rating: a shoreline owner moves to higher ground; a year-round coastal property becomes a seasonal vacation property; a municipality is able to aggregate land for levees, revetments, dunes, or sand-replenishing programs; a clearing adds value to a denser property on its perimeter by providing views and water retention. (fig. **3.10.4**)

In any of these transactions, since the trade itself is worth a quotient of flood insurance, and since the mortgage becomes increasingly viable, the exchange could draw investment from insurance companies and banks. Both institutions could also incentivize the transaction with lower rates and streamlined deals. In many cases, a simple rating that accounts for a number of factors would simplify mortgage and exchange transactions, stripping away much of the quantitative technical language, and replacing it with qualitative indicators. Deadlocked and devalued properties could then be revalued and released into circulation.

How Growth and Subtraction Can Coexist

Perhaps most important is the idea of interplay itself, as an art and as a goal of design. Rather than restricting architects and urbanists to the more familiar, singular object form or master plan, designing active forms or leveraging relationships and interdependencies would allow them to organize a stream of objects. New habits of mind about counterbalancing interplay could inform the design of many spaces and territories.

Subtraction is not necessarily the disposal of failure, an error, or the eradication of contradiction. Rather, it can be a deliberate tool for managing building exchanges. Different from the tabula rasa, these sorts of subtractions do not erase information but rather release a flood of information and association. Architects might view the phenomena of subtraction as an operative principle of practice, rather than as a by-product of destructive forces. It is both a tool and a new territory. Like the cultivation of crops or the use of

one microorganism to counteract another, subtraction may be a productive technique for changing not only the shape but the constitution or organizational disposition of space. Subtraction can be growth.

Mooikloof Ridge, Pretoria, Gauteng, South Africa

Sunninghill, Sandton, Gauteng, South Africa

4

HARNESSING ECOLOGICAL POTENTIAL

4.1
REDISCOVERING THE NATURE OF SUBURBS

Christopher Sellers

ANTISUBURBAN CRUSADES

ECOLOGICAL FUNCTION

Along the edges of American cities in the 1980s, nature-minded residents turned abandoned railroad rights-of-way into trails and wove together strings of forest patches with pathways.[1] Thus was born the Greenbelt Trail in New York's Nassau County, crossing that most iconic of post–World War II suburban landscape. There on Long Island, a half-hour's drive from Manhattan, you can now walk a continuous twenty-two miles through more or less secluded patches of woodland and meadow that are the fruits of long-standing public and private preservation efforts as well as this land's sheer ecological resilience. To the hiker, the Greenbelt reveals a suburban diversity that is a far cry from the customary imagery of suburbia, not just socioeconomically, but also ecologically.

Throughout its southerly length it stays within a strip of state park at most a quarter mile (0.4 kilometer) wide, as it courses just east of Levittown. This huge subdivision is mass suburbia's prototype, and while its trees have matured, its lawns remain little changed from when the town was founded as an all-white community for the middle to working classes. West of the trail lies North Amityville, a postwar suburban haven for blacks banished from Levittown. There, amid smaller lawns and lesser trees, the rural surrounds have also long since been lost.

Once the path crosses the island's central axis, more fulsome woods and greenery flourish. Forest preserves abound on both sides of the trail, courtesy of the county, the township of Oyster Bay, and the Nature Conservancy. A tree cover more dense and extensive than sixty years ago envelops villages like Upper Brookville and Cold Spring Harbor; nurseries and farms thrive. There, New York's wealthy continue to find suburban landscapes suitable to their pocketbooks and liking.

That patches of forest and meadows have survived here over decades of suburbanizing, intentionally as well as inadvertently, is a reminder of what many other residents of today's suburbs encounter daily. But when you mention suburbia, for most Americans, a reflexive imagery kicks in that is in stark contrast to a forest or meadow. The term connotes a place dominated by roads, houses, and malls; an almost entirely built environment, furbished only with the manicured greenery of lawns and shrubs. It's also a place often seen from outside or beyond. In the opening shot of the movie *American Beauty*, a modern tale of dystopian suburbia, the camera zooms down from outer space into a neighborhood alongside Chicago and a home lot.[2] That's how our culture frames this kind of place, largely through imagery that nearly begs our alienation from it. Part of the reason is that this and other inherited notions of suburbia turn a conspicuously skewed or blind eye to the presence of nature in the suburbs. This invisibility of nature in the suburbs has its own history, going back to when and how suburbia first acquired its modern prominence and meaning. Kenneth Jackson's classic history of suburbanization aside, that moment was not during the nineteenth or early twentieth century, when in the United States, as in Britain and other of its former colonies, suburbs began to branch out from denser downtowns.[3] Instead, the notion of suburbia arrived in a big way in the United States only just after World War II, when people began talking of suburbs as having a typical, definable character and way of life.

That modern stereotype remains influential. In the first depictions of suburbia by media and social scientists, the countryside in which so many suburbs were set suddenly became difficult to imagine, even as it continued to beckon migrants. A nascent environmental

1   Rails to Trails Conservancy, "History of RTC and the Rail-Trail Movement," accessed September 2014, http://www.railstotrails.org/about/history/; Long Island Greenbelt Trail Conference, "Long Island Greenbelt Trail Conference," accessed January 15, 2015, http://www.hike-li.org/ligtc/.

2   *American Beauty*, directed by Sam Mendes and Alan Ball (Los Angeles: DreamWorks Home Entertainment, 1999), VHS.

3   Kenneth T. Jackson, *Crabgrass Frontier: The Suburbanization of the United States* (New York: Oxford University Press, 1987); Robert Fishman, *Bourgeois Utopias: The Rise and Fall of Suburbia* (New York: Basic Books, 1989).

movement then added another reason to dislike suburbia: its urbanizing "sprawl" erased a preexisting natural world. Where sprawl intruded, local nature of any sort became far more difficult to see—if not entirely absent.

In many ways, sprawl offered an apt description of what builders did in the course of suburban development: they razed trees, slashed into farms, and filled in wetlands.[4] Moreover, many of those who bought suburban homes hardly contemplated their own environmental impacts, even as habits from driving to lawn watering to pesticide usage imposed tremendous tolls on their surroundings. Especially as the environmental agenda evolved to also take on an energy crisis and global warming, the antienvironmental reputation of suburbia grew. With it emerged an attendant fantasy: that for America to become a "green" society, we have to somehow get rid of our suburbs entirely—the very places where a majority of Americans have come to live.

Part of what makes this vision so fantastical—and not a little ominous for what the economist Thomas Piketty has dubbed a "patrimonial middle class"—is its disconnect from two veins of history. This fantasy of a green America is disconnected from the environmentalist movement from which it originated and from suburbs themselves, those places it proposes to abolish.[5] In truth, the mass movement that environmentalism became in the United States arose mainly in suburbs. And once you delve into the actual history of what postwar critics limned as "suburbia," once you look closely at what drew people there, you find many motives that are well-nigh environmental in tone. A less dismissive and more evenhanded approach to this postwar era of America's suburbanization reveals that its impacts on the natural world, and on suburbanites themselves, were considerably more diverse—and environmentally

inspiring—than most talk of suburbia or of sprawl has made them out to be.[6]

How can we find ways past long-standing assumptions that suburbia or sprawl are inevitably, or even typically, hostile to nature or the environment? A first step is to set aside those misleading or questionable stereotypes that suburbia has accrued, and to develop a working notion of suburbs that is more strictly locational and geographic. Ongoing trends in many environmental fields, not least in ecology, offer some helpful tools for doing so. A few decades ago most serious ecologists concentrated on studying rural locales; more recently, they've become much more interested in metropolitan areas. A case in point is their development over the past couple of decades of the notion of an "urban-rural gradient."[7] Instead of just assuming that natural ecosystems stopped where suburbs began—mirroring the earliest renditions of sprawl—this idea posits a gradual and continuous transition from those lands most densely packed with buildings and people to those where humans and their edifices are sparser. It's a notion that opens the door to appreciating the ecological diversity of those many in-between landscapes that make up our suburbs. Of course, the physicochemical and biological dimensions of a place, emphasized by these ecologists, intertwine with its human sociocultural and economic features. In place of the environmental pipe dream of wishing our suburbs away, I propose a steadier and more evenhanded look at them, one that reveals their variety and also their considerable environmental promise. Not just our downtowns but also our suburbs can be springboards toward a greener future.

How Media Defined Suburbia

To understand just how and why nature got left out of post–World War II depictions of suburbia, it helps to appreciate how differently people saw suburbs in

4   Adam Ward Rome, *The Bulldozer in the Countryside: Suburban Sprawl and the Rise of American Environmentalism* (Cambridge: Cambridge University Press, 2001); Robert Bruegmann, *Sprawl: A Compact History* (Chicago: University Of Chicago Press, 2006).

5   Thomas Piketty, *Capital in the Twenty-First Century*, trans. Arthur Goldhammer (Cambridge, MA: Belknap Press of Harvard University Press, 2014).

6   Christopher Sellers, *Crabgrass Crucible: Suburban Nature and the Rise of Environmentalism in Twentieth-Century America* (Chapel Hill: University of North Carolina Press, 2012).

7   Mark J. McDonnell and Steward T. A. Pickett, "Ecosystem Structure and Function along Urban-Rural Gradients: An Unexploited Opportunity for Ecology," *Ecology* 71, no. 4 (August 1990): 1232; Mark J. McDonnell and Amy K. Hahs, "The Use of Gradient Analysis Studies in Advancing Our Understanding of the Ecology of Urbanizing Landscapes: Current Status and Future Directions," *Landscape Ecology* 23, no. 10 (December 2008): 1143–55.

the late nineteenth and early twentieth centuries. As the potential for suburban living opened up along many urban edges via streetcars and commuter rail in the United States, suburban places were often considered rural or countryside. When the well-known agriculturalist Liberty Hyde Bailey in 1906 founded the magazine *Country Life*, he envisioned a widening readership for it through "the growth of suburbanism." A competitor published out of Boston even called itself *Suburban Country Life*.[8] In this time, places where genuine country living was to be had—suburbs—were places where nature was far easier to find and see.

A case in point was the 1925 depiction in the first book-length US publication on the subject, *The Suburban Trend*, written by the journalist and New Jersey resident Harlan Douglass. He described a "distinct suburban psychology" arising from the "simple and subtle appeals" of the "sky and landscape, unobstructed," which made one (and these are his words) a "lover of nature." He suggested that this "psychology [of]…nature love" might more easily accrue to adults with means—a suburban "upper middle class." As for children, "with no more of nature than the suburban house lot affords," he said, they might find "not merely space for play, but a certain environmental content and feeling for life." In contrast to many later writers, he noted a racial and ethnic diversity to the suburban experience, observing that it could be different in colonies of "Negroes" or the "foreign-born." Douglass looked beyond the residential subdivisions of affluent commuters to those who lived along urban edges because of fewer resources, who grew their own food, and also to the many who operated market farms and dairies not so far away. His perspective on these places was tinged with a distinctly agrarian romanticism. He considered it "one of the most heartening evangels of future civilization…

[that] the expanding city may permanently overflow into village forms and contain cattle as well as men."[9]

Already, a notion of suburbia was beginning to crystallize, as more people moved into such places. The idea also drew on the way in which, from the 1890s, fiction writers began to craft suburban plots and characters. As with so much of suburban history, the earliest flourishing of the place as a descriptor came from Britain. Britain's garden cities of the 1920s and especially the public, working-class housing built on urban outskirts during the 1930s provided the templates for suburban places. Across the Anglo-Saxon world, Australia, Canada, and the United States subsequently appropriated them. They applied them especially to communities created during the rapid expansion of housing experienced after World War II, as newly created government programs of support stoked pent-up demand for home building. (figs. **4.1.1–2**)

Around 1950, the nation's suburbs suddenly surged into the headlines in the United States. They began with a story about builders heroically stepping up their projects around New York and other cities to relieve a postwar housing shortage. Returning veterans and their families had been living in cramped apartments or even chicken coops. Now, huge low-cost developments like Levittown afforded a chance for homeownership. Coverage of suburban mass builders quickly evolved into something more: a story about suburbia, an entirely new slice of the world where a youthful middle class was moving. The business media led in the discovery of these places. Reporters from other fields, novelists, and social scientists soon joined the throng, fleshing out these suburbs' uniqueness as a social milieu, as exhibit A in the arrival of a new, mass-consumerist society.

Once coverage of suburbs and suburbia took off, media and social scientists

8   Sellers, *Crabgrass Crucible*, 18–19.
9   Harlan Paul Douglass, *The Suburban Trend: The Rise of Urban America* (New York: Arno Press, 1970), 248 ("lover of nature"), 249 ("environmental content"), 304 ("evangel").

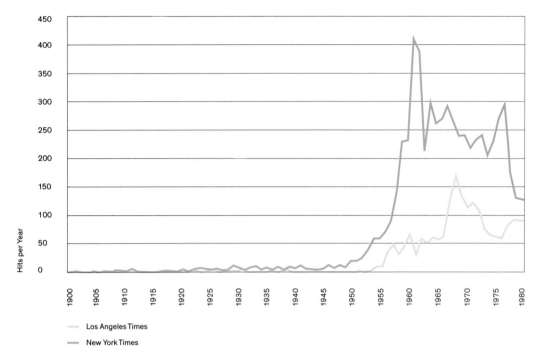

4.1.1 "Suburbia" in American newspapers, 1920–1980

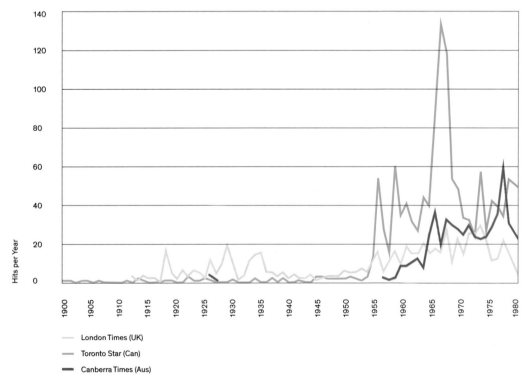

4.1.2 "Suburbia" in other Anglophone newspapers, 1920–1980

looking outward from traditional downtowns were inclined to see the suburbs as dominated by houses and the human hand. To them, suburbia harbored only the most meager of rural reminders, like the "little sapling outside the picture window" that the journalist William Whyte noted in a mass suburb featured in *The Organizational Man*.[10] New demographic and observational tools just becoming available bolstered the tacit commitment of mass-suburbia portraitists to write the countryside or nearby nature out of what they saw.

Press coverage drew, for instance, on the US Census's first adoption of "suburbs" as a working category, in 1950. For the census takers, suburbs were essentially urban places: outside city limits, but still part of a metropolitan area. Suburbs registered a 33 percent gain in population from 1940, as opposed to a 9 percent gain inside city limits, and thus counted as a growth of metropolitan—as opposed to rural—America. Aerial photography, just coming into its own in the news magazines of the 1940s and 1950s, bolstered this exclusively urban categorization of suburbs. Taken from several thousand feet up, the bird's-eye views tended to erase much. Differences in houses vanished when seen from on high, as did the faces or even bodies of those who lived there, isolated trees and forest patches, and street-level landscapes of shrubs and lawns. What stood out were the larger patterns crafted by developers: the similar house sizes and placement, and the squared-off, uniform grids that underlay most neighborhoods. To elaborate the lives of mass suburbia's residents, journalists such as Whyte at *Fortune* and Harry Henderson at *Harper's* borrowed from relatively novel social science techniques like the community study. Their localized, sociological preoccupations often confirmed that the new suburbanites were excessively social and, like their houses, conformist in bent.

These observers steered away from any nature-related questions.[11] (fig. **4.1.3**)

Coverage of this new suburbia lost track of what earlier in the twentieth century had been easier to remember: that suburban migrants often sought the countryside. Instead, via a subtle but decisive shift in emphasis, they found suburban migrants to be fleeing the city. Many reasons propelled this supposed revulsion in the contemporary analysis: high taxes, crime, declining services, pollution, noise, and of course, overcrowding, often an anodyne way of referring to an increased nonwhite presence. Older, positive aspirations of suburban migrants to live near nature and countryside now rarely figured in to the coverage. Suburbanites were now city folk who did not pointedly seek rural surroundings so much as places where cities and buildings were not: where there was more open space. Suburbs became nearly synonymous with an entire way of life for a rising middle class.

A closer look at those many couples who sought new homes on postwar Long Island suggests how a suburban country vision still found traction among new suburban homebuyers, seeking the prospect of a recognizable natural landscape nearby. It was easiest to see among migrants to upscale suburbs, such as Long Islanders Robert and Grace Barstow Murphy, who moved into a 6-acre property in the village of Old Field, just as Robert was retiring from his position as ornithologist with the American Museum of Natural History in 1952. What appealed to the Murphys in particular were the "good trees" and a "spring pond a good place to feed and tame waterfowl," and also that the house was "completely hidden from the highway." He figured it was "likely to keep for many years to come the spacious residential seclusion it now enjoys."[12]

Pursuit of countryside also inspired migrants to working-class housing,

10 William H. Whyte, *The Organizational Man* (New York: Doubleday & Company, 1957).

11 Sellers, *Crabgrass Crucible*, 40.

12 Robert Cushman Murphy, "'April 5–6, 1952,' in Volume 'Long Island and Elsewhere 1950–52,'" Robert Cushman Murphy journals, 1907–1971, American Philosophical Society Library, Philadelphia, PA.

13 Julian Kane and Muriel Kane, interview by Christopher Sellers, April 2005; Eugene and Bernice Burnett, interview by Christopher Sellers, January 2004.

4.1.3 Aerial photograph of Levittown on Long Island, New York, in 1954

including to the first Levittown. Julian and Muriel Kane, for instance, who bought their Levitt house in 1952, had already developed an interest in nature and rural settings, despite growing up mostly in Brooklyn and Queens. When they decided to buy a home, the nearby fields and farms made Levittown more attractive; as Julian Kane put it, more of a "real suburb"; "we had our countrified area." Though African American families who sought suburban residences were fewer in number and less successful than their white counterparts, they acted on similar aspirations. Turned away from Levittown, Bernice and Eugene Burnett nevertheless found a country-like inspiration there that led them to the purchase of a house in North Amityville's Ronek Park, a few miles farther out. Bernice was struck by the "airiness" of the place, and that it recalled the outskirts of Charlotte Amalie, the capital of the US Virgin Islands where she had lived until age nine, a contrast to "overcrowded" Harlem.[13]

If there were some resemblances in what each of these three families found in their respective purchases, the stark ecological differences in the lots and neighborhoods into which they moved reflected the fragmentation, socioeconomically, of postwar suburbanization. The Old Field area into which the Murphys moved was the most privileged of the three; an incorporated village of the rich and well-to-do, where the country-like ambience came from the zoning of smaller lots, subdivisions, or commerce. As for Levittown, it had much smaller lots and homes, and never incorporated or exerted zoning controls over surrounding properties. Though Levitt and Sons cut corners in other ways, they did plant lawns and an unusual number of trees in the yards, and established neighborhood recreation areas and parks. In North Amityville, the Burnetts and other new African American homeowners had to undertake most of this planting and park making themselves, after the developers had left. Across this

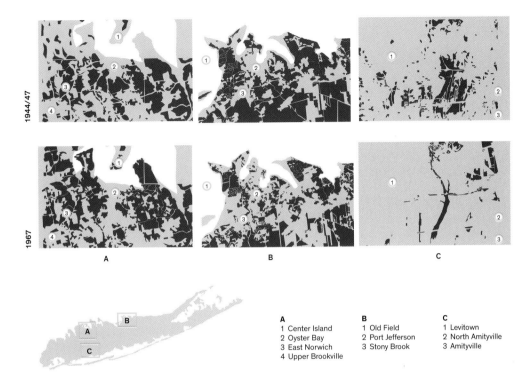

A

B

C

A
1 Center Island
2 Oyster Bay
3 East Norwich
4 Upper Brookville

B
1 Old Field
2 Port Jefferson
3 Stony Brook

C
1 Levittown
2 North Amityville
3 Amityville

4.1.4 Changing forest cover in select corners of Long Island, 1944 versus 1967

14 Meyer Liebowitz, "'Migratory' Fowl Find a Home in Diminishing L.I. Wetlands," *New York Times*, February 7, 1957, http://search.proquest .com.proxy.library .stonybrook.edu /hnpnewyorktimes /docview/114152117 /abstract/5B44E33 E8711401FPQ/1 ?accountid=14172; Irvin Molotsky, "Berle Signs Orders to Protect State's Tidal Wetlands," *New York Times*, September 15, 1977, http://search .proquest.com.proxy .library.stonybrook .edu/hnpnewyorktimes /docview/123081210 /abstract/5B44E33 E8711401FPQ/29 ?accountid=14172.

15 Elizabeth A. Johnson and Michael W. Klemens, *Nature in Fragments: The Legacy of Sprawl* (New York: Columbia University Press, 2005).

wide range of suburban microenvironments, the combined impact of zoning development and new homeownership was cumulative. The suburbs invited in a vast newly domesticated ecology from lawns and shrubbery to dogs and cats; a biotic multitude that made this version of the city more than just the sum of its buildings and human inhabitants.

In the classically environmental way of seeing such suburbs as sprawl, we hear little or nothing about these new arrivals, and much more about the resulting destruction of preexisting land, plants, and animals. As subdivisions sprawled across Long Island, as many as half of its wetlands were filled in during the postwar years.[14] Not just its farmland but also its suburban forest continued to shrink, receding to those corners where developers were stymied or restricted. What early notions of sprawl did not include, and what ecologists have recently begun to highlight, is how those plant communities that remained were fractured. Chopped up by roads and highways, many passages through which wildlife as well as human pedestrians could freely roam were lost.[15] By the early 1960s, the fragmentation and diminishment of forests and other older habitats reached a critical point in Nassau and western Suffolk counties.

Attentiveness to the diversity of suburban ecology reveals how differently these impacts were experienced. Over the first two decades of the postwar period, Old Field and other incorporated villages, as well as the northerly reaches of Oyster Bay, had zoned lots for a minimum of two acres. Not only did they keep their existing trees, but their overall forest cover expanded. By contrast, those clumps of trees and forest patches that had dotted the Levittown and Amityville areas prior to suburbanization were wiped out. In these parts of Long Island, the only substantial woods to hold were those placed in public reserves. (fig. **4.1.4**) Especially when it came to having a wilder and more diverse ecology nearby, the suburban rich were getting richer, and the suburban middle or working class, poorer. Not surprisingly, a 1960 Audubon bird count in wealthy Oyster Bay, led by the ornithologist Robert Cushman Murphy himself, yielded some forty-six species, three more than a count conducted along the same route some fifty years early—with twenty species not found in 1910. To tell from recent studies, many new arrivals may have been pushed there by all the home building in other parts of the island.[16]

If ecological differences between richer versus poorer suburbs widened over the post–World War II years, they have gotten even more marked with the growth of America's wealth gap over the past few decades. As middle-class suburbs have been struggling and as our poorer suburbs have supplanted our cities as homes to the greatest share of our nation's poverty, suburbs have become more likely to be targeted for new urbanizing projects than for additional parks. The wealthiest suburban residents, meanwhile, remain enveloped by ample space and greenery, even as their consumption of fossil fuels and other resources far outstrips those of less affluent suburbanites. The recent drought in California has illuminated some of these inequities, as we've learned just how much more water Los Angeles's wealthiest communities have lavished on their landscaping.[17]

These changes are heading us toward a future in which not just the poor but our middle class will be increasingly deprived of all those benefits of having recognizable nature nearby, documented by forty years of research. We now know that far more than aesthetics is at stake. Having trees and green spaces close by helps maintain clean air and water, enables physical activity and stress reduction, and demonstrably improves health, from raising birth weights to lowering mortality in the elderly to fostering emotional as well as physical healing.[18] Do we really want to reserve these advantages only for the wealthiest of our suburbanites?

The Suburban Roots of the Greens

Once we look more broadly and even-handedly, we can see that the ecological reshuffling wrought by suburbanization encompasses not just neighboring forests and meadows but also nearby farms. Many of them do not so much vanish as adapt, seeking out suburban consumers with nursery crops, vineyards, and farm stands. Rather than seeing post–World War II Long Island, for instance, as a suburbia where nature was utterly lost to sprawl, we'd do better to see it as an informal commons, an interconnected, regional habitat of land, water, and air shared by a host of new, small property owners. Like the village greens of eighteenth-century Britain, suburban commons became threatened by overuse. In the case of Long Island, however, the threat of overuse did not come from sheepherders but from the aerospace industry and other businesses, aided by a housing market for their employees that was arguably the freest and most financially lubricated in the Western world. This commons was informal in the sense that it as yet had minimal government oversight; neither regional planning nor environmental regulations had much foothold, especially in the early postwar decades. But many who shared this commons became ever more disturbed about what was happening to it. Precisely out of this dynamic in suburbia, far more so than out of concern for the national parks or wilderness, a modern popular environmentalism was born.

The Nature Conservancy was an invention of the suburban East Coast. Its first two chapters formed in suburban Washington, DC, and in New York's suburban Westchester County; in 1954, a third chapter coalesced on Long Island, with Old Field resident Robert Cushman Murphy at its helm. Chapter organizing culminated in a private preservation initiative that had already begun among

16 Ira Henry Freeman, "Group Retraces Route President Took in Walk Fifty Years Ago," *New York Times*, June 11, 1960; John M. Marzluff, Reed Bowman, and Roarke Donnelly, "An Historical Perspective on Urban Bird Research: Trends, Terms, and Approaches," in *Avian Ecology and Conservation in an Urbanizing World*, ed. John M. Marzluff, Reed Bowman, and Roarke Donnelly (Norwell, MA: Kluwer Academic Publishers, 2001), 1–18; John M. Marzluff, *Welcome to Subirdia: Sharing Our Neighborhoods with Wrens, Robins, Woodpeckers, and Other Wildlife* (New Haven, CT: Yale University Press, 2014).

17 Michael Miller et al., "California's Wealthy Lagging in Water Conservation," *Los Angeles Times*, April 5, 2015, http://www.latimes.com/local/lanow/la-me-ln-wealthy-cities-lag-in-conservation-20150404-story.html; Caroline Mini, "Residential Water Use and Landscape Vegetation Dynamics in Los Angeles" (Los Angeles: University of California, 2013); Céline Kuklowsky, Stephanie Pincetl, and Terri Hogue, "Residential Water Consumption in Los Angeles: What Are the Drivers and Are Conservation Measures Working?," policy brief written for the California Center for Sustainable Communities at UCLA (Los Angeles, 2015), http://sustainablecommunities.environment.ucla.edu/residential-water-consumption-in-los-angeles/.

18 Kathleen L. Wolf and Alicia S. T. Robbins, "Metro Nature, Environmental Health, and Economic Value," *Environmental Health Perspectives* 123, no. 5 (May 2015): 390–98; Wendy Y. Chen and Chi Yung Kim, "Assessment and Valuation of the Ecosystem Services

well-to-do property owners on the island's north shore, as well as on Fire Island along its south edge.

These stirrings developed into a mass movement with a broad social base. Across the nation in California, the Sierra Club underwent an extraordinary boost in membership once it began to address those problems afflicting western suburbanites. By the mid-1960s, the Levittowner Julian Kane had become a key player in the local politics of ecological preservation, and environmental advocates took the original ecosystem on which Levittown now sat as a major rallying point. The Long Island Environmental Council, the umbrella for some sixty groups, held its first picnic in 1969 at the site of the last remnants of the Hempstead Plains, the sole naturally occurring prairie east of the Alleghenies. Support for land preservation had spread across class lines, from north shore elites to residents of Long Island's largest working-class suburbs.[19]

The fight against pollution—the single-most important issue for US environmentalists by the late 1960s—was largely led and supported by suburbanites. When the ozone-ridden haze christened as smog first arrived in Los Angeles, suburbanites inaugurated the push to address it. From the new science that established how smog derived from the burning of petroleum to the new laws that created and empowered the nation's first regional air control district, those in the Los Angeles suburbs innovated those very approaches to air pollution control that by the early 1970s would be applied nationwide. Groundwater contamination by phosphate detergents was another newly discovered and controlled route of pollution in this era. Suburban Long Island was among the first corners of the nation to confront this problem, launching its health officials into a similarly pioneering role.[20]

Protests over pesticides also had largely suburban roots. In 1957 the Department of Agriculture sent out planes that dumped DDT wholesale across the Long Island suburbs in an effort to stop the spread of the gypsy moth. A dozen Long Islanders launched a lawsuit against the spray campaign. That suit, which nearly went to Supreme Court, caught the attention of the environmentalist Rachel Carson herself; its transcript and contacts spurred the writing of her famous book, *Silent Spring*.[21] Less than a decade later, a Long Island lawyer and his wife launched another suit against DDT, this time to protest its use by the local mosquito commission. Joining with other local citizens and scientists, they and their fellow suburbanites created what became known as the Environmental Defense Fund, one of two new national groups to emerge from the environmental mobilizations of the 1960s and 1970s.[22]

Environmentalism arose around America's greatest cities, then, not in retreat from the suburbs but in their defense. The environmental political project defended a nature that was not remote, pristine, or "out there." It was, more accurately, suburban nature. Arguably, the suburbs around our largest cities served as the chief templates through which a new politics of the modern environmental movement came to be imagined and organized.

Even as the ecological and human diversity of suburbs has in many fields become ever more apparent, many urban planners, designers, and environmental professionals cling to the stereotypical ways of seeing suburbs that coalesced over the 1950s. You see it in a New Urbanism that declares walkability, multi-use, and mass transit—the watchwords!—to be utterly opposed to a suburban nation. You see it in sweeping declarations of suburbia's coming end. You see it, as well, among those environmentally minded

Provided by Urban Forests," in *Ecology, Planning, and Management of Urban Forests*, ed. Margaret M. Carreiro, Yong-Chang Song, and Jianguo Wu (New York: Springer, 2008), 53–83; G. N. Bratman, J. P. Hamilton, and G. C. Daily, "The Impacts of Nature Experience on Human Cognitive Function and Mental Health," *Annals of the New York Academy of Sciences* 1249 (n.d.): 118–36.

19 Sellers, *Crabgrass Crucible*.
20 Ibid., chaps. 4 and 7.
21 Rachel Carson, *Silent Spring* (Boston: Houghton Mifflin, 1962).
22 Sellers, *Crabgrass Crucible*.

who can't even begin to consider how suburbanites might actually join the battle against global warming—short of picking up and moving to a Brooklyn or a San Francisco.

The legacy of over a century of suburban metropolitan growth has made suburbs an ineradicable part of our landscapes and lives. Environmentally speaking, that's hardly as bad a thing as much planning literature would have you believe. Moreover, suburbs remain major founts of environmental support and activism. Smart growth and New Urbanist initiatives on Long Island today are rooted primarily in the work of locals—themselves suburbanites. Recent environmental triumphs in New York, from the People's Climate March (which drew four hundred thousand to the streets of New York City in September 2014) to America's first statewide ban on fracking, owe much to how many Long Islanders and other suburbanites joined in these campaigns.[23] If you penetrate the suburbia stereotype to consider the actual land, communities, and aspirations in our suburbs, in all their variety, you will find much potential, and much promise.

23 Christopher Sellers, "Beyond Environmentalism: Marching toward Climatism," The Energy Collective, accessed November 4, 2014, http://theenergy collective.com/chris -sellers/2151521/beyond -environmentalism -marching-toward -climatism.

4.2
THE COSMOPOLITAN ECOLOGY OF SUBURBIA

Sarah Jack Hinners

ECOLOGICAL FUNCTION

PRODUCTIVE SUBURBS

4.2.1 In Salt Lake City, Utah, a residential neighborhood hugs the lower slopes of Mount Olympus, a designated wilderness area

1   Richard J. Hobbs, Eric S. Higgs, and C. Hall, *Novel Ecosystems: Intervening in the New Ecological World Order* (West Sussex, UK: Wiley, 2013).

2   Erle C. Ellis and Navin Ramankutty, "Putting People in the Map: Anthropogenic Biomes of the World," *Frontiers in Ecology and the Environment* 6, no. 8 (2008): 439–47.

3   Jan Zalasiewicz et al., "Are We Now Living in the Anthropocene?," *GSA Today* 18, no. 2 (February 2008): 4–8.

The words *suburbia* and *diversity* are not often positively associated with one another. Suburbs are generally thought to exemplify the opposite of diversity: the homogenization of architecture, of retail and commercial sectors, and of demographics; places of mass-designed and mass-produced buildings, generic infrastructure, middle-class white populations, and national chains. If you were to ask an ecologist, she would probably share the above associations and add some further descriptive terms such as *biotic homogenization* and *loss of habitat*. The entire field of ecology—defined as the study of the relationships between organisms and their environment—is based on the study of pristine ecosystems that have experienced as little human influence as possible, so as to allow us to understand how they work and self-organize. With this background, it is difficult for an ecologist to contemplate suburbia without a certain disdain, not to mention befuddlement. How does an ecologist even study a system in which humans clearly play such a dominant role? In order to understand suburban landscapes as ecosystems, ecologists will instinctively compare suburbs to "natural" ecosystems in which they have a stronger understanding of the components and processes at work.

Ecologists, reluctantly rising to the challenge of the human-dominated modern world, have recently coined the term *novel ecosystems* to describe ecosystems that have never existed before, that is, novel assemblages of species, with a unique set of ecosystem processes and dynamics.[1] In fact, science is gradually coming around to recognizing the global-scale human effects on the biophysical world, as reflected in new terminology. "Anthrome"—based on the ecological term *biome*—is a classification of ecosystem types based on history and intensity of human use.[2] "Anthropocene" is the proposed name of a new geologic era in which human activities drive ecological, climatological and even geologic processes.[3] These nomenclature developments are reflections of a deep shift in the way natural scientists approach research, and our methodology must also shift to recognize and incorporate human agency in studying ecological systems.

I would argue that suburbs are an example of a particular pattern, a distinct category of novel ecosystems, although the pattern may manifest in any number of different ways. The key characteristic of this pattern is the blending of anthropogenic and natural processes, of locally native and exotic, of wild and cultivated. These species combine in nonrandom ways to create a landscape-scale experiment in human habitat. Whether this is a good thing to be celebrated, or an ecological disaster to be bemoaned, is not necessarily relevant here. It is happening, and it is interesting. In order to create suburbs, there is certainly destruction and disruption of ecological systems. No one who has witnessed the bulldozing phase of new development can deny this or feel good about it. However, there is also creation, and self-organization of novel ecological systems with new sets of components and processes, and new sets of parameters and constraints. Life does go on. My interest in suburban ecology stems from an ongoing fascination with the relationship between humanity's presence in landscapes and the ecology of those landscapes—the interaction of human, domestic, and wild elements. (figs. **4.2.1–2**)

Suburban ecosystems, in general, are more heterogeneous and dynamic over space and time than natural ecosystems.[4] In a natural ecosystem, the plant community that exists in a particular location is the product of ecological processes over long timescales: seed dispersal, establishment, and reproduction under the local set of climate and soil conditions, and interactions with other species. In contrast, plant diversity in suburban landscapes is a function of human choices—what to species to plant, how to manage and maintain private landscaping—in addition to, and in interaction with, natural processes and uncultivated species (i.e., weeds). Even abiotic

4.2.2 Wildlife wandering into Salt Lake City via City Creek Canyon may have as much direct access to their state legislators as human residents; the Utah Capitol is the dome to the right

conditions, such as soil properties and precipitation, are manipulated by human property owners through applications of soil amendments and irrigation practices.

Thus each individual residential yard is a subsystem with a unique history and management regime, embedded within a mosaic of other yards, parks, and remnant fragments of preexisting land uses. The suburban landscape mosaic exhibits nesting temporal and spatial scales. In other words, the choices of individual property owners are nested within the overall design of a subdivision, which was probably designed by a different firm than the neighboring subdivision. Subdivisions of different ages also each have their own ecological identity, based on factors such as design trends, changing zoning codes, and landscaping choices. The result is that design processes are spatially discrete but also hierarchically nested. In the matrix between these designed spaces, natural processes flourish, at scales ranging from cracks in the concrete of a sidewalk to the network of wild habitat patches that remains in unbuildable areas, such as steep slopes,

4 Nancy B. Grimm et al., "Integrated Approaches to Long-Term Studies of Urban Ecological Systems." *BioScience* 50, no. 7 (2000): 571–84; Steward T. A. Pickett et al., 2008, "Beyond Urban Legends: An Emerging Framework of Urban Ecology, as Illustrated by the Baltimore Ecosystem Study," *BioScience* 58, no. 2 (2008): 139.

riparian zones, or conserved open space. (fig. **4.2.3**)

To further complicate the ecological picture, we humans import plant and animal species from all over the world to populate our little pieces of suburban paradise.[5] In so doing, we are building our own human habitat, rather than seeking out a place with appropriate existing habitat, as most species do. The resulting ecosystems are cosmopolitan agglomerations, in which species meet other species from around the world that they have not met before, in a physical setting that does not exist in the natural world, and they figure out a new set of relationships. Just as is the case for humans, the suburban life is not for everyone. In this great mixing, some species will thrive, others will survive only with constant human care, and others will fail to gain a foothold at all.

In the suburbs of Denver, Colorado, a strong open space preservation ethic combines with some steep and unbuildable terrain, resulting in the wide-scale conservation of bits and pieces of native short-grass prairie, interspersed with suburban residential development. Wild sunflowers, Indian paintbrush, and buffalo grass coexist within inches of well-watered Kentucky bluegrass lawns and hybrid roses. Domestic dogs and coyotes encounter one another on a daily basis, for better or worse, and certainly exchange critical canid information via mutual sniffing of scat. This suburban landscape is much more biologically diverse than the short-grass prairie it replaced, for to the original palette of native species has been added a global selection of ornamental and cultivated species associated with human habitat, including plants that feed or shade us, plants that increase our homes' value, and plants that make us happy. (fig. **4.2.4**) If open space was not preserved in the quantity that it is in the Denver area, this

4.2.3 Wild grassland abuts a flower-filled suburban backyard in Colorado

biodiversity would be much less rich, because the smallest patches of native habitat are often overrun by the human-associated species that escape across white picket fences. Smaller patches of open space sustain smaller and less viable populations of native species and less diverse ecological communities.[6]

In this suburban Denver landscape, I spent three summers studying wild bees. Not honeybees, although they were present, but wild bees. Most people don't realize how many species of bees there are, most of which do not make honey, and a good many of which are not social but solitary. Just among the hundred wild bee species encountered in my research, sizes ranged from a couple of millimeters in length to about half the size of my thumb, and color ranged from black to red, yellow, brilliant metallic copper, green, and blue. Some burrow their nests into the ground, some look for exposed mud banks, and others nest in hollow stems and crevices. My hypothesis in studying

5   Peter del Tredici, 2014, "The Flora of the Future," in *Projective Ecologies*, ed. Chris Reed and Nina-Marie Lister (New York: Harvard University Graduate School of Design and Actar Publishers, 2014), 238–57; Michael L. McKinney, "Urbanization as a Major Cause of Biotic Homogenization," *Biological Conservation* 127, no. 3 (2006): 247–60; Franz Rebele, "Urban Ecology and Special Features of Urban Ecosystems," *Global Ecology and Biogeography Letters* 4, no. 6 (1994): 173–87.
6   Sarah J. Hinners, unpublished data.

4.2.4 Wild coneflowers in remnant prairie outside Denver, Colorado

7   John B. Dunning, Brent J. Danielson, and H. Ronald Pulliam, "Ecological Processes That Affect Populations in Complex Landscapes," *Oikos* 65, no. 1 (1992): 169–75.

8   Sarah J. Hinners, Carol A. Kearns, and Carol A. Wessman, "Roles of Scale, Matrix, and Native Habitat in Supporting a Diverse Suburban Pollinator Assemblage," *Ecological Applications* 22, no. 7 (2012): 1923–35.

these bees was that the addition of all the human-associated elements—flowers, trees, supplemental water, built structures—would provide such an abundance of new resources, both for foraging and for nesting, that these areas of remnant habitat in the suburbs would actually support more abundant and diverse communities of wild bees than open native prairie, a process known as habitat supplementation or complementation.[7] (fig. **4.2.5**)

In the end, this was more or less what I found.[8] But there was an important scaling factor involved. Small patches of conserved habitat of less than 20 acres (less than 8 hectares in this study) exhibited degraded habitat quality, as well as dramatically impoverished bee fauna. Larger patches, however, had a similar number of bee species to the numbers that would be expected on undeveloped open prairie. This indicates that a certain balance in quantity between the native and the domesticated is necessary to obtain the maximum benefit of both. Furthermore, and in some ways most interesting, there was a greater *density*

of species in all of the suburban sites, compared to what was found on the open prairie. That is, each time we collected a sample of suburban bees, it had more species on average than a sample taken in open prairie. Like humans, these suburban bees are living in closer contact with fellow bees than their rural counterparts. Or, to look at it another way, a given unit of native prairie surrounded by suburbia supports more bee species than the same unit of native prairie surrounded by more native prairie. But you have to have enough of those native units, or you still won't have many bee species.

About 20 acres (8 hectares) seems like rather a large area for an organism as small as a bee, and in areas where development pressure is strong the likelihood of 20 acres of native habitat escaping the bulldozer is small. Areas with more unbuildable land, for example, steep slopes or wetlands, have a better chance of keeping some of these open spaces, and thus their rich biological diversity. In the coastal suburbs of San Diego, steep canyons make home building impractical,

4.2.5 A member of the bee genus *Agapostemon* bearing a full pollen load; these beautiful emerald-colored pollinators are common suburban flower visitors

9   Kevin R. Crooks, "Relative Sensitivities of Mammalian Carnivores to Habitat Fragmentation," *Conservation Biology* 16, no. 2 (2002): 488–502; Kevin R. Crooks, Andrew V. Suarez, and Douglas T. Bolger, "Avian Assemblages along a Gradient of Urbanization in a Highly Fragmented Landscape," *Biological Conservation* 115, no. 3 (2004): 451–62.

10 Michael E. Soulé et al., "Reconstructed Dynamics of Rapid Extinctions of Chaparral-Requiring Birds in Urban Habitat Islands," *Conservation Biology* 2, no. 1 (1988): 75–92.

so developments are located atop mesas, dissected by linear ravines containing primarily native vegetation and providing habitat for a variety of wild creatures. In the early 2000s, a landscape and wildlife ecologist named Kevin Crooks chose the area for a series of detailed investigations of the ecology of this complex suburban landscape. He and his team booby-trapped trails with motion-detector cameras and laid down special clay pans to capture tracks left by the secretive wildlife of the canyons. They studied mammalian predators such as weasels, skunks, raccoons, bobcats, and coyotes, and also looked at birds.[9] They found a pattern similar to the one I have observed for bees: a certain amount of nativeness is critical in the landscape for supporting species diversity, but given that base amount, the new resources provided by the presence of human dwellings diversifies the habitat resource base. It also supports greater species diversity, and more species within a smaller area. However, Crooks found that not all wild species thrive in this more heterogeneous environment. Some just disappear from these environments when the available native habitat drops below a certain threshold. This highlights the critical issue of scale in ecology, as well as in planning and design—it is essential to consider the various scales at which different species (including humans) operate within a landscape.

I want to add an important qualification here that reflects conventional ecological wisdom. Although suburban landscapes clearly have the potential to support a surprising number of species, there are many native species of birds, bees, and predators (and this would be true of pretty much any taxonomic group) that cannot live in the suburban landscape. In the 1980s, a couple of decades before Kevin Crooks worked in San Diego, the famed conservation biologist Michael Soulé studied the birds in these canyons, focusing on species that require native chaparral habitat.[10] He found that as chaparral habitat patches became smaller and more isolated, these birds disappeared—no great surprise. These are urbanization-sensitive species with habitat requirements that simply are incompatible with suburbia. We can't convert everything to suburbs and pat ourselves on the back saying we've done something good for biodiversity. In the broader picture, efforts must be made on behalf of these sensitive species as well, by preserving wildlands of sufficient area and connectivity. This is a tremendous challenge in growing regions, and one that cannot and must not be put off until there's nothing left to conserve.

Habitat preservation aside, from an ecological and evolutionary perspective, suburbs are, in many ways, loci of novelty and innovation. A relatively new land-use type, their ecology is not static or fixed. We don't have all the answers yet, because we're still in the middle of the experiment. It takes a while for local species to try out life in this landscape and see whether they can make it. As wild habitat diminishes, species that have not been found in suburban or urban areas may appear there. Like urban humans, urban species are cosmopolitan; they are drifters—rootless, resourceful, and innovative. Like urban humans, they are moving from a rural life lived for their species' entire natural history to a new experiment in habitat, mingling with new species, exploiting new resources, and learning new patterns of resource availability.

Another research project in San Diego, this one at the turn of this century, is significant for a different reason. Sometime in the 1980s, a population of dark-eyed juncos (*Junco hyemalis*) became established on the campus of the University of California, San Diego. Juncos are a small, gray species of sparrow that is widespread across North America. In Southern California, juncos have established breeding ranges in the mountains, but historically there were no native year-round populations in the Mediterranean climate zone along the coast. Presumably, one year, some overwintering individuals just decided to stay for the breeding season and see if they could make a go of it. The ecologists Pamela Yeh and Trevor Price studied the resulting coastal population from the late 1990s to the early 2000s—by then it was a stable population of approximately two hundred birds.[11] The key feature of this

4.2.6 An opportunistic junco builds a nest and raises a brood of young in a bike helmet

population's adaptation to its new habitat was the species' behavioral plasticity, which allowed the birds to extend their reproductive season in response to the milder coastal climate, thereby fledging more young. Furthermore, Yeh went on to demonstrate that the novel conditions in the new habitat were leading to genetic changes in the population, specifically, a decrease in the amount of white feathers in their tails, a sexual signaling trait in this species.[12] Thus, as natural selection would lead us to expect, in a different set of environmental conditions the genetics of the population began shifting to adapt. (fig. **4.2.6**)

Returning to bees, we also see native species finding new and enhanced opportunities in this suburban domestic-wild landscape. *Peponapis pruinosa*, also called the squash bee, is a North American bee species not-too-distantly related to honeybees (which are Eurasian in origin) and bearing a superficial similarity in appearance. (fig. **4.2.7**) Unlike her honeybee relative, *Peponapis pruinosa* is a specialist. While honeybees will collect pollen and nectar from pretty much any abundant floral source (they are motivated by quantity), *P. pruinosa* only visits flowers of the squash family (*Cucurbitaceae*). In the native short-grass prairie of the western United States, there are some wild cucurbits, but not a lot, and they are spatially rare. However, in backyard suburban gardens, there is an abundance of cucurbits, including zucchini, pumpkins,

11 Pamela J. Yeh and Trevor D. Price, "Adaptive Phenotypic Plasticity and the Successful Colonization of a Novel Environment," *American Naturalist* 164, no. 4 (2004): 531–42.

12 Pamela J. Yeh, "Rapid Evolution of a Sexually Selected Trait Following Population Establishment in a Novel Habitat," *Evolution: International Journal of Organic Evolution* 58, no. 1 (2004): 166–74.

4.2.7 *Peponapis pruinosa*, a western US native specialist on flowers of the squash family

13 Yolanda Van Heezik et al., "Do Domestic Cats Impose an Unsustainable Harvest on Urban Bird Populations?," *Biological Conservation* 143, no. 1 (2010): 121–30; Christopher A. Lepczyk, Angela G. Mertig, and Jianguo Liu, "Landowners and Cat Predation across Rural-to-Urban Landscapes," *Biological Conservation* 115, no. 2 (2010): 191–201.

14 Will J. Peach et al., "Reproductive Success of House Sparrows along an Urban Gradient," *Animal Conservation* 11, no. 6 (2008): 493–503; J. Denis Summers-Smith, "Is Unleaded Petrol a Factor in Urban House Sparrow Decline?," *British Birds* 100 (September 2007): 558–60.

15 Paula C. Dias, "Sources and Sinks in Population Biology," *Trends in Ecology & Evolution* 11, no. 8 (1996): 326–30.

cucumbers, and melons. In my Denver study, while I didn't find huge numbers of *P. pruinosa*, they were fairly well distributed among my various suburban study sites, but I didn't find a single one in the open prairie to which they are native.

Critics have pointed out that urban populations of suburban-dwelling species live a very different existence than their country cousins, since they are generally subject to increased levels of noise, pollution, predation by housecats, disease, parasitism, and suboptimal diets (except for the predation/parasitism part, many say this about humans as well).[13] Even raising two broods a year, the San Diego junco population has stayed stable in size, but not grown. In Britain, a series of studies has documented the mystery of a decades-long decline in the population of urban and suburban house sparrows (*Passer domesticus*). This is a species that, as its name suggests, lives in close association with human settlements, so it should be thriving in the modern world, yet it may be overwhelmed by pollution and poor nutritional quality of its diet.[14]

Some argue that urban and suburban habitats serve as population sinks, that is, individuals can survive there, but populations do not grow or thrive and are maintained only by immigration from source populations.[15] These habitats are where dispersing individuals go to eke out a meager living and die. Again, we are midexperiment here. Certainly, urban and suburban populations of any species experience a different set of stressors and opportunities than rural or wild land populations. But we have an opportunity here to recognize that we are creating habitat for more than just ourselves, and to do it better.

To date, urban ecologists have worked to document the ecology of suburbia as they have found it, treating suburbia phenomenologically, as a section of the gradient between rural and urban. But because suburban landscapes are in large part the product of human decisions, there is the potential for conscious intent, for design, to shape these ecosystems. From an ecologist's perspective, there are all sorts of interesting questions that arise. What ecological outcomes might we design for? What kinds of ecosystems do we want to build for ourselves? How much wildness is welcome in our backyards? To what extent do we stay true to the local native ecosystem, or try to preserve or restore it? How might suburban (human) culture change in the future, and how might those changes influence suburban ecosystems? For example, with increases in ecological awareness, might we see a shift in aesthetic preferences toward more native or natural landscaping in yards and parks? Might we begin to systematically embrace conservation of native and wild areas as part of the suburban landscape tapestry?

Having taken the step of asserting that we can design the ecology of suburban landscapes, I will take a further step in proposing that those landscapes be designed to more comprehensively fill the role of human habitat. Suburbs are commonly criticized from a social perspective for being socially and architecturally homogeneous, and for lacking a sense of place that, it's argued, the human psyche needs. Ecology, however, is inherently place-based. What if suburbs were allowed—or even designed—to reflect and celebrate the native ecology of their place? That, even if nothing else were changed in a housing development, would make tremendous strides toward alleviating "placelessness." It would involve close collaboration between conservationists (who are generally reluctant to have anything to do with development) and developers and landscape architects (who often prefer to work with a blank slate). It involves recognizing and intentionally combining those forces of nature and culture that are already at work.

To build with intent, to cultivate these spontaneous, complex systems of people and place, means reinventing our construction process and redesigning the subsystem of the economy in which it

takes place. The Anthropocene has reinvented the world, but we have yet to adapt our way of doing things to this reality of our own making; we have yet to accept the responsibility of our own power. In the words of Erle Ellis:

> We have never had more power to do great things, to design better landscape ecologies both for sustenance and for nature, to create beauty, and to manage a biosphere that will nurture, please and honor our children, ourselves, and our ancestors. And with creation comes both opportunity and responsibility.[16]

Thus far, without any intent at all, we have created in suburbia a landscape type that is full of intense ecological, and even evolutionary, change and activity. What might we do if we actually stop and think about it?

16 Erle C. Ellis, "Anthropogenic Taxonomies: A Taxonomy of the Human Biosphere," in *Projective Ecologies*, ed. Chris Reed and Nina-Marie Lister (New York: Harvard University Graduate School of Design and Actar Publishers), 180–81.

Fairview, Texas, United States

Cary, North Carolina, United States

4.3
METABOLIC SUBURBS, OR THE VIRTUE OF LOW DENSITIES

Susannah Hagan

DESIGN
MODELS

FLEXIBLE
REGULATION

PRODUCTIVE
SUBURBS

TECHNOLOGY

Over 80 percent of the present-day populations of the United Kingdom and the United States find the suburbs "attractive places to live."[1] This is a startling figure, given the hostility that suburbs provoke in most advocates of sustainable development. Does that mean 80 percent of these populations want to live "unsustainably"? If so, in what sense?

What if the suburban landscape, with its plentiful open spaces, were to be reconfigured as one energy-efficient, sustainable system? Today's planning community still largely gives its allegiance to the "compact city" model of ever more dense urban centers, combined with efforts to rein in the open, suburban spaces known—and censured as—"sprawl." But there is a question that planners have raised all too infrequently: Could suburbia, with its low-density way of life, offer environmental advantages?

What Are Suburbs?
Defining *suburbs* is vexing (as in, a vexed question). There are large differences in age, typology, density, and demography to choose from or to try to include. However broad or narrow one's definition, however, suburbs have been the subject of much hostility from planners. In the United Kingdom (as elsewhere), planners typically advocate the "compact city" model for regional sustainability and rely almost exclusively on transport energy analysis to justify the raising of low residential densities by the insertion of higher density dwellings within them. Higher densities mean more people per unit area, which makes public transportation more economically viable, which then cuts down on car use, which saves transport energy. This causal chain has been convincingly challenged by subsequent academic research, not for its logic, but for the assumption that its occurrence is inevitable.[2] Nonetheless, the compact city remains the dominant

influence on planning policy internationally, the one cited in planning documents to ensure "sustainable development."

As a result, the qualities that draw people to suburbs are diminished by increasing congestion: "Relatively spacious, low density suburban areas (the archetypal leafy suburbs) are coming under increasing development pressure... Current levels of change increase the potential for local distinctiveness and historically significant features to be lost."[3] What is also being lost is an opportunity to include suburbs within sustainable development, rather than remain prodigally outside it. The Greater London Authority has recognized the consequences of disinvestment in, and neglect of, the urban fringe: of suburbs that are deprived areas, rather than the plump houses and tended gardens of popular imagination. As a result, the more recent London plans take a more inclusive approach to settlement conditions, with the suburbs now seen as part of the city and therefore entitled to the same regeneration investment, though that may not translate into cash in the current economic and political climate.[4]

A Modest Proposal
Within the framework of sustainable redevelopment, low densities are perceived to be socially isolating and environmentally—and therefore economically—wasteful, a description that may fit some, but certainly not all, suburbs. Turning the compact city model on its head, however, frees us to ask what the environmental advantages of low densities might be. In other words, if the minuses of compaction and densification are admitted—increased stress on citizens, increased expenditure on increased maintenance of infrastructure and services, increased energy demand for more vertical living—then the pluses of lower densities can be entertained as well. What are these, and how can they be

1   Department of the Environment, Transportation and the Regions, *Living in Urban England* (London: DETR, 2000).

2   See Michael Breheny, "Sustainable Development and Urban Form: An Introduction," in *Sustainable Development and Urban Form* (London: Pion Limited, 1992); Michael Jencks and M. R. Burgess, *Compact Cities* (London: Spon, 2000).

3   Simon G. Potts et al., *London's Suburbs: Unlocking Their Potential, A Report Accompanying the London Assembly's Enquiry into London Suburbs* (London: BURA & URBED, 2007); English Heritage, *The Heritage of Historic Suburbs* (London: HELM, 2007).

4   Greater London Authority, "Consultation Draft Replacement London Plan," accessed June 10, 2015, http://www.london.gov.uk/ shaping-london /london-plan/docs /chapter2.pdf.

Habitat	Income	Metabolism	Energy

Living Machine
- For black water cleaning
- Use when there is a 10m × 30m strip of land available for 60m3/day of sewage (300 people)

Aerobic Digester
- For producing compost from agricultural and household waste to sell to growers
- Size: For 500 households 6 × 1.5m × 1.5m3
- Cheaper option than anaerobic digester
- Use when brownfield site can't be dug
- Use when open space is less than 1ha

Hedgerows/Thickets
- Use when soil isn't good enough for trees

Market Gardens 1
- Use when soil is good
- Use when water is available
- Use when there is one open space or a collection of open spaces in proximity of not less than 1.6ha/person to ensure a living
- Use in combination with orchards

Rainwater Harvesting 1
- Collection of rainwater for growers' land
- Use when buildings are adjacent to land used for income

Anaerobic Digester
- For producing heating gas from agricultural and household waste
- Use when this digester becomes affordable to a district
- Use when Brownfield site can't be dug
- Use when open space is less than 1ha

Trees
- Use when market gardens and orchards cannot thrive
- Use species appropriate to climate and soil, e.g., willows on polluted soil

Beehives
- For honey to sell
- Use when soil is unsuitable for food growing
- Use on open space of any size, where there are flowers/wildflower ares within striking distance

Rainwater Harvesting 2
- Collection of rainwater for growers' storage pond
- Use where there are vacant, nonporous sites

CHP
- For producing heat and electricity when there is simultaneous demand for electricity and heating over 24-hour cycle (e.g., for hospitals, swimming pools)
- Use when Brownfield ground can't be dug
- Use when open space is less than 1 ha

Marshes/Bogs
- Use where there is existing unpolluted water or new water storage

Market Gardens 2
- Use when soil is unsuitable for food growing, greenhouses for vegetable or flower growing
- Use on open space of any size

Storage Pond
- Constructed wetlands for gray-water cleaning and storage for growers' land. Surface flow/storage pond
- Use where water or marsh exist already, or where they can be introduced near gray-water harvesting
- Use where there is open space of a minimum of 20m2
- Will also contribute to habitat

Coppicing
- For heating energy only. 1ha heats 4 houses/year
- Use when rainfall is 1200mm or more
- Use when soil is polluted

Habitat	Income	Metabolism	Energy

Wildflowers
—Use bee-friendly species
—Can be used with hedgerows and/or marsh agent

Orchards
—For cash crop orchards
—Use when soil is good, water is available
—Use when there is one open space or a collection of open spaces in close proximity of not less than 1.6ha/person to ensure a living
—Use combination with market gardens

Reed Bed
—Constructed wetlands for gray-water cleaning subsurface flow
—Use where water or marsh exists already, or where it is suitable to introduce them
—Use where there is open space of 5–10m2
—Use where cost is less of an issue, and efficiency needs to be high
—Will also contribute to habitat

Solar Water / PV
—For solar hot water and/or electricity
—Use when subsidies are available for solar water panels or photovoltaics
—Use when roof inclination and solar orientation are productive

4.3.1 A context- and climate-responsive catalog insertions to economically beneficial "Income" insertions

achieved? Will they enhance or will they undermine the current desirability of suburbs to a majority of the population in many countries?

The one commodity that many suburbs have in abundance is open land. Land is valuable. It can do things: grow food and fuel; collect, purify, and recycle water; modify harsh microclimates; save energy; generate energy. The "performative" potential of the suburban landscape can potentially transform suburbs into "organic extensions of the urban system."[5] (fig. **4.3.1**)

This requires an expansion of focus from urban centers, which exclude suburbs and the countryside beyond, to urban regions, which include both. Suburban landscapes can and should be a key component of a grown infrastructure, "a multifunctional resource capable of delivering a wide range of environmental and quality of life benefits for local communities, [and include] parks, open spaces, playing fields, woodlands, allotments and private gardens."[6] Among these environmental benefits are metabolic capacities latent within suburban open space, capacities that can contribute to the reduction of the overall environmental impact of the city region. For example, certain wastes can be imported into suburban open spaces from the center to metabolize. The center, on the other hand, can import any surplus suburban renewable energy,

locally grown organic food, or recycled water. In this way, the suburb becomes part of an artificial ecosystem, rather than a parasite, and is perceived as a contribution to the metropolis rather than as a drag on it. (fig. **4.3.2**)

Public Goods in Private Ownership
The suburban landscape is a complex patchwork of privately and publicly owned land. The private backyard or garden is ground zero, however, whether it is a few trees behind a terraced house or a rolling couple of acres, and its privacy is potentially an obstacle to the collectivity of an environmentally productive landscape. (fig. **4.3.3**) Natural system boundaries do not observe ownership boundaries. They ride right over them, or stop short of them, or include some privately owned land but not all, thus unfairly distributing the metabolic work to be done. There is also a cultural resistance to one's hard-earned property being dragooned into a communal undertaking for which the immediate personal benefit remains elusive. Real estate tax breaks are one possible carrot to dangle in front of potential contributors to the system, as are reductions in energy and/or water tariffs.

The integration of different kinds of green space, with their different forms of ownership, into one integrated energy-saving suburban landscape system therefore requires research into governance

5   Local Futures, *State of the Suburbs Local Futures* (London: Leadership Centre for Local Government, 2007).

6   South East Green Infrastructure Partnership (SEGIP), *South East Green Infrastructure Framework—From Policy into Practice* (London: Land Use Consultants, 2009).

Phase 1	Low LA Investment	Low LA Investment	Higher LA Investment
	open source audit: how many spaces? who owns them? how large are they?	grower audit: market gardeners? bee keepers? composters? willing to train others / be trained?	soil tests: polluted open spaces unpolluted open spaces
Phase 2	No LA Investment	Low LA Investment	LA Incentives
	polluted soil (PS): leave wild unpolluted soil (US): allow allotments	PS: plant wildflowers US: plant trees	bee-keeping
Phase 3	LA Incentives	LA Incentives	LA Incentives
	US: market gardens (quicker yield) PS: market gardens in raised beds	US: orchards (slower yield) PS: coppice (slower yield)	PS: greenhouses (more expensive)
Phase 4	LA Incentives	LA Incentives	LA Incentives
	aerobic digestion (compost for sale)	anaerobic digestion (gas for sale)	CHP heat + power for sale
Phase 5	LA Incentives	Higher LA Investment	Higher LA Investment
	domestic rainwater harvesting	US: constructed wetlands for black-/ gray-water filtration	Infrastructure to move filtered water back to + from residential and/or arable land

4.3.2 Local authorities (LAs) or communities wanting to minimize risk can begin with cheaper ecosystem elements and progress to more expensive ones as affordable interventions start to produce income

and participation, as well as into environmental strategies, appropriate techniques and technologies, and appropriate scales of intervention (from the individual house to the district). How is a top-down "push" on energy saving, for example, converted into community "pull"? How can people be helped to reconcile what the majority of them moved to the suburbs for—space and independence—with the increasing number of ethical and practical challenges to that space, if not that independence? Conceptually, one needs to stand at the "intersection between social and bio-physical dimensions to [sub]urban space."[7] Technology is not enough. No amount of anaerobic digesters, "living machines," and wind turbines will have much impact until they are embraced by a public that understands their importance: "Public education is a prerequisite to public participation."[8]

In this case, however, public education could be accomplished through participation. These new performative landscapes would have to be designed, and this could allow a process of codesign, in which lay and expert knowledge are viewed as equally important to the process of developing place-specific strategies. Residents and other stakeholders would collaborate with designers and engineers. The practice requires a commitment on the part of the designer to work in this way, something not often encouraged by his or her training, and the space and time (and therefore money) to engage in a genuine collaboration. This range of collaboration could "provide a wealth of information regarding the appropriateness of a technology in a given setting, along with any potential barriers to its implementation."[9] As environmental interventions in the suburbs would require new legislation to deal with the complexities of using public and private land, local planners and politicians are also vital to successful codesign sessions. Hydrological systems cross political boundaries and would often require interdistrict or even interregional cooperation between appropriate levels of government, probably nudged by a nationally legislated requirement to comply. Environmental legislation already works

7   Matthew Gandy, "Rethinking Urban Metabolism: Water, Space and the Modern City," *CITY* 8, no. 3 (December 2004).

8   Roland Burkhard, "A Review of Rainwater Management Techniques and Their Integration in Planning," *Urban Water* 2 (2006): 197–221.

9   Carole Pateman, *Participation and Democratic Theory* (Cambridge: Cambridge University Press, 1970).

like this anyway in both the United States and the member states of the European Union.

Ornamented Performance

What the resulting designs looked like would vary according to suburb, residents, and local government. New suburbs in which such systems could be built in from the beginning are obviously much easier to configure without controversy than to convert existing suburbs. New residential cluster developments are particularly easy to deal with, as there is a much larger proportion of land commonly owned by the cluster than there is commonly owned by local government or the county in older house-and-garden suburbs. That land could be put to work without having to poach too much from private yards. (fig. **4.3.4**)

How the result will look also depends on soil, climate, density, and typology. Where there is unpolluted and fertile soil, a reasonable growing season, and worthwhile dimensions of open land, then (sub) urban agriculture may be appropriate in the form of market gardens, commercial orchards, and a greater provision of sought-after allotments. If the land is flat and subject to high winds, stands of trees could be planted to improve the microclimate and reduce heating fuel consumption. "Living machines" to clean gray or even black water, ponds for storing rainwater, and systems for delivering it from, and redistributing it to, surrounding buildings would appear where there was the space. Water systems might be in a park or at the bottom of a line of private yards, their extremities donated to make a communal collection point in return for free recycled water (desirable once all water is metered). Seasonal heat storage systems could be installed under parking lots and tennis courts. Neighborhood combined heat and power (CHP) plants might be deployed and so might anaerobic

4.3.3 "Public" land between private suburban plots can become communal land, used for leisure and environmental activities

digesters, with their gas used to produce electricity. (fig. **4.3.5**)

Codesign would ensure that residents understood the reasons for such moves and had a direct influence on the location of metabolic processes. Underused or ornamental open land could be extended to social as well as environmental uses: for instance, the area around a collecting pond at the end of some yards could also serve as a semiprivate gathering place shared by a group of houses, a typology one finds in some areas of London, where the private gardens at the rear of the houses open onto an interior communal garden, accessible only to residents. This delivers an immediate and familiar benefit—the opportunity to socialize in a protected space—and provides a double use for these landscapes, one social and the other environmental.

The Question of the Car

This artificial ecology folded into the public-private patchwork of suburban open land does not, of course, address the problems raised by the compact city critique of low-density settlements: their car dependency. But it would be difficult to increase the density of every low-density settlement in order to create enough travelers to justify public transportation. This assumes that people would then abandon their cars and use trains or buses, as ticket prices for overcrowded public transport rise inexorably.

10 Robert Fishman,
    Bourgeois Utopias
    (New York: Basic Books,
    1987); Joel Garreau,
    Edge City (New York:
    Anchor Books, 1991).

4.3.4 The introduction of ecosystem catalog elements is highly sensitive to initial conditions and will produce very different patterns of land use in response to the social and physical characteristics of a particular suburb. As the artificial ecosystem evolves, it begins to respond to its own, as well as found, conditions, increasing in impact both environmentally and economically.

Nor can one extend public transport infrastructure so that it provides a convenient access point for every suburban user. Cars are unavoidable for the foreseeable future, but fossil fuel and status-driven ones are not. Small solar and biomethane vehicles, or hydrogen-powered ones, could be used to travel in existing low-density suburbs and the countryside. If metabolic landscapes were introduced into suburbs, their residents' thinking about the environment might change sufficiently for them to independently assess their relationship with cars or at least with the car as it is presently constituted.

The Necessity of Planning

Is the hostility of urban planners toward the suburbs driven entirely by what is perceived to be a waste of land and energy, or is there also a desire to preserve traditional distinctions between city and noncity, inside and outside, each defined in opposition to the other?

Such hard-edged differentiations started to lose meaning when towns first expanded past their Renaissance fortifications, sliding over the walls and into the countryside, obscuring the sharp demarcations between town and country. This sprawl was largely unplanned and freely chosen. The majority of people who moved to the suburbs moved because they wanted to. In the twentieth century, corporations relocated because they wanted to, because there was a skilled workforce in the hinterlands. Such a mix transformed suburbs into "technoburbs" and "edge cities" economically, if not environmentally, into self-sustaining settlements.[10]

What was defended as democracy in action in the late 1960s had become neo-conservative free market dogma by the 1980s, but the point, oddly, was the same: suburbs equal liberty; suburbs equal freedom from top-down state planning. Writing in the journal *New Society* in 1969, Paul Barker, Reyner Banham, Peter Hall,

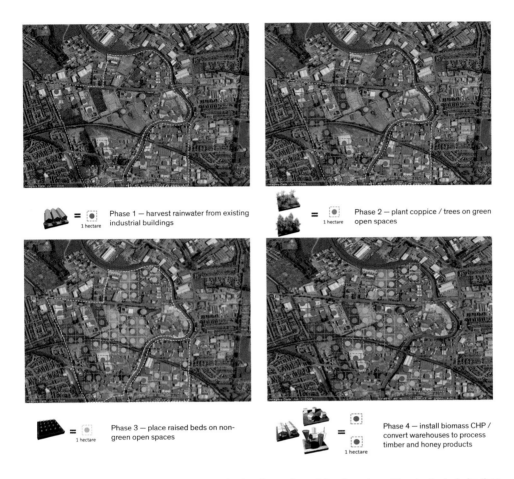

Phase 1 — harvest rainwater from existing industrial buildings
= 1 hectare

Phase 2 — plant coppice / trees on green open spaces
= 1 hectare

Phase 3 — place raised beds on non-green open spaces
= 1 hectare

Phase 4 — install biomass CHP / convert warehouses to process timber and honey products
= 1 hectare

4.3.5 A more detailed illustration of the phased introduction of ecosystem catalog elements, and the rules for deploying them

and Cedric Price declared things couldn't be any worse if planners were relieved of their powers and we were left with what they called "Non-Plan." [11] In their article of the same name, they made several provocative connections between land use, social exclusion, and democratic choice:

> As people become richer, they demand more space; and because at the same time they become more mobile, they will be able to command [more space]. They will want this extra space in and around their houses…To impose rigid controls in order to frustrate people in achieving the space standards they require, represents simply the received personal or class judgements of those who are making the decisions. [12]

But the concept of Non-Plan is simply nostalgia, a longing for the 1970s, when the architecture critic Reyner Banham defended the unplanned, self-organizing supersprawl of Los Angeles as the way forward from oppressive and unsuccessful postwar planning. [13] Two subsequent decades of neoconservative deregulation have made it abundantly clear that Non-Plan is equally oppressive, but oppresses the weak rather than occasionally thwarting the strong (the weak being the economically vulnerable and the environment). Non-Plan allows the free market to devour the unfit and overexploit natural resources that belong to the community. Planning ostensibly protects both and needs now to allow the retooling of the suburbs' open spaces. The suburban picturesque should turn toward an eighteenth-century landscape paradigm

11 Paul Barker et al., "Non-Plan: An Experiment in Freedom," *New Society* 338 (March 20, 1969).
12 Ibid., 338.
13 Reyner Banham, *Los Angeles: The Architecture of Four Ecologies* (Berkeley and Los Angeles: University of California Press, 2001).

of ornament and performance: husbanded woods that bore timber to sell, remolded hills that fed profitable wool-producing sheep.

This is not, however, a call to a return to European postwar planning in all its statist glory. Whichever political party or combination of parties is in power, necessary environmental re-formation will not happen without social acceptance, and social acceptance will not happen without education and participation, especially in privatized realms such as suburbs. This suggests that design may become crucial, not as an arm of an arm of the state, but as a medium of public education and lay-professional collaboration. Is the architectural profession ready, not only to overcome its traditional antipathy toward the suburban, but to help suburban communities produce neighborhood development plans that radically reconsider their open spaces?

A slightly different version of "Metabolic Suburbs, or The Virtue of Low Densities" was first printed in arq: Architectural Research Quarterly *16, no. 1 (2012): 9–13. Reprinted with kind permission of Cambridge University Press.*

4.4
SUBURBAN
WETLANDIA

Celina Balderas Guzmán

ECOLOGICAL FUNCTION

PRODUCTIVE SUBURBS

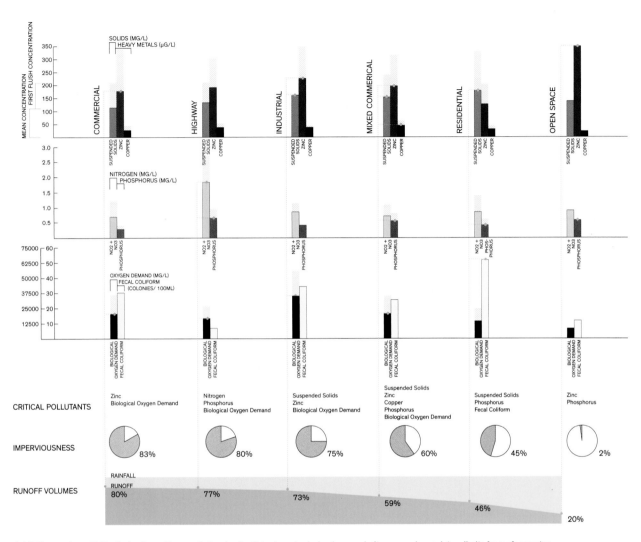

4.4.1 Stormwater pollution by land use. Stormwater's mix of pollutants varies by land use and often exceeds regulatory limits for surface water

Stormwater has become an increasing threat to cities, suburbs, and the natural systems that protect them. City dwellers can routinely see it run off rooftops, streets, and parking lots when it rains. But not always as visible are the pollutants—the trash, heavy metals, fertilizers and pesticides, bacteria, and sediment—that stormwater commonly carries through the urban environment. (figs. **4.4.1–2**)

Urbanization entails paving over natural areas that once had a greater capacity to capture and absorb this stormwater. But as urbanization expands, a region's natural hydrologic system of rivers, streams, lakes, and, most significantly, of wetlands, is slowly degraded if not entirely destroyed.

Thus, cities are in need of a new paradigm for managing stormwater. The best solutions will be those that shift away from monofunctional, centralized infrastructure. Since the 1990s, constructed wetlands have arisen as a promising multifunctional, decentralized, and low-cost solution to stormwater problems and, more broadly, to climate change. These artificial systems are designed to mimic natural wetlands by using the same physical, biological, and chemical processes to treat water. Besides treating stormwater pollution and detaining floodwaters, constructed wetlands can, among other functions, boost ecosystem services at large (such as biodiversity),

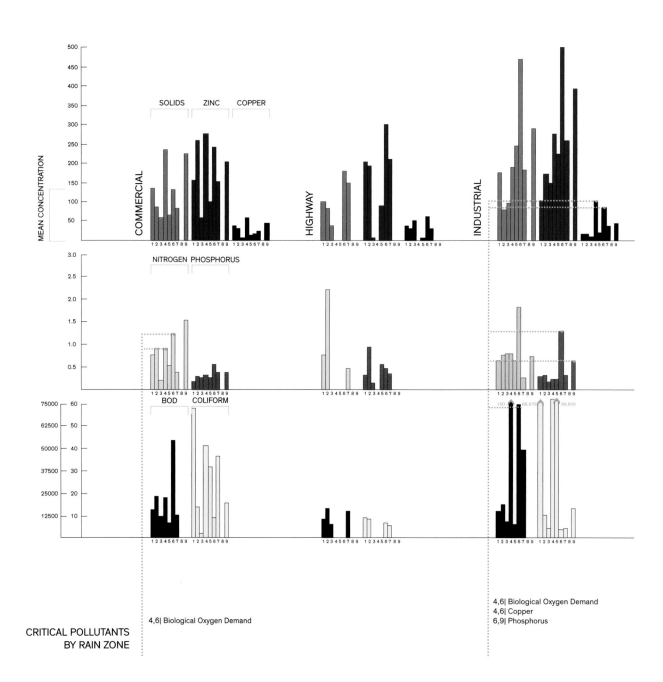

CRITICAL POLLUTANTS
BY RAIN ZONE

4,6| Biological Oxygen Demand

4,6| Biological Oxygen Demand
4,6| Copper
6,9| Phosphorus

4.4.2 Stormwater pollution varies greatly by land use and rain zone (continues on overleaf)

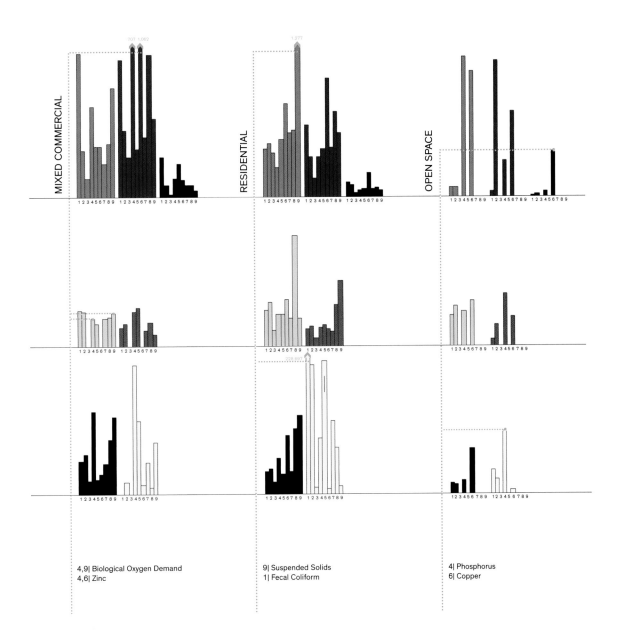

4,9| Biological Oxygen Demand
4,6| Zinc

9| Suspended Solids
1| Fecal Coliform

4| Phosphorus
6| Copper

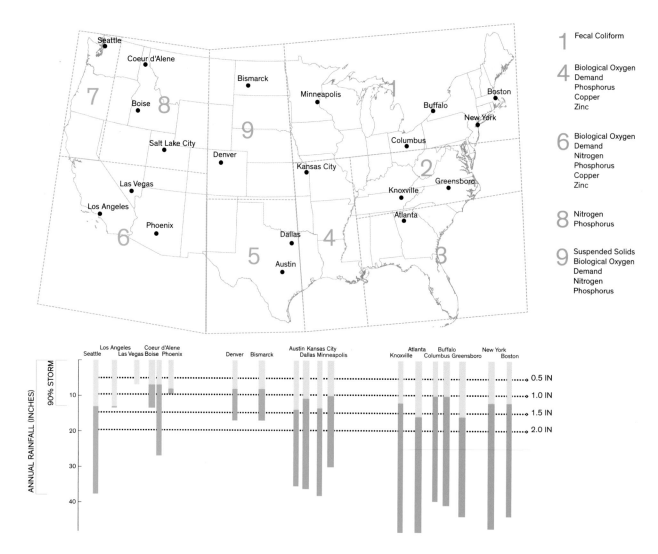

4.4.2 Stormwater pollution varies greatly by land use and rain zone

and provide urban amenities (such as recreation).

However, to be most efficient and productive, a constructed wetland must cover multiple acres and have a sizable watershed. For that reason, the rapid pace of suburban expansion that continues today provides an opportunity for a fundamental change in our approach to coping with stormwater and, simultaneously, rethinking urban infrastructure.

The Stormwater Problem
Hundreds of American cities function with limited-capacity water treatment plants for stormwater. When untreated water enters natural water bodies, it degrades the natural environment; when it floods urbanized areas during large storms, it causes physical damage.[1] In 2008 the cost of flooding in the United States was estimated at around $2.7 billion annually.[2] In many areas worldwide, the increased intensity of storms will heighten the risk of urban floods. The two effects—flooding and degradation of the environment—are intimately related.

As urbanization increases, streams are channeled or buried, and the conveyance patterns of water through underground pipes are changed. (fig. **4.4.3**) The negative effects are felt

1   United States Environmental Protection Agency, "Greening CSO Plans: Planning and Modeling Green Infrastructure for Combined Sewer Overflow (CSO) Control," March 2014, 5. Seven hundred American cities still have combined sewer systems.
2   Stanley A. Changnon, "Assessment of Flood Losses in the United States," *Journal of Contemporary Water Research & Education* 138, no. 1 (April 1, 2008): 43.

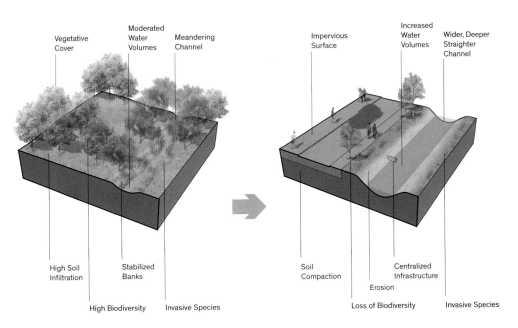

Vegetative Cover · Moderated Water Volumes · Meandering Channel · High Soil Infiltration · Stabilized Banks · High Biodiversity · Invasive Species

Impervious Surface · Increased Water Volumes · Wider, Deeper Straighter Channel · Soil Compaction · Erosion · Centralized Infrastructure · Loss of Biodiversity · Invasive Species

4.4.3 Illustration of the changes in natural hydrologic systems as a result of urbanization

in four broad ways: stream hydrology (more runoff and floods), channel morphology (more erosion and widening of streams), ecology and habitat (destruction of habitat), and water quality (more pollution).[3] The United States, according to the Environmental Protection Agency (EPA), has thousands of impaired rivers and streams that are "too polluted or otherwise degraded" to meet water quality standards.[4]

Natural wetlands are a particularly important feature of natural hydrologic systems. Urbanization, and especially suburbanization, has been responsible for large amounts of wetland loss including, historically, outright destruction. This has proceeded despite the fact that wetlands serve essential functions needed by metropolitan areas, especially in times of climate change: water treatment, flood protection, aquifer recharging, soil conservation, urban heat island reduction, biodiversity maintenance, and more.[5] Wetlands are the most valuable terrestrial biome in the world, with ecosystem services worth an estimated $5 trillion per year worldwide or about $6,000 per acre ($15,000 per hectare) per year.[6] Their productivity stems from being a liminal

ecosystem between land and water, a rich and constantly changing environment.

Unless cities and, most important, new suburbs are developed differently than they have been in the past, degradation of natural hydrologic systems, including wetlands, will continue as urbanization accelerates rapidly around the world. The urban expansion expert Shlomo Angel and colleagues estimate that cities in developing countries could more than quadruple in size between 2010 and 2050.[7] In spite of being a developed country, even the United States continues to grow significantly, with development reaching into new watersheds. Based on population projections, an estimated 54 million acres (22 million hectares) of previously undeveloped land will become effectively suburbanized between 2003 and 2030, especially in the southeast and south-central regions.[8] Another study estimates that 97 million acres (39 million hectares) of land will become effectively suburbanized between 2000 and 2050.[9] These expansions would be equivalent to building eight new Houston metropolitan areas by 2030, and fifteen by 2050.

3 Elizabeth A. Brabec, "Imperviousness and Land-Use Policy: Toward an Effective Approach to Watershed Planning," *Journal of Hydrologic Engineering* 14, no. 4 (April 2009): 426.

4 United States Environmental Protection Agency, "Total Maximum Daily Loads (TMDLs) and Stormwater," accessed February 14, 2015, http://water .epa.gov/lawsregs /lawsguidance/cwa/tmdl /stormwater_index.cfm.

5 Amanda M. Nahlik et al., "Potential Indicators of Final Ecosystem Services in Wetlands" (paper presented at the Society of Wetland Scientists Annual Meeting, Salt Lake City, Utah, June 28–July 2, 2010).

6 Robert Costanza et al., "The Value of the World's Ecosystem Services and Natural Capital," *Nature* 387, no. 6630 (May 15, 1997): 253.

7 Shlomo Angel et al., "Global Urban Expansion," in *Infinite Suburbia* (New York: Princeton Architectural Press, 2017).

8 The density of development used in this study corresponds to single-family homes on roughly a quarter-acre lot (900 square meters): Eric M. White, Anita T. Morzillo, and Ralph J. Alig, "Past and Projected Rural Land Conversion in the US at State, Regional, and National Levels," *Landscape and Urban Planning* 89, nos. 1–2 (January 30, 2009): 37–48.

9 David J. Nowak and Jeffrey T. Walton, "Projected Urban Growth (2000–2050) and Its Estimated Impact on the US Forest Resource," *Journal of Forestry* 103, no. 8 (December 2005): 383–89.

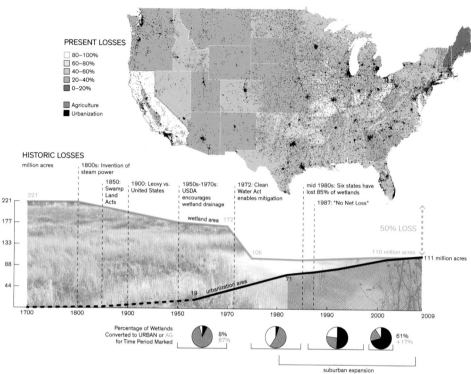

4.4.4 Timeline of wetland losses and urbanization in the United States along with present-day map

10　Thomas E. Dahl and Gregory J. Allord, "History of Wetlands in the Conterminous United States," accessed September 26, 2012, https://water.usgs.gov /nwsum/WSP2425 /history.html.

11　Thomas E. Dahl and US Fish and Wildlife Service, *Status and Trends of Wetlands in the Conterminous United States 2004 to 2009* (Washington, DC: US Department of the Interior, US Fish and Wildlife Service, Fisheries and Habitat Conservation, 2011), 16.

Wetlands versus Cities

Our present-day recognition of urban stormwater problems and the value of wetlands, follow a long history of wetland destruction. Before European settlement, the contiguous United States had an estimated 221 million acres (89 million hectares) of wetlands, covering about 11 percent of the country.[10] Today, there is an estimated 110 million acres (45 million hectares) of wetlands, half the amount present in colonial times.[11] (fig. **4.4.4**) During the country's early expansion, wetlands were seen as an impediment to development and travel, as sources of disease, and, overall, as a waste of land. In the nineteenth century, this attitude led to large-scale campaigns, sanctioned by the federal government, of wetland removal, to make way for urbanization and agriculture, and to control natural hydrologic systems with engineered systems.[12] Policy makers and engineers viewed the natural hydrologic system as "disorderly but knowable" and strove

for a technological redesign that would make rivers function "in orderly, predictable ways."[13] Ironically, by eliminating natural systems and introducing a high degree of engineered infrastructure, the vulnerability of cities to risks such as flooding was increased, rather than reduced.

Many of our nation's greatest cities were at least partly created by filling wetlands. The island of Manhattan was originally about 10 percent wetlands of a wide variety, such as near-shore eelgrass beds, salt marshes, shrub swamps, red maple swamps, and Atlantic cedar bogs (which are particularly unique ecologically). There were about fifty different ecosystems on the island at the time Europeans first arrived.[14] Today, none of the original Manhattan wetlands remain, and many of those in surrounding areas, such as the Meadowlands in New Jersey and Flushing Meadows in Queens, have been significantly and irreparably altered. These ecological alterations have exacerbated damage from storms. As the scholar Ted Steinberg has written about New York City's development, "In trading in its tidal wetlands for land development, the city had denied itself a frontline defense that, if the sedimentary record is any guide, kept all but the most vicious flooding at bay."[15] As a result, New York is the third-most vulnerable port city in the world, according to a 2013 report by the Organisation for Economic Co-operation and Development, a truth borne out by the devastating effects of Hurricane Sandy in 2012.[16]

Los Angeles, commonly thought of as being a naturally arid landscape, had more water prior to the channelization of rivers and streams. Specifically, historical ecologists have found that in the second half of the nineteenth century the Ballona Creek watershed—which includes downtown Los Angeles, Hollywood, Beverly Hills, Culver City, Baldwin Hills, and parts of Santa Monica—was composed of 174 unique wetlands, ranging from salt marshes to freshwater marshes to wet meadows, covering 14,149 acres (5,470 hectares).[17] Only 4 percent—600 acres (240 hectares)—of wetlands remain in this watershed today.[18] The obliteration of these wetlands was part of a regional urbanization strategy that included hardening the natural hydrologic system through paving over floodplains and burying streams, channeling and concretizing rivers and streams, and building dams, debris basins, and flood-control basins. This strategy put more people and property in risky areas and added many engineered elements that could fail to the hydrologic system, and indeed many did. As the environmental historian Jared Orsi put it, "Technology, city growth, and nature joined to make Los Angeles a hazardous metropolis."[19] Besides the flood risks, Los Angeles also faces acute water scarcity, because the widespread elimination of natural hydrologic features

from the landscape has served to move water out and into the ocean more rapidly, as opposed to capturing it for reuse or attempting to recharge groundwater.

While urbanization and suburbanization alike have contributed to wetland loss, unfortunately, no study exists to clearly attribute the gross losses, the types of wetlands lost (not all wetlands are created equal), and the wetland gains (in some cases) to each form.[20] Given that suburbanization is a more spatially extensive phenomenon than the urbanization patterns of dense city cores, we can assume that the greatest wetland losses probably were and continue to be the result of suburban development.

Wetlands were reduced specifically so that cities and suburbs could be created, but the loss of wetlands has exposed cities to numerous risks. In addition to flooding and the loss of biodiversity and habitat, there have been consequences for water-based industries. Negative impacts on multiple scales have resulted from water scarcity, poor water quality, and microclimactic changes. Climate change is accentuating the risks cities face through increased flooding, heat, and other factors. But as much as it threatens urban areas, climate change (with its resulting sea-level rise, air and water temperature changes, and variations in rainfall and storms) is also a threat to wetlands.[21] It's estimated that coastal wetlands—even taking into account their movement inland—will decrease by 68 percent globally with a 3-foot (1-meter) sea-level rise, with disproportionate losses in China, Vietnam, Libya, Egypt, Romania, and Ukraine.[22] The wetlands remaining in cities will face new challenges, if not total demise.

New Infrastructure Paradigms

The nation's stormwater infrastructure needs are significant. In 2008 the EPA estimated that $42 billion—almost

12 Bryony Coles and John M. Coles, *People of the Wetlands: Bogs, Bodies, and Lake-Dwellers* (New York: Thames & Hudson, 1989); Samuel P. Shaw and C. Gordon Fredine, "NPWRC: Wetlands of the United States—Their Extent and Their Value to Waterfowl and Other Wildlife," accessed November 19, 2012, http://www.npwrc.usgs.gov/resource/wetlands/uswetlan/index.htm.

13 Jared Orsi, *Hazardous Metropolis: Flooding and Urban Ecology in Los Angeles* (Berkeley: University of California Press, 2004), 52.

14 Eric W. Sanderson, "Urban Legend: Discovering Manhattan's Wetlands," *National Wetlands Newsletter* 27, no. 1 (February 2005): 14; see also Theodore Steinberg, *Gotham Unbound: The Ecological History of Greater New York* (New York: Simon & Schuster, 2014).

15 Ted Steinberg, "Development of a Disaster," *Discover* 35, no. 4 (May 2014): 50–54.

16 Stephane Hallegatte et al., "Future Flood Losses in Major Coastal Cities," *Nature Climate Change* 3, no. 9 (September 2013): 802–6, doi:10.1038/nclimate1979.

17 Shawna Dark et al., "Historical Ecology of the Ballona Creek Watershed" (Southern California Coastal Water Research Project, n.d.), iv, http://www.ballonahe.org/downloads/on_geo_data/ballona_report%5Bemail%5D.pdf.

18 "Early History," *Friends of Ballona Wetlands*, accessed November 19, 2015, http://www.ballonafriends.org/history.html.

19 Orsi, *Hazardous Metropolis*, 79.

20 Wetland gains have been reported in significant numbers since the 1998 to 2004 period. These gains are related to wetland mitigation policies or stormwater rules introduced during that time. Though it is not known how much

certainly an underestimate—is needed for stormwater management infrastructure over the next twenty years, an increase of $17 billion from 2004. Concurrently, $64 billion is needed to correct combined sewer overflows.[23] What if cities and regions spent this money on a type of infrastructure that would not lock them into confined limits and had multiple functions and benefits?

Cities are making the difficult choices about how to upgrade their aging, often-outdated infrastructure and avert disasters while facing climate change risks, less funding, and more stringent regulations. Planners and politicians must choose not only the most effective infrastructure to build but also the best value. The possibilities include green infrastructure options such as bioswales, detention ponds, filter strips, or green roofs, for example, which generally focus on reducing the amount of stormwater generated by an area. Or cities can choose more expensive options: upgrading gray infrastructure by increasing the convey-ance capacity of pipes or the capacity of water treatment plants, or by separating combined sewage systems. Often, cities choose a mixed portfolio of green and gray infrastructure options. But, as two urban drainage engineers recently wrote, "Notwithstanding all advancements in the design of urban drainage systems due to new technologies and ongoing research, drainage systems are still facing break-down in their function in the twenty-first century."[24] A new infrastructure paradigm is needed for stormwater.

While green infrastructure options are increasingly popular, it is not clear exactly how effective they are. In a 2009 review of green infrastructure strategies for stormwater in the United States, the EPA recognizes that their effectiveness is unknown, due to lack of data.[25] Green strategies are typically undertaken on a project-by-project basis, and studies often find that water quality and biotic health at the scale of the watershed are not greatly improved by small-scale retrofits.[26] Instead, cities need green infrastructure at both site and regional scales, to create a hybrid system of both centralized and decentralized infrastructures that work together. Of course, research that quan-tifies the costs and benefits of green infrastructure at all scales is still needed.[27]

Constructed wetlands are likely to be the most significant green infrastruc-ture solution and could be the backbone of a new infrastructure system. Built near or adjacent to natural streams, con-structed wetlands could be the collectors of stormwater for urban subwatersheds, intercepting stormwater before it reaches natural streams and rivers. If used in this manner, these wetlands could be aggre-gated into a regional network. Constructed wetlands could be built as part of new developments, and older suburbs could be retrofitted with them at the same time. In this way, constructed wetlands could support centralized facilities, such as water treatment plants, and collect water from smaller, decentralized strategies, such as bioswales from streets.

Constructed wetlands have been shown to effectively clean water at a lower cost than conventional water treatment plants.[28] These wetlands, along with bioswales, are the only green infrastruc-ture strategies that are carbon negative when considering construction and maintenance.[29] They offer more carbon sequestration, vegetative diversity, and cultural opportunities than detention ponds.[30] Used in rural areas since the 1970s to treat agricultural and industrial wastewater, constructed wetlands began to be used for stormwater treatment in the 1990s. While the application to stormwa-ter is relatively new, constructed wetlands show promise as infrastructure that has the potential to reap both site-scale and regional-scale benefits.

of these gains are attributed to urbaniza-tion exactly, the gains are mostly in the form of freshwater ponds, which wetland scientists do not consider ecologically equivalent to wetlands. See Tiffany Wright et al., "Direct and Indirect Impacts of Urbanization on Wetland Quality," *Wetlands & Watersheds*, Article 1 (Center for Watershed Protection, December 2006), 16, http://www.northinlet .sc.edu/training /media/resources /Article1Impact%20 Urbanization%20 Wetland%20Quality.pdf.

21 Brian Blankespoor, Susmita Dasgupta, and Benoit Laplante, "Sea-Level Rise and Coastal Wetlands," *Ambio* 43, no. 8 (March 22, 2014): 997.

22 Ibid., 997–98.

23 United States Environmental Protection Agency, "Clean Watersheds Needs Survey 2008, Report to Congress," 2010, 2–18, http://water .epa.gov/scitech/datait /databases/cwns/upload /cwns2008rtc.pdf.

24 Zeinab Yazdanfar and Ashok Sharma, "Urban Drainage System Planning and Design—Challenges with Climate Change and Urbanization: A Review," *Water Science & Technology* 72, no. 2 (July 15, 2015): 166.

25 Committee on Reducing Stormwater Discharge Contributions to Water Pollution, National Research Council, *Urban Stormwater Management in the United States* (Washington, DC: National Academies Press, 2009), 1.

26 Allison H. Roy et al., "How Much Is Enough? Minimal Responses of Water Quality and Stream Biota to Partial Retrofit Stormwater Management in a Sub-urban Neighborhood," *Plos One* 9, no. 1 (January 17, 2014): e85011–e85011, http://journals.plos.org /plosone/article/asset ?id=10.1371%2Fjournal .pone.0085011.pdf.

4.4.5 Rendering of a wetland with recreational components

The advantage of constructed wetlands over other green infrastructure options is that they are large enough to fulfill ecological and urban design goals at the same time that they treat stormwater. If the potential for serving multiple functions is fully exploited by design, constructing wetlands networks in cities can maximize their cost-effectiveness. For example, an urban network of constructed wetlands can be used to develop areas for economic activities such as food production, biomass production, fishing, aquaculture, or game hunting. It can support features for climate change resiliency, including detention areas for floodwaters, and it can ensure water security (through water reuse and groundwater recharge) and create ecological conservation areas. Finally, it can create recreational systems of walking trails or floodplains that double as sports fields, foster public health benefits (such as cleaner air and opportunities for exercise), and through aesthetics, raise nearby real estate values.[31] In the future, wetlands may even be able to generate electricity via microbial fuel cells.[32] (fig. **4.4.5**) In these ways, constructed wetlands can become a powerful stormwater solution that strengthens not only the ecological function of watercourses, and thereby the critical ecosystem services cities need, but also boosts the amenity value of cities.

A network of constructed wetlands could be the first truly multifunctional large-scale infrastructure system in modern cities. By being inherently multifunctional, the network's resiliency surpasses that of our current large-scale infrastructure system, which is primarily made up of engineered structures that are expensive to build and upgrade, have high carbon footprints, and are completely monofunctional. Pipes have no other function than transporting water.

The idea of a suburban wetland network is not a proposal to erase conventional infrastructure. Rather, it would be an infrastructure system working with and in parallel to conventional systems. Beyond the myriad of functions a wetland system could provide, it could also help organize and structure new suburban developments, connect these places to older suburbs and downtowns via recreational trails, and bring value to surrounding areas. All of these benefits cannot be achieved by conventional infrastructure alone.

The performance of a wetland depends on its age, size, and complexity.[33] In theory, if we implemented a systemic wetland infrastructure network, its performance might improve over time as the system matured, vegetation grew, and complexity increased. Although this idea has never been tested, it stands in sharp contrast to our traditional, engineered infrastructure, whose utility and performance declines with time. As hard infrastructure ages, its conveyance capacity diminishes, it can leak or break, and it must be replaced, rebuilt, or repaired. Often, capacity limits are reached, necessitating bigger pipes to be installed or

27 William L. Allen, "Advancing Green Infrastructure at All Scales: From Landscape to Site," *Environmental Practice* 14, no. 1 (March 2012): 23.

28 Robert H. Kadlec and Scott D. Wallace, *Treatment Wetlands* (Boca Raton, FL: CRC Press, 2009).

29 Trisha L. C. Moore and William F. Hunt, "Predicting the Carbon Footprint of Urban Stormwater Infrastructure," *Ecological Engineering* 58 (September 2013): 44–51.

30 Trisha L. C. Moore and William F. Hunt, "Ecosystem Service Provision by Stormwater Wetlands and Ponds—a Means for Evaluation?," in "Stormwater in Urban," special issue, *Water Research* 46, no. 20 (December 15, 2012): 6811–23.

31 "Economic Benefits of Runoff Controls" (report by the US Environmental Protection Agency, Office of Wetlands, Oceans, and Watersheds, Washington, DC, 1995).

32 Liam Doherty et al., "A Review of a Recently Emerged Technology: Constructed Wetland–Microbial Fuel Cells," *Water Research* 85 (November 15, 2015): 38–45.

33 William J. Mitsch and James G. Gosselink, *Wetlands* (New York: Van Nostrand Reinhold, 1993), 539.

treatment facilities to be expanded. Hard infrastructure's performance declines because it is inflexible, so major changes to the system require a complete revamping of every piece in the system.

It would be revolutionary to build urban infrastructure with performance that actually increased as time passed. While a wetland network would certainly require constant maintenance of the landscape, it would never have to be completely rebuilt or replaced, and capacity limits would not be reached as a metropolitan area expanded, as long as new wetlands were built to connect to the system. Moreover, hard infrastructure has been constructed with the notion that future population growth and resource consumption can be precisely predicted.[34] History has shown us that demographic predictions have often been wrong, and with climate change advancing, predictions are becoming even harder to calculate. Instead, a better method of building infrastructure may be one that does not depend on future projections; rather, it builds capacity on a modular, as-needed basis that fosters self-sufficiency within an area to decrease downstream impacts. In this way, constructed wetlands may be a "no-regrets" strategy: one that is "beneficial in addressing current stormwater management needs regardless of whether or not climate may change in the future."[35]

One challenge to constructed wetlands is that they need to be large to treat water effectively.[36] Although the exact size depends on treatment goals, stormwater volumes, and site availability, constructed wetlands are typically multiple acres in size. In dense urban cores, it would be expensive to buy large sites for wetland development. As a result, constructed wetlands at an infrastructural scale are more viable in suburban areas.

Suburban Wetlandia

It is projected that millions of acres of watersheds will be developed into suburbia in the coming years. Before this construction is fully underway, what are the planning options that would avoid exacerbating stormwater problems and environmental degradation, and at the same time improve metropolitan resiliency as a whole?

While suburban development has been part of the problem, it could also be part of the solution. Constructed wetlands at an infrastructural scale are most viable in suburban areas where sufficient inexpensive land is available. Plus, since suburban areas are typically upstream of urban cores, they could play an important role in hydrologic protection, potentially becoming indispensable for the entire metropolitan infrastructure. A networked system of constructed wetlands in suburbia as a spine for recreational and economic activities would also help structure and protect future metropolitan expansions.

Continued suburbanization presents an opportunity to rebuild wetland systems that urbanization and suburbanization previously destroyed. The expansion of new suburbs in metropolitan areas could be accompanied by corresponding constructed wetland areas in new developments, at the same time that older suburbs are retrofitted with wetlands along local streams and rivers. For each subwatershed, a constructed wetland would, with community input, be designed for specific goals determined by water treatment needs, level of flood protection required, and suitability for groundwater recharge.

Compared to urban areas, suburbia's availability of inexpensive land offers not only space but also higher-quality ecosystems in streams and rivers. Because suburbs have less impervious surfaces than cities do, suburban streams may be

34 Christian Urich and Wolfgang Rauch, "Modelling the Urban Water Cycle as an Integrated Part of the City: A Review," *Water Science & Technology* 70, no. 11 (December 15, 2014): 1858.

35 Christopher Pyke et al., "Assessment of Low Impact Development for Managing Stormwater with Changing Precipitation Due to Climate Change," *Landscape and Urban Planning* 103, no. 2 (November 30, 2011): 167; originally from Edward Means et al., "Decision Support Planning Methods: Incorporating Climate Change Uncertainties into Water Planning," report prepared for the Water Utility Climate Alliance, January 2010, 9, http://www.wucaonline.org/assets/pdf/pubs-white paper-012110.pdf.

36 Celina Balderas Guzmán, "Strategies for Systemic Urban Constructed Wetlands" (master's thesis, Massachusetts Institute of Technology, 2013), 74–78, http://hdl.handle.net/1721.1/80907.

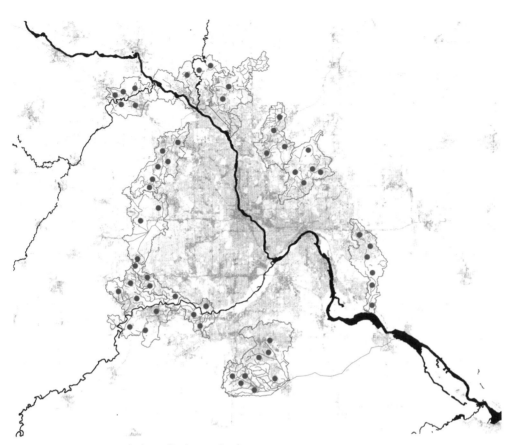

4.4.6 Diagram of upstream suburban wetlands as a network

37 Tom Schueler, "The Importance of Imperviousness," *Watershed Protection Techniques* 1, no. 3 (1994): 100–111.

38 Hannah Prior and Penny Johnes, "Regulation of Surface Water Quality in a Cretaceous Chalk Catchment, UK: An Assessment of the Relative Importance of Instream and Wetland Processes," *Science of the Total Environment* 282–83 (2002): 159–74; Ranran Yang and Baoshan Cui, "A Wetland Network Design for Water Allocation Based on Environmental Flow Requirements," *CLEAN— Soil, Air, Water* 40, no. 10 (2012): 1055.

39 Ying-zi Wang et al., "Application of Landscape Ecology to the Research on Wetlands," *Journal of Forestry Research* 19, no. 2 (2008): 168.

40 Clay H. Emerson, "Watershed-Scale Evaluation of a System of Storm Water Detention Basins," *Journal of Hydrologic Engineering* 10, no. 3 (2005): 237–42; Sue J. Powell, "Modelling Floodplain Inundation for Environmental Flows: Gwydir Wetlands, Australia," *Ecological Modelling* 211, nos. 3–4 (2008): 350–62.

41 Wang et al., "Application of Landscape Ecology to the Research on Wetlands," 168.

42 Matthew J. Cohen and Mark T. Brown, "A Model Examining Hierarchical Wetland Networks for Watershed Stormwater Management," *Ecological Modelling* 201, no. 2 (February 24, 2007): 179–93.

less affected than urban ones, especially at levels of imperviousness below 25 percent.[37] Constructed wetlands in or near these higher-quality ecosystems could have better functionality. In addition, because suburban areas are typically upstream of downtowns, constructed wetlands in suburbia could serve as an important upstream control for flooding, water quality, and moderation of water flows in times of drought.[38] In landscape ecology, the theory of landscape hierarchies claims that landscape features that are higher in the hierarchy (e.g., upstream wetlands) will "constrain and mediate the dynamics of lower hierarchical levels."[39]

As a systemic network, instead of as isolated projects, constructed wetlands can reap their maximum potential benefit. Unfortunately, most stormwater wetlands are designed as isolated, site-scale projects with little consideration to the larger hydrologic network.[40] In urban areas, the larger hydrologic network often has lost its original hierarchy of wetlands, streams, and rivers, and the flow convergence that it once created.[41] The hierarchy had maximized the mitigation of flood pulses and the reduction of sediments and nutrients.[42] Systemic constructed wetlands can reintroduce hierarchy into the hydrologic network and bolster many of its existing, degraded functions. (fig. **4.4.6**)

Constructing the Future

Imagine leaving your house in suburbia and being able to walk, jog, or bike all the way downtown, following a system of interconnected wetlands and streams leading down to the major regional river. (fig. **4.4.7**) You would pass community gardens, urban agricultural areas, recreational spaces such as sports fields, and ecological conservation areas, as well as functional facilities such as water recycling plants, areas for sediment capture,

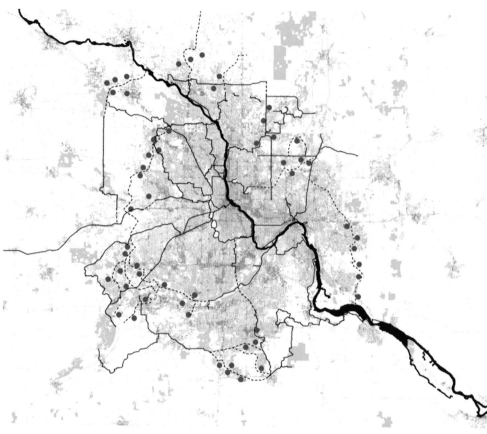

4.4.7 Diagram of upstream suburban wetlands as a recreational system

and maybe even electricity-generating facilities. You might see multiple types of ecosystems: forested wetlands, freshwater emergent wetlands, or ponds. Markers along streams would display information from sensors about the water quality, water volume, or carbon sequestration in real time.

Down every reach of stream or river there would be individualized constructed wetlands that served specific functions, as dictated by local geography and by the needs of surrounding communities, giving each wetland a unique identity. In a wetland system that is spread across a large area, there is more likely to be heterogeneity of conditions. This heterogeneity would make the system more resilient to disturbances such as climate change, and more ecologically productive.[43] To turn this vision into a reality, constructed wetlands have to be designed with not just scientific and engineering knowledge but with the

urban design and urban planning sensitivity that will expose the potential of constructed wetlands as multifunctional infrastructure. Much work remains to be done: because stormwater wetlands are relatively new, design guidance is lacking.[44] And the majority of research examines individual wetlands, providing methods for assessing their function and condition. There are few methods for assessing wetland systems.[45] Without such methods, it is difficult to understand the ecosystem functions, interactions and effects of wetlands on the hydrologic network, although such effects do exist.[46] As a result, there are few studies examining the potential of systemic wetlands for urban stormwater management or for their ecological potential.[47]

Overall, we need further research to develop a truly urban constructed wetland system. Significant policy changes would be required to implement

43 Baoshan Cui, Zhiming Zhang, and Xiaoxia Lei, "Implementation of Diversified Ecological Networks to Strengthen Wetland Conservation," *CLEAN—Soil, Air, Water* 40, no. 10 (October 1, 2012): 1021.

44 James N. Carleton et al., "Factors Affecting the Performance of Stormwater Treatment Wetlands," *Water Research* 35, no. 6 (April 2001): 1552–62. For a few existing design guidelines, see Thomas R. Schueler and Anacostia Restoration Team, *Design of Stormwater Wetland Systems: Guidelines for Creating Diverse and Effective Stormwater Wetlands in the Mid-Atlantic Region* (Washington, DC: Anacostia Restoration Team, Department of Environmental Programs, Metropolitan Washington Council of Governments, 1992). This is an update of Schueler's work: Karen Cappiella et al., "The Next Generation of Stormwater Wetlands" (Center for Watershed Protection, February 2008). For landscape architects, there are two guidelines for wetlands generally, although they focus on the aesthetic and wildlife habitat functions of wetlands: Craig S. Campbell and Michael Ogden, *Constructed Wetlands in the Sustainable Landscape* (New York: Wiley, 1999); and Robert L. France, *Wetland Design: Principles and Practices for Landscape Architects and Land-Use Planners* (New York: W. W. Norton, 2003).

45 Xufeng Mao and Lijuan Cui, "Reflecting the Importance of Wetland Hydrologic Connectedness: A Network Perspective," *Procedia Environmental Sciences* 13 (2012): 1316.

46 Robert R. Christian et al., "Ecological Network Analyses and Their Use for Establishing Reference Domain in Functional Assessment

stormwater-constructed wetlands, too. And the expertise of multiple disciplines would have to be included: hydrology, engineering, ecology, planning, design, and policy, to name a few. Yet, despite obstacles, the future holds the potential to create a whole that is greater than the sum of all of these parts.

This essay is adapted from the author's master's thesis: Celina Balderas Guzmán, "Strategies for Systemic Urban Constructed Wetlands," Massachusetts Institute of Technology, 2013, http://hdl.handle .net/1721.1/80907. The thesis was advised by MIT professors Alan M. Berger, Andrew Scott, and Heidi Nepf, as well as CH2M Technology Fellow James S. Bays.

of an Estuary," *Ecological Modelling* 220, no. 22 (November 24, 2009): 3113–22.

47 David R. Tilley and Mark T. Brown, "Wetland Networks for Storm-water Management in Subtropical Urban Watersheds," *Ecological Engineering* 10, no. 2 (June 15, 1998): 133; Cui, Zhang, and Lei, "Implementation of Diversified Ecological Networks to Strengthen Wetland Conservation," 1016.

Aberdeen, Palm Beach County, Florida, United States

Pembroke Pines, Broward County, Florida, United States

4.5 DESIGNING BACKWARD FOR SUBURBIA

Margaret Grose

DESIGN MODELS

FLEXIBLE REGULATION

PRODUCTIVE SUBURBS

At a recent conference about streetlights, I was one of the few designers and perhaps the only ecologist present. What was I doing there, you might ask, since streetlights are surely the territory of road and systems engineers, lighting and energy experts, and planners? Many of the participants were curious when I approached street lighting from the point of view of human population health, and were eager to know more. Specialization and confinement into narrow disciplinary territories is a problem of our times and reveals itself in suburban design. Yet the central conundrums of suburbia range across disciplines: density versus sprawl, too much light at night, too much noise, too little privacy, loss of and lack of greening, the impacts of blanket policies rather than site-specific designs, single-issue policies, and climate and population change impacts on future greening, water, and human stress. Added to this is the failure of design to do more than incremental changes and to produce overwhelmingly bland suburbs. None of these issues belong in one discipline, but urban design needs to deal with all of them—spatial form, public health and safety, public open space, transport, indigenous values, historical and cultural underlays, planning, and current and future management practices. In suburbs, barriers exist between the decision-making territories that govern these areas. Likewise, planning, spatial form, urban heat island effect, public health and safety, and other myriad points of interest about suburbia should not be considered without ecology.

There has been and will be vast increases in people living in suburbia, representing rapid changes in human social relationships, our material culture, and our relationships to the environment. How do we attempt better ecological suburbs as designers? We would like to think that ecology sits at the heart of our ambitions for the future of suburbia,

yet the environment often plays second fiddleand is taken as just another piece to address, another tick in the box. Suburban design poses a particular problem in that the development of suburbs is often driven by those who are not educated in ecological systems, the ecologies and ambiguities of sites, systems or holistic thinking, data use, incomplete data, or the strong conceptual ideas found in ecology that can underpin design.[1] Instead, those who develop suburbs often work in isolation from other disciplines and are trained with guidelines, minimum standards, land-parcel by land-parcel decision-making, and design exemplars as set pieces rather than as examples of answers to site-specific questions.

Is the environment seen as important enough for more designers and planners to place it centrally in suburban design? Many landscape architects incorrectly conceive of ecology as data alone, to be abandoned at some stage in the process of designing the suburb. Yet in science, the emerging revolution in genetics will lead to a broader conceptual change, placing far more importance on what we do with our suburban environments where so many people live. It is now considered that we do not live by genes alone and that genes, and their expression, are an extension of the environment: "The gene has emerged from the environment."[2] This great paradigm shift places the environment in a new relationship to us; we are environmental constructs. It also places the design professions at the forefront of how we interact with our environments and how they affect us; this is taking us beyond ideas of landscape and health, and highlights the importance of suburban landscapes.

How, then, can we think about designing ecologically rich suburbs? As in animal breeding, where best outcomes are gained by considering combinations of traits that maximize fitness of the animal,

1   Margaret Grose, "Thinking Backwards Can Inform Concerns about 'Incomplete' Data," *Trends in Ecology and Evolution* 29, no. 10 (2014): 546–47; Margaret Grose, "Inverse Problem-Solving Helps Us to Collect the Needed Data: A Reply to Falcy," *Trends in Ecology and Evolution* 30, no. 6 (June 2015), 295–96.

2   Rama S. Singh, "Darwin's Legacy II: Why Biology Is Not Physics, or Why It has Taken a Century to See the Dependence of Genes on the Environment," *Genome* 58 (2015): 62. See also Kevin N. Laland, "On Evolutionary Causes and Evolutionary Processes," in "Cause and Function in Behavioral Biology: A Tribute to Jerry Hogan," ed. J. J. Bolhuis and O. Lazareva, special issue, *Behavioural Processes* 117 (August 2015): 97–104.

the best ecological outcomes in suburbs involve examination and testing of multiple traits and their expression within suburbs.[3] In this essay, I discuss three theoretical ideas that can help us to think more explicitly about suburbs and to deal with the multiple traits within them: first, inverse problems and thinking backward for best ecological outcomes; second, the strength of weak ties; and third, the tyranny of small decisions—ideas borrowed from the disciplines of mathematics, sociology, and finance. These ideas can assist in removing barriers between decision-making territories and lead to more complete answers to the questions arising in designing a new suburb or retrofitting an old one.

Thinking Backward and Inverse Problems

In suburbs, the final design usually grows out of client, planner, and designer imperatives, site-specific needs, theoretical considerations, and ecological and social ambitions for the site.[4] The starting point of suburban design has been dominated by site analysis, while in planning it is dominated by planning codes and nodes of development. Site analysis is often taught as a sifting of site issues to arrive at a solution, but this approach can leave a difficult gap between analysis and design that is sometimes referred to by students as "analysis paralysis."[5] Site analysis is often done through spatial overlays to give direction or "best fit" to site works and can result in suburbs that are very similar spatially. This problem can be alleviated by thinking differently.

Site analysis for suburb design is inherently a linear analysis and a forward problem. In a forward problem, all of the components are known, and we need to work out the answer.[6] However, design is constricted by linear analysis because it allows little fluidity in thinking about the components that make up the answer

or their interactions; further, linear design can be dominated by planning ideas of opportunities and constraints, or by prescriptive types of information (maps, overlays, topography).

Design can be seen with new eyes as an "inverse problem," a curious term from mathematics that is also used in engineering.[7] It is the opposite of a normal linear problem and is particularly appropriate when applied to suburban design because of the multiple components that make up a suburb. For suburbs, the answer to the problem is a design ambition, which might be, for example, to increase biodiversity; create a functioning wetland; preserve or remediate local green areas; link public open space; sequester carbon through the planting of an urban forest; or a combination of these. In short, we often know what we want to achieve in a suburb, but how do we get it with the best outcomes?

Using the idea of an inverse problem, we can think backward from the desired outcome for our suburb. The difference between normal problems and inverse problems, or thinking backward, can be seen in the following way:

The problem of $2 \times 2 = x$ is a normal, or a forward, problem: the answer is agreed by all of us; the components give us only one solution; and we think in the forward direction to compute the answer.[8] The French philosopher Henri Bergson, who noted that "to do philosophy is to reverse the habitual direction of thought," put forward the idea of thinking backward about problems.[9] With an inverse problem, we know the desired answer, but have to work backward to get there: we might use $2 + 2$, 2×2, $3 + 1$, $3.5 + 0.5$, or $1 + 1 + 4 - 2$ to arrive at a desired answer.[10] In other words, while we know the answer, we cannot really know the precise components of the answer; we can consider a whole range of variations to get to the known answer. For suburbs, this means that we

3　Wilco C. E. P. Verberk, C. G. E. Toos van Noordwijk, and Alan G. Hildrew, "Delivering on a Promise: Integrating Species Traits to Transform Descriptive Community Ecology into a Predictive Science," *Freshwater Science* 32, no. 2 (2013): 531–47.

4　Margaret J. Grose, "Practice Wisdom from Planners, Developers, Environmentalists, and Other Players Finding the 'True Debates' in Suburban Development in South-Western Australia," *Australian Planner* 47 (2010): 26–36.

5　Ian L. McHarg, *Design with Nature* (New York: American Museum of Natural History, 1969).

6　Ibid.

7　Jacques S. Hadamard, "Sur les problèmes aux derivees partielles et leur signification physique," *Bulletin Princeton University* 13 (1902): 49–52.

8　For forward problems, see Richard C. Aster, Brian Borchers, and Clifford H. Thurber, eds., *Parameter Estimation and Inverse Problems* (Amsterdam: Elsevier Academic Press, 2013).

9　Henri Bergson and T. E. Hulme, *An Introduction to Metaphysics* (New York: Putnam's, 1912); Margaret J. Grose, "Thinking Backwards Can Inform Concerns about 'Incomplete' Data," *Trends in Ecology and Evolution* 29, no. 10 (2014): 546–47.

10　As an example, see Nick Polydorides, Eskild Storteig, and William Lionheart, "Forward and Inverse Problems in Towed Cable Hydrodynamics," *Ocean Engineering* 35, nos. 14–15 (2008): 1429–38.

can test a range of variations of the components making up a suburb.

For suburbs, we might debate which components are more robust, resilient, or doable, and test the components through digital scenario examinations, digital modeling, and working with scientific knowledge on end-point results. By thinking backward in a nonlinear, reverse manner, we can test the importance, relationships, and impacts of components in any scheme, which allows us to develop a thorough understanding of the components within our design. Additionally, a feature of inverse problems is that, unlike a forward problem, there are multiple answers that can be seen as variations on our ecological ambition, and multiple ways of getting to the answer. In getting to the answer, designers have the opportunity to articulate, examine, test, and experiment with components of a proposed suburb while still in the plastic stage of design (i.e., before construction).

Testing of components of the suburb can be done by factorial experiments. Factorial experiments are the foundations of experimental science because they enable the testing of various parameters (or factors) to see what impacts different levels of specific factors have on a set of measurable outcomes or responses. They can be seen as carefully thought-out questionnaires, where we can ask questions of systems or, for suburbs, questions of design possibilities.[11] Factorial experiments can be done on a wide range of versions, states, moieties, or levels of components that make up the issues for the suburban design and allow us to identify the impacts of any potential design or action before we build. Digital modeling can give us many permutations of factors at various levels and reveal how impacts occur, and where. Testing can also help us identify the important structures, policies, or design moves in a suburb on a particular site that are key to determining suburban outcomes and that might be targeted for alteration. We can also learn which important interactions occur between the suburb's components or traits. Such interactions can provide strong links between ecological science, the physical sciences, and design.

The factorial experiment is a different method to "data-scaping," which is a graphic representation of spatiotemporal data and spatiotemporal relationships of landscape phenomena; data-scaping is a visualization and not an active engagement with site, and does not deal with systems and the performance of systems. In contrast to the techniques of data-scaping, GIS analysis, and the overlay method of site analysis developed by the landscape architect Ian McHarg, factorial testing enables an examination of the performance of the components (factors) in the systems making up an ecological ambition.[12] We might, for example, examine the impacts of two or three changes to simple factors such as footpath width, setback of houses from road, and road width. Through digital modeling, we can specifically test the impacts of these factors (e.g., wide vs. small setbacks) on street trees (and on shade and heat reduction), on carbon biomass, exposed soil (a carbon sequester), and on front and back garden size and planting opportunities. Factorial testing with digital modeling will (in this example) allow us to ascertain which combinations of footpath, house setback from street, and setback from road give the best outcomes for our ambition without having to do the tedious and expensive job of building and then testing, or relying on precedents in design that might be specific for other landscapes and not ours.

In this way, factorial testing enables the articulation of the impacts of specific factors within a site through simulation of processes and interactions, and allows us to test scenarios in three dimensions and as living systems; interrogating the site in

11 Ronald Fisher noted the "Questionnaire" of factorial Eeperiments in "The Arrangement of Field Experiments," *Journal of the Ministry of Agriculture of Great Britain* 33 (1926): 503–13.

12 Lubos Mitas, William S. Brown, and Helena Mitasova, "Role of Dynamic Cartography in Simulations of Landscape Processes Based on Multivariate Fields," *Computers and Geosciences* 23, no. 4 (1997): 437–46.

this way also allows us to incorporate data from ecological processes into our modeling. This parametric modeling removes the gap between site analysis and design as is found in overlay site analysis, moves us away from the domination of planning and guidelines, and moves us forward to a new factorial testing and rethinking of design, as well as working in three dimensional processes. Factorial design testing is a perfect driver for suburban design because of the clear sets of traits or factors involved in suburban development, their complex interactions, and their site-specificities.

By digital testing of factors, we can also anticipate otherwise unforeseen impacts in other arenas. For example, the issue of house lot size has been important in the argument that our suburbs need to be denser to avoid urban sprawl. Densification, however, will lead to a grievous reduction in the numbers of large trees, and an increase in impervious surfaces, leading to consequences for carbon sequestration, shade and heat, biodiversity, and increased stormwater runoff. These interactions might be missed in simpler, normal forward problem solving that does not test for interactions.

Testing of factors or parameters can be done with physical models and digital modeling, such as those for stormwater testing in suburbs, and changes to topographic landforms, or testing impacts of street-tree greening on heat and shade.[13] Testing can be mapped and captured in digital forms.[14] These sorts of tests suggest that data can be combined from different fields. For example, plant data from ecological science, water flow and heat data from engineering science, along with conceptual ideas from landscape ecology and general ecology (such as connectivity, biodiversity, and carbon sequestration), can be used purposely and at a finer and more specific scale within landscape design.[15] Further, testing in this way

allows a purposeful exploration of processes that engage with both environmental flux and trophic cascades.

Interactions between factors can occur in cascades. Trophic cascades in ecology are usually associated with predator-prey relationships and cascading effects in a food web; the word *trophic* is used as meaning "feeding." However, the verb from which the adjective trophic is derived in the ancient Greek, τρέφω (*trepho*), has many meanings, including "to thicken" (as in density), "to have within oneself," "to maintain or support," or "to turn constantly." The ideas of trophic cascades are finding uses outside experimental ecology. Trophic cascades are context-dependent and can be nonlinear.[16] It is not unreasonable, then, to refer to trophic cascades in suburban design, where road widening, for example, will have a cascading impact on street trees, green verges, the percentage of impervious surfaces, heat island effects, and biodiversity. Urban trophic systems differ from the more natural habitats in which they are embedded.[17] However, as in ecological systems, changes in suburban trophic cascades can bring dramatic shifts in both the appearance and the properties of suburbs.[18] Factorial testing of various levels of design components will reveal "trophic interactions" between suburban components just as in ecological systems. For example, at what point does road size negatively or positively affect street tree size? Factorial testing will give us the answer to this and other ecological questions that are site-specific to a suburban area at quite small scales. This is important, since current suburban design typically suffers from being poorly aligned with the landscape because it is not driven by site-specific testing but by general, widely applied guidelines. The essential question of "how will *this* site respond?" remains untested. Guideline-driven suburban development has led

13 Enriqueta Llabres and Eduardo Rico, "Proxi Modelling: A Tacit Approach to Territorial Praxis," *Journal of Space Syntax* 5, no. 1 (2014): 50–67.

14 Ibid.

15 Jillian Walliss and Heike Rahmann, "Future Directions," in *Landscape Architecture and Digital Technologies: Re-conceptualising Design and Making* (London: Routledge, 2015).

16 Michael L. Pace et al., "Trophic Cascades Revealed in Diverse Ecosystems," *Trends in Ecology and Evolution* 14, no. 12 (1999): 483–88.

17 Stanley H. Faeth et al., "Trophic Dynamics in Urban Communities," *BioScience* 55, no. 5 (2005): 399–407.

18 This point is noted in relation to ecosystems in Pace et al., "Trophic Cascades Revealed in Diverse Ecosystems," 483–88.

to precedent-driven suburban design, which can only change design thinking by incremental innovation build by build. This conundrum suggests that landscape architects are not using the full capacities available to them of the revolution in the tools of design—digital modeling and testing of parameters, traits, and possibilities.

Factorial experiments and thinking backward as an idea do not give us a neat answer of the kind we would see when we shake out soil in a series of sieves for particle size. We also need knowledge of our own processes of decision making to enable us to ask ourselves, "Does this satisfy the ambition we have for this site from thinking backward?" and importantly, "Is our ambition *ambitious*?"

The Strength of Weak Ties

The social scientist Mark Granovetter first put forward the idea of "the strength of weak ties" in 1970. In a study of how people changed their jobs, he found that most people obtained information about jobs from the "weak ties" of their associates, not from the "strong ties" of their closer friends.[19] As the basis of network theory, the original idea comes from the micro-scale interaction of personal ties. It is very relevant to the workplace as a community.[20] This sociological theory is that our acquaintances—our weak ties—are less likely to be socially involved with one another than are our strong ties, that is, our close friends. People with few weak ties will be confined to a more limited set of information than people with many weak ties, because weak ties provide us with information from diverse sources. In contrast to weak ties, strong ties are usually joins between like-minded people or organizations, and breed a "local cohesion."[21] The idea of weak and strong ties encourages us to think about how we get information, and on what information we usually base decision making; often

it is only from strong ties to like-minded people in our own professional sphere. Such cohesion in groups leads to fragmentation into disciplinary or knowledge groups, such as the kind that occurs in disciplines of ecologists, planners, and designers, where cohesion and agreement are reinforced by guidelines, agreed minimal standards, and exemplars applauded by the particular disciplinary group. Such cohesion can lead to narrow views.

This point was brought home to me during a recent visit from a person promulgating broad-leafed exotic trees being planted in preference to eucalypts in Melbourne, the city where I reside, on the basis of heat island reduction; yet no consideration had been given to the ecological impacts of exotic tree species that give little or no support to local wildlife, as opposed to local trees, which give a great deal of support. It was an example of how single-issue interrogations and single-issue guidelines based on one set of strong professional ties can lead to poor ecological outcomes.

Importantly, weak ties can assist us to consider information outside our usual strong disciplinary ties and assist us to rethink or reimagine design. The sociologists William Liu and Robert Duff pointed out in the 1970s that "although communication may take place more easily among people who share similar attributes and have similar attitudes and beliefs, such communication may be in large measure redundant: no new information enters the system."[22] In short, when considering suburbia, if we rely on close, strong, ties, we are likely to be working with only part of the information relevant to the systems of the suburb. Worse, some ties might be absent altogether, even when of vital importance. Despite absences and poor weak ties, recommendations are often made to decision makers such as local government based purely on ideas and knowledge generated solely among strong ties.

19 Mark Granovetter, "The Strength of Weak Ties," *American Journal of Sociology* 78, no. 6 (1973): 1360–80.
20 Mark Granovetter, "The Strength of Weak Ties: A Network Theory Revisited," *Sociological Theory* 1 (1983): 201–33.
21 Granovetter, "The Strength of Weak Ties," 1378.
22 William T. Liu and Robert W. Duff, "The Strength in Weak Ties," *Public Opinion Quarterly* 36, no. 3 (1972): 361–66.

Streetlighting in suburbs is also an example of the impacts of failed or absent weak ties. Decisions made about new generation suburban streetlights have focused on energy saving, because the main players are lighting experts, energy providers, and financial and management experts, and because streetlighting is a major expense for local government. However, knowledge beyond energy and costs would provide information about the negative health impacts of streetlights and other artificial light at night on circadian rhythm, increased obesity and breast and prostate cancer, the importance of the color spectrum of the lamps on health, ecological impacts on animals, impacts of glare into the night sky, and astronomical pollution.[23] Because of the isolation between weak and strong ties, none of these factors are currently incorporated in most decisions about street lighting, and artificial light at night has been absent from discussions about healthy suburbs.[24] When we fail to accommodate weak ties in suburban discourse, we are not seeing the whole picture and are in danger of missing important traits.

Other examples abound. For example, outer suburban houses have been held up as higher users of energy in comparison with inner cities, and these studies are used as arguments for policies of densification.[25] However, as authors of those studies have noted, their research was limited to energy consumption for suburban dwellings and for road usage, and were not a whole-of-city analysis that might or might not support densification. This type of study does not take into account loss of greening and heat island impacts, impermeable and permeable surfaces, or levels of exposed soil for carbon sequestration. Such information would come from weak ties beyond the construction and energy sectors, and, when considered, might give very different, and certainly more complex, pictures

of energy use and environmental impacts in suburban and urban typologies, and hence different advice guidelines.

The Tyranny of Small Decisions
The tyranny of small decisions is an idea from business put forward by the economist Alfred Kahn in the 1960s and taken up by the American ecologist Bill Odum, who described the concept in regard to the piece-by-piece destruction of the wetlands of the US East Coast.[26] Although no one intended the mass destruction of these wetlands, they were lost because each small decision was taken without reference to the whole region or situation.[27] Examples of small decisions in suburban design include plant selection, the limiting of public open space to minimum standards, street tree removal, lighting selections, increasing paving, and infill development reducing green cover. All can lead to an accumulation of the small decisions that give an ecologically poor end result.[28] The tyranny of small decisions is particularly important in suburban design where there is parcel-by-parcel work on suburban sites, which often leads to disjointed public open space or failed biological or social connectivity across the scale of the wider region. Such small decisions have led to design outcomes divorced from living systems.

Decisions might also be considered "small when they have arisen from the strong ties of like-minded people found within single disciplines. In this situation, design guidelines for suburban development are made for single issues or traits of a suburb, such as roads or public safety, without reflecting on complex impacts of these ideas, and their interactions. Public safety and walkability offer two examples of how this has occurred. Issues of public safety have led to design guidelines supporting long view lines and no large bushes, yet these restrictions have a negative impact on biodiversity by

23 Margaret J. Grose, "Artificial Light at Night: A Neglected Population Health Concern of the Built Environment," *Health Promotion Journal of Australia* 25 (2014): 193–95; Kevin Gaston, "A Green Light for Efficiency," *Nature* 497 (2013): 560–61; Abraham Haim and Boris A. Portnov, *Light Pollution as a New Risk Factor for Human Breast and Prostate Cancers* (Dordrecht: Springer, 2013); Richard G. Stevens et al., "Meeting Report: The Role of Environmental Lighting and Circadian Disruption in Cancer and Other Diseases," *Environmental Health Perspectives* 115 (2007): 1357–62; Richard G. Stevens, "Light at Night, Circadian Disruption, and Breast Cancer: Assessment of Existing Evidence," *International Journal of Epidemiology* 38 (2009): 963–70; Chris DeFrancesco, "AMA: Health Implications of Light at Night 'Serious,'" *UConn Today*, June 20, 2012, accessed November 13, 2014, http://today .uconn.edu/blog/2012/06 /ama-health-implica tions-of-light-at-night -serious/; Russel J. Reiter et al., "Light at Night, Chronodisruption, Melatonin Suppression, and Cancer Risk: A Review," *Critical Reviews in Oncogenesis* 13, no. 4 (2007): 303–28; Catherine Rich and Travis Longcore eds., *Ecological Consequences of Artificial Night Lighting* (Washington, DC: Island Press, 2006).
24 Grose, "Artificial Light at Night: A Neglected Population Health Concern of the Built Environment," 193–95.
25 R. J. Fuller and Robert H. Crawford, "Impact of Past and Future Residential Housing Development Patterns on Energy Demand and Related Emissions," *Journal of Housing and the Built Environment* 26 (2011): 165–83.
26 Alfred E. Kahn, "The Tyranny of Small

neglecting the midstory level of vegetation; however, the disciplines of safety and biodiversity are rarely considered together and no single decision or guideline addresses the them both.[29] Likewise, the concept of walkability arose from the idea of people living in suburbs being able to walk to amenities, including the public park. Yet the widespread promulgation of walkability in Australia is now leading to densification (more people close to amenities), with infill housing and loss of private open space, trees, and greening; this was surely not anticipated by those who wanted more people to walk to the park to experience some green space. In this way, single issues have acted as tyrannies.

In the processes of suburban design, the "tyranny of small decisions" also suggests constraint in thinking, or even professional coercion to think in a like-minded manner as to the processes of suburban design and what is achievable. Limited views can arise due to the confines of thinking within disciplines or fields of inquiry that are constrained by knowledge, custom, and levels of information.[30]

Questioning, Experimenting, and Predicting Suburbias

The three main ideas of thinking backward, weak and strong ties, and the tyranny of small decisions assist the endeavor to design future suburbias better by focusing not only on what we are asking and doing but also on *how* we are asking and doing. The perspectives outlined here suggest that there are many opportunities to organize the clarity of our thinking, by inverse problem solving, by considering knowledge and expertise held in weak and strong ties, and by assuming that a small decision has impact. Importantly, we need to be more aware of decision making and the ways of thinking that might lead us to exclude from suburbs inter-relationships

that we need to include for a comprehensive understanding of the site and better ecological designs. These are significant challenges for us in an age where specialization into disciplinary territories and narrowed curriculums of experience have become disciplinary tyrannies. However, with awareness, these impediments need not remain.

There are two challenges in our current thinking. First, we should abandon the common thinking of design as a linear process whereby we tease out a design from a largely two-dimensional descriptive site analysis. As outlined in this brief theoretical discussion, linear guideline-driven processes in thinking about suburbs are unhelpful and confine us to the forward problem, which produces a most likely solution that is most likely to be bland. In contrast, design interrogations that come out of thinking backward expose the interrelated decisions, and nonlinear systems within suburbia, and suggest that we can test for the performance of multiple design ideas to arrive at suites of ecologically sound possibilities that give opportunities for flair, intuition, and unique places. In the future, landscape design and planning will move into the greater use of specific environmental data for the ecological design of suburbs, perhaps echoing architecture's move into the "ecotectural" analysis of the building.[31]

Second, digital technologies now available allow designers to test factorial combinations and levels of factors to explore and critique design possibilities in suburbs while the design is still in plastic form; ideas such as sprawl, density, light, noise, privacy, greening, road impacts, and stormwater movement across suburbs can be tested by digital modeling at various scales. These new important creative tools can assist us to move beyond the techniques of description and decoration, and to move toward thinking differently, to testing designs and experimenting, and

Decisions: Market Failures, Imperfections, and Limits of Economics," *Kyklos* 19 (1966): 23–47.

27 William E. Odum, "Environmental Degradation and the Tyranny of Small Decisions," *Bioscience* 32, no. 9 (1982): 728–29.

28 Margaret J. Grose, "Small Decisions in Suburban Open Spaces: Ecological Perspectives from a Hotspot of Global Biodiversity Concerning Knowledge Flows between Disciplinary Territories," *Landscape Research* 35, no. 1 (2010): 47–62.

29 Ibid. Several examples of planning policy with other absences are given, and with images.

30 Ibid.

31 Jin-Ho Park, *Designing the Ecocity-in-the-Sky: The Seoul Workshop* (Mulgrave, Victoria, Australia: Images Publishing, 2014).

then to predicting suburban performance
to enable us to enliven our suburbs and
bring more variety and ambition to
the solutions of how to design a better
suburb. How we tackle these challenges
of thinking and digital testing will define
the ecological and social outcomes we
achieve in future suburbias, and these
created environments will even set the
stage for modulating our future genes.

4.6
GREENING SPRAWL
LAWN CULTURE AND CARBON STORAGE IN THE SUBURBAN LANDSCAPE

Joan Iverson Nassauer

Suburban residential landscapes are popularly understood to be socially and environmentally homogeneous places where expanses of mown lawn appear in an alternating rhythm of driveways and predictably similar houses. Much has been made of suburban social pressures for conformity, epitomized by the pressure to have a perfect lawn: even, green, and weed-free.[1] More recently, the environmentally detrimental effects of lawn irrigation, pesticides, fertilizers, leaf blowing, and mowing have been widely discussed.[2] Beyond these immediate environmental impacts of lawn culture, the more insidious societal costs associated with car-dependent suburban transportation systems are of growing concern. Social and health effects of sedentary lifestyles and long commuting times, social equity effects of jobs beyond the reach of public transportation, as well as climate effects of greenhouse gases emitted by cars—all contribute to arguments for adopting more dense urban settlement patterns as alternatives to suburbia.

Yet suburban development is massive and growing. In the United States, large-lot residential development covered a total area fifteen times larger than did dense urban settlement in 2000, and suburbs have continued to grow more quickly than cities.[3] The market for suburban residential development remains a vital driver of metropolitan landscape patterns. Even if market demand for new suburban development were to disappear today, the legacy effects of the more than 5 percent of the US land area in suburban development would remain.[4] This reality suggests that, rather than only critiquing suburbia, we should consider how low-density suburban development patterns can provide broader societal benefits.

Viewed through another lens, the lawn culture landscape of suburban "sprawl" looks like "greening." In city neighborhoods, greening means bringing maintained turf, trees, and gardens back into a largely paved landscape. In contrast, suburban neighborhoods, typified by expansive lawns, canopy trees, and flowers and shrubs, *are* green. But suburban green landscapes could provide far more substantial ecosystem services related to human health, biodiversity, stormwater management, and carbon storage to contribute to climate change mitigation. How do we "green" sprawl to deliver these societal benefits? Could design and planning guide the resources expended on keeping suburbia green differently—to achieve a stronger balance in favor of ecosystem services compared with environmental costs?

Understanding the vernacular aesthetics of suburban landscapes as part of the land development process can suggest some answers. Respecting what residents want their landscapes to look like could help planners and designers devise development patterns that nudge suburban residents and developers to want landscapes that provide greater ecosystem services. To make suburban sprawl a deeper shade of green, designers can use the nudge concept that has become familiar in the fields of psychology and behavioral economics: giving people what they want in a landscape pattern that also embodies what society needs.[5]

This essay examines how suburban residential landscape patterns could be designed to give developers and residents what they want and also mitigate climate change by storing more carbon. It synthesizes findings from several of our past studies in metropolitan southeastern Michigan, in the United States, to identify social drivers of sprawl and suburban lawn culture that suggest clues about how and where carbon can be stored in suburban residential landscapes.

Ecosystems store carbon in soil and vegetation including wood, litter, foliage,

1　Sally Bayley, *Home on the Horizon: America's Search for Space, from Emily Dickinson to Bob Dylan* (Oxfordshire, UK: Peter Lang Ltd., 2010); Jo Gill, *The Poetics of the American Suburbs* (New York: Palgrave Macmillan, 2013); Michael Pollan, *Second Nature: A Gardener's Education* (New York: Dell, 1992).

2　Elizabeth Kolbert, "Turf Wars," *New Yorker*, July 21, 2008; Paul Robbins and Julie T. Sharp, "Producing and Consuming Chemicals: The Moral Economy of the American Lawn," in *Urban Ecology: An International Perspective on the Interaction between Humans and Nature*, ed. John M. Marzluff et al. (Boston: Springer US, 2008), 181–205.

3　Daniel G. Brown et al., "Rural Land-Use Trends in the Conterminous United States, 1950–2000," *Ecological Applications* 15, no. 6 (2005): 1851–63; William H. Frey, *Population Growth in Metro America since 1980: Putting the Volatile 2000s in Perspective* (Washington, DC: Brookings Institution, 2012), 27.

4　Cynthia Nickerson et al., *Major Uses of Land in the United States, 2007*, EIB-89 (US Department of Agriculture, Economic Research Service, 2011).

5　Richard H. Thaler and Cass R. Sunstein, *Nudge* (New Haven, CT: Yale University Press, 2008).

or roots. Importantly, landscape management also critically affects how much carbon is stored and for how long. Because the wood of trees lasts many years—sometimes centuries—it is particularly helpful in storing carbon to mitigate climate change. Mature trees that were in place before development, retained during land development, and maintained by homeowners, for example, store much more carbon than more recently planted trees. Similarly, relatively undisturbed soils have proportionately larger carbon stores than more recently cultivated or graded soils. In temperate forest biomes that were formerly used for agriculture, as in much of southeastern Michigan, if trees volunteer as early successional vegetation or are planted as part of the development process, carbon storage increases in vegetation as well as in associated soil, and in litter such as leaves or needles mulched in place.[6]

Suburban landscapes that have all these characteristics—more mature trees, more area in dense trees with shrubs, more area of undisturbed soil, more area with litter left in place—are likely to store more carbon. The higher the proportion of the suburban landscape that has trees, especially mature trees or dense trees, the more carbon will be stored.[7]

Our past studies in southeastern Michigan have shown us that we can learn about ecosystem services in suburban landscapes by examining exurbia, a particularly extensive type of suburbia where lots are larger in order to accommodate private wells and septic systems. It may be surprising to consider exurbia, the most sprawling type of suburbia, as having great potential to mitigate climate change by storing carbon. However, exurbia by its very nature has more extensive areas of unused landscape. Our studies have found that, in the temperate forest biome that characterizes Michigan, larger lots have more trees and a disproportionately larger

area in dense trees and shrubs that store carbon at a level approaching that of trees in mature northern hardwood forests.[8] By giving exurban homeowners larger lots, designers and planners may be able to nudge the suburban development process to store more carbon in the landscape. Are larger lots what homeowners want?

Homeowner Preferences
Describing homeownership—an overarching cultural reality of the suburban development process—the geographer Richard Walker says that the planning of suburbia must aim "to reconcile private property as a commodity circulating in a full-blown land market (bent on realizing rents and investors' profits), and private property as personal possession (for the enjoyment of one's riches)."[9] Developers largely determine what property characteristics are available to homebuyers in the suburban residential land market. Designing suburban landscapes to increase carbon storage would require understanding differences among various developers' and homeowners' perceptions of market values and homeowners' preferences for enjoying their own property. Homeowners' own aesthetic preferences (what they would personally enjoy) may be different from what they believe to be reflected in the value of their home as a commodity (what they believe future buyers for their home would prefer). In addition, developers may believe that buyers will not be willing to pay for certain landscape characteristics regardless of their preferences.

To find enduring suburban landscape patterns that will foster more trees, tactics must be found to reconcile these sometimes-contradictory perspectives. The suburban home landscape that developers offer must be a landscape that will have enough buyers. The landscape that homeowners enjoy must also be a landscape that they are sufficiently confident

6   Cinzia Fissore et al., "The Residential Landscape: Fluxes of Elements and the Role of Household Decisions," *Urban Ecosystems* 15, no. 1 (2012): 1–18; Cristina Milesi et al., "Mapping and Modeling the Biogeochemical Cycling of Turf Grasses in the United States," *Environmental Management* 36, no. 3 (2005): 426–38.

7   William S. Currie et al., "Multi-Scale Heterogeneity in Vegetation and Soil Carbon in Exurban Residential Land of Southeastern Michigan, USA," *Ecological Applications* 26, no. 5 (July 1, 2016): 1421–36.

8   Ibid.

9   Richard A. Walker, "Book Review Essay— Suburbia Reconsidered: When American Became Suburban," *Urban Geography* 28, no. 8 (2007): 809–15.

they can sell. Preserving, planting, and maintaining trees over time may not motivate the commodity calculus of either the homeowner or the developer, so designers and planners must find tactics that complement the calculus.

What have my collaborators and I learned about the cultural realities that can contribute to finding design tactics to store more carbon in suburban landscapes? First, everyday landscape aesthetics powerfully affect suburban landscape patterns and management. Furthermore, the design and management of a homeowner's yard may be affected more by the appearance of neighbors' yards than by broader cultural norms for lawn culture. Where neighbors have many trees, individual homeowners may be more likely to have many trees. This tendency to mimic aesthetic characteristics of neighbors' yards in one's own yard may reflect the overriding power of the conception of the suburban home as commodity. Designing and managing the yard for personal enjoyment is typically subordinate to ensuring its acceptability to neighbors, whose apparent landscape preferences may be interpreted as representing broader market preferences. Second, developers recognize the value that homeowners place on trees in their neighborhood, but they believe that the cost of protecting or planting trees often is greater than what homebuyers are willing to pay. Last, both developers and homeowners recognize the value of and market demand for the larger lots that typify exurbia. Importantly, in the forest biome of southeastern Michigan, these larger lots nudge developers and homeowners to retain more trees, homeowners to plant more trees, and, compared with smaller lots, result in a disproportionately larger area of dense trees. Very large lots, greater than one acre, have the largest proportionate area in dense trees and have more trees. Consequently, they store the largest amount of carbon to mitigate climate change.

Homeowners' Cultural Aesthetic of Care and Neighborhood Norms

Homeowners want their home landscapes and their neighbors' home landscapes to look well cared for. The appearance of care is both an aesthetic preference (a pleasurable response to the appearance of the landscape) and a cultural norm (an understanding that the character of the homeowner can or will be judged by the care that is apparent in the landscape). Neatness is an essential aspect of the cultural aesthetic of care because it conveys an immediately recognizable sense of order and because it displays regular human presence and the intention to invest time or other resources in a place.[10] In suburban landscapes, care is conveyed by elements that I have described as "cues to care," for example, mown turf, trimmed trees, hedges in rows, and colorful flowers.[11] These cues connote marketability or productivity, civility or neighborliness, and safety. Suburbia epitomizes the aesthetic of care as displayed by neatness.

To some suburban homeowners, trees and woodlands do not look sufficiently neat, at least not on their own property. Trees growing on a mown lawn may be beautiful, but the seeds, fruits, leaves, and branches that fall look messy and require maintenance. Dense trees and shrubs lacking a mown understory, particularly with the weedy appearance and uneven growth habits of early successional vegetation, can dramatically violate norms for neatness. While many studies have found that canopy trees contribute to the aesthetic value of a neighborhood, homeowners may prefer to see trees beyond their own property—as borrowed scenery or a "natural area" that does not require their own care.[12] Such a preference suggests that planning for trees and woodlands to predominate in the public

10 Joan Iverson Nassauer, "The Aesthetics of Horticulture: Neatness as a Form of Care," *Journal of the American Society for Horticultural Science* (1988); Joan Iverson Nassauer, "Cultural Sustainability," in *Placing Nature: Culture and Landscape Ecology,* ed. Nassauer, Joan (Washington, DC: Island Press, 1997).

11 Joan Iverson Nassauer, "Messy Ecosystems, Orderly Frames," *Landscape Journal* 14, no. 2 (1995): 161–70; Joan Iverson Nassauer, "Care and Stewardship: From Home to Planet," *Landscape and Urban Planning* 100, no. 4 (2011): 321–23.

12 Zhifang Wang et al., "Different Types of Open Spaces and Their Importance to Exurban Homeowners," *Society & Natural Resources* 25, no. 4 (2012): 368–83.

Design Alternatives	Price Range	Subdivision 1	Subdivision 2
Conventional	Higher		
Ecological Open Space	Higher		
Ecological Private Yards	Higher		

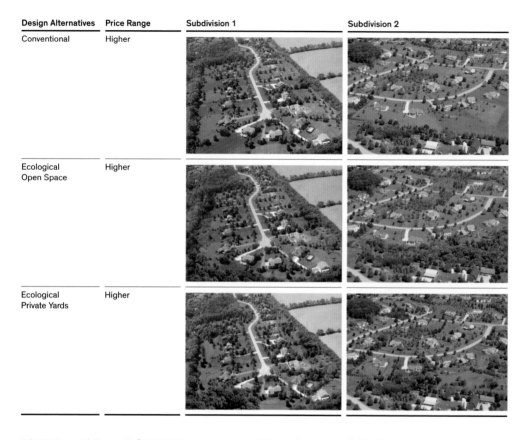

4.6.1 Higher-priced homes (> $450,000) in conventional subdivision designs compared with alternative designs that would store more carbon

13 Joan Iverson Nassauer, Zhifang Wang, and Erik Dayrell, "What Will the Neighbors Think? Cultural Norms and Ecological Design," *Landscape and Urban Planning* 92, no. 3 (2009): 282–92.

14 Joan Iverson Nassauer et al., "Parcel Size Related to Household Behaviors Affecting Carbon Storage in Exurban Residential Landscapes," *Landscape and Urban Planning* 129 (2014): 55–64; Rachel Stehouwer Visscher et al., "Exurban Residential Household Behaviors and Values: Influence of Parcel Size and Neighbors on Carbon Storage Potential," *Landscape and Urban Planning* 132 (2014): 37–46.

15 Solomon E. Asch, "Effects of Group Pressure upon the Modification and Distortion of Judgments," *Groups, Leadership, and Men* (1951): 222–36; Sushil Bikhchandani, David Hirshleifer, and Ivo Welch, "A Theory of Fads, Fashion, Custom, and Cultural Change as Informational Cascades," *Journal of Political Economy* (1992): 992–1026; B. Douglas Bernheim, "A Theory of Conformity," *Journal of Political Economy* (1994): 841–77.

and quasi-public open spaces of suburbia should be a core tactic for enhancing carbon storage in suburban landscapes.

Our studies suggest that another tactic is to plan for trees at the scale of neighborhoods rather than individual properties. In their own yards, homeowners' preferences may be more influenced by what they see in their neighbors' yards than by broader cultural norms of lawn culture. They may be more likely to prefer trees for their own properties in neighborhoods where neighbors have trees or are planting trees. In an experiment with nearly five hundred southeastern Michigan exurban homeowners, we found that they adjusted their choice of an "ideal" home landscape to match images of hypothetical neighbors' yards.[13] When they saw images of neighbors' yards that exemplified lawn culture, they chose a turf-dominated yard as their own ideal. When they saw images of neighbors' yards that had less turf, they chose a yard with less turf as their own ideal. In subsequent in-depth interviews and surveys of exurban homeowners, we found that their own yard styles actually tended to match those of nearby neighbors.[14] Possibly, suburban homeowners see their neighbors' landscapes as market signals, suggesting the preferences of future buyers for their homes. Perhaps they are matching neighbors' behavior or preferences for other more immediately social reasons, a tendency that has been examined in the fields of behavioral economics and psychology.[15]

Design Alternatives	Price Range	Subdivision 5	Subdivision 6
Conventional	Lower		
Ecological Open Space	Lower		
Ecological Private Yards	Lower		

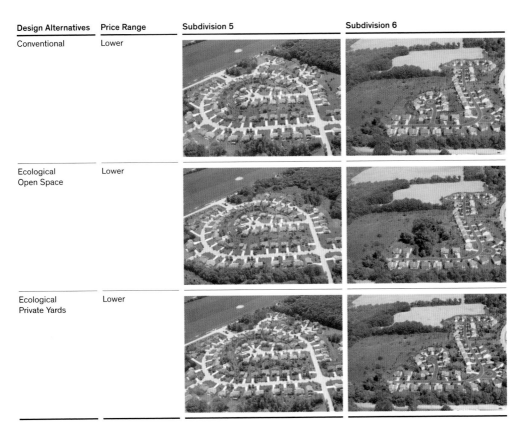

4.6.2 Lower-priced homes (<$450,000) in conventional subdivision designs compared with alternative designs that would store more carbon

16 Troy Bowman and Jan Thompson, "Barriers to Implementation of Low-Impact and Conservation Subdivision Design: Developer Perceptions and Resident Demand," *Landscape and Urban Planning* 92, no. 2 (2009): 96–105; Troy Bowman, Jan Thompson, and John Tyndall, "Resident, Developer, and City Staff Perceptions of LID and CSD Subdivision Design Approaches," *Landscape and Urban Planning* 107, no. 1 (2012): 43–54; Timothy Carter, "Developing Conservation Subdivisions: Ecological Constraints, Regulatory Barriers, and Market Incentives," *Landscape and Urban Planning* 92, no. 2 (2009): 117–24; Z. Aslıgül Göçmen, "Barriers to Successful Implementation of Conservation Subdivision Design: A Closer Look at Land Use Regulations and Subdivision Permitting Process," *Landscape and Urban Planning* 110 (2013): 123–33.

17 Susan Elizabeth Westbrook, "Residential Developers' Perceptions of Ecological Alternatives for Exurban and Suburban Development" (master's thesis, University of Michigan, 2010).

Developers' Perceptions of the Market for Suburban Homes

Providing ecosystem services is not yet a leading aim of residential developers in suburban America. Developers and their financial backers may see market demand, local regulations, zoning ordinances, and financial risks as limiting their capacity to provide ecosystem services. However, several studies have concluded that suburban and exurban residential developers underestimate homebuyers' interest and willingness to pay for ecological design features.[16]

We investigated developers' perceptions of homebuyers' market preferences in one-on-one in-depth interviews with representatives from twenty development firms in southeastern Michigan.[17] Each firm had constructed more than two subdivisions per year between 2000 and 2002 for a range of homebuyer market segments in both suburban and exurban settings. During the interviews, the developers described how they thought homebuyers would perceive four different subdivision design alternatives, depicted in visualizations. Then, we compared developers' responses with the actual perceptions of southeastern Michigan homeowners in their market segment, in which we defined homes priced over $400,000 in 2002 as higher priced.

The four subdivision design alternatives could be described as conventional, ecological open space (emphasizing increased public or quasi-public open space), ecological private yards

Design Alternatives	Price Range	Subdivision 3	Subdivision 4
Ecological Remnant	Higher		

4.6.3 Higher-priced homes (> $450,000) sited to retain remnant areas of dense trees that store more carbon than turf or agricultural land uses

(emphasizing less turf) or ecological remnants (emphasizing protection of existing trees and woodlands). (figs. **4.6.1–3**) Compared with conventional designs, ecological open space designs reduced lot size and/or the number of lots in order to increase the amount of shared open space. Ecological private yard designs did not vary in lot size or the number of lots but changed the landscape pattern and composition within each private lot to increase the number of trees or area in prairie gardens. Ecological remnant designs avoided removing woodlands, streams, or wetlands, and consequently had road and lot configurations different from the other alternatives.

We found that developers' perceptions of homebuyers' preferences generally matched homebuyers' actual preferences. They ranked all of the "ecological" designs higher than they ranked conventional alternatives. The developers believed these subdivision characteristics were desired by homebuyers: larger lots, lower density, nearby woodlands or wooded lots, and homes that back up to open space.

Concerning trees, one developer noted about the ecological design alternatives for subdivision 6, "Trees definitely improve the value of the neighborhood." Developers for the higher-priced market noted that subdivision 3 where remnant woodlands were retained "is more desirable because of vegetation…[it] gets

a premium for trees." Of subdivision 2, one developer said, "[Homebuyers] like trees, and trees bring in some extra money." However, another developer described "a trade-off between vegetation and density."

Although homeowners ranked some ecological private yard designs higher than ecological open space alternatives, many developers not in the higher-priced market discussed potential problems with the trees and prairie gardens in private yards: One said that it "would be too expensive to do all the plantings." Another said, "The [homebuyer] prefers the vegetation, but I don't want to deal with the landscape requirement." Developers who built higher-priced subdivisions stated: "Natural buffers [like those shown in private yards] are preferred…but not appropriate for a traditional buyer [meaning those who are not in a higher-priced market]."

In our study, developers who did not build for the higher-priced market recognized homebuyers' preference for ecological designs, but they did not perceive these alternatives as profitable in their markets. One explained, "More profit [comes with] with more density," and another said, "The one with the most number of units will have the most profits." Developers for higher-priced markets, however, believed that remnant woodlands, wooded open spaces, or more trees

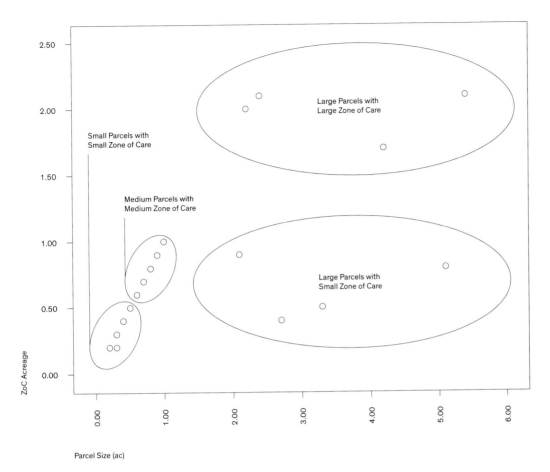

18 Derek T. Robinson, "Land Cover Fragmentation and Configuration of Ownership Parcels in an Exurban Landscape," *Urban Ecosystems* 15 (2012): 53–69.

4.6.4 The zone of care, where all vegetation is visibly maintained, occupies the entire lot if lots are smaller than one acre. Larger lots have an area that is untended, beyond the zone of care.

on private lots throughout the neighborhood would be profitable in their markets.

Our study suggests that developers do know that many homebuyers prefer more trees in their neighborhoods. However, the developers we interviewed tended to believe that subdivisions that were designed to retain areas of dense trees or to consistently incorporate more trees on private lots throughout the neighborhood were suitable only for the higher-priced market. This may be partly a failure of imagination, as well as a lack of sufficient precedents for affordable wooded residential developments. It raises the question: how can the very large lots where more expensive homes are located deliver more carbon storage as a broad societal benefit?

Lot Size: Nudging Suburban Landscapes toward More Trees

Larger lot sizes may include a proportionately larger treed area because, as the geographer Derek Robinson has suggested, there are "limits to anthropogenic management of land within parcels with increasing size."[18] Examining land cover in three southeastern Michigan townships, he found that the proportion of the lot in turf or impervious surfaces decreased with increased lot size. He also observed that large lots with large proportions of forest were likely to be adjacent to similar lots, and as lot size increased, connected habitat patch size increased. Looking at large lots from the perspective of property owners' attitudes and behavior, another study found that Vermont exurban homeowners with

4.6.5 The zone of care is very small in the backyard of this large lot (> 1 acre), and there are more trees beyond the zone of care

19 Daniel L. Erickson, Sarah Taylor Lovell, and V. Ernesto Méndez, "Landowner Willingness to Embed Production Agriculture and Other Land Use Options in Residential Areas of Chittenden County, VT," *Landscape and Urban Planning* 103, no. 2 (2011): 174–84.
20 Nassauer et al., "Parcel Size Related to Household Behaviors"; Visscher et al., "Exurban Residential Household Behaviors and Values."
21 Rachel Stehouwer Visscher, Joan Iverson Nassauer, and Lauren L. Marshall, "Exurban Residential Household Behaviors and Values: Influence of Parcel Size and Neighbors on Carbon Storage Potential," *Landscape and Urban Planning* (2015–submitted).

larger properties were more willing to have forests than were those with smaller properties.[19] What social drivers might help to explain the effect of lot size on the area in trees?

Our studies suggest that larger lots have proportionately more trees partly because social norms for visible care to residential landscapes are limited to an area of approximately 1 acre including the house, which we described as the "zone of care."[20] (fig. **4.6.4**) Beyond that threshold, homeowners are unlikely to regularly mow or prune. Dense trees and shrubs, dead wood, and leaves characterize the area beyond the zone of care in southeastern Michigan, and this type of land cover tended to be similar throughout neighborhoods of large lots. Since most exurban lots are larger than 1 acre and have an area beyond the zone of care, they inherently store proportionately more carbon per area.

Large lots may have an area beyond the zone of care because the lot size exceeds homeowners' management capacities, but large lots also may relieve social pressures of neighborhood norms. The size of the zone of care varies little on smaller lots, where the entire lot is visibly maintained, but varies dramatically on lots larger than one acre, where the zone of care sometimes is smaller than on small lots (fig. **4.6.5**). Since much of a large property may not be visible to neighbors and the public passing by, homeowners may feel relieved of social norms for neatness. Supporting this interpretation, our studies and many others suggest that social norms allow the backyard, which often is not visible to passersby, to be maintained more casually than the front yard—even on small properties.[21] In addition, social pressure to visibly maintain a large area may be relaxed because of apparent neighborhood norms for the landscape aesthetics of care. Owners of large lots tend to live in neighborhoods of other large lots that have an area beyond the zone of care where dense trees and shrubs can grow.

4.6.6 Trees were planted within the zone of care of this mid-sized lot (.5–1 acre)

Planting trees also contributes to carbon storage, and we found that more trees were planted on large lots. In our studies, owners of lots even as small as 0.5 acre planted more trees than owners of smaller lots. (figs. **4.6.6–7**) Lots 0.5–1.0 acre typically were in neighborhoods with very neat landscape styles and little or no area beyond the zone of care. On lots of this size, trees were planted to exhibit norms for neatness, in canopied lawns and border plantings.

Our studies suggest that lot sizes larger than the zone of care (1 acre in southeastern Michigan) may effectively nudge developers and homeowners to behaviors that result in more trees. The larger the lot, the larger the area beyond the zone of care, and the more carbon stored in densely wooded areas in suburban landscapes of forest biomes. Our studies also indicate carbon storage benefits of lots as small as 0.5 acre, where homeowners plant more trees than in smaller lots. Social mechanisms may drive behaviors that result in more trees on large lots, where social pressure for neatness may be relieved by visual privacy and neighborhood yard care norms that incorporate an area beyond the zone of care.

Tactics for Greening Sprawl by Storing Carbon in the Suburban Landscape
The sprawling suburban development that continues to expand across America can be more truly "green" by storing more carbon in trees. While mown lawns dominate much of suburbia, larger areas of tree cover, especially mature trees and dense trees with shrubs, would provide the essential ecosystem service of climate change mitigation. Our studies suggest the following tactics for increasing tree cover in suburban residential landscapes.

Make lot size larger than the zone of care. Especially in exurban areas, where local governments commonly require large minimum lot sizes to protect potable water supplies from septic system pollution, protect agricultural land uses, or protect "rural character," minimum lot sizes larger than the zone of care (about 1 acre in southeastern Michigan) would nudge homeowners to store more carbon in trees. The size of the zone of care may vary with regions and cultures, but the concept of a zone of care surrounding the dwelling may be generally useful wherever residential landscapes can provide more ecosystem services beyond the zone of care. On very large lots, relief from social norms for visible maintenance may nudge carbon storage by leading developers to clear smaller areas of trees and undergrowth and by leading homeowners to retain trees and allow dense trees and shrubs to grow beyond the zone of care.

Deeper understanding of the physical characteristics of the zone of care and social motivations for homeowners to maintain it may help to shrink it by design. Shrinking only the zone of care in low-density development would allow for a larger area in dense trees and shrubs. Shrinking both the zone of care and lot size to achieve higher-density development could reduce other inevitable societal costs of suburban sprawl as well.

What might nudge developers and homeowners to incorporate more trees on private lots of different sizes? Plans for higher density neighborhoods could replicate "nudge" characteristics of more treed large lots: visual screening to promote a smaller zone of care and neighborhood yard care norms that include areas beyond a zone of care. This can happen in subdivision designs that shrink the front yard, allowing for a much smaller requisite zone of care in the front and more private backyards, designed to have a small zone of care within an armature of dense trees and shrubs that connect lots throughout the block.

Change neighborhoods, not individual lots. In the suburban landscape, a more wooded landscape will be more acceptable to homeowners if it is introduced at the scale of neighborhoods, where landscapes

4.6.7 Each of these small lots (<.5 acre) is managed entirely as within the zone of care.

with more trees and dense woodlands can be the norm for the neighborhood. The implications for design and planning are clear: make wooded areas predominate in suburban open space systems and bring trees into yards and streetscapes at the scale of neighborhoods. While developers may be more inclined to include wooded open spaces rather than wooded yards in new subdivisions (and some homeowners are, in fact, reluctant to maintain trees in their own yards), consistency across a neighborhood is likely to make trees on private lots desirable to more homeowners. Governance (e.g., local government requirements, homeowners' association rules), subdivision design, or a particular landscape ethos within the neighborhood could tip the balance to nudge homeowners to have more trees because they are surrounded by neighbors who have more trees.

Promote innovation by residential developers. From the standpoint of developers, suburban landscapes are a product that they manufacture for sale at the right price. From the standpoint of homeowners, a suburban landscape is a commodity to occupy as they anticipate its sale as well as a home to enjoy. These commodity values of suburban residential landscapes may appear to create little incentive for developers to provide ecosystem services like carbon storage in trees. Climate change mitigation has rarely been incorporated in land-use law in the United States so far. However, government regulations by a few states and local governments as well as more informal incentives like certification programs can and do affect whether developers innovate to produce larger societal benefits.

Developers, who understand smaller lots as suitable for less expensive homes, may be nudged to innovate further by new design conceptions of suburban residential development featuring smaller lots in a predominantly wooded landscape. While the developers we interviewed thought that homebuyers desired nearby woodlands or wooded lots and homes that back up to open space, they thought that most homebuyers could not afford these characteristics. There is a need for sufficient, replicable precedents to demonstrate that wooded residential developments can be affordable.

Expect societal benefits from large suburban lots. In our studies we examined sprawl from the perspective of those who live in exurban homes and those who develop exurban subdivisions. From that perspective, the most immediate way to "green" sprawl is to fully use the legacy pattern of large exurban lots to accommodate more ecosystem services, including more trees to store carbon. Even if, going forward, new suburban development reformed to consist solely of affordable homes on smaller lots in thickly wooded neighborhoods, the legacy of very large lots would remain significant for carbon storage in biomes like southeastern Michigan, where untended areas become successional woodlands and most development occurs on former agricultural land. It may seem counterintuitive to recognize that large lots—the larger the better—do provide a societal benefit by storing carbon in trees. But where very large lots characterize a landscape, the societal benefit of carbon storage should be recognized and expected. More could be done on large lots. The way in which homeowners manage their forests

could be more fully explored for all their potential ecosystem services: for example, reducing fire risks, managing hydrologic systems, absorbing airborne pollutants, and building biodiversity. Governance incentives and certification programs may be helpful.

What we learned suggests how suburban development patterns could be changed and adapted to store more carbon in trees and contribute to mitigating climate change. Exurban residential landscapes may be the epitome of sprawl, but they are also the realization of certain societal desires and values, and they may be a buffer against some environmental risks. If design and planning can use those desires and values to nudge suburbia to store more carbon in trees, society benefits.

In this essay, I draw on my colleagues' work in our collaborative project, Spatial Land Use Change and Ecological Effects, from the National Science Foundation's (NSF) program on the Dynamics of Coupled Natural and Human Systems (grants #GEO-0813799 and #GEO-0814542). I have been very fortunate to learn from them over the past decade of our work together, and we all benefited from the outstanding leadership of Dan Brown. In addition, Rachel Visscher's Environmental Protection Agency Science To Achieve Results (EPA STAR) STAR Fellowship (Assistance Agreement FP91750901-1) supported her work. I am grateful for the support of the NSF and EPA. In addition to my coauthors whose work I cite here, I thank Cristy Watkins, whose work in my lab advanced our understanding of the superb developer interview data gathered by Liz Westbrook.

Durham, North Carolina, United States

Durham, North Carolina, United States

4.7
BELTING FUTURE SUBURBIA

Alan M. Berger

DESIGN
MODELS

FLEXIBLE
REGULATION

PRODUCTIVE
SUBURBS

4.7.1 Agriculture Reserve, Delray Beach, Florida. Greenbelt edges can take many forms. This new planned unit development is directly adjacent to an agricultural reserve. No new development is permitted in the reserve landscape.

For centuries, cities have used containment policies to define their edges. The goal has been to prevent any suburban expansion that would enable the development of a polycentric metropolitan structure. One of the most pervasive and restrictive types of urban containment is the "greenbelt": a circular band of landscape at the edge of a city, with low-intensity programming (passive recreation, conservation, agriculture, and forestry areas, for example) or no programmed purpose at all.[1] The modern greenbelt concept originated with Ebenezer Howard and Raymond Unwin in their garden city movement during the late nineteenth century, although variations of the idea—sometimes conceived as a void or a "green lung"—have been around for hundreds of years.[2]

From a city planning perspective, greenbelts have several key characteristics (fig. **4.7.1**). They are intended to restrict urban growth and are often preplanned to designate a city's future urban boundary. They can also be retrofitted around urbanizing territories to redirect unplanned or speculative growth. Greenbelts are also intended to reinforce the visual or aesthetic separation of urban and rural landscapes, further hardening the dualities of city versus nature, urban versus rural.[3]

They are intended to be static, immutable forms. But, as history shows, they inevitably succumb to unplanned change, especially when they are implemented on the fringe of a city. The fringe is one of the most dynamic, complex, and frequently misunderstood manifestations of urbanization. By extension, the greenbelt concept should be reexamined as a fringe tool, especially since, over the past decades, greenbelts around the world have lost much of their effectiveness. New development and unforeseen uses have eroded their boundaries and disrupted their intended uses, while

1   David N. Bengston, Jennifer O. Fletcher, and Kristen C. Nelson, "Public Policies for Managing Urban Growth and Protecting Open Space: Policy Instruments and Lessons Learned in the United States," *Landscape and Urban Planning* 69, nos. 2–3 (August 15, 2004): 271–86.

2   Ibid. These authors also reference thirteenth-century greenbelts from the following sources: Leslie Ginsburg, "Green Belts in the Bible," *Journal of the Town Planning Institute* 42 (May 1956): 129–30; Robert Freestone, "Greenbelts in City and Regional Planning," in *From Garden City to Green City: The Legacy of Ebenezer Howard,* ed. Kermit C. Parsons and David Schuyler (Baltimore: Johns Hopkins University Press, 2002), 67–98; and Ebenezer Howard, *Garden Cities of Tomorrow* (1898; repr., London: Faber & Faber, 1946).

4.7.2 Leapfrog development along Diagonal Highway, Boulder, Colorado, just outside Boulder's restrictive greenbelt

unchecked suburbanization has leap-frogged beyond them. (fig. **4.7.2**)

Despite a clear failure to achieve the proposed goals, especially at the fringe, the use of greenbelts has proliferated. Why do planners uncritically default to the creation of greenbelts as a means of controlling growth? Which, if any, green-belt strategies have been successful? Is the concept of greenbelting flexible enough to receive new meanings and new programming as cities change over time?

These questions are critical. Rapid urban expansion and population growth, combined with a number of other cultural, environmental, and economic factors, will continue to place enormous pressure on cities to reconsider how to control their leading suburban fringes. Greenbelts have not adapted to the realities of these changes. They no longer work well as urban containment tools, but they can be reconceptualized to serve other crucial functions. For example, biodiversity, water storage and purification, energy production, food cultivation and process-ing, affordable housing, and recreational networks can all be explored in new, interesting ways at the suburban fringe. Today's overreliance on unsustainable, engineered, and expensive solutions to provide cities with natural resources doesn't make sense when greenbelts can perform some of these holistic func-tions more effectively. Ecological function needs to become a fundamental priority in metropolitan land-use decisions, and greenbelts are the vehicle for this to change to be initiated. Parallel with this change will be a paradigmatic shift in the way we teach and practice planning and design to prioritize future ecosystem services and dynamic ecological perfor-mance in urbanism. Reconceiving the dynamics of metropolitan edges, where land conversion, degradation, ecosys-tem service losses, and social equity are perhaps at their most extreme, should be one of the central research ambitions of urbanism itself. Contemporary urbanism

3   John Herington, *Beyond Greenbelts: Managing Urban Growth in the Twenty-First Century* (London: Jessica Kingsley Publishers and Regional Studies Association, 1990), 6–13; Marc Antrop, "Landscape Change and the Urbanization Process in Europe," *Landscape and Urban Planning* 67, nos. 1–4 (March 15, 2004): 9–26.

desperately needs a new model for imagining the outer edges of cities—the suburban fringes where the dynamics of land conversion, environmental systems, economic production, and technological innovation can merge into new conceptions of how we live on a landscape.

The Static Greenbelt at the Dynamic Fringe

From a theoretical perspective, a greenbelt transforms the space that surrounds it in unplanned ways because planners have not considered, or planned for, the services and functions a greenbelt can provide. Its capacity to enhance surrounding areas is rarely considered. It is created, fundamentally, as "negative" space, defined more by what it is not than by what it is in and of itself.[4] The greenbelt is viewed as generic green space—the opposite of development—and what matters to planners is its status as "non-development."[5] As a result, greenbelts are often reduced to being aesthetically managed agrarian landscapes that provide recreation and food for the city.[6]

Most important, the dynamics of the suburban fringe are rarely factored into the greenbelt scheme. Urbanists are only recently recognizing the importance of the fringe. Previously, as the geographer David Simon notes, there was a significant perception that the fringe was unimportant because of its short-term, transitory nature. Thus, when development pressures mounted at the fringe, there wasn't any framework in place for the greenbelt to ensure flexibility and the continued high performance of the landscape. However, the fringe is now recognized as a major (and persistent) phenomenon, which exists globally, has lasting effects, and is a critical site for confronting growth challenges.[7]

The suburban fringe—I use the term to describe a hybrid of suburb and fringe—is by nature a place of change.[8] It is more or less the zone that transitions from suburban to rural land use; from a majority of housing-based uses to landscape-based uses; from recreational to industrial to fully agricultural zones.[9] (fig. **4.7.3**) It is a no-man's-land of random, disaggregated, and often uncomplimentary, informal, and uncontrolled land uses. Unlike incorporated towns and cities with clearly marked edges, the suburban fringe lacks spatial distinction. It is defined more by process than form, by flows rather than boundaries. There are many types of local, regional, national, and international flows that cross each other at the fringe: people, goods, income, capital, natural resources, waste, and more. The suburban fringe is widespread globally, and as a result, there are innumerous territorial theories, terms, and concepts by academicians to describe it. Outside the United States, scholars often refer to this phenomenon as "peri-urbanization" or the "peri-urban landscape."[10] Neither urban nor rural, the suburban fringe or peri-urban landscape desperately needs the environmental stewardship capabilities and conceptual organizational capacities of landscape architects and planners. Why?

The fringe is facing massive environmental pressures, such as the need for wastewater treatment and disposal, and the threat of potable water contamination, especially in the developing world.[11] Another major environmental issue at the fringe is land conversion, especially in regard to its impacts on open space preservation and agriculture production. (figs. **4.7.4**–**5**) Additional concerns include the rate and scale of resource use, and the siting and adequacy of waste infrastructure.[12] Lower-income groups often find more affordable residency on the fringe, and so are disproportionally affected by environmental degradation.[13]

It is significant that the suburban fringe is proliferating worldwide, especially in Asia, Latin America, and Africa.

4   Manfred Kühn, "Greenbelt and Green Heart: Separating and Integrating Landscapes in European City Regions," *Landscape and Urban Planning* 64, nos. 1–2 (2003): 26.

5   Herington, *Beyond Greenbelts*, 28–30.

6   Kühn, "Greenbelt and Green Heart," 20; Marco Amati, "From a Blanket to a Patchwork: The Practicalities of Reforming the London Green Belt," *Journal of Environmental Planning and Management* 50, no. 5 (2007): 579–94; Carol Harrison, "Countryside Recreation and London's Urban Fringe," *Transactions of the Institute of British Geographers* 8, no. 3 (1983): 295–313.

7   David Simon, "Urban Environments: Issues on the Peri-Urban Fringe," *Annual Review of Environment and Resources* 33, no. 33 (January 1, 2008): 168.

8   This is a combinatory term meant to describe areas that have characteristics of suburbs and fringes. I have used Kurtz and Eicher's 1958 definition to create this hybridization. See Richard A. Kurtz and Joanne B. Eicher, "Fringe and Suburb: A Confusion of Concepts," *Social Forces* 37 (October 1958): 32–37.

9   German Adell, "Theories and Models of the Peri-Urban Interface: A Changing Conceptual Landscape," Development Planning Unit, University College London, March 1999, 9; another frequently used term is the "Rural-Urban Fringe." Scott et al. describe this term as "Deconstructing the RUF," which "is a complex undertaking and can become a self-defeating exercise." Indeed, there is a burgeoning number of terms advanced in the pursuit of a definitional "holy grail"; ranging from landscapes at the edge; places of transition; heterogeneous mosaics; landscapes of disorder;

4.7.3 Suburban fringe at south edge of Lincoln, Nebraska

According to the East Asian planning scholar Douglas Webster, "In East Asia, the magnitude and impact of the phenomenon is, and will be, more important than in any other world region."[14] During the twenty-five years from 2002 to 2027, it is estimated that the population of peri-urban areas in East Asia will increase by approximately 200 million people, accounting for 40 percent of urban population growth in that region. In Bangkok, 53 percent of population growth from 2002 to 2022 is expected to occur outside the city proper. For Jakarta, the equivalent is 70 percent. In China, 40 percent of future urban population growth in extended urban regions that are service-oriented (Beijing, Shanghai, and Hangzhou), and over 60 percent of future urban population growth in more industrial cities (Chongqing, Chengdu, and Ningbo), is forecasted to occur in peri-urban areas. Moreover, peri-urban areas are increasingly important as sites of investment, making "the actual importance

of the process in East Asia, in terms of local, national, and global impacts… even more significant than implied by the demographics."[15]

New Spatial Patterns on the New Fringe

Because of its unclassifiable spatial qualities and fast rate of growth, the suburban fringe has been difficult to understand and conceptualize, yet its dynamics have been radically reshaping cities.

    Suburban fringe dynamics have produced unprecedented spatial patterns and landscape typologies around the world. These in-between landscapes, neither rural nor urban, with their heterogeneous built forms, are often characterized by transport infrastructure to support automobiles. (figs. **4.7.6**–**7**) Moscow, the largest city in Europe, has a suburban fringe composed of proliferating single-family homes in a unique, formal arrangement that concentrates along the highways and ring roads.[16] In Western Europe, the fringe of Brussels is described as having an "urban

chaotic landscapes; new geography of urban sprawl; the last frontier; ephemeral landscapes; edgelands; and forgotten landscapes. Collectively, these terms all signify an implicit "otherness," heavily laden with negative overtones, implying that it is a "space waiting for something better to come along." See Alister Scott et al., "Disintegrated Development at the Rural-Urban Fringe: Re-Connecting Spatial Planning Theory and Practice," *Progress in Planning* 83 (July 2013): 9.
10 The peri-urban landscape is a mosaic of agricultural and urban ecosystems affected by material and energy flows demanded by urban and rural areas: Adriana Allen, "Environmental Planning and Management of the Peri-Urban Interface: Perspectives on an Emerging Field," *Environment & Urbanization* 15, no. 1 (April 2003): 135–47.

4.7.4 Water pollution at the edge of a Mumbai slum, India

4.7.5 Water treatment plant, eastern edge of Bakersfield, California

4.7.6 Planned unit development along western edge of Port St. Lucie, Florida

4.7.7 New suburban development north of Denver, Colorado. Layout and organization is based on single mode of automobile transportation

4.7.8 Polycentric growth in and around Houston, Texas. Three nodes are visible: downtown in the foreground, Uptown/Galleria in the upper right, and Rice/Medical Center in the upper left.

shadow," which forms when star-shaped urban development occurs in combination with transportation infrastructure that is overly focused on connecting urban centers, leaving "wedges" of countryside.[17] Similarly, the Belgian city of Flanders has been called a new fringe prototype, resembling "neither countryside, nor cityscape, but in fact something 'in between.'"[18]

In Latin America, the fringes of megacities such as Mexico City, Buenos Aires, Santiago, and São Paolo contain a side-by-side mix of dissimilar activities, such as agriculture, housing, industry, recreation.[19] In Southeast and East Asia, the fringe, termed *desakota* (city-village), is characterized by complex mosaics of juxtaposed activities previously regarded as incompatible. For example, computer assembly workshops are adjacent to rice paddy fields or coconut groves; urban-oriented activity centers such as golf courses abut rural villages; and industrial estates or themed gated communities extend into formerly agricultural lands.[20] Although marginal in location, the *desakota* is surprisingly significant in economic terms and is evidence of the shift toward multiple urban nodes. For example, in Jakarta since the year 2000, the bulk of foreign investment has occurred at the fringe.[21]

Spatially, the most important phenomenon produced by fringe dynamics is the development of new urban high- and medium-density nodes, containing clusters of housing, employment, and commercial development. Instead of the traditional monocentric pattern of a high-density center that declines toward the edges, metropolitan areas that are polycentric are an inverted tent, in contrast to the tentlike density of compact European cities.

Polycentrism has emerged as the prevailing form of large metropolitan areas worldwide and is likely to continue until well into the next century.[22] We define the polycentric form as a metro area consisting of a principal city along with many other spread-out nodes of density, all contributing to the regional economy. (fig. **4.7.8**) For example, Mediterranean Europe's urban areas are increasingly experiencing a change toward growth that is dispersed and horizontal, rather than vertical. Examining the Barcelona metropolitan region from 1993 to 2000, researchers concluded that widespread growth of single-family housing at the edge of metropolitan areas was linked to "high dependence on the private automobile, a strong filtering process by the property market, and [a] lack of planning," adding, "in Barcelona and in other Mediterranean cities, the mononuclear compact city and the accompanying continuous metropolis are losing its previous and almost absolute dominance. Instead, we find a network of interrelated cities with different potentialities."[23] In Latin American megacities, the phenomenon of increasing polycentrism and the growth of secondary cities has been termed "polarization reversal." Latin American urban form has also been described as "urban archipelagos," characterized by diffuse boundaries and often-weak planning oversight and control.[24] In Southeast Asia and East Asia, a new form of metropolitan urbanism was coined the Extended Metropolitan Region (EMR), which describes the polycentricism and expansion of urban activities into rural zones that has been occurring since the 1960s.

Greenbelts, originally conceived for the monocentric city model, need to be readapted, given the push toward polycentrism that has become evident worldwide. Some planners have taken up the question of how new greenbelt forms could more effectively adapt to today's metropolitan structure and see the answer as including the support of new regional functions. For example, the regional planner Manfred Kühn draws on the concept of the regional

11   Douglas Webster, "On the Edge—Shaping the Future of Peri-Urban East Asia" (discussion paper, Stanford University, Institute for International Studies, Asia/Pacific Research Center, Stanford, California, 2002): 32–33, accessed July 20, 2015, http://aparc.fsi.stanford.edu/sites/default/files/Webster2002.pdf.

12   Simon, "Urban Environments," 167–85.

13   Adell, "Theories and Models of the Peri-Urban Interface," 1.

14   Webster, "On the Edge," 6.

15   Ibid., 6; Douglas Webster, Jianming Cai, and Larissa Muller, "The New Face of Peri-Urbanization in East Asia: Modern Production Zones, Middle-Class Lifestyles, and Rising Expectations," *Journal of Urban Affairs* 36 (2014): 315–33.

16   Robert J. Mason and Liliya Nigmatullina, "Suburbanization and Sustainability in Metropolitan Moscow," *Geographical Review* 101, no. 3 (July 2011): 317, 319.

17   Antrop, "Landscape Change and the Urbanization Process in Europe," 16.

18   Steven J. Meeus and Hubert Gulinck, "Semi-Urban Areas in Landscape Research: A Review," *Living Reviews in Landscape Research* 2 (January 2008): 9.

19   Adrian G. Aguilar and Peter M. Ward, "Globalization, Regional Development, and Mega-City Expansion in Latin America: Analyzing Mexico City's Peri-Urban Hinterland," *Cities* 20, no. 1 (February 2003): 7.

20   Simon, "Urban Environments: Issues on the Peri-Urban Fringe," 169–70; Andre C. Ortega, "Desakota and Beyond: Neoliberal Production of Suburban Space in Manila's Fringe," *Urban Geography* 33, no. 8 (November–December 2012): 1119.

21   Delik Hudalah and Tommy Firman, "Beyond Property: Industrial Estates

city to consider how the greenbelt serves to connect, not separate, the different components of metro areas across Europe. Specifically, he has contrasted the greenbelt and the "green heart":

> Whereas the Greenbelt approach operates in a *monocentric* city and its surrounding countryside, the Green Heart approach operates in a *polycentric* city region…In the first case, landscape is an outside zone, forming a belt around the city. In the second case, landscape is an inside zone, forming the core of a city region.[25]

Kühn's insights point out the need for strategic greenbelt forms that deal with the dynamics, flows, and exchanges that take place at the regional scale.

Austria's Viennese greenbelt is an exemplary model that adapted to these changes, and went from static form to a flexible, regional mosaic of environmental services. In 1905 the town council formally established the Viennese Forest and Meadow Belt, which has evolved over the century:

> In times of crisis, such as the early post-War periods, the Vienna green belt was a major source of the supply of fuel wood and emergency food and enabled large parts of Vienna's population to survive. In times of abundance, the needs are primarily directed toward recreation and to environmental services like providing clean water and clean air and the provision of high biodiversity in and around Vienna.[26]

As nearby cities have grown closer together, planners are now thinking regionally and considering how to integrate Vienna's greenbelt into a larger, transnational greenbelt system for all of lower Austria, enabling polycentric sharing of environmental and other services.[27] In this way, Vienna offers one

example of how this trend to multicentrality opens up new opportunities for belting innovations.

In addition to new opportunities, fringe schemes pose novel challenges. One of these, as the planner Adriana Allen notes, is the complex governance at the fringe resulting from institutional fragmentation. "No district is able to apply a single isolated approach when supplying the comprehensive water and energy flows required by its population, or to manage the wastes and pollution generated by that population within its jurisdictional limits," says Allen.[28] (Fig. **4.7.9**) Because of the shifting economic and social conditions, it is hard to create stable institutional landscape discourse for optimizing the peri-urban interface: "institutional arrangements or areas of responsibility tend to be either too small or too large, too urban or too rural in their orientation."[29] Taking up similar themes, other urban scholars refer to the fringe as a place of "policy disintegration," calling it "a 'messy' yet opportunistic space in policy and decision-making processes, [that] remains confused and 'disintegrated,' lacking sufficient understanding and explicit attention for sustainable management as [a] place in [its] own right."[30]

The Developer's Greenbelt
Given the intense pressures at the fringe and the emergence of polycentrism, it is not surprising that the realization of conventional retrofits for greenbelts is drastically different than the original designs. One classic example is Metropolitan London's greenbelt, the world's first modern greenbelt. As its critics contend, its strict use as a containment tool renders it unresponsive to dynamic urbanization and expansion processes, including changing economic conditions, demographic fluctuations, development pressures, and other human and ecological adaptations.[31] The result is that

and Post-Suburban Transformation in Jakarta Metropolitan Region," *Cities* 29, no. 1 (February 2012): 40–48.

22 Alan M. Berger et al., "Where Americans Live: An Environmental and Geographical Tally," *Harvard Journal of Real Estate—Navigating Investments with Ethical Risk* (June 2013): 39–50. Future estimate is based on my own research projections using US Census data. Using current polycentric conditions across the United States, developed land consumes about 3.9 percent of total US land in 2015, including transportation and urban areas. Urban areas consume about 2.7 percent of total US land. It would take until 2130 to develop the nonconservation land inventory of the Bureau of Land Management, if land develops in step with current population growth. It would take an additional 120 years, until 2250, to develop the nonconservation land inventory of the Bureau of Land Management plus 50 percent of all grazing lands, if population growth remained steady. Calculation assumes land transfers do not include lands conserved for recreation or wilderness and a developed land growth rate that equals the population growth rate of the United States, from Cynthia Nickerson et al., *Major Uses of Land in the United States, 2007*, EIB-89, US Department of Agriculture, Economic Research Service, December 2011, accessed December 2, 2015, www.ers.usda.gov /publications/eib89.

23 Bibiana Catalan, David Sauri, and Pere Serra, "Urban Sprawl in the Mediterranean? Patterns of Growth and Change in the Barcelona Metropolitan Region 1993–2000," *Landscape and Urban Planning* 85, nos. 3–4 (April 30, 2008): 176, 181–82.

24 Julio Dávila, "Falling between Stools? Policies,

London's greenbelt has morphed from an agrarian concept to a landscape sink for multiple urban functions far from the original idea: public utilities, reservoirs, gravel pits, and transportation infrastructure.[32]

Attempting to balance development pressures with greenbelt preservation demands, local authorities around the area have used different interpretations of greenbelt regulations to allow additional development around built-up areas. Namely, when greenbelt land has been taken for development, land was added to the greenbelt elsewhere to compensate. Thus, the total amount of greenbelt land remained the same, setting the precedent for land as interchangeable and rendering London's greenbelt as a landscape constantly shifting to give way to development pressures and land conversions.[33]

There is currently a strong debate over the future of the greenbelt in Britain. The planner and housing specialist Nick Gallent suggests this debate is closely bound up with a larger dialogue about urban growth and its potential movement into the countryside.[34] The government has identified a need for three million new homes as a result of both population growth and reduction in average household size, with much of the need concentrated in southeast England. Importantly, infill will not be sufficient to meet this demand.[35] In 2008 the British government approved the largest redrawing of greenbelt boundaries in decades, allowing potential development to meet government housing and construction targets.[36] Astonishingly, in a recent economics competition to rethink England's garden cities, the highly coveted Wolfson Prize was awarded to a proposal to add hundreds of thousands of new homes in London's greenbelt areas, based on a platform that argued greenbelt towns should have new development imposed on them![37]

Since World War II, many cities worldwide have been retrofitting their greenbelts. Tokyo and Sydney established greenbelts after the war, but recently eliminated them because of strong population growth and resistance from landowners wanting to exercise their development rights.[38] In India, the Bangalore Development Authority's 2015 master plan revision includes opening up parts of its greenbelt for industrial development, even as continual ad hoc shrinkage of the greenbelt has been registered over the past decade.[39] In Hong Kong, the government has struggled to preserve land inside a greenbelt that functions more as a land bank than as a conservation area.[40]

In South Korea, Seoul's greenbelt (modeled in 1971 after London's) doubly served conservation purposes and security buffering from North Korea. It has expanded four times since its inception and has eroded only moderately as upward pressure on land and housing prices forced the release of marginal land for development. Seoul's greenbelt, however, also serves as an example of tremendous social inequity, as land is simply taken from owners without any reciprocity for lost development rights.[41] The greenbelt was established by a dictatorship, and landowners were not compensated for their loss of development rights. As a result, landowners seeking compensation have been the primary drivers of greenbelt reform.[42]

In post-perestroika Moscow, fringe dynamics have put the greenbelt under increasing pressure. From 1996 to 2006 it lost about 11 percent of greenbelt forests to housing (seasonal dachas and permanent suburban homes, many in gated communities); vegetable gardens; transport infrastructure (roads, parking lots); retail establishments (big box stores and strip malls); and postsocialist industry (food processing and printing plants,

Strategies, and the Peri-Urban Interface," in *The Peri-Urban Interface: Approaches to Sustainable Natural and Human Resource Use*, ed. Duncan McGregor, David Simon, and Donald Thompson (New York: Earthscan, 2006), 44–56.

25 Manfred Kühn, "Greenbelt and Green Heart: Separating and Integrating Landscapes in European City Regions," *Landscape and Urban Planning* 64 (2003): 25–26.

26 Meinhard Breiling and Gisa Ruland, "The Vienna Green Belt: From Localised Protection to a Regional Concept," in *Urban Green Belts in the Twenty-First Century*, ed. Marco Amati (Burlington, VT: Ashgate, 2008), 181.

27 Ibid., 167.

28 Allen, "Environmental Planning and Management of the Peri-Urban Interface," 138.

29 Ibid., 135–38.

30 Scott et al., "Disintegrated Development at the Rural-Urban Fringe," 1.

31 Robert L. Gant, Guy M. Robinson, and Shahab Fazal, "Land-Use Change in the 'Edgelands': Policies and Pressures in London's Rural-Urban Fringe," *Land Use Policy* 28, no. 1 (2011): 266–79.

32 Ibid., 272.

33 Ibid., 267; Marco Amati and Makoto Yokohari, "The Establishment of the London Greenbelt: Reaching Consensus over Purchasing Land," *Journal of Planning History* 6, no. 4 (November 2007): 311–37.

34 Nick Gallent, "The Rural-Urban Fringe: A New Priority for Planning Policy?," *Planning Practice & Research* 21, no. 3 (August 2006): 383–93.

35 Simon, "Urban Environments: Issues on the Peri-Urban Fringe," 167–85.

36 Gant, Robinson, and Fazal, "Land-Use Change in the 'Edgelands,'" 276.

37 Robert Booth, "Prize-Winning Designer Says Double Size of

4.7.9 Wellington, Florida, edge next to the Everglades Wildlife Management Area. Stormwater retention and treatment areas are engineered for precise control.

4.7.10 Seagate Technologies in Longmont, Colorado. Many industries do not rely on centrality in the new tech economy.

furniture factories, gravel pits, concrete mixing plants, and landfills). The greenbelt has become increasingly fragmented, experiencing a net conversion rate of 14.6 percent between 1991 and 2001.[43] In 2005 the Ministry of Economic Development released a draft of the Forest Code that would effectively eliminate the protected designation of forests in the greenbelt.[44]

The Not-So-Smart Greenbelt

When greenbelts are not designed with the intelligence and flexibility to adequately manage fringe dynamics, they inevitably provoke significant unintended consequences. For example, when greenbelt restrictions are too tight, development leapfrogs to areas directly beyond the restrictions, thus reversing the effects of containment. Land speculation follows this same trajectory when supply is inelastic—constrained—inside the urban core.[45] Greenbelts in London, Seoul, and Boulder, Colorado, have seen widespread leapfrog expansion just outside their greenbelt perimeters. Nonetheless, planners and designers continue to uncritically adopt greenbelts as antisprawl tools.[46] Ironically, planners' rational intentions for greenbelts—to reduce the effects of land speculation, horizontal spreading, unchecked growth, and long commutes—often produce worse outcomes, as leapfrog development relocates development well beyond the belt's borders. Critics of the use of greenbelts to contain suburban expansion say that by reducing the supply of developable land, the greenbelt creates economic and social havoc within constrained urban areas inside the greenbelt and particularly promotes crises in housing affordability.

The criticism has some truth to it. In the United States, one of the best examples of the negative effects of greenbelts on housing affordability is Boulder, which initiated the Boulder Valley Service Area in 1977 as a growth control zone to contain urban development and preserve rural edges. The growth controls did slow expansion, but they also caused an affordability crisis for people in Boulder. Today, Boulder's median home price is $480,000; downtown it is a whopping $700,000. In contrast, nearby Denver's median home price is about $270,000. As a result, 66 percent of Boulder employees live outside Boulder and must commute (mostly by car).[47] The same result can be seen elsewhere. Scholars found that if Seoul had the flexibility to release more greenbelt land, housing prices and congestion would significantly decrease across the whole metropolitan area.[48] Without intelligent flexibility, the greenbelt loses its efficiency as a policy tool.[49]

As the United States and other locations have recently experienced, housing affordability brings a diverse mixture of people to the suburban fringe. The entry of new ethnicities, incomes, backgrounds, and experiences will be changing old urban and rural dichotomies.[50] New spatial patterns (dispersion, decentralization, and polycentrism with multiple nodes of higher density) are increasingly prevalent in global economies in both industrial and service-based contexts, as opposed to historical concentric urban patterns built from local and regional strengths. (fig. **4.7.10**) Furthermore, critical new environmental concerns about climate change adaptation/mitigation, and about ecosystem services, have intensified over the past decades.

As London, the world's first greenbelt system, reveals, a lack of spatial and programmatic flexibility combined with urban growth pressures is leading to drastic changes in greenbelt policy and use. Early greenbelts were intended to control urban growth, prevent cities from merging into each other, and keep urban and rural environments distinct, but they absorbed other functions over time to justify their continued existence.[51] The unsettled

Forty English Towns," *Guardian*, September 3, 2014, accessed July 17, 2015, http://www .theguardian.com/ society/2014/sep/ 03/wolfson-winner- green-belt-development.

38 Amati and Yokohari, "The Establishment of the London Greenbelt," 311–37.

39 Harini Nagendra, Suparsh Nagendran, Somajita Paul, and Sajid Pareeth, "Graying, Greening, and Fragmentation in the Rapidly Expanding Indian City of Bangalore," *Landscape and Urban Planning* 105, no. 4 (April 30, 2012): 400–406.

40 Bo-sin Tang, Siu-wai Wong, and Anton King- wah Lee, "Green Belt in a Compact City: A Zone for Conservation or Transition?," *Landscape and Urban Planning* 79, nos. 3–4 (March 2, 2007): 358–73.

41 Chang-Moo Lee, "An Intertemporal Efficiency Test of a Greenbelt: Assessing the Economic Impacts of Seoul's Greenbelt," *Journal of Planning Education and Research* 19, no. 1 (1999): 41–52; Chang-Hee Christine Bae, "Korea's Greenbelts: Impacts and Options for Change," *Pacific Rim Law & Policy Journal* 7, no. 3 (1998): 479–502.

42 David N. Bengston and Youn Yeo-Chang, "Seoul's Greenbelt: An Experiment in Urban Containment," in *Policies for Managing Urban Growth and Landscape Change: A Key to Conservation in the Twenty-First Century*, ed. David N. Bengston (St. Paul, MN: Department of Agriculture, Forest Service, North Central Research Station, 2005).

43 Mason and Nigmatullina, "Suburbanization and Sustainability in the Metropolitan Moscow," 316–33.

44 Mikhail Blinnikov et al., "Gated Communities of the Moscow Green Belt: Newly Segregated Landscapes and the Suburban Russian

relationship between the concepts of greenbelt and green infrastructure, and the functions that each are programmed to perform, is evidence of this.[52]

Innovative Approaches to Belting

There are many examples of the integration of green infrastructure and the original greenbelt idea. Within Belgium, the Brussels Capital Region is trying to create a "blue and green network" to embed biodiversity into as many infrastructural and landscape systems as possible.[53] Hamburg, Germany, also has a "green network" of variably scaled green rings at different distances from the city center that allows people and wildlife to recreate and circulate easily.[54] Portland, Oregon's Environmental Services Department launched the "Grey to Green" initiative in 2008 and invested $55 million to "help manage stormwater runoff more naturally, control invasive plants, restore native vegetation, protect sensitive natural areas, and restore Portland's streams."[55] London is now trying to implement a "Green Grid" and "Blue Ribbon" network as part of its efforts to create green infrastructure.[56] The Chicago Wilderness program formed in April 1996 as an effort to use restoration ecology in the Chicago region to conserve biodiversity and promote ecological health.[57] Chicago Wilderness activities led to the creation of the Green Infrastructure Vision to identify opportunities to support biodiversity and provide habitat through green infrastructure.[58] These are just a few ways in which regional authorities, metropolitan agencies, cities, and municipalities are retrofitting greenbelt concepts and trying to increase the infrastructural capacities of landscape as new growth and increased costs for environmental services mount.

Those innovations, and others around the world, came about because the theoretical idea of the greenbelt has

Environment," *GeoJournal* 66, nos. 1–2 (2006): 65–81.

45 Stephen Malpezzi and Susan M. Wachter, "The Role of Speculation in Real Estate Cycles," *Journal of Real Estate Literature* 13, no. 2 (July 2005): 143–64, accessed December 11, 2015, http://libproxy.mit.edu/login?url=http://search.ebscohost.com/login.aspx?direct=true&db=bth&AN=17560639&site=eds-live.

46 Robert Bruegmann, "Urban Sprawl," in *International Encyclopedia of the Social & Behavioral Sciences*, 2nd ed., ed. James D. Wright (Oxford: Elsevier, 2015), 934–39.

47 Peter Pollack, "Controlling Sprawl in Boulder: Benefits and Pitfalls," *Land Lines* 10, no. 1 (1998), accessed December 11, 2015, http://www.lincolninst.edu/pubs/435_Controlling-Sprawl-in-Boulder---Benefits-and-Pitfalls; Joseph N. de Raismes III et al., "Growth Management in Boulder, Colorado: A Case Study" (unpublished policy paper from Boulder City Attorney's Office), accessed December 11, 2015, http://www.bouldercolorado.gov/files/City%20Attorney/Documents/Miscellaneous%20Docs%20of%20Interest/x-bgmcs1.jbn.pdf; Katherine J. Jackson, "The Need for Regional Management of Growth: Boulder, Colorado, as a Case Study," *Urban Lawyer* 37, no. 2 (2005): 299–322.

48 Myung-Jin Jun, "The Effects of Seoul's Greenbelt on the Spatial Distribution of Population and Employment, and on the Real Estate Market," *Annals of Regional Science* 49, no. 3 (December 2012): 619–42; Casey J. Dawkins and Arthur C. Nelson, "Urban Containment Policies and Housing Prices: An International Comparison with Implications for Future

Research," *Land Use Policy* 19 (2002): 6–7.

49 Chang-Moo Lee and Peter Linneman, "Dynamics of the Greenbelt Amenity Effect on the Land Market—the Case of Seoul's Greenbelt," *Real Estate Economics* 26, no. 1 (March 1, 1998): 107–29; Lee, "An Intertemporal Efficiency Test of a Greenbelt," 41–52.

50 Michael Gregory Lloyd and Deborah Peel, "Green Belts in Scotland: Toward the Modernisation of a Traditional Concept?," *Journal of Environmental Planning and Management* 50, no. 5 (2007): 639–56; Joel Kotkin, *The Next 100 Million: America in 2050* (New York: Penguin Press, 2010).

51 Kühn, "Greenbelt and Green Heart," 19–27; Marco Amati and Makoto Yokohari, "Temporal Changes and Local Variations in the Functions of London's Green Belt," *Landscape and Urban Planning* 75 (2006): 138; Tang, Wong, and Lee, "Green Belt in a Compact City," 364.

52 Michael Hough, "Nature as Infrastructure: Strategies for Sustainable Regional Landscapes," *Places—a Forum of Environmental Design* 19, no. 1 (Spring 2007): 54–58; Wenping Liu, Jirko Holst, and Zhenrong Yu, "Thresholds of Landscape Change: A New Tool to Manage Green Infrastructure and Social-Economic Development," *Landscape Ecology* 29, no. 4 (April 2014): 729–43; Pierre Bélanger, "Landscape as Infrastructure," *Landscape Journal* 28, no. 1 (March 2009): 79–95; Margaret Bryant, "Urban Landscape Conservation and the Role of Ecological Greenways at Local and Metropolitan Scales," *Landscape and Urban Planning* 76, nos. 1–4 (April 30, 2006): 23–44.

53 Belgian National Focal Point to the Convention on Biological Diversity,

ed., "Biodiversity 2020, Update of Belgium's National Biodiversity Strategy" (Brussels: Royal Belgian Institute of Natural Sciences, 2013): 29, accessed December 11, 2015, https://www.cbd.int/doc/world/be/be-nbsap-v2-en.pdf.

54 "Hamburg—European Green Capital 2011," accessed August 17, 2014, http://ec.europa.eu/environment/europeangreencapital/wp-content/uploads/2011/04/Doku-Umwelthauptstadt-engl-web.pdf.

55 "City of Portland's Grey to Green Program: Grey to Green Accomplishments," *The City of Portland, Oregon, Environmental Services*, accessed August 17, 2014, http://www.portlandoregon.gov/bes/article/321331.

56 "The London Plan—Blue Ribbon Network," City of London, accessed August 17, 2014, https://www.london.gov.uk/what-we-do/planning/london-plan/current-london-plan/london-plan-chapter-7/blue-ribbon-network-0.

57 "Chicago Wilderness and Its Biodiversity Recovery Plan," *Chicago Wilderness*, accessed August 17, 2014, http://c.ymcdn.com/sites/www.chicagowilderness.org/resource/resmgr/Publications/biodiversity_recovery_plan.pdf.

58 Dennis Dreher, "Chicago Wilderness Green Infrastructure Vision: Challenges and Opportunities for the Built Environment," *Journal of Green Building* 4, no. 3 (Summer 2009): 72–88.

not optimally performed in practice, generating costs and negative social consequences. As greenbelts erode under the pressures of urbanization and the rapid transformation of the suburban fringe, antiquated conceptions of them as "containment vessels" for urban expansion, "aesthetic voids" to preserve rural landscape qualities, or "ecological tools" to separate people and nature are in dire need of revision and "reimagination." (figs. **4.7.11–12**) Moreover, the demographic, economic, and environmental contexts of rapidly growing metropolitan regions have changed. Major new forces at the suburban fringe include neoliberalism (trade liberalization), and globalization. Economic restructuring—the rise of consumption, service, and/or leisure economies; manufacturing decentralization; and farming consolidation and intensification—also are playing a role. To those changes, add political decentralization, improved transportation and communication technologies that enable greater mobility and dispersion, environmentalism and the emergence of the international development industry.[59] (figs. **4.7.13–14**)

As the geographer John Herrington asserts, "Green Belts have become an outmoded and irrelevant mechanism for handling the complexity of future change in the city's countryside." The greenbelt must go beyond containment—growth control—to provide real recreation and tourism opportunities, ecological biodiversity, infrastructural systems such as waste and water management, productive agriculture and forestry, and economic place competitiveness and development activities.[60]

New concepts of belting at the suburban fringe, where intense growth pressures collide with environmental services, can change the balance of metropolitan scale sustainability. The unique fringe location and the rapid rate of

conversion that is already in effect there, together with the environmental degradation accumulating at the urbanizing edges of metro areas, is a generational design challenge that opens up unlimited opportunities for greenbelts. Greenbelts could provide fringe areas with new infrastructural projects and with open space. They could lower land prices, which in turn could support new multifunctional development.[61] In an embrace of polycentrism, greenbelts could also increasingly connect to each other within a region, revealing a dynamic zone of new, fluid landscape opportunities in ways that completely avoid the bureaucratic trappings of the core city.

Process-Based Ways to Belt the Suburban Fringe

How do we reconceive the greenbelt? Unfortunately, the planning field currently lacks a deep reservoir of methods and tools for regulating and managing dynamic, evolutionary landscape processes such as those found at the suburban fringe. Nonetheless, some scholars have theorized ways in which the fringe can have its own unique, open-ended process-based form. The resilience researcher Johan Colding has suggested that suburbs begin to use what he calls "ecological land use complementation" to better support ecosystem services.[62] This concept clusters different types of green patches together to improve connectivity, taking habitat size and heterogeneity into consideration by establishing buffers to mitigate the negative effects of proximity and to provide refuge for species in habitat reserves during times of stress.

The geographer Jeremy Whitehand has elucidated the concept of fringe belts at the edges of metropolitan areas, with objects and stasis as the primary drivers of urban form: "The fringe belt concept embraces two major categories of processes: first, the structuring of urban

59 Cecilia Tacoli, "Rural-Urban Interactions: A Guide to the Literature," *Environment & Urbanization* 10, no. 1 (April 1998): 147–65.

60 Herington, *Beyond Greenbelts: Managing Urban Growth in the Twenty-First Century*, 51–53.

61 Ward S. Rauws and Gert de Roo, "Exploring Transitions in the Peri-Urban Area," *Planning Theory & Practice* 12, no. 2 (June 2011): 269–84.

62 Johan Colding, "'Ecological Land-Use Complementation' for Building Resilience in Urban Ecosystems," *Landscape and Urban Planning* 81, nos. 1–2 (May 29, 2007): 46–55.

4.7.11 Soledad, California, urbanization at the edge of Estancia Estates Winery grape fields

4.7.12 Edge of Oildale, 3.5 miles (5.6 km) north of Bakersfield in Kern County, California, adjacent to Kern River Oil Field

4.7.13 Golf Club at La Quinta, south of Palm Springs, California

4.7.14 Mission Viejo, California, in Orange County

growth and the urban area in terms of alternating zones of residential accretion and fringe belts; and, second, subsequent processes of change."[63] Others have emphasized the theoretical dimensions of fringe development. The planners Ward Rauws and Gert de Roo describe complex, nonlinear processes of change in effect at the fringe. For this reason, they suggest that planners need to plan, but at the same time to also be adaptive.[64]

The landscape architect and urbanist James Corner also stresses the importance of ecological and urban processes, arguing, "The processes of urbanization—capital accumulation, deregulation, globalization, environmental protection, and so on…are much more significant for the shaping of urban relationships than are the spatial forms of urbanism in and of themselves."[65] From this perspective, form is not irrelevant, but it is also not sufficient to understand urban systems. He recommends a paradigm shift from conceiving of objects to conceiving of systems, encompassing a broad range of actors, forces, exchanges, and activities.[66] Corner suggests that ecology can play a critical role in this, writing, "in conceptualizing a more organic, fluid urbanism, ecology itself becomes an extremely useful lens," because of its focus on dynamism, interconnectedness, inclusivity/continuity, and complexity.[67]

The role of ecology in planning and design should become a fundamental priority in making decisions about land-use conversion and metropolitan sustainability, particularly as suburbia expands and the fringe is transformed.[68] This can be approached from many analytical and conceptual perspectives, from ecological economics to urban metabolism to landscape urbanism. But what these movements all have in common—and, unfortunately, have working against them—is the lack of a process-based discourse that can be adopted by institutional

decision makers. As the fledgling fields of landscape urbanism and so-called ecological urbanism have shown, process-driven design remains isolated from academic discussion.[69]

To move such a discourse into the real world of practice will require a paradigmatic shift of the way we teach and practice planning and design. Such a shift must borrow more from (dynamic) target-based environmental standards than from (static) zoning and planning codification protocols that are already deeply entrenched in governing structures, and uncritically regurgitated by academic institutions and biased groups alike.[70] In his research, the landscape ecologist Sybrand Tjallingii identifies two ecological discourses about nature that structure notions of fringe landscapes: "nature as object" and "nature as process," the former being deeply rooted in current planning practice, and the latter having promising prospects but weak institutional traction.[71]

Some designers and planners are making a concentrated effort to bring process-based ecological forms and performance measurement to the forefront of decision making. The landscape architect and planner Joan Nassauer has argued that we need to build new, innovative, ecological processes into forms that we already live with and recognize: "In the everyday landscape, rather than simply designing to enhance ecological quality or even to express ecological function as form, we must design *to frame ecological function within a recognizable system of form*."[72]

If greenbelts are to evolve they must have a new purpose. Over the past four decades, the suburban fringe has increasingly transformed from the locus of rural poverty to the burgeoning crest of middle class expansion. (figs. **4.7.15**–**18**) New, wealthier residents at the fringe are demanding more accountability for

63 Jeremy W. R. Whitehand and Nick J. Morton, "Fringe Belts and the Recycling of Urban Land: An Academic Concept and Planning Practice," *Environment and Planning B: Planning and Design* 30, no. 6 (2003): 820; Jeremy W. R. Whitehand, "Fringe Belts: A Neglected Aspect of Urban Geography," *Transactions of the Institute of British Geographers* 41 (1967): 223–33.

64 Rauws and de Roo, "Exploring Transitions in the Peri-Urban Area," 272, 280.

65 James Corner, "Terra Fluxus," in *The Landscape Urbanism Reader*, ed. Charles Waldheim (New York: Princeton Architectural Press, 2006), 28.

66 Alan Berger, *Systemic Design© Can Change the World* (Netherlands: SUN Architecture, 2009).

67 Corner, "Terra Fluxus," 29.

68 Alexander J. Felson, Steward T. A. Pickett, "Designed Experiments: New Approaches to Studying Urban Ecosystems," *Frontiers in Ecology and the Environment* 10 (2005): 549–56.

69 Sybrand P. Tjallingii, "Ecology on the Edge: Landscape and Ecology between Town and Country," *Landscape and Urban Planning* 48, nos. 3–4 (May 1, 2000): 104; Charles Waldheim, "Landscape as Urbanism," in *The Landscape Urbanism Reader*, ed. Charles Waldheim (New York: Princeton Architectural Press, 2006) 35–54; Richard Weller, "Landscape (Sub) Urbanism in Theory and Practice," in *Landscape Journal* 27 (2008): 2–8; Chris Reed, "The Agency of Ecology," in *Ecological Urbanism*, ed. Moshen Mostafavi and Gareth Doherty (Zurich: Lars Muller Publishers and Harvard Graduate School of Design, 2010), 324–29; Robert Costanza et al., "The Value of the World's

protection of natural resources and protection from environmental risks through sustainable planning and design practices.[73] An enormous opportunity has emerged in landscape innovation for these new constituents, with the role of planners and designers to orchestrate the larger systems of productive ecology, innovative sustainable technologies, and experimental suburban belting typologies.

There is a growing chorus of urbanists suggesting that cities move toward sustainability by actually supporting horizontal growth and polycentrism, all the while integrating resource exchanges between urban cores and their functional suburbs and hinterlands through systemic ecological thinking.[74] The landscape ecologist Sarah Taylor Lovell even suggests that instead of just focusing on preserving and restoring small, high-quality patches and connecting corridors, planners' designs should incorporate heterogeneity, as a way to improve the quality of the overall matrix in agricultural and urban landscapes. This heterogeneity can be achieved with multifunctional landscape features that improve ecosystem function, such as vegetative buffers, natural and constructed wetlands, edible gardens, stormwater infiltration systems, and waste treatment systems.[75]

Today's suburban fringe, where metabolic urban-suburban exchanges are their greatest, is dynamically changing. Its social and environmental issues, along with its economic growth zones, have become high priorities for metropolitan areas. But for planners and designers to have agency in imagining the future of the suburban fringe, they must be prepared to engage with much more than just physical form. The anemic greenbelt typology, used ineffectually to control the fringe, can be reimagined to combine the potentials of ecology, infrastructure, and landscape.

Suburban areas can perform many of the environmental services that expanding urban metro areas need, but only if both existing form-based codes and zoning that privileges the building of objects over designing for dynamic ecological processes are diminished. Until the planning and design professions develop a process-based discourse for institutional use, the potential of the fringe as a major contributor to overall metropolitan environmental services and its other landscape opportunities will remain unfulfilled.

If, on the other hand, the greenbelt were to be opened to new interpretations, it could house full metabolic exchanges that balance the entire metropolitan resource demands, resulting in truly sustainable urban conditions.[76] Beyond formal machinations and design rhetoric, this should be one of the central ambitions of urbanism itself.

The "Wastebelt" Vision

Waste in myriad forms—solid, liquid, surface, and so forth—should be the foundation for a new kind of belting mechanism on the suburban fringe: the "wastebelt." As the base for the construction of this process-based discourse, the wastebelt is where regional-scale resource management and visionary representational models begin. These models can capture the imagination of policy makers and citizens who may see the suburban edge only as a place for singular uses, speculation, and low value.

Wherever humans exist, waste exists. This is especially true in metropolitan areas where waste is concentrated by increased population density and consumption. The fringes of metro areas have historically been considered the locations of accumulated waste disposal from the city itself.[77] Perhaps the best example of waste at the fringe emerged in Victorian society. Starting in the mid-eighteenth

Ecosystem Services and Natural Capital," *Nature* 387 (1997): 253–60; Judith Layzer, *Natural Experiments: Ecosystem-Based Management and the Environment* (Cambridge, MA: MIT Press, 2008), 103–36.

70 See Congress for New Urbanism's highly self-referential *Form-Based Code Institute* at http://formbasedcodes .org/organizations.

71 Tjallingii, "Ecology on the Edge," 103–19.

72 Joan Nassauer and Paul Opdam, "Design in Science: Extending the Landscape Ecology Paradigm," *Landscape Ecology* 23, no. 6 (July 2008): 633–44; Joan Nassauer, "The Appearance of Ecological-Systems as a Matter of Policy," *Landscape Ecology* 6, no. 4 (March 1992): 239–50; Joan Nassauer, "Messy Ecosystems, Orderly Frames," *Landscape Journal* 14, no. 2 (1995): 162.

73 Lloyd and Peel, "Green Belts in Scotland," 641–42.

74 André Botequilha-Leitão, "Eco-Polycentric Urban Systems: An Ecological Region Perspective for Network Cities," *Challenges* 3, no. 1 (June 2012): 1–42; Richard T. T. Forman and Michel Godron, *Landscape Ecology* (New York: John Wiley & Sons, 1986); Berger, *Systemic Design© Can Change the World*; Zev Naveh, "What Is Holistic Landscape Ecology? A Conceptual Introduction," *Landscape and Urban Planning* 50 (2000): 7–26; Steward T. A. Pickett and Mary L. Cadenasso, "Linking Ecological and Built Components of Urban Mosaics: An Open Cycle of Ecological Design," *Journal of Ecology* 96, no. 1 (2008): 8–12; Mark J. McDonnell and Steward T. Pickett, "Ecosystem Structure and Function along Urban-Rural Gradients: An Unexploited Opportunity for Ecology," *Ecology* 71, no. 4 (1990): 1232–37; Michael I. W.

4.7.15 Southern leading edge of Lincoln, Nebraska

4.7.16 Southern edge of Papillion, Nebraska, on the southern edge of the Omaha metropolitan area

4.7.17 Southern Oaks neighborhood on southeast edge of Bakersfield, California

4.7.18 Broward County, Florida, new planned unit developments surrounded by agricultural reserve land

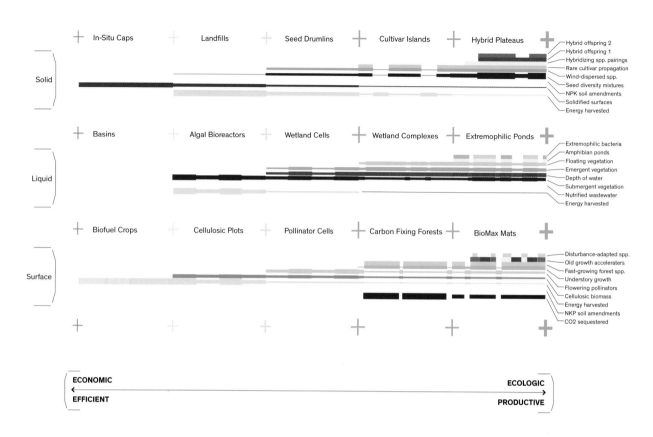

4.7.19 Wastebelts optimization gradients, the waste matrix

century, the United Kingdom's major cities, including London, Manchester, Liverpool, and Glasgow, rapidly urbanized as a result of massive population growth. The population surge, combined with inadequate infrastructure, economic inequity, and industrial pollution, produced a housing shortage and unsanitary conditions, especially in relation to improper sewage treatment. The Sanitary Movement of the 1840s and 1850s included a new, strongly hostile attitude toward urban waste.[78] Initially, the Victorians focused on just getting waste out of the city—dumping it on the fringe or into the sea, rather than on effectively treating it. But sanitary mapping and health-related statistical improvements led to modern sewage infrastructures that reinforced the city's outer edges as a waste dumping ground.

In the United States, colonial towns dumped solid waste at their outskirts and fluid waste into rivers that flowed outward. In the 1850s, cities started to designate specific outer areas for disposal. There was no organized waste disposal system until the mid-nineteenth century, when urbanization generated significant new volumes of waste. The landscape architect Mira Engler contends, "In the first few decades of the twentieth century, American cities' automated, centralized sanitation networks were pushed outside city limits, screened, or buried beneath the streets."[79] Boston dumped its waste on Columbia Point; New York discarded its trash into the ocean; Chicago used Lake Michigan.[80] Moreover, Chicago built a great deal of new land from waste, with refuse used to reclaim property and expand the amount of usable terrain, either by establishing a dry base on marshland or by filling quarries and clay pits on the fringe.[81] New York City has had a waste crisis since the 1960s. By the early 1990s, it had been forced to shut down ten

Hopkins, "The Ecological Significance of Urban Fringe Belts," *Urban Morphology* 16, no. 1 (2012): 41–54; Kevin Thomas and Steve Littlewood, "From Green Belts to Green Infrastructure? The Evolution of a New Concept in the Emerging Soft Governance of Spatial Strategies," *Planning, Practice & Research* 25, no. 2 (2010): 203–22; Simon, "Urban Environments," 170.

75 Sarah T. Lovell and Douglas M. Johnston, "Designing Landscapes for Performance Based on Emerging Principles in Landscape Ecology," *Ecology and Society* 14, no. 1 (2009): 44; see also Richard T. T. Forman, "Basic Principles for Molding Land Mosaics," in *Urban Regions* (Cambridge: Cambridge University Press, 2008), 223–42.

76 Susannah Hagan, "Metabolic Suburbs, or the Virtue of Low

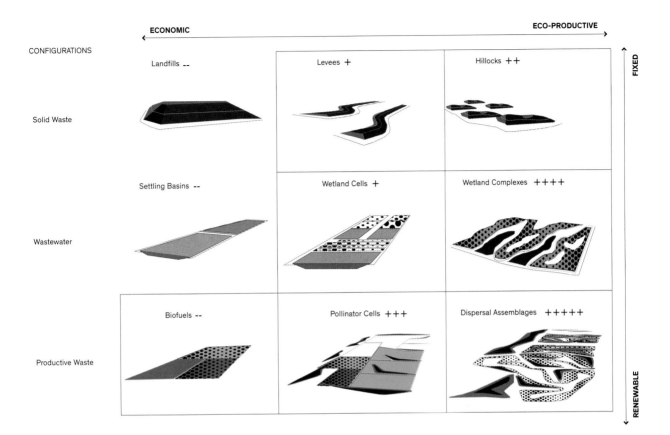

ECONOMIC ⟶ ECO-PRODUCTIVE

FIXED

RENEWABLE

CONFIGURATIONS

Solid Waste

Landfills −−   Levees +   Hillocks ++

Wastewater

Settling Basins −−   Wetland Cells +   Wetland Complexes ++++

Productive Waste

Biofuels −−   Pollinator Cells +++   Dispersal Assemblages +++++

4.7.20 Wastebelts modular plug-ins

out of eleven incinerators and six landfills. In 2001 it closed Fresh Kills on Staten Island, the world's largest disposal facility. According to the landscape architect Pierre Bélanger, New York City's experience shows that society "[can] no longer deal with the magnitude and complexity of urban waste streams in big cities." He has argued that society must cope with waste by developing new strategies that offer less centralized and more diversified systems of materials recovery.[82]

The examples that follow show how wastebelts could function, beginning with a "waste matrix" that visualizes a way to optimize trade-offs between economic and ecologic potentials of the wastebelt concept. The matrix could be accompanied by modular plug-ins, representing potential configurations of form and program on the basis of matrix decisions. New belting strategies for wastewater, energy, and "drosscape" are represented, using the matrix to guide optimization and landscape programming potential.[83]

The Waste Matrix

When creating new types of wastebelts, trade-offs between economic and ecological benefits to a region must be considered. By distributing various design options across a gradient from the economical to the ecological, planners and designers could better communicate the trade-offs to their stakeholders, hopefully leading to more optimal mix of outcomes. The waste matrix represents a menu of solid, liquid, or surface treatments that contain or treat forms of urban waste. (fig. **4.7.19**) For example, landfills generally contain energy resources such as off-gassing methane (created from the organic liquids and entombed solids). The same landfills could also contain energy infrastructure such as solar or wind farms. In addition, they have surfaces

Densities," *Architectural Research Quarterly* 16 (2012): 9–13.

77 Lloyd and Peel, "Green Belts in Scotland," 641–42.

78 Michelle Elizabeth Allen, *Cleansing the City: Sanitary Geographies in Victorian London* (Athens: Ohio University Press, 2008).

79 Mira Engler, "Waste Landscapes: Permissible Metaphors in Landscape Architecture," *Landscape Journal* 14, no. 1 (1995): 24; Mira Engler, *Designing America's Waste Landscapes* (Baltimore: Johns Hopkins University Press, 2004); Alan Berger, *Drosscape: Wasting Land in Urban America* (New York: Princeton Architectural Press, 2006).

80 Craig E. Colten, "Chicago's Waste Lands: Refuse Disposal and Urban Growth, 1840–1990," *Journal of Historical Geography* 20, no. 2 (April 1994): 124.

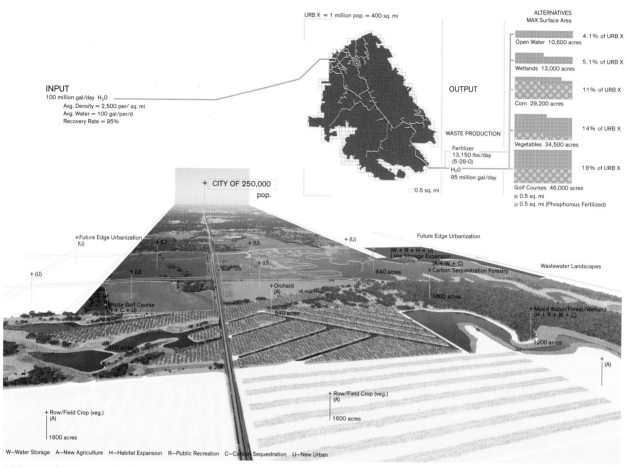

4.7.21 Wastewater-supported landscapes

that could be programmed for social and recreational activities. Stacking and mixing these uses could greatly amplify a site's productive outputs and efficiencies without sacrificing its ecological integrity or recreational benefits. The matrix offers an experimental view of waste landscape by agglomerating and hybridizing waste, ecological, and recreational programs.

Modular Plug-ins

There are many ways to treat and contain solid, liquid, and surface wastes. (fig. **4.7.20**) Endless new configurations can be imagined, linked, and layered in the new wastebelt system. Some formations are designed to be fixed and static (like landfills), while others evolve and mature (like vegetative colonies) as wastes are recovered and ecology flourishes. The total

amount and configuration of these modular components are dependent on the needs of the urban area and the amount of waste needing containment or treatment. Different plug-ins can be added over time as the metro area grows, depending on the waste output.

Wastewater-Supported Landscapes

In the areas between the advancing suburban fringe and the agricultural hinterlands, new wastebelts can be supported by the wastewater flows derived from the city population and from agricultural runoff.[84] (fig. **4.7.21**) As an example, consider a typical city with a population of 250,000, surrounded by areas used for agriculture. The resultant waste outputs support about 6,400 acres (about 2,590 hectares) of new landscapes of types.

81 Ibid.
82 Pierre Bélanger, "Landscapes of Disassembly," *Topos: The International Review of Landscape Architecture & Urban Design* 60 (2007): 83–91.
83 Berger, *Drosscape*.
84 Celina Balderas-Guzmán, "Strategies for Systemic Urban Constructed Wetlands" (master's thesis, MIT, 2013), accessed July 21, 2015, http://hdl.handle .net/1721.1/80907; Chandigarh Administration has launched initiative to recycle wastewater (treat effluent received from secondary treatment plants to tertiary levels, so it can be used to irrigate greenbelts): "Chandigarh Master Plan 2031," Chandigarh, accessed December 15, 2015, http://chandigarh .gov.in/cmp_2031.htm.

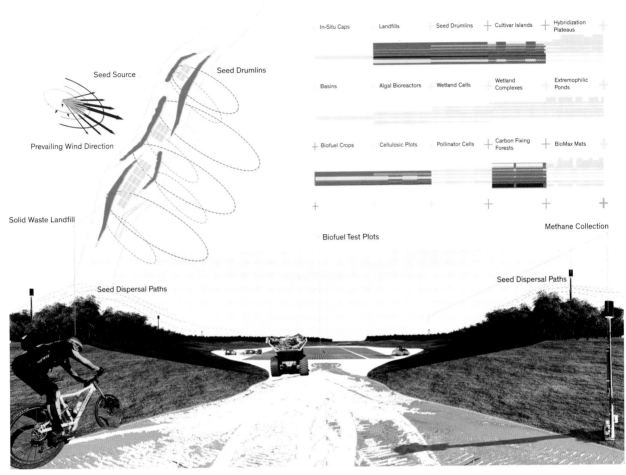

4.7.22 Wastebelts Energybelts

Lake water storage could be expanded, as a way to buffer irrigation needs and as a recreational amenity. These waters could feed wetlands and support both forestry (for carbon sequestration) and extra-capacity agriculture such as orchards or more row crops. Amenity-driven locations like golf courses, running trails, leisure parks, and aquatic centers could all benefit from their adjacency and coursing water features. These new productive zones, habitat zones, and recreational zones could intermix with the encroaching housing edge. Cleansing wetlands could buffer and improve even more runoff from the new development and/or new agricultural areas. In this scenario, these land uses are mixed and hybridized to extract maximum benefit from the waste outputs of city inhabitants

and the agricultural sector. The collectively produced positive feedback enhances the value and productivity of each landscape zone.

For an urban area of one million people, about 95 million gallons per day of wastewater (360 million liters per day) can be captured and treated for reuse. The wastewater generated from urban and agricultural uses would contain nitrates and phosphates that could be recycled and used as fertilizer. For example, golf courses require an average of 750,000 gallons per acre (7 million liters per hectare) for the support of turf grass (which makes up about 50 percent of total golf course area) and 65 pounds per acre (58 kilograms per hectare) of phosphate fertilizer. Given the wastes generated by the one-million-person city over the

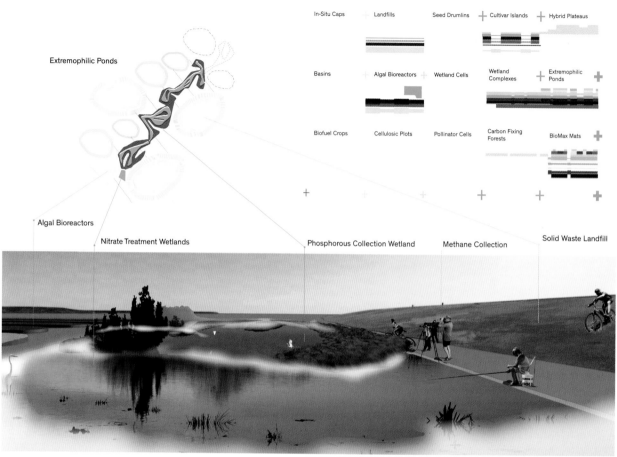

Extremophilic Ponds

In-Situ Caps   Landfills   Seed Drumlins   Cultivar Islands   Hybrid Plateaus

Basins   Algal Bioreactors   Wetland Cells   Wetland Complexes   Extremophilic Ponds

Biofuel Crops   Cellulosic Plots   Pollinator Cells   Carbon Fixing Forests   BioMax Mats

Algal Bioreactors

Nitrate Treatment Wetlands   Phosphorous Collection Wetland   Methane Collection   Solid Waste Landfill

4.7.23 Wastebelts Wetbelts

180-day growing period, 46,000 acres (about 18,600 hectares) of golf course could be irrigated with wastewater, with about half of it fertilized. That amounts to about 18 percent of the size of the hypothetical one-million-person city itself, which is a significant economic and ecological impact.[85]

Energybelts

This design concept illustrates a wastebelt configuration for maximizing energy production opportunities.[86] (fig. **4.7.22**) Landscape elements include "seed drumlins"—long, extruded hills that accommodate incoming waste while serving as dispersal pads for wind-dispersed vegetation species to populate the surrounding lands. When these seed drumlins are added to the tops of standard municipal landfills, the landscape is no longer one mono-functional cavity. With a large enough surface area, either cellulosic or oil-based biofuel crops would provide an additional biomass for energy revenues. Over time, the "energybelt" grows by accepting regional waste for landfill expansion, thus producing more methane and biofuel production areas for the energy needs of the growing population. The energybelt would become an attractor for tech energy experimentation and innovation. Trails are interwoven throughout the complex to provide unique recreational experiences.

Wetbelts

This design concept illustrates a wastebelt configuration for maximizing the potential of high rainfall regions. (fig. **4.7.23**) The wetbelt takes advantage of abundant stormwater to grow algae in bioreactor

85   Notes for wastewater nutrient recovery calculations: Ostara, a Canadian company, built technology that can turn 1 million residents' wastewater into 2,400 tons/yr of phosphorous and ammonia-rich fertilizer (5-28-0 + 10 percent Mg).

Open Water
95 percent recovery of used water for 1 million residents would yield, on average, 95 million gal/d
10,600 acre lake at average depth of 10 feet (drought protected)

Corn
9,000 gal/acre/d—peak, high-yield corn water use (can be reduced by 70 percent due to rain input)
390,000–1,080,000 gal/acre for 1 growing season (120 days)
95 percent wastewater

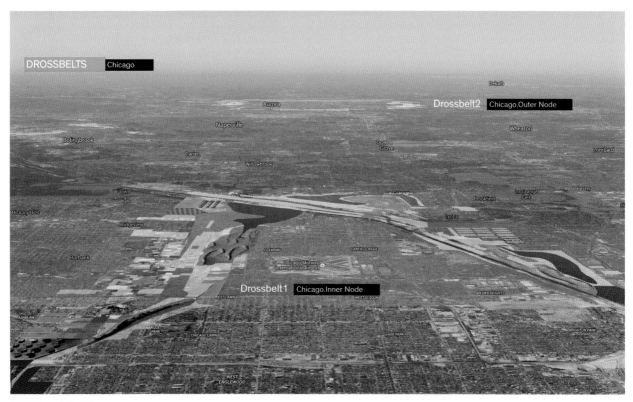

4.7.24 Drossbelts Chicago

ponds for biofuel production. It is designed to form complex islands that encourage microclimatic variation and ecological experimentation. As the habitat assemblages develop, targeted recreational access could be granted for particular types of fishing and birding, or for aquaculture. If the wetbelt has access to suburban or agricultural runoff, the nutrient-rich water could be mined for nitrogen and phosphorous. The collected nutrients could be repackaged as standard fertilizer or algae feed. Extreme conditions of polluted water could be tested for various cleanup methods utilizing extremophilic bacteria and algae. Novel landscape-based systems like these are needed to advance treatment technologies and reclamation methods for waste-affected lands.

Drossbelts
Wastebelts can also be aggregated within the deindustrialized urban fabric.[87] (fig. **4.7.24**) Many Rust Belt cities still contain large industrial parcels and polluted legacy sites. On the south side of Chicago, extensive abandoned tracts sit alongside railroad corridors and watercourses. The drosscape sites could be strung together and reprogrammed with new energy. The abundant space could also host the necessary landfills, staging areas, dirty soil processing sites, and seeding mounds necessary to rehabilitate the legacy sites and halt the potential pollution migration. Retention basins could capture runoff and serve as recreation zones and potential wetland filtering stations.[88] Utilizing city databases to locate abandoned or inactive sites, and then matching them with unmet economic and environmental needs, could provide a potent model for reinvigorating entire urban sectors. The system of sites may provide the space and environmental flexibility to reinvent land use in stagnating areas.

recovery could produce 29,200–10,600 acres of corn
140 lbs/acre for nitrate and 60 lbs/acre for phosphate
Phosphorous from wastewater nutrient recovery could fertilize 22,400 acres of corn

Vegetables
5,500–7,000 gal/acre/d—most vegetables and grain crops 330,000–840,000 gal/acre for 1 growing season (60–120 days)
95 percent wastewater recovery could produce 34,500–13,600 acres of vegetable crop
240 lbs/acre for nitrate and 170 lbs/acre for phosphate (averages for lettuce, USDA)
Phosphorous from wastewater nutrient recovery could fertilize 7,900 acres of vegetables

Wetland Habitat
Hydraulic loading rate of 7,000–70,000 gal/acre/d
95 percent recovery

Conclusion

The anemic greenbelt typology, used ineffectually for decades to control the fringe, can be reimagined to combine the potentials of ecology, infrastructure, and production in a new landscape ensemble. New concepts of belting at the suburban fringe, where intense growth pressures collide with environmental and ecosystem services, can change the balance of metropolitan scale sustainability. The unique fringe location and the rapid rate of conversion that is already in effect there present a generational design challenge that opens up unlimited opportunities for innovative greenbelt solutions.

There is a growing chorus of urbanists suggesting that cities move toward sustainability by actually supporting horizontal growth and polycentrism. As this is already naturally occurring, the role of ecology in planning and design needs to become a more fundamental priority in making decisions about land-use conversion and metropolitan sustainability, particularly as suburbia expands and the fringe is transformed. A process-based discourse needs to be articulated and adopted by institutional decision makers in order to drive such an ecological approach. Such a shift must borrow more from (dynamic) target-based environmental standards than from (static) zoning and planning codification protocols that are already deeply entrenched in governing structures. Suburban areas can perform many of the environmental services that expanding urban metro areas need, but not until mindlessly repetitive form-based codes and zoning, which privilege the superficial building of objects over designing for dynamic ecological processes, are removed from the intellectual and professional planning and design culs-de-sac they helped create.

Reconceiving the dynamics of metropolitan edges, where land conversion, degradation, ecosystem service losses, and social equity are perhaps at their most extreme, should be one of the central research ambitions of urbanism itself. Contemporary urbanism desperately needs a new model for imagining the outer edges of cities—the suburban fringes where the dynamics of urban expansion and resource consumption most visibly collide—and where the greenbelt could be reinvented to perform ecosystem services through innovative and intelligently designed landscape complexes.

Sara E. Brown assisted in the initial research of major elements in this essay. Casey L. Brown assisted in ideation and design of the wastebelts concept with the author.

could support 1,300–13,000 acres of constructed wetlands

Golf Course
Typical course is 110–200 acres (including water features and out-of-play areas)
375,000 gal/acre for 1 growing season of turf or 750,000 gal/acre for 50 percent of area (Colorado)
95 percent wastewater recovery for 1 growing season (180 d) could support 230 golf courses
About as many as Colorado has (243)
Phosphorous from nutrient recovery could support 20,700 acres of golf course at 65 lb/acre

86 Diane Cardwell, "Fuel from Landfill Methane Goes on Sale," October 2, 2013, accessed October 2, 2013, http://www.nytimes.com/2013/10/03/business/energy-environment/the-swamp-gas-station-fuel-from-landfill-methane-goes-on-sale.html; Jad Mouawad and Diane Cardwell, "Farm Waste and Animal Fats Will Help Power a United Jet," *New York Times,* June 30, 2015, accessed July 21, 2015, http://www.nytimes.com/2015/06/30/business/energy-environment/farm-waste-and-animal-fats-will-help-power-a-united-jet.html?ref=topics.
87 Berger, *Drosscape.*
88 Base data for mapping from the "Land Use Inventory," Chicago Metropolitan Agency for Planning (CMAP), accessed December 15, 2015, http://www.cmap.illinois.gov/data/land-use/inventory.

4.8
THE HORIZONTAL METROPOLIS

Paola Viganò

DESIGN
MODELS

PRODUCTIVE
SUBURBS

TRANSPORT
INFRASTRUCTURE

The form of the contemporary city has changed. The *città diffusa* of northern Italy, the *desakota* system in China, Japan, Thailand, or Vietnam, the fine-grain settlement dispersion in Flanders, and the *Zwischenstadt* in Germany all describe a new urban condition: the horizontal metropolis. It is the product not of conventional suburbanization but of territorial constructions occurring over time and accumulating as layers. The result is a varied set of conditions over entire regions, made up of an original mix of agricultural and nonagricultural economic activities, dispersed infrastructure, housing, and fragments of nature over entire regions. It is a "city-territory" that cannot be described as simply suburban or peri-urban.[1] These characteristics make the horizontal metropolis, both in Europe and in other global contexts, a reserve of spatial capital, an agent of transformation, and a place with great potential for facing contemporary urban challenges.

In the foreword to *The Suburb Reader*, Kenneth T. Jackson, author of the influential *Crabgrass Frontier: The Suburbanization of the United States*, still associates the idea of the European city with "dense urban environments even in small towns" and "sharp divisions between rural and urban areas."[2] The persistence of this caricature is one reason a different conceptualization is essential.

Roots of the Horizontal Metropolis in Europe

Horizontality is part of the time-honored political construction of Europe and the nation-state. One of its roots is the Roman-Burgundian region: an impressive north-south section of Europe from the Netherlands, including a swathe of Belgium to Switzerland and northern Italy, and Provence in the south of France.[3] This region comprises multiple countries, medium-sized cities, and dense infrastructure networks, but no large

capitals.[4] Cities were not just places of consumption and surplus extraction but centers of trade and industry, investing in land reclamation, the improvement of infrastructure, and dispersed industrial production. In this vast space, a scattered system of inhabited places has been the root of a long-term process of dispersion.

More recently, without intensity and without density, the horizontal metropolis emerged for various reasons: the enhancement and democratization of the quality of housing, the development of small-sized industries (or the restructuring of heavy industry in the 1970s), the flight out of the city by the urban population (in a quest for better living conditions or better economic opportunities), as well as concentration and the demand for services.

Horizontality of social and functional relations and multidirectionality of flows characterize the horizontal metropolis, where agriculture, hydraulic solutions, recreational purposes, energy production, slow mobility, public space, and facilities blend into each other in multifunctional areas.

The horizontal metropolis has its own unique character, different from the traditional metropolis. And in the last few decades, this phenomenon of dispersion and horizontality has accelerated greatly in Europe. As a result, it is now being recognized not only as worthy of research but also as worthy of specific policies and design.

Foundational Research

The concept of the horizontal metropolis has come to the fore at different times throughout the history of city and territorial design. Since the end of the nineteenth century and especially during the twentieth century, many authors have tried to describe, conceptualize, and interpret this new form of urbanization. Yet the first attempt to reflect on the emerging territories of dispersion on the

1   Giorgio Piccinato, Vieri Quilici, and Manfredo Tafuri, "La città territorio, verso una nuova dimensione," *Casabella Continuità* 270 (1962); André Corboz, "Vers la ville-territoire," in *Erganzungen* (Bern-Stuttgart: Paul Haupt, 1990), 633.

2   Kenneth Jackson, foreword to *The Suburb Reader*, ed. Becky M. Nicolaides and Andrew Wiese (New York: Routledge, 2006); Kenneth Jackson, *Crabgrass Frontier: The Suburbanization of the United States* (New York: Oxford University Press, 1985), xxi.

3   Norman Davies, *Vanished Kingdoms: The History of Half-Forgotten Europe* (London: Allen Lane, 2011).

4   George Brugmans et al., "Lessons Learned," in *Megacities: Exploring a Sustainable Future*, ed. Steef Buijs, Wendy Tan, and Devisari Tunas (Rotterdam: 010 Publishers, 2010); Bénédicte Grosjean, *Urbanisation sans urbanisme: Une histoire de la ville diffuse* (Wavre, Belgium: Mardaga, 2010).

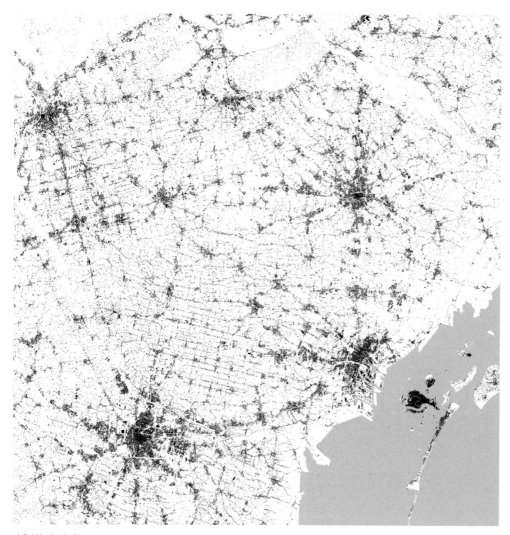

4.8.1 Venice built areas   ⌐————⌐ 5 km

5   *The Transformation of the Urban Habitat in Europe* was research coordinated by Bernardo Secchi at IUAV Venice in 1992–94 involving different schools in Europe and authors such as André Corboz, Marcel Smets, Nuno Portas, and Bernardo Secchi, "Le trasformazioni dell'habitat urbano in Europa: Alcuni appunti," *Quaderno Della Ricerca Sulle Trasformazioni dell'Habitat Urbano in Europa* (Venice: Università Iuav di Venezia, 1993): 7–15. See also Paola Viganò, "Una ricerca Europea," *Cronache Cà Tron* 1 (1993); Fabrizio Paone, "Le trasformazioni dell'habitat urbano," *Urbanistica* 103 (July–December 1994): 6–30.

6   Paola Viganò, ed., *New Territories: Situations, Projects, Scenarios for the European City and Territory* (Rome: Officina Edizioni, 2004). See also Stefano Munarin, and Maria Chiara Tosi, *Tracce di Città* (Milan: Franco Angeli, 2001); Paola Viganò, ed., *Territori della nuova modernità /Territories of a New Modernity* (Naples: Electa, 2001).

7   "The Horizontal Metropolis: A Radical Project" is research held at the EPFL by the Laboratory of Urbanism (Lab-U) coordinated by Paola Viganò.

European scale was the research study "The Transformation of the Urban Habitat in Europe" (1992–94), coordinated at Università Iuav di Venezia (IUAV Venice) by the urbanist Bernardo Secchi.[5] The objective of the research was to describe the diffuse city on the European scale and the urban elements constituting the city, with particular attention to recent, decentralized small-to-medium-scale industrial production. Years after, this research was followed by investigations of various scenarios, resulting in a comparative framework: "New Territories."[6]

Ongoing research builds on this foundational research in order to explore new design strategies, images, and tools to tackle the horizontal metropolis.[7] We need to critically reflect on the radical nature of the change that is underway, making reference to this past research and to the larger tradition of studies on the dispersed urban condition in Europe and beyond, connecting it to design experiences of the horizontal metropolis. In our present research, we explore how this complex form of urbanity can be a renewable resource under certain conditions. A few themes are explored in the following examples from Venice, Belgium, and Switzerland, which show the power of water, transportation, and energy networks in driving horizontality and creating new hybrid, multifunctional spaces.

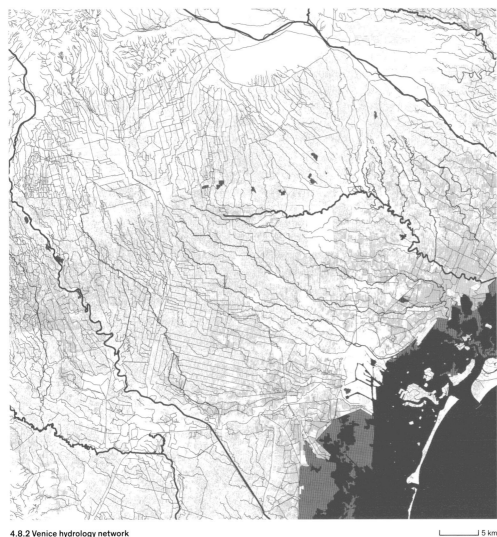

4.8.2 Venice hydrology network	⊢————⊣ 5 km

8	Francesco Indovina, ed., *La città diffusa* (Venice: Dipartimento di Analisi Economica e Sociale del Territorio, Istituto Universitario di Architettura, 1990).

9	Ibid., 42.

Isotropy: The Logic of Water Networks in the Horizontal Metropolis

Today's diffuse urbanization around Venice is definitively part of a horizontal metropolis; the metropolitan area of Venice can be read as an isotropic space, that is, a space that develops the same conditions in all directions. The phenomenon is not unique in Italy. Starting in the 1960s, the need to develop new concepts around this peculiar character of the urban transformations became clear. Yet it was important to avoid the misunderstanding generated by similarities with the North American suburb. In contrast to the North American suburb, the "diffuse city" around Venice, as described by the urbanist Francesco Indovina, comprises both ancient and distributed forms of urbanization, where small urban centers can become nodes, and yet spatial hierarchies are often complex and undefined.[8] At the beginning of the 1990s, the diffuse city was the result of a long-term territorial construction that slowly densified its scattered rural pattern, restructuring the industrial production outside the city and welcoming waves of urban core population leaving the city in search of better living conditions. Thus, the "diffuse city" was imagined to take "a balanced and balancing role, both in terms of production (innovation) and in terms of the social quality of life."[9] Yet to capture this

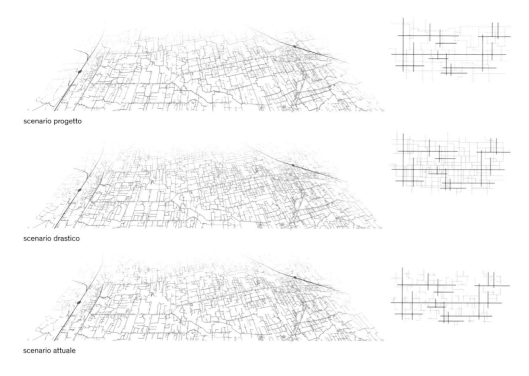

scenario progetto

scenario drastico

scenario attuale

4.8.3 Venice Low Inten[City]: dirt roads microinfrastructures, a reconfiguration

potential, the diffuse city had to become more than the expression of individual and fragmented choices, but an explicit collective project. Our "project of isotropy" is a planning and design agenda that proposes to valorize the low presence of hierarchies and lay the groundwork to support the contemporary need of diffused infrastructure in the horizontal metropolis of Venice.[10]

Water revealed itself to be a key element in understanding the structure of the Venetian metropolitan area and reimagining its dispersed and diffused settlement organization. In different parts of the world, we can recognize the importance of water in structuring urban expansion, since water is related to the exploitation of fertile areas and the reclamation of otherwise unproductive and uninhabitable land. The architecture of water management, water accessibility, and agriculture has been the basic support of the hybrid development of horizontal metropolises around the world. Both in

the Western world and in Asia, water and road networks are often conceived as one unique infrastructural body: from Thailand to Holland, roads, canals, paths, and ditches run parallel. Consequently, they produce fine-grained landscapes that are the product not only of autocratic civilizations (that imposed large works irreplicable today) but also of the distribution of responsibilities within the community to maintain those systems. Water management contributed to the construction of horizontal social relations.[11] Thus, the term *horizontality* alludes to horizontal space and horizontal power relations as well.

This is the case in the Veneto region, where the building of infrastructure is related to soil and landscape conditions. For example, dry plains become the sites of artificial irrigation systems, springs become water sources to be tapped, and wet plains become the sites of vast drainage projects. However, issues such as climate change adaptation, extensive

10 The research "Water and Asphalt, the Project of Isotropy" (the publication is forthcoming) has been led by Bernardo Secchi and Paola Viganò, first exhibited at the X Architecture Biennale in Venice in 2006, then developed thanks to national funds (PRIN 2008), with Lorenzo Fabian and Paola Pellegrini, and in the frame of EMU (European Master in Urbanism) and students of the Università IUAV di Venezia. See Paola Viganò, "Water and Asphalt, the Project of Isotropy in the Metropolitan Region of Venice," *Architectural Design* 78, no. 1 (2008).

11 On autocratic civilizations, see Karl August Wittfogel, *Oriental Despotism: A Comparative Study of Total Power* (New Haven, CT: Yale University Press, 1957); On water management, see Piero Bevilacqua, *Venezia e le acque: Una metafora planetaria* (Rome: Donzelli Editore, 1995).

impermeable surfaces, technological transformations of irrigation systems, fragmented water and ecological networks, flood risk, and energy scarcity all raise the need to reexamine conventional methods of urban and infrastructural planning and design. The issues we face today cannot be solved by a few large-scale investments in infrastructure. Instead, decentralized adaptations are needed. During the last decade, we have developed a countertheory "about the 'capability' of a diffuse territory, highly industrialized without immense investments in major mobility infrastructures, to adapt and integrate the transition toward a sustainable future."[12]

This countertheory is particularly applicable to water infrastructure, which is an immense network realized over centuries for multiple functions, including drainage, irrigation, and storage, and industrial uses (e.g., for the heavy industry of Porto Marghera for which big dams and transmission network were created). The spongy and capillary system of water and road networks, associated with hedgerows and wetlands, establishes osmotic relations between different territorial components and can be the basis of a project of isotropy, an extended project of mitigation and adaptation to climate change and to the new demographic and economic conditions.[13] (figs. **4.8.1–4**)

Brussels: Transportation Networks in the Horizontal Metropolis

Another example of a European horizontal metropolis is Belgium, where the continuum between urban and rural not only has been driven by scattered individual choices but has been constructed by explicit policies. In this case, the horizontal metropolis is intentional. It is the result of public investment in the realization of an alternative to the compact city, which suffers from congestion and from social and political conflict.

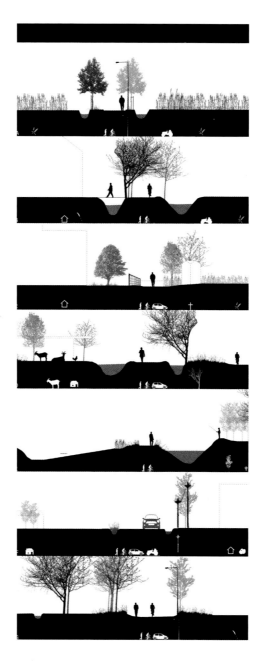

4.8.4 Venice Low Inten[City]: dirt roads micro-infrastructures, sections

12 Paola Viganò, "Micro Infrastructures," in *Scaling Infrastructure*, ed. MIT Center for Advanced Urbanism (New York: Princeton Architectural Press, 2016).

13 Bernardo Secchi, ed., *On Mobility* (Venice: Marsilio, 2010); Lorenzo Fabian and Paola Viganò, eds., *Extreme City* (Venice: Università IUAV di Venezia, 2010); Lorenzo Fabian, Emanuel Giannotti and Paola Viganò, eds., *Recycling City: Lifecycles, Embodied Energy, Inclusion* (Pordenone: Giavedoni Editore, November 2012); Emanuel Giannotti, Paola Viganò, eds., *Our Common Risk* (Milan: Edizioni et al., 2012).

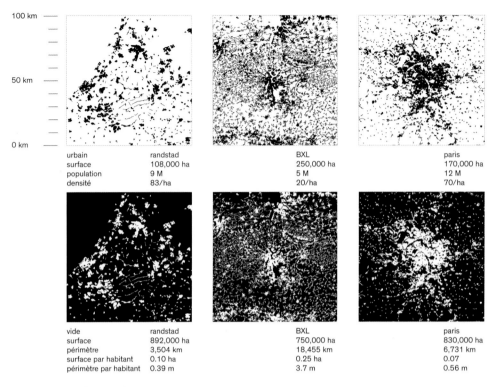

urbain	randstad		BXL		paris
surface	108,000 ha		250,000 ha		170,000 ha
population	9 M		5 M		12 M
densité	83/ha		20/ha		70/ha

vide	randstad		BXL		paris
surface	892,000 ha		750,000 ha		830,000 ha
périmètre	3,504 km		18,455 km		6,731 km
surface par habitant	0.10 ha		0.25 ha		0.07
périmètre par habitant	0.39 m		3.7 m		0.56 m

4.8.5 Brussels 2040: linear of contact

In response to this problem, a new urban model was created, which the urbanist Marcel Smets terms "Radiant Periphery" (*banlieue radieuse*), countering the Corbusian idea of the Radiant City. A strong appreciation of this spatial organization was already in Benjamin Seebohm Rowntree's report on labor and land in Belgium, published in 1910.[14] As an English sociologist and author of *Poverty: A Study of Town Life*, Rowntree wrote the report with the purpose of contributing to the solution of poverty in Britain by studying the systems of land tenure in Europe.[15] The author connects the possibility of working in the city and living in the countryside to the existence of a dense network of railways, light rails, and tramways. In his opinion, the transport facilities in Belgium were the best in the world.

The specific shape that the Industrial Revolution assumed in Belgium was to disperse the working class outside the city while connecting the peasants to the new dispersed industrial economy without fomenting a rural exodus. This strategy was supposedly a more pacifying and lower-cost solution. The construction of an infrastructure at the regional scale to organize a dispersed industrial city was "the logical answer to a specific problem."[16]

Today, the dense network of public transport remains a fundamental layer of territorial organization in Belgium. The term *campagnes urbanisées* was used by Emile Vandervelde, a socialist exponent and professor in Brussels, when alluding to the then fledgling new system of transportation. Vandervelde discusses the negative separation of rural activities from industry, a situation that could be overcome by expanded transport mobility and accessibility.[17] With this improved transport, the invention of new hybrid urban areas would be made possible; farms, factories and town houses would reconfigure the old villages as a *composé*—a combined entity. Meanwhile, single-family homes inserted throughout the urban space would bring airiness

14 On the *banlieue radieuse*, see Marcel Smets, *La Belgique ou la banlieue radieuse* (Paysage d'Architectures, Brussels: Fondation de l'Architecture, 1986), 33–35; Benjamin Seebohm Rowntree, *Land and Labour: Lessons from Belgium* (London: Macmillan and Co., 1910).

15 Rowntree, *Land and Labour*; Benjamin Seebohm Rowntree and Bryan S. Turner, *Poverty: A Study of Town Life* (London: Routledge/ Thoemmes, 1997).

16 Smets, "La Belgique ou la banlieue radieuse," 33.

17 The "trains ouvriers," with the incredibly low-cost ticket, are in Émile Vandervelde's opinion the "the most unconsciously revolutionary decision" (*la plus inconsciemment révolutionnaire*) taken by the Belgian government in the thirty years prior to his book *L'exode rural et le retour aux champs*, and after the Franco-Prussian War: Émile Vandervelde, *L'exode rural et le retour aux champs* (Paris: F. Alcan, 1903), 203, accessed December 1, 2015, http://gallica .bnf.fr/ark:/12148 /bpt6k55341938.

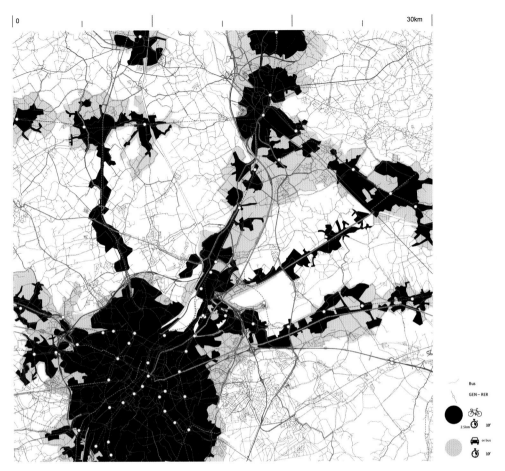

4.8.6 Noordrand, Brussels: no car scenario A

18 Ibid., 9. The hybrid character of the Belgian territory has been deeply investigated in the recent years. See Bruno de Meulder, Jan Schreurs, Annabel Cock, and Bruno Nottebom, "Patching Up the Belgian Urban Landscape," *Oase* 52 (1999): 78–113; Michiel Dehaene, *Tuinieren in het Stedelijk Veld— Gardening in the Urban Field* (Ghent: A & S Books, 2013).

19 Rowntree, *Land and Labour*, 107.

20 Bernardo Secchi and Paola Viganò, "Bruxelles et ses territoires, plan régional de développement durable: Elaboration d'une vision territoriale métropolitaine à l'horizon 2040 pour Bruxelles," unpublished (2011).

and greenery. This hybridization was intended to spread the *matériel de la civilisation*—the "material of civilization," then unique only to urban centers—to the countryside.[18]

Nevertheless, it is important to clarify that agricultural organization (Belgium is a country of small holdings) constituted the underlying structure of villages and cottages on top of which, by a process of stratification, the new, original industrial system was laid.[19] The soil of Flanders was not highly fertile, but it was frequently manured and nothing was wasted. It provided some of the most intensive agriculture of Europe: a poor soil able to maintain a dense population and proving the capacity of smallholdings to benefit from organized crop rotation. Indeed, the dispersed character has been inherently present for centuries.

In the vision for Brussels 2040 proposed by Bernardo Secchi and me, the horizontal metropolis is defined as "a typologically differentiated and well-provisioned extensive urban condition."[20] Its region includes three valleys and a dense and well-connected public transportation network. It is organized by a series of urban and regional elements— historic centers, parks, forests, new central places, and so forth. This horizontal metropolis is rich in natural capital yet heavily modified by the industrial canal connecting Antwerp, Brussels, and Charleroi.

To describe its main quality, we created a metric to capture the very rich and complex relationship between built space and open space. We called this metric the "linear of contact"; it measures the per capita length of urban to rural interface.

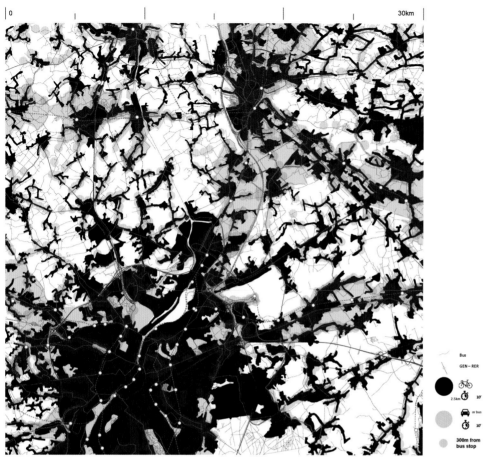

0 | | | | | | 30km

21 Paola Viganò, "The Horizontal Metropolis and Gloeden's Diagrams: Two Parallel Stories," *Oase* 89 (2013): 94–111.

Bus

GEN – RER

2.5km 10'

or bus 10'

300m from bus stop

4.8.7 Noordrand, Brussels: no car scenario B

It is much higher in Brussels than in other metropolitan areas in Europe: 12 feet (3.7 meters) per inhabitant, compared to 2 feet (0.56 meters) per inhabitant in the greater Paris region, which is an icon for the compact metropolis. In comparison, in the Dutch Randstad, with its large-scale urban fragments, the indicator is 1.3 feet per inhabitant (0.4 meters per inhabitant).

Moreover, the close relation with open green or cultivated space is appreciated even in low-income, low-density areas, such as those south of the Brussels region. The denser and degraded areas remain inside the cities. The issue is how to connect the metropolis's poorest and densest part—the industrial and polluted strip along the canal—to the more porous and permeable parts. One proposal contained in our vision for Brussels 2040 is the West Gardens, which is an idea for adding value

to the most fertile areas of Brussels by coupling urban agriculture, new educational spaces, and flood protection along the secondary network to gain space for water.

The regional rail system is gradually evolving to create an increasingly connected mesh. "Leaving behind the hub-and-spoke concept, and imagining systems that cross the city (in addition to the already dense urban networks): the horizontal metropolis becomes a prototypical context for imagining a "no-car" scenario and a regional system of public space along the valleys, revealing the metropolis's spatial structure."[21] The space gained for other uses by creating car-free islands and strong public transport corridors to connect them is the first step toward the transformation and requalification of the horizontal

4.8.8 The western gardens: education, agriculture, flooding risk A

4.8.9 The western gardens: education, agriculture, flooding risk B

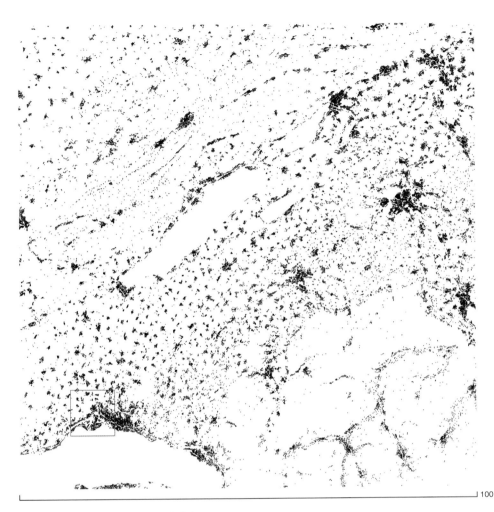

22 Pierre Joseph Proudhon is the author of *Du Principe Fédératif* (1863).
23 Peter Kropotkin, *Fields, Factories, and Workshops Tomorrow* (London: Colin Ward & Freedom Press, 1998), 25.

100 km

4.8.10 Lausanne and the swiss plateau, built form

metropolis. Reinforcing the regional railway will enhance this intense, albeit diffuse urban condition. No-car scenario in a horizontal metropolis can become an innovative spatial construct; however, its implementation necessitates cooperation across the highly fragmented administrative and political system of Brussels. (figs. **4.8.5–8**)

Switzerland: Energy Networks and Diffused Production in the Horizontal Metropolis

At the beginning of the twentieth century, cities grew rapidly as a result of the agrarian crisis of the previous decades, namely, the depletion of the European countryside as a result of intense agricultural competition from the rest of the world. Large numbers of people pouring into cities created problems of overcrowding, pollution, disease, social unrest, infrastructural shortfalls, and so forth. These problems compelled several authors (Vandervelde among them) to revive the idea of power redistribution and territorial rebalance, already proposed by the philosopher and politician Pierre Joseph Proudhon and others, to alleviate the mass migration into urban centers.[22] Peter Kropotkin wrote a manifesto about the industrialization of agriculture and the implantation of new "industries in the fields." Kropotkin was in favor of recovering the "most varied texture of soils and climates," a variety that can exist only within "a variety of occupations."[23] This theme of integration of activities, against division of labor,

4.8.11 Lausanne view

24 Jean-Jacques Rousseau, "Lettre 87: Au Maréchal de Luxembourg [Môtiers, January 20, 1763]," in *Lettres: [1728–1778]*, ed. Marcel Raymond (Lausanne: La Guilde du Livre, 1959), accessed November 26, 2015, http://classiques.uqac.ca/classiques/Rousseau_jj/lettres_1728_1778/lettres_tdm.html.

25 Thomas Bender, *Toward an Urban Vision: Ideas and Institutions in Nineteenth-Century America* (Lexington: University Press of Kentucky, 1975).

of maintaining a productive landscape, is still crucial in the horizontal metropolis.

At the end of the nineteenth century, the decentralization of industrial production became a means of territorial rebalancing. It was made possible thanks to electricity and hydropower, known as *houille blanche* ("white coal"), best exemplified in the case of Switzerland. It was the presence of dispersed energy production in the mountains that fed the philosopher Jean-Jacques Rousseau's imagery when he described Switzerland, at the end of eighteenth century, as a unique city with workshops distributed in the valleys, close to the streams and river, and its neighborhoods along the slopes.[24] In the Pyrenees or in the Alps, workshops could be positioned along and powered by the watercourses, the same as electric tramways running along the valleys and remote alpine villages. Just as the American factories were drawing their power from New England's waterfalls, European hydropower was the rural counter to the steam-power engines fueling the crowded European factory cities.[25] In this way, the widespread availability of energy and easy distribution through the network produced the isotropic dispersal of industrial production.

Today, European industrial space is dramatically changing. West of Lausanne, Switzerland, in between cultivated agricultural plots and the remains of forest, large infrastructural nodes, former orchards, and villages transformed into dormitory neighborhoods merge with heterogeneous and highly fragmented industrial fabric. The current approach is to increase housing and office space by reusing former industrial areas. Possibilities emerge to reverse this model: to maintain, recycle, and integrate industrial production designing the new productive landscape of the horizontal metropolis. (figs. **4.8.9–11**)

A Revolution in Land Use: Another Broadacre City

The "Revolution in Land Use," the title of the second part of Jean Gottmann's *Megalopolis*, is the fundamental trait of the conurbation described in his research on the East Coast of the United States. In *Megalopolis* Gottmann observes the symbiosis and the mixture of urban and rural in the megalopolitan land use. The mix of functions is repeatedly recognized as a characteristic feature of the territories of dispersion (as in the *desakota* system described by McGee or in

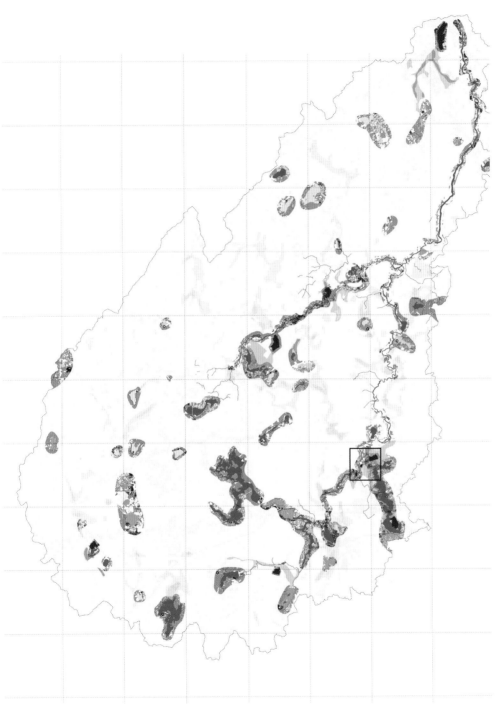

4.8.12 Boston watershed buffer network

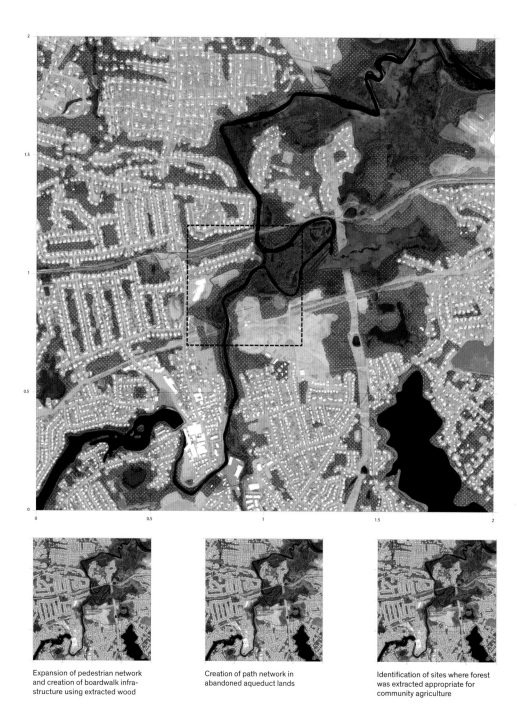

Expansion of pedestrian network and creation of boardwalk infra-structure using extracted wood

Creation of path network in abandoned aqueduct lands

Identification of sites where forest was extracted appropriate for community agriculture

4.8.13 Boston proposed territorial buffer system

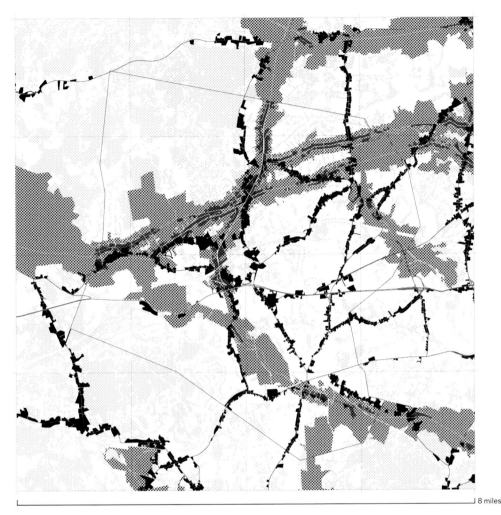

4.8.14 Boston superimposition, existing forest and proposed forest corridors

8 miles

26 Jean Gottmann, *Megalopolis; the Urbanized Northeastern Seaboard of the United States* (New York: Twentieth Century Fund, 1961); Indovina, *La Città Diffusa*; Bernardo Secchi, "La Periferia," *Casabella* 583 (1991); Terry G. McGee, "The Emergence of Desakota Regions in Asia: Expanding a Hypothesis," in *The Extended Metropolis: Settlement Transition in Asia* (Honolulu: University of Hawaii Press 1991), 3–25.

27 In the frame of a design studio at the GSD, Harvard. See Paola Viganò and Lauren Abrahams, *Territorialism 1: Inside a New Form of Dispersed Megalopolis* (Cambridge, MA: Harvard Graduate School of Design, 2013).

28 John L. Thomas, "Holding the Middle Ground," in *The American Planning Tradition: Culture and Policy*, ed. Robert Fishman (Washington, DC: Woodrow Wilson Center Press, 2000), 38.

29 Peter G. Rowe, *Making a Middle Landscape* (Cambridge, MA: MIT Press, 1991).

the *città diffusa* by Indovina, Secchi and others).[26] From this point of view the American suburb bears stronger and stronger similarities with the dispersed urbanizations of Europe.

But inside this symbiosis, the continuity of the megalopolis is broken by spatial, economic, and social fractures that destroy the continuity of the suburban ground, the ever-changing core of the American city. Strategies of territorialism, that is, of appropriation of a certain territory and self-limitation of movements inside a precise area, develop, constantly adapting and defining boundaries of inclusion and exclusion inside it. Given the impossibility of externalizing the problems of the megalopolis, interior peripheries grow in it.

In metropolitan Boston, for example, the reclamation of rivers, abandoned railways, and reservoirs in the highly contaminated Sudbury, Assabet, and Concord watersheds has revealed astounding disconnects in the megalopolis structure.[27] In the lower plains, the big mobility infrastructures fragment the territory where polluted and degraded areas concentrate, creating higher environmental and social risks. The metamorphosis of the "Middle Ground" touches all its elements: the prefabricated one-floor, single-family ranch houses, the commercial strip, the roads, the parking lots, and the dead-end streets.[28] The unfinished project of the middle landscape today is an open structure to reimagine.[29]

30 Viganò and Abrahams,
Territorialism 1.

4.8.15 Boston frame

A few statements can synthesize the reflection on the metropolitan area of Boston and territorialism: continuity and accessibility of space are crucial in a territory where social differences and processes of distinction are so strong. Meshing the metropolis goes beyond the hub-and-spoke logic of public transport: recycling former infrastructures of rail lines, aqueducts, canals, and rivers reinforces horizontal relations among the territories of the metropolis beyond the center-periphery paradigm. The "democratic deficit" in the low-lying areas, the lower quality of space, justifies an exploration of new forms of urbanity and soil productivity, reintroducing agriculture and varied typologies of recycling. The interior peripheries of the megalopolis are spatial, as well as social exceptions in search of radical reinterpretation. Porosity, permeability, and connectivity of space are issues in this form of city to react against extreme forms of territorialism and exclusion.[30] To imagine another Broadacre City—Frank Lloyd Wright's never-built project—as our current research is developing in different contexts, underlies the attempt and the urgency to revise the suburban model. This approach contextualizes Wright's proposal in time and place, and continues to expand the designer's reflection on the spatial consequences of a revolution in land use: in search of new coexistences and more inclusive spaces. The recycling of suburbia is only at its beginning. (figs. **4.8.12**–**15**)

Beyond Suburbia
Now, the task is to enlarge the frame of what we examine in contemporary forms of urbanity, including its roots, interpretation, and future challenges. These are the starting points of research on a new urban space: the horizontal metropolis. Building on past research and on the understanding of long-term processes of urban and territorial rationalization, the horizontal metropolis project works on reinforcing or establishing isotropic conditions on territorial infrastructures and on the coexistence of their different rationalities, as in the case of Venice, and on spatial hybrids, learning from the diffuse heterogeneous condition that has formed through time, valorizing a diffuse network of public transport as in the case of Brussels. Add to that the horizontal metropolis project's work against the extreme specialization of space and the division of labor, and on new continuities, accessibility, porosity, and integration, as in the cases of Switzerland and Boston metropolitan area. Europe is facing dramatic changes: the horizontal metropolis is the writing of both a legacy and a possibility.

Redlands, California, United States

Fowler, California, United States

4.9
SPRAWL IS DEAD!
LONG LIVE THE LOW-DENSITY CITY

Alex Wall

DESIGN
MODELS

PRODUCTIVE
SUBURBS

ECOLOGICAL
FUNCTION

Rapidly expanding cities, especially megacities, are experiments in human settlement undertaken without a clear goal. The urbanization process continues to be driven by late twentieth-century economic determinism, powered by fossil fuels, and built using generic real estate typologies, with little regard for environmental consequences. These include changes in the spatial and temporal variability of resources, effecting direct and subtle changes in climatic, hydrologic, and biogeochemical processes and biotic interactions.[1] Nonetheless, the city is part of nature, dependent on the ecosystem services provided by a robust urban ecology.

The low-density city is a theoretical proposal to reconceptualize urban development, ecosystem function, and human activities to create sustainability and resilience for today's seemingly endlessly spread-out cities. Why a low-density city? In a recent essay, the *Economist* declared that we are not in an age of urbanization but rather in the age of suburbanization.[2] Despite its continuing popularity, suburbia is typically labeled the most ecologically destructive form of urbanization.[3] Many urbanists believe the only way forward is to shrink the footprint of urbanization as a whole, and correct the suburbs using traditional urban tools to establish density, coherence, legibility, and human scale. Without negating New Urbanism, smart growth, or transit-oriented development, the low-density city instead folds these urban models into a new resilient, heterogeneous settlement concept that includes urban cores, infrastructure, open spaces, and adjoining suburbs and small towns.

In fact, heterogeneity in urban form can ensure resiliency. Researchers at the Urban Ecology Research Laboratory at the University of Washington argue that there is insufficient empirical evidence to confirm the effect on ecological function of different urban forms, densities, land-use mix, and infrastructure.[4] As yet, the effect on ecological conditions of monocentric versus polycentric urban structure is not yet clear. Thus, no single urban pattern is consistently more resilient than another.[5] For these reasons, diversifying urban form through variations in centrality, building density, road connectivity, and ecological features can build resilience by expanding a region's capacity to adapt to a variety of possible future conditions.[6]

Returning to the claim made by the *Economist*, the result is not the triumph of suburbia but rather a different kind of urban settlement altogether. What can make it new is the constant negotiation between the needs of urban development and ecosystem function, guided by citizens, communities, and governments wielding new values that inform their activities and choices.

An Archaeology of Urban Expansion
Over the last half-century, architects and planners have devised critical formulations to understand dispersed urbanization. Taken together, these formulations—like the map of the overlaid layers of Troy—represent an archaeology of urban concepts on which the low-density city can build. Three precedents worth mentioning are Jean Gottmann's megalopolis, Peter Calthorpe and William Fulton's arguments for the regional city, and Thomas Sieverts's concept of the *Zwischenstadt*, which I translate as the "city in-between cities."

In 1961 the French geographer Jean Gottmann published *Megalopolis*, a study of the 450 miles of contiguous settlement between Washington, DC, and Boston.[7] The scale of the megalopolis was geographic, and Gottman believed that it was "a cradle of a new order in the organization of inhabited space, a laboratory of urban growth, a space at the threshold of a

1 Marina Alberti, *Advances in Urban Ecology: Integrating Humans and Ecological Process in Urban Ecosystems* (New York: Springer, 2009), 252–53.

2 "Places Apart: A Planet of Suburbs," *Economist*, no. 8916 (2014): 49–54.

3 Reid Ewing, Rolf Pendall, and Don Chen, *Measuring Sprawl and Its Impact: Volume I* (Washington, DC: Smart Growth America, 2002), accessed November 3, 2015, http://www .smartgrowthamerica .org/documents /MeasuringSprawl Technical.pdf.

4 Alberti, *Advances*, 252–23: "Emerging models of urban ecology still cannot effectively take into account the complex interactions between humans and ecology… We lack an understanding of the mechanisms linking emerging urban ecosystem patterns to ecosystem processes and controlling their dynamics."

5 Marina Alberti, "Planning under Uncertainty: Regime Shifts, Resilience, and Innovation in Urban Ecosystems," *The Nature of Cities*, last modified January 22, 2013, 17, accessed November 3, 2015, http:// www.thenatureofcities .com/2013/01/22 /planning-under -uncertainty-regime -shifts-resilience-and -innovation-in-urban -ecosystems/.

6 Marina Alberti, "Maintaining Ecological Integrity and Sustaining Ecosystem Function in Urban Areas," *Current Opinion in Environmental Sustainability* (2010): 182.

7 Jean Gottmann, *Megalopolis; the Urbanized Northeastern Seaboard of the United States* (New York: Twentieth Century Fund, 1961).

30 miles

4.9.1 Megalopolis in 1961

30 miles

4.9.2 Megalopolis today

4.9.3 Houston

8   Ibid., 9.
9   Richard Florida,
    "The Megaregions
    of North America,"
    *Martin Prosperity
    Institute*, University
    of Toronto, Rotman
    School of Management,
    last modified 2005,
    accessed November 3,
    2015, http://martin
    prosperity.org/media
    /Mega%20Regions
    _Insight_14-03-05.pdf.
10 Stefano Boeri Architetti,
    "BIOMILANO—Six
    Transition States," last
    modified February 12,
    2011, accessed November
    3, 2015, http://www
    .stefanoboeriarchitetti
    .net/en/news/b-i-o-m-i
    -l-a-n-o-six-transition
    -states/; see also
    Tancredi Capatti,
    "Metrobosco and Co.:
    The Trend of Urban
    Afforestation," *Topos:
    European Landscape
    Magazine*, no. 66 (2009):
    80.

new way of life…beyond urban and rural and a multipurpose concept of land use."[8] (figs. **4.9.1**–**2**) At the time, this linear cluster of cities was unique; today, depending on the parameters, there are between seven and twelve such agglomerations in the United States alone.[9]

The blanketing of a region with urban development doesn't obliterate the national parks, forests, farmlands, lakes, or rivers but rather reduces them to fragments, some large but many more that are small. The idea of the low-density city is to both expand and link these spaces—including sites that are polluted and forgotten—into an evolving and productive network of ecosystem habitats. We are looking for a counterfigure

to the megalopolis, with a new ecosystem at the superregional scale. A current example of this thinking is Stefano Boeri's Metrobosco plan for Milan, which envisages about 74,000 acres (30,000 hectares) of linked urban forests, using fast-growing trees such as poplar to offset increasing emissions, noise, and dust in the "city-region."[10] A second example, to be described later, is the "Green Vision for Orange County" plan, which links mountain and coastal habitats using river and stream corridors.

By the 1970s, cities began to spread into their surrounding region. Geographers began to characterize the everyday pulse of US cities as a "daily urban system," demarcated not by political boundaries but by traffic and logistics flows that are critical to prosperity, health, and social cohesion.[11] Examples of regional cities include Greater Los Angeles, multicentered Houston and Atlanta, and global cities such as London and Istanbul. Regional cities can be characterized by "dispersed concentration," a term that aptly describes the variations in density of the historic core, edge city employment centers, and the low-density urbanization and open spaces surrounding them.[12] (fig. **4.9.3**)

In their 2001 book, *The Regional City*, the urbanists Peter Calthorpe and William Fulton argued that the most important settlement scales had become the region and the neighborhood, recognizing the importance of spatial and transportation links between them.[13] In a demonstration of integrated multiscale design and planning, Calthorpe was commissioned to undertake the Region 2040 plan for the Willamette Valley, Oregon. The plan included the growth boundary for Portland, identified the centers, districts, and corridors for Portland Metro, and later, envisioned the transformation of a former regional shopping center site into the Clackamas mixed-use urban neighborhood.[14] (figs. **4.9.4–5**) Thinking at regional scale, both Calthorpe's plan guiding development in the Willamette Valley and the New York Regional Plan Association's 1996 Regional Plan for New York, New Jersey, and Connecticut sought to use future urban development to establish place and support equity, as well as create prosperity and meet the needs of their diverse communities. At the scale of the regional city, questions of place, identity, and equity are as important as the economy and infrastructure. Human agency expressing new values will be critical in creating a living city where urban development and ecosystem function evolve together.

One indicator of postwar economic success in Europe is that cities have

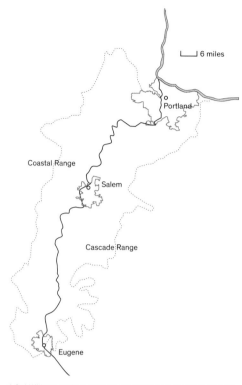

4.9.4 Willamette Valley Basin, adapted from Peter Calthorpe and William Fulton, *The Regional City* (Washington, DC: Island Press, 2001)

spread out into expansive regional settlements. In 1997 the German urban planner Thomas Sieverts published *Zwischenstadt*, which set out to define and name the sprawling low-density urbanization around the historic centers of European cities. Sieverts described the *Zwischenstadt* as a new kind of city altogether, which reflected changes in economics, culture, transportation, and communication. He argued further that its presence confirmed the build-out of the city region, the dissolution of the compact European city, and the end of the golden age of planning from above.[15] *Zwischenstadt* challenges us to see and read this nontraditional city in new ways. Its fragmentation and unconventionally ordered mixture of urban and landscape areas does not mean the end of "city" but rather the existence of an urban structure open to many new visions and experiments: popular, elite, infrastructural, and purely commercial. Sieverts's thesis challenges architects and planners

11 John S. Adams, Ronald Abler, and Ki-Suk Yi, *A Comparative Atlas of America's Great Cities: Twenty Metropolitan Regions* (Minneapolis: University of Minnesota Press, 1976), 2.

12 Arnd Herbert Motzkus, *Dezentrale Konzentration—Leitbild für eine Region der kurzen Wege?* (Sankt Augustin: Asgard-Verlag, 2002).

13 Peter Calthorpe and William B. Fulton, *The Regional City: Planning for the End of Sprawl* (Washington, DC: Island Press, 2001), 6.

14 Ibid., 139–43.

15 Thomas Sieverts, *Zwischenstadt: Zwischen Ort und Welt, Raum und Zeit, Stadt und Land* (Braunschweig: Vieweg, 1997). Sieverts's *Zwischenstadt* was published in German in 1997, and translated into English as *Cities without Cities: An Interpretation of the Zwischenstadt.*

4.9.5 Portland, adapted from Calthorpe and Fulton, *The Regional City*

16 Peter Baccini and Paul
    H. Brunner, *Metabolism
    of the Anthroposphere:
    Analysis, Evaluation,
    Design* (Cambridge, MA:
    MIT Press, 2012), 17.

17 Ibid., 60. They write that
    nested scales of urban
    development correspond
    to effective levels of
    governance, for example,
    states and countries
    must deal with policy
    and regulation, while
    local governments at the
    level of cities and towns
    can deal with individual
    actors and specific
    projects. The smallest
    scale is management of
    households and small
    businesses.

to meet contemporary popular culture on its own terms as a prerequisite for a new design and planning.

At the time of *Zwischenstadt*'s initial publication, the need to integrate urban development with local and regional ecosystems was not an urgent priority. Acknowledging the anthropogenic transformation of terrestrial and aquatic ecosystems, and benefiting from recent research in urban ecology, the goal of the low-density city is that future urban growth and ecosystem function evolve together.

Megalopolis, *The Regional City*, and *Zwischenstadt* describe the strategic value of thinking at the large scale. A region encompasses all of the metabolic systems of the anthroposphere: settlement patterns, traffic congestion, air quality, and terrestrial and aquatic ecosystem function, as well as socioeconomic patterns, such as economic enterprises, political and cultural institutions, social coherence demographic change, and the geography of wealth and poverty.[16]

The academics Peter Baccini and Paul H. Brunner have argued that only by looking at nested scales will planners be able to create the relationships necessary to achieve sustainable development.[17] In urban ecology, the dynamic of nested scales is both vertical and horizontal. The ecoregion is the scale for measuring climate, precipitation, and biodiversity, while cities and towns need to manage hydrology, soils, and wildlife with urban climate. The smallest collective unit is local habitat, its function, resilience, and disturbances.

A Precedent for the Low-Density City

Are there working examples that could serve as a starting point for the gradual transformation of sprawling American settlement into a resilient low-density city? Orange County, California, has a profile in the popular media as a form of paradigmatic suburbanism based on its consumption culture, automobile lifestyle, and the deed restrictions of its exclusive subdivisions. Located between Los Angeles and San Diego, it is in fact a major employment center for jobs in the high technology, defense, services, and financial industries. Bounded by the Pacific Ocean to the west and the Santa Ana Mountains and Cleveland Hills to the east, the county's salubrious climate has made it a magnet for retail, tourism, and sports and athletic centers.

Orange County has multiple urban centers; its suburban subdivisions are punctuated by three cities with populations over 200,000, Santa Ana, Anaheim, and Irvine; and the smaller cities of Fullerton, Huntington Beach, and Orange. Between the 1960s and the 1980s, edge city employment centers formed around the large and successful regional shopping centers in Irvine, Newport Center, and South Coast Metro. Today, Orange County has a population of 3 million, making it the sixth-most populous county in the United States. With a net inhabited area of 791 square miles (2,048 square kilometers), the population density is approximately 3,900 people per square mile (1,500 people per kilometer), making Orange County more densely settled than Portland, Oregon.[18] (fig. **4.9.6**)

In the 1996 critical review of Irvine and Orange County, "The City Which Does Not Imitate the City," the architect Alessandro Rocca betrayed the fascination of European architects with the experiment in settlement taking place at the scale of the territory in Southern California. In contrast to the concentration, plurality, and complexity claimed for the European city, Rocca questioned the destiny of an urban landscape composed of models from commercial development and resort planners, marketed using the most sophisticated media tools, reflecting the taste culture and revenue goals of residential and retail development companies.[19] Indeed, Orange County has been an experiment, with notable planning at the regional, city, and subdivision scales. The original vision for Orange County was underpinned by three high-profile projects, Disneyland in Anaheim (1955), a regional airport in Santa Ana named for the actor John Wayne (1964), and William Peireira's 1961 master plan for Irvine, a new town centered on the campus of a new branch of the University of California.

Twenty years after Rocca's critical review, it remains to be seen if subsequent planning and development will enfold social, economic, and ecological equity and resilience as part of a transformed "brand." The "Green Vision for Orange County" plan, which seeks to create stream and river corridors linking coastal with mountain habitats, is an ambitious long-term strategy to protect and enhance biodiversity and especially to support county watersheds in maintaining coastal pressure against saltwater intrusion.[20] (fig. **4.9.7**)

The Grammar of the Low-Density City

How might architects and planners conceptualize the elements of urbanization with those of local and regional ecosystems? One answer was given by the 1996 publication of the ecologists Wenche Dramstad, James D. Olson, and Richard T. T. Forman's *Landscape Ecology Principles*, which described the structural pattern of a region as a

18 Scott Martell and Dan Weikel, "Orange County Urban, Not Suburban," *Los Angeles Times*, last modified March 6, 2003, accessed November 3, 2015, www.articles.latimes.com/2003/mar/06/local/me-commute6. Since 2000, growth in daily commuter flows into county employment centers shows the growing economic independence of Orange County, further evidence that the county is not suburban.

19 Alessandro Rocca, "Irvine Ranch of Orange County: The City Which Does Not Imitate the City," *Lotus* 89 (1996): 53–102.

20 "Green Vision Map," *Friends of Harbors, Beaches, and Parks*, accessed November 3, 2015, http://www.fhbp.org/publications/green-vision-map.html.

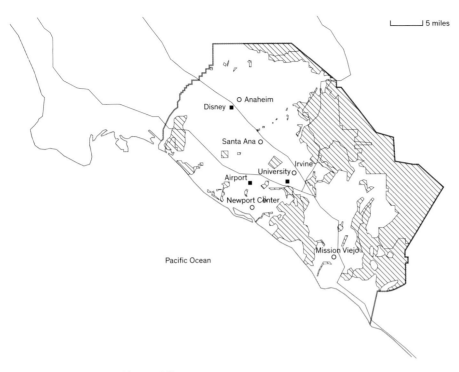

4.9.6 Orange County: Regional fragmentation

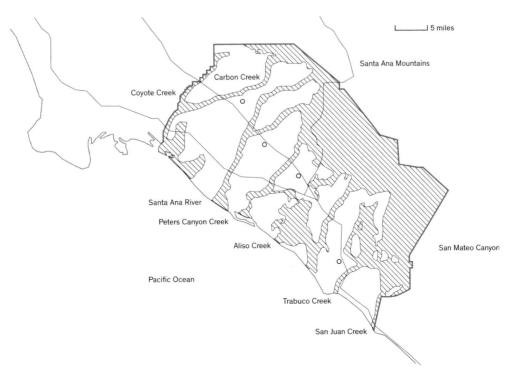

4.9.7 Orange County: Regional unity

landscape mosaic composed of patch, edge, corridor, and matrix, of either natural or human origin.[21] Immediately taken up by many designers and planners, the terms were striking for their metaphorical power to describe the built elements of urbanization.

Landscape Ecology Principles was not conceived for working in pristine or decorative landscapes. The authors accepted fragmentation and coexistence of ecology within urban and suburban settlement patterns. To bring the functional elements of regional ecosystems into architectural or urban projects, their system was developed at three scales that explicitly integrate nature and humans: regional, landscapes and site. Foreman describes a region as a broad geographical area with a common macroclimate and sphere of human activity and interest. A landscape, in contrast, is a mosaic where the mix of local ecosystems or land uses is repeated in a similar form over a wide area. Where parts of a region may be ecologically quite dissimilar, a landscape manifests an ecological unity throughout its area.[22] A site, defined by its local ecosystem or land use, for example, a wood or forest patch, is a relatively homogeneous element with distinct boundaries within a landscape.

To give emphasis to the interaction between buildings, ensembles, and adjoining ecosystems, I adopt the *patch*, *edge*, *corridor*, and *matrix* terms from landscape ecology. Patch, used by landscape ecologists to describe plant and animal habitats, describes repetitive elements of the low-density city, such as subdivisions, edge city employment centers, commercial retail areas, and office or light industrial parks. For ecologists, porous or hard edges are the active boundary between multi-scaled habitat patches. Edges are also an attribute marking the shifting boundaries of settlement. Rather than a line demarcating buildings from natural landscapes, Edge describes a linear zone of variable depth and conditions. In the low-density city, institutional buildings, residential complexes and transportation infrastructure should be designed with an active edge, a zone where people, built elements, and ecosystem functions are integrated. Nature corridors—essential to support regional ecology and biodiversity—allow animals, birds, seeds, and marine wildlife to migrate and disperse. In the lowdensity city, infrastructure corridors help structure and nurture the evolving urban pattern. Rail and highway rights-of-way include uncountable fragments of space, some of them quite large. These rights of way trace linear paths across regions and continents, disrupting animal migration routes at the same time as offering myriad sites for hybrid and novel ecosystems. The elements of the spread-out city and the ecological region need to be considered together to enable designers, planners, and urban ecologists to create new patterns for the coevolution of the city with changing local and regional ecosystems.

What could be a model for a flexible urban form that offers potential for adaptation and mitigation while providing amenity and comfort? Useful precedents exist at two scales. At the beginning of the twentieth century, the Finnish planner Eliel Saarinen believed that the dense European city was no longer an effective model for new living standards. His concept for the organic decentralization of cities, developed between 1911 in Helsinki and the late 1930s at Cranbrook Academy of Art near Detroit, showed the dense cores of cities broken up into islands separated by an irregular lattice of open space. At Cranbrook, Saarinen directed his students to diagram the decentralization of American cities such as Hartford, Detroit, and Chicago. Each city was reimagined as an archipelago of urban islands. Saarinen's concept relies on a decades-long process of selective

21 Wenche E. Dramstad, James D. Olson, and Richard T. T. Forman, *Landscape Ecology Principles in Landscape Architecture and Land-Use Planning* (Washington, DC: Island Press, 1996).

22 Richard T. T. Foreman, *Land Mosaics: The Ecology of Landscape and Regions* (New York: Cambridge, 1995), 12–13. Foreman argues that the landscape is basically composed of only three types of spatial elements—patch (edge), corridor, and matrix— and these may be of natural or human origin.

demolition and decisions not to rebuild. The result suggests a syncopated rhythm of dense but spacious built fabric and open spaces, which can be used to locate new traffic infrastructure, sport, and landscape.[23] (figs. **4.9.8–9**)

In 1987 this concept of ordering settlement form with a structure of unbuilt space was revisited in the Office for Metropolitan Architecture (OMA)'s plan for the new town of Melun-Senart south of Paris. Here, a figure of intersecting bands of open space was programmed with different functions, such as leisure, sport, infrastructure, and all those uses which don't fit in either dense urban districts or settled low density areas.[24] (figs. **4.9.10–11**) Today, Saarinen's lattice or OMA's bands might be programmed with nature corridors, urban forest, biomass production, and urban farming. They would follow closely the city's watershed, a contemporary version of Frederick Law Olmsted's engineered "necklaces" of parks and water features making a green infrastructure through the city and suburbs of Boston. Future cities may be archipelagoes of density in a far larger field of low-density settlement, all structured by a network of highly productive open spaces.

Ecosystem Services, Cycles, and Actors
As urbanization continues, we blithely assume that the ecological capacity of a particular region can sustain cities that cover an enormous area. Los Angeles, London, Beijing, and São Paulo, for example, all cover between 450 and 700 square miles (1,165 to 1,812 square kilometers), much of which is impervious.[25] The extent of impervious surfaces affects both the structure and function of ecosystems by altering biophysical processes and habitat, and by modifying major biogeochemical cycles, resulting in the heat island, aquifer depletion and increased runoff flows. Ultimately the ecosystem's capacity to deliver important services to the human population and support well-being is threatened.[26] To limit urbanization's damage to the environment, we need to create an urban metabolism that is consistent and coproductive with the natural cycles of ecosystems. Three fields of action enable the low-density city to function as a living system.

The first field of action is to engage the ecosystem services provided by the sun, wind, rain, plants, and animals. To achieve a more true cost and benefit analysis in the assessment of proposed urban development, the economist Robert Costanza proposes setting an economic value to these services. Rather than a commodification or privatization of nature, he argues that many ecosystem services are "public goods or common pool resources," and need new "common asset institutions to better take these values into account."[27] Acknowledging the value of ecosystem services has not only economic and ecological benefits; Costanza argues that "the rights of people and nature are not two different things, but are concurrent, and that the biosphere is part of the public commons."[28] In the low-density city, human agency can evolve from the unconscious alteration of earth's systems to a collective stewardship. Buildings are no longer inert objects reliant on energy, water, and artificial lighting but may become partly sentient as they engage their local microclimate and weather.

The second field of action is the transformation of energy and substance flows within cities from a linear to a cyclical urban metabolism. Material and nutrient flows take place at many interrelated scales: from the inputs and outputs of individual households to the city itself as a recycling system, and finally to the metabolism of the region. In the low-density city, there will be sufficient spaces for cycling, recycling, and transformation of materials. Rather than secondary

23 Eliel Saarinen, *The City: Its Growth, Its Decay, Its Future* (New York: Reinhold Publishing Co., 1958).

24 Rem Koolhaas et al., *Small, Medium, Large, Extra-Large* (New York: Monacelli Press, 1998), 972–90.

25 "The Largest Cities in the World by Land Area, Population, and Density," *City Mayors Running the World's Cities*, last modified January 6, 2007, accessed November 3, 2015, http://www.citymayors.com/statistics/largest-cities-area-125.html. Size of cities: for example, Los Angeles—498 m2 (1,290 km2), New York—468 m2 (1,214 km2), Istanbul—707m2 (1830 km2), Beijing—532 m2 (1377 km2), London—607 m2 (1572 km2), Sao Paulo—582 m2 (1509 km2), Mexico City—573m2 (1485km2).

26 Alberti, "Maintaining Ecological Integrity and Sustaining Ecosystem Function in Urban Areas," 178.

27 Robert Costanza et al., "Changes in the Global Value of Ecosystem Services," *Global Environmental Change* 26 (May 2014): 152.

28 Ibid., 154.

3 miles

4.9.8 Chicago: aggregate of urban districts, adapted from Eliel Saarinen, *The City: Its Growth, Its Decay, Its Future* (New York: Reinhold, 1958). Original drawing by Saarinen and Hutchinson Jr., 1935–36, Cranbrook Academy of Art.

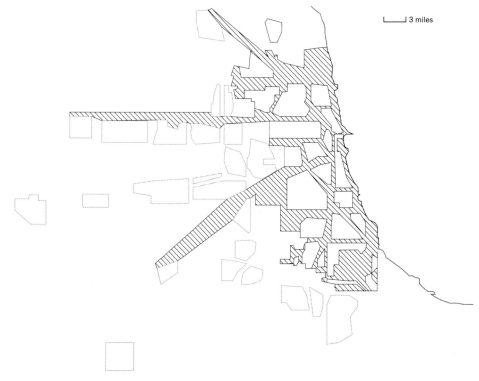

3 miles

4.9.9 Chicago: irregular landscape lattice of open spaces, adapted from Saarinen, *The City: Its Growth, Its Decay, Its Future*. Original drawing by Saarinen and Hutchinson Jr., 1935–36, Cranbrook Academy of Art.

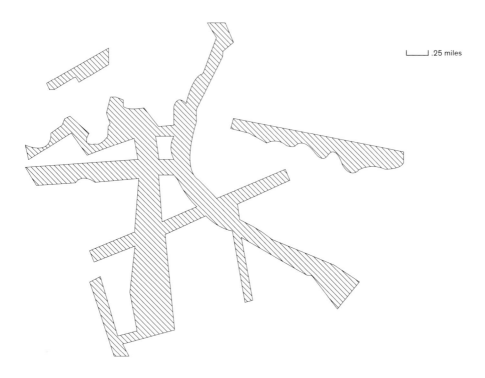

4.9.10 Melun Senart: irregular landscape lattice, adapted from Rem Koolhaas and Bruce Mau, *Small, Medium, Large, Extra-Large*

4.9.11 Melun Senart: aggregate of urban districts, adapted from Koolhaas and Mau, *Small, Medium, Large, Extra-Large*

.25 miles

.25 miles

service spaces, these should be considered an active and didactic realm that represents the spirit and intention of the low-density city.

The linear urban metabolism, developed during the Industrial Revolution, consists of inputs of food, water, energy, and goods, with outputs of organic and inorganic waste, including emissions of carbon dioxide, nitrous oxide, and sulfur dioxide, the practice of sea dumping, and the use of landfills. One result of linear material flows is that the hinterland has to cope with the waste of anthropogenic activities.[29] The use of fossil fuels is a typical linear flow. In contrast, renewable energy and the recycling of water and waste are part of a cyclical metabolism of a city, which repairs, cleans, and reuses input materials and resources. In cases where these are returned to the environment, they are, after treatment, as close as possible to their original state.

Effective discussions about urban development, the natural environment, and risks from changing climate and weather patterns have proved ineffective at a societal scale. As urbanization continues accompanied by rising emissions and perceptions of growing inequality, the lack of social cohesion in the face of uncertainty threatens the goals of sustainability and resilience. The study of urban metabolism should not be limited to the accounting of energy and materials but must also consider social contexts. The engineer Sabine Barles argues that societies and the biosphere can be considered two interdependent systems in coevolution. A holistic urban metabolism must evolve from the agriculture-industry-city triptych to include spatial, social, and ecological contexts and processes.[30]

The third field of action is fostering empathy and building consensus to solve conflicts politically and peacefully. It supports the human disposition to cooperate, to do justice, and to fight for values.[31] The

goal of a low-density city can never be achieved without integrating local actors to build social resilience across urban communities. Combining informal tactics with new forms of governance and participation produces a "midway up" future. Midway up integrates everyday urbanism practices of cities in the Global North with the development tactics, that have emerged in informal settlements in the Global South. It fuses top-down capacities and bottom-up activism; it is based on empathy and engaging local knowledge and innovation to generate user-based ideas on creating cities.[32]

Each of the three fields of action described above has spatial manifestations. The benefit of ecosystem services at a regional scale includes the living structure of urban rivers, forests, parks, and food production. A cyclical metabolism implies buildings and spaces for staging recycling, storage, and remanufacture of materials. They are visible parts of the urban landscape, not hidden in pipes or underground. Empathy and social sustainability require a variety of collective spaces for confrontation, negotiation, and resolution from the city plaza to shared spaces in new residential typologies. Together they amount to a visible and narrative infrastructure of technical, ecological, and social spaces. The three fields of action provide strategies and tools to build equity and resilience in the low-density city.[33]

Embracing Instability and Uncertainty
In the section above, renewable energy and the recycling of water and waste were described as part of a cyclical metabolism of a city. Urban ecologists, however, have moved beyond the notion of circularity, balance, and order.[34] A new paradigm understands the natural world as a setting of dynamic change and uncertainty, as first described in 1971 by C. S. Holling and M. A. Goldberg. Ecological systems are not

29 Baccini and Brunner, *Metabolism of the Anthroposphere,* 50.

30 Sabine Barles, "Urban Metabolism: Persistent Questions and Current Developments," in *Grounding Metabolism,* ed. Daniel Ibañez and Nikos Katsikis (Cambridge, MA: Harvard University Press, 2014), 62–63.

31 Jeremy Rifkin, "The Empathic Civilization– Rethinking Human Nature in the Biosphere Era," *Huffington Post,* last modified March 18, 2010, accessed November 3, 2015, http://www.huffington post.com/jeremy-rifkin /the-empathic-civili zation_b_416589.html. For Rifkin, empathy is different than sympathy, which is passive. "Empathy," he explains, "conjures up active engagement, the willingness of an observer to become part of another's experience, to share the feeling of that experience."

32 Sabine Mueller and Alex Wall, "Actors: Who Builds the City?," chap. 10 in "Urbanisms and Sustainabilities" (unpublished manuscript, 2011).

33 Ibid., "Chapter 1: Welcome to the Anthropocene."

34 Elizabeth Rapoport, "Interdisciplinary Perspectives on Urban Metabolism: A Review of the Literature" (working paper, University College London, Environmental Institute, London, UK, 2010): 10.

in a state of delicate balance. Even "normal" geophysical processes and changing climate subject ecosystems to trauma and shocks.[35]

The low-density city goal of linking urban development with its ecological region depends on complex interactions between humans and ecosystems over multiple scales. Academics like Marina Alberti argue that the effects of changing climate, such as extreme weather and sea-level rise in addition to shocks from floods, fire, or aggressive land-use change, creates instability that systems react to, evolve, and effectively learn from. Rather than optimizing a single set of supposedly ideal circumstances, the goal should be to support greater variety across scales to increase urban resilience to inevitable shocks.[36]

Alberti proposes that the new model of dynamic change is regulated by three properties of ecosystems: the potential for change, the degree of connectedness, and system resilience.[37] These attributes are also useful for assessing the resilience of the low-density city in adapting to the risks of changing climate and could involve different urban patterns, diverse social groups, and a variety of communication and transportation modes in producing a flexible, redundant, and resilient urban system. The cycling of energy, resources, materials, and waste by diverse communities evolves with habitat and ecosystem function. Material and resource flows are measured against the changing carrying capacities of evolving ecosystems.[38] The coevolution of the urbanization process and ecosystem function is an outcome of human agency guided by new values.

From this perspective, as Roger Keil writes, urbanization does not distance humans from nature but rather is "a process by which new and more complex relationships of society and nature are created."[39] In the low-density city, these interlinked processes can be represented by a simple triangular figure, which links urban development, ecosystem function, and human activities and choices.

Hampton Roads, Virginia: Experimentation and Preparedness

Many cities need to transform their structure and pattern to evolve more closely with the needs and limits of their regional ecosystems. One example is urban development in low-lying coastal areas, which continues unabated. The fate of shorefront summer homes in New Jersey and Long Island, New York, after Hurricane Sandy seems to have eclipsed the meaning of the devastation of Katrina on the Gulf Coast. Elsewhere, in Miami, which the Organisation for Economic Co-operation and Development (OECD) in 2008 placed as the number one city with the most investment directly at risk, waterfront condominium and hotel construction is booming.[40] High-profile world cities may command federal and state financial support for rebuilding and defense, but there are many other cities that may have to rely on experiments in design, planning, and community preparedness and action as their best defense.

The cluster of cities in the Hampton Roads region of Virginia is only the thirty-sixth-largest metropolitan statistical area in the United States by population. This low-density urban settlement is built along rivers and saltmarshes, and often on filled creeks and wetlands. The land is sinking, or still settling after a prehistoric meteorite impact created the Chesapeake Bay.[41] The suburban build-out, completed in the 1980s, leaves few remaining development sites other than polluted postindustrial areas along the rivers. Hampton Roads is, however, one of the largest sheltered deepwater ports in the world and home to the United States Navy Atlantic Fleet, a dominant employer in the region. The clash between urban development,

35 Crawford S. Holling and Michael A. Goldberg, "Ecology and Planning (1971)," in *Projective Ecologies*, ed. Chris Reed and Nina-Marie Lister (Cambridge, MA: Harvard University Graduate School of Design, 2014) 106–25.
36 Alberti, *Advances*, 72.
37 Ibid., 10.
38 Peter W. G. Newman, "Sustainability and Cities: Extending the Metabolism Model," *Landscape and Urban Planning* 44 (January 1, 1999): 219–26.
39 Roger Keil, "Urban Political Ecology," *Urban Geography* 26, no. 7 (2005): 729.
40 R. J. Nicholls et al., "Ranking Port Cities with High Exposure and Vulnerability to Climate Extremes: Exposure Estimates," OECD Environment Working Papers, no. 1, OECD Publishing.
41 Hillary Mayell, "Chesapeake Bay Crater Offers Clues to Ancient Cataclysm," *National Geographic News*, last modified November 13, 2001, accessed November 3, 2015, http://news.nationalgeographic.com/news/2001/11/1113_chesapeakcrater.html.

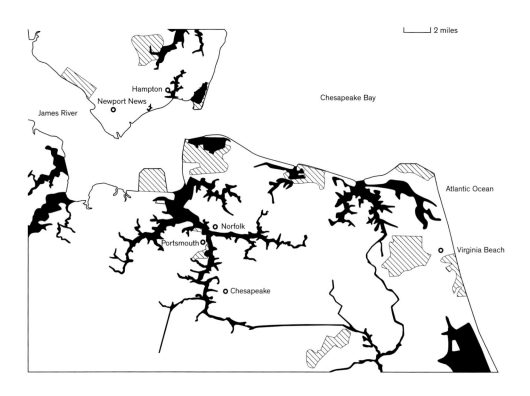

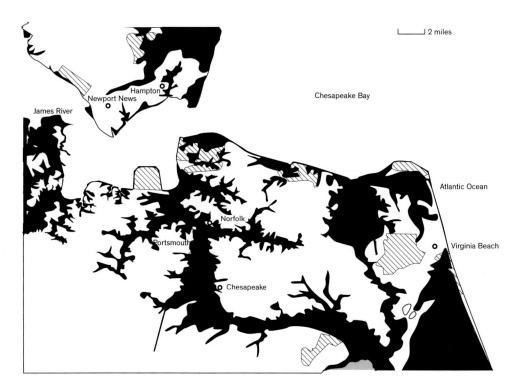

4.9.12 Hampton Roads, Virginia 2100

the navy's operations, and ecosystem function in the face of questions of resilience is becoming urgent.[42]

What will be the urban form and typologies of a low-density city in managed retreat from recurrent flooding, and how will the evolving settlement pattern relate to an expanding zone of shallow tidal inundation? What new bioaquatic functions and human activities might appear and take hold in this new watery landscape? Especially if they are on elevated ground, what role should decommissioned military sites and post-industrial areas play with regard to no longer viable first-generation suburban subdivisions nearby? Where can communities gather in the face of an approaching storm, but also, what will be the spaces where they can meet, strategize, and demonstrate for policy changes? And how can the succession from sweet water to brackish and tidal ecosystems be managed to continue to provide ecosystem services, one habitat replacing the other. Can cities change their sites in an orderly fashion? (fig. **4.9.12**)

The future of the Hampton Roads cities and landscapes is one site where the proposition of the low-density city, discoveries in urban ecology, and new typologies of living and working will make the transition from theory to everyday reality.

Shifting Centrality across the Low-Density City

How long will it take to achieve a low-density city? At the end of his 1943 book, *The City: Its Growth, Its Decay, Its Future,* Eliel Saarinen included an abstract diagram of the organic decentralization of a dense city over fifty years. Starting with an abstract "solid" urban form, the figure fragmented and expanded into an archipelago of islands following a spatial logic given by scale, function, and landscape. Today, this logic would yield space for diverse habitats leading to highly

productive urban ecosystems. In the diagram, each of the islands is not an individual building but a complete quarter, ensemble, or institutional complex with its own internal open spatial structure integrated with the larger scale spaces.[43] (fig. **4.9.13**)

In contrast, for many sprawling landscapes, an opposite strategy can take place. With the goal of building a new urban culture, spaces of centrality can be assembled over time by adding new functions and buildings. Upgrades of concepts such as pedestrian pockets, walkable urbanism, or smart growth, these infill projects can be finely tuned to the needs and attributes of their local environment. (fig. **4.9.14**)

The low-density city can be the social and spatial settlement form for a more equitable use of limited resources in the open system of the contemporary city. It can be the experimental field for the evolution from unbounded urbanization to more strategic development form in constant negotiation with local ecosystems, a transformation that is nothing less than a reimagining of growth. Rather than endless suburbia or the "triumph of sprawl," the twenty-first-century low-density city can be a platform for diversity rather than homogeneity, integration rather than segregation, transformation rather than renovation, and local pragmatism and invention rather than international idealism. It requires not a new urbanism but many urbanisms; not sustainability, but many sustainabilities.

42 David Malmquist, "VIMS Researcher Briefs Capitol Hill on Coastal Flooding," *Virginia Institute of Marine Sciences*, News and Events, last modified March 30, 2015, accessed November 3, 2015, http://www.vims.edu /newsandevents/top stories/nuisance _flooding.php.

43 Saarinen, *The City*, 288–89.

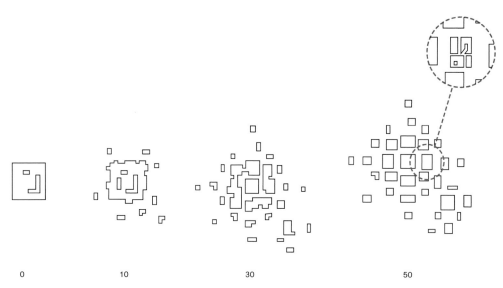

4.9.13 The organic decentralization of a dense city over fifty years, adapted from Saarinen, *The City: Its Growth, Its Decay, Its Future*

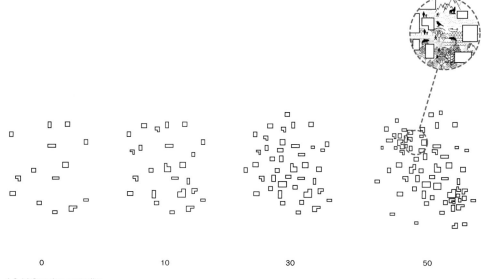

4.9.14 Creating centrality

4.10
WILLOW POND
TECHNOLOGIES FOR A FUTURE SUBURBAN FORM

Bruce Tonn and Dorian Stiefel

FLEXIBLE REGULATION

PRODUCTIVE SUBURBS

TECHNOLOGY

This is a scenario about a plausible future world in which an imaginary community has become a sustainable suburb. This scenario was developed to consider the social, technological, economic, environmental, and political contexts that make current suburban form unsustainable and to identify the attendant technological solutions.

This scenario is "set" in the year 2050 and based on a fictional community called Willow Pond. The name, Willow Pond, was completely fictional, too, in that the subdivision had neither willow trees nor a pond. Built during the 1990s, the original, imaginary Willow Pond had all the characteristics of a typical US "sprawling" residential development: single-family homes situated on partial acres of land; two-car garages; lawns in the front and back; invasive ornamentals dominating the landscaping; no sidewalks; a confusing layout of streets and culs-de-sac; and no commercial establishments.

These characteristics lead to a number of problems commonly associated with suburbia, yet many can be alleviated by existing and future technologies as exemplified by this scenario. One is the social issue of reduced community interaction, which future technology can address by increasing collaboration and reducing the need to leave the community to earn an income. Economic issues such as poor government budget choices are offset in this scenario by decisions informed by artificial intelligence. Environmental issues such as overreliance on nonrenewable natural resources are handled in this scenario by reduced use of energy overall and increased use of energy-efficient and renewables-based technologies. Political issues such as general public distance from the political process are offset by technologies for community engagement. Finally, emerging technologies that are not yet ready for production or implementation are assumed in this scenario to be ready by 2050.

By 2050, Willow Pond has become more self-sufficient and sustainable. Residents increased the energy efficiency of their homes and altered their behaviors to reduce their ecological footprints. Redesigned homes and yards support individual activities from telework to distance education. The redesigned community supports wildlife patches, self-sufficiency zoning, and indoor growing environments.

When we consider any plausible future world, we must distinguish the underlying assumptions and the decision points that are revealed in the scenario.[1] Underlying assumptions common to all scenarios include determining which key factors affect the outcome (e.g., creating a sustainable suburban form); identifying the relevant trends (e.g., multiyear changes in the same directions); determining the relative importance and uncertainty of the key factors and trends; and considering the implications.

Decision points are revealed when we reflect on how we might change our current behavior for future invention and planning.[2] Considering this plausible future creates a roadmap for anyone to follow, especially designers, planners, and policy makers. The new future might be achieved by understanding the roles of technological adaptation, productivity, and personal relationships in developing sustainable suburban forms. Considering the future also helps us create proactive polices and make real implementations of change.

In the sections that follow, we address the technological adaptations necessary to achieve this plausible future; the trends that will ease those transitions; the barriers to be overcome; and the benefits of overcoming those barriers. We close by revisiting this sustainable suburban form from the perspective of the systems of technologies that can make it real.

1　Jib Fowles, *Handbook of Futures Research* (Westport, CT: Greenwood Press, 1978), 807.
2　Peter Schwartz, *The Art of the Long View: Paths to Strategic Insight for Yourself and Your Company* (New York: Random House, 1996).

Sustainable Suburban Form

Willow Pond's sustainability is a function of self-sufficiency in which the majority of the food and materials needed by the community are grown or manufactured in the community. This is a necessary feature, as it eliminates the transportation energy costs and emissions wrought by specialization in which different areas have different capabilities but the food and materials have to be transported between each. Specialization, for example, in agriculture, is no longer necessary because technological innovations such as indoor farming offset issues with the local soil or climate.

Technological adaptation facilitated major redesigns of homes, yards, communities, and the commercial sector in Willow Pond. Homes are now designed to support diverse activities, from telework to distance education. Areas are set aside for 3-D printing and other household manufacturing activities. Kitchens have been redesigned for cooking fresh foods and recycling and reusing all kitchen wastes. The homes are constructed entirely of renewable, reusable, and recyclable materials. Drywall is gone, replaced by structural and polarizing glass in some places; carbon "fabricate anything blocks" (much like Legos but made of nanomaterials) in others. Many homes feature greenhouses with endangered flowering plants, crops to meet the particular tastes of the household, and other agriculture that produces income streams for the household. The insides and outsides of homes now have niches for wildlife such as bats and spiders.

Yards have been repurposed. In place of manicured lawns, bushes, and flowerbeds, residents grow biofuel crops, hemp for fibers, and fruit trees. Chickens and animals such as sheep and goats make their homes in these new yards. Most yards have dedicated patches of prairie that are homes for wildlife.

The entire subdivision has been rethought with respect to the local ecology, the regional ecosystem, and the interrelated economic considerations. The wildlife patches are coordinated throughout the development to expand the area's supporting ecology, including support for once-endangered species.

Residents rethought local land-use regulations and even homeowners' association agreements. Self-sufficiency zoning was invented to allow a mixture of agriculture and other work activities in a residential setting. Gone are the setback requirements and design overlays. Also gone are ordinances that inhibited residential renewable energy. Planners now see sprawl farms and vertical farms as central aspects of urban design rather than peripheral interests. Agricultural specialization as a function of land type is unnecessary because technologies are aiding all agricultural development, and most agriculture is being handled in a controlled facility.

The commercial sector has fewer grocery, clothing, department, and other stores because most items are consumed where they are produced. Many buildings have been repurposed as vertical farms. Appropriate spaces now house community 3-D printers, assembler/disassemblers, and associated materials for items too large to print, assemble, or disassemble at home. The community primarily uses distance education, distance medicine, and telecommuting, thereby reducing the need for central spaces previously devoted to schools, hospitals, and office buildings.

The newly intertwined residential and commercial sectors are an important aspect of the sustainable suburban form. Key features such as indoor growing environments, ubiquitous Internet, and a system for both centrally storing energy and dispatching everything are integral to both sectors in order to leverage time and resources.

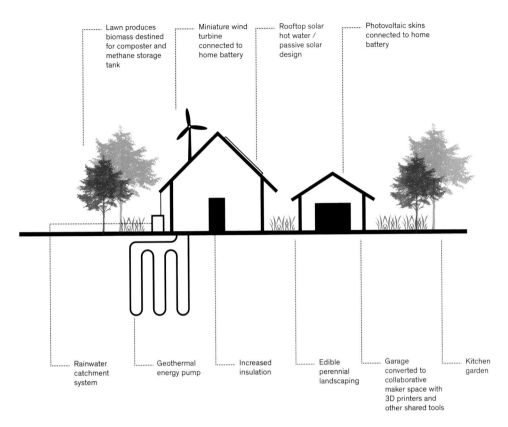

Lawn produces biomass destined for composter and methane storage tank

Miniature wind turbine connected to home battery

Rooftop solar hot water / passive solar design

Photovoltaic skins connected to home battery

Rainwater catchment system

Geothermal energy pump

Increased insulation

Edible perennial landscaping

Garage converted to collaborative maker space with 3D printers and other shared tools

Kitchen garden

4.10.1 A typical Willow Pond home

Technological Adaptations:
New Energy Systems

Technologies must converge on homes and communities to make this self-sufficiency a realistic goal. The foundations for these adaptations are advances in nanotechnology, biotechnology, information technology, and cognitive technologies. With respect to community self-sufficiency, these technologies can be grouped into seven categories. (figs. **10.1–2**)

Energy-efficient technologies help these communities and homes increase local manufacturing and local production. Due to tremendous decreases in costs of individual components, and major improvements in integrating residential energy system components into an efficient whole, the typical home features technology for producing energy, storing energy, and managing the energy system.

To produce energy, residents depend on solar, wind, geothermal, and biomass

technologies. Rooftops feature fabric photovoltaic (PV) skins and solar hot water heaters.[3] Mini wind turbines produce a few kilowatts toward energy self-sufficiency.[4] The geothermal energy pump and hydrogen-producing algae trays produce power for the fuel cells, while lawns now produce biomass that nearby composter and methane storage tanks process into energy.[5]

To store energy, residents primarily use fuel cells and other battery technologies.[6] Fuel cells store energy from the photovoltaic cells and small-scale wind turbines, and also produce electricity using hydrogen or methane.[7] Homes also use passive thermal energy storage techniques, such as heat-storing fluid and water tanks, home siding, and floor tiles.[8] Flywheels, which provide continuous energy even if the energy source is discontinuous; compressed air energy storage, which stores energy produced during off-peak times for use during

3   Martin A. Green, "Photovoltaics: Technology Overview," *Energy Policy* 28, no. 14 (2000): 989–98.

4   Paul Gipe, *Wind Energy Basics: A Guide to Home and Community-Scale Wind-Energy Systems* (White River Junction, VT: Chelsea Green Publishing, 2009); Lidula Nilakshi Widanagama Arachchige and Athula D. Rajapakse, "Microgrids Research: A Review of Experimental Microgrids and Test Systems," *Renewable and Sustainable Energy Reviews* 15, no. 1 (2011): 186–202.

5   Henrik Lund and Georges Salgi, "The Role of Compressed Air Energy Storage (CAES) in Future Sustainable Energy Systems," *Energy Conversion and Management* 50, no. 5 (2009): 1172–79; Younes Ghasemi et al., "Microalgae Biofuel Potentials (Review)," *Applied Biochemistry and Microbiology* 48, no. 2 (2012): 126–44; Chris Perry et al., "Increasing Productivity in Irrigated Agriculture: Agronomic Constraints and Hydrological Realities," *Agricultural Water Management* 96, no. 11 (2009): 1517–24; Yoshito Yuyama, Masato Nakamura, and Masaru Yamaoka, "Development of a Pilot-Scale Biomass Refinery System for Suburban Agricultural and Livestock Industrial Areas," *Japan Agricultural Research Quarterly* 44, no. 1 (2010): 93–100.

6   Haisheng Chen et al., "Progress in Electrical Energy Storage System: A Critical Review," *Progress in Natural Science* 19, no. 3 (2009): 291–312.

7   "Fuel Cell Basics," *Fuel Cell & Hydrogen Energy Association*, accessed November 1, 2015, http://www.fchea.org /fuel-cells/.

8   Atul Sharma et al., "Review on Thermal Energy Storage with Phase Change Materials and Applications," *Renewable and*

Stem cell meat manu-facturing | Sprawl farms | Vertical farms | Electric vehicles | Natural & edible land-scaping | Assembly / disassembly centers | Permeable paving | Fish farms | Water tower | Methane digester

4.10.2 A view of the Willow Pond community

peak times; and other mechanical storage such as springs, which allow energy to be stored more densely than in traditional energy storage devices such as lithium-ion batteries, are found throughout the community.[9]

Energy production, storage, and consumption are managed by whole-house and community artificial intelligence systems to ensure comfort per resident preferences and sustainability for the community.[10] Connected wireless sensors are located throughout the homes and community to measure temperature, humidity, air flows, carbon monoxide (CO), volatile organic compounds (VOCs), and radon. To simplify grid management, the Willow Pond development transmits major blocks of energy to the grid from its storage system at appointed times, or draws on the grid as needed.

Almost all personal and commercial vehicles are now electric. This suits residents of Willow Pond, as their home and community-based systems are designed to produce and store energy that can be easily transformed into electricity. Residents of Willow Pond make many fewer work, school, shopping, and entertainment trips than their counterparts in the twentieth century because life is essentially home- and community-based.

All of the technologies mentioned in this section are available in some form now, although they are each in varying stages of research, development, and deployment. Artificial intelligence and nanotechnology-based systems are primarily in the research stages, whereas energy production and energy storage systems are in the development and deployment stages. Autonomous electric vehicles exist now, but with limited electricity storage

capacity, the related limited range, and limited autonomous abilities.

More Adaptations:
Recycling Water and Materials
Willow Pond has a closed water system. Each home and commercial facility is equipped with a sophisticated nanotechnology-based water filtration system that purifies wastewater for reuse, whether for drinking or washing. Rain barrels collect water to supplement household water supplies and nourish the household plants and animals. Willow Pond's water tank provides water pressure for the fire hydrant system and doubles as an energy storage system. Substantial energy is saved because water is rarely pumped from place to place.

The industrial ecology is now dominated by the IR-3 concept: All materials used in the manufacture of goods are either Infinitely Reusable, Recyclable, or derived from Infinitely Renewable resources.[11] Advances in nanotechnology, biotechnology, and materials engineering support this industrial ecosystem with steel, glass, aluminum, and wood.

Reusable carbon "fabricate anything blocks" can be robotically assembled into large-scale construction and manufacturing for structures, vehicles, and furniture, and then robotically disassembled for reuse. Smaller-scale manufacturing of items such as clothes, rope, and electronics is supported with recyclable plastics; transgenic silk (e.g., spider silk produced by genetically modified silk worms); nanotechnological fibers and yarns; and graphene technology.[12] The IR-3 industrial ecology combines with 3-D printing and robotic assemblers/disassemblers to decentralize manufacturing.

Sustainable Energy Reviews 13, no. 2 (2009): 318–45.

9   Rafael Peña-Alzola et al., "Review of Flywheel Based Energy Storage Systems" (paper presented at the Power Engineering, Energy and Electrical Drives [POWERENG] International Conference, 2011); Henrik Lund and Georges Salgi, "The Role of Compressed Air Energy Storage (CAES) in Future Sustainable Energy Systems," *Energy Conversion and Management* 50, no. 5 (2009): 1172–79; Jeffery B. Greenblatt et al., "Baseload Wind Energy: Modeling the Competition between Gas Turbines and Compressed Air Energy Storage for Supplemental Generation," *Energy Policy* 35, no. 3 (2007): 1474–92.

10   Rafael Del-Hoyo et al., "Virtual Agents in Next Generation Interactive Homes," in *Trends in Practical Applications of Agents and Multiagent Systems* (Dordrecht, Neth.: Springer, 2012): 9–17.

11   Bruce Tonn et al., "Toward an Infinitely Reusable, Recyclable, and Renewable Industrial Ecosystem," *Journal of Cleaner Production* 66 (2014): 392–406.

12   Ibid.; Hongxiu Wen et al., "Transgenic Silkworms (*Bombyx Mori*) Produce Recombinant Spider Dragline Silk in Cocoons," *Molecular Biology Reports* 37, no. 4 (2010): 1815–21; Katherine Bourzac, "Spinning Nano Yarns: A Method for Turning Powders into Fibers Has Many Potential Applications," *MIT Technology Review*, last modified 2011, accessed November 1,

Concepts like carbon "fabricate anything blocks," nano-scale robotic assembly, transgenic silks, nanotechnological fibers and yarns, and graphene technologies are primarily in the research stages, whereas 3-D printing and robotic assemblers/disassemblers are in the development and deployment stages.

Sustainable Agriculture: Creating Food, Medicine, and Information

Willow Pond is sustainably self-sufficient with respect to food and medicine. The sprawl farm is located where the community center and pool used to be. It produces more than enough vegetables and fruits annually for the community of approximately 150 people. The sprawl farm's stem-cell meat production vats provide protein, and sprawl farm fishponds supplement the fishponds in the former swimming pools. A special area houses the genetically modified silk worms that produce industrial-strength spider fibers. The sprawl farm also has a special area devoted to "agriceuticals," which are genetically modified plants that produce a range of over-the-counter and prescription medicines.

Information technology is seamlessly embedded throughout Willow Pond. Facilitated by microphones and speakers located everywhere, residents use natural dialogue with the system and each other. The system also communicates through images, words, and 3-D holographic images that appear within or on objects.

Humans are always connected to the ubiquitous Internet via implanted devices that enhance cognition, and handle all information through neural paths, rather than input/output devices. All systems and interfaces are tailored to optimize human control of important home functions and facilitate education, work, and entertainment.

Cognitive technologies represent the vast knowledge base developed to improve the interaction between humans and technology, and to help humans deal with their technologically infused families and communities. Smart clothes regulate body comfort when, in order to save energy, buildings are warmer in the summer or cooler in the winter than might be desired otherwise. Cognitive technologies provide the interface between the humans and the clothing system. Cognitive technologies also support custom home system interactions with specific individuals, both children and adults. They operate regardless of whether the recipient is hearing or vision impaired by working with their cognitive styles. Language preferences and capabilities for understanding data and graphics are taken into account when explaining a 3-D printing design, for example, or a complex issue facing the community.

Stem-cell meat production; communication through images, words, and 3-D holographic images; implanted devices to enhance cognition; and other cognitive technologies are primarily in the research stages, whereas sprawl farms and vertical farms are in the development and deployment stages. By deploying and leveraging these technologies, residents redesigned their homes, yards, community, and commercial sector to be sustainable. And yet, trends in technology, politics, economics, and environmentalism also eased this transition.

Trends That Eased the Transition

Willow Pond of the early twenty-first century was completely unsustainable. It did not produce food, generate energy, or manufacture products. Water was piped in, and waste was not recycled. Residents generally did not work from their homes or in the neighborhood. They rarely walked or biked in the neighborhood because there were no interesting local destinations. In short, like other suburbs of that time, the old Willow Pond

2015, http://www.technologyreview.com/news/422311/spinning-nano-yarns/; Andre Konstantin Geim, "Graphene: Status and Prospects," *Science* 324, no. 5934 (2009): 1530–34.

had an enormous ecological footprint and was not socially, technologically, economically, environmentally, or politically sustainable.

Fortunately, a new and distinctive path toward sustainability emerged in the suburbs, guided by a critical question: What is the best way to accomplish sustainability? The major social, technological, economic, environmental, and political trends that were leveraged to produce a sustainable Willow Pond community ranged from increasing collaboration and self-reliance to declining political trust in the national system.

The Willow Pond grassroots movement toward community-based self-sufficiency is the culmination of a host of driving forces and technologies whose roots can be traced to the turn of this century but are only now, in 2050, having a truly distinct and disruptive impact on society. Increasing collaboration and self-reliance, for example, is not a new trend in American politics. However, information technology has made collaboration easier through encyclopedia sites like *Wikipedia* or crowd-sourced funding sites like Kickstarter.[13] Doing things on your own is easier now with additive manufacturing (e.g., 3-D printing) and access to instructions on the Internet.

Increasing information-technology ubiquity and capability means that decision support systems, complex adaptive systems, and artificial intelligence can be used in every aspect of the community, especially community governance.[14] Of course, technology and technological adaptation were also factors in the other trends. Increased understanding about the anthropogenic impacts on everything from ecology to climate meant that humans knew to begin working together to withstand the effects. At a minimum, it required careful planning and conservation, not to mention resources.

Climate change is taking a severe toll on the agricultural sector and, as a result, consumers. Global warming, combined with frequent and destructive extreme weather events, is negatively affecting crops and livestock. These effects reverberate throughout the economy. Increasing fluctuations in food prices and supplies are unpredictable and frustrating. Many people choose food self-sufficiency to reduce their vulnerability to price and supply shocks.[15]

The world hit its peak production of oil decades ago, yet the demand for energy continues to increase. In these exceptionally volatile energy markets, supplies of energy and electricity from the grid are regularly reduced. Again, many people choose energy self-sufficiency to reduce their vulnerability to these prices and supply shocks.[16]

Increasing employment uncertainties are driven by several factors. Modular factories and the supporting manufacturing jobs move around the globe, temporarily settling in locations that offer the best economic incentives. Spendthrift countries teeter on the brink of economic collapse, resulting in perpetual global economic crises. Government-financed economic development programs are chronically underfunded. Available jobs offer little security, low wages, and no benefits. Income disparities throughout the country are visible; resentment among the have-nots is running high.[17] To these alienated Americans, economic self-sufficiency honors the important values of hard work and self-reliance.

Consistent with declining trust in the national political system, the public mood has shifted from benign resignation to the strong belief that self-reliance and self-sufficiency are necessary in order to secure happy and healthy futures. Willow Pond uses a strong democracy system that features intensive dialogues about day-to-day operations of the community's local

13 Don Tapscott and Anthony D. Williams, *Wikinomics: How Mass Collaboration Changes Everything* (New York: Penguin Press, 2008); Bruce Tonn and Dorian Stiefel, "The Future of Governance and the Use of Advanced Information Technologies," *Futures* 44, no. 9 (2012): 812–22.

14 Bruce Tonn and Dorian Stiefel, "The Future of Governance and the Use of Advanced Information Technologies," *Futures* 44, no. 9 (2012): 812–22.

15 Hans G. Bohle, Thomas E. Downing, and Michael J. Watts, "Climate Change and Social Vulnerability: Toward a Sociology and Geography of Food Insecurity," *Global Environmental Change* 4, no. 1 (1994): 37–48.

16 Clinton J. Andrews, "Reducing Energy Vulnerability" (paper presented at the International Symposium on Technology and Society Proceedings on Weapons and Wires: Prevention and Safety in a Time of Fear, 2005).

17 Nathan J. Kelly, *The Politics of Income Inequality in the United States* (Cambridge: Cambridge University Press, 2009); Daisaku Yamamoto, "Scales of Regional Income Disparities in the USA, 1955–2003," *Journal of Economic Geography* 8, no. 1 (2007): 79–103.

production facilities but allows the community's information technology system to set production and schedule residents' time.[18]

In short, in order to buffer themselves from crippling price and supply impacts and to better secure their futures, many residents have come to believe that they were better off by themselves. This shift in viewpoint coincided with the slow but steady social reacceptance of collaborative economics, pioneered by *Wikipedia* and Kickstarter; a reemergence of do-it-yourself vigor; and a reinvigoration of the home as the focal point of life for entertainment, telecommuting, distance education, social networking, and gaming.

Barriers Overcome in the Transition

The decentralization of energy and food production, along with manufacturing, was achieved by overcoming major barriers. The most significant barriers had social and economic origins. Communities such as Willow Pond are trailblazing approaches to deal with these types of problems.

One social barrier to the development of Willow Pond was psychological. Although individuals have innate abilities to collaborate with each other, technological development may have exceeded human psychological development, which leads to deficiencies in cognitive skills.[19] Controlling the size of the community lessens this burden, which is why Willow Pond is limited to 150 individuals. Informed by Robin Dunbar's discovery that most functional human organizations—indigenous clans, military companies, and business units—naturally coalesce around this number, residents discovered that this size comfortably supports the strong democratic processes they prefer.[20]

Other social barriers include establishing relatedness and social trust. Willow Pond residents eliminate these barriers with neutral parties, both external facilitators and elders, who facilitate discussions and meetings on a range of topics from deciding color schemes for the sprawl farm to raising children in this new environment.[21] External facilitators are trained in thinking together through dialogue and mediation, whereas elders are an agnostic cross between therapists, ministers, social workers, or sometimes even event organizers who still have an aura of spirituality.[22]

They do not take the place of community leaders and instead accomplish things in neutral ways that leaders cannot. They lead individuals in practices designed to lessen social anxiety (e.g., through high-energy activities designed to reduce social inhibitions) and increase commitment to place (e.g., through new traditions). Facilitators and elders have increased levels of relatedness and trust in the community, which allows residents to productively work together for governance and commerce.[23]

Almost every aspect of the production process can now be automated. Individuals, households, and communities must now balance technology and human capital: How involved should humans be in the production process? External facilitators and elders work with community members to seek answers that are culturally appropriate and individually acceptable. Moderate-to-low-income communities typically rely more on themselves (because it is less expensive) and less on technology, whereas high-end communities like Willow Pond opt for more automation because many residents also have salaried positions. Most of the technologies in the household and community require little human interaction. Where human interaction is required, for example, to kick off a 3-D printing job, it takes just minutes, so it can be managed as part of the household management tasks or can be handled by a designated

18 Benjamin R. Barber, *Strong Democracy: Participatory Politics for a New Age* (Berkeley: University of California Press, 2003).

19 Jerome H. Barkow, Leda Cosmides, and John Tooby, *The Adapted Mind: Evolutionary Psychology and the Generation of Culture* (Oxford: Oxford University Press, 1992).

20 Robin Dunbar, *How Many Friends Does One Person Need? Dunbar's Number and Other Evolutionary Quirks* (London: Faber & Faber, 2010).

21 Although some things never change: Willow Pond mothers still admonish their children for being late to lessons: "I have told you umpteen times to print your new clothes the night before!"

22 William Isaacs, *Dialogue: The Art of Thinking Together* (New York: Random House, 2008).

23 Robert D. Putnam, "Bowling Alone: America's Declining Social Capital," *Journal of Democracy* 6 (1995): 68.

member of the community. Residents with jobs have more than enough time to handle their personal work, the work of the household, and the work of the community.

As noted above, Willow Pond is also characterized by a strong information technology system support. The system does not make the decisions. Instead, the community's system supports Willow Pond's strong democracy by providing customized access to important community information and production and staffing solutions that optimize multiparty decisions criteria. The system also keeps track of individuals' time spent in various production tasks as well as their future commitments.[24]

Members of Willow Pond continue to adjust to yards that are biomass fields; swimming pools that are fish ponds; niches in their homes that are animal homes; and roads made of "fabricate anything blocks" instead of asphalt. Living with wildlife has been a special challenge to residents' fears and preconceived notions. Although Willow Pond residents embrace the concept of wildlife in their community, they still discuss the limits; fish in the pond and bats in the house niches may be acceptable, but what about bears, badgers, buffalo, deer, turkeys, and vultures? Expert facilitation and customized communication continue to be needed in order to ensure safe coexistence.

Community self-sufficiency is balanced against the need to import and export some products and services. For example, the community is too small to provide insurance. Citizens need money to pay the head taxes for infrastructure and to contribute to savings funds.[25] Therefore, a certain percentage of the community's production from its 3-D printers and sprawl farm are for mostly regional export.

The most interesting unintended consequence of this decentralization has been the shift from a cash-based economy to an essentially barter-based one. The absence of prices and the need for intense cooperation have led to an intensely collaborative economy. The community continually addresses issues of wealth disparity such as the time allocated to the house, versus the community or ownership. External facilitators and elders regularly reflect on how much wealth disparity the community can tolerate before it breaks into separate communities or falls apart entirely. They do not consider this issue to be solved, but they do have a better understanding of the issues and relevant approaches than other communities.

Shared resources range from household printers to the sprawl farm; from filament to carbon "fabricate anything blocks." To handle ownership of shared resources, Willow Pond use a variation of the Homeowners' Association Agreements (HOAAs) from the 1990s. The updated HOAA contains provisions on what the HOAA owns (e.g., the sprawl farm); what contributions of resources homeowners must make (e.g., 3-D printers and filament); and the homeowners' rights and responsibilities. When residents sell their home, they also sell their share of the association.

Other key political issues include dealing with controlled substances, addressing poverty, and handling public education. Dealing with controlled substances is necessary because "agriceuticals" can be produced inexpensively within the community, and some are still legally controlled substances. Major discussions focus on what to produce, who can produce them, who can have them, and who will monitor each of these aspects to meet legal requirements.

Addressing poverty is a practical concern when the person in poverty is your neighbor, which is why the community must serve households that do not have

24 Economists are developing new theories based on these systems and the communities they serve. In obligational theory, obligations are the fundamental particles of economics, more basic than money. If an economy has too many obligations in circulation versus the likely ability of the "economy" to meet them, then a bubble is created, and a crash becomes imminent. Community information technology systems are programmed to identify bubble situations; see John C. Harsanyi, "Rule Utilitarianism, Rights, Obligations, and the Theory of Rational Behavior," *Theory and Decision* 12, no. 2 (1980): 115–33.

25 A national head tax for infrastructure was adopted to support the national electricity grid and interstate highway system. This was necessitated because utilities were not able to sell enough electricity to generate enough revenues to maintain the grid (even though most communities still benefited from having access to the grid) and because gas tax revenues disappeared along with the internal combustion engine.

enough food or energy. Handling public education is on the agenda at every public meeting. Given the proliferation of technology and the ease of using the Internet, the community's children learn a great deal about content and social skills from local devices and international interconnectivity.

Willow Pond had to overcome many barriers to transition to this sustainable suburban form. Still, the community has many barriers still to overcome to continue enjoying the benefits of this sustainable suburban form.

A Look at the Benefits

Willow Pond is a great example of community that has created social, technological, environmental, economic, and political sustainability. In addition to sustainability, the residents have achieved quite a few benefits, ranging from increased happiness to increased political empowerment.

Residents are able to control their lives, so they feel happy. However, they also experience substantial ambivalence about being part of a community where everybody knows everybody else's business. They liked the anonymity of life in the early twenty-first century, but they also like the benefits of this decentralized community and a sustainable suburban existence.

Thoughtful reliance on artificial intelligence systems and cognitive technologies led to increased happiness, because the day-to-day effort of life is supported by intelligent systems and the residents have cognitive technologies that allow them to interact as equals with those systems.

Substantial increases in renewable energy production in residential areas as a result of the local energy production and the closed water system are paired with substantial overall decreases in industrial-sector energy consumption. This is because materials are either infinitely reusable, recyclable, or derived from infinitely renewable resources.

Residents enjoy substantial increases in food and medicine self-sufficiency because the majority of the materials are grown or manufactured locally and sustainably. They also enjoy substantial increases in personal health because members have almost-real-time monitoring of their health and access to preventative medicine and therapies. Substantial decreases in transportation costs are possible because most of the vehicles are electric and residents make fewer trips now that work, school, shopping, and entertainment are all local. When residents travel, they travel in semiautonomous vehicles that both plan the trip for the most energy-efficient use of electricity and allow human intervention when necessary for safety.

Substantial increases in political participation are possible because residents feel more empowered to participate. The choices they are making truly affect them.

Is a Sustainable Suburban Form Possible?

Our scenario details a sustainable suburban form that is characterized by community- and household-based sustainable self-sufficiency, made possible by the convergence of advanced technologies that allow the decentralization of production and governance. Several trends were leveraged, and multiple barriers were overcome.

One key trend was the increasing ubiquity and capability of information technology, including advanced information technology support; another was increasing collaboration and self-reliance. A third important factor was reinventing lost social roles with external facilitators, elders, and other people who can facilitate personal relationships and social trust.

Despite these insights, additional research is necessary in order to transition from our current reality to this Willow

Pond. Technology solves the social, technological, economic, environmental, and political problems distinguished above, but human knowledge and will is necessary to research, develop, and deploy these technologies. Moreover, deployment of these technologies requires ongoing human inquiry and reflection about the moral, ethical, and generational impacts. Researchers must therefore answer the following questions as communities like Willow Pond emerge: What is required to ensure long-term sustainability of communities like these? What is the impact of local self-sufficiency and sustainability on national and regional economies? What is the impact of the local self-sufficiency on national culture and politics?

The residents of Willow Pond have established a truly sustainable community that is largely independent of the regional, national, and international economies, and thus highly dependent on technology, productivity, and personal relationships.

4.11
THE POWER OF SUBURBIA

Hugh Byrd

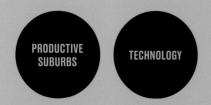

PRODUCTIVE SUBURBS

TECHNOLOGY

Research on the relationship between sustainability and urban form has tended to focus on the connections between urban density, transport fuel consumption, and household domestic energy consumption. One of the most influential studies on transport energy and urban form is the work by the Australian academics Peter Newman and Jeffrey Kenworthy.[1] Their analysis of fuel consumption in different cities graphically illustrated a correlation between the high gross density of a city and low per capita petroleum consumption.

With such clear and measurable correlations between density and energy use, suburbia and urban sprawl were seen to be the culprits of high transport energy, with consequent adverse issues of pollution, poor health, and economic welfare.[2] The compact city was thus advocated as a means of reducing fossil fuel consumption and improving energy efficiency, as well as bettering the environment and health. Intensification of urban form became synonymous with sustainability.

This notion became an integral part of planning policy in Europe, America, and Australia.[3] Over the past two decades, various forms of "compact city" policies have been accepted and implemented around the world. The European Commission was one of the first to promote such a view on environmental and quality-of-life grounds. The United Kingdom incorporated the policy in its Strategy for Sustainable Development to reduce transport energy consumption.[4] Even in the United States, renouncing the American-style urban sprawl and instead promoting growth management policies—smart growth—became the more conventionally accepted theory, with increasing support from urban economists such as David Chinitz and New Urbanists such as James Kunstler.[5] However, for all the attempts to have compact development, it still does not address the fact that suburbia exists and will continue to do so. Thus, what do we do with all the low-density urban form?

Although suburbia has been condemned for its high-energy use due to sprawl, the research that led to this conclusion is based on internal combustion engine vehicles (ICEVs). While research on the impact of emerging technologies on urban form has started, little research has been done on the overall impact of emerging smart energy technologies such as residential distributed energy generation (DG) by solar photovoltaic panels (PV), smart meters, and electric vehicles (EV) that are being developed and are now available for mass deployment.[6] What are the implications if a predominately EV-driven transport system is adopted that, moreover, is fueled by renewable energy sources from DG in suburbia?

An attempt to answer this question might begin with a case study of Auckland, New Zealand, carried out by a cross-disciplinary team at the University of Auckland.[7] At first glance, the experiences of New Zealand would seem appropriate for translation to a wider context, with both its predicted rapid increase in population growth and heavy dependence on imported oil for transport. Almost half of the energy consumed by New Zealand is oil used by the transport industry.[8] This is the case particularly in Auckland, which has become a car-dependent city and experiences the country's greatest growth.[9]

However, New Zealand, and Auckland in particular, have characteristics that differ from other cities and countries. First, with government policy to increase the share of renewable electricity supply from over 70 percent currently to 90 percent by the year 2025, it is important to diversify the sources of renewable energy due to their intermittent nature.[10] There is considerable room for small-scale residential photovoltaic panel deployment.

1   Peter W. G. Newman and Jeffrey R. Kenworthy, "Gasoline Consumption and Cities," *Journal of the American Planning Association* 55, no. 1 (March 31, 1989): 24–37.

2   Karen Witten, Wokje Abrahamse, and Keriata Stuart, *Growth Misconduct? Avoiding Sprawl and Improving Urban Intensification in New Zealand* (Auckland: Steele Roberts, 2011).

3   Arza Churchman, "Disentangling the Concept of Density," *Journal of Planning Literature* 13, no. 4 (May 1, 1999): 389–411.

4   United Kingdom Department of the Environment, *Sustainable Development: The U.K. Strategy* (London: Her Majesty's Stationery Office, 1994).

5   Benjamin Chinitz, "Growth Management Good for the Town, Bad for the Nation?," *Journal of the American Planning Association* 56, no. 1 (March 31, 1990): 3–8; James Howard Kunstler, *The Geography of Nowhere: The Rise and Decline of America's Man-Made Landscape* (New York: Free Press, 1994).

6   Jon Kellett, "More Than a Roof over Our Head: Can Planning Safeguard Rooftop Resources?," *Urban Policy and Research* 29, no. 1 (March 1, 2011): 23–36.

7   Hugh Byrd et al., "Measuring the Solar Potential of a City and Its Implications for Energy Policy," *Energy Policy* 61 (October 2013): 944–52.

8   Ministry of Economic Development, *New Zealand Energy Strategy to 2050: Powering Our Future* (Wellington: Ministry of Economic Development, October 2007).

9   Paul Mees and Jago Dodson, *Bureaucratic Rationality and Public Preferences in Transport Planning* (Brisbane: Griffith University, April 2006).

10 Electricity Authority, *Electricity in New Zealand* (Wellington: Electricity Authority, 2011).

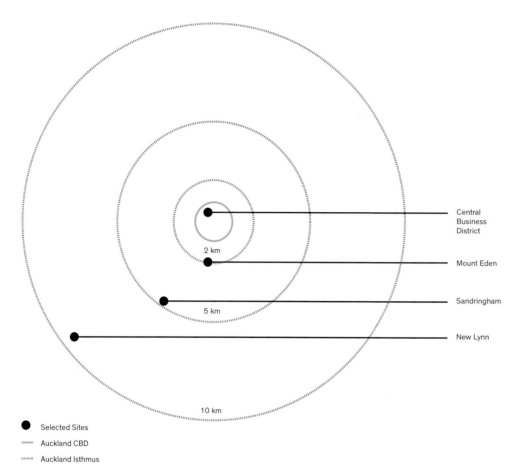

Central
Business
District

Mount Eden

Sandringham

New Lynn

2 km

5 km

10 km

● Selected Sites

— Auckland CBD

···· Auckland Isthmus

4.11.1 Auckland case study site location

11 IT Power Australia and
    Southern Perspective,
    *Assessment of the Future
    Costs and Performance of
    Solar Photovoltaic Tech-
    nologies in New Zealand*
    (Wellington: Ministry of
    Economic Development,
    April 2009).
12 Nathaniel S. Pearre et
    al., "Electric Vehicles:
    How Much Range Is
    Required for a Day's
    Driving?," *Transportation
    Research Part C:
    Emerging Technologies* 19,
    no. 6 (December 2011):
    1171–84.
13 Ministry of Transport,
    Household Travel Survey
    (Wellington: Ministry of
    Transport, 2014).

Second, Auckland receives a significant amount of solar radiation annually, comparable to many high-PV-deployment countries internationally.[11] Electricity produced by residential PVs could reach price parity with the grid by 2017 in Auckland. And third, a US study has disputed the usual argument against electric vehicle uptake, which focuses on range issues.[12] Similarly, statistics suggest that 90 percent of New Zealand private vehicles travel less than 52 miles (84 kilometers) daily, which is well within the current range of EVs.[13] This makes such forms of transport feasible, and with the incorporation of residential PVs with smart grid technology, can facilitate the synergy between PVs and EVs. In this way, we could reduce oil dependence and the environmental harm associated with current transportation modes.

Nonetheless, the focus of this research is on the traditional densities and patterns of suburbia in cities such as Auckland, and their potential to offer surplus solar energy generation that can be harnessed for low-energy electric vehicle transport, which can reduce adverse consequences of air quality, noise pollution, and carbon emissions. Moreover, a significant amount of private transport vehicle journeys in the city do not head toward the center along either existing or potential public transport routes. This indicates an important role that EVs powered by renewable energy can play in the future for both Auckland and for cities with similar characteristics.

The study examined total energy supply and consumption—household and transport—in different residential

Population Density on Selected Residential Blocks

14 Sumita Ghosh, "Simple
Sustainability Indicators
for Residential Areas
of New Zealand" (thesis,
University of Auckland,
2004).

(figures not to scale)	Site Name	Population Density (households/hectare)	Population Density (persons/hectare)	Residents per Household
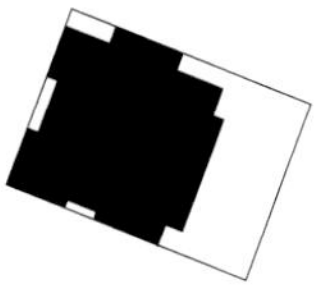	CBD	1,142.2	2,198.3	1.9
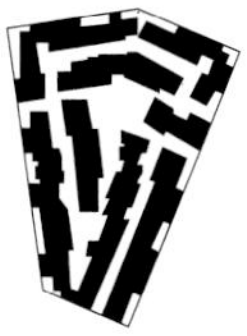	Mt Eden	125.3	321.5	2.6
	Sandringham	29.9	104.2	3.5
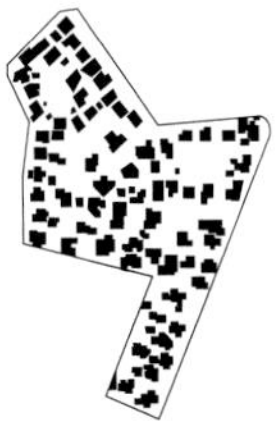	New Lynn	13.5	47.1	3.5

4.11.2 Selected housing site data

densities, and their associated housing typology in various areas of Auckland. Calculation of total energy use takes into account household transport energy consumed and the potential energy supplied by residential roof-mounted PVs. For transportation, by adopting smart energy technologies in the form of electric vehicles benefiting from renewable energy generation by photovoltaic panels, suburbia has the potential to be more energy efficient than compact housing near the city center. Despite this conclusion, it is not our purpose to argue in favor of private transport, or that compact, intensified development should be abandoned.

There are many other issues of importance that must be taken into account in that debate.

Measuring Smart Energy

Four housing sites were selected for the study to test and measure the impact of smart energy technologies on urban form. Sites were chosen on the basis of their distance from the city, their densities, and the detailed data available on these sites from other research.[14] (figs. **4.11.1–2**)

We used net densities that included housing, gardens, and driveways, but did not include public open space, public roads, or nonresidential buildings. New

Daily Average Travel Distance per Vehicle Drivers (km)

Purpose	Major Urban Areas	CBD	Mt Eden	Sandringham	New Lynn
Home	6.4	6.4	6.4	6.4	6.4
Work—main job	4.3	2.5	2.5	5.0	8.0
Work—other job	0.1	0.1	0.1	0.1	0.1
Work—employer's business	0.8	0.8	0.8	0.8	0.8
Education	0.2	0.2	0.2	0.2	0.2
Shopping	1.9	1.9	1.9	1.9	1.9
Personal business / services	1.1	1.1	1.1	1.1	1.1
Medical/dental	0.2	0.2	0.2	0.2	0.2
Social visits	2.2	2.2	2.2	2.2	2.2
Recreational	1.0	1.0	1.0	1.0	1.0
Change mode	0.3	0.3	0.3	0.3	0.3
Accompany someone else	1.1	1.1	1.1	1.1	1.1
Total	**19.4**	**17.8**	**17.8**	**20.3**	**23.3**

4.11.3 Average travel distance per vehicle driver for selected sites

Lynn—the outermost and lowest density area—has a density of 5.7 households per acre (14 households per hectare). New Lynn's density is about half that of Sandringham, the lower-medium density area with 12.1 households per acre (30 households per hectare). In turn, Sandringham has about one-third the density of Mount Eden, the upper-medium density suburb with 50.6 households per acre (125 households per hectare), and about one-tenth the density of the apartment development in the central business district (CBD). These densities represent a typical exponential increase in density from the outer suburbs toward the CBD. (figs. **4.11.3–4**)

Transport Energy Consumption

In order to compare two modes of transport using different forms of energy, we examined analyses of the travel patterns of households, assuming that the patterns would remain the same for both electric vehicles and internal combustion engine vehicles. This assumption does not favor electric vehicles, which actually are likely to encourage more economic travel behavior patterns. However, in the absence of data that show comparative travel

behavior between ICEVs and EVs, we assumed the worst-case situation for EVs.

Detailed information on travel patterns is included in a report by transportation engineers Steve Abley, Michael Chou, and Malcolm Douglass in the "National Travel Profile." [15] This research was commissioned by the New Zealand Transport Agency and is an evaluation of the extensive continuous survey information collected by the New Zealand Household Travel Survey. This report analyzed everyday personal travel such as travel mode, travel purpose, travel by trip purpose, and more. The report separated the data into different types of urban composition. Our four studied sites are within the category "major urban areas, and vehicle drivers within these areas have a mean trip length of 5.0 miles (8.1 kilometers) and an average trip per vehicle driver per day at 2.4 times, which gives an average travel distance per vehicle driver per day of 12.08 miles (19.44 kilometers). Deviations from this average have not been considered as it is a comparative study between three sites that all fall within the category of 'major urban areas.'"

The report also indicated the national mean distance traveled per person per

15 Steve Abley, Michael Chou, and Malcolm Douglass, *National Travel Profiles Part A: Description of Daily Travel Patterns* (Wellington: New Zealand Transport Agency, 2008).

Total Annual Per Person Vehicle Travel Consumption

	Total Vehicle Distance Traveled (km)	Total ICEV Fuel Consumption in Liters of Diesel (L)*	Total ICEV Fuel Consumption in Liters of Petrol (L)*	Total EV Electricity Consumption (kWh)**
High-Density	1,104	9	101	268
Upper-medium Density	2,404	19	219	584
Lower-medium Density	3,631	29	330	882
Low-Density	4,167	34	379	1,012

*Average fuel consumption rate for diesel ICEV – 0.09 L/km, for petrol ICEV – 0.10 L/km. Data from all available models and makes that matches the representative vehicle from fuelsaver.govt.nz, viewed on May 27, 2011.
**Consumption data based on a study by Mike Duke, Deborah Andrews, and Timothy Anderson, "The Feasibility of Long Range Battery Electric Cars in New Zealand," *Energy Policy* 37, no. 9 (January 1, 2009): 3455–62. The study measured the performance of a five-seat family battery electric vehicle capable of over 300km on one battery charge purposely built with LiFePO4 batteries.

4.11.4 Total annual per person vehicle travel consumption for selected sites

16 "Mapping Trends in the Auckland Region-Mapping Commuting," Statistics New Zealand, accessed September 23, 2015, http://www.stats.govt.nz /browse_for_stats /Maps_and_geography /Geographic-areas /mapping-trends-in -the-auckland-region /commuting.aspx.

17 Land Transport New Zealand, *New Zealand Motor Vehicle Registration Statistics 2006* (Palmerston North: Land Transport New Zealand, 2007).

day, categorized by trip purpose and transportation mode. The distance to the main job has assumed travel to the CBD, and the actual travel distance deviations are taken from the Auckland 2006 Census data on the respective areas.[16] This will favor the case for intensifying urban form. It has also been assumed that householders in all three sites will have equal travel distances to other services.

For the purpose of the study, a representative vehicle ICEV was selected for fuel consumption statistics: a 1,801- to 2,000-cylinder capacity light vehicle. This type of vehicle is considered the most appropriate because it represents the greatest percentage among all the vehicles registered in 2006.[17] Also of importance is that, in the same year, 91 percent of light vehicles or cars had gasoline engines, while only 8.5 percent were diesel powered.

Fuel consumption levels per person per year (both gasoline and diesel) for each of the study areas were calculated. The fuel consumption for each area is then converted to electricity consumption assuming that EVs will have the same travel patterns. The final column indicates the energy consumption of a representative electric vehicle for 100 percent of the total distance traveled, assuming the same number of vehicle drivers in each block will travel the same amount in an electric car as they do in a fossil-fueled car.

The results of the research show that by adopting electric vehicles the same travel distance generated much lower energy consumption. In fact, the energy consumption of EVs was four times less than that of ICEVs. On the issue of energy efficiency alone, electric vehicles have a much greater advantage over fossil fuel cars in urban areas. However, the adaptation of this technology will increase the current electricity demand, creating pressure on the supply. This leads to the second part of the study, an investigation of solar energy generation potential in residential households and its relation with EV energy consumption. (fig. **4.11.5**)

Calculating Solar Energy Generation Potential

For residential households, there are several benefits in deploying roof PV modules. They are capable of supplementing some of the household electricity needs or producing income if excess can be supplied to the grid. They can also offer households some degree of resilience should the main electricity supply grid fail.

A synergy could easily exist between operating EVs and utilizing PVs. By integrating these technologies in a residential setting, it could reduce pressure on the electricity transmission grid, improve energy efficiency for households, and reduce fossil fuel reliance on household travel. It could also reduce the peak

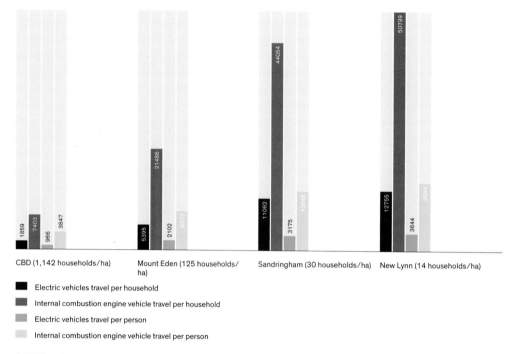

CBD (1,142 households/ha)

Mount Eden (125 households/ha)

Sandringham (30 households/ha)

New Lynn (14 households/ha)

■ Electric vehicles travel per household

■ Internal combustion engine vehicle travel per household

■ Electric vehicles travel per person

□ Internal combustion engine vehicle travel per person

4.11.5 Travel energy consumption in megajoules (MJ) relative to urban density

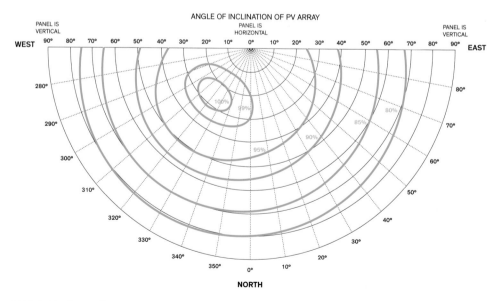

4.11.6 Auckland solar efficiency protractor

	Roof Form	Roof orientation	PV/RA Ratio
	Flat*	na	0.63
	Duo: 1 continuous roof ridge	NE	0.56
		NW	0.47
	complex roof 1: 1 major ridge with slopped ends	NE	0.44
		NW	0.45
	complex roof 2: 2 major ridges	NE	0.42
		NW	0.42
	complex roof 3: 3 or more major ridges	NE	0.33
		NW	0.42

4.11.7 PV over roof area ratio based on roof form and orientation

18 "Powerwall: Tesla Home Battery," Tesla Motors, accessed September 23, 2015, http://www.tesla motors.com/powerwall.

demand for electricity if charging could be done during the daytime. This could be done by storage batteries at home, such as those proposed by Tesla, or by peer-to-peer electricity supply by selling electricity to the location of a vehicle parked away from home.[18]

This synergistic relationship is particularly beneficial for New Zealand households, since the country lacks incentive programs such as a subsidized tariff to allow surplus electricity to be sold back to the grid. Such a policy could be further aided by smart grid technologies that provide for better consumer-side management such as smart meters.

We investigated the solar-efficient roof areas for each house on the four selected residential sites in Auckland. Based on solar data for Auckland, we charted PV angle and orientation in relation to the proportion of maximum radiation that can be received. (fig. **4.11.6**) Only roof areas of 95 percent efficiency or higher were considered in the analysis. From these calculations, we created a three-dimensional digital model of all the roofs in all the sites so that standard panel arrays were arranged on the roof areas that exceeded 95 percent efficiency. The ratio between the PV areas and overall roof areas (RA) was calculated. Overall, we found that the less complicated the roof form, the higher its PV:RA ratio, with some small difference in orientation. (fig. **4.11.7**)

For the purpose of the study, an assumption was made that 43 square feet (4 square meters) of the efficient roof area per household was reserved for solar

Annual Maximum Solar Electricity Generation by PV Per Household

	Maximum PV Avaliable Area (m2)	Annual Solar Electricity Generation by PV (kWh)*	Annual Solar Energy Generation by PV (MJ)**
High Density	—	—	—
Upper-medium Density	15	2,325	3,340
Lower-medium Density	50	2,313	8,325
Low Density	68	3,148	11,333

*Electricity generation based on 0.14kW, 1600mm x 760mm panel, with 7% loss from dust & dirt; 2% loss from wiring; 6% loss to DC conversion.
**Energy conversion based on: Average Electricity – 3.6MJ/kWh. (Barber, 2009: 2)

4.11.8 Solar energy generation potential for selected sites

water heating. This area was excluded in the calculation of the PV electricity generation potential. However, the high-density site (CBD), due to limited solar efficient roof area, had no available PV area after solar hot-water panels were installed. Thus, we adjusted the area reserved for solar water heating to 32 square feet (3 square meters) per household. This is illustrated in each residential site's potential roof PV efficient area, and its corresponding energy generation capabilities. (fig. **4.11.8**)

The relevance of these energy production capacities lies in their association with the different density levels of the studied sites. A positive relation exists between electricity production potential and reduced density of housing. In terms of solar electricity potential, the lower the density the higher the gain. (fig. **4.11.9**) This is in marked contrast with the previous calculations on transport energy consumption of these sites based on internal combustion engine vehicles. But in terms of travel energy expenditure, the higher the density, the less energy used.

Solar Energy Generation Potential and Density

To compare the energy consumed by EVs with the energy supplied by PVs and the relationship with density, three factors are involved: travel energy consumption, solar energy generation, and urban density. By juxtaposing these three factors, we can illustrate the impact they have on each other. Assuming all four residential

sites will utilize their full solar potential, the energy generated could be sufficient to provide all daily travel energy consumption. A caveat: this is applicable only to the three less dense sites, since, due to solar water heating requirements, the high-density site cannot provide any efficient PV areas for energy generation.

The relationship between energy and density for the different selected sites is measured in megajoules of gas equivalent against person per hectare so that it can be directly compared with the graph by Newman and Kenworthy.[19] (fig. **4.11.10**) When EVs powered by PV are included, adequate energy for transport (and even a surplus) is available for the three lower density sites. The curve in negative values indicates the surplus energy for the sites in accordance to their density level. Interestingly, this curve resembles a mirror image of the graph by Newman and Kenworthy, which suggests a reversal of the conventional theory on the relationship between density and travel energy consumption. When EVs are powered by PV generation, an inverse relationship can occur between EV travel energy, consumption, and density.

We also looked at how policy makers could use the relationship between energy use and urban density, taking account of solar hot-water heating, PVs, and EVs. The optimum density to reduce energy consumption in Auckland is in the region of 12 households per acre (30 households per hectare). Below about 247 households per acre (100 households per

19 Peter W. G. Newman and Jeffrey R. Kenworthy, *Cities and Automobile Dependence: A Sourcebook* (Aldershot, UK; Brookfield, VT: Gower Publishing Company, 1990).

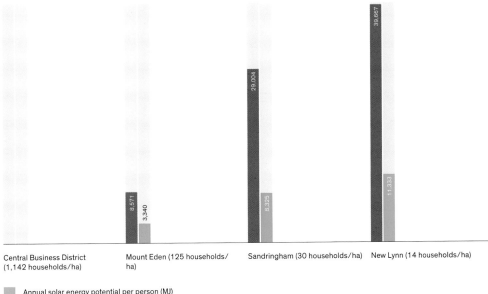

Central Business District
(1,142 households/ha)

Mount Eden (125 households/
ha)

Sandringham (30 households/ha)   New Lynn (14 households/ha)

◼ Annual solar energy potential per person (MJ)

◼ Annual solar energy potential per household (MJ)

4.11.9 Solar energy generation (in megajoules) by PV in relation to density

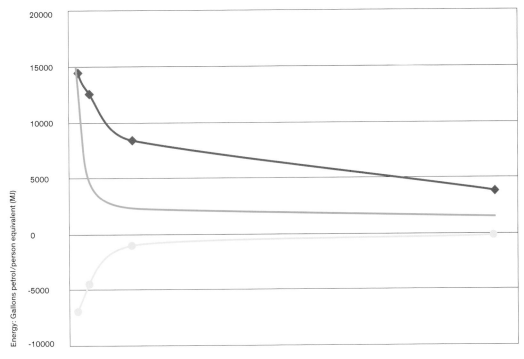

Urban Density (persons/acre)

◆ Internal combustion engine petrol consumption (measured in net density)

— Newman and Kenworthy (measured in gross density)

● Surplus from solar generation after electric vehicle consumption (measured in net density)

4.11.10 Relationship of transport energy and urban density in Auckland for both petrol and electric vehicles

hectare), there is surplus energy from PVs during the daytime that increases until itreaches about 30 households per acre (12 households per hectare). If energy is an important issue in the future of the city, then typical densities found in the existing suburbs are likely to be the most efficient in the future.

Conclusions

Conventional theory on the relationship between urban form and energy suggests that intensifying cities reduces energy consumption for transport. Our case study of four residential sites in Auckland examined the relationship between density, travel energy consumption, and PV electricity generation potential on household roofs.

The results show that an intensive urban form may be more energy efficient, in terms of transport energy use, for vehicles using fossil fuels with internal combustion engines. However, if distributed generation by PVs becomes commonplace in the future, suburbia will have a renewed role as both a collector and supplier of energy, a characteristic that cannot be achieved in the higher density CBD. Through the implementation of smart technologies such as PV, EV, solar water heating, and smart meters, suburbia could be transformed into an energy contributor not only to its own transport needs but also to the city as a whole.

These conclusions are very conservative in their estimation of the extent to which suburbia is likely to become more energy efficient than compact housing form. We have worked under the assumption that travel behavior patterns will remain the same in the future. But the price of fuel is likely to increase, and travel distances are likely to decrease, thus further reducing the energy consumed in suburbia and allowing suburbia to release more PV-generated energy to the grid.

While there are other issues, such as spread of infrastructure and loss of agricultural land, that need to be taken into account when considering policy decisions concerning intensification, transport energy has always been an underpinning argument. The onset of peak oil, the transition to EVs, and the increased cost-effectiveness of PVs is driving a change in private transport options. Suburbia has significant potential for energy efficiency and energy generation. Policy decisions on intensification should be based on the technologies of the future, and not those of the present and past. This issues a call to designers and planners to design for PV and for EVs and the integration with smart meters and other technologies in the home.

San Marcos, Texas, United States

SCALES OF GOVERNANCE

5.1
BETWEEN POWER AND APPEARANCE
THE ENTERPRISE SUBURBS OF SILICON VALLEY

Louise A. Mozingo

ECONOMIC DIVERSITY

FLEXIBLE REGULATION

INNOVATION

Edged by a verge of California live oaks and eucalyptus, Sand Hill Road in Menlo Park, California, gently winds through the last of the coastal range foothills near the north perimeter of the Stanford University campus before leveling out to the flatlands surrounding the San Francisco Bay. Visible through the billowing and swaying trees edging the road are office buildings housing Silicon Valley's most prominent and profitable venture capitalists, deploying the billions that fuel the high technology industry. The Sand Hill offices appear unexceptional, indistinguishable from well-tended beige office buildings containing title companies, tax preparers, and orthodontists in any upper-middle-class suburb in the United States. Surprisingly, these quite unremarkable offices command the most costly rents in the United States, more per square foot than prime Manhattan real estate in a picture-postcard skyscraper.[1]

The offices of Sand Hill Road typify the decades-long custom in Silicon Valley of a relatively modest appearance for the high-technology workplace. This noticeable reserve stands in marked contrast to the extraordinary consequence of Silicon Valley companies that influence large sectors of the global economy and affect how we all conduct our daily lives. The seemingly mystifying mismatch between power and appearance evolved from national trends in suburban development, the postwar pattern of office dispersion in the San Francisco Bay Area, and the particular engineering-based entrepreneurial culture of Silicon Valley. Nevertheless this high-tech, low-key landscape of the Silicon Valley is also now changing noticeably, if not precipitously.

The postwar suburbanization of the San Francisco Peninsula followed national trends in many respects. (fig. **5.1.1**) Speculative developers built retail malls with plenty of parking and subdivisions of single-family houses for homeowners

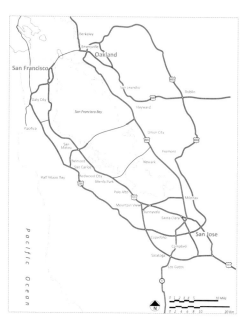

5.1.1 Silicon Valley in the San Francisco Bay Area

commuting to work by automobile. Suburban industrial parks, concentrated along railroad lines before World War II, expanded and proliferated, connecting to the newly completed US 101 Freeway along the eastern side of the San Francisco Peninsula.[2]

In contrast to national trends in the postwar period, the region's administrative offices followed a different pattern of suburbanization. While white-collar businesses in the suburbs of northeast, southeast, and midwestern cities occupied custom-built corporate campuses and estates, these did not appear on the San Francisco Peninsula during the postwar period. (fig. **5.1.2**) Instead, corporate office staffs in the Peninsula suburbs occupied the straightforward utilitarian buildings in industrial parks, sometimes attached to manufacturing plants. Industrial parks had first developed in the 1920s, as industries began moving to suburban peripheries to accommodate single-story, in-line industrial production. Indeed, the Bay Area was one of the places where suburban manufacturing first emerged in the United States.[3] In industrial parks, a master developer subdivided land; laid out lots to be leased or bought by tenant

1   Michael Gerrity, "Sand Hill Road Tops List Most Expensive Office Address in North America," *World Property Channel*, September 7, 2011, accessed June 19, 2014, http://www.worldpropertychannel.com/us-markets/commercial-real-estate-1/most-expensive-office-space-jones-lang-lasalle-john-sikaitis-sand-hill-road-office-space-for-lease-fifth-avenue-office-space-for-lease-greenwich-avenue-office-space-silicon-valley-office-space-4743.php.

2   Donald L. Foley, "Factors in the Location of Administrative Offices with Particular Reference to the San Francisco Bay Area," *Papers and Proceedings: The Regional Science Association Second Annual Meeting, December, 1955*, vol. 2, ed. Gerald A. P. Carruthers (Cambridge, MA: Regional Science Association, 1956); Donald L. Foley, *The Suburbanization of Offices in the San Francisco Bay Area* (Berkeley: Regents of the University of California, 1957).

3   Richard Walker, "Industry Builds out the City: The Suburbanization of Manufacturing in the San Francisco Bay Area," in *Manufacturing Suburbs: Building Work and Home on the Metropolitan Fringe*, ed. Robert Lewis (Philadelphia: Temple University Press, 2004), 92–123.

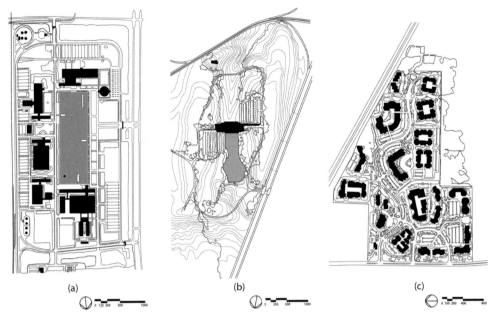

(a)   (b)   (c)

4   Louise A. Mozingo,
     *Pastoral Capitalism:
     A History of Suburban
     Corporate Landscapes*
     (Cambridge, MA: MIT
     Press, 2011), 166–70.
5   Ibid., 153.
6   "Commerce in Menlo
     Park," *Urban Land* 12,
     no. 6 (June 1953): 3–4.

5.1.2 Types of suburban corporate landscapes

industries; installed infrastructure, parking, and circulation for rail; set up trucking and loading docks; and devised basic restrictions on building coverage and size to minimize conflicts and maximize the benefits of the coordinated industrial development.[4] While premier contemporary architects occasionally designed industrial park administrative buildings for office staffs, even then the structures reflected a modernist aesthetic inspired by industrial engineering, pared of extraneous architectural details.[5]

During this same period, the Peninsula city of Menlo Park grasped that expanding suburban offices presented both a challenge and an opportunity. Like many suburban jurisdictions, Menlo Park strived to support the ongoing expansion of single-family neighborhoods through business taxes, as residential development did not generate enough revenue to sustain the services it incurred. Yet local residents and the city officials viewed office buildings as threatening the prevailing suburban aesthetic, incongruous with an ideal middle-class, ranch house California suburb.

In response, the city devised a new zoning strategy, nationally recognized as trendsetting. The 1948 zoning for the new district in Menlo Park set aside 26 acres (11 hectares) limited to "Administrative, Executive, Professional, and Research Institution" uses. An early example of such suburban zoning in the United States, it adapted the aesthetic of a suburban ranch house to office uses. The minimum lots extended to 2 acres (almost 1 hectare), and all parking had to be accommodated in off-street lots at the rate of one parking space for every 250 square feet (22 square meters) of offices, an unprecedentedly high parking requirement. (Downtown offices and main street establishments, at this point, did not have any parking requirements.) The zoning limited the structures to one story, covering a maximum of 40 percent of the lot. Each lot had to provide deep landscape setbacks, creating, essentially, a well-appointed suburban yard around the office building. (fig. **5.1.3**) By 1953, the city expanded the zoning to over 70 acres (22 hectares), as the original tracts covered by the new zoning were built out.[6] The offices along Sand Hill Road, developed in the late 1970s and 1980s, comprise an extension of land-use regulations similar to the original landmark 1948 zoning in Menlo Park.

Thus by the early 1950s, new suburban office uses could be found both in industrial parks clustered along the San Francisco Peninsula and in select, newly zoned office districts in its pleasant, largely white, suburban communities. At this point, Menlo Park's neighbor, Stanford University, developed a third and highly influential addition to the mix of dispersed office uses in the region. Bound not to sell any of the university's over 8,000 acres (3,238 hectares) by the terms of its endowment from Leland Stanford, by the late 1940s, Stanford University deployed this major asset in a new way to generate much-needed income by developing a series of speculative development schemes. Launched in 1951, Stanford Industrial Park belied its name, as the university expected "smokeless" industries to occupy what was basically an office park.[7]

First appearing in the suburbs of cities in the southeast and along Boston's beltway, Route 128, the office park development type evolved from the industrial park. Office parks were coordinated and organized similarly to industrial parks but limited to office uses and located adjacent to polite suburban residential neighborhoods rather than industrial districts. These parks did not include rail or truck access, and depended entirely on the automobile for transportation connections to the metropolitan region. Office park developments contained plenty of parking and extended to a maximum of three stories, or often less in the 1950s. Most important, office parks contained well-landscaped greenswards and setbacks to make them acceptable to surrounding suburban homeowners.[8] Like many office park developers, Stanford provided long-term leases to lots on the sites, and the initial tenants were able to construct custom buildings. With an initial tract of 50 acres (20 hectares), the site expanded to 345 acres (140 hectares)

5.1.3 Typical office building

by 1960, eventually reaching 600 acres (243 hectares) in the 1970s.[9]

By 1960, Stanford Industrial Park attracted national attention. Typical of the hoopla, the editors of *Architectural Forum* declared it was "converting Palo Alto from a suburb to a satellite—without jeopardizing the opportunity to be a garden city."[10] Two leading technology corporations with long-standing ties to Stanford, Varian Associates and Hewlett-Packard, had been among the first tenants, both having relocated from industrial sites elsewhere on the San Francisco Peninsula. Whatever the cachet surrounding Stanford Industrial Park as an opportunity for association with Stanford's growing reputation as an engineering center and prestige university, Stanford Industrial Park was a profit-making enterprise for the university and never an incubator site for start-up tech businesses. Most of the tenants were branch offices of well-established national corporations such as Eastman Kodak, General Electric, Lockheed Aircraft Corporation, and Ampex.[11]

As such, the initial development outcome of the Stanford Industrial Park displayed such notable starkness that by the early 1960s it also garnered the ire

7   "Working in the Suburbs," *Architectural Forum* 114, no. 1 (January 1960): 71; Mozingo, *Pastoral Capitalism*, 166–71.
8   Ibid., 153–58.
9   Ibid., 166–71.
10 "Working in the Suburbs," 57.
11 Mozingo, *Pastoral Capitalism*, 166–71.

5.1.4 Stanford Industrial Park in 1960

12 "Working in the Suburbs," 71.

13 J. Ross McKeever, *Business Parks, Office Parks, Plazas, and Centers* (Washington, DC: Urban Land Institute, 1971), 47.

14 Contrary to many historical accounts, the electronics industry did not start with William Hewlett and David Packard in a Palo Alto garage in 1938 but extended back to early radio and telegraph innovations prior to World War I. See Timothy J. Sturgeon, "How Silicon Valley Came to Be," in *Understanding Silicon Valley: The Anatomy of an Entrepreneurial Region*, ed. Martin Kenney (Stanford, CA: Stanford University Press, 2000), 15–47. On the prestige corporate facilities, see Mozingo, *Pastoral Capitalism*, chaps. 3 and 4.

15 Mozingo, *Pastoral Capitalism*, 53–64.

of local residents, and critiques called it "coarse" and "crowded."[12] Contemporary photographs record the bare ground, free of landscaping, that surrounded the first offices, a condition that would have violated the Menlo Park zoning and in no way matched the grand, Beaux-Arts aesthetic of the Stanford University campus itself. (fig. **5.1.4**) The tenants may have been smokeless, but the industrial aesthetic prevailed.

By 1965, the high-technology industry of the San Francisco Peninsula suburbs was situated in relatively ordinary work settings, where the fundamental aesthetic derived from the modest aesthetic ambitions of industrial buildings and suburban ranch houses. In some cases, industrial park developers simply set aside lots within their developments for office use, to accommodate potential new white-collar tenants.[13] At this point, the region's innovation-driven engineering enterprises (which extended back to the turn of the twentieth century) also reinforced a utilitarian conception of the workplace

in marked contrast to East Coast and midwestern corporations whose suburban emplacements emphasized much grander, prestige-laden ambitions.[14]

The trajectory of William Shockley is an example of the way in which the emerging high-technology industry shaped the postwar workplaces of the San Francisco Peninsula. In 1948 Shockley, along with two colleagues, invented the transistor at AT&T Bell Laboratories in Summit, New Jersey. Designed by topflight East Coast architects and landscape architects, and occupying over 800 bucolic acres (324 hectares) in an upper-middle-class suburban enclave, Bell Labs established the model of the corporate-built research and development campus eventually imitated by countless corporations in the decades to come. Bell Labs generated far-reaching effects in business, high technology, and suburban expansion in the United States and beyond.[15]

In 1955, Shockley left Bell Labs and recruited a group of East Coast engineers to move west with him and start Shockley

Semiconductor Laboratories backed by Beckman Instruments. They set up shop in a prosaic industrial building in Mountain View, just south of Palo Alto. Shockley Labs focused its enterprise on silicon chip technology. Shockley turned out to be an inept and difficult leader, and within a year the eight engineers left to form Fairchild Semiconductor with an infusion of capital from Fairchild Industries. Fairchild Semiconductor eventually built its research and development laboratory in Stanford Industrial Park.

Over the course of the next thirty-five years, the proliferating electronics technology and relatively low start-up costs enabled various engineers to break off from Fairchild and establish over thirty new high-technology firms, including Intel, Advanced Micro Devices, and National Semiconductor. Formed at a rate of almost one new company a year, these "Fairchildren" established a fundamentally new kind of entrepreneurial culture in which colleagues became competitors, though, most often, surprisingly friendly and collaborative ones.[16] This breakaway entrepreneurship did not happen at Fairchild alone but surged through the increasing number of high-technology companies located all along the eastern side of the San Francisco Peninsula, from San Mateo to San Jose.[17]

In 1971, a journalist writing for *Electronic News* would officially name the swath of suburban communities in which this new high-technology business culture thrived as Silicon Valley.[18] The Valley's business culture, fueled by invention, breakaway entrepreneurship, and, by the mid-1970s, venture capitalism, also had implications for the landscape in which it operated. Office parks proliferated, as the fission of early companies created many new companies. Moreover, national and international corporations found that they needed Silicon Valley offices to stay in the game, and new ideas generated at Stanford, Berkeley, MIT, or in local garages found traction as promising start-ups.

Office parks well suited the fluidity of the high-technology industry and the engineering culture of its leaders. The presentable but quite ordinary offices had plenty of parking and were connected to the metropolitan region by a network of freeways that allowed companies to draw workforces from a wide geographic region and easily access airports. Tenants of office parks could choose between several different types of development schemes. If the office park had open lots, developers would build structures to tenant specifications. Developers could build offices on speculation, and tenants could lease a few hundred square feet within a shared building, or occupy an entire building or several buildings within an office park. More successful companies could also buy a large lot within the office park outright and build a custom headquarters all the while occupying or vacating other buildings within the office park, as need be.[19] This kind of ease in tenancy, expansion, contraction, or relinquishment of workspaces complemented the volatile hustle of Silicon Valley businesses.

Beginning in the mid-1960s, office parks expanded in Menlo Park, Palo Alto, Redwood City, Mountain View, Sunnyvale, Cupertino, and northern San Jose. By the 1990s, they filled the remaining agricultural land along the freeways linking these communities. (fig. **5.1.5**) Over the decades, the architecture certainly became more polished and the landscape verges more ample and leafy. Also, more companies built proprietary buildings on corporate-owned office park lots, sometimes creating a compact version of a corporate campus by clustering buildings around a central green space. Even Stanford University realized that Stanford Industrial Park needed to conform to a more generous suburban aesthetic. The

16 Christophe Lécuyer and David C. Brock, *Makers of the Microchip: A Documentary History of Fairchild Semiconductor* (Cambridge, MA: The MIT Press, 2010); Christophe Lécuyer, *Making Silicon Valley: Innovation and the Growth of High Tech, 1930–1970* (Cambridge, MA: The MIT Press, 2005); Annalee Saxenian, *Regional Advantage: Culture and Competition in Silicon Valley and Route 128* (Cambridge, MA: Harvard University Press, 1994); Michael S. Malone, *The Valley of the Heart's Delight: A Silicon Valley Notebook, 1963–2001* (New York: John Wiley & Sons, 2002); Martin Kenney, ed., *Understanding Silicon Valley: The Anatomy of an Entrepreneurial Region* (Stanford: Stanford University Press, 2000).

17 Homa Bahrami and Stuart Evans, "Flexible Recycling and High-Technology Entrepreneurship," in *Understanding Silicon Valley*, ed. Kenney.

18 David Laws, "Who Named the Silicon Valley?," Computer History Museum, accessed January 15, 2015, http://www.computerhistory.org/atchm/who-named-silicon-valley/.

19 Mozingo, *Pastoral Capitalism*, 156–57.

5.1.5 Typical office parks south of US 101 between Sunnyvale and Santa Clara, California, at the core of Silicon Valley

20 Ibid., 170.

university renamed it Stanford Research Park in the early 1970s, adding requirements for higher-quality structures and wider, more abundantly planted landscape setbacks.[20]

The Silicon Valley office park proved quintessentially suburban: single-use, insular, low density, well maintained, adequately verdant, and effortlessly accommodating of the automobile. But its intent was not to project the power or status of the resident firms through the built environment but to accommodate them well enough in an orderly, predictable, and highly functional middle-class suburban setting. In an engineering-based business culture in which a company's cleverest employees would likely set off to pursue the next great idea with foreseeable frequency, or another company's bright idea would make your product abruptly obsolete, investment in extensive and permanent prestige facilities was of marginal interest.

The restraint that marked the Silicon Valley workplace held until the early 2000s. At that point, another set of considerations began transforming the design of Silicon Valley headquarters, and even of speculative office parks. Companies placed new emphasis on distinctive workplaces to project their ascendency in the global high-technology economy, targeting workforces and competitors as well as, for the first time, the public.

This ramped-up emphasis on corporate image stems from a shift in the products of ascendant Silicon Valley companies. During the formative years of the 1950s through the 1970s, hardware companies such as Intel and Hewlett-Packard dominated innovation. In the 1980s and through the 1990s, innovation leaders shifted to software, with such massively successful enterprises as Oracle and Intuit. All of these companies continue to be prosperous and prominent. Oracle, in particular, built some of the more deluxe offices in the valley. In the early 2000s, ascendancy shifted to those companies selling personal devices, most clearly dominated by Apple, and then to Internet platforms such as Google and, later, Facebook. In this latest era, these wide-ranging, consumer-oriented Silicon Valley companies began to emphasize design and visual imagery to an exceptional extent, both to sell their products and to project their corporate persona across the world.

Google's Mountain View headquarters, the Googleplex, forecast the shift

5.1.6 Original Googleplex is upper center of the aerial

21 Peter Burrows, "The Sad
Saga of Silicon Graphics:
The Final Chapter,"
Bloomberg BusinessWeek,
April 1, 2009, accessed
July 26, 2014, http://
www.businessweek.com
/the_thread/techbeat
/archives/2009/04
/the_sad_saga_of.html;
Michael M. Lewis, *The
New New Thing: A Silicon
Valley Story* (New York:
W. W. Norton, 1999).

22 Michelle Martin, "An
Instant Landmark
in Silicon Valley, *World
Architecture* 68 (July–
August 1998): 67–71.

toward a new consciousness in the Valley of how companies could use their workplaces to achieve competitive dominance. Interestingly, the Googleplex began as a recycled headquarters for administration, research, and development of Silicon Graphics Incorporated (SGI). In a rapid turnover typical of Silicon Valley, Jim Clark, a Stanford professor, founded SGI in 1981, and while Clark departed the company in 1994 to establish the Internet browser company Netscape, SGI had a moment of marked preeminence in the late 1990s. The company then began a descent, eventually resulting in an ignominious buyout by anobscure company, Rackable Systems. Nevertheless, for a period, SGI was at the cutting edge of hardware and software development for computer-generated imagery, with a robust set of contracts with both the military and the movie industry.[21]

During its moment in the spotlight, SGI bought a parcel in an office park and built what was an unusually visually arresting assemblage for the Valley, noted by design critics at the time.[22] No doubt reflecting an enterprise in the business of creating virtually vertiginous experiences, the site had a series of structures bouncily canted against each other, with arcing metallic facades around an interior courtyard composed of juxtaposed geometries of planting, paving, and pathways. Like all office park site plans, parking encircled the periphery of the site, carefully bordered by landscaped parkway strips.

In 2003, Google leased the site from the declining SGI and added a playful array of Google-colored umbrellas to the courtyard, solar panels on the roofs and over the parking lots, and, notoriously, playground office accessories such as hammocks, pool tables, and slides between floors. By the time Google bought the site in 2006, the Googleplex, as the old SGI office complex came to be known, had been projected across the world through the medium that Google so unequivocally commanded—the Internet. As Google grew, it followed a strategy of many Silicon Valley companies and took over all the commonplace buildings in the office parks adjacent to the Googleplex. (fig. **5.1.6**) Most of Google's Mountain View employees work in these quite ordinary surrounding office buildings rather than the original Googleplex, where only a small percentage of Google employees actually work. Yet the Googleplex remains very much the flagship corporate image of the company and the touchstone for the design of Google offices across the world.[23](figs. **5.1.7**–**8**)

By the late 2000s, Apple announced it would build a structure never seen in Silicon Valley, a full-out suburban corporate estate in the manner of the postwar titans of American industry. For two decades, Apple's headquarters had been in an office park in Cupertino, where it built the Infinite Loop Campus on its own lot while also occupying the proximate buildings in the office park. Like most Silicon Valley corporations, Apple had seen up and down business cycles since its establishment in 1976, and Apple expanded into or contracted from these office lots as needed. In 2007, Apple officially changed its corporate name from Apple Computers, Inc. to Apple, Inc., a move that underscored its global dominance in selling personal devices. Without question, under the leadership of the now legendary Steve Jobs, Apple had transformed its products—from ear buds to retail stores—by integrating and successfully marketing elegant visual design combined with functionality in a way that outranked all other competitors.

Apple assembled a uniquely large site for Silicon Valley, 175 acres (71 hectares) along the 280 Freeway in Cupertino. The company bought an agglomeration of office buildings from Hewlett Packard (which had seen its fortunes decline) as well as some adjacent office park lots. The Apple 2 campus, designed by the renowned British architect Norman Foster and the Philadelphia-based landscape architect Laurie Olin, is, quite simply, entirely unprecedented for the Silicon Valley. The design sets a sere circle of glass a quarter mile in circumference within a bucolic re-creation of an oak-studded

coastal California grassland, with parking carefully relegated underground or in a separate perimeter structure. The $5 billion price tag is (to use a Jobsian phrase) mind-blowing, the most expensive office building ever constructed. No doubt Jobs's health travails and untimely death in 2011 increased the interest in leaving behind a monumental corporate edifice.[24] Nevertheless, the Apple 2 Campus overturned the decades-long habit of comparative restraint among even the most successful denizens of the Silicon Valley.

If the Apple 2 Campus at least had the justification of being the last act of a legendary leader backed by a corporation with more than $160 billion in cash reserves, the upstart Facebook has no such credentials. Taking a page from the Google playbook, Facebook bought the Sun Microsystems custom-built campus in a Menlo Park office park (Sun had been acquired by Oracle) and transformed its interior garden space into a techie fantasyland—a strolling Main Street complete with a candy store, roll-up garage spaces, diners, bike shop, sushi bar, and large plaza emblazoned with the word HACK, easily read from Google Earth should you happen to search "Facebook Headquarters, Menlo Park."[25] Not pausing, Facebook has forged ahead, buying up additional adjacent office lots and hiring Frank Gehry to design a new headquarters building. With half a million square feet, including one single open-plan office of 100,000 square feet (9,290 square meters), the design wriggles a set of four rectangles over underground parking across a long site, and then tops the structure with an undulating grassy green roof dotted with full-grown trees shading cafes, workbenches, and picnic tables.[26] (fig. **5.1.9**)

The move toward permanence, extravagance, and image has now moved beyond idiosyncratic circumstance and a limited set of companies: the one-upmanship has begun.

23 Adam Lashinsky, "Chaos by Design," *Fortune Online*, October 2, 2006, accessed May 4, 2008, http://money.cnn.com /magazines/fortune /fortune_archive/2006 /10/02/8387489/index .htm; Rob Pegoraro, "Gawking at Google," *Washington Post*, accessed May 4, 2008, http://blog.washington post.com/fasterforward /2008/01/gawking_at _google.html; Carey Dunne, "Eight of Google's Craziest Offices," *Fast Company*, April 10, 2014, accessed July 26, 2014, http:// www.fastcodesign .com/3028909/8-of -googles-craziest-offices.

24 Steve Jobs, "Steve Jobs Presents to the Cupertino City Council," June 7, 2011, YouTube video posted by Cupertino CityChannel, accessed January 15, 2015, https://www .youtube.com/watch?v =gtuz5OmOh_M.; Peter Burrows, "Inside Apple's Plans for Its Futuristic, $5 Billion Headquarters," *Bloomberg BusinessWeek*, April 4, 2013, accessed August 1, 2014, http:// www.businessweek.com /articles/2013-04-04/ap ples-campus-2-shapes -up-as-an-investor-rela tions-nightmare; see also the issue of *CLOG: Apple*, published February 2012, devoted to a series of articles discussing the design elements of the Apple 2, and specifically, Mozingo, "Reaching for the Past: Apple Headquarters as Capitalist Nostalgia," 106–7.

25 Eric Savitz, "Facebook Staffers: Sentenced to Sun Quentin?," *Forbes*, January 1, 2011, accessed August 1, 2014, http:// www.forbes.com/sites /ericsavitz/2011/01/02 /facebook-staffers -sentenced-to-sun -quentin/; Robyn Neck, "Inside Facebook's Headquarters," *USA Today Photos*, accessed August 1, 2014, http://media gallery.usatoday.com /Inside+Facebook's +headquarters/G3949.

26 Bonnie Eslinger, "Facebook Gets OK to

5.1.7 The April 2015 Google proposal to redesign the office park that houses its Mountain View staff

Build Second Campus
in Menlo Park," *San Jose
Mercury News—Peninsula*,
March 28, 2013, accessed
August 2, 2014, http://
www.mercurynews.com
/peninsula/ci_22886654
/facebook-gets-ok-build
-second-campus-menlo
-park; Robert Johnson,
"Exclusive Photos of
Facebook's Sprawling
New HQ, Designed Frank
Gehry," *Business Insider*,
March 19, 2014, accessed
August 1, 2014, http://
www.businessinsider
.com/photos-of-face
book-frank-gehry
-designed-hq-2014-3.

5.1.8 A perspective view of the new Google offices

5.1.9 Facebook West Campus, designed by the architect Frank Gehry and CMG Landscape Architecture

Samsung and Intuit, long-term Silicon Valley tenants, are building new facilities that, while not as extravagant as the Apple 2 campus, certainly aim to convey a singular, urbane appearance with flourishes of green walls and green roofs, underground parking, public spaces opening directly on to roadways, and striking volumetric articulations.[27] More telling, LandBank, a decades-old Silicon Valley–based speculative developer, is demolishing one of its 1970s Sunnyvale office parks to make way for a set of speculative office buildings composed of curvaceous facades, green roofs, and underground parking. Specifically citing the influence of the Apple 2 campus, the LandBank developer stated: "We wanted to look away from what has been."[28]

When Hewlett Packard moved into its Stanford Industrial Park site in 1960, the high-tech workers arrayed along the San Francisco Peninsula were in the process of creating the immersive world of computing within which we all now live. For these workers, what they invented and successfully sold was what mattered most. Where they worked was the happenstance of the company that employed them. For decades, the Silicon Valley workforce was more interested in the circuits on their chips than the swank of their offices. As testified by the offices of the venture capital firms along Sand Hill Road, this is what has been, and still is, operational for many Silicon Valley businesses.

Now, with a few clicks on a laptop or smartphone, anyone on the planet can see any workplace. Silicon Valley corporate valuations and profits are reaching unprecedented levels, billionaires are multiplying, and Silicon Valley as an ideal, and highly influential, entrepreneurial economy permeates political and cultural discourse. In this context, the new epic structures constitute the latest manifestation of a long continuum in human history in which the supremely wealthy

27 Nathan Donato-Weinstein, "Intuit to Start Construction on Mountain View Project," *Silicon Valley Business Journal*, June 26, 2014, accessed August 2, 2014, http://www.bizjournals.com/sanjose/feature/biz-of-408/2014/06/intuit-to-start-construction-on-new-mountain-view.html?page=all; Dara Kerr, "Samsung Breaks Ground on Futuristic Silicon Valley Campus," *CNET*, July 8, 2013, accessed August 2, 2013, http://www.cnet.com/news/samsung-breaks-ground-on-futuristic-silicon-valley-campus/; Catherin Shu, "Samsung Moves on Apple's Turf as Construction on Its New Silicon Valley Headquarters," *Techcrunch*, July 8, 2013, accessed August 2, 2014, http://techcrunch.com/2013/07/08/samsung-headquarters/.

28 Quoted in Nathan Donato-Weinstein, "LandBank Wagers on Chic," *Silicon Valley Business Journal*, June 28, 2014, accessed August 2, 2014, http://www.bizjournals.com/sanjose/print-edition/2013/06/28/landbank-wagers-on-chic.html?page=all; Alia Wilson, "Futuristic Campus for Startups Targeting Site in North Sunnyvale," *San Jose Mercury News*, March 13, 2014, accessed August 2, 2014, http://www.mercurynews.com/business/ci_25331698/futuristic-campus-startups-targeting-site-north-sunnyvale.

and powerful project wealth and power through the built environment—high technology's Versailles moment.

The unacknowledged, long-term risks of this strategy for high-technology corporations, the metropolitan region, and the larger public interest are considerable. Boring, familiar suburban conformity fostered—and continues to foster—a surprisingly intensive, ingenious creative entrepreneurship that is held up as an inspired model of capitalist enterprise. The businesses of Silicon Valley have thrived precisely because of a workplace environment of mobility and flexibility afforded by the very ordinariness of offices parks. Compared to the earlier tech workplaces, the new emplacements are sclerotic, costly commitments, both initially and ongoing, unlikely to be resilient to the buffeted fortunes that are typical of global economies in general, and high technology in particular. They may well suffer the fate of many singular corporate structures of the 1950s through the 1970s, built in the hubris of profitability and dominance, only to be abandoned as obsolete relics by thebeginning of the twenty-first century.[29]

Beyond that, the very success of Silicon Valley has built out a metropolitan landscape whose basic development tenets are now outdated. The new projects do little to address a future in which resources will be significantly more constrained, requiring development patterns that are dense, mixed-use, and oriented to pedestrians, bicycles, and transit. Silicon Valley freeways are appallingly congested, and automobile traffic through the Valley has become a prodigious concern for both the private and the public sectors. The US 101 Freeway between Sunnyvale and Mountain View at about five on weekday afternoons is nightmarish. While a number of the most successful Silicon Valley companies run private bus lines that extend all over the Bay Area to

compensate, they only temporarily obviate a dysfunctional transportation system; the buses still have to run on stop and start freeways. Putting the parking underground may visually evade reality—an appealing prospect to be sure—but functionally, the new projects remain firmly in the metropolitan vision of the middle twentieth century: large enclaves of insular, single-use, auto-dependent suburban development.

The new stupendously expensive and ambitious projects in the Silicon Valley beg the question of how the burden of change in the suburban metropolitan realm will be shared and what the role of private enterprise will be in that equation. Renzo Piano has recently stated: "In the two-thousands—probably for the next three, four, five decades—the real challenge is to transform the periphery. If we fail to do this, it will be a real tragedy."[30] If there was ever a place and a moment to push the boundaries of a new collective vision for both the public and the private realm of the suburbs, it is now in Silicon Valley, where profitability and problems are colliding in breathtaking ways.

29 Mozingo, *Pastoral Capitalism*, 197–201; see also Coral Garnick, "Weyerhaeuser Moving to Seattle's Pioneer Square," *Seattle Times*, August, 27, 2014, accessed July 15, 2015, http://www.seattle times.com/business /weyerhaeuser-moving -to-seattlersquos -pioneer-square/.
30 Quoted in Elizabeth Kolbert, "Postcard from Rome: Civic Duty," *New Yorker*, January 12, 2015, 20.

5.2
CODING PERMANENT FLEXIBILITY

Fadi Masoud

It is no coincidence that some of the most dynamic and complex metropolitan conditions—such as postindustrial sites, historic urban cores, dynamic estuaries, peri-urban fringes, and informal set-tlements—cannot be neatly categorized through the reductive nature of zoning. Despite zoning's regulatory evolution, it remains faithful to its original goal: the well-defined separation of land uses.[1] Such normative divisions have resulted in static conditions that overlook local nuances and are especially unmindful to factors of time and change.[2] In suburbia, this goal is epitomized in the proliferation and inviolability of the "single-family residential" zone as an "end state" zone, which is protected from any transfor-mation. Over time, conventional zoning has proved ineffective in dealing with the "complex and unwieldy reality" of con-temporary urbanism, especially in the face of increased vulnerability created by indeterministic, unknown, and varied environmental forces.[3]

Yet it is in the suburban fringes of the polycentric metropolis where condi-tions become ripe for experimentation in dynamic, process-driven codes and standards that revolutionize traditional zoning's static outcomes. The opportu-nity for innovation is due not just to the abundance of land for ecosystem services but also to the decrease in the complex-ity of regulation and land ownership, as well as the low cost of the development process (as evidenced by the large-scale planned unit developments [PUDs] seen in suburbia). Thus, suburbia represents a latent opportunity to innovate in terms of the flexibility of building programs and building forms, and importantly, the pro-vision of new infrastructure that may be constructed in a sustainable, innovative, and metabolic matter.

Tools of Legibility and Control

Roots of land-use controls develop in North America in the first centuries of settlement due to multiple, interacting factors: an abundance of land coupled with an agrarian economy, a strong belief in private property, and the fear of density and chaos associated with the industrial city.[4] In pursuit of order, legibility, and control of the territory, early survey-ors produced a set of instrumental and reductive tools, such as the Jeffersonian grid, and later, structures of subdivision, land-use provision, building codes, and zoning. These tools were a clear product of the influence of ecological paradigms on American law and policy and were bolstered by Progressive Era judicial pow-ers. Taken together, these tools have been shaping the North American territory in an unimpeded and marginally altered fashion ever since their conception. In fact, zoning remains the most influen-tial and pervasive regulatory tool ever deployed.[5]

It is in the diminution of legislative complexity on the suburban fringes of the polynodal metropolis, where conditions are ripe for the flexibility of program, the affordability of experimentation, and space for formal, infrastructural, and eco-nomic innovation. Yet the standard tools we have inherited, and continue to univer-sally deploy across terrains, remain true to their original purpose of a reductive and inflexible partition of uses—leading to an ecologically derived fallacy of a city in a preferred, "climax, end-state."

The "Climax End-State" Fallacy

For once it is realized that there is no harmony of nature, no divine or other pur-pose hidden beneath the flux and chaos of present planlessness, it becomes immoral to let poverty, ignorance, pestilence, and war continue if they can be obliterated by a "plan."[6]

1   Christopher Serkin and Gregg P. Macey, *Post-Zoning: Alternative Forms of Public Land Use Controls* (Rochester, NY: Social Science Research Network, 2013), accessed January 20, 2016, http://Papers.Ssrn.Com /Abstract=2290256.

2   Rutherford H. Platt, "Land Use Control: Interface of Law and Geography," Resource Paper No. 75–1, January 1976, accessed January 20, 2016, http://Eric .Ed.Gov/?Id=ED155111; Sidney M. Willhelm, *Urban Zoning and Land-Use Theory* (New York: Free Press of Glencoe, 1962); Eran Ben-Joseph and Terry S. Szold, eds., *Regulating Place: Standards and the Shaping of Urban America* (New York: Routledge, 2005).

3   Referring to Judge Sutherland's plea for zoning to be flexible in dealing with the world's "complex and unwieldy reality," *Village of Euclid v. Ambler Realty Co.,* 272 US 365 (1926), accessed April 21, 2015, https://Supreme.Justia .Com/Cases/Federal /Us/272/365/Case.Html.

4   Richard F. Babcock, *Zoning Game: Muni-cipal Practices and Policies,* Underlining/ Highlighting Edition (Madison, WI: Lincoln Institute of Land Policy, 1966).

5   Fred P. Bosselman, "The Influence of Ecological Science on American Law: An Introduction," *Chicago-Kent Law Review* 69 (January 1, 1994): 847; Serkin and Macey, "Post-Zoning"; Sonia A. Hirt, *Zoned in the USA: The Origins and Implications of American Land-Use Regulation* (Ithaca, NY: Cornell University Press, 2014).

6   Dwight Waldo and Hugh T. Miller, *The Administrative State: A Study of the Political Theory of American Public Administration* (New Brunswick, NJ: Transaction Publishers, 2006).

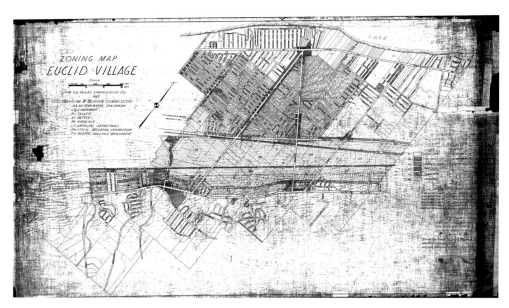

5.2.1 Euclidean zoning is a type of zoning named for the Village of Euclid where zoning was upheld in 1926 as a legitimate governmental power under the police powers of government. Euclidean zoning codes are based on the earliest comprehensive ordinances and the Standard State Zoning Enabling Act (1922).

Ever since ecology was recognized as an essential branch of biological science at the turn of the last century, a fundamental, yet often underplayed, link between ecology, planning policy, and land-use legislation was established.[7] A leading political scientist, Dwight Waldo was a defining figure in American modern public administration during the post–World War II era. Statements such as the one above solidified the ethos of the planning profession as one that could achieve higher objectives as an administrative profession. The notion of an "equilibrium" reached through formulaic standards would abolish "planlessness," increase legibility and control, and eradicate the potentials of indeterministic chaos as a moral public imperative.[8]

Yet as concerns over the environment and its uncertainty propels us to rethink our models of twenty-first-century urbanization, it is crucial to recount the original links between ecological paradigms and planning policy, but more important, allow for the evolution of ecological theories to once again influence the transformation of such policy tools. Four distinct ecological ideas have directly shaped public policy and legal institutions in the United States

during the Progressive Era and created suburbia as we know it.[9]

The first Progressive Era policies were highly influenced by ideas of ecological "empiricism," in which scientific thought comes from factual reasoning rather than abstract principles.[10] The second, which focuses on the concepts of "succession, climax, and equilibrium," developed by the ecologist Frederic Clements, had the most profound impact on American planning and the passing of the Standard Zoning and Enabling Acts during the late 1920s.[11] The third corresponds to the expansion of the concept of "metabolic habitat" and the eventual development of systemic ecology.[12] This is subsequently supplanted by the environmental scientist Daniel Botkin's notions of "non-equilibrium" and open-ended paradigms, which claim that the environment is in a constant state of flux and change, and so our public policy should also be changing.[13]

When ideas around ecological succession (where one biological community replaced another in successive waves) began to take hold, the greatest impact on public planning policy was not the idea of dynamic succession itself, vis-à-vis change, but the contention that succession

7   Bosselman, "The Influence of Ecological Science on American Law"; Daniel B. Botkin, *Discordant Harmonies: A New Ecology for the Twenty-First Century* (New York: Oxford University Press, 1990), accessed January 20, 2016, http://libproxy.mit.edu/login?url=http://search.ebscohost.com/login.aspx?direct=true&db=cat00916a&an=mit.000515749&site=eds-live; Daniel B. Botkin, *The Moon in the Nautilus Shell: Discordant Harmonies Reconsidered* (Oxford: Oxford University Press, 2012); Frank B. Golley, *A History of the Ecosystem Concept in Ecology: More Than the Sum of the Parts* (New Haven, CT: Yale University Press, 1993), accessed January 20, 2016, http://libproxy.mit.edu/login?url=http://search.ebscohost.com/login.aspx?direct=true&db=cat00916a&an=mit.000674054&site=eds-live.

8   Waldo and Miller, *The Administrative State.*

9   Bosselman, "The Influence of Ecological Science on American Law"; Golley, *A History of the Ecosystem Concept in Ecology.*

10 Joseph Postell, "The Anti-New Deal Progressive: Roscoe Pound's Alternative Administrative State," *Review of Politics* 74, no. 1 (January 2012): 53–85.

11 Arnold Valk, "From Formation to Ecosystem: Tansley's Response to Clements' Climax," *Journal of the History of Biology* 47, no. 2 (May 2014): 293–321.

12 Postell, "The Anti-New Deal Progressive."

13 Botkin, *Discordant Harmonies*; Botkin, *The Moon in the Nautilus Shell.*

Los Angeles, California, USA

Land Use (Function)

general sales or services   transportation

residential/accommodations   manufacturing/wholesale

arts/entertainment/rec.   education/public admin.

1:50,000
N↑ └────┘ 1000 m

5.2.2 Existing land-use map of a Los Angeles suburb. Illustrated with reductive land-use primary colors as mandated by the American Planning Association's Land-Based Classification Standards

14 Bosselman, "The Influence of Ecological Science on American Law"; Golley, *A History of the Ecosystem Concept in Ecology.*

15 Hirt, *Zoned in the USA*; Platt, "Land Use Control."

16 Hirt, *Zoned in the USA.*

17 A. Dan Tarlock, "Zoned Not Planned," *Planning Theory* 13, no. 1 (February 1, 2014): 99–112.

18 Thomas Deckker, *The Modern City Revisited* (London: Spon Press, 2000); Babcock, *Zoning Game.*

19 Ruth Knack, Stuart Meck, and Israel Stollman, "The Real Story behind the Standard Planning and Zoning Acts of the 1920s," *Land Use Law & Zoning Digest* 48, no. 2 (February 1, 1996): 3–9; Platt, "Land Use Control."

20 William I. Goodman and Eric C. Freund, *Principles and Practice of Urban Planning*, Municipal Management Series (Washington, DC: Institute for Training in Municipal Administration by the International City Managers' Association, 1968), accessed January 20, 2016, http://libproxy.mit.edu/login?url=http://search.ebscohost.com/login.aspx?direct=true&db=cat00916a&an=mit.000857747&site=eds-live.

21 Ibid.

eventually would reach a "climax state" and then succession would cease into a perfected state.[14] Planners, and the legal system that backed them, believed that if there was a permanent ideal use for every piece of land, then the law ought to give the use a protected status and obstruct any activity that would conflict with that use—calling it "the highest and best use."[15]

RGB (255,255,0) Yellow: The Highest and Best Use Is Zoned—Not Planned

The landmark case of the *Village of Euclid, Ohio v. Ambler Realty Co.* (1926) gave birth to the Standard State Zoning Enabling Act (1926) and, later, the Standard City Planning Enabling Act (1928).[16] (fig. **5.2.1**) The result of both acts was legally mandating zoning for every municipality, but not comprehensive planning per se.[17] This resulted in a rift between the need for immediate enforceable sanction of uses in the present and the evolving needs of the future.[18] As such, this propagated "decades of confusion among officials and planning professionals where municipalities resorted to zoning, an inherently short-term tool, as the primary device for drawing up long-term plans."[19] States enacted laws permitting cities to establish a zoning commission before devising any kind of long-range or comprehensive city plan.[20] As such, this precise administrative planometric policy tool, usually composed of a visually simplified hatch or color representing a future condition, became the exact and immediate legislative spatial blueprint for the development of the land.[21] (fig. **5.2.2**)

Early accounts of "comprehensive planning" practice, before the 1926 Standard State Zoning Enabling Act, reveal a robust form of projective physical planning that took into account a multitude of social, infrastructural, formal, and environmental concerns—to which zoning was envisioned to be an enabling, rather than a restrictive, mechanism.[22] For example, as the environmental ills of the industrial city were becoming more rampant, Frederick Law Olmsted Jr., landscape architect and one of the fathers of professional planning, together with Alfred Bettman, the Cincinnati lawyer amicus in the 1926 case of the *Village of Euclid v. Ambler Realty Co.*, anticipated the development of land-use zoning.[23] They were pivotal in shaping the federal legislation meant to arm physical planners with an "enabling mechanism" to perform comprehensive planning—not as the exception, but as the standard across the country.[24] Yet the comprehensive planning projects of Geddes, Mumford, Burnham, and Olmsted Sr., where park systems, mobility, hydrology, infrastructure, housing, health, society, and development were thought of holistically and comprehensively, remained exceptional cases of planning the industrial city as soon as zoning was mandated.[25] (fig. **5.2.3**) Soon after, the role of land-use zoning in propagating what we consider suburbia today became irrefutable.

It was in the decades immediately following zoning's legalized mandate that its expedited proliferation through federal initiatives such as the 701 Program, the Federal Housing Programs, and the New Deal, further established the link between land-use zoning and the process of suburbanization. (fig. **5.2.4**) The idea of national planning mandated by the Supreme Court was to identify future equilibria and the climax condition of human communities for every part of the country.[26] As zoning became legal, planners were tasked with preparing "plans that projected a future use of every parcel of land in their jurisdiction." Some neighborhoods, mainly established single-family residential ones, were seen as "climax communities"

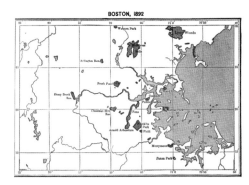

BOSTON, 1892

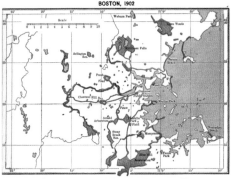

BOSTON, 1902

THE OPEN SPACES OF BOSTON IN 1892 AND 1902 COMPARED

5.2.3 Illustration of the growth of the Metropolitan Park System of Greater Boston between 1892 and 1902 as illustrated by the landscape architect Charles William Eliot. This echoes other plans occurring across the county, such as the McMillan Plan of District of Columbia park system, as proposed by the United States Senate Park Commission in 1902.

that needed protection, while others were in successional transition.[27] Planners issued a "Plan for the year X," to which all processes of change and transformations were assumed to culminate.[28]

In a survey of planning and zoning progress in the United States, published by Harvard University Press in 1929, Theodora Kimball Hubbard and Henry Vincent Hubbard exulted model municipal administrators who were achieving maximum uniformity of land use and the protection of single-family use districts. Madison, Wisconsin, for example, "reported the strictest administration where no variances in use have been granted," and they referenced "the suburban city of Newton, Massachusetts, as "having the most remarkable record of excellent zoning administration…where by 1925 nearly 80 per cent of the city area is zoned for single-family residence."[29]

22 Charles M. Haar, "The Content of the General Plan: A Glance At History," *Journal of the American Institute of Planners* 21, nos. 2–3 (June 30, 1955): 66–70; Goodman and Freund, *Principles and Practice of Urban Planning.*

23 Michael Allan Wolf, *The Zoning of America: Euclid v. Ambler* (Lawrence: University Press of Kansas, 2008).

24 American Planning Association, *Proceedings of the Fourth National Conference on City Planning* (Boston: American Planning Association, 1912); Knack, Meck, and Stollman, "The Real Story." This is similar to how the New Urbanists and smart growth devised "form based codes" and transect planning to enable much of their agendas. These codes have been adopted as law in over 252 municipalities. See Tony Perez, "Misconceptions About Form-Based Codes," Form-Based Codes Institute, October 20, 2014, http://formbased codes.org/articles /misconceptions -form-based-codes.

25 The Plan for Chicago, the McMillan Plan for Washington, and the Emerald Necklace of Boston, among others; Ben-Joseph and Szold, *Regulating Place*; Deckker, *Modern City Revisited.*

26 Haar, "The Content of the General Plan."

27 Bosselman, "The Influence of Ecological Science on American Law"; Deckker, *Modern City Revisited*; Edward J. Kaiser and David R. Godschalk, "Twentieth Century Land Use Planning: A Stalwart Family Tree," *Journal of the American Planning Association* 61, no. 3 (September 30, 1995): 365–85.

28 Peter J. Taylor, "Technocratic Optimism, H. T. Odum, and the Partial Transformation of Ecological Metaphor after World War II," *Journal of the History of*

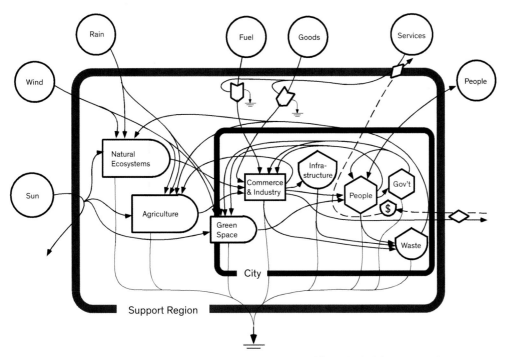

5.2.4 Model adapted from City as a System Diagram, showing energy system and flows of a city in its support region

Biology (1988); Babcock, *Zoning Game.*

29 Theodora Kimball Hubbard and Henry Vincent Hubbard, *Our Cities Today and Tomorrow: A Survey of Planning and Zoning Progress in the United States* (Cambridge, MA: Harvard University Press, 1929), 175.
30 Hirt, *Zoned in the USA.*
31 Tarlock, "Zoned Not Planned"; Sonia Hirt, "Form Follows Function? How America Zones," *Planning Practice and Research* 28, no. 2 (2013): 204–30; Hirt, *Zoned in the USA.*
32 Hirt, *Zoned in the USA.*
33 Tarlock, "Zoned Not Planned."
34 Taylor, "Technocratic Optimism."
35 Ibid.; Golley, *A History of the Ecosystem Concept in Ecology.*
36 Taylor, "Technocratic Optimism."
37 Bosselman, "The Influence of Ecological Science on American Law."

It was the exclusivity and sanctity of this category that was one of the primary reasons of public support for zoning in twentieth-century America.[30] In contrast to multifamily dwellings, which were seen as unhealthy urban tenements, along with incompatible industrial uses, the single-family residential zone was viewed as salvation from the problems of health, safety, and morality.[31] In other words, it was to be a protected "climax end state condition," the rationale behind providing more of these zones across the once agricultural edge, and the justification of state control over private property. This established the basis of land use as the reflection of the value orientations of those decision makers at a specific moment in time.[32] Now long lost to the process-based bureaucratic milieus of practice and the single-function municipal plans, it is argued that the North American continent is zoned, and not planned.[33]

Ecology Evolving Policy
Many of the failings of the top-down modernist planning schemes evolved when ecosystem thinking took place.[34] For example, when the Odum brothers developed the building blocks of contemporary ecology as webs and chains of food, trophic levels, productivity, energy flows, and metabolism, the emphasis placed on "communities" rather than "individuals" meant that the habitat (neighborhood, district, community) rather than the individual (private property) must be thought of holistically and systemically.[35] Bureaucrats began to understand the idea that if one exerted control on a certain coefficient, such as food, water, or energy, one could then affect metabolism, growth, and dominant species in that ecosystem.[36] Economists, engineers, and environmental policy makers quickly adapted these basic principles from ecology, understanding their consequence on human activity and natural resources by passing environmental laws at a national scale.[37]

While the federal government enacted a series of national policies that influenced the built and natural environments, such as the National Environmental Policy Act 1969 and the Clean Water Act 1972, such acts remained expensive, inefficient, and ill-suited to shaping local policy at the planning scale.[38] As the suburban model ceaselessly burgeons, the role of an evolved paradigm of ecology in planning and design should become a fundamental priority in making decisions about land use and built form.[39]

The most contemporary ecological paradigm with the greatest potential of affecting planning standards today is best described by the environmental scientist Daniel Botkin. Botkin was the first to challenge the prevailing view that the environment remained constant over time and "achieves a form and structure that would persist forever" unless disturbed by human influence. Many still believe that "if left undisturbed, nature would recover, returning to a state of perfect balance."[40] In his seminal texts *Discordant Harmonies* (1990) and *The Moon in the Nautilus Shell: Discordant Harmonies Reconsidered* (2012), Botkin makes the claim that while human action is both a predictable and a random principal powerful force operating on the world, "it is impossible to return to an ideal nature, because ecosystems are patches or collections of conditions that exist for finite periods of time" and are inherently in a state of flux.[41] He further contends that ecosystems may only be managed, but never truly restored or preserved. Typical land-use zoning still hinges on the previous equilibrium and successional paradigms that are driven by a notion of a perfected universal end-state. This static end image continues to influence much of planning practice and master-planned proposals and documents, when in fact we require a dynamic view of the environment, and therefore dynamic tools and policies for the profession.[42]

What then of the role, instrumentality, and agency of urban designers and physical planners in light of a paradigm that doesn't end in "climax end-state"? These questions are becoming extremely evident and timely when dealing the horizontal, expansive polycentric metropolis, as well as places that are highly vulnerable to climatic risks, such as coastal areas.

From Object to System-Based Codes

The wider performative, or process-based, aspects of infrastructure remain at the helm of a centralized core of knowledge within engineering.[43] As such, physical planners are left with the object-based, descriptive metrics of separating the land into sections or zones with different rules that govern the structures on them. Existing standards begin by describing the primary use of the land or its function. This determines the kinds of programmatic activities that are allowed to occur inside the structure(s) built on the parcel (such as residential, commercial, institutional, industrial). The second parameter is the shape of the structure in its two- or three-dimensional configuration (height, setback, etc.). The third parameter is the bulk (how much building can be placed on a unit of land (floor area ratio, maximum build-out, maximum number of buildings per unit land, maximum or minimum density, etc.).[44]

The first to recognize the opportunity of transforming contemporary suburbia using a set of innovative codes and standards were the New Urbanists. By recognizing the instrumentality of standards, "form-based codes" were institutionalized at the scale of the domineering suburban PUD.[45] The New Urbanists saw an opportunity in the expansiveness and ubiquity of PUDs as an occasion to construct a neotraditional narrative around pedestrian-oriented, dense, compact, and nostalgia-themed neighborhood patterns by mutating the code of suburban development. Density was assumed as sufficient in offsetting environmental concerns of suburban sprawl, especially that of carbon emission.[46] Yet it is precisely because

38 Virginia S. Albercht, "Role of Environmental Regulation in Shaping the Built and Natural Environment," in Ben-Joseph and Szold, *Regulating Place*, 271.

39 Alexander J. Felson and Steward T. A. Pickett, "Designed Experiments: New Approaches to Studying Urban Ecosystems," *Frontiers in Ecology and the Environment* 3, no. 10 (2005): 549–56.

40 Botkin, *Discordant Harmonies*; Botkin, *The Moon in the Nautilus Shell*.

41 Botkin, *Discordant Harmonies*.

42 Ibid.; Botkin, *The Moon in the Nautilus Shell*.

43 Pierre Bélanger, "Landscape as Infrastructure," *Landscape Journal* 28, no. 1 (January 1, 2009): 79–95.

44 Jerold Kayden and Charles Haar, *Zoning and the American Dream* (Chicago: Planners Press, 1989).

45 Hirt, "Form Follows Function?"

46 Eran Ben-Joseph, *The Code of the City: Standards and the Hidden Language of Place Making* (Cambridge, MA: MIT Press, 2005); "Center for Applied Transect Studies," accessed December 7, 2015, http://transect.org/transect .html; "Form-Based Codes Defined," *Form-Based Codes Institute*, accessed December 7, 2015, http://formbased codes.org/definition.

neotraditional code starts with the static "form" and aggregation of objects (buildings, building use, style, laneways, awnings, and porches), rather than dynamic "process" of environmental functions (flow, fluxes, change, transformation), as the foundation of codes that their efforts have only resulted in a kind of permanent "inflexibility" with negligible shifts at the metropolitan scale, especially from an environmental perspective.[47]

In fact, form-based codes go a bit further in advocating for the delineation and clear separation of "environmental" services from what New Urbanists traditionally associate with the "city." Andrés Duany, the architect and founder of New Urbanism, argues, "Environmentalism inadvertently enforces and leads to suburbanization."[48] Rather than interweaving the environment as a foundational and structural aspect of the built environment, New Urbanists claimed that many of the environmentally driven regulations, such as groundwater recharge, on-site storm-water detention, minimum permeable square footage for tree planting, protection of wetlands, greenways, wildlife corridors, "all favor 'dendritic' street patterns characteristic of conventional suburbia."[49]

Using the notion of "transect" zoning, New Urbanists claim that natural wilderness "successionally" evolves into an urban "climax" expressed mainly through building density and their ideal city-form. As such, environmental regulations requiring space would remain on the fringe of the metropolitan region. (fig. **5.2.5**) In the conceiving of a set of novel codes for "permanent flexibility," however, the artificiality of such boundaries and segments are futile. Systems, such as water flow, biodiversity, ecosystem services, and metabolic transfers, are never neatly contained within predefined segments; instead the opportunity is there for them to become generative of complimentary and relational built forms and land uses at the metropolitan scale.[50]

By revisiting what constitutes a land use or a zoning code, by including probability and uncertainty as a parameter, by allowing it to "expand and contract," evolve and become dynamic, such tools may become enabling, contextual, and responsive—rather than restrictive or reactionary measures derived through contextual, and process-driven protocols.[51] A way of opening up future coding and standards of planning starts by coupling dynamic process-driven language from landscape and ecology with land use to create open-ended, yet quantifiable, scenario-driven plans.

Opportunistic Suburbia

Suburbia and the exurban fringe are the ideal location for the advancement of novel types of process-driven standards and codes. This is due not just to the abundance of land for ecosystem services but also to the decrease in the complexity hurdles and cost of the development process. The fastest rates of conversation in the metropolitan region is highly associated with the developer's decisions to build homes in the suburbs or exurbs to offset the cost of land brought on by heavy regulations closer to the urban core and established neighborhoods.[52]

Suburbs are also an opportunistic space in policy- and decision-making processes. Many forms of regional control such as greenbelts and growth boundaries for environmental or conservation decisions assume that land is being "wasted" for development purposes. Various studies have showed, however, that no more than 6 percent of the total land area of the United States (excluding Alaska) is devoted to urban land uses.[53] Yet it is precisely the separation of land uses into reductive categories (such as residential and conservation areas) that make it illegal for tapping into the coupling of uses and the

47 Garnett, "Redeeming Transect Zoning?"
48 Andrés Duany and David Brain, "Regulating as If Humans Matter: The Transect and Post-Suburban Planning" in Ben-Joseph and Szold, *Regulating Place*, 305.
49 Ibid.
50 Sybrand P. Tjallingii, "Ecology on the Edge: Landscape and Ecology between Town and Country," *Landscape and Urban Planning* 48, nos. 3–4 (May 1, 2000): 103–19.
51 Alan Berger, *Systemic Design Can Change the World* (Amsterdam; Baarn: Sun Architecture, 2009).
52 Bernard H. Siegan, "The Benefits of Non-Zoning," in Ben-Joseph and Szold, *Regulating Place*.
53 Ibid., 223.

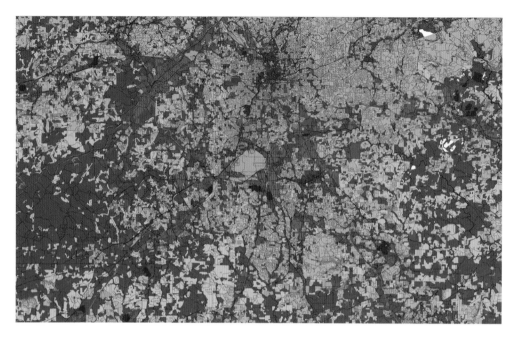

54 Richard D. Tabors, Michael H. Shapiro, and Peter P. Rogers, *Land Use and the Pipe: Planning for Sewerage* (Lexington, MA: Lexington Books, 1976).

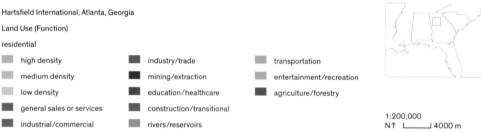

Hartsfield International, Atlanta, Georgia

Land Use (Function)

residential

high density	industry/trade	transportation
medium density	mining/extraction	entertainment/recreation
low density	education/healthcare	agriculture/forestry
general sales or services	construction/transitional	
industrial/commercial	rivers/reservoirs	

1:200,000
N↑ ⊢————⊣ 4000 m

5.2.5 Existing land-use map of the Atlanta region using the American Planning Association's Land-Based Classification Standards. Residential enclaves are nestled in between large swaths of open space and forests that hug infrastructural routes.

creation of feedback mechanisms from an infrastructural (wastewater cycling, water storage, and energy generation, for example) and programmatic (agriculture, recreation, environmental, and employment) point of view. Such restrictions further limit the potentials of innovative forms of subdivision and housing typologies, as it perpetuates the excessive use of land for singular purposes, which some critics condemn as "sprawl" and "leap frogging." (fig. **5.2.6**)

The process of land subdivision has followed the same standards adopted by the Federal Home Finance Agency since the late 1930s, and many of the obstacles for innovation often appear in the administration of street layout and their associated grading and drainage.

"Sewerage, not planning, dominates the growth game" declare the sanitary engineers to county planning staff.[54] The opportunity, however, for novel types of land uses and standards leading to "permanent flexibility" may emerge by strategically intervening in three uniquely suburban development approvals processes. The first is the benefit of working on PUDs, which streamline large swaths of land ownership, and then continues to manage and oversee the agreed covenants and rules of the individual owners once the property has been purchased. The second is the provision of brand-new infrastructure, especially water and wastewater, to be constructed in a sustainable, innovative, and metabolic matter. And third is in the process of large-scale grading and earth work, in favor of net-positive ecosystem service at the watershed scale. (fig. **5.2.7**) Once such a system is in place, the buildings' floor area ratios, foundations, setback, density, height, and use emerge as a reflection of the bigger systemic and environmental process-based coding on the suburban fringe. (figs. **5.2.8**–**9**)

Conclusion

Newer ecological theories vary, but tend to see the environment in a process of constant change and flux, rather than one with a stable end-state. Environmental law may have adapted to new paradigms, but planning policy derived during the Progressive Era remains embedded in the static concept of a future condition tied to the "end-state planning." This essay proposes that in the diminution of regulatory planning tools and the erosion of code in certain contexts, such as the suburban edges of the polynodal metropolis, brownfields, coastal areas, and estuaries, that we may propose novel land uses and forms of occupation. As such, zoning remains the most prolific and powerful tool at the purview of urbanists and planners, as the starting point for such transformations. In the most ubiquitous condition of urbanization, potential new models could arise in the suburban fringe, where the privation of overregulation and the abundance of space allow for transformative innovation and experimentation in code, process, and form.

Ultimately, this condition establishes an opportunity for policy planning to be a part of the design process and a progeny of it. This brings design thinking into the powerful domain of public decision making by including it in the precise edicts of urbanism, and not acting as the exception to it.

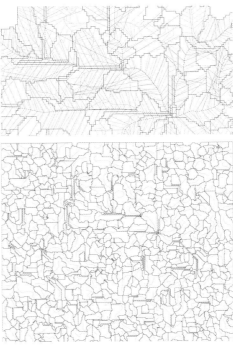

5.2.6 A propositional subdivision scheme that uses the natural drainage patterns to clearly demarcate micro-watersheds that run along and through the site. This acts as the first step in decentralizing hydrological infrastructure on greenfields or the exurban edge.

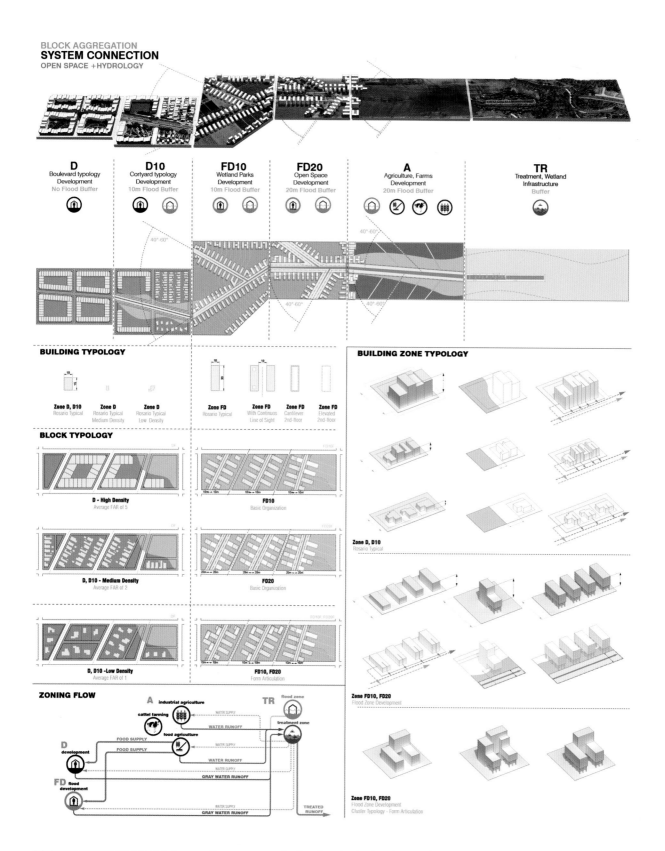

BLOCK AGGREGATION
SYSTEM CONNECTION
OPEN SPACE +HYDROLOGY

D
Boulevard typology
Development
No Flood Buffer

D10
Cortyard typology
Development
10m Flood Buffer

FD10
Wetland Parks
Development
10m Flood Buffer

FD20
Open Space
Development
20m Flood Buffer

A
Agriculture, Farms
Development
20m Flood Buffer

TR
Treatment, Wetland
Infrastructure
Buffer

BUILDING TYPOLOGY

Zone D, D10 — Rosario Typical
Zone D — Rosario Typical Medium Density
Zone D — Rosario Typical Low Density

Zone FD — Rosario Typical
Zone FD — With Continuos Line of Sight
Zone FD — Cantilever 2nd-floor
Zone FD — Elevated 2nd-floor

BLOCK TYPOLOGY

D - High Density
Average FAR of 5

FD10
Basic Organization

D, D10 - Medium Density
Average FAR of 2

FD20
Basic Organization

D, D10 -Low Density
Average FAR of 1

FD10, FD20
Form Articulation

BUILDING ZONE TYPOLOGY

Zone D, D10
Rosario Typical

Zone FD10, FD20
Flood Zone Development

Zone FD10, FD20
Flood Zone Development
Cluster Typology - Form Articulation

ZONING FLOW

A — industrial agriculture
cattel farming
food agriculture
TR — flood zone
WATER SUPPLY
WATER RUNOFF
treatment zone
D — development
FOOD SUPPLY
FOOD SUPPLY
WATER SUPPLY
WATER RUNOFF
FD — flood development
WATER SUPPLY
GRAY WATER RUNOFF
WATER SUPPLY
GRAY WATER RUNOFF
TREATED RUNOFF

5.2.7 The built form (objects) and their aggregation emerge as a reflection of novel systemic and process-based coding such as flooding, soil, and solar variables

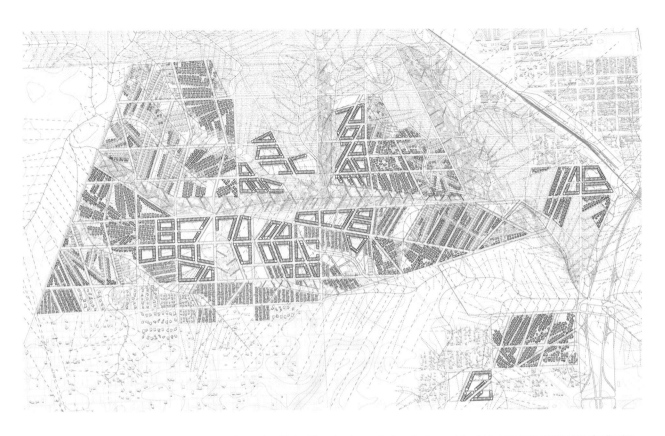

5.2.8 A future planned unit development that protects the most arable land from development, allows for the most floodable areas to become points of collection and treatment, and imagines novel forms and patterns of urbanization on the suburban edge.

5.2.9 Rendered detail of one possible segment of the PUD showing various density variables and land-use conditions.

Arrowcreek, Reno, Nevada, United States

Weston, Florida, United States

5.3
CITIES, SUBURBS, AND THE CHALLENGE OF METROPOLITAN GOVERNANCE

Richard Briffault

GOVERNANCE & POLICY CHALLENGES

REGIONAL GOVERNANCE

SOCIAL INEQUALITIES

SUBURB-CITY INTER-DEPENDENCIES

A defining feature of American metropolitan areas is the lack of effective metropolitan governance. Our metropolitan areas are fragmented into dozens, and sometimes hundreds, of local governments, each with its own tax base, interests, and policies. As a result, there are frequently significant interlocal fiscal and service inequalities, and the sheer number of local governments makes it difficult for them to work with one another to address regional concerns. Yet these many local governments—and their residents—cling to their independence and have long resisted the formation of effective regional political institutions.

Part of the problem arises out of the disconnect between the socioeconomic idea of the suburb and the suburb's legal status. According to a popular dictionary definition, a suburb is "an outlying part of a city or town" and "a smaller community adjacent to or within commuting distance of a city."[1] Other definitions add the concept of residential, as in "a usually residential area or community outlying a city."[2] These definitions also stress the economic connection to the city: "It is... often dependent upon the nearby city for employment opportunities and other benefits."[3] Although today the suburbs are no longer purely residential and some are commercial and employment centers, these definitions and the thinking that underlies them assume both a certain distinction between cities and suburbs and a certain relationship between them. The suburb is not a city and is often separate from a city, yet it is also closely linked economically and socially to a city.

Legally, however, many suburbs actually are cities. As a matter of law, a city is a municipal corporation, that is, an entity formally established by the state and endowed with certain governmental powers. The specific powers vary from state to state and, sometimes, even within a state. But a municipal corporation typically can levy, collect, and spend tax dollars; provide traditional public services, particularly in the areas of public safety, public health, and public streets and roads; and regulate private behavior, including land use.

More important, although both classic cities and suburban "cities" have legal and political independence from each other, economically and socially they are not independent at all but interdependent constituents of metropolitan regions. Regions, not the separate cities and suburbs within them, function as labor and housing markets. Businesses look to regions, rather than the particular localities in an area, for employees, suppliers, and customers. In the global economy, metropolitan regions are "the units of economic competition," with the prosperity of the component localities rising and falling with the overall economic health of the region.[4] Cultural, sports, educational, and health institutions—museums, orchestras, stadiums, universities, and hospitals—play important roles in regional life and interregional competition. Infrastructure, environmental and natural resources—airports, transit systems, air and water quality, water supply, waste removal, and open space—transcend local boundaries and affect interregional competition as well. Cities and suburbs have "shared fortunes."[5] Although they may compete with each other, they—and the regions that they constitute—grow, or fail to grow, together.[6] As David Rusk, the former mayor of Albuquerque, New Mexico, once put it, "The real city is the total metropolitan area—city and suburb."[7] Yet there are few, if any, metropolitan governments of regional scope. A central challenge for twenty-first-century America is how to effectively govern the many metropolitan regions that are composed of large numbers of legally distinct cities and suburbs.

1   *Merriam-Webster OnLine,* s.v. "suburb," accessed August 1, 2015, http://www.merriam-webster.com/dictionary/suburb.
2   *The Free Dictionary,* s.v. "suburb," accessed August 1, 2015, http://www.thefreedictionary.com/suburb.
3   *BusinessDictionary.com,* s.v. "suburb," accessed August 1, 2015, http://www.businessdictionary.com/definition/suburb.html.
4   Theodore Hershberg, "Regional Cooperation: Strategies and Incentives for Global Competitiveness and Urban Reform," *National Civic Review* 85, no. 2 (Spring–Summer 1996): 25.
5   Jordan Rappaport, "The Shared Fortunes of Cities and Suburbs," *Federal Reserve Bank of Kansas City Economic Review* (Third Quarter 2005): 33.
6   Stephanie Shirley Post and Robert M. Stein, "State Economies, Metropolitan Governance, and Urban-Suburban Economic Dependence," *Urban Affairs Review* 36, no. 1 (September 2000): 56.
7   David Rusk, *Cities without Suburbs,* 2nd ed. (Washington, DC: Woodrow Wilson Center Press, 1995), 3.

The Legal Structure of Metropolitan Areas

The term *city* suggests a relatively large, densely populated urban center. Although many states require certain population or population density minimums as a condition for the incorporation of a city, these requirements can be quite low— 300 people in Kentucky, 200 people in Georgia or Arkansas, 150 people in New Mexico or Oregon.[8] The number of municipalities in the United States has grown steadily in recent decades, with roughly 450 added between 1982 and 2012.[9] Moreover, particularly in older parts of the country, many small municipalities were formed decades, if not centuries, ago, before the enactment of general incorporation laws and before massive urban growth swept these communities into expanding metropolitan areas and turned them into suburbs of larger cities. As a result, many relatively small communities are legally cities, including those that fit the dictionary definition of a suburb due to their primarily residential character and commuting proximity to larger cities.

In 2013, the vast majority of the municipalities in the United States—16,494, or roughly 85 percent of all cities—had fewer than ten thousand people, and another 2,239 incorporated places (11 percent of the total)—had between ten thousand and fifty thousand people.[10] These smaller municipalities may not fit the traditional image of the "city" as a large, densely populated central place, but they are home to 40 percent of the population that the Census classifies as urban. Some of these smaller, legal "cities" are freestanding communities outside a metropolitan area, but socially and economically many are suburbs. Yet, as cities, they typically enjoy the taxing and regulatory powers of larger, more stereotypical "cities" and are authorized to provide the same types of public services.

Many suburbs that are not incorporated as cities also may have their own local governments. The largest category of local government in the United States today is the special purpose district, which provides one or a small number of specific governmental functions, such as fire protection, water supply, sewerage, solid waste management, parks, libraries, and health and hospitals. Although some of these districts overlap incorporated municipalities, many are created in unincorporated areas that, due to population growth, need public services but do not want to bear the costs of a full-fledged general-purpose government.[11] Some special districts, such as community services districts, community development districts, or stewardship districts, play a key role in providing physical improvements, basic infrastructure, land-use planning, and public services in unincorporated but developing areas in states like California, Florida, and Texas. Many special districts, like cities, can borrow money and impose assessments to cover the costs of the services they provide. Although not technically cities, these districts, like cities, function as relatively autonomous local governments for suburbs.[12]

Cities and suburbs together form metropolitan areas or regions. The people of the United States are increasingly and overwhelmingly concentrated in metropolitan areas. More than 83 percent of Americans lived in metropolitan areas in 2010, and more than 90 percent of population growth in the 2000 to 2010 decade occurred in metropolitan areas.[13] Typically, the people who live in a metropolitan area do not confine their daily lives to their home locality, which, after all, takes up only a small fraction of the area. A person is likely to live in one locality, work in another, shop in a third, seek entertainment in a fourth, and move through a large number of others in the course of a day.

8   Kentucky: Baldwin's Ky. Rev. Stat. Ann. § 81.060 (1)(a); Georgia: West's Code of Ga. Ann. § 36–31–3; Arkansas: West's Ark. Code Ann. § 14–38–101 (a)(1); New Mexico: West's N.M. Stat. Ann. § 3–2–2 A(3); Oregon: West's Ore. Rev. Stat. Ann. § 221.020.

9   "General Purpose Local Governments by State: Census Years 1942 to 2012—United States—States 2012 Census of Governments," U.S. Census Bureau, American FactFinder, accessed July 31, 2014, https://www.census.gov /govs/cog/.

10   Darryl T. Cohen, Geoffrey W. Hatchard, and Steven G. Wilson, *Population Trends in Incorporated Places: 2000 to 2013; Population Estimates and Projections; Current Population Reports* (US Department of Commerce, Economics and Statistics Administration, US Census Bureau, March 2015), 3, 1–19.

11   Nancy Burns, *The Formation of American Local Governments: Private Values in Public Institutions* (New York: Oxford University Press, 1994), 80.

12   Nadav Shoked, "Quasi-Cities," *Boston University Law Review* 93 (December 1, 2013): 1971–2032.

13   John Rennie Short, "Metropolitan USA: Evidence from the 2010 Census," *2012 International Journal of Population Research,* Article ID 207532, accessed July 29, 2015, http://www.hindawi .com/journals /ijpr/2012/207532/.

Unlike *city*, which has a legal meaning, and *suburb*, which is often either a legal city or part of another local government, *metropolitan area* or region usually has no legal significance. The US Census employs the term *metropolitan statistical area* (MSA) to refer to areas with an urbanized core of at least fifty thousand people, plus adjacent territory that has a high degree of social and economic integration with the core, as measured by commuting ties.[14] But few if any metropolitan areas fall within a single local government with full governing authority. Instead, as a result of the proliferation of cities and special districts in the suburbs and the lack of an all-encompassing metropolitan area government, a defining feature of our metropolitan areas is highly fragmented local governance.

About half the metropolitan areas in the United States have 200 or more local governments, and some areas have far more than that.[15] Metropolitan Chicago has an estimated 1,500 local governments, and the Houston, Philadelphia, and Pittsburgh metropolitan areas each have more than 800 local governments.[16] Fragmented governance is particularly common in the Midwest and, albeit to a lesser degree, the Northeast.[17] As many Americans learned during the nationwide controversy over police behavior and community relations in Ferguson, Missouri, in 2014, St. Louis County, with barely one million people, has ninety municipalities—or one city for every eleven thousand people—and that does not count the special districts within the county.[18] The greatest recent increases in the number of local governments have occurred in highly suburban or suburbanizing states like Maryland and Colorado.[19]

The Costs of Fragmentation

A multiplicity of relatively small local governments within a metropolitan area is not necessarily a bad thing. Indeed,

for many years the leading model of local government law was built on the benefits of fragmentation. Based on the work of the economist Charles Tiebout, scholars emphasized that with a large number of relatively small local governments near each other, residents and firms could, simply by moving a short distance (or staying put), choose the local government that offered them the most attractive package of public services, taxes, and local regulations.[20] A large number of nearby local governments with the legal power to adopt different service delivery, budget, and regulatory priorities would permit households and businesses to sort themselves according to their individual preferences, thus maximizing overall satisfaction with local government in the region. Moreover, given the mobility of residents and firms within the metropolitan area, local governments would have an incentive to hold down costs, improve their services, and make sure their regulatory programs satisfied local needs lest their "consumer-voters" exercise the "exit" option and decamp to a neighboring community.[21]

But fragmentation has its costs. Fragmented regions have difficulty cooperating to address issues of regional concern, such as the creation or expansion of critical physical infrastructure. In one fascinating case study, two adjacent Connecticut suburbs squabbled over the location of a new commuter rail station. Both would have been better off if the new station had been located in either town. But because each sought to win it and could not agree, the opening of the new station was delayed for years.[22] Because local governments are largely dependent on their own tax bases to finance the services they provide their residents, metropolitan localities "engage in competitive fiscal mercantilism," deploying zoning rules, eminent domain, low-interest loans, infrastructure investments, and tax incentives to attract or retain net

14 "Metropolitan and Micropolitan: About Metropolitan and Micropolitan Statistical Areas," *United States Census*, accessed July 29, 2015, http://www.census.gov/population/metro/about/.

15 Michael J. Rich, "The Intergovernmental Environment," in *Cities, Politics, and Policies: A Comparative Analysis*, ed. John P. Pelissero (Washington, DC: CQ Press, 2002), 35–36.

16 Ibid.

17 Carma Hogue, *Government Organizations Summary Report: 2012, Government Divisions Briefs* (US Department of Commerce, Economics and Statistics Administration, US Census Bureau, September 26, 2013), 2.

18 Emily Badger, "What Happens When a Metropolitan Area Has Way Too Many Governments," *Washington Post Wonkblog*, last modified February 18, 2015, accessed July 29, 2015, http://www.washingtonpost.com/news/wonkblog/wp/2015/02/18/what-happens-when-a-metropolitan-area-has-way-too-many-governments/.

19 Hogue, *Government Organizations Summary Report: 2012*, 4.

20 Charles M. Tiebout, "A Pure Theory of Local Expenditures," *Journal of Political Economy* 64, no. 5 (October 1956): 416–24.

21 Ibid., 418.

22 Minor Myers III, "Obstacles to Bargaining between Local Governments: The Case of West Haven and Orange, Connecticut," *Urban Lawyer* 37, no. 4 (Fall 2005): 853–92.

revenueproducing land users. These activities may be pursued without regard to the noise, traffic, congestion, or other disamenities and negative competitive effects they may impose on neighboring communities.[23] Thus when one suburban Chicago community rezoned land to permit the development of an open-air music theater "in close proximity to residentially developed areas within the corporate limits" of two adjacent communities, those communities sued, claiming that the project would burden them with noise, safety, and environmental costs.[24] Similarly, when New Rochelle, New York, sought to stimulate its economic redevelopment by using its eminent domain power to provide land for a new Ikea superstore, the neighboring town of Mamaroneck, which abutted the planned Ikea site, sought to use its own legal powers to block New Rochelle's action, claiming it would "create serious traffic congestion" in Mamaroneck.[25]

By the same token, many local governments also try to exclude net service-consuming users, such as low-income residents, from within their municipal boundaries. With municipal finances heavily dependent on revenues generated within local boundaries, fragmentation leads to enormous disparities in tax bases, tax rates, and the quality and quantity of locally provided services. |Generally, the more fragmented the region, the greater the intraregional differences in tax base, with the most affluent areas able to levy lower tax rates and still finance better services, while the poorest areas—which often include old, inner suburbs as well as fiscally strapped central cities—charge the highest tax rates for the worst services.[26]

Fragmentation tends to encourage sprawl.[27] Local governments can use their land-use powers to require large lots, limit or block multifamily structures, or impose development impact fees or other exactions that reduce the amount of affordable housing within the locality. This is particularly true in residential suburbs, which are politically dominated by homeowners who have most of their wealth invested in their homes and so are particularly attentive to any changes that might reduce property values. These "home voters" may see growth as leading to a loss of amenities and an increase in local public service costs, while not recognizing the benefits to the region of more affordable housing for people who may be employed by firms in nearby cities. As a result, suburban residents often will support local land-use policies that have the effect of pushing new development farther out, thereby extending commuting times, consuming open space, and increasing the region's environmental impact.[28]

Due to the ability of many local governments to exercise land-use powers, fragmentation can have an adverse impact on regional productivity, wages, and the economy. The economic essence of a city is agglomeration, that is, the concentration of people and firms in a relatively dense place. Agglomeration reduces transportation costs, creates deeper and more specialized labor and consumption markets, and promotes innovation. This benefits both firms and workers within the region, and the economy as a whole.[29] But fragmentation, and particularly the increased local land-use regulation that results from it, interferes with agglomeration and undercuts its benefits.[30] By pushing new development to the periphery of the metropolitan area, suburban land-use regulation tends to reduce density and the economic benefits that come with it. The Organisation for Economic Development and Co-operation (OECD) recently surveyed its thirty-four member nations and concluded that for each doubling in the number of municipalities per one hundred thousand inhabitants within a metropolitan area, labor productivity in that area decreased by 5 to 6 percent.[31]

23 On competitive fiscal mercantilism, see David Y. Miller, *The Regional Governing of Metropolitan America* (Boulder, CO: Westview Press, 2002), 109; Myers, *Obstacles to Bargaining*, 872–75.

24 *Village of Barrington Hills v. Village of Hoffman Estates*, 410 N.E.2d 37 (Ill. 1980).

25 *City of New Rochelle v. Town of Mamaroneck*, 111 F.Supp.2d 353 (S.D.N.Y. 2000).

26 Myron Orfield, *American Metropolitics: The New Suburban Reality* (Washington, DC: Brookings Institute, 2002), 85–95.

27 Hank Savitch, "Dreams and Realities: Coping with Urban Sprawl," *Virginia Environmental Law Journal* 19, no. 3 (2000): 345.

28 William A. Fischel, *The Homevoter Hypothesis: How Home Values Influence Local Government Taxation, School Finance, and Land-Use Policies* (Cambridge, MA: Harvard University Press, 2001).

29 Edward L. Glaeser, "Are Cities Dying?," *Journal of Economic Perspectives* 12, no. 2 (Spring 1998): 141–50.

30 Nestor M. Davidson and Sheila R. Foster, "The Mobility Case for Regionalism," *UC Davis Law Review* 47, no. 1 (November 2013): 81–102.

31 OECD, *The Metropolitan Century: Understanding Urbanisation and Its Consequences* (Paris: OECD Publishing, 2015), 55–56.

The equality, efficiency, and environmental cases for metropolitan area government are strong, but since at least the middle of the last century, the cause of regional government has had little political traction and has, instead, experienced considerable and successful regional resistance. Municipal mergers are extremely rare. City-county consolidations in which a central city government is combined with the surrounding county but the other cities within the county maintain their legal independence are only slightly more common. Although there are more than three thousand counties in the United States, there have been fewer than three-dozen city-county consolidations.[32] Academic critics have derided regionalism as little more than a "push by elite groups" to supplant grassroots decision making in small local units by adding a new layer of unaccountable bureaucracy.[33] And the public has not been much more supportive. When proposals for the merger or consolidation of smaller cities into larger, more metropolitan units have been put before the voters, the voters have generally said no. "Over the last 40 years, nearly 100 referenda and initiatives have proposed city-county consolidations, but voters have rejected three-fourths of them."[34] People appear to like keeping their governments small and closer to home, and will reject consolidation into a larger unit in the absence of either a strong concern about the quality of local government services or some crisis in local government performance.[35] And, admittedly, given the size of some of our metropolitan areas, a local government that is metropolitan in scope would scarcely be "local" at all.

From Regional Government to Regional Governance

With true regional *government* out of reach, some modest progress has been made on regional *governance*. Through changes to incorporation and annexation laws, the creation of regional special districts, special funding mechanisms, interlocal agreements, enhanced county powers and partial city-county combinations, and public-private partnerships, states and local groups have sought to facilitate metropolitan area-wide approaches to metropolitan area-wide problems while leaving preexisting local governments in place. There is resistance to some of these measures, too, but because they are likely to preserve some considerable measure of local autonomy, they have a better chance for success.

One approach has been to prevent increased fragmentation by making it more difficult to incorporate new municipal corporations in the suburbs. A number of states either bar new incorporations within a certain distance of an existing city or use state or county administrative boards to oversee, and potentially reject, proposed new incorporations.[36] Some states have also made it easier for existing cities to expand by annexing adjacent suburban land, thereby preventing that area from incorporating. Most states require a city to obtain the consent of the landowners or residents of the area the city would like to annex as a condition for annexation, but a handful of states permit unilateral or involuntary annexations that dispense with the need for that consent.[37] Such regionalist incorporation and annexation rules in some of the most rapidly growing areas in the South and West have produced much less fragmented and less internally unequal regions, with greater opportunities for cooperation and, perhaps not coincidentally, better economic performance. Thus Albuquerque mayor David Rusk found that relatively less fragmented metropolitan areas like Houston, Nashville, or Albuquerque were less segregated, enjoyed higher rates of job creation and greater gains in real income, and had

32　"City-County Consolidations," National League of Cities, accessed July 21, 2015, http://www.nlc.org/build-skills-and-networks/resources/cities-101/city-structures/city-county-consolidations.

33　Robert Bruegmann, *Sprawl: A Compact History* (Chicago: University of Chicago Press, 2005), 145.

34　"City-County Consolidations."

35　Dagney Faulk and Michael Hicks, *Local Government Consolidation in the United States* (Amherst, NY: Cambria Press, 2011), 32–34.

36　About Texas barring new incorporations near cities, see Vernon's Texas Stat. & Codes Ann. § 42.041; about using administrative boards to review new incorporations, see Richard Briffault, "Our Localism: Part I—The Structure of Local Government Law," *Columbia Law Review* 90 no. 1 (January 1990): 83.

37　Christopher J. Tyson, "Localism and Involuntary Annexation: Reconsidering Approaches to New Regionalism," *Tulane Law Review* 87, no. 2 (December 2012): 303–25.

narrower city-suburb income gaps than more fragmented metropolitan areas that were comparable in size.[38]

Working with existing local governments, most states now authorize interlocal agreements that enable cities and their suburbs to buy services from each other or pool their resources and provide some public services more efficiently. These agreements are voluntary and generally steer clear of politically fraught issues like affordable housing or fiscal resources, and instead focus on the creation and maintenance of physical infrastructure.[39]

Similarly, some states have strengthened the powers of their counties to enable them to govern more effectively in unincorporated areas, thereby reducing the need for new incorporations. Most states are divided into counties, but traditionally counties had relatively few governing responsibilities, and served more as a basis for the local performance of basic state functions like maintaining roads, providing criminal justice, keeping vital statistics, and running the courts. In many metropolitan areas, counties have been strengthened to take on more service delivery and regulatory responsibilities in unincorporated areas. In a small number of places, primarily in the South, counties have even entered into partial mergers with their largest cities, creating so-called two-tier governments, like Jacksonville–Duval County Florida, Nashville–Davidson County, Tennessee, and Louisville–Jefferson County Kentucky. These entities better coordinate their services and reduce costs.[40] Typically these two-tier consolidations preserve the independence of the other preexisting municipalities within the county and so do not fully address interlocal tax and spending differences or the spillover effects of local regulation.

Many major metropolitan areas use regional special-purpose districts to finance, construct, or operate key aspects of their physical infrastructure, particularly regional transportation systems, including mass transit, airports, ports, water supply, irrigation, flood control, wastewater treatment, and power supply. These systems and facilities can offer significant economies of scale when provided on a regional basis; some, like commuter transit systems, by their very nature must serve multiple communities. Financed by user charges and/or regional taxes, such as a metro area surcharge on the sales tax, they are also usually run by appointees selected by the component local governments or by the state, rather than candidates elected by the voters. Overlaid on top of existing local governments, these entities typically provide a single function and constitute a limited form of regional organization. Metropolitan Portland, Oregon, is the rare case where the regional special district has multiple responsibilities. The Portland "metro" manages the region's solid waste system, parks, and open spaces. It also coordinates regional land-use planning with local governments; oversees the zoo, convention center, and other cultural facilities; and is the rare regional district whose officers are elected by the voters. Thus, the district does provide a form of regional governance.[41]

Special districts have also been used to provide metropolitan-area financial support to local activities with regional benefits. Perhaps the most striking example is metro Denver's Scientific and Cultural Facilities District (SCFD). Authorized by voters in a four-county region, it imposes a modest surcharge on the state sales tax to support a range of cultural facilities in Denver itself—the Art Museum, Botanic Gardens, Museum of Science and Nature, and the zoo—as well as smaller cultural institutions throughout the metro area. The SCFD, and the metro area voters' approval of a subsequent increment to the sales tax to

38 Rusk, *Cities without Suburbs*, 27–48.
39 Clayton P. Gillette, "The Conditions of Interlocal Cooperation," *Journal of Law and Politics* 21 (Spring–Summer 2005): 365–95.
40 Rusk, *Cities without Suburbs*, 93–98.
41 "What Is Metro?," Oregonmetro.com, accessed August 1, 2015, http://www.oregonmetro.gov/regional-leadership/what-metro.

finance a baseball stadium in downtown Denver, reflects the judgment of suburban residents that they have a stake in the flourishing of cultural and entertainment institutions located in the central city, and that the region as a whole would benefit from more secure financing of these programs.[42]

Finally, even in areas where there are no formal governmental organizations of regional scope, informal public-private partnerships that link local governments, businesses, and major nonprofits like universities and hospitals can play a useful role in regional planning and in recruiting and retaining industry.[43]

Shortfalls of Regional Governance Mechanisms

These are all positive developments, but regional governance has fallen short in the two areas where it is most needed: land-use regulation and fiscal equity. In our fragmented metropolitan regions, local land-use regulation inevitably affects other nearby communities and the region as a whole. Sometimes the spillover effects are relatively clear-cut, as when local recruitment of a new industrial facility, shopping mall, big box store, or entertainment center imposes traffic, noise, or congestion costs on nearby communities. Some states, such as Florida, have taken steps to provide for some regional oversight of local developments that have such regional impacts.[44]

The more common problem, particularly in the northeast and in rapidly growing areas in the west, is the opposite: restrictive local zoning that, by requiring larger lots, barring multifamily dwellings, or imposing exactions, drives up the cost of housing and has the effect of excluding people from the community. The New Jersey Supreme Court put it well in its landmark *Mount Laurel* decision, writing, "This pattern of land use regulation has been adopted for the same purpose in developing municipality after developing municipality. Almost every one acts solely in its own selfish and parochial interest and in effect builds a wall around itself to keep out those people or entities not adding favorably to the tax base, despite the location of the municipality or the demand for varied kinds of housing."[45] These restrictive housing measures reduce affordability, increase sprawl, and make whole regions less attractive to firms and prospective residents alike.

In some states, most prominently New Jersey, the courts have imposed limits on the ability of developing communities to exclude low- and moderate-income housing. Other states, such as California, have required communities to include low- and moderate-income housing elements in their zoning plans.[46] In Oregon, the Urban Growth Boundary around metro Portland has curbed sprawl, and a regional administrative agency oversees local land development.[47] But these actions are relatively unusual and underscore the lack of a regional approach to land-use decision-making in most metropolitan areas.

The lack of fiscal regionalism is even more striking. Local governments are largely dependent on their own resources to fund their programs. This means that more affluent communities can provide better services at lower tax rates, while poorer communities have to tax themselves at higher rates; even so, they can only afford to provide inferior services. As mentioned earlier, local fiscal dependence also affects local land-use regulation, causing localities to use zoning to try to attract firms and affluent residents while excluding lower-income people who may cost more in local services than the taxes they pay. In this way differences in local fiscal capacity create unequal tax rates and services, and promote class and income segregation. Moreover, interlocal inequality within a metropolitan area tends to correlate with slower growth.

42 Bruce Katz and Jenifer Bradley, *The Metropolitan Revolution: How Cities and Metros Are Fixing Our Broken Politics and Fragile Economy* (Washington, DC: Brookings Institution, 2013), 41–63.

43 Ibid., 64–87.

44 Fla. Stat. Ann. § 380.06.

45 *Southern Burlington N.A.A.C.P. v. Township of Mount Laurel*, 336 A.2d 713 (N.J. 1975).

46 In the Matter of the Adoption of N.J.A.C. 5:96 and 5:97 by the New Jersey Council of Affordable Housing, 221 N.J. 1 (Supreme Court of New Jersey, March 10, 2015); Cal. Gov't Code §§ 65580 et seq.

47 Norman Williams and John M. Taylor, "§ 171:21 The Oregon Act—Urbanization (Goal 14)," in *American Land Planning Law: Land Use and the Police Power*, vol. 7 (Eagan, MN: Thomson/West, 2003).

Some form of regional tax base sharing could address this. Some part of the tax base of more affluent communities could be treated as a tax base for the entire metropolitan region, and thus available for use to fund services in the region's poorer communities. The regional taxes used to support regional facilities are a step toward this, but they are usually closely focused on physical infrastructure and do not involve direct aid to poorer communities or redistribution from one community to another. Over many decades, the school finance reform movement has sought to alleviate interlocal fiscal disparities by having the states play a greater role in financing local public schools, but with mixed success at best.

A rare instance of regional tax base sharing was adopted by Minnesota for the greater Minneapolis–St. Paul area. A portion of the incremental revenue resulting from increases in the value of commercial and industrial property value in the region is placed in a fund for redistribution to localities in the region based on local need.[48] By making the precise location of new economic development in the metro area less important, such a fiscal regionalist measure can damp down the ferocity of interlocal fiscal competition and promote greater interlocal equality while leaving local decision-making autonomy in place. But the Twin Cities tax base sharing program has not been emulated by other regions.

These examples of tax base sharing, regional financing, infrastructure districts, two-tier city-county consolidations, and the like indicate that there is no shortage of ideas on how to revamp our governance structures to address the regional nature of life in metropolitan America. Nor is there any question that the states have the legal authority to create regional bodies with significant powers. But their limited use, especially for pressing matters like controlling exclusionary land regulation and promoting greater fiscal equity, suggest that the real issue is persuading metropolitan area residents that a regional perspective and regional institutions are needed.

Persistence and leadership are required. Typically multiple efforts over a period of years have been needed for city-county consolidations. Of the seventeen successful consolidation attempts made between 1970 and 2003, "six (35.3 percent) had multiple referenda (up to five attempts) before the consolidation was approved."[49] Local leaders, including members of the business community, civic organizations, and not-for-profit institutions need to be involved. Most important, the states need to take a leading role. States could use carrots like increased state aid or additional infrastructure investment in areas that create more cooperative mechanisms or, perhaps, sticks of reduced aid to areas that fail to do so. Further, new forms of regional governance may be needed that better combine opportunities for local or neighborhood input with decision making by regional bodies.

Perhaps this requires a return to the definition of the *suburb* with which this essay began. The defining feature of the suburb is its simultaneous distinction from and connection to the city. Suburbanites seem well aware of their separation from the city. But they need to give greater attention to their underlying connection to it and to the shared city-suburban—in other words, regional—fate that connection entails. By the same token, the ongoing appeal of the relatively small residential suburb is a reminder of the need for some neighborhood-level political institutions in city and suburb alike.

Cities and suburbs rise and fall together in metropolitan areas. But until we have legal and political institutions

48 Myron Orfield and Nicholas Wallace, "The Minnesota Fiscal Disparities Act of 1971: The Twin Cities' Struggle and Blueprint for Regional Cooperation," *William Mitchell Law Review* 33, no. 2 (2007): 591–612.

49 Faulk and Hicks, *Local Government Consolidation in the United States*, 18–19.

that better reflect this underlying economic and social reality, we will be unable
to effectively address the inefficiencies
and inequalities that mark so many of our
metropolitan areas.

5.4
SUBURBAN GOVERNMENT AND THE VIRTUES OF LOCAL CONTROL

Howard Husock

In his definitive book *Crabgrass Frontier: The Suburbanization of the United States*, the historian Kenneth Jackson noted that "it is almost a truism to observe that the dominant residential pattern is suburban."[1] As undeniable as the trend toward suburbanization has been, however, it is one that has long faced criticism. Jackson may have characterized suburban housing as "affordable homes for the common man."[2] Yet in her song "Little Boxes," the folk music and protest singer-songwriter Malvina Reynolds scoffed at them, as "little boxes made of ticky-tacky…and they all look just the same." Although far from narrowly negative about the phenomenon, Jackson offered the view that suburbs reinforced urban problems, as the affluent moved to suburbia and central cities became associated with social problems—indeed, that "the new houses of the suburbs were a major cause of the decline of the central cities."[3] To this he added the overarching American tendency to sort residentially by socioeconomic status, which he cast as an implicit negative.

Similarly, the localized suburban political model is often contrasted—unfavorably—with the aspiration of broad, regional governance, which its advocates believe offers gains in both efficiency and fairness across the metropolitan area. The urban scholar and one-time Albuquerque mayor David Rusk made the quintessential case for regional governance in his 1993 book, *Cities without Suburbs*. As Rusk wrote, "Segregating poor urban Blacks and Hispanics has spawned physically-decaying, revenue-strapped, poverty-impacted, crime-ridden 'inner cities.' These inner cities are isolated from their 'outer cities'—wealthier, growing, largely-white suburbs."[4]

An even more nuanced discussion of a positive role for greater regionalization of American public services is that of David Miller of the Graduate School of Public and International Affairs at the University of Pittsburgh. In *The Regional Governing of Metropolitan America* (which concedes that "externally imposed solutions, although often seen as the visible form of regionalism, seldom work"), Miller nonetheless advocates that the deep American tradition of relatively small local government should evolve.[5] As Miller writes, "I do not want to convey that I am a cheerleader for the existing system of relationships among local governments in metropolitan areas. Indeed, I will demonstrate that those relationships are fundamentally flawed."[6]

Unremarked on, however, in most literature about suburbs and their governance, are some notable political features that drove and continue to drive and explain suburbanization: much smaller units of government, more local political control, and greater accountability to smaller electorates. Such desires, this essay argues, are evident in historical accounts of post–World War II suburbanization and continue today—not without good reason.

This essay takes the view that the demonstrated preference across the socioeconomic spectrum for smaller units of government should not be dismissed as a vestige of an antiquated, agrarian-era system. Instead, I argue that local government, particularly as practiced in small jurisdictions such as suburbs, merits appreciation and protection. It should be seen as an aspect of American federalism worth defending, one that should be considered a fundamental building block of the nation's governance, a key to political accountability, and even a spur to economic development. One simply cannot dismiss the fact that Americans in great numbers, have chosen, and continue to choose, such governmental units. Some aspects of suburban home-rule might even be brought, to good effect, to central cities.

1 Kenneth T. Jackson, *Crabgrass Frontier: The Suburbanization of the United States* (New York: Oxford University Press, 1985), 4.
2 Ibid., 116.
3 Ibid., 244.
4 David Rusk, *Cities without Suburbs* (Washington, DC: Woodrow Wilson Center Press, 1993), 1.
5 David Y. Miller, *The Regional Governing of Metropolitan America* (Boulder, CO: Westview Press, 2002), 5.
6 Ibid., 5.

The Suburban Preference

There is simply no way around the fact that Americans in large numbers have voluntarily migrated to suburban jurisdictions. One cannot assume, to be sure, that this migration is solely and mainly the result of the more localized government structures of suburbs; housing choices, public-school quality, and perceived quality of life, among a market basket of factors, surely matter (as reflected, for instance, in a 2012 survey commissioned by the National Association of Homebuilders).[7] The numbers of those effectively voting with their feet are notable. As reflected in data from the US Census of Governments, between 1952 and 2012 the number of US municipalities increased significantly, from about 16,500 to 19,500. Between 1950 and 2010, the population of core US cities (in metropolitan areas where boundaries remained intact) declined by more than five million, while surrounding suburban area populations increased by thirty-two million. Moreover, as would be expected, those jurisdictions to which Americans were moving had smaller populations, per municipality, than those places that they were leaving behind. The 2010 population of some 4,300 noncore jurisdictions averaged 11,604 people (median, 3,632), while that of historic core municipalities averaged 961,000 (median 584,000).[8] The suburban population shift included the emergence of predominately African American and Hispanic suburbs, from Prince George's County, Maryland, to Hempstead, Long Island. Minorities, it turns out, are not necessarily against living in smaller, more localized jurisdictions.

We should not be surprised by this. Traditional US local government is a strongly expressed American preference with deep historical roots. Woodrow Wilson observed, in 1898, "our local areas are not governed. They act for themselves. The large freedom of action and broad scope of authority given to local authorities is the distinguishing feature of the American system of government."[9] As even Rusk has conceded, the efforts of cities to annex additional area are typically defeated when voters have a choice.

It's important to define what is meant here by "local government." It is one which, in the United States, can be directed in a variety of ways: by an elected executive (e.g., mayor or county executive); by a legislature (e.g., city council); by a city manager chosen by elected officials; even, as in New England, by direct or representative town meetings that make collective spending decisions.

Such governments provide a recognizable market basket of services, such as police and fire protection, street cleaning, garbage pickup, library service, and, in many parts of the country, public education, although schools are often overseen by independent school district boards. In addition, local governments typically perform a variety of regulatory functions, particularly in the realm of zoning and other land usage.

In addition, these municipalities often fund infrastructure projects, including those for locally controlled or owned roads, bridges, and buildings, through the proceeds of tax-advantaged municipal bonds. To a great extent, this leaves decisions about the rate of taxation and how revenues should be spent to be made locally. Thus US local government is decentralized both in its provision of services and in its funding of those services. This characteristic distinguishes it from most of the world, in which taxes are collected by a central government and only then disbursed to localities. This difference is no small matter and can even be characterized as a critical aspect of American exceptionalism.

7   "David Crowe et al., "What Home Buyers Really Want," National Association of Home Builders, 2014, http://ebooks.builderbooks.com/product/what-home-buyers-really-want.

8   US Census Bureau, "Metropolitan and Micropolitan: Core Based Statistical Areas (CBSAs) and Combined Statistical Areas (CSAs)," last modified February 1, 2013, accessed November 14, 2015, http://www.census.gov/population/metro/data/def.html.

9   Woodrow Wilson, *The State: Elements of Historical and Practical Politics*, rev. ed. (Boston: D.C. Heath & Co., 1898), 501, 506; as quoted by Martha Derthick, "Federalism," in Peter H. Schuck, *Understanding America: The Anatomy of an Exceptional Nation* (New York: PublicAffairs, 2008), 125.

The Benefits of Local Governance

There is historical evidence that a desire for localized control over the quality and character of public services helped, among other factors such as the desire for single-family homeownership, to drive post–World War II suburbanization. Indeed, the desire for localized government was among the findings of one of the classic analyses of the great postwar wave of American suburbanization. The sociologist Herbert Gans, in *The Levittowners: Ways of Life and Politics in a New Suburban Community*, studied households moving into what was known as Levittown, New Jersey. Gans's survey research found that, for a significant group of men (not women)—5 percent—the "principal aspiration for life in Levittown" lay in a "desire to have influence in civic affairs."[10] That was almost as high a percentage as those who chose having a better family life (6 percent). They ranked it higher than a desire to be active in churches and clubs (2 percent), and five times as high as decorating the new house. The highest ranking—18 percent—was given to "privacy and freedom of action in new home," which, arguably, is not unrelated to the fundamental localist sentiment.[11] The strong, evinced preference for residing in places within a small government jurisdiction can be explained in many ways, but one can look first to the nature of such governments. Their functions are intensely local and touch the lives of residents in a far more direct and personal way than those of other levels of government. What if the streets are dirty, or school buildings are in disrepair; if police are lax and crime is rampant; if major new residential or commercial developments are built; if traffic is congested or chaotic because of poor signals or signage? All these factors will have ongoing effects on the quality of life as experienced by residents every day of their lives.

But why choose a suburb as the venue for exercising such control? Put another way, why would those quintessential, original post–World War II suburbanites in Levittown—and their waves of successors over two generations—have seen the opportunity for participation in civic affairs as part of the attraction of the place? The reasons are numerous and help explain the ongoing popularity of America's suburbs.

There is the matter of sheer numbers. As noted above, those moving from central cities to suburbs are moving to jurisdictions in which electorates are far smaller. One's vote—and voice—has greater weight in an election for local office in a community of fifty thousand (or often much less) than it does in a big city. One inevitably has a sense that local officials are more accountable to local electorates. It is simply not as daunting a task to elect, or defeat, candidates in smaller jurisdictions.

In larger jurisdictions, spending and operating decisions are made at a distance from individual voters or even from specific neighborhoods. Under such circumstances, it makes sense for interest group politics to develop. It becomes more difficult to organize on behalf of the general interest (e.g., lower taxes) and easier to advocate for more narrow interests.

A teachers' union in a big city accumulates dues and makes campaign contributions and lobbies. It inevitably has more power than a small parent group, which cannot devote the same level of time and resources to advancing or defending its own perceived interests. Thus, not only is an individual vote more greatly weighted in a smaller electorate, it is relatively easier for groups of voters to organize for specific goals and be less likely to face what amounts to professional, interest group opposition.

The potential to influence elections extends, of course, to the greater influence

10 Herbert J. Gans, *The Levittowners: Ways of Life and Politics in a New Suburban Community* (New York: Pantheon Books, 1967), 39.
11 Ibid., 39.

voters can have in the most crucial matter decided at the local level: the specific mix of public goods that the local government will provide and the extent to which a jurisdiction will direct more resources toward one group of public goods (e.g., schools, parks) compared to others (e.g., law enforcement, services for the elderly). This was the essential point made by Charles M. Tiebout in his classic essay, "A Pure Theory of Local Expenditures," in which he wrote: "The consumer-voter may be viewed as picking that community which best satisfies his preference pattern for public goods. This is a major difference between central and local provision of public goods."[12]

Preference for Suburbs: Quality of Education

The establishment of suburban households by young families should not be viewed as a phenomenon confined to the immediate post–World War II era. The ongoing movement of many such households to suburban jurisdictions reflects the preference for what are often perceived to be higher-quality suburban public school systems. Multiple studies have demonstrated that public school districts located in suburban neighborhoods—where administration of education is most localized—are generally associated with better outcomes for children in terms of student achievement, access to gifted and accelerated programs, and preparation for success in college and employment.[13] Although it has been argued that this disparity in educational outcomes arises due to the higher concentration of poverty in urban areas, the superior performance of most suburban education systems holds even when comparing suburban and urban areas with equal poverty rates among school-attending children, according to the National Center for Education Statistics.[14] It may be that suburban school systems

are often showing outcomes that one would expect with students of higher socioeconomic status, but control and accountability of officials matter in this regard as well. Strong local government units allow households greater ability to prioritize public education in their own community—and crucially, to discipline elected school officials—such as members of local boards of education—through the ballot box, when quality is perceived to fall or other types of preferences (curricular or extracurricular) are not delivered. There can be little doubt that those choosing suburban life value this combination of quality and accountability. The National Association of Realtors' 2013 Community Preference Survey revealed that 74 percent of households considered high-quality public schools to be important or very important in their decision about where to live, signaling a strong demand for suburban neighborhoods.[15] Perhaps this would explain why millennials, who are entering the prime years of household formation and having children, are showing strong preferences for living in the suburbs.[16] Put another way, the movement to US suburbs should not be seen as a limited post–World War II, Levittown-era phenomenon but as an ongoing part of American life.

Although there remain a great many suburban school districts that serve as population magnets, it is worth noting that regional consolidation of school districts has broadly taken place in the postwar era. There were more than fifty thousand independent school districts in 1957, compared with just over thirteen thousand in 2007.[17] The consolidations have coincided with a steady increase in education costs and national concern over educational achievement. The existence of suburban school districts continues to offer a geographic version of school choice—and Americans avail themselves of it. The dynamics on display with regard

12 Charles M. Tiebout, "A Pure Theory of Local Expenditures," *Journal of Political Economy* 64 (1956): 418.

13 Suzanne E. Graham and Lauren E. Provost, "Mathematics Achievement Gaps between Suburban Students and Their Rural and Urban Peers Increase over Time," The Carey Institute—University of New Hampshire, June 1, 2012, accessed November 14, 2015, http://scholars .unh.edu/cgi/view -content.cgi?article= 1171&context=carsey; Paul Emrath and Natalia Siniavskaia, "Household Type, Housing Choice, and Commuting Behavior," National Association of Home Builders, last modified December 1, 2009, accessed November 14, 2015, https://www .nahb.org/en/research /housing-economics /special-studies/house hold-type-housing -choice-and-commuting -behavior-2009.aspx.

14 "Urban Schools: The Challenge of Location and Poverty," National Center for Education Statistics, last modified June 1, 1996, accessed November 14, 2015, http://nces.ed.gov/pubs /web/96184ex.asp.

15 "National Community Preference Survey October 2013," *National Association of Realtors* website, last modified October 1, 2013, accessed November 14, 2015, http://www.realtor .org/sites/default/files /reports/2013/2013 -community-preference -analysis-slides.pdf.

16 Kris Hudson, "Generation Y Prefers Suburban Home over City Condo," *Wall Street Journal*, January 21, 2015, accessed November 14, 2015, http://www.wsj .com/articles/millen nials-prefer-single -family-homes-in-the -suburbs-1421896797.

17 US Bureau of the Census, *U.S. Census of Governments: 1957*, vol. 3, no. 1, *Finances of School Districts* (Washington,

to education have multiple implications related to local government. Local governments can best reflect specific voter-consumer preferences, and local governments must compete with other local governments, both in the types of public goods they offer and in the cost-effectiveness of their provisions. As Gans wrote of the "political-decision making process" in Levittown, "Although Levittown's public decisions were made by a handful of elected officials, responding principally to demands and pressures from a small number of citizens and interest groups, many decisions were remarkably responsive to the rest of the citizenry, particularly the lower middle-class majority."[18]

Thus suburban voters have the potential, in the classic economist Albert Hirschman formulation, for both voice and exit. Indeed, within the suburban framework, they enjoy the possibility of exit as their life circumstances change. For instance, elderly voters may choose a jurisdiction that invests less in education and more in meals-on-wheels. At the same time, they may realize that a robust public education system is more likely to help maintain the value of their property. If they can afford to do so, they may be willing to continue pay relatively high property taxes for public schools even after their own children have grown.

Development and Local Governance

The role (and attraction) of local government goes beyond the choice of existing services in different municipalities. One of the most powerful aspects of US local government is its control over land use and development (as per Gans on Levittown). The power of local zoning, planning, and architectural review boards—many staffed by local professionals serving as volunteers—is frequently cast as the power to restrict. And, indeed, there are a small number of affluent communities that can afford to require homes to be built on 2-acre lots and such. But this emphasis on NIMBY-ism (Not In My Backyard) and restrictive zoning ignores the fact that, in marked contrast to the calculus faced by neighborhood groups in big city settings, suburban voters have good reason to approve new projects. Suburban jurisdictions have far greater assurance that they will not just endure the costs, but also enjoy the benefits of new economic development, whether commercial or residential.

New development, after all, brings new revenue through property taxes, the lifeblood that makes possible the delivery of suburban public goods. New development may bring additional traffic, or more public school children, but it will also build the tax base. A small jurisdiction, moreover, can be confident that it will realize (and be able to choose) the benefits of that more robust tax base, whether in the form of a new wing on a high school (at least in those cases where municipalities control schools), road resurfacing, or a new recreation center. Communities in big cities, in contrast, must face the prospect of negative impacts from new development, such as a major new apartment complex, at the same time knowing full well that tax proceeds that accrue from it will flow to the center of government, to be disbursed based on a wide array of factors and influenced by many interest groups distant from any one community.

One should not be surprised, for instance, that in New York City, local community boards—which must be consulted in the context of development decisions but have no legal veto or approval power—are known as obstacles to development. They have, after all, no good reason to believe their neighborhoods will be the ones to enjoy additional public goods and amenities, which might be financed by additional tax revenues. The umbilical

DC: US Government Printing Office, 1958); US Bureau of the Census, "Local Governments and Public School Systems by Type and State," 2007, accessed November 14, 2015, http://www .census.gov/govs/cog /GovOrgTab03ss.html.

18 Gans, *The Levittowners*, 336–37.

connection between public goods and the property tax, so central to suburban government, is broken in larger jurisdictions.

To be sure, local control may lead to large-lot zoning in some jurisdictions, but hardly in all. US suburban municipalities are characterized by tremendous variety. Some may zone out multifamily housing, but many others welcome industrial parks and garden apartments, based on the preferences and, of course, the incomes of their residents. Thus local control can and has fostered economic development. Although it is true that, in recent years, localities have received revenue from state and federal, as well as local, sources, their relative fiscal autonomy is profoundly disciplining and provides incentives to assess the relative costs and benefits of development, as well as the affordability of services and employee compensation.

Moreover, the fact that individual units of government have the capacity to borrow via tax-advantaged bonds exposes local decision making—via ratings agencies—to the discipline of financial markets. This is internationally atypical and differs in a positive way from a norm in which localities that are untethered to their own sources of revenue have an incentive to spend in undisciplined ways.

Critics of existing suburban government arrangements such as Rusk have argued that regional governance better encourages economic growth, in part as a result of the efficiency of such government. There is reason, however, to be skeptical of such analyses. The emergence of the San Francisco Bay Area as an economic powerhouse—in which governance is shared amongt San Francisco, Oakland, and San Jose, as well by many smaller jurisdictions from Palo Alto to Sunnyvale—would seem to belie the Rusk thesis. One of the few major North American examples of local government consolidation is that of metropolitan Toronto in 1998, which had the goal of efficiencies and cost-savings. Critics, however, estimate that Toronto's government costs have actually increased post-consolidation.[19] It is not my point or purpose, however, to make the case for local government on narrowly utilitarian grounds, based on its relative efficiency, or to rule out the possibility that, for some purposes, regional governance cooperation makes sense and saves dollars. The most obvious example is the mutual aid system for firefighting. It is in the interest of small municipalities to maintain local fire and emergency medical units in proximity to residences, but it surely does not make sense to own and maintain a large fleet of fire engines to fight a potential five-alarm blaze.

But a defense of local government virtues in the United States also extends to more philosophical issues and the nature of community. Those Levittowners who aspired to be "active in local affairs" understood that there is camaraderie and shared purpose to be had through such involvement. More newcomers were interested in civic affairs than in clubs, suggesting the possibility that the former was seen, in part, as a substitute for the latter. Those who run for modest local offices, like those who volunteer to serve on a range of possible boards—planning, zoning, tax assessment, libraries, even tree planting—are jointly engaged in a kind of a virtuous conspiracy to maintain and improve the place in which they live. That they have a financial interest in protecting their property values there is no doubt. Still, in the process, they learn to know and trust each other, and simply to enjoy each other's company, though local politics can be fractious, as well.

The collateral benefits of these relationships are impossible to calculate. They include everything from helping a household in need to offering advice to the children of a fellow board member. Such

19 Wendell Cox, "Local and Regional Governance in the Greater Toronto Area: A Review of the Alternatives," PublicPurpose.com, January 10, 2007, accessed November 14, 2015, http://www .publicpurpose.com /tor-demo.htm.

are the bonds of American communities, and local government helps forge them. There is joy and satisfaction to be found in civic participation.

Balancing Governance and the Need for Services

Rather than seeking ways to diminish or dilute the role of local government through merger or subordination into regional structures, reform-minded urbanists should look for ways that residents of central cities can enjoy some of the benefits of local government that are now denied to them. Breaking up the large, unwieldy school districts of New York, Chicago, and Los Angeles has been proposed. Let many smaller districts compete for students on the same basis that suburban municipalities now compete with each other through a reputation for high quality. This would begin to level the playing field between parents and publicsector labor unions, as well as to provide a sense for residents that increased property tax revenues could lead to specific improvements in nearby educational offerings or physical plants. This is a long way from the sort of "community control" that was bandied about in the 1960s, relative to inner-city minority communities. The term was never defined to include the sort of fiscal control, which suburban jurisdictions have.

Of course these calculations are the norm in suburban jurisdictions, and not just in the most affluent ones. In comparison to their suburban counterparts, central city residents are disenfranchised (or, at least, less enfranchised, as it were). The reasons for their disconnect from local decisions include a lost connection between local taxes and spending decisions, whether for schools or other public goods, and the fact of their relatively diluted votes.

Such discussion opens the door to the concern that some communities are better off than others and, as a result, will have the capacity to spend more on public services. This is a discussion that can be analogized to the larger contemporary discussion about income inequality and what, if anything, should be done as a matter of public policy to reduce it.

The benefits of localism are not just for the wealthy but also for a very wide swathe of the American public. Nor is it accurate to suggest that large governments serve egalitarian ends. Research shows that our largest cities tend to be the most unequal. Many large cities are widely accused by poorer residents of using city resources to force them out. A smaller town may be less tempted to do this, particularly if working-class residents have a strong say.[20]

Some jurisdictions are able to finance what amount to luxury public goods, whether public swimming pools or golf courses, while others make do with less. But, as spending patterns have demonstrated, relatively less-affluent jurisdictions may spend as much or more per student for education as higher-income areas, with poor results. Similarly, employee compensation levels, fringe benefits such as pension and health insurance, can be high in poor communities. A classic case is Detroit. The once proud Motor City, prior to the adjustments wrought by municipal bankruptcy, exemplified all these points.

The fact that it is easy to cite isolated examples of poor communities with dysfunctional governments does not detract from the fact that the potential exists, even in such communities, for self-correction over time. Welcoming new development that more affluent communities might reject is one obvious approach. What may be acceptable in a blue-collar community may not be in a more affluent place. Residents of poorer communities, like those of poorer nations, can derive benefits from development—say a port

20 Alan Berube, "All Cities Are Not Created Unequal," Brookings Institution, February 20, 2014, accessed November 14, 2015, http://www.brookings.edu/research/papers/2014/02/cities-unequal-berube; Thomas Sowell, "Race and Rhetoric," Creators.com, 2012, accessed November 14, 2015, http://www.creators.com/conservative/thomas-sowell/race-and-rhetoric.html; Nikole Hannah-Jones, "In Portland's Heart, 2010 Census Shows Diversity Dwindling," *Oregonian*, April 30, 2011, accessed November 14, 2015, http://www.oregonlive.com/pacific-northwest-news/index.ssf/2011/04/in_portlands_heart_diversity_dwindles.html; Henry W. McGee Jr., "Gentrification, Integration, or Displacement? The Seattle Story | The Black Past: Remembered and Reclaimed," BlackPast.org, 2007, accessed November 14, 2015, http://www.blackpast.org/perspectives/gentrification-integration-or-displacement-seattle-story; David Price, "Home Matters! Seven Policies That Could Prevent Roxbury's Gentrification," *Nuestra Ciudad Development Corporation*, April 14, 2014, accessed November 14, 2015, http://www.nuestracdc.org/blog/2014/04/14/15-home-matters-seven-policies-that-could-prevent-roxburys-gentrification.

expansion or the placement of a new factory or warehouse—that can directly improve the lives of local citizens and expand the tax base in order to improve services. This is not to say, of course, that they should be forced to accept environmentally dangerous uses—nor that oversight in that regard from higher units of government should be lax.

Does this mean that all public services should be provided on a strictly local basis or that assistance should never be offered to communities facing sharp declines in their fortunes and tax revenues? Not at all. Localities faced with needs that cross borders, whether flood control, pollution abatement, or fire protection, have every reason to cooperate, as they do when building a regional library collection more extensive than any one community could afford. These sorts of regional arrangements are better by virtue of their voluntary nature. Miller argues that this sort of regionalism is, indeed, taking shape. The measures differ profoundly from a "city without suburbs" approach, which would, in effect, redistribute tax revenues across a wider geography and in the process sacrifice the proximity of voters to spending decisions. It is better for areas that have declined to have the incentive to improve their fortunes by offering a hospitable development climate.

Might there be occasions—for instance, following the loss of a major employer—in which a municipality might justifiably look for help to maintain its schools, parks, and police? Indeed, yes. But emergency assistance is quite a different matter than an ongoing cycle of grants-in-aid, as, for instance, those distributed through the federal Community Development Block Grant program.

Emergency assistance can come in the form of a loan from state government, or a one-time grant, tied to what might, in the international context, be referred to as structural adjustment (reductions in cost commensurate with reductions in populations and required services). Grants-in-aid, often available only for select purposes, are viewed as "free" money and come without the accountability relationship that makes government most effective.

The broad point here is this: ensure that an adequate level of public goods can be best met within the overall US tradition of local governance. Fostering irresponsibility from "the commanding heights" is no way to promote better communities; that work is best done at the local level.

It is tempting to describe local US government as a patchwork, with the implication of inefficiency, ineffectiveness, and redundancy. But if there is any wisdom in crowds, Americans are convinced of the virtues of small units of government—and have voted, quite literally with their feet, in favor of them. Their common sense decision deserves our respect and should neither be dismissed as the choice of those merely fleeing urban problems nor patronized as that of the middle-brow.

Addison, Dallas, Texas, United States

Hickory Creek, Denton County, Texas, United States

5.5
OLD SUBURBS MEET NEW URBANISM

Nicole Stelle Garnett

ANTISUBURBAN CRUSADES

FLEXIBLE REGULATION

HOUSING AFFORDABILITY

In recent years, America's older suburbs—sometimes called "inner ring" or "first" suburbs—have become the focus of a tremendous amount of popular and scholarly attention.[1] A sense of doom pervades much of the commentary on these communities, which are home to approximately one-fifth of the nation's population.[2] Since the publication of Myron Orfield's *Metropolitics* in 1997, a steady stream of reports have emerged warning that many of our inner-ring communities are on a path of decline that will lead inevitably to the social and economic crises facing inner-city communities.[3] Inner-ring suburbs are, according to these accounts, our next ghettos. The 2014 riots in Ferguson, Missouri—a poor, predominantly African American suburban community—heightened these anxieties about the future of the inner ring, leading some to warn that the unrest in the St. Louis suburb was reflective of a pervasive and deep suburban dysfunction resulting from failed public policies at all levels of government.[4]

Among many scholars of metropolitan America, inner-ring suburbs have assumed a symbolic role previously reserved for struggling urban communities. They have become the poster children for all of the land-use and local government reforms *du jour*, including regional growth controls, redistributive tax policies and—most recently—the various tools in the New Urbanists' regulatory tool kit. A complete discussion of all of these regulatory options would consume (and has, indeed, consumed) volumes. But the most interesting and perhaps the most significant of these options is the argument that New Urbanist regulatory tools, specifically transect zoning and form-based codes, are uniquely suited to the task of renewing older suburbs.

The Inner Ring Today

Generalizations about the current state of inner-ring suburbs are risky, given the stark regional and intrametropolitan variation among inner-ring communities. The inner-suburban communities of the Sunbelt are quite distinct from those in the "old and cold" metro regions of the Northeast and the Midwest. Moreover, while some older suburbs, like Ferguson, Missouri, are poor, majority-minority communities, others are extremely affluent. Indeed, many of the wealthiest communities in the United States are tony older suburbs. That said, despite the gloom pervading much of the commentary, inner-ring suburbs, compared to the national median, continue to be relatively wealthier, and have a better-educated workforce, lower rates of unemployment, and higher housing values.[5]

Still, inner-ring suburbs unquestionably have undergone dramatic demographic transformations in recent decades. To begin, as the demographer William Frey recently observed in the *New Republic*, these suburbs are "not just for white people anymore."[6] Many inner-ring communities that were once exclusively or almost exclusively white are today racially diverse. A majority of racial minorities in the nation's largest metropolitan areas now live in suburbs.[7] In the past decade and a half, the lion's share of suburban population gains was attributable to minority migration to suburbs, primarily inner-ring suburbs. These demographic shifts include unprecedented "black flight" from cities, dramatic increases in Hispanic suburban population share, and the emergence of new suburban immigrant gateways and "ethnoburbs."[8] In 2014 61 percent of immigrants lived in suburbs (up from just over 50 percent in 2000), with increasing numbers of new Americans shunning traditional "gateway" cities and settling directly in suburbs, especially in inner-ring communities.[9]

1   Robert Puentes and David Warren, "One-Fifth of America: A Comprehensive Guide to America's First Suburbs," Brookings Institution, Metropolitan Policy Program, February 2006, 1, accessed April 7, 2015, http://www.brookings.edu/research/reports/2006/02/metropolitanpolicy-puentes.

2   Myron Orfield, *American Metropolitics: The New Suburban Reality* (Washington, DC: Brookings Institution Press, 2002); Bernadette Hanlon, *Once the American Dream: Inner-Ring Suburbs of the Metropolitan United States* (Philadelphia: Temple University Press, 2010); William H. Hudnut III, *Halfway to Everywhere: A Portrait of America's First-Tier Suburbs* (Washington, DC: Urban Land Institute, 2003); Elizabeth Kneebone and Alan Berube, *Confronting Suburban Poverty in America* (Washington, DC: Brookings Institution Press, 2013); William H. Lucy and David L. Phillips, *Confronting Suburban Decline: Strategic Planning for Metropolitan Renewal* (Washington, DC: Island Press, 2000).

3   Orfield, *Metropolitics*, 23–65.

4   Peter Dreier and Todd Swanstrom, "Suburban Ghettos like Ferguson Are Ticking Time Bombs: The Protests There Might Be the First in a Wave of Suburban Riots," *Washington Post*, August 21, 2014; Daniel J. McGraw, "Ferguson: Race and the Inner-Ring Suburb," *Belt Magazine*, August 14, 2014, accessed April 7, 2015, http://beltmag.com/ferguson-race-inner-ring-suburb/; Pete Saunders, "The Death of America's Suburban Dream: The Events in Ferguson, Missouri Reveal the 'Resegregation' of America's Once-Aspirational Inner Suburbs," *Guardian*, September 5, 2014, accessed April 30, 2015,

Many inner-ring suburbs also are facing new economic strains, with relative poverty more prevalent than it was a generation ago. A comprehensive study of the economic and demographic profiles of sixty-four inner-ring suburban counties undertaken by the Brookings Institution scholars Robert Puentes and David Warren in 2006 found that, while the median income in inner-ring suburbs remains about 25 percent higher than the nation's median, income levels in inner-ring suburbs were stagnating and poverty rates were increasing, even as national income levels rose and poverty levels declined.[10] The number of high-poverty inner-suburban neighborhoods is mirroring the decline in concentrated urban poverty.[11] In another Brookings study, Elizabeth Kneebone and Alan Berube found that during the first decade of the twenty-first century, the number of poor individuals living in the suburbs rose by more than half, which was more than twice the 23 percent rate of increase in cities. Kneebone and Berube also found that the number of poor individuals living in suburban neighborhoods where poverty rates exceed 40 percent rose by 63 percent between 2001 and 2010, mostly heavily concentrated in inner suburban communities.[12]

Inner-ring suburbs also are growing more slowly than their outer suburban cousins. Puentes and Warren found, for example, that while inner-ring suburbs were growing faster than central cities, their rate of growth was only half that of newer suburbs. The slowing of growth is frequently coupled with an aging population and stagnating or declining housing values.[13]

The Inner Ring as a Distributional Problem

Most academics consider the challenges facing inner-ring suburbs that are a result of these demographic shifts—such as a declining tax base, strains on public education, aging infrastructure, increasing crime, and a heavier social service burden—to be a distributional problem. According to this view, inner-ring suburbs are victims of a local government system that enables suburban sprawl and exclusionary zoning, encourages better-resourced communities to lure wealthier residents, and deprives older suburbs of access to a fair share of the regional tax base. According to these critics, the fragmentation of American metropolitan regions enforces intrametropolitan inequalities, leaving older struggling suburbs to play a constant and futile game of catch up. Unable to finance improvements in local services without raising taxes, imposing tax increases in turn makes inner-ring suburbs less attractive places to live. As the suburbs scholar Bernadette Hanlon has argued, "The 'push factors' of deteriorating schools and poor services combined with relatively high tax rates encourage further population loss, particularly of any remaining high income families."[14]

Critics who view the problems of the inner-ring suburbs in distributional terms tend to endorse redistributive policy solutions: Growth management is promoted as a means of redirecting populations that might otherwise locate in outer suburbs into older, built-up areas. These critics endorse tax-base sharing mechanisms to ensure what they consider the fair distribution of fiscal resources across municipalities in a metropolitan region. They also propose new regional government structures to tame the excesses of intermunicipal competition for resources and residents, allocate the inputs required for new development (such as infrastructure funds), and foster intrametropolitan collaboration.[15]

Commentators such as Richard Briffault and Orfield specifically link the need for regional policy solutions to the plight of inner-ring suburbs. As Briffault

http://www.theguardian.com/cities/2014/sep/05/death-america-suburban-dream-ferguson-missouri-resegregation; Jeff Smith, "In Ferguson, Black Town, White Power," *New York Times*, August 17, 2014.

5 Puentes and Warren, "One-Fifth of America," 5–7.

6 William H. Frey, "The Suburbs: Not Just for White People Anymore," *New Republic*, November 24, 2014.

7 Ibid.

8 Frey, "The Suburbs"; Wei Li, *Ethnoburb* (Honolulu: University of Hawaii Press, 2009); John Iceland, *Where We Live Now: Immigration and Race in the United States* 38 (Berkeley: University of California Press, 2009); Lucy and Phillips, *Confronting*, 26–30.

9 Janie Boschma, "America's Immigrants are Moving to the Suburbs: They're Drawn There for the Same Reasons That the Rest of Us Are—Affordability, Jobs, and Schools, *National Journal*, December 11, 2014, accessed April 7, 2015, http://www.nationaljournal.com/next-america/america-s-foreign-born-population-is-increasingly-moving-to-the-suburbs-20141208; Jill H. Wilson and Nicole Prchal Svajilenka, "Immigrants Continue to Disperse, with Fastest Growth in the Suburbs," Brookings Immigration Fact Series, no. 18, October 29, 2014, accessed April 7, 2015, http://www.brookings.edu/research/papers/2014/10/29-immigrants-disperse-suburbs-wilson-svajlenka.

10 Puentes and Warren, "One-Fifth of America," 5.

11 Ibid., 11.

12 Kneebone and Berube, *Confronting*, 16–20. These trends are arguably related, with increased suburban poverty being the unintended consequences of policies seeking to break up pockets of urban

has argued, "For many poorer urban municipalities—especially the older, declining suburbs, which lack even the business districts, housing stock, and cultural amenities of older cities…[a] regionalist strategy that recognizes the relationships and connections among localities in a metropolitan area is essential."[16] These arguments are not without intuitive appeal, although, as I have written elsewhere, it is unclear whether the costs of policies designed to tame the woes of metropolitan fragmentation will sacrifice too many of the benefits of the intermunicipal competition predicted by the economist Charles Tiebout.[17]

The Inner Ring as an Aesthetic Problem: Enter the New Urbanism

Briffault hints at a related, but distinct, concern about inner-ring suburbs, one that is framed in aesthetic rather than distributional terms. Observers frequently refer to the built environment in many older suburbs as aging, unattractive, and unappealing, and contrast the housing and commercial stock (tract, ranch, and split-level houses and strip malls) to the older, more architecturally appealing homes and commercial buildings found in central cities and select early suburbs. This critique is primarily directed not at the true first suburbs, as inner-ring suburbs are sometimes called, but at what more accurately might be called the second suburbs. The first American suburbs were developed prior to the Great Depression and tend to have the older housing stock and traditional street-front commercial districts that are favored by elite opinion. The second wave of suburbia, which was developed on a massive scale in the postwar period, lacks such amenities. These homes and communities are considered by many to be aesthetically challenged timepieces with little to offer in the frenzied metropolitan competition for wealthier residents.[18]

The distributional view of inner-suburban problems suggests policy solutions that would minimize competition between municipalities. The aesthetic view suggests a slightly different approach that seeks to overcome impediments to competition imposed by the presumably unappealing built environment of postwar suburbs. Critics raising aesthetic concerns assert that inner suburbs cannot be expected to compete because they lack the inputs needed to fuel successful regeneration, especially the types of residential and commercial structures attractive to would-be gentrifiers. In a recent book, for example, the New Urbanists Ellen Dunham-Jones and June Williamson argue that suburbs need to be "retrofitted" to reflect contemporary architectural and urban design preferences and accommodate modern land-use patterns. That is, "isolated privately owned malls and aging office parks" need to be demolished and replaced by "multiblock, mixed-use town centers," "edge center agglomerations of suburban office and retail…interlaced with residences and walkable streets," "ambitious new public transit networks… proposed, constructed and integrating into rapidly developing suburban contexts," and "archaic zoning ordinances… thoroughly overhauled to permit higher-density, mixed-use development.[19]

Not surprisingly, New Urbanists embrace the view that inner-ring suburbs face many problems as the result of aesthetic challenges. From its inception, the New Urbanism has been, in important respects, an aesthetic critique that views American suburbia as an affront to good urban design—one that can only be remedied by implementing better, more urban, design principles. New Urbanists believe, in other words, that suburbs need to be urbanized.[20]

Some of the development tools promoted by New Urbanists could conceivably serve older suburban communities well.

poverty.; Hanna Rosen, "American Murder Mystery," *Atlantic*, July–August 2008, accessed April 8, 2015, http://www.theatlantic.com/magazine/archive/2008/07/american-murder-mystery/306872/.

13 Puentes and Warren, "One-Fifth of America," 8–9.

14 Hanlon, *American Dream*, 54.

15 Richard Briffault, "Our Localism, Part I: The Structure of Local Government Law, *Columbia Law Review* 90 (January 1990): 18–24; Richard Briffault, "Beyond City and Suburb, Thinking Regionally," *Yale Law Journal Forum* 116, December, 11, 2006, accessed April 30, 2014, http://www.yalelawjournal.org/forum/beyond-city-and-suburb-thinking-regionally; Orfield, *American Metropolitics*, 85–150.

16 Briffault, "Beyond City and Suburb," 18–24.

17 Nicole Stelle Garnett, "Suburbs as Exit, Suburbs as Entrance," *Michigan Law Review* 160 (November 2007): 277; Nicole Stelle Garnett, "Unbundling Homeownership: Regional Reforms from the Inside Out," *Yale Law Journal* 119 (June 2010): 1905; Charles M. Tiebout, "A Pure Theory of Local Expenditures," *Journal of Political Economy* 64, no. 5 (October 1956): 416–24.

18 D. Jamie Rusin, Sean Slater, and Ryan Call, "New Suburbanism: Reinventing Inner Ring Suburbs," *Urban Land Magazine*, July 8, 2013, accessed April 15, 2015, http://urbanland.uli.org/planning-design/new-suburbanism-reinventing-inner-ring-suburbs/; Garnett, "Suburbs as Exit, Suburbs as Entrance," 282–85.

19 Ellen Dunham-Jones and June Williamson, *Retrofitting Suburbia: Urban Design Solutions for Redesigning Suburbs* (Hoboken, NJ: John Wiley & Sons, 2011).

20 Ibid., 3.

For example, "dead" malls can be flipped, unused parking lots filled, and one-way streets rerouted and lined with sidewalks to achieve greater connectivity and walkability. The challenge for inner-ring suburban leaders, however, is that many New Urbanist redevelopment efforts are pricey—well beyond the reach of many cash-strapped local governments.

In this context, the allure of using land-use regulations to require alterations in the urban landscape is apparent. Land-use regulations appear costless, since they theoretically only set the stage for the desired development and redevelopment, which will in turn be undertaken by private parties. The difficulty is—as decades of social science research demonstrate—that land-use regulations are far from costless. And, unfortunately, their costs all too frequently are borne by those of modest means.[21] Proponents of the distributional approach to inner-suburban challenges acknowledge the costs of land-use regulations. Indeed, their proposals flow in important respects from their critique of prevailing regulatory practices. They also acknowledge that their proposed alternatives are not costless, although, in my view, they may underestimate those costs. Proponents of the New Urbanist alternatives to current land-use regulations tend to ignore or downplay the costs, frequently billing them as cost-saving devices that will free communities from the constricting grip of traditional zoning tools, when in reality, compliance costs can be extraordinarily high.

New Urbanists argue that cities should reject use-based zoning regulations in favor of a system of form-based aesthetic controls. This regulatory alternative to zoning flows from the assumption that urban development proceeds naturally from more dense areas to less dense ones. Andrés Duany called this progression the "urban transect," and New Urbanists urge local governments to replace traditional

use zoning with regulations on building form appropriate to the various "transect zones" along the progression. The extent of the New Urbanists' influence is reflected in the fact that local governments are increasingly supplementing or supplanting traditional land-use regulations with transect zoning laws and the form-based codes that inevitably accompany them.[22] The extent of this trend is difficult to gauge, but the fact that it is a trend is verifiable. Local governments as large as Miami, Denver, and Cincinnati and as small as one-hundred-person villages have enacted these devices into law.[23] Transect zoning and form-based codes may be particularly attractive to inner-ring suburban leaders, since they are billed as a way to remedy the aesthetic challenges that prevent their communities from competing with their suburban neighbors, both older and newer. A good example of such a community is Arlington, Virginia, an inner-ring suburb of Washington, DC, which adopted a form-based code to govern its Columbia Pike corridor in 2013.[24]

Countering Costlessness of New Urbanist Codes

Despite their allure, however, the adoption of these codes may prove counterproductive, especially in inner-suburban communities, for four related reasons.

First: Transect zoning is billed as embracing a simple theory about how to regulate urban development, which is that buildings appropriate for the city center should go in the city center, regardless of their use, and suburban buildings should look suburban, again, regardless of their use. In its implementation, however, transect zoning is anything but simple. As a practical matter, New Urbanists favor replacing traditional zoning with very meticulous and exhaustive aesthetic regulations, found in the form-based codes that fill the ubiquitous gaps in transect

21 Edward Glaeser and Joseph Gyourko, "Zoning's Steep Price," *Regulation* (Fall 2002); Edward Glaeser and Joseph Gyourko, *Rethinking Federal Housing Policy: How to Make Housing Plentiful and Affordable* (Washington, DC: AEI Press, 2008); Peter Ganong and Daniel Shoag, "Why Has Regional Convergence in the US Stopped?," Working Paper RWP12–028, Kennedy School of Government, Harvard University, Cambridge MA, 2012, accessed April 30, 2015, http://dash.harvard.edu/handle/1/9361381.

22 Nicole Stelle Garnett, "Redeeming Transect Zoning," *Brooklyn Law Review* 78 (Winter 2013): 571.

23 In 2008, Hazel Borys and Emily Talent found that 279 form-based codes had been enacted by local governments and that about 200 additional were being considered. See Hazel Boyrs and Emily Talent, "Form-Based Codes, You're Not Alone," accessed April 14, 2015, http://www.placemakers.com/how-we-teach/codes-study/.

24 "Arlington County Adopts Innovative Tools to Increase Affordable Housing on Columbia Pike," last modified November 16, 2013, accessed April 15, 2015, http://news.arlingtonva.us/releases/arlington-county-adopts-innovative-tools-to-increase-affordable-housing-on-columbia-pike.

Example of inappropriate facade expression

Example of appropriate facade expression

5.5.1 Illustrative example of appropriate facade expression in form-based code

zoning regimes. To varying degrees, these codes dictate the architectural details (e.g., the form) of buildings appropriate for the various zones in the urban transect. These details can consume dozens, even hundreds, of pages of regulations. As an alternative, some codes, including the Columbia Pike form-based code, provide illustrative "examples" of "appropriate" building and design styles, and require architectural review of all but the smallest projects. (fig. **5.5.1**) Both forms of regulation raise development costs, and the vagueness of the second approach raises its own serious concerns.[25]

Second: The concept of the "urban transect" is ill suited to many suburban communities. The foundational planning principle of New Urbanism is that urban development naturally proceeds from more to less dense—from urban, to suburban, to rural. After decades of zoning, however, the urban transect frequently reflects New Urbanists' preferences and aspirations for urban development more than the actual facts on the ground in American communities. Rather than proceeding neatly along the transect, the densities of many metropolitan areas are either flat or proceed from less dense to more dense, to less dense again.[26] While New Urbanists would like to reverse this trend, they have not satisfactorily addressed how to confront communities with development patterns that fail to approximate the urban transect. In fact, transect zoning has been imposed in

locales where development patterns are entirely divorced from predictions of how the urban transect would develop. Columbia Pike is, again, a case in point. Consider, for example, the regulating plan for Baileys Crossroads, a neighborhood along the Columbia Pike corridor. (fig. **5.5.2**) Not surprisingly, in suburban places like this, the transect is defined to fit existing development patterns, rather than the ideal progression New Urbanists prefer.

Third: Transect zoning and form-based codes seek to impose, by law, a particular urban aesthetic. Real estate developments governed by transect zoning and form-based codes look and feel very different from the developments—both urban and suburban—that preceded them for decades. This is because form-based codes have as their goal the reversal of over a century of planning practices that reflect what the New Urbanists consider wrongheaded aesthetic preferences. I happen to share the New Urbanists' aesthetic preferences in large part. This fact, however, does not alleviate my concerns about using the law to impose aesthetic preferences on the built landscape. On the contrary, if the New Urbanists' critique of twentieth-century planning practices teaches anything, it is that using public land-use regulations to impose architectural fads on the urban landscape can lead to unfortunate, even socially damaging, results. This may be particularly true in inner-ring communities, where recent

25 Garnett, "Redeeming Transect Zoning," 579–85; "Columbia Pike Neighborhoods Special Revitalization District Form Based Code," accessed April 15, 2015, http://arlingtonva .s3.amazonaws.com /wp-content/uploads /sites/31/2014/07 /CP_FBC_Res_Complete -Code.pdf.

26 Robert Brueggman, *Sprawl: A Compact History* (Chicago: University of Chicago Press 2005): 19–20; Léon Krier, *The Architecture of Community* (Washington, DC: Island Press: 2009), 11–13. Krier argues that the "fiasco of the suburbs is the tragic illustration" of "erroneous [urban] planning" and architectural design.

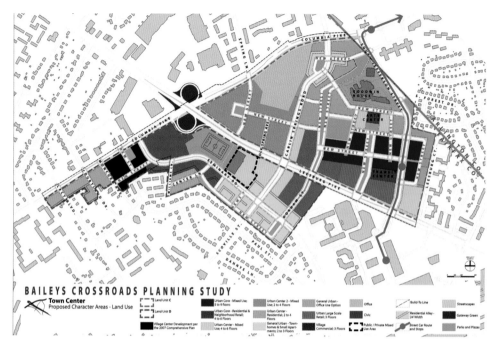

BAILEYS CROSSROADS PLANNING STUDY

5.5.2 Transect example, Baileys Crossroads Planning Study

27 Kaid Benfield, "As We Remake Suburbia, Should We Guard against Gentrification?," *Switchboard Natural Resource Defense Council,* accessed June 11, 2013, http://switchboard.nrdc .org/blogs/kbenfield /as_we_remake_sub urbs_should_th.html; Nicole Stelle Garnett, *Ordering the City: Land Use, Policing, and the Restoration of Urban America* (New Haven, CT: Yale University Press, 2010), 44–48.

28 Julian Conrad Juergensmeyer and Thomas Roberts, *Land Use Planning and Development Regulation Law,* 2nd ed. (St. Paul, MN: West Academic Press, 2007), 101.

29 Robert Steuteville, "Survey: Combine New Code with Activities and Investment," *New Urban News,* last modified April 1, 2010, accessed April 15, 2015, http://bettercities.net /article/survey-combine -new-code-activities -and-investment; Mark Simpson, "Cost and Business Resistance Kill Orlando Suburb Beautification and Traffic Calming Effort," Transportation Nation, last modified April 2, 2011, accessed April 15, 2015, http://transporta tionnation.org/2011/04 /02/cost-and-business -resistance-kill-orlando -suburb-beautification -and-traffic-calming -effort; Ed Tombari, "The Future of Zoning?," *Land Development Magazine* 22 (2009): 25.

demographic shifts have led to the adaptive reuse of commercial structures considered obsolete by many New Urbanists. For example, many inner-ring suburbs feature many strip malls filled with stores serving newly arrived immigrant populations, including this one in suburban Indianapolis. (fig. **5.5.3**) Although these uses do not match the aesthetic preferred in most form-based codes, they can serve the residents of the community surrounding them well. As a result, just as the modernists' wrecking balls destroyed functional urban communities during the postwar urban renewal period, so might the New Urbanists' codes target suburban communities that function well for the thousands of newcomers who are discovering them.[27]

Fourth: Finally, at least in the inner ring, the goal of form-based codes is to "upscale" communities. Form-based codes are in many respects the equivalent of highly technical performance-zoning schemes. (Performance zoning regulates land use by establishing parameters designed to limit the negative impact of the use. Although performance zoning is more flexible than conventional zoning, it is often prohibitively difficult to administer.)[28] Anecdotal evidence suggests that compliance costs have stalled many redevelopment efforts governed by form-based zoning.[29] But even the successful implementation of form-based codes carries a risk of driving up housing costs, as well as the costs of running businesses like the ones shown in the image. Critics of inner suburbia frequently lament that many residents move up and out to newer suburbs with more attractive housing styles (read: McMansions, not split-levels). That is undoubtedly true, but it not necessarily lamentable. Not only is the economic mobility reflected in such moves, generally speaking, a good sign, but these moves also free up quality housing stock for families and individuals of more-modest means. The reality is that the housing filtering process has, for generations, been one of the most important sources of affordable housing in the United States. The goal of the New Urbanist retrofit of inner suburbs essentially is to stop the filtering process, with the result being gentrification that prices out many potential new suburban residents. Pulling up the suburban ladder at a time when immigrant and minorities are finally reaching its rungs raises serious transitional fairness issues. It also threatens to deplete the reservoir of vitality and diversity that can enliven and enrich struggling inner-suburban communities.[30]

Rethinking the Older Suburbs

Local leaders in older suburbs rightly want to promote economic growth by infusing an aging physical infrastructure with new life. The New Urbanists promise that this goal not only can be accomplished, but can be micromanaged through public land-use regulations. The promise is undoubtedly attractive to local leaders who feel trapped by the geographic footprint imposed by zoning, but are wary of land-use deregulation. Nonetheless, inner-ring suburban leaders would do well to resist the deceptive allure of controlled diversity. A different vision of regulatory reform—one that embraces the goal of abandoning the regulatory straightjacket of single-use zoning but eschews the desire to control the aesthetic details of the transition from single-use to multi-use communities (which I have previously called "mixed use zoning without the strings")—would better enable these communities to promote growth, maintain a stable supply of affordable housing, and harness the entrepreneurial energies of the individuals, families, and business who now call older suburbs home.[31]

5.5.3 Sign advertising occupants of suburban strip mall

30 Thomas Bier, "Moving Up, Filtering Down: Metropolitan Housing Dynamics and Public Policy," Discussion Paper: Brookings Institution Center on Urban and Metropolitan Policy, September 2001, http://www.brookings.edu/~/media/research/files/reports/2001/9/metropolitanpolicy%20bier/bier.pdf; Matthew Yglesias, "Filtering: How to Get Growth without Gentrification," *Moneybox* (blog), *Slate*, December 11, 2012, accessed April 15, 2015, http://www.slate.com/blogs/moneybox/2012/12/11/filtering_vs_gentrification_how_to_get_urban_growth_without_displacement.html.

31 Garnett, *Ordering the City*, 200–201.

5.6
BEYOND SUBURBIA?
URBAN TRANSITIONS ACROSS THE GLOBAL SOUTH

Adriana Allen

GOVERNANCE & POLICY CHALLENGES

ECOLOGICAL FUNCTION

NEOLIBERAL PROPERTY MARKETS

SOCIAL INEQUALITIES

Suburbia is sometimes romanticized as a landscape where urban life can take place in harmony with nature. At other times, it is heavily criticized for its exclusionary social makeup or its destructive impact on the environment. But in both cases, the concept of suburbia fails to capture the actual complexity of contemporary urbanization across the Global South. Over time, the notion of suburbia has become closely associated with a North American pattern of urbanization and a North American way of life. But numerous scholars now suggest that suburbanization is less and less an operation of centrifugal expansion from urban cores into suburban landscapes. Instead, today it often resembles a lumpy rural-urban continuum that challenges conventional distinctions of the city, suburbia, and the countryside.[1]

Across the Global South—Africa, Asia, Latin America and the Caribbean, and the Middle East—peri-urbanizing areas will house approximately 45 percent of the 1.4 billion people who will join the world's urban population by 2020.[2] Unlike suburban landscapes, peri-urban areas are physically and socioeconomically distinctive not only for their rural-urban ambiguity but also for the coexistence of extreme poverty and wealth.[3]

Peri-urban areas can play a crucial role in regulating the inputs and outputs that sustain the ecology of urban regions. Affected by both the productive economic growth generated by cities and the valuable natural environment that is crucial for urban living, they are subject to constant tensions between the two. But planning policies don't integrate their treatment of urban space and ecologically important space, and don't unify the need to support the environment with the need for social development. Inadequate infrastructure and housing for the poor isn't addressed by environmental regulation, and protecting ecosystems isn't included in urban development plans.

I've previously argued that peri-urban areas are characterized by two distinctive features, in addition to the physical, social, and economic issues mentioned earlier.[4] The first concerns their heterogeneous and fast-changing socioeconomic makeup. The continuous but uneven process of urbanization is generally accompanied by (and often produced by) land speculation, informal land transactions, and a shift in economic activities, while residual pockets of farming, and clandestine abattoirs and mining activities, for example, still remain.

The second distinctive feature concerns their governance. Typically, these areas are regulated by overlapping institutions that simultaneously treat these areas as the "backyard of the city," where unwanted activities such as landfills are located, or as a "buffer zone" to accommodate future expansion. At the same time, the peri-urban area is often seen as a depository of environmental capital and attributes that regulate cities' food, energy, and water security, with the capacity to mitigate pollution and absorb carbon dioxide emissions. Moreover, because of competing claims and institutional gaps, the needs of the peri-urban poor for adequate water, sanitation, food, and energy are often ignored, making them particularly prone to environmental injustices. Thus peri-urban areas are subject to intense struggles over space, but also, increasingly, treated as a blank canvas on which to experiment with sustainable urban transitions.

In the past, the struggle over the "city-to-be" was either regulated by the state or controlled by the market. The state would make infrastructural and housing investments to relocate the poor or to decentralize industrial production away from core inner areas. The market would allocate space on the basis of the highest bidder. In contrast, today's debates over peri-urban development

1   See John Friedmann, "Modular Cities: Beyond the Rural-Urban Divide," *Environment and Urbanization* 9, no. 1 (1996): 129–31; Adriana Allen, "Understanding Environmental Change in the Context of Rural-Urban Interactions," in *The Peri-Urban Interface: Approaches to Sustainable Natural and Human Resource Use*, ed. D. McGregor, D. Simon, and D. Thompson (London: Earthscan, 2005), 30–43; Kenny Lynch, *Rural-Urban Interaction in the Developing World* (London: Routledge, 2005); Duncan McGregor, David Simon, and Donald Thompson, eds., *The Peri-Urban Interface: Approaches to Sustainable Natural and Human Resource Use* (London: Earthscan, 2006).

2   Douglas Webster, *Summary of Peri-Urbanization: The New Global Frontier* (Enschede, Netherlands: International Institute for Geo-Information Science and Earth Observation, 2004).

3   Adriana Allen, "Neither Rural, Nor Urban: Service Delivery Options That Work for the Peri-Urban Poor," in *Peri-Urban Water and Sanitation Services: Policy, Planning, and Method*, ed. Mathew Kurian and Patricia McCarney (London: Springer, 2010), 27–61.

4   Adriana Allen, "Environmental Planning and Management of Peri-Urban Interface: Perspective on an Emerging Field," *Environment and Urbanization* 15, no. 1 (2003): 135–48.

are increasingly formulated in relation to focused on environmental value, often placing an overriding priority on averting any unplanned urbanization that might squander peri-urban natural capital and ecosystem services.

Thus, throughout the peri-urbanizing Global South, urban transitions are increasingly being pursued under various conditions of "differential sustainability," that is, being designed to accommodate different ecological thresholds that have each been adjusted to meet the needs and wants of certain privileged social groups and territories at the expense of others. Furthermore, more often than not, the ecological thresholds designated by the elite are far from those truly functional for nature. In this context, the unclear or fuzzy regulation of land and ecosystem services that often characterizes change in peri-urban areas assists, in practice, in unleashing urban economic expansion, sacrificing the sustainability of vital ecosystem services and reinforcing the invisibility of the peri-urban poor, both as producers and as rightful citizens.

Drawing from primary research conducted in a range of contexts, I trace three distinctive and dominant planning mechanisms that produce and reproduce differential sustainability across different peri-urbanizing areas in the Global South.

Containment Strategies

For several decades, urban containment policies—often under the rubric of smart growth—have been applied in the Global North as a land-rationing strategy, forbidding development on large swathes of land that would otherwise be developable.[5] In the peri-urbanizing areas of the Global South, this approach has evolved into new policy objectives to contain informal growth in valuable environmental areas. Advocates of the compact city look to limit peripheral urban development,

assuming that peri-urban borders can be controlled through regulatory land-use planning instruments, often ignoring the politically supported economics that drive peri-urbanization in the first place and the inability of urban policies to secure adequate access to land, housing, and services for the urban poor. The popularization of containment measures marks the end of various degrees of governmental tolerance for peri-urban informality, legitimizing the eviction of the poor to enable the preservation of selective ecological functions.

For example, in Lima, Peru, peri-urban informal expansion has historically been not just tolerated but actively enabled by local governments through provisions, outside formal mechanisms, to occupy urban land.[6] Between the 1970s and the 1980s, this process of informal urbanism produced orderly neighborhoods in the periphery of the city and over time became the main means for the poor to access land and housing in Lima. However, during the 1990s, the government stopped supporting incremental participatory urbanization, favoring instead a market approach.

Driven by the unmet demand for affordable housing and land elsewhere in the city, the poor are now increasingly forced to occupy the steep slopes on the outskirts of the city, in the natural environment of the *lomas costeras* (desert coastal ridges with seasonal vegetation). This unique but fragile ecosystem helps to trap humidity and generates seasonal meadows, acting as a buffer to climate variability and supporting the recharging of Lima's underground aquifers. The first wave of informal settlements, the outcome of planned invasions in the 1980s, occupied the bottom of the hills. Today, the logic propelling the occupation of the steep slopes coinciding with the *lomas* is different, and compounded with issues of risk, water injustice, land trafficking,

5   Gregory K. Ingram, Armando Carbonell, Yu-Hung Hong, and Anthony Flint, eds., *Smart Growth Policies: An Evaluation of Programs and Outcomes* (Cambridge, MA: Lincoln Institute of Land Policy, 2009).

6   Martim O. Smolka and Adriana de A. Larangeira, "Informality and Poverty in Latin American Urban Policies," in *The New Global Frontier: Urbanization, Poverty, and Environment in the Twenty-First Century*, ed. George Martine, Gordon McGranahan, Mark Montgomery, and Rogelio Fernandez-Castilla (London: Earthscan, 2008), 99–114.

and the constant renegotiation of the border of the city.[7] (fig. **5.6.1**)

The landscape generated through the endless building of "stairways up to the sky" operates through two fundamentally different but converging processes. On the one hand, organized land trafficking mafias are driving the commodification of the slopes, actively operating on the upper part of the hills, opening new roads and selling plots in areas of high risk to rockslides and mudslides that lack any provisions for basic services. On the other hand, the leaders of existing informal settlements unwillingly mimic this process in the hope of generating revenue by leasing new plots. In the absence of public investment to ameliorate their residency costs, the revenue obtained from carving new plots is perceived by local settlers as the only means to collectively face the costs of risk mitigation due to the occurrence of episodic but repetitive small-scale disasters. Furthermore, rushing to develop the slopes before land traffickers do so is seen by local leaders as a strategy to gain some form of control over the conditions on which newcomers will co-inhabit the area. Meanwhile, the pursuit of compact development puts a high priority, in planning circles, on Lima's municipal plans to regulate the borders of the city through the creation of an eco-corridor of *lomas* parks. These initiatives, however, only address those few areas where public land has not been encroached or is subjected to titling conflicts, thus leaving aside most of the expansion frontier of Lima and the conflictive dynamics of peri-urbanization shaping this urban region.

The containment of informal growth is increasingly being pursued not just through land-use planning mechanisms but also by using regulations as a means to deny services. Research we conducted in the peri-urban interface of metropolitan Mexico, Caracas, Chennai, Dar

5.6.1 The endless expansion over the steeps slopes of peripheral Lima.

es Salaam, and Cairo found that the peri-urban poor are outside networked infrastructures for water and sanitation.[8] But, contrary to what is often expected, we found that for the poor, living far from "the pipes" is a permanent condition, not a transitory one. When members of local governments and service utilities were asked why this is the case, the most frequent answer from those interviewed was that once infrastructure was provided, the full urbanization of peri-urban areas would be unstoppable, threatening the maintenance of vital ecosystem services for the sustainability of the city as a whole. To avoid such a scenario, seemingly consensual border pacts between existing settlers and the authorities are often sought to discourage further informal land transactions and sprawl over peri-urban land.

This is visible in the peri-urban district of Milpa Alta in Mexico City's Metropolitan Area. With the aim of protecting both forested land and the aquiferous reserve in this area from the perceived threat posed by increasing informal settlement, a census was carried out in 1997 throughout the district. It divided the population into two groups: those recorded in the census, and those who settled after it had been conducted. A Zero Growth Pact (ZGP) was developed upon this distinction, unilaterally establishing that only those who settled before 1997 could access water provided by public tankers (although not piped infrastructure). In return, those included

7   Rita Lambert and Adriana Allen, "Mapping the Contradictions," in *Environmental Justice and Urban Resilience in the Global South*, ed. Adriana Allen, Liza Griffin and Cassidy Johnson (London: Palgrave McMillan, forthcoming.

8   Adriana Allen, Julio Dávila, and Pascale Hofmann, "The Peri-Urban Water Poor: Citizens or Consumers?," *Environment and Urbanization* 18, no. 2 (2006): 333–51.

9   Martha Schteingart and
    Clara Eugenia Salazar,
    *Expansión urbana, socie-
    dad y ambiente* (Mexico
    City: Editorial El Colegio
    de México, 2005).
10 Adrian Guillermo
    Aguilar and Clemencia
    Santos, "Informal
    Settlements' Needs
    and Environmental
    Conservation in Mexico
    City: An Unsolved
    Challenge for Land-Use
    Policy," *Land Use Policy*,
    28 (2011): 649–62.

5.6.2 Weekly water entitlement for those within the ZGP

in the ZGP are expected to police the area and denounce any new settlers, who are to be denied any access to the public water supply. Despite this, informal land-use change continues, with dwellers accessing water through different mechanisms, and often forced to resort to illegal practices at higher unit costs. Meanwhile, local politicians intervene at their discretion to ensure the supply of free water to those outside the ZGP. (fig. **5.6.2**)

In the name of environmental protection, the ZGP has created a new landscape of contradictions that fosters differential sustainability. While unable to stop the land conversion of forested areas, the pact enforces various forms of illegality to both long-established and more recent settlers. While the former appear to enjoy comparatively better water provision, the right of both groups to water is still only partially guaranteed by an arbitrary date. At that point, it will be determined whether limited recognition will be granted or denied. This is a case where, under the cloak of supporting sustainability, coercive regulations are used to curb informal expansion by limiting access to water. This

forces the peri-urban poor to resort to coping through bribes and vote selling.

Similar agreements to the ZGP have been implemented throughout the country as a means to avoid further urban expansion over areas of high ecological value.[9] The Mexican scholars Adrian Aguilar and Clemencia Santos argue that a key shortcoming of containment policies over peri-urban land is not only the fact that conservation land is overregulated—which often results in no enforcement at all—but that urban space and environmentally valued space are treated as two separate realities.[10] As such, environmental regulation ignores the reality of insufficient housing and land for the poor, as much as urban development policies ignore the importance of preserving vital ecosystem functions that support urban life. Thus, mechanisms to protect environmentally sensitive areas, and de facto interventions to regularize informality in such areas, continue to reproduce counterproductive differences between peri-urban and urban sustainability standards, while failing to meet their respective ecological and social objectives.

Payment for Ecosystem Services

Because policies such as the ZGP are increasingly under attack in Mexico, there has been a shift to market-based mechanisms, which are regarded as more efficient for safeguarding ecologically valuable land. These methods seek an economic framework, using objective knowledge and the creation of incentives to promote environmental stewardship and capture the value of the natural world. The proliferation of economic approaches such as Payment for Ecosystem Services (PES) reflects an effort to replace punitive measures to control negative environmental behavior with voluntary transactions expected to promote care for the environmental.

The conquest of nature through an understanding of its economic benefits is certainly not new, but only in the new millennium did its operation start to gain popularity as a plausible contemporary planning strategy in the Global South. Traditionally applied to rural areas, the application of PES is gradually expanding to the peri-urban area, expected to control urban sprawl and deliver a win-win situation for both conservation and sustainable development. Examples range from applications to reduce vulnerability to climate change in peri-urban Durban to the preservation of the CO2 absorption capacity of peri-urban forests in Abeokuta, Nigeria.[11] The Payment for Environmental and Hydrological Services (PSAH) program initiated in 2003 and administered by Mexico's National Forestry Commission (CONAFOR) also illustrates this trend.

Following the neoliberal restructuring of environmental policy in Mexico over the last two decades, the PSAH program works on the assumption that water users should pay forest owners for the positive environmental effects of peri-urban forests in preserving aquifer recharging areas, mitigating runoff, and ensuring clean drinking water for cities. As almost 80 percent of Mexico's forests exist on communally owned lands—*ejidos* or *comunidades*—the program includes mostly communally owned forests.

A decade of internationally driven experiments set the scene for the adoption of the PSAH in Mexico in the first years of Vicente Fox's presidency. By 2008, Mexico had one of the world's largest national PES programs.[12] In its original design, PSAH targeted payments toward noncommercial forest to preserve ecosystems relevant to national interests, instead of those attractive to the international market. The program was initially conceived as both an antipoverty measure and an environmental preservation strategy, aimed at developing local markets in which payments were to be linked to existing municipal water bills and used to support impoverished communal forest managers. In order to address the growing scarcity of water, PES planned to focus on both overexploited watersheds and on cloud forests, the latter playing a key role in preserving hydrological services.[13] In practice, however, the targeted areas did less to preserve threatened aquifers than originally intended, as the establishment of a payment system between individual service consumers and forest managers was deemed more viable in forested land near cities.[14]

After much controversy and negotiation, PSAH was finally framed to target peri-urban forests near large cities, incorporating about 9,880 acres (4,000 hectares) of communal land. An evaluation conducted by the American researcher Nicholas DuBroff characterizes the program as a promising mechanism to tackle "the perennial threat of illegal urbanization to Mexico City's ecological conservation lands… precluding new irregular settlements in these same areas."[15]

PSAH incorporated about 46 percent of the last remaining forests in

11 For more details on the application of PES in Durban, see, James Waters, "The Role of Ecosystem Services in Peri-Urban Vulnerability to Climate Change," *Imperial College London—Centre for Environmental Policy*, last modified September 2009, accessed November 15, 2012, https://workspace.imperial.ac.uk/environmentalpolicy/public/Executive%20Summary-James%20Waters.pdf; to learn more about the application on PES in urban forest preservation, see Humphrey Kaoma and Charlie M. Shackleton, "Homestead Greening Is Widespread amongst the Urban Poor in Three Medium-Sized South African Towns," *Urban Ecosystems* 17, no. 4 (2014): 1191–207.

12 Kathleen McAfee and Elizabeth N. Shapiro, "Payments for Ecosystem Services in Mexico: Nature, Neoliberalism, Social Movements, and the State," *Annals of the Association of American Geographers* 100, no. 3 (2010): 579–99.

13 Isabel García Coll, "Potencial de recarga de acuíferos y estabilización de ciclos hídricos en areas forestadas," INE-DGIPEA Research Report, Mexico, 2002.

14 Jennifer Alix-García, Alain de Janvry, Elisabeth Sadoulet, and Juan Manuel Torres, "An Assessment of Mexico's Payment for Environmental Services Program," Rome: United Nations Food and Agriculture Organization, last modified 2005, accessed October 12, 2012, http://ftp.fao.org/es/ESA/Roa/pdf/aug05-env-mexico.pdf.

15 Nicholas DuBroff, "Curbing Informal Urban Growth with Ecosystem Services in Mexico City," MSC Report, El Colegio de Mexico and Massachusetts Institute of Technology, 2009, accessed December 19, 2012, http://siteresources.worldbank.org/

metropolitan Mexico between 2003 and 2009, from which only 12 percent were at high deforestation risk. The payment scheme established by the federal government estimated what an appropriate price might be based on social and ecological risk factors.[16] In the case of Milpa Alta, participating communities received about $57 per acre ($23 per hectare)— an incentive too small to deter community members from deforesting their land for agricultural purposes or from subdividing the common forest for informal development.[17]

In a Center for International Forestry Research (CIFOR) publication, the economist Sven Wunder reflects on other PES experiences across the world and argues that it is almost impossible to beat market-based pressures for land. Instead, he says, "payments for environmental services are most effective in marginal lands where a modest payment can "tip the balance" in favor of conservation."[18] But if that is the case, what is the actual role of PES in addressing fair distribution while preserving areas of high ecological value vis-à-vis other land market pressures?

PES schemes operate under the assumption that environmental degradation and social vulnerability can be reversed through the creation of markets that internalize the costs and benefits of preservation into production and consumption decisions. When scrutinized from an environmental justice perspective, this logic appears to have two fundamental flaws. First, PES automatically excludes marginalized groups as service providers, such as those occupying or working the land without title or regularized tenure. And service consumers, such as individuals paying water tariffs or buying charcoal or regionally produced food, are likely to face higher costs when peri-urban land is set aside for conservation under PES schemes. Second, through the commodification of ecosystem services, PES schemes inevitably create unsolvable trade-offs between conservation and fairness.

Green Enclaves

A third distinctive planning mechanism that produces differential sustainability across peri-urbanized areas is the greening of elite residential enclaves— or "eco-enclaves"—as described by the renowned scholars Mike Hodson and Simon Marvin.[19] This is manifested in a new generation of sustainable master planning products aiming to address the ecological aspirations of privileged groups while in effect reproducing differential sustainability.

Whether adhering strictly to "hard" sustainability design parameters ("zero carbon" or "100 percent recycling"), or adopting a more cosmetic approach, elite residential enclaves are increasingly being marketed in terms of their green credentials. They promise a refuge away from the undesirable experiences of cities (slums, crime, etc.), and an opportunity for residents to live an environmentally sustainable life. Here, green citizenship aspirations meet real estate development greed in a marriage that offers the possibility of realizing eco-living dreams for a minority of urbanites.

Since the 1990s, green enclaves have proliferated across most metropolitan regions in the Global South, driving the conversion of large chunks of primary agricultural land, previously the food source of adjacent urban areas and the livelihood of small subsistence farmers. Paradoxically, the adoption of stricter Environmental Impact Assessment requirements has driven up the cost of new developments and has been seized by the real estate sector as an opportunity to capture a fast-growing niche in the market through the construction of green enclaves. Peri-urbanization becomes ruled not just by the private-sector model

INTURBANDEVELOPMENT/Resources/336387-1272506514747/Dubroff.pdf.

16 Carlos Muñoz-Piña, Alejandro Guevara, Juan Manuel Torres, and Josephina Braña, "Paying for the Hydrological Services of Mexico's Forests: Analysis, Negotiations, and Results," *Ecological Economics* 65 (2007): 725–36.

17 DuBroff, "Curbing Informal Urban Growth with Ecosystem Services in Mexico City."

18 Sven Wunder, "Payments for Environmental Services: Some Nuts and Bolts," Occasional Paper, Center for International Forestry Research, Jakarta, 2009, 9.

19 Mike Hodson and Simon Marvin, "Urbanism in the Anthropocene: Ecological Urbanism or Premium Ecological Enclaves?," *City* 14, no. 3 (2010): 298–313.

of urban growth but also by the alignment of public urban planning with market forces. The result is increased sociospatial segregation.

In Ghana, the Accra Metropolitan Area (AMA) provides an example of how green enclaves are rapidly transforming the urban face through the commodification of peri-urban land. In an insightful characterization, the geographer Richard Grant points out that about twenty-three gated communities were at varying stages of development in 2004, representing an investment of almost $435 million, but only about 3 percent of AMA's total housing stock.[20] He describes the mushrooming of gated communities as the "globalizing of Accra from above," a process fueled by the restructuring of foreign direct investment, the expansion of international lending and mortgage programs, and the diffusion of global residential aspirations.[21] The rapid emergence of gated communities is driving up food prices in the city, as it has a direct impact on the shrinking of agricultural land. This is particularly evident in the northeastern AMA, in the area of La—a traditional site of subsistence farming that up until the late 1980s supplied most perishables consumed in Accra.

In La, large areas of land are rapidly entering the real estate market as gated communities, church and college complexes, and individual unapproved structures. Signs threatening individual structures with demolition pepper the area, but local capacity to enforce planning regulations is weak. This, alongside other factors, has given weight to calls to grant the La district municipal status, though it remains to be seen whether greater decentralization of powers will be used to protect local agricultural practices or instead to accelerate commodification through more luxury housing. (fig. **5.6.3**)

Within the area under study, an international company, Finali Ltd, secured

5.6.3 Farming land lost to mushrooming residential developments in peri-urban Accra

20 Richard Grant, *Globalizing City: The Urban and Economic Transformation of Accra, Ghana* (Syracuse, NY: Syracuse University Press, 2009).
21 Ibid., 18.
22 Adriana Allen and Alexandre Apsan Frediani, "Farmers, Not Gardeners: The Making of Environmentally Just Spaces in Accra," *City* 17, no. 3 (2013): 1–17.

land in 2008 to develop over 400 acres (160 hectares) into a large-scale luxury-housing compound named Airport Hills. Exclusive developments such as this have proliferated, forming a new boundary around one of the sites to which La farmers are shifting when they are displaced from the areas where they previously worked the land. Displacements are also often caused by the rush to build unapproved structures by individual families and traditional authorities. These practices are officially regarded as a negative but unstoppable trend, fueled by attempts to capture the increasingly valuable land before others do. Upmarket-gated communities like Airport Hills, though, are seen in a more benevolent light.[22]

Since 2010, the Millennium City Initiative led by the Earth Institute at Columbia University has worked with the metropolitan authorities to address Accra's most pressing environmental challenges. However, despite this intended green credential, the city's current development strategy stipulates that urban agriculture will be pushed to surrounding municipalities, where competition for land is lower. Furthermore, peripheral land within AMA is to be acquired not for subsistence agriculture but for large-scale, export-oriented schemes. Under this model, the prospect for protecting the role of peri-urban agriculture in supporting local livelihoods and contributing to Accra's food security appears to be slim.

Plans to create green areas for organic food production within gated communities are emerging in a small number of large-scale real estate developments. These initiatives, however, appear to be paying lip service to the purported benefits of urban agriculture, in that they are unlikely to stop the disappearance of local food production systems. Meanwhile, green enclaves such as Airport Hills are celebrated by the local authorities as a potential way of creating a "new and orderly Accra," where the city expands in harmony with nature while maximizing the economic potential of its land.

Green enclaves constitute a large and fast-growing industry claiming to offer plausible options for smart forms of urbanization. These complexes are being produced in a highly internationalized environment, in which sustainability design principles are increasingly being exported by a handful of large, multinational architecture and engineering consultancies working for a diverse set of consumers, ranging from state clients to public-private partnerships to private developers. Green enclaves create an exclusive, exclusionary dream of the city-to-be, while disrupting the previous social and economic integration of peri-urban areas.

However, such enclaves should not be understood merely as part of the gentrification of peri-urban territories. Above all, green enclaves actively attribute new meanings to such spaces and to the political agency of their inhabitants. In short, green enclaves enable differential

sustainability through by segregating green citizens away from "the other."

Differential Sustainability at Work

The planning mechanisms discussed throughout this essay are widely regarded as acceptable means, in effect normalizing the production and reproduction of differential sustainability in the peri-urban area as a desirable outcome. Land-use management at the peri-urban interface is highly contested, with communal and traditional land systems increasingly transformed by formal and informal markets. Public agencies, unable to apply the repertoire of institutional mechanisms usually deployed in core urban areas, are, not surprisingly, experimenting with innovative yet one-dimensional solutions that aim, paradoxically, to regulate conflict by rendering invisible the multiple driving forces that propel such conflict in the first place.

Analysis reveals that the sprawl of informal settlements over ecologically valuable peri-urban land cannot be regulated successfully without a simultaneous consideration of environmental, social, economic and political factors. In particular, it's necessary to consider the elements that drive the peri-urbanization of poverty and the erosion of the poor's right to the city and to the natural environment across the Global South. Past experiences that succeeded in addressing such challenges include the multiple supports, social and environmental, for viable strategies of incremental urbanism, such as the ones that took place in Lima, Peru, in the 1970s and 1980s. In those cases, informal urbanization was approached not as a problem but as a collective ensemble of a multitude of practices that produce the city and need to be supported by the state.

In all three mechanisms analyzed in this essay, a fundamental tension lies in the proposition that sustainable urban futures might be achievable, but only at the expense of the less privileged, thus inevitably endorsing the reproduction of social and environmental differences. Mechanisms such as the ones reviewed here have been described by the Swedish political ecologists Henrik Ernstson and Sverker Sörlin as "technologies of globalization," which provide standardized diagnoses and remedies that environmentally shape spaces.[23] These mechanisms—often imported from the Global North—frame the pursuit of sustainability as a normative domain in which ordinary citizens are reduced to either green consumers, to second-class citizens paternalistically protected or coerced to act on behalf of the common good, or to individuals economically incentivized to keep their actions within preestablished thresholds. Those living and working informally in peri-urban territories are outside the vision and environmental practices prescribed as desirable, and therefore further displaced or marginalized both from current urban development and from the city-to-be.

The practice of environmental planning is not inevitably geared toward the reproduction of differential sustainability. However, by and large, analyses and normative prescriptions of what sustainability might entail in an increasingly urban world continue to contain an implicit assumption of universality that is blind to the specific ways in which social and natural processes coproduce in different contexts. The discussion highlights the urgent need to bring the notion of environmental justice to the fore, as a means to analyze critically the political aspects of sustainability planning and to produce a more nuanced understanding of differences across the urbanizing Global South.

The contemporary urban transition has its epicenter in the Global South and will continue to be associated with peri-urbanization in the decades to come. The challenge ahead is to repoliticize the way in which planning is responding to an urban future beyond reproducing islands of reform and difference that undermine the prospects for just and environmentally sustainable transitions.

This essay is based on a longer piece titled "Peri-Urbanization and the Political Ecology of Differential Sustainability," in The Routledge Handbook on Cities of the Global South, *edited by Susan Parnell and Sophie Oldfield (London: Routledge, 2014): 522–38.*

23   Henrik Ernstson and Sverker Sörlin, "Ecosystem Services as a Technology of Globalization: On Articulating Values in Urban Nature," *Ecological Economics* 86 (2013): 274–84.

Bunsucesso, Rio de Janeiro, Brazil

Mankhurd, Mumbai, Maharashtra, India

5.7
BRAZILIAN SUBURBS
MARGINALITY, INFORMALITY, AND EXCLUSIVITY

Martin Coy, Simone Sandholz,
Tobias Töpfer, and Frank Zirkl

In the Global North, suburbia is the result of processes of vertical and horizontal mobility that proceeded throughout the twentieth century. It is a product of what is thought to be socioeconomic progress, increased income, individual well-being, private property, and the changing perception of quality of life in the city and its outskirts. Suburbia represents the idealization of a quiet life away from the city, and it corresponds in many cases to a manifestation of the garden city concept.

In contrast, in the Global South (especially in Latin America and Brazil), the word *suburbia* does not have such a positive connotation. Historically, the gradient of Latin American and Brazilian cities always declined, in terms of income and density, from the city center toward the urban peripheries. Thus, in Brazilian scientific and planning discussions, the terms *peri-urbanization* and *urban periphery* are much more common—and more appropriate—than the term *suburbia* to describe the outskirts of the cities, which is associated with stigmatization of peripheral areas. Until recently, to live in the suburb in Brazil meant to belong to the lower classes and often to be marginalized in Brazilian society.[1] When Brazilians talk about *suburbio*, they tend to associate the term with working-class residential areas on the urban fringes that have precarious housing conditions, lack of infrastructure, the predominance of informal rules, and the presence of social conflict, delinquency, and violence. This stigma permeates suburbia's representation in Brazilian media, for example, how suburbs are portrayed in the extremely popular *telenovelas*, as well as the self-perception of its suburban residents.

This stigma has begun to change since the 1970s with the emergence of gated communities at the urban outskirts. Gated communities are luxurious and highly protected housing estates, developed by real estate companies.[2] Under the described sociospatial conditions of peri-urban areas, gated communities constitute veritable islands of wealth in oceans of poverty. Gated communities are the main reason why in recent years peri-urban areas in many Brazilian agglomerations might be characterized best by socioeconomic and spatial fragmentation. Nevertheless, the persistent stereotypes produce the still dominant image of peri-urban areas in Brazil as distant, poor, segregated, precarious, highly informal, or even illegal, ungoverned, in permanent transformation, and dangerous. In order to better understand the structure, dynamics, and recent transformations of Brazilian peri-urban areas, we must uncover the socioeconomic and political driving forces of urban development and sociospatial differentiation over the past decades.

Today 160,925,792 Brazilians (corresponding to almost 85 percent of the total population) live in urban areas.[3] In 1940 only around 31 percent of Brazilians were considered to be urban. These numbers indicate a complete inversion in Brazil's population distribution. Due to the increasing industrialization and the accompanying modernization, Brazil has passed, since the 1940s, through deep economic, social, political, and cultural transformations, as well as transformations of its settlement structures.[4] Brazil's urbanization and peri-urbanization processes have gone through several phases of growth, internal differentiation, housing production, and infrastructural policies, as well as governance and self-organization.

Early Peri-Urbanization (until the 1960s)

From the 1940s onward, Brazil's development strategies and policies were increasingly characterized by an urban bias. Emerging industries and growing

1   Celso Athayde, "Periferia: Favela, beco, viela agenda Brasileira," in *Agenda Brasileira; Temas de uma sociedade em Mudança*, ed. André Botelho and Lilia Moritz Schwarcz (São Paulo: Companhia das Letras, 2011).

2   Martin Coy and Martin Pöhler, "Gated Communities in Latin American Megacities: Case Studies in Brazil and Argentina," *Environment and Planning B* 29 (2002); Martin Coy, "Gated Communities and Urban Fragmentation in Latin America: The Brazilian Experience," *GeoJournal* 66 (2006).

3   "Censo demográfico 2010: Características da população e dos domicílios; Resultados do universo," Instituto Brasileiro de Geografia e Estatística, accessed May 22, 2015, http://biblioteca.ibge.gov.br/visualizacao/periodicos/93/cd_2010_caracteristicas_populacao_domicilios.pdf.

4   Ermínia Maricato, "Metrópoles desgovernadas," *Estudos Avançados* 25, no. 71 (2011); for the case of the agglomeration of São Paulo, see Lúcio Kowarick and Eduardo Marques, eds., *São Paulo: Novos percursos e atores; Sociedade, cultura e política* (São Paulo: Editora 34, 2011).

cities became constitutive elements of a modern Brazilian society. The promise of a better life, and work, education, health, and shelter, worked as the main pull factors of an increasing rural-urban migration. In particular, the rapidly growing major cities of the southeast (e.g., the urban and industrial agglomerations of São Paulo, Rio de Janeiro, and Belo Horizonte, the economic core region and growth engine of the country) saw massive inflows from the rural regions of the Brazilian northeast. During this phase, the centers of the urban agglomerations were still able to receive large amounts of incoming people. Subsequently, city centers became denser and more vertical, as planned quarters for middle- and upper-class inhabitants emerged, expanding the traditional inner-city areas such as Jardins in São Paulo or the Zona Sul in Rio de Janeiro. Poor immigrants were to a large extent absorbed in informal squatter (*favelas*) and degraded inner-city dwellings (*cortiços*), abandoned by those people who moved to new middle- and upper-class quarters. The *cortiços* are mostly former upper-class villas and office or commerce buildings. These were subdivided into very small and precarious residential units consisting of one single room per family with shared substandard sanitary facilities. In Rio de Janeiro, the first favelas emerged through the occupation by the poor of the hilly areas unsuitable for regular construction. They constructed shanties first, which then were gradually improved to small simple houses.

New industries—predominantly in the fields of automotive, consumer goods, machinery, and the like—were localized in municipalities at the urban outskirts, such the ABC Paulista (part of the São Paulo Metropolitan Region, named after the municipalities of Santo André, São Bernardo do Campo, and São Caetano do Sul) in the case of São Paulo, and the Baixada Fluminense in the case of Rio de

Janeiro. This stimulated the migration of workers and their families to those particular peri-urban areas.

Peak Peri-Urbanization (1960s to 1980s)
The ongoing rapid increase of rural to urban migration and the concomitant natural increase of urban population reached its peak in most major Brazilian cities in the 1970s and early 1980s. However, the housing deficit became more and more perceptible, especially for the lower-income groups. As a consequence, the authoritarian regime that ruled Brazil from 1964 to 1985 installed several institutions to reinforce the public housing sector, implementing a far-reaching system for finance, construction, and distribution of social housing. The most important of these institutions is the Federal Housing Bank BNH (Banco Nacional de Habitação). Large-scale social housing schemes were constructed in all major Brazilian agglomerations. Here, the Cidade de Deus (City of God) in Rio de Janeiro serves as one example. This 1960s public housing project—at that time far from the city center—consisted of nearly six thousand small, detached houses of 375 square foot (35 square meters) each as well as of five-story apartment dwellings. Later housing projects of that kind, like the São Paulo Cidade Itaquera and Cidade Tiradentes, are huge bedroom communities of numerous multistory apartment blocks, lacking—at least initially— almost any form of social infrastructure. (fig. **5.7.1**) During this period overall 1,428,498 dwelling units were built throughout Brazil.[5]

The responsible public institutions and the contracted construction firms usually preferred the outskirts of the cities or even peri-urban municipalities to accommodate such large-scale social housing projects due to higher availability and lower prices for land. By making these location choices, the state itself

5   Katharina Kirsch-Soriano da Silva, *Wohnen im Wandel: Mutationen Städtischer Siedlungsstrukturen in Recife/Brasilien* (Vienna: Lit, 2010).

6   Maricato, "Metrópoles
    desgovernadas."

5.7.1 Social housing and informal settlements in peri-urban São Paulo

proliferated and supported significantly the ongoing peri-urbanization. As a consequence, sociospatial segregation sharpened between the centers of the urban agglomerations and the outskirts. The dwellers of the peri-urban areas became more and more disadvantaged due to large distances between their homes and the (mainly informal) work places in the cities, their distance from transport and other infrastructure, and so on. Nevertheless, during this period the peri-urban population in all Brazilian agglomerations increased much faster than the population of the central cities.

Fragmented Peri-Urbanization (1980s to 2000)
All in all, the Brazilian public housing policy never fulfilled its tasks.[6] The housing deficit continued to be high, although urban growth decelerated from the 1980s onward. In parallel to the Brazilian economic crisis, public housing policies also plunged into crisis. Traditional social housing projects were increasingly substituted for low-cost housing schemes. This new model was usually realized in extremely peripheral localizations due to affordable access to land. Low-cost housing, sites and services, and slum-upgrading programs have dominated this period of housing policies in Brazil, based on the principles of the 1976 United Nations Human Settlements Program (UN-Habitat) conference and the subsequent Vancouver Declaration on Human Settlements. The results have been increased discrimination against their residents and proliferating marginalization trends in peri-urban areas. Marginalization is often manifested in the absence of workplaces and subsequently long commutes mostly in precarious buses, as one example. This phenomenon can be observed not only in the major urban agglomerations of the country but also in smaller- and medium-sized agglomerations, which were then growing more dynamically than the major ones. A good example is Cuiabá, the extremely fast-growing capital of the state of Mato Grosso, where low-cost housing projects were realized during this time on a large scale in peri-urban areas like Morada da Serra and Pedra 90. (fig. **5.7.2**) While the former still consisted of small, detached houses, the latter was an example of sites-and-services projects, where lots are provided with minimal infrastructure.

Selected metropolitan regions (RM), and urban agglomerations (AU)	Population	Population	Annual growth rate	Share (%) in relation to the country	Share (%) of the peri-urban munici-palities in relation to the core municipalty
	2000	2010	2000–2010	2010	2010
RM do Vale do Rio Cuiabá (MT)	726,220	833,766	1.39	0.44	33.90
MM Paulista (SP)	27,315,142	30,623,808	1.15	16.07	63.25
RM São Paulo (SP)	17,878,703	19,683,975	0.97	10.32	42.83
RM Campinas (SP)	2,338,148	2,797,137	1.81	1.47	61.39
RM do Vale do Paraíba e Litoral Norte (SP)	1,989,692	2,264,594	1.30	1.19	72.18
RM Baixada Santista (SP)	1,476,820	1,664,136	1.20	0.87	74.80
AU Sorocaba (SP)	1,225,020	1,447,331	1.68	0.76	72.11
AU de Piracicaba (SP)	1,169,891	1,307,256	1.12	0.69	47.03
AU de Jundiaí (SP)	580,065	698,724	1.88	0.37	59.47
Microregião Bragança Paulista (SP)	424,522	498,171	1.61	0.26	70.54
Microregião São Roque (SP)	232,281	262,484	1.23	0.14	69.97
Brazil, Regiões Metropolitanas—RM, Regiões Integradas de Desenvolvimento—Rides e Aglomerações Urbanas—AU	92,697,653	106,377,043	1.39	55.77	
Brazil, urban	137,755,550	160,925,792	1.57	84.36	
Brazil	169,799,170	190,755,799	1.17	100.00	

5.7.2 Key figures of selected metropolitan regions and urban agglomerations

Approximately nine thousand rudimentary urbanized lots were offered for self-build housing.[7]

Yet the most important driving force of peri-urbanization at that time was the proliferation of illegal allotments by private landowners and real estate companies, as well as the spontaneous invasion of private or public land at the urban and peri-urban peripheries. In the case of illegal allotments, supposed or actual owners subdivided the still predominantly rural land and sold these plots without formal permission. The new owners started to build their houses within the limits of their financial resources, expanding their structures over time. This caused a long-lasting process of urbanization starting with a small building and often resulting in a consolidated house of more than two floors. Informal urban development, such as this incremental self-help housing or the proliferation of *favelas*, and urban and peri-urban migration triggered by expulsion, came to characterize peri-urban areas to a large extent.

But this was only one side of the coin. On the other side, the peri-urban realm had been discovered by new actors: large private developers and construction firms, whose interest is the realization of huge gated communities—the so-called *condomínios fechados*—for a growing clientele of privileged people seeking a private Arcadia. These large, walled estates are equipped with all kinds of infrastructures and services, including leisure facilities and shopping centers. Self-governed by the developers and the residents, the entities are protected by private security. In Brazil, the emblematic examples are the Alphaville complex at the northwestern outskirts of São Paulo (municipalities of Barueri, and Santana do Parnaíba), on the one hand, and the gated communities of Barra da Tijuca in the southern zone of Rio de Janeiro on the other.[8] Alphaville consists of several residential areas, each separately walled, with only one guarded access. Within these areas there are huge single-family homes mostly equipped with individual leisure facilities like pools or

7   Martin Coy, "Stadtentwicklung an der Peripherie Brasiliens" (habilitation treatise, University of Tübingen, 1997).

8   Coy and Pöhler, "Gated Communities"; Coy, "Gated Communities."

sports grounds, separately protected by walls and fences as well as CCTV. The complex includes a vertical commercial zone, which offers services and commodities needed by the local population.

Every large or medium-sized agglomeration in Brazil has its own Alphaville, and the gated community lifestyle has turned out to be most important in Brazil's high-ranking housing trends. Ongoing marginalization, increasing land appropriation by privileged actors, and the absence or at least the weaknesses of public steering are the characteristics of this phase of fragmented peri-urbanization. As a result, a gap is apparent between the spaces occupied by the wealthy and the marginal classes, with upper classes preferring to settle in suburban luxurious high-rise complexes.[9]

Reorganized Peri-Urbanization (ince 2000)

In the course of the 1980s, the Brazilian redemocratization process (aimed specifically at the elaboration of the new constitution in 1988) played an important role in urban politics and planning due to the activities of the National Urban Reform Movement.[10] For about the past two decades, underprivileged groups have been increasingly organized in such social urban-reform movements, in particular the provision of urban infrastructure in poorer quarters, the construction of housing facilities, and the option to purchase parcels. The major policy result was the Estatuto da Cidade (City Statute), passed in 2001, and the establishment of the Ministry for Urban Affairs in 2003. The City Statute mandates that Brazilian municipalities with more than twenty thousand people have to issue a master plan (Plano Diretor) at least every five years. In addition, it provides legal support for municipalities to promote land tenure and legitimatizes different new legal instruments for urban

areas.[11] Although these attempts have been very promising in theory, in practice the outcomes are limited. Participatory instruments, even if mandatory by law, remain unused or are treated as processes for legitimizing decisions of urban authorities.[12]

The most recent phase of urbanization and peri-urbanization is characterized above all by a general decline of urban growth. In relative terms, the population share of the major Brazilian agglomerations in national urbanization trends has decreased, in particular in São Paulo and Rio de Janeiro, whereas the share of northern and midwestern Brazilian agglomerations increased. Yet urban poverty and sociospatial marginalization have still increased throughout the country, perhaps as a consequence of the neoliberal politics that shaped Brazil at different levels, among other factors. For urban agglomerations, neoliberal politics corresponded to a reinforcement of social and sociospatial inequalities, as well as to aggravated violence and security problems at the urban margins.

In urban and peri-urban areas, the driving force of private capital interests (such as real estate developers) and the resulting proliferation of gated communities, shopping centers, and private business complexes ran counter to spontaneous informal dynamics (such as squatter settlements) and to civil society-driven processes such as neighborhood initiatives and participatory budgeting. These opposing forces continued to be the most important factors of development and change, and exceeded, certainly, the ruling capacity of public authorities.[13]

During the latest phase of peri-urbanization, however, the national government as well as the federal states and the municipal authorities recognized the need for change and action in the urban and peri-urban realms. As a consequence

9   Lawrence A. Herzog, "Barra da Tijuca: The Political Economy of a Global Suburb in Rio de Janeiro, Brazil," *Latin American Perspectives* 40, no. 2 (2013).

10 Martin Coy, "Stadtentwicklung und Stadtpolitik: Sozioökonomische Fragmentierung und Beispiele Zukunfts-orientierter Planung," in *Brasilien Heute: Geographischer Raum-Politik-Wirtschaft-Kultur,* ed. Sérgio Costa et al. (Frankfurt: Vervuert, 2010).

11 Mozart V. Serra et al., "Urban Land Markets and Urban Land Development: An Examination of Three Brazilian Cities: Brasília, Curitiba and Recife," *IURD Working Paper Series,* Institute of Urban and Regional Development, University of California at Berkeley, 2004.

12 Kirsch-Soriano da Silva, *Wohnen im Wandel.*

13 Maricato, "Metrópoles desgovernadas."

of the 1988 constitution and the accompanying National Urban Reform Movement, several innovative elements of urban policy and governance, such as participatory budgeting, were implemented. Strengthening of the municipal and the state level can be considered as one of the main outcomes of the constitutional process in the 1980s and its follow-ups in the 1990s and 2000s. Additionally, overall awareness for new governance rules for major urban agglomerations became a subject of major importance.

However, the most important impacts on recent urban and peri-urban development stem from the federal investment programs PAC 1 and PAC 2 (Growth Acceleration Programs 1 and 2), which can be considered the main public reaction to the challenges of the global financial crisis 2007 and 2008. In 2007 Brazil's housing deficit was as approximated to 7.2 million housing units. The highest deficit in absolute numbers occurred in the metropolises of Rio de Janeiro and São Paulo, but in relative numbers the north and northeast of the country were most affected, with more than 60 percent of the shortages concerning poor households.[14]

In order to alleviate this high housing deficit, in 2009, the national government initiated the housing program Minha Casa Minha Vida (MCMV; My House My Life). It can be considered the first significant public measure in the housing sector after a long crisis of respective public policies. The ambitious program aimed at building one million housing units in each of its two phases. Almost 90 percent of the above-mentioned national housing deficit corresponds to the poorest target group of the MCMV program—those earning up to three times the minimum wage. However, the MCMV program dedicated only 40 percent of its housing units to that group, although this group makes up the majority of the housing need.[15] In the metropolitan region of São Paulo,

the MCMV program completed almost six hundred social housing projects by 2013, totaling more than 107,000 dwellings. Out of that, 34 percent are for the poorest target group, 39 percent for the target group between three and six minimum wages, and 27 percent for the wealthiest target group (between six and ten minimum wages).[16] In this context, it is interesting to note that the MCMV sites for the poorest strata are located in the most peripheral areas of the metropolitan region of São Paulo, whereas the sites of middle- and upper-income target groups are significantly more central.[17] This aspect shows that, at least in this case, the MCMV program does not reverse the long-lasting tendencies of sociospatial segregation.

Emerging Polycentricity: Macrometrópole Paulista

All over the world, finding adequate, efficient, and legitimate formats and rules of governance for suburban or peri-urban areas is a major challenge. The same is true for Brazil, where rapid and uncontrolled urban expansion in the 1960s and 1970s caused many problems in housing, land regulation, and infrastructure provisioning, especially in the field of urban and peri-urban transport and waste and water management. In the long run, these issues could certainly not be resolved within the boundaries of the existing municipalities. In 1973 the Brazilian military government installed nine metropolitan regions (Regiões Metropolitanas, or RMs) around the major urban agglomerations of the country: São Paulo, Rio de Janeiro, Belo Horizonte, Salvador, Recife, Fortaleza, Belém, Curitiba, and Porto Alegre. The main idea of this centralistic top-down measure was to instate, by law, mechanisms of centralized coordination, macro planning, monitoring, and control of processes and potential conflicts in the urban and peri-urban context.

14 Kirsch-Soriano da Silva, *Wohnen im Wandel.*
15 Eduardo Marques and Leandro Rodrigues, "O programa Minha Casa Minha Vida na metrópole paulistana: Atendimento habitacional e padrões de segregação," *Revista Brasileira de Estudos Urbanos e Regionais* 15, no. 2 (2013).
16 Ibid.
17 Ibid.

In reality, however, the RMs never fulfilled their original tasks.[18] Although specific institutions of planning and management have been installed in some RMs, the metropolitan region as an important player in the very dynamic and contested field of urban and peri-urban governance disappeared rapidly from the political scene.[19] The main reasons were the institutional weaknesses, struggles about responsibilities, political conflicts between different levels, and, last but not least, a total lack of democratic legitimization.

Meanwhile, the original number of nine metropolitan regions has grown significantly. Today, 106,377,043 Brazilians live in the 920 municipalities belonging to what are now sixty-three metropolitan regions. This corresponds to 55.8 percent of Brazil's total population and 66.1 percent of its urban population. Out of these, the RM São Paulo—with 19,683,975 inhabitants in thirty-nine municipalities—is the largest, and the RM Sul de Roraima with 21,633 inhabitants in three municipalities is the smallest, indicating the different spatial and socioeconomic contexts and political positions among the RMs. Though plans for a Metropolitan Statute as a legal framework equivalent to the City Statute were not realized, several important issues in metropolitan area governance were recently addressed, resulting in new legal frameworks for intermunicipal consortia and public-private partnerships, for example.

It is notably the agglomeration of São Paulo where the question of appropriate boundaries, transitions, or the amalgamation between different metropolitan regions is more than ever on the agenda of regional policy, planning and research.[20] The RM of São Paulo is by far the biggest urban and peri-urban agglomeration of Brazil and South America. The core region is increasingly coalescing with its neighboring metropolitan regions and agglomerations of Campinas, Santos, Jundiaí, and other more distantly located cities and their fringes, such as São José dos Campos, Sorocaba, and Piracicaba, forming a veritable city region called Macrometrópole Paulista (MM Paulista). It constitutes 173 municipalities with more than thirty million inhabitants, corresponding to 74 percent of the population of the state of São Paulo and 16 percent of Brazil as a whole. The Macrometrópole generates 83 percent of the gross domestic product of the state of São Paulo, which is 8 percent of Brazil's GDP. Within the Macrometrópole some of the most dynamic and wealthiest science and technology poles, like Campinas or São José dos Campos, converge with declining industrial areas, such as parts of the ABC Paulista, agro-industrial centers like Sorocaba, or agglomerations of poverty, unemployment, and marginalization like Guarulhos. Despite the continuing single dominance of the São Paulo core city, more than 60 percent of the Macrometrópole population lives in peri-urban municipalities today. Over the last years, the peripheries of the core cities and the municipalities at the outskirts of the Macrometrópole Paulista grew generally faster than the core cities. These different growth patterns between core cities and peripheral and/or peri-urban areas contributed to the strengthening of the polycentric structure of this urban region and, to some extent, caused more and more diffuse centralities. No clear "gradient" of wealthier or poorer parts of the Macrometrópole can be identified. Its sociospatial as well as its functional and economic structure increasingly reflects a patchwork of urban/peri-urban fragments. (fig. **5.7.3**) The economic, social, and infrastructural linkages between fragments are predominantly informal, mostly unplanned, and characterized by open or implicit conflicts for the control over land. In this context

18 Maricato, "Metrópoles desgovernadas"; Jeroen Johannes Klink, "Novas governanças para as áreas metropolitanas; O panorama internacional e as perspectivas para o caso Brasileiro," *Cadernos Metrópole* 22 (2009).

19 See, e.g., the Empresa Paulista de Planejamento Metropolitana [EMPLASA; Paulista Metropolitan Planning Company] in the RM of São Paulo, an institution for metropolitan planning.

20 EMPLASA, *Plano de ação da macrometrópole Paulista 2013–2040: O futuro sas metrópoles Paulistas* (São Paulo: Governo do Estado de São Paulo, 2013).

21 EMPLASA, *Plano De Ação.*

5.7.3 Fragmented peri-urban landscape in São Paulo

of prevalence of private capital interests (at least for the case of the wealthier fragments) and/or informal rules of local governance, the strengthening of public steering at local and specifically at intermunicipal levels becomes highly relevant. This is one of the major tasks for the Macrometropolitan Action Plan (Plano de Ação da Macrometrópole PAM 2013–2040), which was elaborated and implemented by the regional planning body EMPLASA (Empresa Paulista de Planejamento Metropolitano) and the state government of São Paulo in 2013.[21] Three strategic "axes" define the priorities of the PAM concerning the further development and internal structure of the MM Paulista: (1) to enhance territorial connectivity and economic competitiveness; (2) to strengthen territorial cohesion and inclusive urbanization; and (3) to establish (macro) metropolitan governance. Concrete areas of future public action are more cooperation and coordination between the corresponding municipalities as well as between municipalities, the Macrometrópole and the state; the creation and structuration of new centralities; the improvement and the expansion

of public housing (e.g., by the Minha Casa Minha Vida program); and last but not least, in the adaptation and more coherent application of urbanistic instruments offered by the Estatuto da Cidade. Infrastructure implementation and improvement projects (mainly expansion and modernization of the highway system, railroad, airport, and port infrastructures) are of central importance but also dominate politics. The official debate in the Macrometrópole Paulista is oriented toward economic development, instead of toward social, socioecological, or participatory governance.

The Future of Brazilian Suburbs

Current processes and challenges that Brazil's peri-urban areas have to face are manifold. (fig. **5.7.4**) Growth dynamics are shifting toward urban outskirts and are coming along with an increasing pressure to locate industries or services on vacant peri-urban land, augmenting environmental concerns. The growing number of commuters between center and periphery and within the periphery continues to conflict with fragmentation and persistent infrastructural deficiencies. The search

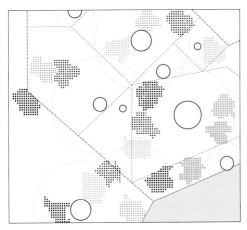

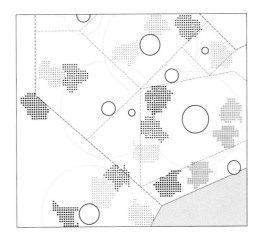

22 Martijn Koster, "Mediating and Getting 'Burnt' in the Gap: Politics and Brokerage in a Recife Slum, Brazil," *Critique of Anthropology* 32, no. 4 (2012).

○ urban center   ░░ social housing

○ peri-urban area   ░ gated communities

--- federal state border   ░ business locations

--- municipality border   ▦ modern industries

▦ favela   ░ declining industries

○ urban center

○ peri-urban area

⌐ migration

⤢ commuting

— highways

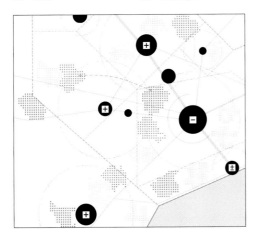

● urban center

○ peri-urban area

federal state border

--- municipality border

— highways

⊞⊟⊞ decreasing/stagnating/increasing urban dynamics

5.7.4 Schematic illustration of peri-uban structures and processes in Brazil

for adequate governance arrangements, with strong or weak forms of institutionalization, continues to overcome shortcomings in sharing regional metropolitan administrative tasks. Increasingly, Brazilian cities develop specific innovative strategies to resolve these major challenges for the future.

A main feature of the municipalization has been the testing and establishment of forms for more popular participation in urban management since the end of the 1980s. The most popular one is participatory budgeting, implemented by local governments under the guidance of the Partido dos Trabalhadores (Workers' Party or PT) counteracting old clientele politics and enabling local municipalities to engage with slum dwellers as full citizens.[22] These relatively successful initiatives in several urban agglomerations (Porto Alegre, Belo Horizonte, Belém, etc.) contributed to strengthening the tangible local context of neighborhoods (including peri-urban ones) in urban policies, as well as in discussions about urban problems and solutions. One result was a shift in cognition away from the more abstract and anonymous level of metropolitan regions toward the peri-urban realm of each municipality.

Another example for innovative urban development is the case of Curitiba, capital of the state of Paraná. This fast-growing metropolitan area is well known for alternative solutions in urban planning, building up infrastructure like a modern public transport system, as well as in guiding the architectonical urban development. The physiognomy of the core as well as that of peripheral areas changed significantly due to decisions made by city hall by means of a master plan, the first already released in the 1960s. The combination of special corridors for a bus rapid transit system and the opportunity for real estate developers to build high-rise apartment buildings alongside these bus lanes changed the urban physiognomy and had a certain influence on its architecture. Municipal housing programs in suburban areas as well as the establishment of social and other infrastructure changed Curitibas's vast and fast-growing outskirts during the 1980s and 1990s. Nowadays these areas are definitely in better shape than most Brazilian or Latin American cities.

Summing it up, all these efforts are leading to a better quality of life for people living in suburban areas. Today, the cities of Curitiba and Porto Alegre are considered as two of the most innovative urban conglomerations and serve as best practices for sustainable urban development even on a global scale. This is showing the innovative potential of Brazilian cities on their path to overcome suburban marginality and disparity.

5.8
DACHASCAPES AND DYSTOPIAS

Robert J. Mason and Lilya Nigmatullina

ECOLOGICAL
FUNCTION

GOVERNANCE
& POLICY
CHALLENGES

Had there been a Cold War suburban sprawl race, the United States would have won hands down. In contrast to the United States, Soviet metropolitan development was tightly constrained by the central government, which limited migration to the city proper and provided modest but serviceable high-density housing for workers. Thus suburban housing was undesirable due to its lack of services and infrastructure. Yet in spite of the controls on migration, people still flocked to the metropolitan area, creating an inverted spatial structure with densities that were higher at the edge than in the center. The desires of the people for suburban living, although suppressed, still played out through dachas (summer houses) on the government-allocated lands in Moscow's peripheries.

But in the post-Soviet era of privatization and lax regulation, people's suppressed desires for suburban living led to massive suburbanization, which increasingly symbolized luxury. Today's Moscow is characterized by American-style sprawl, massive highway congestion, growing inequality, and limited urban and regional planning controls. However, the traditional dacha model could be reinvented as a new paradigm for sustainable suburbanization.

The Soviet Era
The Soviet Union inherited a predominantly rural population from czarist Russia. Small, wooden, single-family houses predominated, with only Moscow and Leningrad having populations in excess of one million. Under the Stalinist politics of rapid industrialization and collectivization of rural land, millions of people moved from the countryside to the industrializing urban centers. Housing was in short supply, since investments in industries outpaced those in housing production. Even as recently as the 1976 to 1980 period, industrial investment

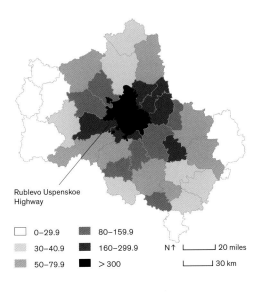

Rublevo Uspenskoe Highway

☐ 0–29.9	▨ 80–159.9	
▨ 30–40.9	▨ 160–299.9	N↑ └────┘ 20 miles
▨ 50–79.9	■ >300	└────┘ 30 km

5.8.1 Moscow Oblast population density

exceeded housing investment by 150 percent.[1] Moreover, World War II had brought severe deterioration in housing conditions, leaving more than twenty-five million people homeless.[2]

Still, through much of the twentieth century, the powerful central government endeavored to keep cities compact and well served by public transportation. Urban growth was concentrated mainly in the suburban reaches of large metropolitan areas, in satellite cities of twenty thousand to one hundred thousand residents containing urban infrastructure, industries, and institutions.[3] In the 1980s and 1990s, as Moscow expanded, some of the nearest satellite cities were incorporated into the capital. (fig. **5.8.1**) People who did reside in suburban single-family houses often lacked access to infrastructure and services—such as running water, electricity, and gas—that were available in cities. For these reasons, most Soviets favored high-rise apartment living; moreover, the directives of the State Committee on Construction Affairs, the main institution responsible for planning and construction, greatly circumscribed their choice.[4] Indeed, in the Soviet Union, housing was a strictly controlled public good rather than a commodity that could be bought and sold.[5]

1 Ed A. Hewett, *Reforming the Soviet Economy: Equality versus Efficiency* (Washington, DC: Brookings Institution Press, 1988), 314.
2 Eric Martinot, *Investments to Improve the Energy Efficiency of Existing Residential Buildings in Countries of the Former Soviet Union* (Washington, DC: World Bank Publications, 1997), 21.
3 Gregory D. Andrusz, *Housing and Urban Development in the USSR: Urban Public Policy* (Albany: State University of New York Press, 1984), 240.
4 Blair A. Ruble, "Housing the Citizens in Soviet Russia, 1955–90: The Tyranny of Technology," in *The European Cities and Technology Reader: Industrial to Post-Industrial City*, ed. Colin Chant and David Goodman (London: Routledge, 1999).
5 Michael Alexeev, "Market vs. Rationing: The Case of Soviet Housing," *Review of Economics and Statistics* 70, no. 3 (August 1988): 414–20.

The hasty and extensive construction practices of the Khrushchev era produced a distinct form of urban sprawl within large cities.[6] Apartment buildings constructed in the 1970s and 1980s, by contrast, were typically taller than their predecessors, preventing cities from sprawling. With the accelerated construction of multistory houses, single-family homeownership declined rapidly. At the same time, populations in satellite towns built in and around major cities were increasing. By the 1980s, the country's urban population share had increased to 64 percent, and the number of cities with a population of more than one million rose to twenty-three. People migrated because urban life provided not only employment opportunities but also free housing.[7]

Since 1860, Moscow's official borders have expanded six times, with high-rise apartment buildings covering much of the annexed territory.[8] In contrast, the area occupied by the Moscow Forest and Park Protection Belt—or greenbelt—did not expand proportionally. (fig. **5.8.2**) The 1935 General Plan of Moscow Reconstruction initially set the greenbelt area at 556 square miles (1,440 square kilometers). Though its area has not changed much since then, the greenbelt has become increasingly fragmented, experiencing a net conversion rate of 14.6 percent (into uses such as farms, parks, and forests) between 1991 and 2001.[9] Yet the greenbelt does retain extensive forested areas; these swaths are valued principally for their recreation areas and water resources. Timber harvesting is very limited.[10]

With its official population of 11.5 million in 2010, Moscow is the largest city not only in Russia but also in Europe. Moreover, Moscow is Russia's primary city, leading the nation in politics, economics, culture, and education, and capturing almost 14 percent of the country's GDP, 29 percent of all retail sales, and 30 percent of direct foreign

5.8.2 Dacha and garden outside Moscow

investment and tax receipts.[11] Given its overwhelming primacy, Moscow experienced tremendous in-migration through much of the twentieth century. The Soviet government tried to limit Moscow's growth by introducing a system of residence permits; however, the authorities did not limit the increase in population beyond the city limits.[12] As a result, migrants who were unable to obtain permits often settled in nearby satellite cities and commuted to workplaces in Moscow. By 1973, Moscow's daytime population had grown to 9 million, compared with only 7.4 million at night. The maximum radius of daily commuting varied between 18 to 24 miles (29 to 39 kilometers) from the center. Railways were the most widespread means of commuting, with suburbanites accounting for 91 percent of all rail passengers.[13]

With its extensive high-rise satellite developments near the urban edge, Moscow's suburbanization could be characterized as multinodal peripheral development. Although such patterns can be found in European and North American cities, Moscow's nodes tend to be larger and more densely populated. In contrast with most major European metropolitan areas, such as Paris, average population densities in Moscow's built-up areas generally increase as one moves outward from the city center to a radius of 20 miles (32 kilometers).[14]

Suburban locales that did not host satellite cities suffered from underinvestment

6 Henry W. Morton, "Housing in the Soviet Union," *Proceedings of the Academy of Political Science* 35, no. 3 (1984): 73.

7 Basile Kerblay, *Modern Soviet Society* (London: Methuen, 1983).

8 Grigory Ioffe and Tatyana Nefedova, "Environs of Russian Cities: A Case Study of Moscow," *Europe-Asia Studies* 50, no. 8 (1998): 1327; Olga Gritsai and Herman Van Der Wusten, "Moscow and St. Petersburg, a Sequence of Capitals, a Tale of Two Cities," *Geojournal* 51, nos. 1–2 (May 2000).

9 John P. Boentje and Mikhail Blinnikov, "Post-Soviet Forest Fragmentation and Loss in the Green Belt around Moscow, Russia (1991–2001): A Remote Sensing Perspective," *Landscape and Urban Planning* 82, no. 4 (October 2007): 208–21.

10 Andris Kleinhof, Lars Carlsson, and Mats-Olov Olsson, *The Forest Sector in Moscow Oblast* (Laxenburg, Austria: International Institute for Applied Systems Analysis, 1999).

11 Robert Argenbright, "Moscow on the Rise," *Geographical Review* 103, no. 1 (January 2013): 20–36; Mikhail Blinnikov et al., "Communities of the Moscow Green Belt: Newly Segregated Landscapes and the Suburban Russian Environment," *GeoJournal* 66, nos. 1–2 (June 2006): 66.

12 Pavel Polyan, Tatyana Nefedova, and Andy Treyvish, *Gorod I Derevnya v Evropeyskoy Rossii: Sto Let Peremen* [City and Village in European Russia: One Hundred Years of Changes] (Moscow: OGI, 2001).

13 Kerblay, *Modern Soviet Society*, 59.

14 Jesicca K. Graybill and Beth A. Mitchneck, "Cities of Russia," in *Cities of the World: World Regional Urban Development*, ed. Stanley D. Brunn, Maureen Hays-Mitchell, and

and often lacked basic utilities and services, such as schools and kindergartens, accessible public transportation, and grocery stores. For these reasons, most Soviets did not covet a privately owned house in a suburban area, and suburbanites were considered the least favored segment of society. The Soviet ideal home was an apartment in a modern high-rise near a subway or bus station: what American planners term *transit-oriented development*. Because of poor living and housing conditions, suburbanites often wanted to move to cities. But the government restricted movement of people into the largest cities, such as Moscow and Leningrad, in order not to overcrowd them with provincial migration.[15]

Living beyond the city limits was quite desirable in summer, however. Tired of being confined inside their small apartments, Soviet people fled the cities as soon as their summer vacations started. Before the 1950s, only a small group of Soviet elites had access to private dachas, which their employers or the state provided for them. Dachas were usually comfortable, two-story houses built on lots ranging in size from 0.30 to 1.25 acres (0.1 to 0.5 hectares).[16] The majority of Soviet citizens had to seek places in state sanatoria or rustic pioneer camps, or rent houses in small villages. Convinced that additional income made rural homeowners less enthusiastic about their jobs, the government banned the leasing of suburban houses, but then reversed course in the face of strong public dissatisfaction.[17]

In the 1950s, the government started to allocate land for collective orchards. Employees of state ministries and enterprises received parcels of land within the collectives to use for gardening, though not for constructing dwellings.[18] By the late 1960s, though, with loosened regulations and Soviet adoption of a two-day weekend, people started building small houses in the orchards.

Government regulations dictated the style, as well as size, of these seasonal residences. Although they were not convenient for permanent living, these tiny dwellings (which usually lacked electricity) were comfortable enough for weekends. In the 1980s, 189 collective orchards existed in the Moscow region, and by the 1990s, about 648,000 families had parcels of land in collective orchards. Most of the orchards were 5 to 25 miles (8 to 40 kilometers) from the city center. Initially, people usually commuted by train or bus, however, by the 1980s and 1990s, automobile commuting was very much on the rise. This seasonal, recreational suburbanization became a distinctively Soviet style of low-density living.[19]

That cities practically emptied during summer indicated that Soviet people preferred their tiny suburban parcels, with their small houses, to city apartments. Orchards and dachas provided fruits and vegetables for fall and winter consumption, thus shoring up family food supplies during the chronic Soviet food shortages. These places also represented a distinctive style of living, bringing contrast to monotonous lives and a sense of belonging to a local community. Dacha or orchard neighbors typically enjoyed stronger mutual ties than did neighbors in city apartments, for they were linked by a common sense of place that encompassed residence, land, and shared activities. The Soviet people's strong attachment to their dachas indicates that Western-style year-round suburban living might have proliferated had it been affordable and allowed by the government.

Post-Soviet Suburbanization Trends

Because the Soviet command-and-control economy had no need for a legal framework to guide planning and development, none was in place when the centrally planned economy collapsed. (In fact, an urban development code would not be

Donald L. Zeigler, 4th ed. (Lanham, MD: Rowman & Littlefield, 2008), 271.

15 Morton, "Housing in the Soviet Union."

16 Ioffe and Nefedova, "Environs of Russian Cities," 1336.

17 Aron J. Katsenelinboigen, *The Soviet Union: Empire, Nation, and System* (New Brunswick, NJ: Transaction Publishers, 1990).

18 Ioffe and Nefedova, "Environs of Russian Cities," 1337.

19 Stephen Lovell, *Summerfolk: A History of the Dacha, 1710–2000* (Ithaca, NY: Cornell University Press, 2003); Oleg Golubchikov and Nicholas Phelps, "Post-Socialist Post-Suburbia? Growth Machine and the Emergence of 'Edge City' in the Metropolitan Context of Moscow" (paper presented at the Third International Workshop on Post-Communist Urban Geographies for Actors Shaping Urban Change, Tartu, Estonia, 2009).

adopted until 1998.)[20] The stage was thus set for the Law on Privatization of Housing Stock, adopted in 1991, and the Basic Law on Housing Reform, adopted eight months later, to significantly change the economic, social, demographic, and aesthetic character of Russian cities. In just ten years, two-thirds of the housing stock was privatized, and the vast majority of dachas and collective orchards shifted into private ownership. In only six years, the number of families possessing parcels of land in collective orchards in the Moscow region had doubled, and the land area occupied by orchards increased from 75,000 acres to 270,000 acres.[21]

After 1992, Muscovites started purchasing houses in all accessible rural areas, even in such remote zones as Tver and Kaluga oblasts, situated 111 and 118 miles (179 and 190 kilometers) away from Moscow, respectively. But in contrast with most of their counterparts in the West, people who purchased suburban residences usually retained their apartments in Moscow. Moreover, and in contrast with other parts of Russia, most homeowners in the Moscow region gained ownership of their homes, but not of the land beneath them.

Among all types of Russian suburban dwellings, "cottages"—mass construction of these commenced in the 1990s—most closely resemble American single-family houses.[22] These structures hardly resemble the modest rural dwellings that the English word *cottage* typically connotes; rather, they are suburban, often very luxurious, single-family houses. Located mainly beyond the city limits, most of them are permanent residences, though some wealthy owners use them as second homes. These cottages do not replace dachas, although they occasionally occupy former dacha lands or are built within dacha communities. However, these cottages are year-round dwellings.

Initially, cottages were relatively cheap houses, built on 0.20 to 0.25 acre (0.08 to 0.10 hectare) plots of land, usually inside existing dacha settlements or on the edges of fields.[23] With the emergence of Russia's new wealth, however, cottages increased in size and value, and started to be grouped in clustered settlements with common infrastructure. The geography of cottages in the Moscow region reveals the sharp economic segmentation of post-Soviet Russian society. Suburban housing has become a matter of prestige, and an important part of the self-identification process for elites.[24] Increasingly, Moscow's suburban zones are hosting exclusive gated communities that contain the wealthiest Russians.[25]

Although the vast majority of suburban dwellers still live in comparatively affordable high-rise apartments, suburban settlements with single-family cottages and townhouses are proliferating in the Moscow region. Overall, regional population distribution has become increasingly uneven. Spatial concentration of suburban settlement is highest along highways and roads radiating from the Moscow Ring Road. With its concentration of cottage and townhouse communities, the west has become Moscow's most extensively suburbanized region. Suburban settlement also is very evident in other directions, particularly to the city's east and southeast. But in these areas, construction that is compact, high-density, high-rise, and more environmentally sustainable still predominates over single-family housing. In recent years, population densities in the west—a region characterized by lower-density residential developments—have not increased significantly compared to those in the east.

Businesses as well as residents are moving out of Moscow. In the suburbs, the increase in wealthy residents is playing a major part in the suburbanization of commerce. Two decades ago, suburbanites

20 Oleg Golubchikov, "Urban Planning in Russia: Toward the Market," *European Planning Studies* 12, no. 2 (2004):229–47.

21 Ioffe and Nefedova, "Environs of Russian Cities," 1337.

22 L. Alexander Norsworthy, *Russian Views of the Transition in the Rural Sector: Structures, Policy Outcomes, and Adaptive Responses* (Washington, DC: World Bank Publications, 2000).

23 Ioffe and Nefedova, "Environs of Russian Cities."

24 Alla Makhrova, "Dorogaya moya Moskva: Tsena prestija" [My Expensive Moscow: The Cost of Prestige], *Demoscope Weekly* 247–48 (March 22, 2006), accessed May 26, 2015, demoscope.ru /weekly/2006/0247 /tema01.php.

25 Blinnikov et al., "Gated Communities of the Moscow Green Belt."

typically commuted to the city for shopping. Now they have their own shopping centers, most of them situated close to highways. From 2000 to 2012, planning permissions for new shopping centers and other commercial facilities were readily granted, with a resultant nine hundred developments now lining the heavily congested, 68-mile-long (109-kilometer) Ring Road.[26]

Elite Highway Suburban Development

Surrounded by secluded developments comprising old dachas of the Soviet elite and new single-family houses and townhomes, Rublevo Uspenskoe Highway is one of the shortest federal highways radiating from the Moscow Ring Road. Its suburban developments form a residential area 18 miles (29 kilometers) long and about 4 miles (6 kilometers) wide.[27] Rublevo Uspenskoe Highway, or simply Rublevka, is one of Russia's best-known suburban areas.

Rublevka symbolizes the start of consumer-oriented lifestyles and Western-style suburbanization in Russia. The first of the new suburbanites—people with rapidly increasing incomes during the 1990s—fled Moscow to Rublevka. Since then, the area has become synonymous with wealth and prestige. Indeed, Rublevka's landscapes capture the rapid transformation of social structure in Russia, from a relatively egalitarian, classless society in Soviet times to a consumer-oriented society with sharp divisions between rich and poor.

Rublevka's distinct status has a long history. In 1664 Czar Alexey Romanov issued a decree prohibiting industrial enterprises in the upwind area to Moscow's west. As a result, Rublevka remains an area of the highest environmental quality in the Moscow region. Exceptional air and water quality, extensive green space, and access to the Moscow River and several reservoirs all have played key parts in securing Rublevka's elite residential status.

Today, Rublevo Uspenskoe Highway is the second-most-developed suburban area in the Moscow region after Novorizhskoe Highway.[28] Fifty percent of Rublevka's communities are inside a 12-to-18-mile (19 to 29 kilometers) band around the Moscow Ring Road. Rublevka is the most expensive residential area in the Moscow region. Land prices, which are not fixed, depend on such criteria as distance from Moscow and proximity to forest and water amenities. In September 2008 the value of 0.025 acres (0.01 hectares) of land in Barvikha, which is considered the most elite region of Rublevka, reached a record equivalent to $420,000, while the average price of 0.025 acres (0.01 hectares) in West Moscow Oblast was only $30,000.[29] The average size of an individual plot of land in Rublevka is 0.75 acres (0.30 hectares); the average house size, about 7,500 square feet (697 square meters). The minimum value of a cottage is $1 million; the maximum is $45 million.[30] Currently, the Rublevka real estate market is saturated, with a considerable portion of profits earned locally now coming from construction and operation of elite clubs, restaurants, fitness centers, and other businesses that serve its wealthy residents.

Rublevka is referred to as the "golden community" or "golden ghetto" because of its isolation from other residential areas. Fences and walls, often more than 10 feet (3 meters) high, surround houses protected by elaborate security systems. As land values started to increase in the 1990s, many residents sold their parcels and moved away; thus the vast majority of Rublevka's current inhabitants are the new elite. Residents include Russia's most well-known businesspeople and politicians, including President Vladimir Putin. Rublevka functions essentially as a highly select, closed club. Rapid devaluation

26 Anna Sokolova, "Podmoskovye: Torgovyi ray, stroitelniy bum, transportniy kollaps" [Moscow Oblast: Retail Heaven, Construction Boom, Transportation Collapse], *Forbes*, June 14, 2012, accessed May 26, 2015, www.forbes.ru /node/83124.

27 Yuri Medvedkov and Olga Medvedkov, "Upscale Housing in Post-Soviet Moscow and Its Environs," in *The Post-Socialist City: Urban Form and Space Transformations in Central and Eastern Europe after Socialism*, ed. Kiril Stanilov (Dordrecht, Netherlands: Springer, 2007), 256.

28 Alla Makhrova, "Organizovannye kottedzhnye poselki: Novyi tip poseleniy (na Primere Moskovskoy Oblasti)" [Organized Cottage Settlements: A New Type of Settlements (following the Example of the Moscow Area)], *Regionalnye Issledovaniya* 3.2, no. 17 (2008), www.shu.ru /pages/mag/RI_2008 _02(17).pdf.

29 "Tsena zemli na Rublevke dostigla $420 tysyach za sotku," [The Price of Land in Rublevka Reached $420,000 per 100M2], *Nedvijimost*, September 12, 2008, accessed May 26, 2015, https:// realty.newsru.com /article/12Sep2008/land.

30 "Stoimost' samogo dorogogo uchastka na Rublevke sostovlyaet $45 mln" [The Most Expensive Plot of Land in Rublevka Costs $45 Million], *Cottage. ru*, August 20, 2009, accessed May 26, 2015, www.cottage.ru /news/?id=211256.

of the ruble in 2014, resulting from decreasing oil prices and Western sanctions imposed upon Russia, significantly affected real estate values.

Middle-Income Suburbanization

Since the 1990s, migration to Moscow's new suburbs—those consisting principally of comfortable cottages—has been a privilege mainly of high-income elites. Single-family suburban housing remains costly and inaccessible because of high land value, developers' ambitions to gain as much profit as possible by constructing expensive dwellings on already expensive land, and potential buyers with very limited access to consumer credit. An additional barrier to middle-class home ownership is that residents are unable to claim income tax deductions for mortgage and real estate tax payments.

Who constitutes Moscow's middle class? The National Research University Higher School of Economics defines the average middle-class household as a three-person family where the head of household earns at least 180,000 rubles ($2,900), residing in a two-bedroom apartment, having a car less than eight years old, and possessing savings sufficient to support them for at least six months in case of loss of the main source of income.[31]

Recently, middle-income Muscovites have been provided greater opportunities to move to the suburbs. One of the most important factors driving this trend was the 2008 economic crisis, which dramatically lowered profits from suburban housing sales. As demand for expensive suburban houses dropped sharply, construction of many elite cottage settlements froze, and some projects halted sales.[32] In turn, real estate developers began to direct attention to "economy-class" suburban housing.[33]

Housing quality is directly related to price. Inferior construction materials

and poor insulation are typical in houses costing less than $200,000, while more expensive economy-class houses meet relatively higher construction standards and have access to more developed infrastructure, including roads, electricity, water, sewers, and social and educational facilities.[34]

Other important characteristics of middle-income suburban housing are distance from the city limits and dwelling size. Middle-class suburban housing is generally concentrated in areas more than 20 miles (32 kilometers) from Moscow city. The average size of an economy suburban dwelling generally does not exceed 1,180 to 1,620 square feet (110 to 150 square meters).[35]

Notable government housing programs include the Affordable and Comfortable Housing for Russian Citizens project. Designed to increase the proportion of suburban single-family housing, it provides funding for new housing, as well as favorable loan rates and other subsidies for young families[36] This and other government programs are in part prompted by the rather perplexing belief that a slowdown in high-rise construction will help alleviate traffic congestion. Middle-income, single-family-home suburbanization indeed has accelerated, suggesting that once they have the means to do so, many people are prepared to leave the center city. As a consequence, within a 30-mile (48 kilometer) radius of the central city, the amount of land available for new housing construction is decreasing rapidly.

Future Metropolitan Development

By the mid-1990s, Russia had entered a period of what the environmental studies expert Jonathan Oldfield characterized as government "de-ecologization."[37] Many critics of Russia's recent environmental policies are now concerned principally with natural resources management,

31 Marina Selina, "Tret' Moskvichey popala v sredniy klass" [Third of Muscovites Considered Middle-Class], *Open Economy*, April 10, 2014, accessed May 26, 2015, opec.ru/1693333 .html.

32 "Krizis ubil Rublevku" [Crisis Has Killed Rublevka], *1RRE, Pervyi Vserossiyskiy Analiticheskiy Portal O Nedvizimosti*, March 23, 2009, accessed May 26, 2015, www.1rre .ru/news/doc/32653.

33 Isolde Brade, Alla Makhrova, and Tatyana Nefedova, "Suburbanization of Moscow's Urban Region," in *Confronting Suburbanization: Urban Decentralization in Postsocialist Central and Eastern Europe*, ed. Kiril Stanilov and Luděk Sýkora (Chichester, UK: Wiley-Blackwell, 2014).

34 "Tseny na elitnuyu zagorodnuyu nedvizhimost Podmoskovya: Kottedzhy, taunhausy na novorizhskom Shosse" [Prices of Elite Suburban Real Estate in the Moscow Region: Cottages, Townhouses in Novorizhskoye Highway], *V Poselke*, last modified 2010, accessed May 26, 2015, www.vposelke.ru.

35 "Sredniy klass menyaet kvartiry v 'rezinovoy' Moskve na domiki v prigorode" [Middle Class Replaces Apartments in 'Rubber' Moscow with Houses in Suburbs], *B MOCKBE*, March 3, 2009, accessed May 26, 2015, newsmsk.com /article/03mar2009 /zagorod.

36 Komitet Podderzhki Reform Prezidenta Rossii, "Pochemu my govorim o nacionalnom proekte v jilishnoy sfere?" [Why Are We Talking about National Project in Housing?], Komitet Podderzhki Reform Prezidenta Rossii, December 21, 2007, accessed May 26, 2015, comreform.ru /projects/nacionalnyj -proekt-zhile.

37 Jonathan D. Oldfield, "Russia, Systemic

industrial pollution, and national parks and protected areas.[38] Our focus, by contrast, is on urban sustainability. Recent trends in Moscow's metropolitan development tend to affirm the historian Robert Bruegmann's thinking—that when given a practicable choice, the majority of citizens will choose to live in a suburban locale.[39] Jack Underhill, writing during the perestroika era, put it this way: The old spatial order was being supplanted by a new pattern that reflected "the long-suppressed and diverse aspirations of many peoples each striving to attain their own unique historic identity and 'sense of place.'"[40] Increasing wealth, widening income disparities, and limited government planning have yielded growing housing inequalities, and increased both traffic congestion and suburban sprawl.

Russia's urban land use—the compactness of its cities and its public transport services—has been compared favorably with that of Europe and Japan.[41] But this is the Soviet legacy: Moscow has hardly embraced forward-looking municipal actions like greater energy efficiency, improved public transportation, and reduced emissions of greenhouse gases. Russia has not, for example, followed France's lead in emphasizing sprawl reduction as a key component in reducing future greenhouse-gas emissions. Nor has it embraced the European practice of imposing substantial gas taxes; indeed, Russia's gas prices are among the lowest in the world outside the Organization of Petroleum Exporting Countries. And the Soviet Union's exemplary recycling and reuse practices—a response to the scarcity of many consumer goods—has been replaced by an increase in per capita waste generation and a looming landfill crisis for the Moscow metropolis.[42]

Russia—and metropolitan Moscow—is taking an approach that may not do nearly enough to contain American-style suburbanization and "exurbanization."

One sustainability bright spot is the redevelopment of brownfields as a means for meeting real-estate demands close to the central city.[43] But since the early 1990s, Moscow planning has been almost entirely about roads and hardly about expanding its historically magnificent, but now inadequate, mass transit system.[44] Indeed, Moscow's 2025 plan, approved in 2010, sets the stage for another construction boom, with historical buildings to be replaced by dozens of new high-rises. The plan provides for two million new parking spaces, but gives little weight to expanding public transportation.[45] In 2011 a 250 percent expansion of the City of Moscow's territory was authorized, through annexation of land to its southwest. While the full consequences of this development are yet to unfold, it raises significant questions about infrastructure, transportation, and potential erosion of the area's ecological function as the city's "green lungs."[46]

Conceivably, citizen concerns about development may become powerful enough to force changes in the planning system, moving it toward greater transparency and fairness. Moreover, given democracy's messiness and unpredictability, increased citizen engagement—which in any case is not the direction in which the central government is trending—would not necessarily ensure more ecological protection or more robust sustainability planning.

In contrast with this rather dystopic suburban planning trajectory is the unique Russian role of dachas as second homes and family farmlands, a distinctive phenomenon characterized variously as "seasonal suburbanization," "quasi-suburbanization," and "exurbanization."[47] Family-based agriculture is deeply embedded in Russian culture; with more than 40 percent of the Russian urban population having access to a dacha and up to 70 percent with access to some sort of agricultural plot, including those at dachas.[48]

Transformation, and the Concept of Sustainable Development: Environmental Politics," *Environmental Politics* 10, no. 3 (2001): 94–110.

38 Laura A. Henry, "Thinking Globally, Limited Locally," in *Environmental Justice and Sustainability in the Former Soviet Union*, ed. Julian Agyeman and Yelena Ogneva-Himmelberger (Cambridge, MA: MIT Press, 2009).

39 Robert Bruegmann *Sprawl: A Compact History* (Chicago: University of Chicago Press, 2005).

40 Jack A. Underhill, "Soviet New Towns, Planning and National Urban Policy: Shaping the Face of Soviet Cities," *Town Planning Review* 61, no. 3 (July 1, 1990): 263.

41 Jean Mercier, Long Term Transportation Policy in Russia in Response to the Kyoto Agreement (Kalingrad, Russia: Consortium for Economic Policy Research and Advice, 2004), accessed May 26, 2015, http://www.ibrarian.net /navon/paper/Long _Term_Transpor%C2 %ADtation_Policy _in_Russia_in_Resp .pdf?paperid=5382165.

42 Sally McGrane, "As Moscow's Landfills near Limits, Recyclers Do Whatever It Takes," *New York Times*, September 19, 2014, accessed May 26, 2015, www.nytimes. com/2014/09/19/world /europe/as-moscow -landfills-near-limits -recyclers-do-whatever -it-takes.html.

43 Isolde Brade, Alla Makhrova, and Tatyana Nefedova, "Suburbanization of Moscow's Urban Region," in *Confronting Suburbanization: Urban Decentralization in Postsocialist Central and Eastern Europe*, ed. Kiril Stanilov and Luděk Sýkora (Chichester: Wiley-Blackwell, 2014).

44 Keith Gessen, "Letter from Moscow: Stuck: The Meaning of the City's Traffic Nightmare,"

Dachas protect agricultural lands, provide local food, and serve as a comparatively low per capita land consumption alternative to American-style seasonal second homes or year-round suburban homes. But if dacha regions continue being converted to sprawling suburbs, as is already happening in some places, then the implications for sustainability are not encouraging. Yet there is encouraging recent evidence that the tide is turning back toward planting new gardens, as opposed to tearing out existing ones.[49] Metropolitan land-use planning that seeks to restrict low-density sprawl and also support family farming—by keeping dacha lands productive and well served by public transportation—can be a powerful means for promoting sustainable "dachascapes." Still, dachas and small farms must compete not only with housing sprawl but also with commercial agriculture, including large hog and poultry farms, with their attendant environmental impacts and local undesirability.[50]

Moscow's potential as a sustainable twenty-first-century metropolis is great indeed, precisely because suburban sprawl, though becoming pervasive, is still in its relatively early stages. Should the national and local governments choose to promote sound urban and regional planning, aggressively reduce greenhouse-gas emissions, expand public-transportation infrastructure, and support small-scale local food production, then Moscow may well distinguish itself as a leader in sustainable metropolitan development.

This essay is adapted from Robert J. Mason and Liliya Nigmatullina, "Suburbanization and Sustainability in Metropolitan Moscow," Geographical Review *101, no. 3 (2011): 316–33.*

New Yorker, August 2, 2010, 24–28, accessed May 26, 2015, www.newyorker.com/magazine/2010/08/02/stuck-3.

45 Kevin O'Flynn, "Critics Say Moscow's New Construction Plan a 'Death Sentence,'" *Radio Free Europe/Radio Liberty*, last modified May 25, 2010, accessed May 26, 2015, www.rferl.org/content/Critics_Say_Moscows_New_Construction_Plan_A_Death_Sentence/2032517.html.

46 Nikolai Volovich and Yevgenia Nikitina, "The Conflicts between the Systems of Public and Private Land Law," in *Land Management: Potential, Problems, and Stumbling Blocks*, ed. Erwin Hepperle et al. (Zurich: vdf Hochschulverlag AG, an der ETH, 2013), 195–210.

47 Golubchikov and Phelps, "Post-Socialist Post-Suburbia?," 4.

48 Melissa L. Caldwell, *Dacha Idylls: Living Organically in Russia's Countryside* (Berkeley: University of California Press, 2011); Louiza M. Boukharaeva and Marcel Marolie, *Family Urban Agriculture in Russia* (Cham, Switzerland: Springer, 2015), 23, 96.

49 Boukharaeva and Marolie, *Family Urban Agriculture in Russia.*

50 Grigory Ioffe and Tatyana Nefedova, "Land Use Changes in the Environs of Moscow," *Area* 33, no. 3 (September 2001): 273–86.

Residencial Genesis, Santana de Parnaíba, São Paulo, Brazil

Tamboré, Santana de Parnaíba, São Paulo, Brazil

5.9
TURBO-SUBURBANISM IN LUANDA

Anne Pitcher and Sylvia Croese

GOVERNANCE & POLICY CHALLENGES

NEOLIBERAL PROPERTY MARKETS

SOCIAL INEQUALITIES

TRANSPORT INFRASTRUCTURE

In the United States, suburbanization on the peripheries of cities from Detroit to Birmingham is linked to the rise of the middle class. Similarly, cities in the developing world appear to be replicating this process as the outskirts grow faster than the cores.[1] In sub-Saharan Africa, new suburban upper- and middle-class "landscapes of privilege" are sprouting up across the continent.[2] At the same time, governments from South Africa to Angola have embarked on social housing provision on city peripheries as well.

Several distinct features of suburbanization in Africa differentiate it from the United States and Europe. First, unlike the compartmentalization of residential and commercial spaces evident in Europe and the United States, these spaces are often interlaced and interwoven on the peripheries of Africa's rapidly growing cities. Although the initial purpose of a new suburb may be simply to provide housing, other activities such as beauty salons, small supermarkets, and street traders hawking cigarettes and SIM cards will likely appear within months after construction. Second, older suburban spaces are rapidly transforming from single-story, colonial buildings to the high-rises of today, while new residential or industrial developments contribute to emerging suburban centers beyond the city core. Third, as in China, the state (increasingly in partnership with the private sector) is often a central actor in shaping suburban growth, for instance, through the financing and design of suburbs for the purpose of relocating middle class as well as poor residents out of rapidly reconfiguring city centers.[3]

Urban Growth in Postconflict Luanda

The suburbanization of Luanda, the capital of Angola, exemplifies the larger processes occurring across Africa. Heterogeneous suburbs increasingly characterize Luanda's landscape, radiating north, south, and east from the city's historic center on Africa's west coast. A decade ago, Luanda's suburbs largely consisted of sprawling informal settlements—*musseques*—that were the result of an influx of displaced people from the countryside, owing to a long period of civil conflict following independence in 1975. Replicating the pattern seen in cities of other developing countries, there was little urban planning, or property and land management, in these areas during the war. The construction industry collapsed, and investment in the maintenance of the colonial housing stock or the construction of new houses came to a standstill. (fig. **5.9.1**)

Considered a safe haven during the war, the capital of Luanda saw its urban population grow from approximately 500,000 residents at independence to over 3 million inhabitants by 2002. Since the end of the war, this growth has continued unabated, reaching 6.5 million out of a total population in Angola of 24.4 million by 2014.[4] Between 2005 and 2010, estimates indicate that average urban growth of 5.79 percent per year in Luanda was higher than in any other southern African city.[5] Luanda is currently the fifth-largest metropolitan area in Africa after Cairo, Lagos, Kinshasa, and Johannesburg. The pressure that population growth has put on the city's precarious infrastructure and services means that 75 percent of city dwellers still live in unplanned informal housing and depend on the informal sector for their survival.[6]

Following the end of the war in 2002, political stability and an economic boom have attracted a growing number of skilled, educated foreigners and contributed to an emerging Angolan urban middle class. Until recently, increasing levels of oil production in Angola coupled with a rise in global oil prices from 2002 to 2008 and again from 2010 to 2014 allowed the government to rely on oil

1   "A Planet of Suburbs," *Economist*, last modified December 6, 2014, accessed May 1, 2015, http://www.economist.com/suburbs.

2   James S. Duncan and Nancy G. Duncan, *Landscapes of Privilege: The Politics of the Aesthetic in an American Suburb* (New York: Routledge, 2004).

3   Alan Mabin, Siân Butcher, and Robin Bloch, "Peripheries, Suburbanisms, and Change in Sub-Saharan African Cities," *Social Dynamics: A Journal of African Studies* 39, no. 2 (2013): 167–90.

4   Government of Angola, "Resultados preliminares do recenseamento geral da população e da habitação de Angola 2014" (Luanda: National Institute of Statistics, 2014).

5   UN-Habitat, *The State of African Cities 2008: A Framework for Addressing Urban Challenges in Africa* (Nairobi: UN-Habitat, 2008), 137.

6   Development Workshop, "The Case of Angola: Strengthening Citizenship through Upgrading of Informal Settlements Cross Country Initiative," Final Synthesis Report TF 0901110 presented to the World Bank, Luanda June 2011, 1.

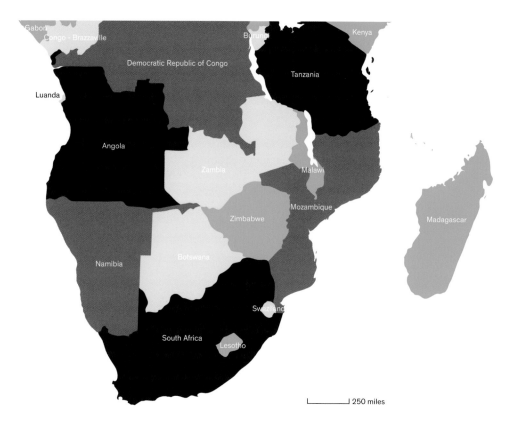

7   Sylvia Croese, "1 Million Houses? Angola's National Reconstruction and Chinese Engagement," in *China and Angola: A Marriage of Convenience?*, ed. Marcus Power and Ana Cristina Alves (Oxford: Pambazuka Press, 2012), 124–44.

8   Lucy Corkin, *Uncovering African Agency: Angola's Management of China's Credit Lines* (London: Ashgate, 2013).

9   M. Anne Pitcher, "Geo-Coded Dataset of Luanda's Suburban Developments" (unpublished maunscript, 2014).

10 Kai Voeckler, with Archis Interventions, *Prishtina Is Everywhere: Turbo-Urbanism: The Aftermath of a Crisis* (Berlin: Parthas, 2008).

250 miles

5.9.1 Map of Luanda, the capital of Angola, on the West African coast

revenues to invest in housing and public infrastructure projects as part of postwar reconstruction. In an effort to improve urban living conditions and to address a substantial housing backlog in the context of massive urban growth, the government pledged in 2008 to build one million houses across the country.[7] Over the past few years, an assemblage of international and national private-sector actors have arisen to acquire land, plan developments, undertake construction, and conclude real estate transactions.

The presence of Chinese companies and workers in housing investment and construction is particularly noteworthy, but other foreign companies are also engaged in urban and suburban development. More than fifty state-owned and four hundred private Chinese companies were operating in Angola by 2010, with sixty thousand to seventy thousand Chinese workers, shopkeepers, traders, managers, and company directors residing in the country. By 2011, China had provided about US\$14.5 billion US dollars in credit to Angola through the China Export Import Bank, the China Development Bank and the Industrial and Commercial Bank of China, largely to finance infrastructure and construction projects.[8] In return, almost half of Angola's oil production is exported to China, making it China's second-largest oil supplier after Saudi Arabia.

Other countries have also extended lines of credit to Angola for housing, infrastructural development, and reconstruction. As of 2015, firms from China, Brazil, Portugal, Israel, and elsewhere were financing, designing, and building nearly ninety housing or mixed residential, office, and commercial projects in Luanda's center and suburbs.[9] In that sense, Luanda's postwar growth mirrors the "turbo-urbanism" that characterized Prishtina after the end of the war in Kosovo.[10]

11 Government of Angola,
 *Angola 2025: Angola,
 a Country with a Future:
 Sustainability, Equity,
 and Modernity* (Luanda:
 Ministry of Planning,
 2007).

5.9.2 The redeveloped Bay of Luanda in Luanda, the capital of Angola

Suburban Planning and Antiplanning

In theory, postwar city planning largely perpetuates colonial plans for the expansion and deconcentration of city growth. It is rooted in functionalist, growth-pole thinking and driven by top-down, technocratic approaches to city planning, with little regard for the needs of the poor. This viewpoint is illustrated in "Angola 2025," Angola's official vision for the future, which largely follows a late-colonial master plan, adopted just before independence in 1975, for the expansion of the capital into small satellites around the city center. The urban vision articulated by "Angola 2025" is expected to transform Luanda into a true world-class city, or "a modern, efficient, creative and unified metropolis" that connects the country to the outside world.[11] To realize this aspiration, urban redevelopment has consisted of the establishment of the old colonial center on the coast as the political and business heart of the city. Dozens

of skyscrapers occupied by oil companies, banks and government ministries, have arisen in the city's *baixa*, the old colonial city center, over the last decade. Redevelopment of the bay of Luanda was mostly completed in 2012. A four-lane bridge links up a new, walkable seaside promenade lined by palm trees with the Island of Luanda, a peninsula historically home to a fishing community, followed by the informal settlement of internally displaced people during the war. Following their removal, the island mainly sports trendy beach bars and restaurants for a high-end clientele. (fig. **5.9.2**)

Farther down the coast, the dome of the new National Assembly building and a gigantic rocket-shaped mausoleum honoring the first president of Angola, Agostinho Neto, telegraph the importance of political power across the landscape. Both are part of the politico-administrative center that is being redeveloped. In the future, it will be connected by road to the southern part of the city, Luanda Sul. A new ring road extends the city toward the southeast, accompanied by the construction of large-scale housing settlements, officially designated as new *centralidades*—centralities—such as Kilamba, Zango, and Cacuaco, while the government is targeting the northern part of the city for a large-scale upgrading program.

Whereas an overarching modernist vision appears to drive urban redevelopment, in practice, planning decisions regarding where to locate peripheral sites for housing or commercial development follow multiple disconnected logics. Politically, housing policy reflects the state's desire for legitimacy in the aftermath of a destructive civil conflict. On the one hand, this is articulated through the construction of new suburbs in order to serve a growing, ill-housed but politically strategic middle class. On the other hand, the government has chosen to upgrade—rather than clear—older, dilapidated areas such as Cazenga and Sambizanga, because they were the birthplaces of urban resistance against the Portuguese during the colonial period. Economically, new suburbs also embody the efforts of domestic business interests and political elites with international connections to profit from housing provision. Here, low land values and informal land occupation by the poor favor the selection of peripheral sites for clearance and new construction. Spatially, the location of the new suburbs to the east and southeast of the new ring road reflects the redesign of the outdated colonial politico-administrative borders of the city and greater metropolitan area. Moreover, the locations, compositions, and socioeconomic conditions of suburbs embody indigenous influences and preferences, as well as design styles from abroad and the influence of New Urbanism. Thus, despite the existence of a modernist planning agenda,

these multiple logics, actors, and interests have produced a polycentric, highly differentiated, and unequal city, which the urbanists Stephen Graham and Simon Marvin have termed "splintering urbanism" in their examination of other cities.[12] The landscape of Luanda now boasts highly networked luxury enclaves, business parks, financial hubs, and special economic zones, but informal settlements, ordinary spaces, and internet deserts also define the city.

Luxury Housing Compounds

Working in tandem with the private sector, the Angolan state has spearheaded the expansion and construction of high-end suburban developments with diverse housing models and residential designs. Under a public-private partnership with the Provincial Government of Luanda, the Brazilian construction and engineering firm Odebrecht built the country's first luxury residential compound, Atlântico Sul, in Talatona, as part of the development of Luanda Sul.[13] The construction of Angola's first shopping center, Belas Shopping, and the residential and business complex, Belas Business Park, followed.[14] Smaller, gated communities that mimic locations worldwide then proliferated. We now see the single-family homes with matching garages and swimming pools in the back garden associated with Alphaville (outside São Paulo, Brazil) or Kendall (in Florida) reflected in Talatona, which is becoming its own city. Condominiums in this zone replicate the exclusivity that typifies gated communities in Brazil, Dubai, or the United States. They resegregate urban space in Angola along class lines, rather than the racial lines of the colonial period.[15] (fig. **5.9.3**)

Purchase prices for high-end units in some exclusive gated enclaves in Talatona can run into the millions of dollars. Admission to these luxury developments is limited to those who have a car and

12 Stephen Graham and Simon Marvin, *Splintering Urbanism: Networked Infrastructures, Technological Mobilities, and the Urban Condition* (London: Routledge, 2001).
13 Paul Jenkins, Paul Robson, and Allan Cain, "Luanda City Profile," *Cities* 19, no. 2 (2002): 139–50.
14 "Global Presence: Talatona Residencial," *Odebrecht*, accessed December 31, 2014, http://www.odebrecht.com/presenca-no-mundo/en/home.
15 Cristina Udelsmann Rodrigues, "Angolan Cities: Urban (Re) Segregation?," in *African Cities: Competing Claims on Urban Spaces*, ed. Francesca Locatelli and Paul Nugent (Leiden: Brill, 2009), 37–53.

5.9.3 Talatona, a luxury enclave development south of the capital

16 Anne Pitcher and Sylvia Croese, field work in Luanda, Angola, June 2014.
17 Sylvia Croese, "Post-war State-Led Development in Angola: The Zango Housing Project in Luanda as a Case Study," (PhD diss., Stellenbosch University, 2013).

work for oil companies or the state. Of course, to purchase a freestanding home with a landscaped yard or a condo with amenities such as a pool or fitness center, buyers must also be able to finance their purchases either through their employers, from their own savings, or through access to credit.[16] However, credit is extremely rare, as mortgages are not yet common in Angola, even among those with formal jobs.

Social Housing and the Chinese Pop-Up Model

The growing differentiation in residential property markets evidenced in Luanda Sul is reinforced by the government's housing policy. There is little effort to make subsidized financing available to low- and middle-income families in order to assist with self-help building. Instead there is a focus on direct housing provision to the poor; for the middle class, state subsidies for housing purchase are restricted to a very limited number of buyers. Moreover, many new government-sponsored housing

projects are consciously targeted at different socioeconomic strata of society, as illustrated by the examples of social housing in Zango and middle-class housing in Kilamba.

In Zango, the largest social housing project in Luanda financed by the state, thirty thousand houses have been built to accommodate residents displaced from areas in the city targeted for urban redevelopment. Odebrecht has also been the main contractor for the construction of this social housing southeast of the city. In terms of its typology, social housing in Luanda resembles the semidetached housing units provided by the South African government to house South Africa's poor under the Reconstruction and Development Programme. Lined up row after row, quarter after quarter, houses in Zango are painted in different colors from green to yellow and orange to purple as they stretch out for miles along the main road.[17] (fig. **5.9.4**)

Apart from social housing, which mainly consists of basic shelter for low-income groups, there has been an increasing focus on the construction of mixed-use developments following the Chinese mass housing model. Several of these are designed to serve the middle class. Perhaps the most infamous is Kilamba, located some 16 miles (25 kilometers) from the historic city center. When fully occupied, Kilamba will house nearly one hundred thousand middle-class Angolans in a small city that mimics many of the Chinese instant cities on which it was modeled. Funded by a $3.5 billion oil-backed line of credit and built by CITIC, a Chinese state-owned construction firm, Kilamba follows a standard, modernist grid pattern of development. Initially ridiculed by journalists as a ghost city when it remained empty for a year after its grand opening by the president of Angola, the project's twenty thousand three- to five-bedroom units are now filling up after the government lowered prices and made houses available through a state-subsidized mortgage scheme designed for Kilamba. Currently, fifty-three thousand residents live in twenty-four blocks containing a total of 710 buildings of four, eight, and twelve stories, as well as schools, basketball courts, and common green space.[18] Shops and restaurants have already started to occupy the ground floors of designated buildings in each block.[19] (fig. **5.9.5**)

5.9.4 Zango, a social housing development south of the capital, designed and constructed by Odebrecht, a Brazilian firm

18 Joaquim Israel Marques, president of Kilamba, interviewed by Anne Pitcher, Casimiro Costa, and José Tiago, Kilamba, Luanda, Angola, June 19, 2014.
19 Allan Cain, "African Urban Fantasies: Past Lessons and Emerging Realities," *Environment and Urbanization* 26, no. 2 (2014): 1–7; M. Anne Pitcher and Marissa Moorman, "City Building in Post-Conflict, Post-Socialist Luanda: Burying the Past with Phantasmagorias of the Future," in *African Cities Reader III: Land, Property, Value,* ed. Ntone Edjabe and Edgar Pieterse (Vlaeberg: Chimurenga and African Centre for Cities, 2015).
20 Paul Robson and Sandra Roque, *Here in the City There Is Nothing Left Over for Lending a Hand: In Search of Solidarity and Collective Action in Peri-urban Areas in Angola* (Guelph, Canada: Development Workshop, 2001).

Informal Settlements

Yet the majority of city and suburban dwellers still live in overcrowded but vibrant informal settlements, which pepper the landscape in and around the old city core and the new suburbs. Initially, many occupied the empty houses left behind by the Portuguese settlers, as well as land in informal settlements predating independence. Over time, new arrivals to the city built their homes at increasing distances from the city center on whatever vacant space they could find: farm land, but also on former waste dumps, such as those in Boavista, an informal settlement close to the harbor of Luanda.[20]

Thus different typologies of informal settlements can be distinguished in Luanda, depending on when and where they emerged. Some are laid out according to minimal planning regulations; those houses are built with permanent construction materials such as blocks and cement, or have been expanded or upgraded over time. More recent peripheral settlements are less formally organized, with

5.9.5 Kilamba, a new mixed-use, suburban development 30 kilometers (18.6 miles) from Luanda, built by the Chinese Firm, CITIC

21 Development Work-shop and Centre for Environment and Human Settlements, "Terra Reforma Sobre a Terra Urbana em Angola no Period Pós-guerra: Pesquisa, Advocacia e Políticas de Desenvolvimento, Development Workshop," Occasional Paper, no. 6, Development Workshop, Luanda, 2005.

22 Sandra Roque, "Cidade and Bairro: Classifi-cation, Constitution and Experience of Urban Space in Angola," *Social Dynamics* 37, no. 3 (2011): 332–48.

23 Development Workshop, "The Case of Angola: Strengthening Citizen-ship through Upgrading of Informal Settlements Cross Country Initiative."

24 Chloé Buire, "The Dream and the Ordinary: An Ethnographic Investigation of Sub-urbanisation in Luanda," *African Studies* 73, no. 2 (2014): 290–312.

more flimsy construction materials. In the absence of public support or public goods provision, all city dwellers—whether in the center or on the periphery—have had to adopt private solutions to address the deficiencies in public services. In the city center, residents have come to rely on purchased generators and water pumps to make up for the degraded colonial electricity and water networks. In more peripheral settlements, an ever-growing number of residents accesses water and electricity through informal connections and private vendors at high cost.[21]

These informal settlements "inter-rupt" the city rather than exist in confined, enclosed spaces, separate from the central business district or the suburbs. In spite of efforts to create zones of exclusivity for the wealthy, Luanda's rich and poor live closely together, with luxury air condi-tioned office buildings and new apartment blocks often standing side by side with dilapidated colonial villas or informal shacks. During their daily commutes, drivers of the newest, most expensive SUVs buy goods from vendors standing on potholed roads or alongside major new expressways. Like many governments elsewhere, the Angolan government prefers the eradication of informal settle-ments and their replacement by orderly new cities, rather than the in situ upgrad-ing of services and infrastructures in what are perceived as disorderly and unorga-nized slums.[22] This approach means that most residents of informal settlements have benefited little from urban develop-ment interventions, with local land and property markets remaining largely informal, and access to affordable housing finance limited.[23] (fig. **5.9.6**)

Life in Luanda's New Suburbs

Suburban development in Luanda is far-reaching in scale and very ambitious. While it has not met the desperate need for housing by low-income residents, it has produced new forms and imagi-naries of suburban life.[24] As in Brazil, the association of homeownership with a dream come true is a ubiquitous trope.

5.9.6 *Musseques* (lit. "sandy places"), informal settlements near Luanda

25 Allan Cain, Sylvia
    Croese, and Anne
    Pitcher, "New Housing
    in Luanda," Household
    Survey, Development
    Workshop and the
    University of Michigan,
    June–August 2014.
26 M. Anne Pitcher, "Cars
    Are Killing Luanda:
    Cronyism, Consumerism,
    and Other Assaults
    on Angola's Post-War,
    Capital City," in *Cities
    in Contemporary Africa*,
    ed. Martin J. Murray
    and Garth A. Myers
    (New York: Palgrave
    Macmillan, 2007),
    173–200.

Television and newspaper advertisements extol the virtues of marble entrances and five-bedroom mansions in exclusive neighborhoods. Even at the highest levels, the official housing policy is called "My dream, my house." In a recent survey, residents in the new middle-class suburb of Kilamba, when asked why their new apartment was "better" than where they lived before, answered that one reason was "it's mine," "I own it." Kilamba residents were also overwhelmingly satisfied with the quality of their new homes, the neighborhood, the proximity to schools and the schools' quality, the availability of electricity and water, and other amenities.[25]

But the enchantment declined when asked about commute times. While the majority of respondents expressed satisfaction or partial satisfaction with the distance to work, the majority of them commuted more than an hour each way. Twenty percent spent between two and three hours to get to work. Owing to the lack of investment in public transportation, most suburban development is predicated on and privileges the car.

Yet traffic jams and hours lost in the car undercut the fantasy of middle-class suburban living.[26] As the urban core gets redeveloped, those with sufficient funds might drift back to the historic city center, while those without will continue to pursue their dream for a house of their own.

Future Challenges
Suburbs across the African continent are rapidly transforming. Economic and natural population growth, aided by government intervention, increasingly reconfigures urban peripheries into a mix of sprawling formal and informal development. The accelerated suburban development that has taken place in Luanda over the last decade reflects both the diversity and the demand exhibited elsewhere in cities such as Lagos, Accra, Maputo, and Nairobi. The pace, location, and timing of construction in the suburbs do not represent a rejection or abandonment of the inner city as they did in the United States during the 1960s. Rather, they are a consequence of overcrowding and insufficient housing in the city center.

In that respect, the redesign of the urban core currently proceeds in tandem with expansion of the peri-urban and suburban areas. Owing to the delays in urban infrastructural expansion occasioned by Angola's long conflict, demand for decent housing by all socioeconomic groups is likely to remain high for the foreseeable future.

Top-down and state-led suburban growth has improved the quality of life for some by increasing the formal housing stock and providing packaged subdivisions with amenities from basketball courts to health clinics for the middle class. These new, organized suburban spaces are contributing to the emergence of new imaginaries and "consumption-related identities" for elites and the middle class.[27] Cellphones are ubiquitous; cars, televisions, and computers are common in middle-class neighborhoods, and access to the internet is rapidly expanding, aided by the efforts of skilled computer technicians from Spain, Portugal, and other European countries who have moved to Luanda looking for work in the wake of the 2008 global financial crisis.

Revenue from the sale of oil has allowed the Angolan state to drive and reshape suburban expansion in unprecedented ways; yet the assumption that these efforts adequately address the postwar needs of urban residents is misplaced. Current levels of social housing provision, or state financing for Chinese-style pop-up cities are both inadequate and unsustainable over the long term. Even in Luanda, where most expenditure is targeted, no more than a small fraction of the population is experiencing the benefits of new suburbs and centralities. The majority of urban residents encounter much more precarious living conditions, with inadequate shelter and insecure rights to housing and land. In addition, residents in many other cities of Angola confront similar or worse conditions.

Unless the provision of housing can be distributed more widely, the heterogeneous, fragmented nature of suburbs will continue.

Importantly, the investment in suburban residential development needs to be matched by investments in infrastructure and services, such as public transport. As in the past, Luanda's suburbs continue to be plagued by limits to the capacity of public utility companies and local governments to deliver basic services and manage local land and property markets. The low levels of autonomy, capacity, and resources of local governments mean that requests for services or adequate infrastructure by those without connections get snarled up in bureaucratic backlogs and red tape. The lack of a formal property market, the scarcity of affordable housing finance, and long commute times often mean that only the well-connected fully enjoy the advantages and amenities of new housing developments.

Furthermore, oil prices are volatile and, at the time of writing, just experienced precipitous decline. Oil revenues, therefore, may not provide a reliable source of financing in the future. The Angolan government has made repeated pledges to diversify the economy away from oil, but as the African politics expert Ricardo Soares de Oliveira notes in a recent publication, "There is no sign of structural transformation and the economy's full possibilities remain untapped."[28] Angola so far does not have a strong domestic construction industry and continues to import most of its cement from abroad. In the absence of alternative revenues, state-led housing provision will likely slow down considerably. Going forward, the way that the government addresses these issues will determine the degree to which residents must rely on private and informal solutions to address public failure, and to fulfill the aspirations of suburban living.

27 Paul Knox, "Vulgaria: The Re-Enchantment of Suburbia," *Opolis: An International Journal of Suburban and Metropolitan Studies* 1, no. 2 (2005): 33–46.

28 Ricardo Soares de Oliveira, *Magnificent and Beggar Land: Angola since the Civil War* (London: C. Hurst and Company, 2015), 210.

5.10
THE DARK SIDE OF SUBURBIA
ISRAELI SETTLEMENTS OF THE WEST BANK

Rafi Segal

GOVERNANCE
& POLICY
CHALLENGES

SOCIAL
INEQUALITIES

The bright lights of the Jewish hilltop suburbs shine above the darkened Palestinian villages and towns in the valleys of Samaria and Judea. (fig. **5.10.1**) In its contrast of light and darkness, the Samarian night reveals more than it hides: the illuminated urban layout of the Israeli settlements and their connected road systems shows itself as a network cast onto the mountains and hilltops of the occupied territories of the West Bank. This network is one of power and surveillance, of one population's control over another. At night, the other side of what by day might seem like a harmless suburban environment of single-family detached homes is exposed as an invasive and violent intrusion on the landscape and livelihoods of the Palestinians it seeks to suppress.

In 2003 Eyal Weizman and I published *A Civilian Occupation: The Politics of Israeli Architecture*, a collection of essays, photos, and plans that explore how architecture, urban planning, and landscape design have had a hand in shaping the Israeli-Palestinian conflict.[1] The project viewed the landscape and built environment of the occupied territories of the West Bank through the conventional tools of urban development: infrastructure and housing. It construed the landscape as a battlefield—a spatial matrix of forces in a continuous process of transformation, adaptation, construction, and obliteration. We argued that in this environment, where architecture and planning had been systematically instrumentalized as executive arms of the Israeli state, planning decisions directly serviced national and geopolitical objectives to seize land and exercise control over the Palestinian population. Unfortunately, these arguments remain relevant today. Some of these issues, and a description of a selection of settlement plans, follow. (fig. **5.10.2**)

5.10.1 Night view of the Cross-Samaria Highway with the settlement Barkan on the hilltop in the background

The Suburban Model on the West Bank

The first Jewish settlements of the West Bank were established in the Jordan Valley during the early years of Israel's occupation, 1967–77. Fifteen agricultural villages (kibbutzim and moshavim) were then built under the Labor government's rule to establish a secure border with Jordan. Following the political turnabout of 1977, which saw the right-wing Likud Party rise to power, the political climate in Israel changed. Settlements began to be established in the mountain region in and around the Palestinian cities and villages, with the intention of annexing the area to prevent territorial concessions. It was during this time that a suburban model replaced the agricultural settlement as the occupation's prevailing urban typology. These communities were designed, and often marketed, as extended suburbs of the larger Jerusalem metropolitan area. Much of the West Bank began to be considered a part of the sacred, biblical landscape associated with Jerusalem. As Weizman explains, "The extension of the city's 'holiness' to the new suburbs was conceived as part of Israeli attempts to generate widespread public acceptance of the newly annexed territories."[2]

The mountain peaks of the West Bank easily lend themselves to state seizure. Land ownership has been hard to ascertain ever since the Ottoman rule of Palestine, when residents paid tax only on the lands they cultivated. These lands later reverted to private ownership. Areas determined to be under

1   Rafi Segal and Eyal Weizman, eds., *A Civilian Occupation: The Politics of Israeli Architecture* (London: Verso and Babel, 2003).
2   Eyal Weizman, "The Subversion of Jerusalem's Sacred Vernaculars," in *The Next Jerusalem: Sharing the Divided City*, ed. Michael Sorkin (New York: Monacelli Press, 2002), 132.

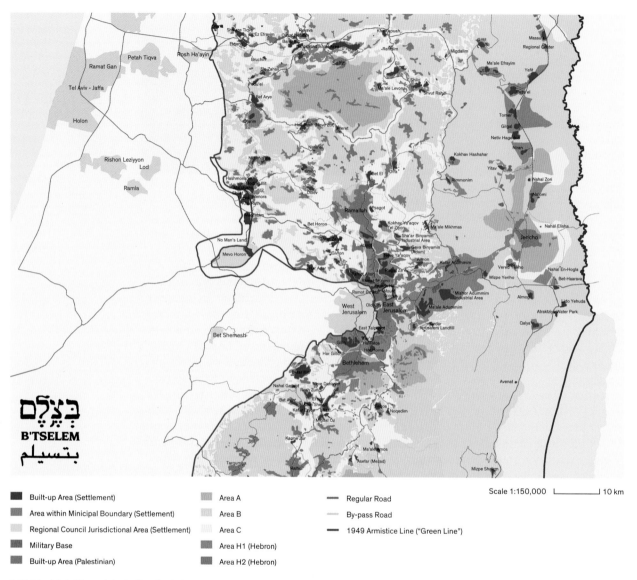

■ Built-up Area (Settlement)	▨ Area A	━ Regular Road
▨ Area within Minicipal Boundary (Settlement)	▨ Area B	━ By-pass Road
▨ Regional Council Jurisdictional Area (Settlement)	▨ Area C	━ 1949 Armistice Line ("Green Line")
▨ Military Base	▨ Area H1 (Hebron)	
▨ Built-up Area (Palestinian)	▨ Area H2 (Hebron)	

Scale 1:150,000 ⊢————⊣ 10 km

5.10.2 Jewish Settlements in the West Bank, Built-up Areas and Land Reserves, May 2002. Section from map of Israeli settlements in the West Bank. B'Tselem, Eyal Weizman. Reprinted from Rafi Segal, Eyal Weizman, *A Civilian Occupation: The Politics of Israeli Architecture.*

continuous cultivation remained in private Palestinian ownership, and the rest was declared state property. Since Palestinian-cultivated areas are mainly located in valleys and along mountain slopes where agriculturally suitable soils exist, the barren hilltops, along with isolated plots and discontinuous islands around the mountain peaks, became easy targets for annexation by the state.[3]

These hilltop areas became the sites of Jewish settlements, usually as dormitory communities. Assisted by

considerable government subsidies, a settler could purchase a newly built, single-family detached home for the price of a small apartment in Tel Aviv. These suburbs offered newly constructed homes and roads, along with plenty of space, clean air, and panoramic hilltop views. It was all less than half an hour away from the city centers of either Jerusalem or Tel Aviv.

Most of these settlements are structured in a concentric layout, with the topographical contours of the mountain

3   Yehezkel Lein and Eyal Weizman, *Land Grab: Israel's Settlement Policy in the West Bank* (Jerusalem: B'tselem, 2002).

retraced as lines of infrastructure. The roads are laid out in rings around the summit, with water, sewage, and electricity lines buried beneath them. Land is divided into equal, repetitive lots, each containing a single-family house sited along the road, and facing the landscape. While the ideal form for these suburbs is the circle, in reality the plan is distorted, as it has had to adapt to irregular topography and the form and extents of available state land.

Vision plays a key role in every aspect of the design. The arrangement of homes around the summits directs the residents' gaze outward. This produces sight lines for surveying the landscape to attain different forms of power: strategic, in overlooking main traffic arteries; controlling, by watching over Palestinian towns and villages; and defensive, in overlooking the immediate surroundings and approach roads. The settlements are, in effect, optical devices designed to exercise control through supervision and surveillance.

The spatial layout of these settlements—the arrangement of infrastructure and distribution of house lots—reveals the design principles and strategies at play. (fig. **5.10.3**) The diagrams presented here are abstracted urban plans of West Bank Jewish settlements in which the roads are rendered in black, housing lots in dark gray, and commercial or public land uses in medium gray (these only appear in a few settlements) and the lightest gray. A contour line depicts the extent of the municipal boundaries of each settlement; included within these borders are areas that have already been designated for future expansion as part of the master plan. The light gray areas reveal where these settlements will grow in the future. The three primary urban elements that have created this typology—roads, single-family lots, and developable land—are the core elements that make up suburbia.

The Suburb as Civilian Fortification

When examined as a series, these plans further highlight the adaptability of this typology to diverse topographical conditions and the availability of land. The concentric layout of ring roads and culs-de-sac, where the roads tend to follow the horizontal topographical lines or the mountain ridges, allows a maximum outer exposure to the house lots; the plans act as two-dimensional imprints of the spatial form of the hilltops they occupy. From a planning perspective, their design is not efficient as an attempt to minimize the ratio between infrastructure and the number of houses, or to concentrate residential development in one area. On the contrary, the roads often far exceed what's required. Housing lots are scattered along the edges of settlements to grab and occupy as much land as possible, and to maximize the settlers' field of vision over the territory below.

Through their shared road system and geographic location, the settlements form a large-scale network of civilian fortifications that tactically survey territory and enact national security goals under the guise of suburban living. By placing settlers across the landscape, the Israeli government administers power not only through agencies of state power and control such as the police and military; it also "drafts" civilians to inspect, control, and subdue the Palestinian population.

On the West Bank, the suburb, that most ubiquitous of urban typologies, rears its dark side. It transforms the landscape into a terrifying weapon of suppression that permits one world to impose its power on another. As this visual and physical network continues to expand, multiple separations and boundaries are continuously imposed on the world below (the Palestinians), while strengthening the connections between the Israeli hilltop settlements above. And as individual settlements expand, their presence gradually

Tapuah
Area: Nablus
Population: 350
Established: 1978
Location on map: F6
Latitude: 650
Type: Community
    Settlement
Planner: M. Ravid

Giva'at-Ze'ev
Area: Ramallah
Population: 10300
Established: 1983
Location on map: E9
Latitude: 760
Type: Local Council
Planner: Nehemya Gorali

Mizpe-Yeriho
Area: Jericho
Population: 1200
Established: 1978
Location on map: G9
Latitude: 160
Type: Community
    Settlement
Planner: The Settlement
    Planning Department

Talmon
Area: Ramallah
Population: 1200
Established: 1989
Location on map: E8
Latitude: 560
Type: Community
    Settlement
Planner: A. Wilenberg,
    Gile'adi

Na'aran

Ma'on
Area: Hebron
Population: 250
Established: 1981
Location on map: E14
Latitude: 770
Type: Community
    Settlement

Ofarim

Qedar
Area: Jerusalem
Population: 450
Established: 1985
Location on map: G10
Latitude: 440
Type: Community
    Settlement
Planner: The Settlement
    Planning Department

Tomer
Area: Jordan Valley
Population: 300
Established: 1976
Location on map: H7
Latitude: -220
Type: Moshav
Planner: Yiga'al Levy

Oranit
Area: Jenin
Population: 5000
Established: 1985
Location on map: D6
Latitude: 140
Type: Local Council

Noqedim
Area: Bethlehem
Population: 600
Established: 1982
Location on map: F11
Latitude: 570
Type: Community
    Settlement
Planner: The Settlement
    Division of the Jewish
    Agency

Sal'it
Area: Tul Karem
Population: 500
Established: 1977
Location on map: D4
Latitude: 260
Type: Moshav

Kochav-Ya'acov
Area: Ramallah
Population: 2200
Established: 1984
Location on map: F8
Latitude: 765
Type: Community
    Settlement
Planner: Eyal Itzki

Na'ale
Area: Ramallah
Population: 150
Established: 1985
Location on map: D8
Latitude: 430
Type: Community
    Settlement
Planner: A. Wizenthal

Yafit
Area: Jordan Valley
Population: 150
Established: 1980
Location on map: H2
Latitude: -245
Type: Moshav

Ma'ale Levona
Area: Nablus
Population: 500
Established: 1982
Location on map: F6
Latitude: 734
Type: Community
    Settlement
Planner: Rachel Walden

Bet-Horon
Area: Ramallah
Population: 750
Established: 1977
Location on map: E8
Latitude: 620
Type: Community
    Settlement
Planner: The Settlement
    Planning Department

Rimmonim
Area: Jericho
Population: 500
Established: 1977
Location on map: G8
Latitude: 680
Type: Moshav
Planner: The Settlement
    Planning Department

Ateret
Area: Ramallah
Population: 300
Established: 1981
Location on map: E7
Latitude: 720
Type: Community
    Settlement
Planner: S. Melman, A.
    Kaplan

Zufim
Area: Tul Karem
Population: 850
Established: 1989
Location on map: D5
Latitude: 145
Type: Community
    Settlement
Planner: Eilon Meromi,
    Gertner-Gibor-Koms

Rechan
Area: Jenin
Population: 120
Established: 1977
Location on map: E2
Latitude: 375
Type: Community
    Settlement
Planner: A. Inbar, M. Ravid

5.10.3 Plans of settlements in the West Bank, reprinted from Segal and Weizman, *A Civilian Occupation*

Revava
Area: Salfit
Population: 500
Established: 1991
Location on map: E6
Latitude: 415
Type: Community
    Settlement
Planner: M. Ravid

Nofim
Area: Nablus
Population: 400
Established: 1980
Location on map: E5
Latitude: 380
Type: Community
    Settlement
Planner: Rachel Walden

Elazar
Area: Bethlehem
Population: 200
Established: 1975
Location on map: E11
Latitude: 910
Type: Community
    Settlement
Planner: The Settlement
    Planning Department

Hamra
Area: Jordan Valley
Population: 150
Established: 1971
Location on map: H15
Latitude: -55
Type: Moshav

Ro'i
Area: Jordan Valley
Population: 150
Established: 1976
Location on map: H4
Latitude: 30
Type: Moshav

Hinanit
Area: Jenin
Population: 500
Established: 1980
Location on map: E2
Latitude: 385
Type: Community
    Settlement
Planner: A. Inbar

Elon-Moreh
Area: Nablus
Population: 1000
Established: 1979
Location on map: G4
Latitude: 640
Type: Community
    Settlement
Planner: M. Ravid

Mechora
Area: Jordan Valley
Population: 150
Established: 1973
Location on map: H5
Latitude: 225
Type: Moshav

Geva Binyamin
Area: Ramallah
Population: 1000
Established: 1984
Location on map: F9
Latitude: 640
Type: Community
    Settlement
Planner: The Settlement
    Planning Department

Hermesh
Area: Jenin
Population: 300
Established: 1982
Location on map: E2
Latitude: 270
Type: Community
    Settlement
Planner: Shahar Yehoshua

Mehola
Area: Jordan Valley
Population: 300
Established: 1968
Location on map: H3
Latitude: -180
Type: Moshav

Geva'ot

Eli
Area: Nablus
Population: 2500
Established: 1984
Location on map: F6
Latitude: 700
Type: Community
    Settlement
Planner: The Settlement
    Planning Department

Ganim
Area: Jenin
Population: 100
Established: 1983
Location on map: G2
Latitude: 280
Type: Community
    Settlement
Planner: M. Ravid, A. Inbar,
    Ya'ad Architects

Kfar-Edumim
Area: Jerusalem
Population: 1700
Established: 1979
Location on map: G9
Latitude: 360
Type: Community
    Settlement
Planner: Samach-
    Abramowitz,
    Moshe Goldwasser,
    Gideon Harlap

Shaqed
Area: Jenin
Population: 500
Established: 1981
Location on map: E2
Latitude: 410
Type: Community
    Settlement
Planner: Gonen Architects

Gittit
Area: Jordan Valley
Population: 100
Established: 1972
Location on map: G6
Latitude: 305
Type: Moshav

Karmei-Zur
Area: Hebron
Population: 500
Established: 1984
Location on map: E11
Latitude: 940
Type: Community
    Settlement
Planner: The Settlement
    Division of the Jewish
    Agency

Nili
Area: Ramallah
Population: 700
Established: 1981
Location on map: D8
Latitude: 360
Type: Community
    Settlement
Planner: Bina Nudelman

Elqana
Area: Qalqilia
Population: 3000
Established: 1977
Location on map: D6
Latitude: 235
Type: Local Council

Dolev
Area: Ramallah
Population: 900
Established: 1983
Location on map: E8
Latitude: 600
Type: Community
    Settlement

Na'ama
Area: Jordan Valley
Population: 130
Established: 1982
Location on map: H3
Latitude: -200
Type: Moshav

closes in, more and more, on any possibility of future Palestinian urban growth.

The Walls of Suburbia

The barrier wall constructed by Israel in the past decade is yet another element of control. The wall further expands what the settlements have been doing: isolating and fragmenting the fabric of Palestinian towns and villages while enhancing the physical and visual space between the disparate Jewish settlements. In this case, the wall does not act as a single binary divide between sovereign entities. Rather, it serves as a series of cuts, barriers, and roadblocks that subdivides and entraps part of the landscape and its population—the Palestinians—while it allows maximum "free" space for the other part, the Jewish settlers. In this territorial conflict the Jewish suburbs of the West Bank are presented by the state as the raison d'être for all security measures.

For what is the single-family home suburban development, if not the urban typology most emblematic of the freedom to own land, of mobility, and of the right to access space? (fig. **5.10.4**)

The flight of the middle class from the cities to the "protective" walls of suburbia gains new meaning in the context of the occupation of the West Bank. In a daunting reversal, the act of retreat from the "conflicts" of the city has become an intrusive act, perpetuating a conflict on a much larger scale. The adaptability and flexibility of the suburban typology makes it an effective tool of territorial control that can be implemented in a range of scales, to comprise a few homes or an entire neighborhood, and flexible enough to conform to the specific topographical conditions of different sites.

Moreover, the social homogeneity that is characteristic of this suburban population serves the political aim of the occupation: that of acting as a single, unified front against the local hostile

5.10.4 Jewish hilltop suburbs near Bethlehem

population. The monotonous architecture of the settlement typology, which reflects this homogeneity, turns urban sprawl in the West Bank settlements into a well-coordinated and fully planned strategic project to effect a maximum level of territorial control, using the most rudimentary element of domestic space: the single-family detached house.

Sandton, Gauteng, South Africa

Parel, Mumbai, Maharashtra, India

List of Contributors

Alan M. Berger
Alan M. Berger is professor of landscape architecture and urban design at the Massachusetts Institute of Technology in the Department of Urban Studies and Planning, where he teaches courses open to the entire student body. He is codirector of the Norman B. Leventhal Center for Advanced Urbanism and founding director of P-REX lab at MIT. All of his research and work emphasizes the link between urbanization and consumption of natural resources, and the waste and destruction of landscape, to help us better understand how to proceed with redesigning around our wasteful lifestyles for more intelligent outcomes. He coined the term *systemic design* to emphasize the importance of linking local and regional systems throughout the design process. In addition to his award-winning books *Drosscape: Wasting Land in Urban America* (Princeton Architectural Press, 2006) and *Reclaiming the American West* (Princeton Architectural Press, 2002), his other books include *Designing the Reclaimed Landscape, Nansha Coastal City: Landscape and Urbanism in the Pearl River Delta* (with Margaret Crawford), *Systemic Design © Can Change the World,* and *Landscape + Urbanism around the Bay of Mumbai* (with Rahul Mehrotra). Prior to working at MIT, he was associate professor of Landscape Architecture at Harvard Graduate School of Design, 2002–2008. He is a Prince Charitable Trusts Fellow of the American Academy in Rome.

Joel Kotkin
Joel Kotkin is the Presidential Fellow in Urban Futures at Chapman University in Orange, California, and the executive director of the Houston-based Center for Opportunity Urbanism. He is the author of eight books including *Tribes: How Race, Religion, and Identity Determine Success in the New Global Economy* (1993), *The City: A Global History* (2006), *The Next Hundred Million: America in 2050* (2009), and *The New Class Conflict* (2015). His most recent book, *The Human City,* was published in spring 2016. Kotkin writes regularly for *Forbes,* the *Orange County Register,* the *Daily Beast,* and RealClearPolitics.

Celina Balderas Guzmán
Celina Balderas Guzmán is an urban designer and urban planner with expertise in the environmental challenges facing cities. She is a researcher at the Norman B. Leventhal Center for Advanced Urbanism (LCAU), where she currently leads a project to design constructed wetlands for stormwater in urban areas in collaboration with civil engineers. For LCAU's Future of Suburbia biennial theme, she led and managed this publication and collaborated on the exhibition and conference that took place in the spring of 2016. She has three degrees from MIT, including a bachelor of science in architecture, master of city planning, and master of science in architecture studies, urbanism.

Martha de Alba
Martha de Alba is a senior lecturer of social psychology at the Universidad Autónoma Metropolitana—Iztapalapa Campus, Mexico City, and a fellow at the European/International Joint PhD on Social Representations and Communication. Her research interests include social representations, experiences, and memory of urban spaces.

Adriana Allen
Adriana Allen is professor of development planning and urban sustainability at the Development Planning Unit (DPU), University College London, where she leads the DPU's Research Cluster on Environmental Justice, Urbanization and Resilience. Originally trained as an urban planner, she has specialized, over the years, in the fields of urban environmental planning and political ecology. She has almost thirty years of international experience in research and consultancy undertakings in over nineteen countries in Asia, Africa, and Latin America. Her work as both an academic and a practitioner focuses on the interface between development and environmental concerns in the urban context of the Global South, and more specifically on establishing transformative links between spatial planning, environmental justice, and sustainability in urbanizing and peri-urban contexts. Her most recent publication is *Untamed Urbanisms* (2015), coedited with Andrea Lampis and Mark Swilling.

Shlomo Angel
Shlomo (Solly) Angel is a professor of city planning at the Marron Institute of Urban Management. He leads the Urban Expansion initiative at the NYU Stern Urbanization Project, a joint research center of the Stern School of Business and the Marron Institute. Angel is an expert on urban development policy, having advised the United Nations, the World Bank, and the Inter-American Development Bank (IDB). He currently focuses on documenting and planning for urban expansion in the developing world.

Alejandro M. Blei
Alejandro Blei is a research scholar at NYU's Marron Institute of Urban Management and research coordinator of its Monitoring Global Urban Expansion initiative. He is a coauthor of *The Atlas of Urban Expansion* (2012), which used satellite imagery and historical maps to document global urban expansion over a two-hundred-year period. He is currently an ABD candidate at the University of Illinois at Chicago, with a specialization in urban transportation policy and planning. He has a broad interest in urban spatial analysis with a particular focus on the application of GIS and GPS to studying travel behavior.

William T. Bogart
William T. Bogart is the president of Maryville College, in Maryville, Tennessee. He previously served as dean of Academic Affairs at York College of Pennsylvania and as a member of the economics faculty at Case Western Reserve University. Bogart earned a BA in economics and mathematical sciences from Rice University and a PhD in economics from Princeton University. He has written three books: *The Economics of Cities and Suburbs, Don't Call It Sprawl: Metropolitan Structure in the Twenty-First Century,* and *The False Promise of Green Energy.*

Julian Bolleter
Julian Bolleter is assistant professor at the Australian Urban Design Research Centre (AUDRC) at the University of Western Australia. His role at the AUDRC includes teaching a master's program in urban design and conducting urban design–related research and design projects. Bolleter is an award-winning landscape architect and urban designer and has worked in Australia, the United States, the United Kingdon, and the Middle East on a range of major projects. He has completed a PhD on landscape architecture in Dubai and has published three books: *Made in Australia: The Future of Australian Cities* (with Richard Weller), *Scavenging the Suburbs—* a book that audits Western Australian city of Perth for ~1,000,000 possible urban infill dwellings—and *Take Me to the River: A History of Perth's Foreshore*. In 2014 Bolleter was awarded the Australian Institute of Landscape Architects WA gold medal award (in conjunction with Richard Weller).

Michael Brauer
Michael Brauer is professor in the School of Population and Public Health at the University of British

Columbia. His research focuses on linkages between the built environment and human health, with specific interest in transportation-related and biomass air pollution, the global health impacts of air pollution, and the relationships between multiple exposures mediated by urban form and population health. He has participated in monitoring and epidemiological studies throughout the world and served on numerous advisory committees to international, national, and local public-sector institutions.

Richard Briffault

Richard Briffault is the Joseph P. Chamberlain Professor of Legislation at Columbia Law School. His research, writing, and teaching focus on state and local government law, the law of the political process, government ethics, and property. He is coauthor of the textbook *State and Local Government Law* (7th ed., 2009); principal author of *Dollars and Democracy: A Blueprint for Campaign Finance Reform* (Report of the Commission on Campaign Finance Reform of New York City Bar Association 2000); and author of *Balancing Acts: The Reality behind State Balanced Budget Requirements* (1996) as well as more than seventy-five law review articles.

Casey Lance Brown

Casey Lance Brown directs research for P-REX, an interdisciplinary think tank at MIT. Current projects include strategies for future mobility with Toyota Research Institute as well as future scenarios for land

reclamation, decarbonization, and electrification of urban territories. Independently, Brown conducts long-term research on securitization of international borderlands supported by the Charles Eliot Traveling Fellowship and the geopolitical effects of land speculation originally sponsored by the Rome Prize. Brown is also a fellow of the American Academy in Rome and is currently establishing a carbon neutral research base in southern Appalachia.

Robert Bruegmann

Robert Bruegmann is a historian and critic of the built environment. He received his PhD in art history from the University of Pennsylvania in 1976 and since 1979 has been at the University of Illinois at Chicago, where he is Distinguished Professor Emeritus of Art History, Architecture and Urban Planning. Among his books are *The Architects and the City: Holabird and Roche of Chicago 1880–1918* (1998), *Sprawl: A Compact History* (2005), *and The Architecture of Harry Weese* (2010). His main areas of research are in the history of architecture, urban planning, landscape, and historic preservation.

Hugh Byrd

Hugh Byrd is professor of architecture at the University of Lincoln, United Kingdom, having previously worked at the University of Auckland and the Universiti Sains Malaysia. His research interests are in the future form of buildings and cities around the world as we enter an era characterized by resource depletion and climate change. He

has published widely on issues of environmental performance and energy policy of buildings and cities in various countries. More recent research has focused on disruptive technologies and energy security.

Thomas J. Campanella

Thomas J. Campanella is associate professor of city planning at Cornell University and director of the undergraduate Urban and Regional Studies Program. A recipient of Guggenheim, Fulbright, and Rome Prize fellowships, his books include *Republic of Shade: New England and the American Elm* (2003), *The Resilient City: How Modern Cities Recover from Disaster* (2005), and *The Concrete Dragon: China's Urban Revolution and What It Means for the World* (Princeton Architectural Press, 2008). Campanella has held visiting appointments at Columbia, MIT, Harvard, the Chinese University of Hong Kong, and the Nanjing University School of Architecture and Planning.

Guénola Capron

Guénola Capron is a Franco-Mexican researcher. She worked in the French CNRS and currently teaches as a professor at the Universidad Autónoma Metropolitana campus Atzcapotzalco in the Department of Sociology in Mexico City. She works on urban public spaces and how retailing changes and security issues transform public space in Latin American cities (especially Buenos Aires and Mexico City). Her copublished books include *Quand la Ville se Ferme, Quartiers Résidentiels Sécurisés*, and *Satélite el Libro* (the latter with Martha de Alba).

Bridget Catlin

Bridget Catlin directs the Mobilizing Action Toward Community Health (MATCH) group in the University of Wisconsin Population Health Institute in Madison, Wisconsin, where her work focuses on research and development to support community health improvement. She is codirector of the County Health Rankings and Roadmaps program funded by the Robert Wood Johnson Foundation. Previously she led a number of consumer information and performance measurement projects. Catlin received a PhD in health systems engineering from the University of Wisconsin–Madison, an MHSA from the University of Michigan School of Public Health, and a BA from Clark University in Worcester, Massachusetts.

Daniel L. Civco

Daniel L. Civco is professor of geomatics in the Department of Natural Resources and the Environment at the University of Connecticut. He has nearly forty years of experience as an earth resources scientist specializing in remote sensing and GIS applications. He has been involved extensively in research addressing both inland and coastal wetland resources, land-use mapping and change analysis, impervious surface detection, and natural resources inventory and analysis. Further, he has been involved in algorithm development and refinement for processing remote sensing and other geospatial data. Civco is director of the Center for

Land Use Education and Research (CLEAR), and is the founder of the Laboratory for Earth Resources Information Systems (LERIS).

Christy Collis

Christy Collis is head of entertainment and arts management at Queensland University of Technology in Brisbane, Australia. With Terry Flew, Mark Gibson, Phil Graham, and Emma Felton, she was a chief investigator on the Australia Research Council–funded Creative Suburbia project, which examined the economic and cultural geographies of non-urban creative industries.

Wendell Cox

Wendell Cox is on the Board of Advisors at the Center for Demographics and Policy at Chapman University, and is chair of Housing Affordability and Municipal Policy for the Frontier Centre for Public Policy (Canada), and senior fellow at the Center for Opportunity Urbanism. He is principal of Demographia, an international public policy firm. He was appointed to three terms on the Los Angeles County Transportation Commission by Mayor Tom Bradley and to the Amtrak Reform Council by Speaker Newt Gingrich. He also served as a visiting professor at the Conservatoire National des Arts et Metiers, a national university in Paris.

Martin Coy

Martin Coy is professor for applied geography and sustainability research at the Institute of Geography, University of Innsbruck, Austria. He obtained his diploma

in geography from the University of Frankfurt am Main, Germany, pursued postgraduate studies in social anthropology at the Ècole des Hautes Études Sociales (EHESS) in Paris, France, and holds a PhD and postdoctoral degree in geography from the University of Tübingen, Germany. His regional focus is on Latin America, particularly Brazil and Argentina. In his research, he focuses on mega-urban development (e.g., in São Paulo), urban renewal, sustainable development, human-environment relations, and the regional development of the Amazon region.

Sylvia Croese

Sylvia Croese is a postdoctoral fellow at the Department of Sociology and Social Anthropology at Stellenbosch University. Her PhD thesis, "Post-war State-Led Development at Work in Angola: The Zango Housing Project in Luanda as a Case Study," examined the politics of state-led housing development in postwar Angola. She has written and conducted extensive research in and on Angola as a researcher and consultant and has an interest in issues related to China-Africa relations, housing and urban development, local governance, and electoral politics.

Keller Easterling

Keller Easterling is an architect, writer, and professor at Yale. Her most recent book, *Extrastatecraft: The Power of Infrastructure Space* (2014), examines global infrastructure networks as a medium of polity. Another recent book, *Subtraction* (2014), considers building removal or how to put the development machine into reverse. Her other books include *Enduring Innocence: Global Architecture and its Political Masquerades* (2005) and *Organization Space: Landscapes, Highways and Houses in America* (1999).

Ross Elliott
Ross Elliott has nearly thirty years' experience in the property industry in Australia, including senior leadership roles as state executive director and chief operating officer with the Property Council of Australia and national executive director of the Residential Development Council. His experience spans economic consultancy to business advisory along with being inaugural chief executive of Brisbane Marketing, which succeeded under his leadership in winning the International Downtown Association's award for "Downtown Leadership and Management" in 2003. A respected and active participant in industry affairs, Ross' insights and perspectives are widely shared in Australian forums. Out of hours, he enjoys his family life and chasing cattle on a small rural property south of Brisbane.

Emma Felton
Emma Felton is senior lecturer in the Creative Industries Faculty at Queensland University of Technology and has a background across tertiary teaching, research, and management. Her research and writing is concerned with the cultural sociology of cities, with a focus on the experience of urbanism and its relationship to social and cultural inclusion. Emma

has published in many journals and books, and is coeditor and contributor of *Design and Ethics: Reflections on Practice* (2012).

Robert Fishman
Robert Fishman, professor of architecture and urban planning, teaches in the urban design, architecture, and urban planning programs at Taubman College of Architecture and Urban Planning at the University of Michigan. He received his PhD and AM in history from Harvard and his AB in history from Stanford University. He is an internationally recognized author and expert in the areas of urban history and urban policy and planning. His honors include the 2009 Laurence Gerckens Prize for lifetime achievement of the Society for City and Regional Planning History; the Walker Ames Lectureship, the University of Washington, Seattle, 2010; the Emil Lorch Professorship at the Taubman College, 2006–2009; Public Policy Scholar, the Wilson Center, Washington, DC, 1999; and the Cass Gilbert Professorship at the University of Minnesota, 1998.

Terry Flew
Terry Flew is professor of media and communications at the Queensland University of Technology, Brisbane, Australia. He is the author of *The Creative Industries, Culture and Policy* (2012), *Global Creative Industries* (2013), and *New Media: An Introduction* (2014); coauthor of *Media Economics* (2015); and the founding editor of *Communication Research and Practice*. He

was a member of the Australian Research Council College of Experts for Humanities and Creative Arts from 2013 to 2015, is an International Communications Association Executive Board member, and chairs the Global Communication and Social Change Division.

Ann Forsyth
Trained in planning and architecture, Ann Forsyth is professor of urban planning at the Harvard Graduate School of Design. The big question behind her research and practice is how to make more sustainable and healthy cities. Several issues prove to be the most difficult to deal with in planning better places and provide a focus for some of her more detailed investigations: suburban design, walkability, affordable housing, social diversity, and appropriate green space. In doing this work, she has created several tools and methods in planning— an urban design inventory, GIS protocols, health impact assessments, and participatory planning techniques.

Nicolás Galarza Sanchez
Nicolás Galarza Sanchez is a research scholar at the Urbanization Project, focusing on its Urban Expansion initiative in Latin America. Galarza Sanchez holds a master's of urban planning from NYU Wagner Graduate School of Public Service. Prior to pursuing his master's in New York City, Galarza Sanchez served as adviser to the program director of the National Poverty Alleviation Strategy and to the high presidential commissioner for social action

on civic technology and innovation in his native Colombia.

Nicole Stelle Garnett
Nicole Stelle Garnett is the John P. Murphy Foundation Professor of Law at the University of Notre Dame. Her teaching and research focus on property, land use, urban development, local government law, and education policy. Her numerous publications include *Ordering the City: Land Use, Policing, and the Restoration of Urban America* (2009) and *Lost Classroom, Lost Community: Catholic Schools' Importance in Urban America* (2014; with Margaret F. Brinig). Professor Garnett is a graduate of Stanford University and Yale Law School and served as a law clerk for Judge Morris S. Arnold of the United States Court of Appeals and for Justice Clarence Thomas.

Mark Gibson
Mark Gibson is head of Communications and Media Studies at Monash University, Melbourne, Australia. He has research interests in cultural and creative industries, focusing on geographic factors such as suburban and regional location and, more recently, the crossover between fringe, independent, and avant-garde cultural production and the "mainstream." He is the author of *Culture and Power: A History of Cultural Studies* (2007) and editor of *Continuum: Journal of Media and Cultural Studies*.

David L. A. Gordon
David L. A. Gordon is professor and director of the Queen's University School of Urban and Regional Planning in Canada. He received degrees in engineering and planning from Queen's and a doctorate from Harvard. Gordon teaches planning history and urban development and has also taught at Toronto, Western Australia, Harvard, and Pennsylvania, where he was a Fulbright Scholar. His books include *Planning Twentieth Century Capital Cities* (2006) and *Planning Canadian Communities* (with Gerald Hodge), which won the 2014 Canadian Institute of Planners' National Award. His latest research includes *Town and Crown: An Illustrated History of Canada's Capital* (2015) and a comparison of Canadian and Australian suburbs.

Margaret Grose
Margaret Grose is an Australian ecologist and landscape architect working and publishing between and within design and science. She teaches ecological theory in the Master of Landscape Architecture program and design to undergraduates at the University of Melbourne. Previously, she worked in theoretical biology at the University of Cambridge, and then completed a landscape architecture degree, followed by project work on water systems and suburban design. Her research continues on suburbs, street lighting, teaching ecology to built environment students, and design thinking. She is completing a book, *Constructed Ecologies*, for Routledge in 2017. She is an editor for the *Journal of Urban Ecology*.

Susannah Hagan
Susannah Hagan is professor of architecture at the University of Westminster, London, and is currently leading an AHRC/FAPESP-funded research collaboration with the University of São Paulo called "Public Spaces and the Role of the Architect: a Comparative Study of Influential Modernist and Contemporary Examples in London and São Paulo." Trained as an architect at Columbia University, New York, and the Architectural Association, London, she is also the founder and director of R_E_D (Research into Environment + Design—www.theredgroup.org), a European design research consultancy that specializes in promoting the role of design in making cities more environmentally resilient, with past projects in England, Sweden, and the Baltic cities. She is on the editorial boards of *arq: Architectural Research Quarterly* and the *Architectural Review*, and she is a member of the AHRC Peer Review College and the RIBA Examination Board. She has published extensively on both architecture and urban design, drawing together history, theory, design practice and environmental practice in the books *Taking Shape: a New Contract between Architecture and Nature* (2001), and *Digitalia: Architecture and the Environmental, the Digital and the Avant-Garde* (2008). Her latest book, *Ecological Urbanism: The Nature of the City* (2015) is for students and practitioners, and examines the roles of design and designers in the environmental recalibration of cities.

Michael D. Hais

Michael D. Hais is an author and speaker delivering candid, informed insights on how to engage millennials. His predictions and often pithy analyses have appeared in/on the *New York Times*, the *Today Show*, CNN, *USA Today*, *PBS NewsHour*, NPR, *Barron's*, *Forbes*, Reuters, and Univision. He is the coauthor, with Morley Winograd, of three highly acclaimed books: *Millennial Makeover* (2008), *Millennial Momentum* (2011), and *Millennial Majority* (2015). His earlier career included conducting audience research for Frank N. Magid Associates: hundreds of television stations, cable channels, and program producers in the United States and over a dozen foreign countries.

Espen Aukrust Hauglin

Espen Aukrust Hauglin is assistant professor at the Oslo School of Architecture and Design in Norway. He is an architect specializing in the use of GIS (geographical information systems) and urban planning. His research focuses on how geographic information can reveal specific site correlations and provide insights to planning tasks and large-scale planning processes. His recent work emphasizes findings from various empirical studies in the greater Oslo region as an approach to identify and understand intersections between urban geographic data, urban spatial development, and urban planning systems in Norway.

James Heartfield

James Heartfield has been writing, talking, and campaigning on urban regeneration, housing supply, and rent rises in the United Kingdom since the 1990s. His book *Let's Build! Why We Need Five Million Homes in the Next Ten Years* was published in 2005, though sadly its warning was not heeded by British policy makers.

Sarah Jack Hinners

Sarah Jack Hinners is on the faculty of the Department of City and Metropolitan Planning at the University of Utah and directs the Ecological Planning Center there. She has a BA in geography and environmental studies and a PhD in ecology. She works primarily at the interface of interdisciplinary research (science, social science, etc.) and planning and design in urban systems. Despite having spent several years studying bees in suburban Denver, she has never actually lived in suburbia.

Michael Hollar

Michael Hollar is a senior economist with the US Department of Housing and Urban Development (HUD). He received his PhD in economics from George Washington University and his BA in economics from Wittenberg University. Currently, Hollar works on public finance issues for the Office of Policy Development and Research. His research interests include the determinants of urban growth and the effects of rental housing policy.

Howard Husock

Howard Husock is vice president for publications and research and senior fellow at the Manhattan Institute, where he is also director of the Institute's social entrepreneurship initiative. A *City Journal* contributing editor, Husock has written widely on US housing and urban policy, including in *The Trillion-Dollar Housing Mistake: The Failure of American Housing Policy* (2003) and *Repairing the Ladder: Toward a New Housing Policy Paradigm* (1996). His work has appeared in the *Wall Street Journal*, *New York Times*, *National Affairs*, the *Public Interest*, *Society*, the *Journal of Policy Analysis and Management*, *Philanthropy*, and the *Wilson Quarterly*. He also writes frequently on philanthropy and is the author of *Philanthropy under Fire* (2013) and is a regular contributor to the *Chronicle of Philanthropy* and Forbes.com.

Roger Keil

Roger Keil, Dr. Phil., Political Science, Goethe University, Frankfurt (1992), is York Research Chair in Global Sub/Urban Studies in the Faculty of Environmental Studies at York University in Toronto. A former director of York University's City Institute, he researches global suburbanization, urban political ecology, cities and infectious disease, and regional governance and is principal investigator of a Major Collaborative Research Initiative, "Global Suburbanisms: Governance, Land, and Infrastructure in the Twenty-First Century" (2010–2017). He is the editor of *Suburban Constellations* (Jovis, 2013) and coeditor (with Pierre Hamel) *of Suburban Governance: A Global View* (2015).

Jed Kolko

Jed Kolko was chief economist and vice president of analytics at Trulia at the time of writing. He is now an independent economist and senior fellow at UC-Berkeley's Terner Center. Prior to Trulia, he was associate director of research at the Public Policy Institute of California, and vice president and research director at Forrester Research. He has a PhD in Economics and an AB in social studies from Harvard University. His website is www.jedkolko.com.

Kenneth P. Laberteaux

Kenneth P. Laberteaux, Senior Principal Scientist for the Toyota Research Institute-North America, has worked as a researcher in the automotive and telecommunication industries for twenty-three years. Laberteaux's current research focus is sustainable mobility systems, including US urbanization and transportation patterns, ride sharing, demographics, grid-vehicle interactions, and vehicle electrification feasibility and optimization. Earlier in his time at Toyota, Laberteaux worked on advanced safety systems, leveraging synergies in communication, sensing, and computation. Credited with coining the term VANET, Laberteaux was a founder and two-year (2004, 2005) general cochair of the VehiculAr Inter-NETworking (VANET) workshop. Before joining Toyota in 2002, Laberteaux spent ten years as a researcher at the Tellabs Research Center, working on echo cancellation, data networking protocols, call admission control, and congestion control. While working full-time at Tellabs, Laberteaux completed his MS (1996) and PhD (2000) degrees in electrical engineering from the University of Notre Dame, focusing on adaptive control for communications. In 1992, he received his BSE in electrical engineering from the University of Michigan, Ann Arbor. Laberteaux has produced twenty-five scholarly publications and sixteen patents.

Patrick Lamson-Hall

Patrick Lamson-Hall is a research scholar at the NYU Stern Urbanization Project. His research focuses on trends at the urban fringe, with specific attention to rapidly growing cities in the developing world. This year he established the India Urban Expansion Observatory, a research center for the analysis of high-resolution satellite imagery located in Mumbai, India, and sponsored by NYU and UN Habitat. He is also the coordinator of the Ethiopia Urban Expansion Initiative, a project that is establishing critical urban infrastructure in advance of development. He completed an MUP from the Wagner School of Public Policy in 2013.

Janike Kampevold Larsen

Janike Kampevold Larsen is associate professor at the Institute of Urbanism and Landscape at the Oslo School of Architecture and Design, where she teaches landscape theory. She is project leader for Future North, a research project observing and mapping changes in settlements and territories in the Arctic and Subarctic regions. Her recent publications include *Routes, Roads, and Landscapes* (2012), coedited with Mari Hvattum, Brita Brenna, and Beate Elvebakk; "Global Tourism Practices as Lived Heritage: Viewing the Norwegian Tourist Routes," in *Future Anterior* IX, no. 1 (Summer 2012), edited by Jorge Otero-Pailos; "Imagining the Geologic," in *Making a Geologic Now*, edited by Elizabeth Ellsworth and Jamie Kruse (2013); and "Geologic Presence in the Twenty-First Century Wilderness Garden," in *Studies in the History of Gardens and Designed Landscapes* (2014), edited by John D. Hunt.

Manuel Madrid

Manuel Madrid is a GIS specialist at the gvSIG Association, a non-profit organization whose main objective is the promotion of open geospatial technologies. He completed his master's in valuation, cadastre, and territorial information systems at the Miguel Hernández University of Elche (Spain). He previously completed a bachelor in survey engineering at the Universitat Politècnica de Valencia (Spain). His fields of interest include open geospatial technologies, cartography, urban planning, and education. He has given numerous speeches related with GIS in general and with gvSIG in particular.

Christopher Marcinkoski

Christopher Marcinkoski is an assistant professor of landscape architecture and urban design at the University of Pennsylvania. He is a licensed architect and founding director of PORT, a leading-edge urban design consultancy. Prior to his appointment at Penn, he was a senior associate at James Corner Field Operations, where he led the office's large-scale urban design work, including the Qianhai Water City in Shenzhen, China, and Shelby Farms Park in Memphis, Tennessee. Marcinkoski is the author of *The City That Never Was* (Princeton Architectural Press, 2015) and was coeditor of *Perspecta 38: Architecture after All* (2006). In 2015, he was awarded the Rome Prize in Landscape Architecture from the American Academy in Rome.

Robert J. Mason
Robert J. Mason is professor of geography and urban studies at Temple University. His research and teaching focus on environmental policy making and land-use planning in the United States and Asia. He is the author of *Collaborative Land Use Management: The Quieter Revolution in Place-Based Planning* (2008), as well as a range of additional books and scholarly articles. Current interests include evolving policy responses to environmental shocks, metropolitan growth management, suburban sprawl, watershed issues, and protected areas management.

Fadi Masoud
Fadi Masoud is a lecturer in landscape architecture and urban design at Massachusetts Institute of Technology Department of Urban Studies and Planning, and a research associate with the Norman B. Leventhal Center for Advanced Urbanism. He holds degrees in planning and landscape architecture from the University

of Waterloo, the University of Toronto, and Harvard University's Graduate School of Design. Masoud's current research and design work focuses on establishing relationships between dynamic large-scale environmental systems, landscape design, and the instrumentality and agency of planning standards and codes.

Rahul Mehrotra
Rahul Mehrotra is a practicing architect and educator. He works in Mumbai and teaches at the Graduate School of Design at Harvard University, where he is professor of urban design as well as a member of the steering committee of Harvard's South Asia Institute. His practice, RMA Architects (www.RMAarchitects.com), founded in 1990, has executed a range of projects across India. He has written, coauthored, and edited a vast repertoire of books on Mumbai, its urban history, its historical buildings, public spaces, and planning processes. He currently serves on the governing boards of the London School of Economics Cities Programme and the Indian Institute of Human Settlements.

Ali Modarres
Ali Modarres is director of urban studies at University of Washington Tacoma. He is the editor of *Cities: The International Journal of Urban Policy and Planning.* Modarres earned his PhD in geography from the University of Arizona and holds master's and bachelor's degrees in landscape architecture from the same institution. He specializes in urban geography, and his primary

research and publication interests are sociospatial urban dynamics and the political economy of urban design. He has published in the areas of social geography, transportation planning, and public policy. Some of his recent articles have appeared in *Transport Geography*, *Current Research on Cities*, and *International Journal of Urban and Regional Research*.

Louise A. Mozingo
Louise A. Mozingo is professor and chair in the Department of Landscape Architecture and Environmental Planning at UC Berkeley. Her research concerns American landscape history and sustainable environmental design and planning. Her book, *Pastoral Capitalism: A History of Suburban Corporate Landscapes*, won the 2011 American Publishers PROSE Award in Architecture and Urban Planning, the 2014 Elisabeth Blair MacDougall Prize from the Society of Architectural Historians, and a 2014 American Society of Landscape Architects Honor Award. In 2009, she founded the Center for Resource Efficient Communities, dedicated to interdisciplinary research regarding resource efficient urban design, planning, and policy.

Martin J. Murray
Martin J. Murray is professor of urban planning at Taubman College of Architecture and Urban Planning, University of Michigan, and adjunct professor in the Department of Afroamerican and African Studies of the University of Michigan. His previous appointment was professor of sociology, State University of New York

at Binghamton. He is the author of numerous books and scholarly articles. His most recent books include *Commemorating and Forgetting: Challenges for the New South Africa* (2013); *City of Extremes: The Spatial Politics of Johannesburg* (2011); *Taming the Disorderly City: The Spatial Landscape of Johannesburg after Apartheid* (2008); *Cities in Contemporary Africa: Place, Politics, and Livelihood* (paperback edition, 2011; coedited with Garth Myers). Besides a number of book chapters, his published work has appeared in *International Journal of Urban and Regional Research*, *Environment and Planning A*, and the *Journal of Urban Design*.

Joan Iverson Nassauer

Joan Iverson Nassauer is professor of landscape architecture in the School of Natural Resources and Environment at the University of Michigan. She develops ecological design proposals and investigates how human experience is affected by, and can sustain, environmentally beneficial landscape patterns. She is the author of more than eighty refereed papers and books, and her current design research addresses green infrastructure for highly vacant urban neighborhoods and ecosystem services from suburban landscapes. A fellow of the American Society of Landscape Architects (1992), she was named Distinguished Scholar by the International Association of Landscape Ecology (2007) and Distinguished Practitioner of Landscape Ecology in the United States (1998).

Liliya Nigmatullina

Liliya Nigmatullina is a Washington, DC–based independent scholar focusing on urbanization and suburbanization in Russia and post-Soviet countries. She holds a graduate degree in urban studies from Temple University.

Jason Parent

Jason Parent is assistant research professor at the University of Connecticut's Department of Natural Resources and the Environment. He specializes in the application of remote sensing and geographic information systems to problems involving natural resources. His current research projects include analyzing global urban growth over time, predicting tree hazards to utility infrastructure, and studying how trees adapt to changes in wind exposure.

Nicholas A. Phelps

Nicholas A. Phelps is professor of urban and regional development at the Bartlett School of Planning. Prior to this, he held positions in the Schools of Geography at the Universities of Southampton and Leeds and at the Department of City and Regional Planning at the University of Cardiff. His research interests cover the politics and planning of suburban development and the transformation and economics of urban agglomeration. He is author of *Sequel to Suburbia* (2015), *Post-Suburban Europe* (2006), and *An Anatomy of Sprawl* (2012). He is also an editor of *The Planning Imagination* (2014) and *International Perspectives in Suburbanization* (2011).

Alan E. Pisarski

Alan E. Pisarski is a writer and consultant in the fields of transportation research, policy, and investment. His continuing studies include the Commuting in America series conducted each decade since 1986; *The Bottom Line*, advising Congress on national investment requirements for each of the last five reauthorizations; and working as senior adviser on all of the nation's major transportation surveys and data collection activities. He is frequently invited to testify and consult in both houses of Congress and in state legislatures and international agencies on economic and demographic factors that define travel demand, infrastructure investment requirements, and public policy.

Anne Pitcher

Anne Pitcher is professor of African studies and political science at the University of Michigan. She is also president-elect of the African Studies Association (USA). Her current research focuses on the political economy of urban residential development in Angola, South Africa, and Kenya. Her books include *Politics in the Portuguese Empire* (1993), *Transforming Mozambique: The Politics of Privatization, 1975–2000* (2002), *Party Politics and Economic Reform in Africa's Democracies* (2012). She has also authored and coauthored many articles in scholarly journals and edited collections.

Simone Sandholz

Simone Sandholz is assistant professor at the Institute

of Geography, University of Innsbruck, Austria. After graduating from architecture, she completed a postgraduate degree in conservation and holds a master's in resources management. In her PhD thesis, she focuses on heritage and identity in rapidly changing urban landscapes of the Global South (Brazil, Indonesia, Nepal). She has published on urban regeneration, sustainable development strategies, and risk management in urban areas; authored sessions on urban planning tools for a massive open online course on "Disasters and Ecosystems: Resilience in a Changing Climate"; and managed an international research project on urban green spaces in Brazil.

Rafi Segal

Rafi Segal is an award-winning designer and associate professor of architecture and urbanism at MIT, with projects in Israel, Africa, and the United States. He is coeditor of *Cities of Dispersal* (2008), *Territories* (2003), and *A Civilian Occupation* (2003), and has exhibited his work widely, most notably at KunstWerk, Berlin; Venice Biennale of Architecture; MOMA in New York; and the Hong Kong / Shenzhen Urbanism Biennale. His writings and exhibitions have provided a critical contribution to architecture's role in the peripheries of our cities. Segal holds a PhD from Princeton University and two degrees from Technion—Israel Institute of Technology. Among his current work are the design of a new communal neighborhood for a kibbutz in Israel and the curating of the

first-ever exhibition on the life and work of Alfred Neumann.

Christopher Sellers

Christopher Sellers is professor of history at Stony Brook University who writes and teaches about the environmental histories of cities, suburbs, environmentalism, health, and industry, and their contemporary legacies. Most recently, he is the author of the award-winning *Crabgrass Crucible: Suburban Nature and the Rise of Environmentalism in Twentieth-Century America* (2012), and coeditor of *Dangerous Trade: Histories of Industrial Hazard across the Globalizing World* (2011). He is now writing on, among other things, the historical relationship between suburbanization, race, and environmental politics around Atlanta.

Kanika Arora Sharma

Kanika Arora Sharma is an energy analyst and project coordinator at Brightworks Sustainability. She graduated from Harvard University Graduate School of Design with a master's degree in design studies, specializing in energy and environments. She is passionate about developing sustainable neighborhood revitalization practices that enhance the social value of a community. As a Harvard Community Service Fellow, she worked with the Boston Redevelopment Authority, studying Boston's E+ programs to develop a compilation of "best practices" to promote and advance building practices related to neighborhood development and energy-efficient affordable housing.

Dorian Stiefel

Dorian Stiefel is a postdoctoral researcher at the University of Tennessee's Baker Center for Public Policy. Her research interests include resilience, sustainability, human existential risk reduction, unintended consequences, and government use of emerging and converging technologies. She holds a doctor of philosophy degree in political science from the University of Tennessee; a master's in accounting from the University of Virginia in 1994 (McIntire School of Commerce); and a bachelor of arts in mathematics from Mary Baldwin College in 1992 (Program for the Exceptionally Gifted).

Jon C. Teaford

Jon C. Teaford is professor emeritus at Purdue University. After receiving his PhD from the University of Wisconsin, he began teaching urban history at Iowa State University before moving to Purdue, where he served on the faculty for thirty-two years. He is the author of ten books, including *City and Suburb: The Political Fragmentation of Metropolitan America, 1850–1970* (1979), *The Twentieth-Century American City* (1993), *Post-Suburbia: Government and Politics in the Edge Cities City* (1996), *The Metropolitan Revolution: The Rise of Post-Urban America* (2006), and *The American Suburb: The Basics* (2007). He served as president of the Urban History Association in 2011–12.

Kevin Thom

Kevin Thom is clinical associate professor in the Department of

Economics at New York University. His research focuses on two main areas. The first examines labor market behaviors in developing economies. His work in this area has focused on topics ranging from the dynamics of undocumented migration to the factors that promote the narcotics trade in Mexico. Related to this is an interest in the spatial development of cities and the relationship between rural-urban migration and urban expansion. His second area of research centers on the intersection between biology and economics. Specifically, his ongoing work in this area explores how molecular genetic data can help us better understand heterogeneity in health behaviors such as smoking.

Bruce Tonn

Bruce Tonn is professor in the Department of Political Science at the University of Tennessee, Knoxville, a fellow of the Howard Baker Center for Public Policy, and President of Three3, a non-profit research organization. Tonn's research interests include environmental and energy policy, futures studies, sustainability, and emerging and converging technology. He is an associate editor for the international Elsevier journal *Futures*. Tonn received a BS in civil engineering from Stanford University, a master's in city and regional planning from Harvard University, and a PhD in urban and regional planning from Northwestern University.

Tobias Töpfer

Tobias Töpfer is senior lecturer at the Institute of Geography, University of Innsbruck, Austria.

He has studied geography at the University of Tübingen, Germany, and the Federal University of Rio de Janeiro, Brazil, and completed his studies with a diploma degree in geography. In his recently finished PhD thesis, he focused on the city center of São Paulo, Brazil, and the consequences of rehabilitation measures in public spaces for the inhabitants. In his research he analyzes urban development in metropolises and megacities in the Global South, especially in Brazil. Further research interests are geographical development studies and social geography.

Paola Viganò

Paola Viganò is an architect and urbanist. She has a PhD in architectural and urban composition and is professor in urbanism at the Universita IUAV of Venice. She is also a guest professor at several European schools of architecture (including the Catholic University of Leuven, EPFL Lausanne, and Aarhus, as well as the Harvard Graduate School of Design), serves on the board of the European Masters of Urbanism program (EMU), and is coordinator of the PhD in urbanism at IUAV. In 1990 Viganò founded Studio with the late Bernardo Secchi and has won several international competitions. In 2008 Studio was one of the ten teams selected for the Grand Paris research project and was shortlisted in 2012 for the New Moscow project.

D. J. Waldie

D. J. Waldie is the author of *Holy Land: A Suburban Memoir* (2005), *Where Are We Now: Notes from*

Los Angeles (2004), and other books about suburban Southern California. He is also the author, with Diane Keaton, of two architectural studies: *California Romantica* and *House*. His reviews and commentaries have appeared in the *Los Angeles Times*, the *Wall Street Journal*, the *New York Times*, and other publications. He was formerly the deputy city manager of Lakewood, California.

Alex Wall

Alex Wall, AA Dipl. ARB, is practice professor of architecture and landscape at the University of Virginia, and a former professor of urban design at Karlsruhe Institute of Technology, Germany. He was a partner at UMnet, where together with "asp" Stuttgart, he won several national and international design and planning competitions. His books include *Cities of Childhood* (with Stefano de Martino; Princeton Architectural Press, 1990), *Victor Gruen* 2005), and in preparation with Sabine Mueller, *urbanisms* and *sustainabilities*. His articles include "Programming the Surface" (1999) and, with Susan N. Snyder, "Emerging Landscapes of Movement and Logistics" (1998) and "The Future Is Already Here" (2014). His research focuses on resilience strategies for coastal cities.

Richard Weller

Richard Weller is the Martin and Margy Meyerson Chair of Urbanism and professor and chair of landscape architecture at the University of Pennsylvania. He is also an adjunct professor at the University of Western

Australia and former director of the Australian Urban Design Research Centre and the design firm Room 4.1.3. He has received a consistent stream of international design competition awards at all scales of landscape architecture and urban design. He has published four books and over eighty single-authored papers and is the creative director of the interdisciplinary journal of landscape architecture *LA+*. His current research concerns regions where rapid urban growth and biodiversity are in direct conflict. He was honored with an Australian National Teaching Award in 2012 and is a board member of the Landscape Architecture Foundation.

Morley Winograd

Morley Winograd is a Los Angeles–based author and speaker delivering candid, informed insights on engaging millennials. His predictions and often pithy analyses have appeared in/on the *New York Times*, the *Today Show*, CNN, *USA Today*, *PBS NewsHour*, NPR, *Barron's*, *Forbes*, Reuters, *and* Univision. He is the coauthor, with Michael D. Hais, of three highly acclaimed books: *Millennial Majority* (2015), *Millennial Momentum* (2011), and *Millennial Makeover* (2008). Morley is a senior fellow at the University of Southern California's Annenberg School's Center on Communication Leadership and Policy, and president and CEO of the nonprofit Campaign for Free College Tuition.

Frank Zirkl

Frank Zirkl is assistant professor (postdoc) at the Institute of Geography, University of Innsbruck, Austria. His graduate diploma in geography and PhD were obtained at the University of Tübingen, Germany, with studies about aspects of sustainable urban development in Rio de Janeiro and Curitiba, Brazil. His thematic research focus is on urban geography, sustainability, and tourism, with a regional concentration on Latin America, especially Brazil. Currently, he is working on a postdoctoral thesis in geography—a study about sustainable regional development through tourism in rural areas in Brazil.

Illustration Credits

1.1.1–3: Robert Bruegmann

1.2.1: Courtesy of the National Park Service, Frederick Law Olmsted National Historic Site
1.2.2: Ebenezer Howard, Garden Cities of To-morrow (London: Swan Sonnenschein, 1902)
1.2.3: Courtesy of the Getty's Open Content Program
1.2.4: Everett Historical / Shutterstock.com
1.2.5: Rijksdienst voor het Cultureel Erfgoed
1.2.6: Matthew Niederhauser and John Fitzgerald
1.2.7: Associated Press Photo / Natacha Pisarenko
1.2.8–11: Matthew Niederhauser and John Fitzgerald

1.5.1–2: The J. Paul Getty Museum, Los Angeles
1.5.3: Mary Alice McLoughlin

1.6.1: Michael Waldrep
1.6.2: ©Agencia de Noticias El Universal, October 8, 1950
1.6.3: ©Agencia de Noticias El Universal, October 22, 1950
1.6.4: ©Agencia de Noticias El Universal, August 24, 1958
1.6.5: ©Agencia de Noticias El Universal, September 7, 1958
1.6.6: Gobierno del Distrito Federal, Secretaría de Cultura, Museo Archivo de la Fotografía
1.6.7–8: Michael Waldrep
1.6.9–10: Matthew Niederhauser and John Fitzgerald

1.7.1–2: Ross Elliot; Sourced from Census of Population and Housing, Australia 2011, Table 14 Dwelling Structure by household composition and family composition
1.7.3: Lend Lease Communities
1.7.4: Ross Elliot; Sourced from Macrobusiness, Australian Bureau of Statistics Cat 5202 Table 61, ABS Cat 5204 and Reserve Bank of Australia Financial Statements Table E1
1.7.5: Ross Elliot; Sourced from Urban Development Institute of Australia
1.7.6: Ross Elliot; Sourced from Macrobusiness, Australian Bureau of Statistics Cat 6416
1.7.7: Springfield Land Corporation

1.8.1–2: Lloyds Banking Group
1.8.3: Department for Communities and Local Government (UK)
1.8.4–5: Matthew Niederhauser and John Fitzgerald

1.9.1–2: Public Domain Public Domain

1.10.1–8: Data from Geolytics; mapping and analysis by Ali Modarres

1.11.1: Grorud Espen Aukrust Hauglin
1.11.2: Ivan Brody
1.11.3: City of Oslo
1.11.4: Espen Aukrust Hauglin
1.11.5–6: Janike Kampevold Larsen
1.11.7: Ivan Brody
1.11.8: Alan M. Berger
1.11.9: Dronninga Landskap AS
1.11.10–11: Matthew Niederhauser and John Fitzgerald

2.1.1–3: NYU Stern Urbanization Project
2.1.4: Shlomo Angel, *Atlas of Urban Expansion* (Cambridge, MA: Lincoln Institute of Land Policy, 2012).
2.1.5: NYU Stern Urbanization Project, USGS, NOAA, DeLorme, NPS. Used by permission. Copyright © 2015 Esri and its data providers. All rights reserved.
2.1.6: Yale University, British Arts, Folio A G 11. Geographicus Rare Antique Maps.
2.1.7: David Dowall, (1987) "Technical Report 1: Bangkok Land and Housing Market Study." In *The Land and Housing Markets of Bangkok: Strategies for Public Sector Participation*, ed. Angel et al., Unpublished Report.
2.1.8: 2012 Google / 2012 GeoEye
2.1.9: NYU Stern Urbanization Project. Used by permission. Copyright © 2015 Esri and its data providers. All rights reserved.
2.1.10: NYU Stern Urbanization Project, DigitalGlobe, GeoEye, Earthstar Geographics, CNES/Airbus DS, USDA, USGS, AEX, Getmapping, Aerogrid, IGN, IGP, swisstopo, and the GIS User Community. Used by permission. Copyright © 2015 Esri and its data providers. All rights reserved.
2.1.11: NYU Stern Urbanization Project

2.2.1: Thomas J. Campanella
2.2.2: Thomas E. Segletes
2.2.3–10: Thomas J. Campanella
2.2.11: From Han-Veng Woo, "Design of Streets and the Use of City Walls in the Development of Highway Systems in the Municipalities of China" (unpublished master's thesis, Iowa State College, 1930)
2.2.12–13: Matthew Niederhauser and John Fitzgerald

2.3.1–11: Wendell Cox

2.4.1: Jed Kolko / Trulia
2.4.2: Jed Kolko / Atlantic CityLab
2.4.3: Jed Kolko / Trulia
2.4.4: Jed Kolko
2.4.5–6: Jed Kolko / Trulia
2.4.7–8: Matthew Niederhauser and John Fitzgerald

2.5.1: David L. A. Gordon, image generated by Anthony Hommik
2.5.2: David L. A. Gordon, image generated by Mark Janzen
2.5.3: David L. A. Gordon, Sources: Statistics Canada (2011); Gordon and Shirokoff (2014)
2.5.4: David L. A. Gordon, Sources: Statistics Canada (2011); Gordon and Janzen (2013); Gordon and Shirokoff (2014)

2.6.1–2: Alan M. Berger
2.6.3: P-REX
2.6.4–6: Alan M. Berger
2.6.7–12: P-REX
2.6.13–14: Matthew Niederhauser and John Fitzgerald

2.7.1: Based on figure 4-11 from Brief 4 Population and Worker Dynamics of *Commuting in America 2013: The National Report on Commuting Patterns and Trends*, January 2015, by the America Association of State Highway and Transportation Officials, Washington, DC
2.7.2: Based on figure 4-7 from Brief 4 Population and Worker Dynamics of *Commuting in America 2013: The National Report on Commuting Patterns and Trends*, January 2015, by the America Association of State Highway and Transportation Officials, Washington, DC
2.7.3–4: Alan E. Pisarski
2.7.5: Based on figure 15-8 from Brief 15 of *Commuting in America 2013: The National Report on Commuting Patterns and Trends*, January 2015, by the America Association of State Highway and Transportation Officials, Washington, DC
2.7.6: Alan E. Pisarski
2.7.7: Based on figure 15-4 from Brief 15 of *Commuting in America 2013: The National Report on Commuting Patterns and Trends*, January 2015, by the America Association of State Highway and Transportation Officials, Washington, DC
2.7.8–10: Alan E. Pisarski
2.7.11: Based on figure 15-11 from Brief 15 of Commuting in America 2013: The National Report on Commuting Patterns and Trends, January 2015, by the America Association of State Highway and Transportation Officials, Washington, DC

2.8.1–7: Julian Bolleter / Richard Weller
2.8.8–9: Matthew Niederhauser and John Fitzgerald

2.9.1–2: Michael Brauer

2.10.1–4: Bridget Catlin
2.10.5–6: Matthew Niederhauser and John Fitzgerald

3.2.1–4: Nicholas A. Phelps
3.2.5–6: Matthew Niederhauser and John Fitzgerald

3.3.1: Michael Hollar

3.4.1: Ann Forsyth; draws on: M. Castells and P. Hall, *Technopoles of the World* (London: Routledge, 1994); A. Forsyth and K. Crewe, "Suburban Technopoles as Places: The International Campus-Garden-Suburb Style," *Urban Design International* 15 (2010): 165–82
3.4.2: Ann Forsyth
3.4.3: All photos by Ann Forsyth except Route 128 (Google Streetview), San Francisco, SoMa Area (Ken Lund), and MIT University Park/Kendall Square Areas (Tim Pierce)
3.4.4–5: Ann Forsyth
3.4.6–7: Matthew Niederhauser and John Fitzgerald

3.5.1: Oz Aerial Photos Australia
3.5.2: Emma Felton

3.6.1–10: Roger Keil
3.6.11–12: Matthew Niederhauser and John Fitzgerald

3.7.1–4: Christopher Marcinkoski
3.7.5: 1997 General Plan of Madrid
3.7.6–9: Christopher Marcinkoski
3.7.10: Ricardo Espinosa

3.8.1–5: Alan M. Berger
3.8.6–7: Charles Correa Foundation
3.8.8–9: Matthew Niederhauser and John Fitzgerald

3.9.1–3: Martin J. Murray
3.9.4: Stephanie McClintick
3.9.5–10: Martin J. Murray

3.10.1: Everett Historical / Shutterstock.com
3.10.2: Courtesy of the Georgia Historical Society
3.10.3–4: Keller Easterling
3.10.5–6: Matthew Niederhauser and John Fitzgerald

4.1.1–2: Christopher Sellers
4.1.3: Everett Historical/ Shutterstock.com
4.1.4: Christopher Sellers

4.2.1–2: Allison Spain
4.2.3–4: Carol A. Kearns
4.2.5: Joseph Wilson
4.2.6: Pamela Yeh
4.2.7: Joseph Wilson
4.2.8–9: Matthew Niederhauser and John Fitzgerald

4.3.1–3: R_E_D Research into Environment + Design
4.3.4: Silvio Caputo
4.3.5–6: R_E_D Research into Environment + Design

4.4.1–7: Celina Balderas Guzmán
4.4.8–9: Matthew Niederhauser and John Fitzgerald

4.6.1–3: Joan Nassauer; visualizations by Zhifang Wang
4.6.4–7: Joan Nassauer
4.6.8–9: Matthew Niederhauser and John Fitzgerald

4.7.1–18: Alan M. Berger
4.7.19–24: Alan M. Berger and Casey L. Brown, P-REX

4.8.1–2: W&A B. Secchi, P. Viganò, with L. Fabian, P. Pellegrini, PRIN research
4.8.3–4: Studio Urbanism 2013–2014, Università IUAV, Venezia: P. Viganò with A. Curtoni, A. Pagnacco; students M. Caccin, G. Savegna, J. Scattolin, B. Stallone
4.8.5–7: Studio Bernardo Secchi, Paola Viganò, Milano, 2010–2012
4.8.8–11: Lab-U (Laboratory of Urbanism, EPFL Lausanne), 2014
4.8.12–13: Design Studio Harvard GSD, 2013 (Paola Viganò with C. Cavalieri; student Phoebe White)
4.8.14–15: Design Studio Harvard GSD, 2013 (Paola Viganò with C. Cavalieri; students Ana Victoria Chiari, Simon Willett)
4.8.16–17: Matthew Niederhauser and John Fitzgerald

4.9.1–14: Alex Wall, Rachelle Trahan, and Jingxian Gao

4.10.1–2: Pamela Bellavita, adapted from illustrations by Katie Ries

4.11.1–10: Hugh Byrd
4.11.11–12: Matthew Niederhauser and John Fitzgerald

5.1.1: Amir Gohar
5.1.2: Laura Tepper
5.1.3: Allstate Insurance Company, Menlo Park, CA, 1950; photograph courtesy of Geraldine Knight Scott Collection Environmental

Design Archives, University of California, Berkeley
5.1.4: Palo Alto Historical Association
5.1.5–6: Satellite Imagery Courtesy of TerraServer.com/ Digital Globe
5.1.7–8: Courtesy of Google
5.1.9: Frank Gehry Facebook West Campus, Menlo Park, CA, 2015; photograph © Michael Light

5.2.1: City of Euclid, Ohio
5.2.2: David Burns and Eliza Oprescu
5.2.3: Charles Eliot, 1902
5.2.4: Howard T. Odum, *Systems Ecology: An Introduction* (New York Wiley-Interscience, 1983)
5.2.5: Cassandra Kotva
5.2.6–9: Mariusz Klemens and Fadi Masoud—Effectual Decentralization
5.2.10–13: Matthew Niederhauser and John Fitzgerald

5.5.1: Arlington County, Virginia, Department of Community Planning, Housing and Development
5.5.2: Fairfax County, Virginia, Department of Planning and Zoning
5.5.3: Aaron Renn

5.6.1–3: Adriana Allen
5.6.4–5: Matthew Niederhauser and John Fitzgerald

5.7.1: Tobias Töpfer
5.7.2: IBGE—Censos Demográficos, 2000–2010; Emplasa/VCP/UDI, 2012
5.7.3–4: Tobias Töpfer

5.8.1: Robert Mason and Liliya Nigmatullina
5.8.2: Liliya Nigmatullina
5.8.3: Olga Bochenina
5.8.4–5: Matthew Niederhauser and John Fitzgerald

5.9.1: Peter Carroll
5.9.2–3: Anne Pitcher
5.9.4–5: Sylvia Croese
5.9.6: Ngoi Salucombo

5.10.1: Rafi Segal
5.10.2: B'Tselem, Eyal Weizman; reprinted from Rafi Segal, Eyal Weizman, *A Civilian Occupation: The Politics of Israeli Architecture* (New York: Verso, 2003)
5.10.3: Rafi Segal, Eyal Weizman; reprinted from Rafi Segal, Eyal Weizman,

A Civilian Occupation: The Politics of Israeli Architecture (New York: Verso, 2003)
5.10.4: Milutin Labudovic; reprinted from Rafi Segal, Eyal Weizman, *A Civilian Occupation: The Politics of Israeli Architecture* (New York: Verso, 2003)
5.10.5–6: Matthew Niederhauser and John Fitzgerald

Index

Published by
Princeton Architectural Press
A McEvoy Group company
202 Warren Street, Hudson, NY 12534
Visit our website at www.papress.com

© 2017 MIT Norman B. Leventhal Center
for Advanced Urbanism, Alan M. Berger
(editor), Joel Kotkin (editor), with
Celina Balderas Guzmán

ISBN 978-1-61689-550-1

Project Editor: Barbara Darko
Designer: Project Projects
(Adam Michaels and Siiri Tännler)

Library of Congress Cataloging-in-
Publication Data is available from the
publisher upon request.

Photography for cover, endpapers,
and pp. 4–5: Matthew Niederhauser
and John Fitzgerald

Special thanks to: Janet Behning, Nolan
Boomer, Nicola Brower, Abby Bussel,
Tom Cho, Benjamin English, Jenny
Florence, Jan Cigliano Hartman, Susan
Hershberg, Lia Hunt, Valerie Kamen,
Simone Kaplan-Senchak, Jennifer
Lippert, Kristy Maier, Sara McKay,
Eliana Miller, Wes Seeley, Rob Shaeffer,
Sara Stemen, Paul Wagner, and Joseph
Weston of Princeton Architectural Press
—Kevin C. Lippert, publisher

31192021405475